✳ ✳ ✳

LANGUAGE DEVELOPMENT IN EARLY CHILDHOOD EDUCATION

FOURTH EDITION

Beverly Otto

Northeastern Illinois University

PEARSON

Boston   Columbus   Indianapolis   New York   San Francisco   Upper Saddle River
Amsterdam   Cape Town   Dubai   London   Madrid   Milan   Munich   Paris   Montréal   Toronto
Delhi   Mexico City   São Paulo   Sydney   Hong Kong   Seoul   Singapore   Taipei   Tokyo

Vice President and Editorial Director: Jeffery W. Johnston
Senior Acquisitions Editor: Julie Peters
Editorial Assistant: Andrea Hall
Vice President, Director of Marketing: Margaret Waples
Senior Marketing Manager: Christopher Barry
Senior Managing Editor: Pamela Bennett
Project Manager: Kerry Rubadue

Production Manager: Laura Messerly
Senior Art Director: Jayne Conte
Cover Designer: Suzanne Behnke
Cover Art: Getty Images
Cover Photo: Fuse / Getty Images
Full-Service Project Management: Sneha Pant/ PreMediaGlobal
Composition: PreMediaGlobal
Text Font: 10/12 Melior Lt Std Regular

Every effort has been made to provide accurate and current Internet information in this book. However, the Internet and information posted on it are constantly changing, so it is inevitable that some of the Internet addresses listed in this textbook will change.

Library of Congress Cataloging-in-Publication Data

Otto, Beverly.
  Language development in early childhood education / Beverly Otto, Northeastern Illinois University. — Fourth edition.
    pages cm
  Includes bibliographical references and index.
  ISBN-13: 978-0-13-286755-9
  ISBN-10: 0-13-286755-9
  1. Language arts (Early childhood) 2. Children—Language.
  3. Child development. I. Title.
  LB1139.5.L35O83 2014
  372.6—dc23
                                                                        2012042262

10 9 8 7 6 5 4 3 2 1

PEARSON

ISBN 10:   0-13-286755-9
ISBN 13: 978-0-13-286755-9

To early childhood professionals who make a difference
in the lives of children.

ABOUT THE AUTHOR

Beverly Otto, Ph.D., an early childhood educator for over 30 years, is professor emeritus in the Teacher Education Department at Northeastern Illinois University. She earned her doctorate at Northwestern University in teaching and learning processes, with a focus on emergent literacy. Dr. Otto teaches courses in language and literacy development for preservice and inservice teachers, along with research for classroom teachers. Her major professional goal is preparing teachers to support children's lifelong learning through language and literacy development. Dr. Otto also served as department chair as well as associate dean in the College of Education.

Dr. Otto is the author of *Literacy Development in Early Childhood* (Pearson) and has authored articles published in international, national, and state professional journals. Her field-based research on emergent literacy has been presented at international, national, state, and local conferences. She has served as a consultant to early childhood centers, school districts, and the Illinois State Board of Education.

❋ ❋ ❋

PREFACE

*I*n writing this text, it has been my goal to provide preservice early childhood teachers with a foundation of knowledge they will need to develop classrooms and learning environments where children's language development will be enhanced. *Language Development in Early Childhood*, Fourth Edition, is a book about language development from birth through age 8. It is a foundational text that incorporates theory and research as well as guidelines for enhancing language development in early childhood settings.

This text provides a comprehensive view of language development, focusing on the development of phonological, semantic, syntactic, morphemic, and pragmatic language knowledge. Development of children's knowledge of written language is also included as part of children's language development. Although this text is designed for use as the main text in an undergraduate language development course for majors in early childhood education or child development, it could also be used as a supplementary text in early childhood language arts or reading methods courses.

NEW TO THIS EDITION

For this fourth edition, each chapter has been updated and expanded to reflect recent research and best practice. Revisions in wording and chapter structure have been made to increase the text's readability and improve the reader's comprehension. Also new to this edition are:

- Additional vignettes and examples of children's oral and written language to further illustrate specific aspects of language development
- Updated research on the theoretical foundations of language development
- Increased discussion of the effects of culture on language development and implications for teachers
- Added Family Connection features to Chapters 5, 7, 9, and 11

- Updated Teacher Resources for Chapters 3, 5, 7, 9, 11, and 14
- Added checklists for teachers to use in observing and documenting children's language competencies throughout the kindergarten year
- Updated information on assessment tools and procedures in Chapter 12

The text begins with three chapters that address general language issues: Chapter 1, *Language in Our Lives;* Chapter 2, *Theoretical Perspectives and Contexts of Language Development;* and Chapter 3, *Language Development Among Children of Linguistic Diversity.* Each of these chapters introduces foundational concepts and perspectives that are built on in subsequent chapters.

Chapters 4 to 11 focus on the different ages of children and guidelines for enhancing language development at each age in early childhood settings. At each age, from infancy through primary years, language development is detailed and guidelines are provided for enhancing children's language development. Professors and students will find this feature beneficial, as it strengthens students' understanding of the ways in which children's language develops in early childhood settings. Information and resources on using symbolic gestures and signing with infants and toddlers are included in the revision of Chapters 4 and 5. Specific guidelines for enhancing language development of English language learners are included in Chapters 5, 7, and 9. Chapter 12 emphasizes assessment processes involved in observing, screening, diagnosing, and documenting children's language development. Chapter 13 focuses on language disorders and includes guidelines for teachers working with children with special needs, including autism. Chapter 14 emphasizes the role of school–home connections in enhancing children's language development and learning. The Appendix supplements Chapters 3 and 14 with a listing of common greetings and expressions in different languages for early childhood teachers to use in establishing rapport and school–home connections with families of second language learners.

FOR THE PROFESSOR

In each chapter are three features that will be useful to you and your students. Each chapter opens with Learning Outcomes, which highlight key concepts to guide readers. The Chapter Review section provides questions and terms to use in reviewing chapter content. The Chapter Extension Activities at the end of each chapter provide opportunities to apply chapter content through observation or through interaction with children or practicing teachers. The *Online Instructor's Manual* provides additional suggestions for in-class activities, extension activities, and useful forms, and the *Online Test Bank* includes a variety of assessment items. The *Online PowerPoint™ Slides* present the main concepts from each chapter and can be adapted for your own use.

You can download the electronic *Online Instructor's Manual*, *Online Test Bank*, and *Online PowerPoint™ Slides* from www.pearsonhighered.com. First click on *Educators*, and then click on *Download Instructor's Resources*.

ACKNOWLEDGMENTS

First, I would like to thank my husband and children for encouraging me in this fourth edition. I am also deeply indebted to my nieces and my granddaughter for the privilege of witnessing their language development in all of its passion and joy. I deeply appreciate the support and encouragement from my colleagues, administrators, and students at Northeastern Illinois University. I am also indebted to the many children and teachers whose anecdotes, language examples, and photos appear in this text and to the parents who graciously shared their children with me. A special thanks is extended to Elfriede Weber, director, and the teachers and staff at the Northeastern Illinois University Child Care Center for welcoming me into their center.

In the preparation of this fourth edition, I have deeply appreciated the guidance and insightful contributions of Julie Peters, senior acquisitions editor in early childhood education at Pearson. I would also like to thank the following reviewers for their thoughtful comments: Lisa M. Crane, University of Illinois at Urbana–Champaign; Mary Blake Jones, College of Charleston; Colleen Lelli, Cabrini College; and Kathleen Martin, University of Alabama at Birmingham.

BRIEF CONTENTS

CONTENTS

10 Language Development in the Primary Years   284

13 Enhancing Language Development Among Children with Communicative Disorders   363

CHAPTER 1

LANGUAGE IN OUR LIVES

Learning Outcomes

After reading this chapter you should be able to

- Describe the range of language competencies needed by children
- Explain each of the five aspects of language knowledge
- Distinguish between the three levels of language knowledge
- Identify the receptive and expressive modes of oral and written language
- Explain the critical role of children's oral language competencies in school settings

In the toddler room, Adam and his teacher are sharing a book in the library corner during independent activity time. As his teacher turns the pages, Adam talks about the pictures and responds to questions his teacher asks.

In the preschool room, Kiesha is at the easel, painting a picture. When she finishes, she makes some letter-like forms with her paintbrush and then says, "That's my name."

In the kindergarten room, Juan is participating in "show-and-tell," describing the special rock that he found when he went for a walk with his dad. He is especially fascinated by the silvery sparkles running through the rock and says, "See the sparkles here, and here, and here" as he points to his rock.

In each of these instances, children used language effectively to communicate. Adam was engaged in the storybook sharing, taking an active role in responding to the storybook content. Kiesha showed her awareness that graphic symbols have meaning, representing her name, in this case. Juan communicated the special features of the object he had brought for show-and-tell.

YOUR ROLE AS AN EARLY CHILDHOOD PROFESSIONAL

As an early childhood professional, you will have many interactions with children that are based in oral and written language. You will be talking with children as they interact in your classroom, engaging in the learning activities you provide. As you read books to and with children, you will introduce the children to written language. When you create classroom posters and other displays involving print, you are showing children how written language can be used to communicate. Through these interactions, you will have a significant influence on children's language development. As you prepare for your role as an early childhood professional, it is important that you acquire knowledge of how children develop language competencies. This knowledge will enable you to provide guidance, support, and mediation to enhance children's development. Throughout this text, the emphasis is on increasing your knowledge of language development as well as strategies and activities that will enhance children's language development. This chapter provides an overview of the role of language in our lives and the different aspects of language knowledge. The chapter closes with a description of research that highlights the relationship between oral and written language.

BECOMING SPEAKERS, READERS, AND WRITERS

How did the children in the opening vignette learn to communicate using language? Did it occur automatically without any direct influence from the environment? Is learning to read different from learning to speak? How do children become fluent in more than one language? These questions have sparked intense research and debate for many years. Gradually we are coming to better understand the ways in which children become effective speakers, listeners, readers, and writers. Throughout this text, we will explore the ways in which children become effective communicators and the ways in which we, as teachers, can enhance their development of language. This text differs from other language development texts in its attention to language as communication rather than a focus on speech production and the development of articulation. This approach recognizes that language is a medium of communication with others and within us. The focus here will be on the years from birth through age 8, an age span commonly referred to as the early childhood years. While this text will include descriptions of activities to enhance language development, it is not intended to be a language arts methods text. The language development approach of this text examines the development of both oral and written language within settings in early childhood. Oral language development and written language development are interrelated processes that culminate in children's communicative competencies.

Language is essential to society. It forms the foundation of our perceptions, communications, and daily interactions. It is a system of symbols by which we categorize, organize, and clarify our thinking (Stice, Bertrand, & Bertrand, 1995). Through language, we represent the world and learn about the world. Without language, a society and its culture cannot exist.

To be able to function successfully in a society and its culture (and subcultures), children need to develop a wide range of language competencies. Not only do children need to acquire an oral language, they need to be able to use that language effectively in a variety of settings. Further, in literate cultures, children need to develop competencies in using written language as well. Throughout life, people communicate in a variety of settings: talking on the phone with friends, interacting with a store clerk as they purchase groceries, listening to a radio talk show, and using language in professional or educational settings, such as an attorney in a court of law or a college professor and his students in a university classroom. Our language competencies allow us to participate effectively in a variety of social events and occupational settings and in our daily routines.

There is no one standard of communicative competency that teachers should encourage children to attain. Instead, it is important for teachers to recognize that children will need a wide range of communication competencies to ensure their effectiveness in a variety of settings throughout their lives.

Children's communicative competencies involve both receptive and expressive language. **Receptive language** refers to a child's comprehension of words (oral or written): when a specific word is used, the child knows what it refers to or represents. **Expressive language** refers to a child's production of language to communicate. This develops orally first during social interactions and as a child's speech mechanisms mature allowing the child to gain control over producing specific speech sounds. In literate cultures, children also develop expressive written language as they learn how to communicate using the visual symbol system of their specific culture, e.g., the 26 letters of the English alphabet.

Receptive language development and expressive language development are closely related. While linguists and child development educators agree that receptive language begins to develop prior to expressive language, there is little agreement regarding how long expressive language development lags behind receptive language development (Owens, 1988). The relation between the development of receptive and expressive language appears to be a dynamic one, influenced by a child's specific developmental level, each aspect of language knowledge, and learning environment.

ASPECTS OF LANGUAGE KNOWLEDGE

When children are acquiring language, they are developing five different aspects, or components, of language knowledge: phonological, semantic, syntactic, morphemic, and pragmatic. Each of these aspects refers to a specific domain of language knowledge; however, the aspects do not develop in isolation from each other. Each of these aspects of language knowledge is present in any interaction in which language is used. Initially, a child's knowledge of the aspects or components of language will be only receptive. This means the child will perceive the specific characteristics of language but will not be able to produce language that demonstrates this knowledge. In the sections that follow, each of the five aspects of language knowledge is described, along with examples illustrating each aspect.

Phonological Knowledge

As children hear and perceive oral language, they learn that language is embedded in a sound–symbol system. **Phonological knowledge** refers to knowledge about sound–symbol relations in a language. A **phoneme** is the smallest linguistic unit of sound, which is combined with other phonemes to form words. Phonemes consist of sounds that are considered to be a single perceptual unit by a listener, such as the /m/ sound in the word *mother* (Goodman, 1993; Hayes, Ornstein, & Gage, 1987).

How phonological knowledge develops. Children's development of phonological knowledge is fostered by their perceptual ability to distinguish sounds and also by the ways in which language is used around them. Young infants about 2 months of age have been found to be able to distinguish between a /p/ sound and a /b/ sound long before they are able to produce those sounds. Children's discrimination of sounds precedes their ability to produce those same sounds, due to the complex coordination of the speech mechanism in making those sounds.

In every language, some speech sounds are more important than others. Gradually, young children learn to discriminate and produce the speech sounds that are found in their home language. For example, in English, the sounds represented by the letters /l/ and /r/ are perceived as significantly different phonemes. In contrast, the Japanese language does not distinguish between the /l/ and the /r/. Consequently, when native Japanese speakers learn English, they have difficulty articulating English words such as *rate* and *late.* Another example of the perception of significant differences in similar sounds is found in situations in which native English speakers are learning Spanish. In Spanish, /r/ and /rr/ represent different phonemes, as in *pero* (but) and *perro* (dog). For English speakers learning Spanish, this is confusing when the oral pronunciation of the two phonemes represented by *r* and *rr* seems indistinguishable (Goodman, 1993).

Phonological knowledge does not develop in isolation from other aspects of language knowledge. Learning to distinguish between similar-sounding words, such as *can* and *car*, is facilitated by the different ways in which those two words are used in meaningful contexts. The phonemic differences between the two words become meaningful because the two words are used to refer to different objects and actions.

Children's phonological knowledge during infancy and toddlerhood is evident when children produce and distinguish between the sounds used in their home languages in communicating with those around them. As children move into the preschool years, they may acquire a more conscious awareness of distinct speech sounds in their language and begin to deliberately manipulate their language. This is known as **phonological awareness** (Gillon, 2004). This conscious awareness of speech sounds contributes significantly to children's understanding of the relation between speech and print. The development of literacy skills requires that children be able to use symbols to represent the sounds of their language in writing and to decode the symbols when reading. Children who are unable to consciously focus on or segment the sounds in a word may experience difficulty in learning to read and write (Lieberman, 1973, in Scarborough, 2002).

Prosodic features.   In addition to the perception of sounds in a language, young children notice differences in the way sounds are used in a language to add meaning to what is said. **Prosodic features** in a language represent the way something is said. These features have both acoustic or sound properties and psychological or emotional properties. For example, "they're coming" can be said in different ways to indicate a statement or a question. It can also be said in a way that conveys a sense of boredom, excitement, or dread. Specific prosodic features include intonation, loudness, tempo, and rhythm (Crystal, 1987; deVilliers & deVilliers, 1978; Goodman, 1993; Sandler & Lillo-Martin, 2005).

Young children acquire knowledge of these prosodic features as well as the specific sounds used in a language through interactions with people in their environment. Children's auditory perception of these prosodic features contributes to both their phonological knowledge and their subsequent semantic knowledge. Infants' perception of the speech intonation of those around them is evident when they begin to babble and appear to mimic the intonation of others. Infants learn to sense when their parent or caregiver is happy, excited, calm, tense, or angry from the intonation, loudness, tempo, or rhythm of the adult's speech. Prosodic features are also communicated in sign language, through facial expression, body posture, and rhythmic signing (Sandler & Lillo-Martin, 2005).

Children also become aware of the prosodic features of speech as they interact with their parents and caregivers in storybook sharing. As an adult directs a child's attention to a storybook by reading the text or simply talking about the pictures, each of the prosodic features is employed in sharing the story with the child. For example, when an adult reads the longtime favorite story "Goldilocks and the Three Bears," she typically uses different "voices" for each of the bears: a loud, gruff voice for the papa bear; a gentle, moderate voice for the mama bear; and a tiny, squeaky voice for the baby bear.

Storybook sharing is a very effective way to encourage children to begin to perceive prosodic features in understanding language because the range of language used in storybooks and the range of dramatic expression in story sharing are much greater than in day-to-day conversations. In addition, the pictures in young children's storybooks contribute to the meaning of the shared story, reinforcing the meanings implied in the oral story. Parents and caregivers often tell of instances in which they did not read a storybook with the same intonation or dramatic speech they used previously, and the child stops them and tells them that they need to read the story the "right way," meaning that they need to use the anticipated intonation, loudness, tempo, or rhythm.

Language forms the foundation of our perceptions, communications, and daily interactions.

Semantic Knowledge

In learning that oral symbols, or spoken words, have meaning, semantic knowledge is acquired. The development of semantic knowledge is closely tied to the development of conceptual knowledge (Vygotsky, 1962). **Semantic knowledge** refers to the word labels that specify concepts and also to the semantic networks, or schemata, that represent the interrelations between concepts. Semantic networks—**schemata**—are thought to be cognitive structures in our memory that organize our conceptual knowledge. These semantic networks facilitate new learning and recall and contribute to the reorganization and elaboration of prior conceptual learning.

For example, the English word *ball* references the idea of a round object that has certain properties of rolling and bouncing and that is often used in a game or other physical activity. In acquiring concepts, children learn that objects and actions with similar features or functions can be grouped into the same category or into related categories. For example, when a child learns that a small, round, red plastic object is called a ball, he may see similarities when he sees a white soccer ball and also call it a ball, or he may attempt to roll the soccer ball on the floor. A semantic network, or schema, develops when a child begins to see the relations between concepts. Over time, as a child experiences different types of balls that are used for different purposes, a schema develops for balls. See Figure 1.1 for an example of what adults might have in their *ball*

FIGURE 1.1
Semantic Network or Schema for *Ball*

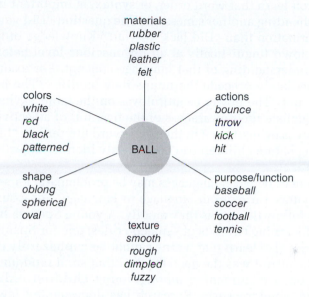

schema. A young child's schema for *ball* will initially be much more limited in complexity and may include only "roundness," "throwing," and "bouncing."

Vocabulary development is closely related to general linguistic competence and to reading comprehension. Children with larger and more developed vocabularies have more options for expressing what they want to say and, thus, have greater linguistic flexibility. One activity that contributes to vocabulary development is storybook sharing, where an adult reads to a child. The vocabulary used in storybooks is often more descriptive and precise than is the vocabulary used in daily conversations. Storybook experiences expand a child's listening vocabulary. A larger vocabulary also increases a child's ability to comprehend written text because reading comprehension is directly related to listening comprehension and oral vocabulary. When a specific word (and concept) is part of a child's oral vocabulary or listening vocabulary, the child can more easily comprehend and decode it when he encounters the word in written text.

Children's development of semantic knowledge is also influenced by their awareness of the grammatical structure in which language is used. This syntactic knowledge is crucial because the grammatical or syntactic structures carry implied meaning. Word order affects the meaning of what is said.

Syntactic Knowledge

To use language effectively, it is necessary to know how to combine words to create meaningful expressions. Each language system has rules or a grammar that prescribes how words are combined to create sentences or meaningful phrases. This aspect of language knowledge is called **syntactic knowledge**.

Children learn that word order, or **syntax**, is important in creating meaning and in comprehending another's message. The question "Did you hit Jack?" asks for different information than "Did Jack hit you?" Knowledge of the importance of word order is known linguistically at an unconscious level before children can verbalize their understanding of that language concept. For example, in English, adjectives immediately precede the nouns they modify: "The beautiful flower was on the table," not "The flower beautiful was on the table." When children are learning to speak English, their awareness of the position of adjectives relative to the nouns they modify is evident even in their two-word utterances: "big ball," "blue car." This occurs long before children can consciously identify adjectives and the words they modify.

Differences between languages may be problematic for second language learners because syntax varies from language to language. For example, in Spanish, some adjectives follow the nouns they modify. A young Spanish bilingual child will have the task of learning two sets of syntactic rules, one for Spanish and one for English.

Children also learn that words cannot be haphazardly combined, as in "flower table the beautiful was the on." The fact that such random combinations of words have not been documented among young children indicates that word order knowledge develops early. Research has documented few instances of children violating syntactic rules simply because utterances that do not observe the specific language's syntax are not comprehendible, useful, or meaningful. To speak in a way that violates syntactic rules dooms the speaker to be misunderstood or ignored.

Morphemic Knowledge

Morphemic knowledge refers to knowledge of word structure. In acquiring syntactic knowledge, children learn that some words have related meanings but are used in different ways in speech and in written language and have different word structure. For example, *happy*, *happiness*, and *happily* have related meanings; however, each word is used in a different way grammatically. *Happy* is an adjective, *happiness* is a noun, and *happily* is an adverb. Thus, each has a different grammatical function. *Walk*, *walking*, and *walked* are related in meaning; however, the location in time or tense is different. In learning how to use words in an appropriate syntactic manner, children also learn that prefixes and word endings change the meaning of a word and its grammatical use.

A word is composed of one or more meaningful linguistic units. The smallest unit of meaning in language is the **morpheme**. There are two types of morphemes: (a) **free morphemes** are used alone as words (e.g., *house*, *turtle*, *book*), and (b) **bound morphemes** must be attached to free morphemes (e.g., the final *-s* in *houses*, the *-ly* in *slow*ly, and the *-ing* in *going*).

Bound morphemes are of two types: derivational and inflectional (Lindfors, 1987; Owens, 1988). **Derivational morphemes** include prefixes, such as *un-* in

TABLE 1.1
Examples of Derivational Morphemes

Using prefixes and suffixes to change meaning and part of speech

Prefix	Stem	Suffix	New Word
un-	*accept* (verb)	*-able*	*unacceptable* (adjective)
im-	*proper* (adjective)	*-ly*	*improperly* (adverb)
dis-	*grace* (noun)	*-ful*	*disgraceful* (adjective)

unhappy, and suffixes, such as *-ness* in *happiness*. These morphemes are added to a root or stem to change the meaning of the word or the grammatical function of the word in the sentence. Table 1.1 provides examples of how derivational morphemes change the meaning and grammatical function (part of speech) of a word.

Inflectional morphemes are word endings added to change verb tense, possession, or plurality or to make comparisons. For example, many verbs add the *-ed* morpheme to show past tense, as in *walk–walk*ed. To show possession, an apostrophe and the letter *s* are added to the end of a noun, as in *Jack–Jack's* hat. Plurality is indicated by adding an *-s* or *-es* to a noun, as in *cat–cats* and *dish–dishes*. To make comparisons, *-er* and *-est* are added, as in *fast*, *faster,* and *fast*est. While many English words are "regular" in the sense that these inflectional morphemes can be used, there are also irregular words that do not follow these patterns. For example, to make a comparison based on the word *good*, you would say *good*, *better*, and *best*, not *good*, *gooder*, *goodest*. To indicate the past tense of *go*, you would say *went*, not *goed*.

The ability to use morphemes appropriately is one of the characteristics of an effective language user. Knowledge of morphology allows children to comprehend others' speech better, such as understanding plural nouns and verb tense. Knowledge that *cat* means one in number and *cats* refers to more than one cat allows more precise communication.

As children's speech progresses beyond the one-word and two-word stages, their understanding of how words are formed is used as they attempt to communicate. Many utterances of young children are novel, not simply repetitions of prior adult speech. In the production of an utterance, children use their knowledge of morphemes to create their messages. As children become more aware of how morphemes are used, their language becomes more precise and meaningful.

Young children acquire morphemic knowledge that is present in their linguistic environments. In settings where a particular dialect is spoken, children will first acquire the morphemic knowledge represented in that dialect. In figuring out how language is used and words are structured, children appear to be looking for patterns and hypothesizing. Children's overgeneralizations of morphological patterns are an example of this.

Children's **overgeneralizations** occur when they assume that a particular word follows a regular pattern when, in fact, it follows an irregular pattern. For example, the past tense of regular verbs is created by adding *-ed* to the present tense. Children who assume that *come* is a regular verb will create the past-tense form by adding *-ed*, resulting in "comed."

Similarly, when children begin to learn comparative forms of adjectives, they may see the pattern of regular comparative forms, which are made with *-er* (*happi*er) and *-est* (*happi*est) endings. However, some children apply this rule to all adjectives, as in *fun, funner, funnest*, or even *best, bester, bestest*. Overgeneralization decreases as language development proceeds and as children have opportunities to interact with adults and older siblings who have acquired more complete morphemic knowledge.

Overgeneralization can also occur in the use of prefixes. For example, children learn that the way to change a word to mean the opposite is to add the prefix *un-*, meaning "not." They understand that *unhappy* means "not happy." Children may create their own words based on their understanding of how prefixes (or suffixes or plural endings) work. To illustrate, a 5-year-old girl was being chided by her mother because a doting aunt had given her another doll during a recent visit to the aunt's home. When her mother asked her why she accepted another doll that she really did not need, the girl replied, "Mommy, Aunty insisted, and I couldn't un-sist!"

Pragmatic Knowledge

Language use is embedded in social–cultural contexts. Different contexts are characterized by differences in the way language is used. Through our social–cultural interactions, we learn when to speak; when not to speak; what to talk about with whom; and when, where, and in what manner to speak (Gleason, 1993). We also learn the specific style of speaking for certain contexts with respect to the expected phonological, semantic, syntactic, and morphemic features. This knowledge or awareness of how to use language differently in different settings and situations represents pragmatic knowledge. This knowledge contributes to appropriate and effective communication (Ninio & Snow, 1999).

Pragmatic knowledge involves the knowledge or awareness of the overall intent of the communication and how language is used to achieve that intent. Pragmatic knowledge encompasses the intent of the speaker, the specific form of the utterance, and the anticipated effect the utterance will have on the listener. The selection of intent or purpose in communication and the way in which language is used contribute to a child's level of communicative competence in early childhood and beyond. Early on in the development of communicative competence, children's efforts appear to have purpose or intent. An 8-month-old child who looks at her mother with outstretched arms and produces strained vocalizations (/uh/ /uh/) is assumed to be communicating that she wants to be picked up. If not initially successful, the child may repeat her request, vocalize louder, or gesture more emphatically (Gleason, 1993).

Conversational skills influence a child's ability to interact with others.

Pragmatic knowledge also contributes to our awareness of how to converse with others, how to participate verbally in various settings, and how to produce connected discourse, such as narratives (Ninio & Snow, 1999). Conversational skills are a critical part of pragmatic knowledge because they affect a child's ability to engage in classroom and social interactions (Ninio & Snow, 1999; Weiss, 2004). Conversational competence depends on the development of specific skills of taking turns, keeping similar or related topics as the focus of the conversation, encouraging participation from the other person(s), and clarifying or repairing areas of confusion. Through children's direct experiences, they become aware of the rules or expected ways in which conversations are initiated, maintained, and discontinued. In a conversation, both people take on the alternating roles of speaker and listener (Clay, 1998). Children who cannot differentiate how to use language in different settings may be "excluded from social interactions with peers or may be unable to request assistance from teachers during classroom activities" (Weiss, 2004, p. 35).

The term **register** refers to the specific ways of using language differently in different settings. For example, face-to-face conversations, classroom discourse, telephone conversations, ritual insults, service encounters, jokes, and doctor–patient talk. Children learn to distinguish different times when quiet voices and loud voices are used, and they pick up social conventions such as saying "please" and "thank you." Children learn how to talk most effectively to adults and to each other by using different interaction styles. For example, a mother of a 5-year-old might discover that the verbal whining she often heard at home from her child never occurred when the child was at school.

Children also acquire knowledge of how language is used in relation to one's gender, or **genderlect** (Kramer, 1974, cited in Warren & McCloskey, 1997; Sheldon, 1993; Tannen, 1990). For example, research has indicated that preschool and kindergarten boys and girls tend to talk about different topics (Haas, 1979, cited in Owens, 2001), with boys talking more about sports and girls talking more about school.

Children also acquire pragmatic knowledge of how language is used to tell story narratives and communicate information through their early experiences

Children acquire pragmatic knowledge of how language is used to tell story narratives and communicate information through their early experiences with storybooks.

with storybooks and information books. Children who have had frequent storybook interactions with a wide variety of types of texts (or genres) will develop an awareness of how language is used in each type of discourse (Otto, 1987). For example, when encouraged to create a fairy tale, preschool children may begin the story with "once upon a time" and conclude their stories with "they lived happily ever after" or "the end."

Relation of Aspects of Language Knowledge to Communication

Development of each of the five aspects of language knowledge is critical to effective communication. Each aspect does not develop in isolation from the other aspects; instead, the aspects are interrelated. For example, phonological knowledge can influence the development of semantic knowledge because perception of sound differences is needed to distinguish between similar words, such as *cat* and *cot*. Syntactic knowledge also influences semantic knowledge because word order implies meaning through grammatical structure. For example, in "The XXX went on a train ride," XXX must be a person or thing capable of being on a train. Morphemic knowledge also influences semantic knowledge because some bound morphemes accompany changes in word meaning (e.g., *happy* vs. *unhappy*). Morphemic knowledge is also related to syntactic knowledge as some bound morphemes change the grammatical function of a word (e.g., *happy* vs. *happiness*). Pragmatic knowledge is influenced by each of the other four aspects because how language is used in different settings is reflected by differences in phonological, semantic, syntactic, and morphemic features.

The complex interrelations of these five aspects of language knowledge to a child's use of language and communication are illustrated in Figure 1.2. The amount of interaction between the five aspects varies with the language or dialect used; however, it is important to remember that no single aspect of language knowledge exists or is acquired in isolation from the other aspects. Each of these five aspects contributes to children's developing competencies in using language. This dynamic interaction is illustrated in Figure 1.3.

FIGURE 1.2

Interrelations Between the Five Aspects of Language Knowledge

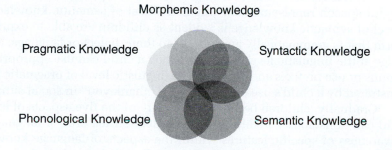

FIGURE 1.3
Components of Communicative Competency

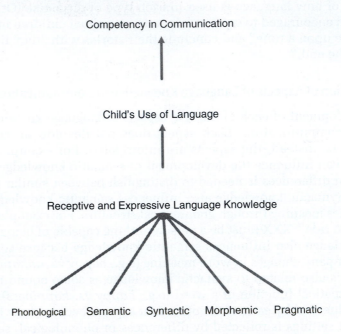

Competency in Communication

Child's Use of Language

Receptive and Expressive Language Knowledge

Phonological   Semantic   Syntactic   Morphemic   Pragmatic

LEVELS OF LANGUAGE KNOWLEDGE

A child's knowledge of language develops at different levels of conscious awareness (Otto, 1982). Children first develop knowledge of language at a **linguistic level**, or usage level. This is the "know-how" of being able to use language in communicative contexts. This linguistic level of language knowledge can be documented in children's development of each of the five aspects of language knowledge. Children's ability to articulate and discriminate different sounds and words when using language to communicate represents their linguistic level of phonological knowledge. Similarly, children's ability to comprehend the semantic meanings of others' speech and to create their own meaningful speech represents their linguistic level of semantic knowledge. The linguistic level of syntactic knowledge is evident as children are able to express their ideas in a form that is grammatically appropriate to their dialect or language. Morphemic knowledge at the linguistic level is evident when a child can use appropriate plural forms of nouns or use prefixes and suffixes. The linguistic level of pragmatic knowledge is demonstrated by a child's use of "please" and "thank you" in social situations.

Gradually, children become more aware of the five aspects of language knowledge and can consciously manipulate and reflect on features of language. This conscious awareness of specific features within the aspects of language knowledge is at a level higher than linguistic knowledge, the **metalinguistic level**. At the metalinguistic level, a child consciously manipulates phonological, semantic, syntactic, morphemic, and prag-matic knowledge to form the desired message. Metalinguistic knowledge is indicated when a child can respond to questions about words and other linguistic concepts, such as sounds, consonants, vowels, and word parts. Children's wordplay in rhyming games is an indicator of their early metalinguistic phonological knowledge. Other evidence of early metalinguistic knowledge has been described by emergent literacy research (Ehri, 1975; Schickedanz, 1981; Sulzby, 1986b; Voss, 1988) that has documented children's spontaneous comments about language, such as "My name starts with a T—Tommy!"

Metalinguistic knowledge acquired through informal interactions with oral and written language develops further when children enter formal schooling. Beginning in kindergarten, many learning activities focus on the conscious manipulation of specific features or concepts of both oral and written language. For example, when a child is asked to give the first sound in the word *bat*, she must not only know how to say the word (linguistic knowledge) but must be able to use her concepts of "sound" and "first" in reflecting on the word and then separating out the sounds.

When children begin to verbalize their metalinguistic knowledge, they are at the most conscious and complex level of language knowledge, **metalinguistic verbali-zation**. For example, when children are asked to explain how the words *cup* and *pup* sound alike, they must be able to verbalize their awareness of the rhyming that is present. This requires talking about their knowledge of a specific feature of lan-guage. Children acquire linguistic knowledge and metalinguistic knowledge as they use language and through interaction with others. Only after oral language is well established can children begin to verbalize their metalinguistic knowledge.

A teacher's awareness of levels of language knowledge is important in determin-ing the developmental appropriateness of language-related tasks in early childhood classrooms. Teachers of young children need to structure their learning activities to involve both linguistic and metalinguistic knowledge; however, it is not appropriate to expect that young children will be able to verbalize their metalinguistic knowl-edge. For example, first-graders may learn to decode words that contain digraphs and blends, but will not be able to explain the difference between a digraph and a blend.

A summary of the three levels of language knowledge is presented in Table 1.2. Linguistic knowledge provides the foundation for higher levels of language knowl-edge. Likewise, the middle level, use of metalinguistic knowledge, provides the basis for the development of the highest level, the ability to verbalize metalinguistic knowledge. For example, children's phonological knowledge during infancy and toddlerhood is at the linguistic level of language knowledge. They are able to pro-duce and distinguish between the sounds used in their home languages. As children move into the preschool years, they may acquire a more conscious awareness of distinct sounds in their language and begin to manipulate their language through this conscious awareness known as phonological awareness. Phonological aware-ness serves as a basis for children to acquire knowledge of **phonics**, which involves learning how alphabetic symbols, letters are used to represent the specific sounds in words used in written language (Eldredge, 2004). This is demonstrated when a second-grade child describes why the initial sounds in *phone* and *paper* are dif-ferent, even though both words start with the letter *p*. Figure 1.4 illustrates the

TABLE 1.2
Levels of Language Knowledge

Level	Definition	Typical Age of First Evidence	Example
I. Linguistic Knowledge	Knowledge of how to use language to communicate	Toddlers and preschoolers	Beginning to use language effectively to communicate needs and intents
II. Metalinguistic Knowledge	Conscious awareness of specific features of language	Preschool and kindergarten	Begins to focus on and manipulate specific sounds in rhyming games or to notice how alphabet letters represent sounds; "Oh, there's a *J*. That's my name, Jon."
III. Verbalization of Metalinguistic Knowledge	Can verbally respond to questions about specific language features	Late kindergarten and primary	Can explain how *cup* and *pup* sound alike

FIGURE 1.4
Developmental Progression of Three Levels of Language Knowledge

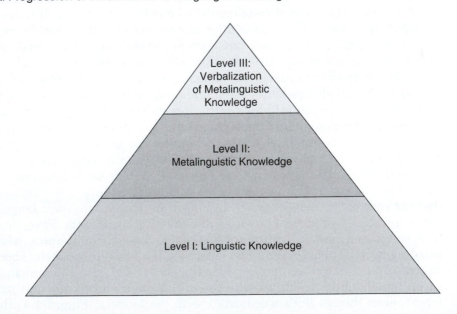

developmental progression of the three levels of language knowledge, beginning with linguistic knowledge as a basis, and continuing on to metalinguistic knowledge, and then to verbalization of metalinguistic knowledge.

ORAL AND WRITTEN LANGUAGE MODES

To become an effective communicator in a literate culture, a child must acquire competencies in using both oral language and written language. Oral language and written language both have receptive and expressive modes. Listening and reading are receptive in nature—receiving and comprehending a message created by another orally (i.e., listening) or in written language (i.e., reading). On the other hand, speaking and writing are expressive in nature. In early childhood and elementary curricula, significant emphasis is placed on providing learning activities that focus on developing children's competencies in these four areas. Table 1.3 provides an overview of these modes and forms of language competencies.

Oral language provides the basis on which knowledge of written language is acquired. As children interact in environments where written language is used to communicate, they acquire knowledge and awareness of how written language is similar to and different from oral language. Written language is not just oral language written down (Purcell-Gates, 1989). Written language uses different vocabulary and a more complex word order or syntax (Chafe, 1982; Purcell-Gates, 1989; Tannen, 1982). In addition, written language must convey meaning through the printed message because it carries the meaning without gesture, facial expression, or immediate contextual situations. For example, when you tell a story orally, you can use gestures, posture, facial expressions, and variations in your intonation to fully communicate your story. For a more formal storytelling event, you might even dress in costume or have story props or puppets. In contrast, a written story relies on only the printed word to communicate the meaning—by the words used, their meaning, the grammatical and morphemic structures, and the pragmatic expectations for a particular genre of story—all of which are communicated through written language.

Awareness and knowledge of the specific ways in which written language works is acquired in each of the five aspects of language: phonological, semantic, syntactic, morphemic, and pragmatic. To be effective communicators, children need to acquire linguistic knowledge in each of the five aspects of language in both oral and written forms of language. Oral language is acquired prior to written language

---

TABLE 1.3

Modes and Forms of Language Competencies

Mode/Form	Receptive	Expressive
Oral language	Listening	Speaking
Written language	Reading	Writing

TABLE 1.4

Comparison of Aspects of Oral and Written Language Knowledge

Aspect of Language	Oral Language	Written Language
Phonological	Sound–symbol system; phoneme-based	Combined oral symbol–graphic system; alphabetic encoding
Semantic	Oral word use accompanied by gesture, facial expression, and intonation	Visual/graphic words; more precise vocabulary since written words are read/decoded without gestures, facial expression, or intonation
Syntactic	Phrase and sentence structure/grammar	Sentence and text structure grammar; more complex than oral language
Morphemic	Inflections and word structure tied to oral pronunciation	Word structure; also adds meaning to words; more critical in written language since meaning of message is carried by the print
Pragmatic	Language used differently in various face-to-face interactions; involves all aspects of language knowledge	Language used differently in various text-based settings; influences writer's assumptions about audience and reader's expectations about text

knowledge; however, as written language knowledge is acquired, oral language continues to develop further; it is refined and elaborated with experiences that involve written language. A summary of the differences between oral language and written language in each of the five aspects of language knowledge is presented in Table 1.4.

CRITICAL ROLE OF CHILDREN'S ORAL LANGUAGE COMPETENCIES

In our classrooms, children who are fluent in oral language are more successful learners than those who are not (Fey, Catts, & Larrivee, 1995). As they learn to read and write, children use their oral language knowledge as a basis for this new knowledge of the written language system when they begin to focus on the features and concepts of written language. Children who are fluent in oral language can communicate their ideas and ask questions during learning activities. In addition, children's oral language competencies influence their development of literacy because reading and writing both involve processing and manipulating language. The basic oral language abilities that are related to subsequent literacy development include vocabulary, syntactic production and comprehension, phonological awareness, and narrative production and awareness (Loban, 1976; Wells, 1986; Windsor, 1995).

Children's oral language competencies develop in both receptive and expressive modes. Listening is a critical receptive language skill because listening is necessary to "receive language." Listening is not a passive activity. Instead, to be effective, listening must be active and purposeful. At school, children spend much of their time listening to their teachers or to their classmates. Their ability to listen and understand their teacher's directions and instruction and the contributions by their classmates influences what and how much is learned; however, explicit attention to developing listening competencies may be absent in many classrooms (Wolvin & Coakley, 1985).

The ways in which children use language to serve different purposes or functions have also been found to predict later language skills. In a longitudinal study, Wells (1986) identified two oral language characteristics that were effective in predicting children's subsequent overall achievement. For 2-year-olds, the use of a range of functions for speech was identified as a predictor of later achievement. For 3½-year-olds, the effective predictor of later achievement was the children's competent use of a range of different sentence types.

Another aspect of school success related to oral language competencies is a child's social-interaction skills (Windsor, 1995). Children who have oral language competencies will be more successful in communicating with both teachers and peers. Their success in carrying on conversations and in responding in learning activities will contribute to further success at school. Children who have difficulty communicating may be ignored by peers or excluded from informal social or collaborative interactions. The inability to participate successfully in a conversation or the inability to clearly articulate the sounds in words may decrease the likelihood that other children will attempt to speak or play with them.

In the section that follows, several research studies will be highlighted to illustrate the importance of oral language development to written language development and the complex ways the two forms of language are interrelated.

Insights from Research on Oral and Written Language

A longitudinal study of oral language development. In an extensive, longitudinal, descriptive study of language development, Loban (1976) followed 211 children from kindergarten through 12th grade. Each year, every child was studied with respect to reading, writing, listening, and other language-related behaviors. After the initial data collection, three subgroups were formed: a high-language-ability group, a low-language-ability group, and a random group representing the total group. Due to the prohibitive constraints on time and money in analyzing this large data collection for the detailed analysis, Loban selected a random subsample of each of the ability groups, along with the initial random (representative) subgroup. Loban's analysis of this random subsample concluded that the children identified as having high language ability in kindergarten were those who consistently exhibited higher

Children's ability to listen and understand their teacher's directions and instruction influences what and how much is learned.

language competencies throughout the 13 years. These specific language behaviors included:

- greater ability and flexibility in the ways in which they expressed their ideas and engaged in conversation
- higher reading and writing competencies
- more extensive vocabularies
- more complex sentences, paragraphs, or both
- more effective listening competencies

Loban's study is significant for the depth of data collected and for the length of time studied. His research documented the importance of oral language ability in kindergarten as a precursor to later competencies in areas of oral and written language with respect to semantic, syntactic, and pragmatic knowledge.

Loban's landmark study was followed by continued exploration of the role of oral language development in children's development of written language and general school performance (Bowey & Patel, 1988; Clay, 1991; Crane-Thoreson & Dale, 1992; Dyson, 1981; Egan, 1996; Fey, Catts, & Larrivee, 1995; Scarborough, 1990; Snow & Ninio, 1986; Sulzby, 1986b).

Additional evidence of the significant role of oral language in the development of literacy comes from the field of emergent literacy research. Since the early 1980s, researchers have focused on the gradual emergence of literacy-related behaviors and competencies. This emergent literacy perspective examines how children acquire knowledge of reading and writing in their daily, informal encounters with written language.

A study of children's early writing. Dyson (1981) closely observed kindergarten children as they interacted in a writing center she had introduced to the classroom. Dyson documented the following ways in which oral language played a significant role in children's early writing:

- Children were observed using talk as they started to write, while they were in the process of writing, and then as a way of explaining or expanding on what they had written.
- Oral language was also used to solicit help from a nearby adult.
- During the process of creating their written messages, children also reread frequently as a way of monitoring what they had written and what part of their message they had yet to put on paper.

In Dyson's study, children used oral language (talk) to guide and facilitate the creation of their written stories. They used oral language as a tool in conjunction with written language to create stories. In addition to using oral language in the process of producing written language, young children are also developing their ability to use language differently in different settings.

Research on children's use of language in literacy-related settings. Sulzby's research (1986b) explored children's use of language in interview settings, story dictation, storytelling, and rereading of their own handwritten compositions. Her research documented the ways children use language differently in those varied settings. She also reported that children appear to be exploring the ways oral language and written language differ. Sulzby noted that some children put written features into their speech, inserted oral language features into their written language, or both. Sulzby (1991a) concluded that young children acquire written language alongside oral language and further stated that oral and written language are interrelated and intertwined in dynamic ways during the developmental process.

A study of children's oral and written narratives. Research by Purcell-Gates (1989) documented children's use of different registers. She concluded that children use language differently in oral narrative than they do in written narrative. Children demonstrated that they "implicitly understood that written narrative is more integrative, involving, literary (stylistically) and decontextualized than oral narrative" (p. 291). Purcell-Gates concluded that children know that the vocabulary and sentence structure of books have a different quality than oral speech. She also noted that children continue to use this knowledge as they become involved in reading and writing.

A longitudinal study of low-income children. Snow, Tabors, and Dickinson (2001) studied low-income, English-speaking children from preschool age through high school in their "School–Home Study of Language and Literacy Development." They concluded that children's receptive vocabulary knowledge in kindergarten was strongly correlated to the children's scores both 5 and 8 years later on specific literacy skills in the areas of receptive vocabulary and reading comprehension. These researchers cautioned that this relation did not predict student achievement without exception. Rather, how children scored in kindergarten indicated how they might score in elementary school and junior high. Other factors that occurred during those years, such as literacy-related experiences at home and at school, appeared to influence how the children actually scored in later years (Tabors, Snow, & Dickinson, 2001).

Research implications. In addition to documenting the importance of oral language development in children, these key research studies have further contributed to our understanding that young children are actively acquiring written language knowledge as their oral language knowledge continues to develop during their early childhood years. Throughout this text, additional research is presented to illustrate the ways in which language develops throughout the early childhood years.

SUMMARY

Children's development of language has been a source of fascination for centuries. Gradually, and without formal instruction, children learn how to communicate. They learn how to express meaning through the use of spoken symbols and through using those symbols (words) in a systematic or structured way.

Language is acquired through knowledge and awareness of the phonological, semantic, syntactic, morphemic, and pragmatic aspects of both oral and written language. Children who are in environments where oral language and written language are used in meaningful ways will gradually acquire competencies in using language to communicate and to solve problems. Knowledge and awareness of each aspect of language knowledge contribute to a child's effectiveness in communicating in both home and school settings. This knowledge and awareness also forms the basis for continued language and literacy development. The development of each of these five aspects of language awareness and knowledge will be explored in future chapters in this text.

✳ ✳ ✳   CHAPTER REVIEW

1. Key terms to review:

receptive language	phoneme	semantic knowledge
expressive language	phonological awareness	schemata
phonological knowledge		syntactic knowledge
	prosodic features	syntax

morphemic knowledge	inflectional morpheme	linguistic level
morpheme	overgeneralizations	metalinguistic level
bound morpheme	pragmatic knowledge	metalinguistic verbalization
free morpheme	register	phonics
derivational morpheme	genderlect	

2. In what ways is language essential to all societies and cultures?

3. How do prosodic features in speech contribute to both phonological and semantic knowledge?

4. When a young child overgeneralizes, what could this tell you about his morphemic knowledge?

5. How are oral language competencies related to the development of literacy? Give examples to support your answer.

✳ ✳ ✳ CHAPTER EXTENSION ACTIVITIES

Observation

1. Observe a group story time in a preschool or kindergarten classroom. Identify examples from the interaction that involve one or more of the five aspects of language knowledge.

2. Observe a kindergarten classroom and describe how the language arts (speaking, listening, reading, and writing) are encouraged by the curricular activities and by the learning resources in the classroom.

3. Observe a first-grade reading lesson. Identify the level(s) of language knowledge encouraged by the reading lesson. Give examples to support your conclusions.

For Research

Using the Internet, locate a professional journal article on preschool, kindergarten, or elementary-aged children on one of the following topics: phonemic awareness, metalinguistic knowledge, and speech and gender roles. Write a summary of the main points of the article. Indicate how the article relates to specific concepts presented in this chapter. Include a copy of the article with your paper.

CHAPTER 2

THEORETICAL PERSPECTIVES AND CONTEXTS OF LANGUAGE DEVELOPMENT

Learning Outcomes

After reading this chapter you should be able to

- Describe four theoretical perspectives of language development
- Explain the brain's role in language development
- Identify and define the seven patterns of interaction
- Explain the role of home environments on language development

Mrs. Frank's preschool classroom was buzzing with the children's talk as they first came into her room. Sarah and Maria were talking about the new doll that Maria had brought in for show-and-tell. Seth, Juan, and Thomas were at the window, talking about the construction equipment that had just passed on the street. The twins, Barton and Jeremy, were asking Mrs. Frank about the new gerbil that was in the pet corner.

The children in Mrs. Frank's classroom provide dramatic evidence of their developing language competencies. The process of language development has intrigued researchers, educators, and parents for decades. How do children learn to talk? How do they learn to participate in conversations? In response to these questions, scholars and researchers have developed theories or sets of interrelated and coherent ideas that explain and make predictions about language development (Santrock, 2001).

LEARNING TO COMMUNICATE: THEORETICAL PERSPECTIVES

During the past 50 years, many linguists and developmental psychologists have studied language development with respect to what is learned, when it is learned, and what variables or factors seem to explain the process of development. These scholars and researchers have documented the amazing complexity of language and the remarkable ability of young children to develop language competencies, regardless of the culture in which they live and the language used at home.

In the field of child study, there has been a long-standing debate about the roles of nature and nurture in influencing an individual's development (Karmiloff & Karmiloff-Smith, 2001; Santrock, 2001). This debate has also been evident in the development of theoretical perspectives on language development. Is a child a "blank slate" at birth, and do the experiences or "nurture" provided in the environment predominantly determine language development? Or is the child already "preprogrammed" for language development in such a way that heredity and maturation are the major influences, with experience and context exerting only limited influence? Several different perspectives have been proposed as theoretical bases for more fully understanding language development. These perspectives have varied in the ways they believe nature and nurture influence language development.

In the first part of this chapter, four theoretical perspectives will be described: nativist, cognitive developmental, behaviorist, and interactionist. While no one theory provides a complete and irrefutable explanation of language development, each theory contributes significant ideas and concepts, which over time have clarified our awareness of the ways language develops. A comprehensive theory of language development would need to consider linguistic complexities and address each of the five aspects of language knowledge. Because the study of languages has occurred concurrently with the emergence of specific theories of language development, earlier theoretical perspectives may not incorporate more recently described linguistic concepts.

While each of the perspectives focuses on the roles of nature and nurture as well as the development of specific language knowledge, there is considerable variation between the theories. The nativist and the cognitive developmentalist perspectives emphasize the contributions of "nature," whereas the behaviorist and interactionist perspectives focus more on the contributions of "nurture." By understanding the contributions of each theory, teachers will better understand the process of language development and will be better able to facilitate language development in their classrooms. (See the summary chart in Table 2.1.)

The discussion of theoretical perspectives is followed by a section on the relation between brain development and language development. In each theoretical perspective, the human brain has a significant role because it is through the brain that stimuli or phenomena are experienced and responses are formed and expressed. The final section of this chapter focuses on the ways in which the contexts of home and school nurture language development and describes specific patterns of interaction that enhance the development of language competencies.

TABLE 2.1
Summary of Theoretical Perspectives of Language Acquisition

Theory	Focus on Nature v. Nurture	Major Theorist(s)
Nativist	Nature	Pinker, Chomsky
Cognitive Developmentalist	Nature	Piaget
Behaviorist	Nurture	Skinner
Interactionist	Nurture	Vygotsky Bruner Halliday

Nativist Perspective

The nativist perspective emphasizes inborn or innate human capabilities (i.e., "nature") as being responsible for language development. Linguist Noam Chomsky and Steven Pinker are the major theorists associated with the nativist perspective.

Chomsky's contributions to our understanding of the acquisition and structure of language have been significant (1965, 1975, 2002; Pinker, 1994). Chomsky contends that all people inherently have the capacity to acquire language due to cognitive structures that process language differently from other stimuli.

A major focus of Chomsky's work has involved identifying grammatical aspects of language and describing the rule systems for using language. Chomsky has defined this rule system, or **universal grammar**, as "the system of principles, conditions, and rules that are elements or properties of all human languages" (1975, p. 29). Semantic knowledge is also considered with respect to its relation to syntax. An example of how different languages structure the same message is shown in Figure 2.1.

Chomsky proposes that this universal grammar is an innate property of the human mind. This component explains the ability of all humans to learn their culture's specific language. The ability to learn language is a quality of the human species because humans obviously are not designed to acquire one language over another. Healthy infants are able "to learn any of the world's 3,000 languages" (Rushton, Eitelgeorge, & Zickafoose, 2003, p. 13). Chomsky's description of the high level of grammatical complexity acquired by young children has contributed to our understanding of the significance of language development among people of diverse language environments.

How, then do children learn a language? Chomsky's description of this process involves an inborn, language-specific mechanism called a **language acquisition device (LAD)** (Chomsky, 1982; Harris, 1992). The LAD enables children to process and acquire language through innate knowledge of grammatical classes, underlying deep structure, and ways in which language can be manipulated.

FIGURE 2.1

Example of Sentence Structures in Different Languages Communicating the Same Message

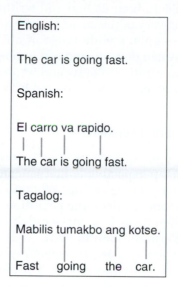

Building on Chomsky's work, Steven Pinker (1994) contended that language is an instinct, not simply a cultural invention: "Language is a biological adaptation to communicate information . . . language is the product of a well-engineered biological instinct" (p. 19). As evidence of the universality and instinctive nature of language, Pinker noted that throughout history, all civilizations, even among primitive societies, have a language. While languages may differ dramatically with respect to linguistic features, the development and use of language in all cultures is universal. Because language exists in every culture, Pinker concluded that it must come from human biological instinct rather than from the existence of the culture. Children are not taught language; rather, "children actually reinvent it, generation after generation" (Pinker, 1994, p. 32). Children are active participants in their language development. In a sense, children teach themselves language. Through the acquisition process, children construct their knowledge of the ways language is used and manipulated. This process is sometimes referred to as **hypothesis testing**. Children test their hypotheses or sets of assumptions of how language is spoken, articulated, used, and manipulated.

In summary, the nativist perspective describes language development as an innate, instinctual process where children develop language by discovering the structure of their language (Cairns, 1996). This discovery process is thought to be aided by an inborn mechanism that is specific for language learning.

Implications of the nativist perspective for early childhood classrooms.   The nativist perspective encourages teachers to use a curriculum that will provide extensive opportunities for children to explore language and engage in hypothesis testing of their developing knowledge of language. By having opportunities to use and explore language in both its oral and written forms, a child's LAD is activated, resulting in his discovery of the structure of his language (syntactic and morphemic knowledge). For example, a wide range of children's literature should be read to children so that they can develop and test hypotheses about how language is used to communicate. Opportunities to draw and write encourage children to communicate and create meaning based on their ideas of how language works.

Cognitive Developmental Perspective

The cognitive developmental perspective is based on the work of Jean Piaget (1955). The emphasis of this perspective is that language is acquired as maturation occurs and cognitive competencies develop. Whereas the nativist perspective emphasizes the inborn language mechanism, the cognitive developmental perspective assumes that cognitive development is a "prerequisite and foundation for language learning" (Karmiloff & Karmiloff-Smith, 2001, p. 5). This perspective also proposes that a child learns language by using the same mechanisms as for other learning. Thus, there is no unique language mechanism. The close relation between cognitive development and language is based on the belief that, for language to develop, specific cognitive growth must occur first.

In the first stage of cognitive development, the sensorimotor stage, children are prelinguistic. According to Piaget, children's understanding of the environment comes only through their immediate direct (sensory) experiences and their motor (movement) activities. An important precursor to the onset of language is the development of object permanence. **Object permanence** involves an awareness that an object continues to exist even when it is out of sight. Further, when the object reappears, it is the same object and has the same properties as before. It is through sensorimotor experiences in infancy that children develop the cognitive ability to understand object permanence. According to Piaget, language appears when children's cognitive growth reaches a point where they use and manipulate symbols (Piaget, 1962, in Paciorek & Munro, 1999). After object permanence is acquired, children begin to use symbols such as words to refer to objects and actions (Santrock, 2001; Sinclair-deZwart, 1969).

Piaget's definition of *language* is narrower than that of other psychologists or linguists. For "language" to exist, Piaget contended, the "capacity for mental representation must be present" (Brainerd, 1978, p. 110). Thus, vocalizations and babbling that occur during infancy are not language, according to Piaget. The development of symbolic representation changes a child's thinking because it is now possible to "invoke objects which are not present perceptually . . . reconstruct the past . . . or make plans for the future" (Piaget, 1961, in Paciorek & Munro, 1999, p. 7).

Symbolic representation is evident when a child uses signs and symbols in response to a new situation, whereas earlier the child would have used trial and error to deal with the situation (Atkinson, 1983). For example, if a child is presented with a new box to open that differs slightly from previous boxes with which the child has played, symbolic representation is evident when instead of simply using trial and error to find a way to open the box, the child appears to use her prior experiences in a symbolic way in "thinking out" a solution to the task before manipulating the box.

At about the age of 1 year, some children begin to represent actions and objects mentally and symbolically. During this time, relations between actions and objects develop and are organized into abstract cognitive structures called **schemata** (Brainerd, 1978). One of the distinguishing features of concepts and schemata is that they reflect experience broader than that of the individual person. This means that concepts and schemata develop from interpersonal interaction and communication. This communication relies on "signs" (Piaget, 1962). Piaget contended that the development of verbal signs or words facilitates cognitive development because it makes possible "the transformation of sensory motor schemas into concepts" (1962, p. 99).

According to Piaget, the second stage of cognitive development is the **preoperational stage**. This stage begins at about 2 years of age and extends to about 7 years of age. Children in this stage "begin to represent the world with words, images, and drawings" (Santrock, 2001, p. 36). Piaget (1955) considered children's initial speech to be egocentric, focused on their own perceptions, which may reflect distorted perceptions or relations. Gradually, as children develop cognitively, their speech becomes socialized, or reflective of more logical thinking.

Because the cognitive developmentalist perspective focuses on the development of schemata and the manipulation of symbols, it contributes to our understanding of how semantic, syntactic, and morphemic knowledge are acquired.

Implications of the cognitive developmental perspective for early childhood classrooms. The cognitive developmental perspective encourages teachers to pay close attention to a child's stage of cognitive development and use that knowledge to appropriately plan learning activities. For example, teachers would implement a curriculum that recognizes the importance of the development of specific cognitive mechanisms as precursors to the onset of language, such as object permanence and symbolic representation. Curricula in infant and toddler centers would have many varied opportunities for very young children to engage in sensorimotor activities. Many opportunities to engage in symbol making and symbol manipulation would also be provided, so children would have activities that encourage them to represent their world using oral and written symbols through speaking, drawing, and writing.

Behaviorist Perspective

The behaviorist perspective emphasizes the role of "nurture" and considers learning to occur based on the stimuli, responses, and reinforcements that occur in the environment. A child is considered to be a "blank slate" (Karmiloff & Karmiloff-Smith, 2001), and learning occurs due to associations established between stimuli, responses, and events that occur after the response behavior. Language is learned as a result of these associations. Reinforcement of a child's verbal and nonverbal responses to language directed at him is responsible for the language learning that occurs. Thus, language is "taught" through situations in which children are encouraged to imitate others' speech and to develop associations between verbal stimuli (i.e., words) and objects (Harris, 1992). Complex speech, such as phrases and sentences produced by a child, is considered evidence that a chain of speech units has been reinforced (Cairns, 1996). Reinforcement often takes the form of attention, repetition, and approval (Puckett & Black, 2001). This type of conditioning (or learning) is called *operant conditioning* (Skinner, 1957). The use of the word *operant* acknowledges the child's active role in the learning process. This type of learning occurs when environmental consequences occur that are contingent on the specific behavior. When a certain behavior is followed by a particular result, that consequence influences whether the behavior will be repeated. This perspective has been used to explain productive speech (Bohannon & Bonvillian, 1997).

For example, when an infant is making sounds while in the presence of a parent and says "ma-ma," the parent may rush to the infant, show signs of delight, and say, "Oh, you said 'ma-ma'!" This positive response from the parent increases the chances that the infant will repeat those sounds. Likewise, speech that elicits no response or is ignored is less likely to be repeated.

Operant conditioning also explains the process of imitation because children's attempts at imitating adult speech are often followed by reinforcement from the communicative environment in which the child is interacting. **Imitative speech** involves the production of speech that approximates the speech of another person. Imitation may occur as a result of direct modeling, such as when an adult tells a child, "Now say 'bye-bye'," and the child responds with an immediate attempt to repeat the specific word(s). Or, it may occur as a result of delayed modeling, when the child approximates previously modeled speech in a similar setting without being prompted. In other instances, imitative speech may occur without the models' awareness that their speech was being learned. A child who hears his parent utter an expletive on accidentally hitting a finger with a hammer or spilling a cup of tea may surprise his parent by using the same word (and intonation) in a similar situation in the child's dramatic play.

Many types of environmental responses serve as reinforcers. Positive reinforcement may come from the excited response of parents to their child's verbal attempts. It may also come from the success of communication to express a want or need. A child who is thirsty and can say "drink" in a way that results in being given a drink is positively reinforced for that attempt. When adults are teaching a child to say "bye-bye," the child's attempts are often followed by positive reinforcement such as a hug, an embrace, or verbal praise.

While the behaviorist perspective does explain how some words and phrases are learned, it does not provide a complete explanation for the development of other language competencies. Specifically, the behaviorist perspective does not explain how children learn to express novel utterances (Harris, 1992), such as their own invented words or phrases that have not been used by the other speakers in their environment.

Using the contributions of behaviorism as a basis, researchers are no longer simply focusing on identifying the stimuli, responses, and reinforcing contingencies that occur in linguistic interactions. Instead, researchers are exploring the dynamic processes that occur in various contexts that support language development where children are actively involved in constructing their knowledge of language. Recent research that has explored the context of young children's language development has identified specific ways in which different contexts and the people in those contexts interact with children who are acquiring language and learning to communicate. This research will be further described in the subsequent section on the interactionist perspective.

Implications of the behaviorist perspective for early childhood classrooms. Teachers who follow a behaviorist perspective would focus on the stimuli and reinforcements that children experience in regard to language use. Activities would be provided that encourage children to communicate verbally through imitation and repetition. Positive reinforcements using attention and approval would be given to encourage children to interact using language. When teaching finger plays and action songs, the focus would be on using repetition, imitation, and positive reinforcement. A teacher's enthusiasm and praise for children's efforts in learning the finger play or action songs would provide further reinforcement.

Interactionist Perspective

The interactionist perspective focuses on the primary role of sociocultural interaction in children's development of language knowledge (Bruner, 1983, 1990; John-Steiner, Panofsky, & Smith, 1994; Schieffelin & Ochs, 1986; Vygotsky, 1978; Wertsch, 1991). This perspective contends that children acquire language through their attempts to communicate with the world around them. This perspective contributes to our understanding of the ways in which children acquire pragmatic language knowledge.

Language is acquired by individuals as they develop awareness of how to communicate and function in society (Halliday, 2007; Tomasello, 2000). The early work of Vygotsky emphasized the role of social interaction in language development (1962, 1978; John-Steiner et al., 1994). Vygotsky's basic premise was that language development is influenced by the society in which the individual lives: "higher mental functions are socially formed and culturally transmitted" (Vygotsky, 1978, p. 126). Speech has social origins. It develops in situations where people are interacting with each other in a communicative context. Tomasello (2000) emphasizes the role of joint attention (i.e., shared reference) as a key part of language develop-ment. As joint attention occurs, children learn they can engage others in communi-cating about ongoing events or entities in their environment.

Another aspect of the interactionist perspective is its focus on the language development *process* rather than on language as a *product* of development. In this way, the interactionist approach builds on each of the three prior perspectives of language development. Specifically, it acknowledges behaviorism's recognition of the environment's responses to young children's communicative attempts, nativ-ism's recognition of the human capacity for processing linguistic information, and the cognitive developmentalist's contention that language development is influ-enced by the nature and sequence of cognitive development.

Extensive research conducted by Bloom and Tinker (2001) has further added to this emphasis on language development and social interaction. In their study of young children between the ages of 9 months and 2 years, Bloom and Tinker found that children expended considerable effort in acquiring language. In recognizing the role of a child as an active learner of language, Bloom and Tinker proposed the Intentionality Model of language development, which has two components:

The interactionist perspective contends that children acquire language through their attempts to communciate with the world around them.

(a) children's active engagement with others as well as other aspects of their environment that provide motivation to develop language competencies and (b) the effort of the language learner in making sense of the "linguistic, emotional, and physical actions" present their environment (p. vii). This challenges earlier assumptions that language development is "natural" and does not require conscious effort. Instead, Bloom and Tinker describe the way in which very young children intentionally expend effort in associating speech sounds with meaning and then begin to use words and phrases. This intentionality for acquiring language also continues well beyond the toddler years as children develop more elaborate language competencies.

The primary role of social interaction in language development is based on the observation that children acquire an awareness of specific communicative functions or intentions (such as indicating, requesting, and labeling) before they are able to express themselves linguistically (Bruner, 1990). This can be seen in the joint attention and verbal turn taking that often occurs between prelinguistic infants and their parents and caregivers. These early understandings of how language functions then provide a foundation on which the linguistic competencies are acquired. The ways in which an environment supports children's language explorations have been referred to as the **language acquisition support system (LASS)** (Bruner, 1983). Environmental supports for language development are present in the interaction patterns found in conversations, such as listening, responding to what has been said, repeating for clarification, and asking questions.

Role of the adult in the interactionist perspective.   In the interactionist perspective, the role of adults in the communication process is crucial in supporting children's language development (Bruner, 1990; Vygotsky, 1978; Wertsch, 1991). Because the child is a novice communicator, an adult in the conversational dyad serves as the expert who often creates conditions that make for effective communication. The difference between what a child can accomplish alone and what she can accomplish with an adult's (or more capable peer's) mediation or assistance is termed the **zone of proximal development** (Vygotsky, 1978). What a child accomplishes independently is her **developmental level**.

For example, the zone of proximal development can be seen in situations in which an adult interprets or mediates a child's attempts at communicating. In this setting, the adult is providing a supportive scaffolding that gives a child opportunities to participate in a conversation. The child's communicative attempts are supported by additions or clarifications by the adult. Harris (1990) pointed out that the success of these scaffolded conversations depends on the adult's sensitivity to and interpretation of the child's communicative attempt. The most effective scaffolding promotes the highest level of functioning with the lowest level of support.

In the example that follows, a mother and her daughter are in a homemade tent in their backyard, which has been constructed of blankets draped over lawn chairs and a rope strung between a tree and a swing set. The daughter, Allison (age 2), has

The zone of proximal development refers to the difference between what a child can accomplish alone and what he can accomplish with an adult's (or more capable peer's) mediation or assistance.

been playing in the tent without her shoes on. Because it is April in the Midwest and a bit cool to be going barefoot, her mother decides it is time for Allison to put her shoes and socks back on. Her mother uses scaffolding to engage Allison in a rhyming song as she puts on Allison's shoes and socks. Not only does this distract Allison from protesting over putting on her shoes and socks, but it provides a way for Allison to learn more about a song that she had heard previously, enabling her to participate in re-creating the rhyming song.

Mother: *Allison, come here and get your socks and shoes on [draws Allison onto her lap, and begins to put her socks and shoes on].*

Allison: *[squirms, resisting] Don't.*

Mother: *Allison, want to sing? How about [begins to sing] Four little ducks went out to play [continues with shoes and socks throughout this singing] over the fields and far away. Mama Duck said, "Quack, quack, quack, quack" and only three little ducks came back. [pause] Three little ducks went out one day over the fields and far away. Mama Duck said [pause]*

Allison: *Quack, quack, quack.*

Mother: *How many ducks came back, Allison?*

Allison:	*One [singing tone] [holds up one finger]*
Mother:	*One. [pause] You sing it. [long pause] One little duck [pause] went out to play . . .*
Allison:	*[joins in, softly] Went out to play . . .*
Mother	
and	
Allison:	*Over the fields and far away . . .*
Allison:	*One little duck, quack, quack, quack . . .*
Mother:	*[nods head]*
Allison:	*One little duck [indecipherable] quack, quack [sings alone, with fingers up on one hand, looking at fingers], four little ducks, four little ducks [indecipherable], three little ducks, quack, quack, four little ducks [pause] four little ducks . . .*

Allison's shoes and socks are now on, and Allison becomes distracted by her 4-year-old sister, who is also playing in the backyard. Allison leaves her mom's lap, and the singing ends. Two minutes later, Allison is observed singing the duck song to herself as she walks in the backyard.

In this segment, the mother's scaffolding took the form of beginning the song and then pausing at predictable points in the song for Allison to participate. The mother verbally faded away when Allison began to sing and accepted Allison's version of the song. This type of linguistic support was effective in initially engaging and sustaining Allison in this routine. The observation of Allison repeating a version of the song to herself only moments later indicated that Allison was then able to sing the song on her own.

Not only does the concept of the zone of proximal development provide us with an idea of development to come, but it emphasizes the crucial role of adults in children's development of language. Adults serve as mediators who introduce children to higher levels of functioning within a supportive scaffolded setting. Psychologists have concluded that it is not possible for children to imitate something that is beyond their respective developmental levels. Thus, when a child such as Allison successfully incorporates some of the new behaviors (i.e., linguistic structures or vocabulary), it is not simply imitated behavior but a reflection of the developmental readiness of the child for acquiring more advanced language knowledge.

Cambourne's work and the role of the environment in facilitating oral language development. The role of the environment in supporting and facilitating children's language development has been further described by Cambourne (1988, 1995). He identified eight conditions that support oral language development: immersion, demonstration, engagement, expectations, responsibility, approximations, employment, and response. In each condition, specific environmental factors are present, along with "particular states of being (doing, behaving, creating)" (1995, p. 184). Cambourne describes these conditions as taking place concurrently and interactively, providing a context that facilitates oral language development (see Table 2.2 for a summary). These conditions are:

- *Immersion.* Young children are surrounded by language as it is used by others in their environment. Beginning at birth, children hear the conversations of their parents, siblings, and others in their environment. Children who are born deaf or who are raised in isolation do not experience this immersion in oral language, and thus their language development is impaired.

- *Demonstration.* As children are immersed in their home language, they see specific demonstrations of how language is used to communicate and how it is used differently in different settings (i.e., pragmatic language knowledge). For example, at the family dinner table, an oral request to pass a serving bowl of salad is likely followed by the response of passing the bowl to the person who requested it. This demonstrates how language can function to serve a particular purpose or meet a specific need.

- *Engagement.* Young children are encouraged to pay attention to the language interactions around them and to become involved in those interactions. When storybooks are shared with toddlers, the book sharing is dependent upon the interest and attention of the toddler. We know that selecting appropriate picture books and welcoming the toddler's questions and comments can actively engage the toddler in the book sharing.

- *Expectations.* Parents, family members, and others in a child's environment communicate to the young child the expectation that he or she will learn to talk. Adults and siblings directly address a young child in conversation-like interactions long before he or she can speak a word. The expectation that children will become "talkers" is very clearly communicated.

- *Responsibility.* Young language learners decide how they will respond to language demonstrations. In taking this initiative, a young child determines what message he wants to send and engages in sending that message. For example, while Mia was out for a walk with her 21½-year-old son, Josiah, she noticed a small black dog and its owner walking toward them. As they approached, Mia said to Josiah, "Look at the little doggie." Just as they met on the sidewalk and passed by, Josiah exclaimed, "No tail!" In this instance, Josiah had decided to comment on what was most important to him—that the little dog did not have a visible tail. Josiah's initiative in responding to his mother's utterance showed that he was active in deciding what aspect of the setting on which to comment.

- *Approximations.* When young children begin to speak, their attempts are approximations of adult words and pronunciations. This "baby talk" is enthusiastically received as "real talk" by parents and others, along with the expectation that these early forms of speech will eventually become more

TABLE 2.2
Cambourne's Conditions Supporting Oral Language Development

Condition	Description	Example
Immersion	Child is surrounded by language used by others.	At home, the child hears conversations of family members throughout the day.
Demonstration	Child witnesses how language is used by others for specific purposes.	At the family dinner table, the child hears a request to pass the salad and listens to a sibling tell about her day at school.
Engagement	Child is encouraged to participate in language interactions.	During storybook sharing, the child is encouraged to name the objects pictured in the book.
Expectations	Beginning in infancy, adults and siblings address child expecting a response.	At snack time, the parent asks the child if he wants a graham cracker or a cheese cracker and waits for the child to respond.
Responsibility	Child creates message in response to language of others.	When her mother says, "it's really chilly today," the child responds, "What does chilly mean?"
Approximations	Child's early forms of speech are accepted as "real communication" by others.	When the child is asked if he wants some juice, the child responds "ju-ju". This is accepted by the parent as "Yes, I want juice."
Employment	Child is given opportunities to "try out" his/her developing language competencies.	During a family mealtime, the child is encouraged to tell about his experiences while playing at the park earlier that day.
Response	Child receives feedback on their use of language to communicate.	While on a walk, the child sees a small, fluffy dog, and calls it a kitty. His mother says, "Oh, it's a small dog, not a kitty. See it does not have a long, fluffy tail like a kitten."

conventional. For example, Scotty, a toddler, referred to his sister Brianna as "Anna." As he progressed through the preschool years, his pronunciation went from Anna, to Banna, and then to Bianna. Finally, when he was in kindergarten, he had mastered the conventional pronunciation of her name, Brianna.

- *Employment.* Young children need to have opportunities to try out their developing language competencies—both with other people and when they are alone. Encouraging young children to participate in conversations at mealtime, while riding in a car, and during picture book sharing provides important opportunities to practice communicating with others. Children also seem to need times when they can talk to themselves, such as before falling asleep or when looking at picture books independently.

- *Response.* When young children are expressing themselves verbally, they need to receive feedback responses from significant people in their environment. This condition is present when a toddler uses an approximation for the word *cracker* and the adult responds by saying, "Oh, you want a cracker?" In this instance, the adult's response confirms the intent of the child's utterance as well as filling in the rest of the words that were implied.

Implications of the interactionist perspective for early childhood classrooms. The interactionist perspective encourages teachers to focus on providing many social interactions in which oral and written language are used. Many "talking" opportunities would be provided from infancy onward so that children can begin to understand the ways in which language functions. In providing these opportunities, the focus would also be on creating a positive emotional context for this communication that provides motivation for continued attempts to communicate with others. Throughout this text, the focus will be on the interactionist perspective. It provides a framework for understanding the complex ways children develop language competencies as they interact with people and objects in their environment. The interactionist perspective also acknowledges that "nature and nurture are inseparably intertwined" (Gopnik, Meltzoff, & Kuhl, 1999, p. 131).

THE BRAIN'S ROLE IN LANGUAGE DEVELOPMENT

This complex interaction between nature and nurture is clearly evident in research that centers on the brain's role in language development (Bergen & Coscia, 2001). In this section, the contributions of both nature and nurture will be explored in understanding the brain's role in language development. The field of research that has focused on the study of "language in the brain" is referred to as **neurolinguistics** (Obler & Gjerlow, 1999, p. xv). This research often incorporates anatomy, physiology, and biochemistry as these areas relate to language processing (Owens, 2001).

The human brain appears to be "prewired" for the development of language (Anderson & Lightfoot, 2002; Chomsky, 2002; Eliot, 1999; Obler & Gjerlow, 1999; Pinker, 1994). As specific regions of the human brain mature, language development occurs. This maturation begins in the womb as the fetus develops. This sets the stage for later complex development of the neural connections in the brain that are involved in receiving and producing language. In addition to brain maturation, a critical requirement for language development is that it needs to occur in environments where language is used in social interaction. In this way, both nature and nurture are involved in language development.

The brain and spinal cord compose the **central nervous system**. The spinal cord begins in the brain stem area and continues down the center of the back, protected by the bone structure of the spine. Communication of brain messages to the rest of the body takes place through the spinal cord and peripheral nervous system (Lamb, 1999; Obler & Gjerlow, 1999). The **peripheral nervous system** involves the nerve pathways that connect the spinal cord with all parts of the body. The peripheral nervous system carries out the actions signaled by the brain not only for language but for movement as well. The focus here will be on the structure of the brain cells along with the main areas of the brain and their relation to language development. (See Figure 2.2.)

FIGURE 2.2

Structure of the Outer Layer of the Left Hemisphere

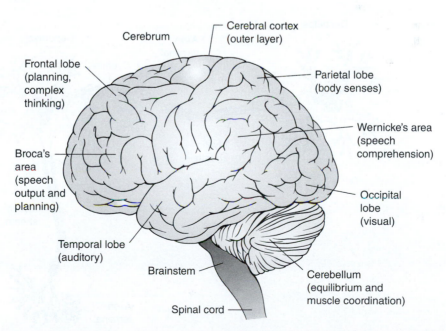

Complex Structure of Brain Cells

The nerve cells (also called **neurons**) in the brain are composed of three main parts: a cell body, axons, and dendrites. **Axons** carry information away from the cell and **dendrites** carry information to the cell body. Each axon is encased in a layer of fat cells called the **myelin sheath**. This protects the nerve cells and makes it possible for the nerve impulses to travel faster (Eliot, 1999). The end of the axon branches out like a tree branch. This branching area, called the **axon terminal**, connects to the dendrites of an adjacent cell body (Santrock, 2001). The area of interconnection between the axon terminal of one cell body and the dendrites of another cell body is called the **synapse** (Puckett & Black, 2001). During prenatal development and early childhood, there is rapid growth of these synapses. Infants' early experiences stimulate the formation of neural connections. In this sensorimotor period, the "sights, sounds, smells, touches, language, and eye contact help the brain connections to take place" (Santrock, 2001, p. 135). Figure 2.3 illustrates the structure of the neuron and synapse.

Main Areas of the Brain

The **cerebral cortex** is the outer layer of the cerebrum. It covers the brain like a cap and accounts for about 80% of the volume of the brain (Santrock, 2001). This area of the brain has a critical role in perception, thinking, and language. The **cerebellum**,

FIGURE 2.3
Structure of Neuron and Synapse

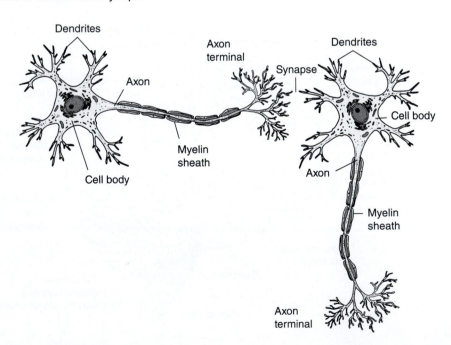

an area in the lower back region of the brain, is associated with movement and coordination (Wolfe, 2001). The cerebellum transmits signals to the muscles that control the various parts of the speech mechanism to produce speech sounds (Lamb, 1999). For example, for a person to speak, the brain must send messages to the lips, tongue, jaw, larynx, pharynx, muscles of the rib cage, and diaphragm to coordinate the production of speech sounds (see Figure 2.4). For a person to write, a message must be cognitively encoded in a writing system, and the muscles of the hand must be coordinated to produce the appropriate written symbols. Therefore, both the cerebral cortex and the cerebellum are involved in comprehending and producing language.

The brain is divided vertically into two sections called **hemispheres**. During the maturation and growth of the brain, each of the hemispheres develops certain cognitive functions. This process is called **lateralization**. Research with young infants has documented more brain activity in the left hemisphere than the right when the infant is listening to sounds of speech (Hahn, 1987, in Santrock, 2001). There is common agreement among neurolinguists that both speech and grammar functions are localized in the left hemisphere; however, neurolinguists also agree that both hemispheres are involved in the more complex forms of communication, such as the use of metaphor and humor, as well as pragmatic knowledge of language (Santrock, 2001).

FIGURE 2.4
The Speech Mechanism

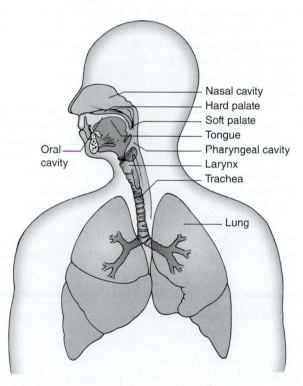

Areas of the Brain Associated with Language Production and Comprehension

The critical role of the brain in language is evident from studies of individuals who have experienced brain damage and subsequently lost specific language capabilities. This general loss of language is called **aphasia** (Obler & Gjerlow, 1999). Studies of children and adults who have experienced brain damage have identified specific areas of the brain associated with language competencies involved in receptive language, productive language, oral language, and written language (Obler & Gjerlow, 1999).

Early research by two neurologists, Paul Broca and Carl Wernicke, reported that damage to specific areas of the brain was associated with specific loss of language capabilities (Crystal, 1987). Broca's research on patients with brain damage in the mid-1800s found that the loss of speech production appeared to be the result of damage to the lower area of the left frontal lobe of the cerebrum. This area is now referred to as Broca's area, and damage to this area can result in a condition is referred to as **Broca's aphasia** (refer to Figure 2.2). Although speech production is slowed and grammatical structures are missing, there is not impairment in the comprehension of speech or in the ability to communicate in written language (Owens, 2001).

About that same time, another neurologist, Carl Wernicke, reported a different type of speech disorder that was associated with damage to a region of the brain in the area to the back and top of the temporal lobe. In this condition, the individual's fluency of speech is normal; however, comprehension and the ability to construct meaningful sentences are significantly impaired. Words that are phonemically similar but that have no semantic relation to what appears to be the message communicated may be substituted. For example, *wine* may be substituted for *why* (Obler & Gjerlow, 1999). This area of the brain is referred to as Wernicke's area, and the condition is referred to as **Wernicke's aphasia** (refer to Figure 2.2).

Additional research has used brain-imaging (metabolic and noninvasive) techniques as well as brain stimulation technology to further document the localization of language functions in the brain (Bergen & Coscia, 2001). Current research in neurolinguistics has also documented the complexity of the brain in language development, leading to the conclusion that the "whole brain contributes to the broad range of language abilities" (Obler & Gjerlow, 1999, p. 12); language abilities are not confined to the left hemisphere of the brain. The exact way the brain mediates between thoughts and linguistic expression is not completely understood. In addition, recent research has documented differences between individuals in how language is localized in specific brain areas (Anderson & Lightfoot, 2002).

The next section will focus on specific interaction patterns occurring at home, in the community, and at school that influence language development.

CONTEXTS OF LANGUAGE DEVELOPMENT

Home, community, and school are the environments in which children's language develops. The important role of social and cultural contexts for language development is the focus of the interactionist perspective discussed earlier in this chapter.

Language is acquired in a social setting; it cannot be acquired in a solitary setting. A language learner must have interaction with another person who is a language user.

By understanding the types of contexts and interaction patterns in which children experience language, teachers are better able to establish classroom settings that foster language development. First, we will consider specific patterns of adult–child interaction. Then we will examine specific features of home, school, and community environments that influence language development. The final section of the chapter provides an overview of the role of teachers in establishing and maintaining contexts that foster language development.

Patterns of Interaction: Overview

In this section, several specific patterns of adult–child interaction will be described. Each of these patterns plays a role in enhancing language development. Each pattern is present in some manner throughout early childhood. Each pattern may be modified in some way to respond to the developmental level of each child, but the characteristic nature of each pattern of interaction is maintained. (See Figure 2.5.)

Eye contact and shared reference. We begin communicating with children through establishing eye contact and **shared reference**. This is a basic interaction pattern (Tronick, Als, & Adamson, 1979). Eye contact is established between an adult and a child and involves jointly focusing on an object or event. Through eye contact and shared reference, objects and events are contemplated and become subjects of conversation. When eye contact and shared reference are not established, communication often breaks down or is not even initiated as there is no clear common focus.

Eye contact is usually established by an adult first looking directly at a child and gesturing (pointing) or speaking a short, attention-getting phrase, such as "Look." It is important for the adult to be close to the child and position herself so that the child can look directly into her eyes (Manolson, 1992). Sometimes the adult touches the child briefly on the shoulder or arm to get his attention. If eye contact and shared reference are not established, the attention-getting phrase and gesture may be repeated. If repeated attempts are not successful, then the interaction may be discontinued as the child may not be interested or sufficiently alert to engage in the shared activity. When this routine has been repeated successfully with infants (6–12 months of age) over time, they begin to respond to the verbal phrase or word by looking at the speaker and then to the location signaled by the adult's gesture. After shared reference is established, communication about the object or event occurs.

Early interactions with children are more individualized, so that eye contact and shared reference with infants and toddlers occur with one child at a time. When classroom activities involve multiple children at one time (such as in preschool, kindergarten, or primary rooms), teachers establish eye contact and shared reference

FIGURE 2.5
Patterns of Interaction-Overview

- Eye contact and
  shared reference
- Communication loop
- Child-directed speech
- Verbal mapping
- Questioning
- Linguistic scaffolding
- Mediation

with several children for a single activity. As teachers interact with more than one child at a time, they spend more time establishing eye contact and shared reference. Though the technique is similar to the one described for infants, the attention-getting language used with toddlers and older children will gradually become more complex and elaborate. Children who do not participate in these contexts of shared reference often lose out on the communication and thus the instruction.

Maintaining shared reference may require constant monitoring and verbal interaction to keep a child focused on the desired object or event. Animated speech or speech with varied intonations and gestures is often effective in maintaining a child's attention. For example, when sharing a storybook with an infant or a toddler, a parent may use animated speech, sound effects, and gestures to maintain the child's attention.

Communication loop.　All patterns of interaction are characterized by a **communication loop**, a circular or cycle-like sharing and exchanging of the roles of speaker and listener (see Figure 2.6). The loop begins with a speaker initiating conversation and continues to a listener, who then becomes a speaker while the first speaker listens. Thus, a conversation may continue through many turns, during which time topics of conversation may be introduced, elaborated, or changed. The communication loop is severed whenever one of the participants fails to continue participating, either by not listening to the speaker or not responding as a speaker. With infants, a communication loop is first initiated through eye contact and shared reference. Rather than a verbal response from the child, the child's eye contact and focus of shared reference serve as active responses in this communication loop. This communication loop can also be thought of as a continuously spiraling loop that changes or develops as the conversation develops because the participation by both as speakers and listeners influence the ongoing interaction.

The notion of a communication loop is also described in Bruner's (1978, 1983) language acquisition support system (LASS). The communication loop is a routinized, repeated interaction between a child and an adult. In this interaction, a series of turns defines the context and creates a structure for further negotiation or clarification of the meaning of actions or objects in the environment. Initially the adult does most of the work in sustaining the interaction. As a child's ability to participate develops, the child assumes more control over the interaction.

FIGURE 2.6
Communication Loop

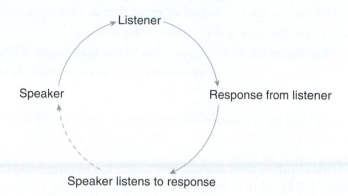

For example, in the following conversation between a teacher and a preschool child, the teacher and child take turns talking first about the child's new snow boots and then moving on to talk about playing in the snow. As the conversation continues, the child initiates a change in the conversation topic with her questions about playing outside and making snow angels.

> *Child:*   *I wore my new snowboots.*
> *Teacher:*   *Yes, those are bright pink snowboots.*
> *Child:*   *I can walk in snow.*
> *Teacher:*   *Yes, because your snowboots will keep your feet warm and dry.*
> *Child:*   *Can we play outside?*
> *Teacher:*   *Yes, we will go outside after snack. What would you like to do outside?*
> *Child:*   *Make angels. Can you make angels?*

Child-directed speech.   The specific language that adults use with young children is also distinctive and serves to enhance language development. This specific language has been termed **child-directed speech (CDS)**.

In a review of research, Pine (1994) identified eight characteristics of speech directed toward children. Because this speech is often in the form of phrases or single words, it is referred to here as "utterances" rather than sentences. When compared to adult-to-adult speech, speech utterances typically addressed to young children are characterized by the following:

1. Utterances are short and well formed.
2. Utterances have fewer false starts than adult-to-adult speech.

3. Utterances are not syntactically complex.

4. Utterances have a higher pitch and intonation is more exaggerated.

5. Utterances are redundant or repetitive in part or in whole.

6. Utterances have a slower rate or tempo.

7. Utterances are more closely tied to the immediate context.

8. Utterances have discourse features that encourage children to participate and to clarify the child's responses.

Researchers have debated whether the existence and use of CDS is a conscious vehicle for "teaching" language or whether it is an intuitive response by adults (or other fluent, though younger, language users) when they are attempting to communicate with children who are just beginning to communicate (Newport, Gleitman, & Gleitman, 1977). This latter position is supported by the observation that speech resembling CDS is often used by English speakers when they attempt to communicate with non-English speakers or their pets (Pine, 1994). CDS has also been observed in settings where older siblings or children are attempting to communicate with younger children.

The role of CDS in language development may be a combination of both informal teaching and communicative necessity. Because these specific characteristics are successful in enhancing communication between fluent and novice or beginning speakers, CDS exposes a novice to aspects of the language and the act of communication that enhance the child's language development. When utterances are short and well formed, a child can process the utterances more efficiently, and a more accurate model utterance is provided to the young language learner. Utterances that have fewer false starts also provide a young child with better language models to facilitate comprehension. Utterances with many false starts would be confusing and impair communication. Utterances that are syntactically simple (few complex sentences and subordinate clauses) would also facilitate young children's linguistic processing.

Speech that has a higher pitch and more exaggerated intonation would hold children's attention more and enhance perception of speech sounds due to the wide variety of intonation. Utterances that are redundant, either in part or in whole, facilitate comprehension of meaning and context through the repetition of key aspects of the utterance. When speech directed to young children is at a slower pace or tempo, it allows for linguistic processing: it takes time to process speech cognitively. If you have ever been in a setting where you were a nonnative speaker, you may have wished that the native speakers would just speak more slowly.

Utterances that are more closely tied to the immediate context foster language development. When utterances refer to objects or people present in the immediate context, a young child can make a visible connection between the oral symbol and its actual referent.

Discourse features of CDS that encourage children's participation include questioning (see the following section) and conversational "rules" such as turn taking, active listening, and maintenance of eye contact. The presence of these features in CDS increases participation by children and furthers their language development.

Adults actively monitor the success of their speech to a young child and change their expectations for a child's responses as the child's levels of language competency increase. Some differences between the interaction styles of mothers and fathers have been noted (Barton & Tomasello, 1994). Mothers typically adjust their speech to young children to a greater extent and in more different ways than do fathers or older siblings. While initially this might seem to indicate that communication is less beneficial when fathers and older siblings are involved, young children's communicative competence might be enhanced in this type of setting, where they must respond or adapt to the communicative demands of others rather than having the style of communication always adapted to them.

Verbal mapping.   The verbal mapping pattern occurs when an adult verbally describes (not just names) an object or action in a level of detail appropriate to the developmental level of the child with whom the interaction is occurring. **Verbal mapping** employs language that fits the situation, providing the symbols for a child's subsequent representation of that event. In most cases, verbal mapping serves to orally identify the concepts being experienced. Shared reference and eye contact are essential for the effectiveness of verbal mapping. Verbal mapping is monologic in nature. The adult provides a verbal description of what is occurring or what is being experienced or seen. The mapping episode may be short, or it may be extended, depending on the situation and the child's attention to the adult's speech.

This pattern of interaction occurs with all ages of children and can enhance development of all five aspects of language knowledge: semantic, syntactic, phonetic, morphemic, and pragmatic. During infancy, verbal mapping provides a narrative to daily routines of dressing, eating, and exploring. At later developmental stages, verbal mapping is crucial during new experiences because it involves modeling, or showing how language is applied to those experiences.

For example, when helping a toddler put on shoes, an adult engages in verbal mapping as she describes what she and the child are doing: "Where are your shoes? [Child gestures.] Yes, those are your shoes. Bring me your shoes. [Child gives shoes to adult.] Let's put this shoe on first. [Holds shoe to child's foot.] Slip your foot into the shoe. [Child responds.] There you go. Now let's tie it up. [Ties shoe.] Now let's put on your other shoe."

As another example, a teacher stops by the classroom's block corner and finds that children are engaged in building a city. Her verbal mapping focuses on describing the types of buildings the children have made. The teacher's mapping continues briefly and is contingent on the children's responses to her. She focuses on providing descriptions of their actions and accomplishments.

Verbal mapping also occurs as children share discoveries with their teachers, parents, and other adults. While outside on the playground, a child might run up to a teacher, holding a caterpillar on a leaf. The teacher's responses might include the following instances of verbal mapping: "What do you have here? Oh, yes, it is a caterpillar. It has yellow and black stripes. Can you see how it moves? Slowly, slowly, little by little. It can even climb up a hanging leaf. See where its eyes are? It looks furry. See the tiny hairs that cover its body? Look at all of its feet."

Verbal mapping is not just idle chatter on the part of an adult. Instead, it involves a conscious focus by the adult on the concepts and vocabulary relevant to the ongoing learning activity. To be effective, verbal mapping needs to take into account the developmental level of children's receptive language skills. Because verbal mapping occurs as action is ongoing, it occurs when the referents for the objects and actions are present. This provides children with important opportunities for conceptual development. As the specific concepts are used in verbal mapping, children are exposed to syntactic, pragmatic, morphemic, and phonemic knowledge related to those concepts. In this way, verbal mapping extends and expands children's receptive language and serves as a basis for their productive–expressive language as well.

Questioning.   Adults ask children questions beginning in infancy. This interaction pattern occurs frequently. Questions asked of very young children are often answered by an adult, who takes both parts in the conversation, because the infant is not yet verbally responding. An infant's nonverbal responses—gestures and facial expressions—may be interpreted by many adults as responses to their questions, even if the child's responses are unintentional or random. The way adults respond to children's unintentional responses, by assuming the verbal or nonverbal behavior as an intended response, sets up an interactive pattern in which the child begins to participate in a dialogue of sorts. The rising intonation that ends a question, the anticipatory facial expression, and gestures of the adult encourage children to respond. Asking questions is a way of "passing the conversational turn" to the child (Pine, 1994, p. 19).

Questioning takes several different roles in communication with young children. Questioning can focus on clarifying something the child said previously. Sometimes questions are used to ask the child to repeat what was said earlier or to rephrase an utterance. At other times, questions are used to determine the child's knowledge or awareness of a concept or an action. This "recitational questioning" is also found in classrooms, where a teacher asks a student a question to which she, the teacher, knows the answer, but is checking to see if the child knows the answer. Informational questioning occurs when an adult seeks information from a child that the adult does not know (e.g., "Where are your shoes?").

Questioning is illustrated in the following example of a conversation between a 4-year-old boy and his teacher. When the child selects a book on trucks and approaches his teacher during the independent activity time, he asks her to read it to him. After they are settled in the book corner, the book sharing begins.

Teacher: [reads title of book] Watty Piper's Trucks. Oh, look, what's happening in this picture?

Child: It's cleaning the street.

Teacher: Yes, that truck is a street sweeper. Let's turn the page and see what's going to happen next. Look at this big red truck. What kind of truck is it?

Child: *A fire truck! [pause] I saw a fire truck today.*

Teacher: *You did? When did you see it?*

Child: *At my house.*

Teacher: *Did the fire truck go by your house?*

Child: *Um-hum. Woo-woo-woo! [sound of fire siren]*

Teacher: *Wow, you can really make the noise of a fire engine siren! Why does this fire truck have a ladder?*

Child: *To help people.*

The teacher's questioning involved the three types of questions. She asked a recitational question when she asked, "What kind of truck is it?" When she asked, "When did you see it?" she was asking for information she did not know. "You did?" was a question that requested clarification of what the child had said.

Children experience responding to these three types of questions—recitational, informational, and clarifying—from early childhood on and gradually begin to incorporate the use of questioning in their productive–expressive speech. At about age 8–9 months, children show intonation patterns accompanied by gestures (pointing) as if they were asking questions. As children acquire more complex language and reach the early preschool years, questioning others becomes one way they find out information.

Linguistic scaffolding.   Using language to provide a scaffold for children's attempts to communicate is an interaction pattern used frequently with infants and older children. **Linguistic scaffolding** refers to a supportive manner in which adults or older children interact with young children in a dialogue (Bruner, 1978; Wells, 1986). This scaffolding assists children in participating at a higher level than they could perform independently. By exploring children's participation in scaffolded interactions, it is possible to see their future learning and development (Dixon-Krauss, 1996; Vygotsky, 1978).

Linguistic scaffolding involves supporting children's speech by recognizing their linguistic capabilities and assisting them in building a conversation. Linguistic scaffolding may include the use of questioning, expansion, repetition, or a combination of these. The questioning used during linguistic scaffolding serves to lead the child ahead in the dialogue or discourse and maintains the verbal interaction. For example, in the following dialogue, questioning is used to maintain the conversation. Without the use of questioning, the dialogue would stop.

Child: *I ate at McDonald's with Grandma and Grandpa.*

Teacher: *Oh, you did?*

Child: *Uh-huh.*

Teacher: *What did you eat?*

Child: *Cheeseburger, Coke, fries.*

Teacher: *Did you go on the playground?*

> Child: Yes.
> Teacher: What did you play on?
> Child: The slide and the horses.

Through the use of questioning, the child became engaged in sharing more complete information about lunch with his grandparents.

Expansion, or **recasting** (Camarata, 1995), is another aspect of linguistic scaffolding. It is used to "fill out" what a child says (Reich, 1986; Wells, 1986). Expansion is also a way to model more complex syntax, morphology, semantics, and correct pronunciation. In the following dialogue, expansion (indicated by roman type) enhances syntax and morphology by creating complete sentences and adding inflectional endings and correct past-tense forms.

> Child: New shoe [looking down at his feet].
> Adult: Oh. You have new shoes.
> Child: [Nods and grins.]
> Adult: What color are your shoes?
> Child: Blue.
> Adult: Yes. Your shoes are blue. Where did you get them?
> Child: Mommy buyed at K-Mart.
> Adult: Oh, your mother bought them at K-Mart.

Repetition is an aspect of linguistic scaffolding. In the previous example, the adult's repetition of specific key words (*shoes, blue, K-Mart*) used by the child served to reinforce pronunciation and to confirm the meaning of what the child said.

Scaffolding often occurs as a result of an adult's intuitive sense that young children need assistance and support in developing and carrying on a conversation. In such instances, adults may not be aware they are engaged in linguistic scaffolding. At other times, they may be aware that they are scaffolding the interaction for a child. **Strategic scaffolding** involves a conscious awareness by an adult that he is teaching or modeling to a child how to carry on a conversation or how to describe an event or object (Beed, Hawkins, & Roller, 1991). Strategic scaffolding provides stronger support for a young child's verbal interactions because it is used consciously by a teacher or an adult and may reflect specific educational or developmental goals for the child. It is important that adults remain sensitive to communication cues from children with respect to topic interest and intended meaning. This involves confirming children's intentions and extending their topic or inviting the children to extend the topic (Wells, 1986). In addition, adults should form and phrase their responses at the level of the child's communication or just beyond that level with respect to syntax, vocabulary, or oral pronunciation to create a zone of proximal development.

Mediation.   Mediation is a type of interaction that focuses on simplifying the learning stimulus or task to facilitate the language interaction with, and comprehension by, the child. The nature of **mediation** appears to be influenced by an adult's awareness of a child's level of comprehension (receptive language) and ability to respond (expressive language). The adult serves as a mediator, a go-between for the child and the learning stimuli, giving the child just enough support to accomplish the task at hand (Gopnik et al., 1999). The importance of this type of interaction in learning was first described by Vygotsky (1978), who emphasized the role of language in transmitting cultural knowledge.

At the preschool level, mediation may be seen in spontaneously altered texts as storybooks are shared orally. When teachers encounter text they feel is too difficult for children to understand, they spontaneously change the text to fit their understanding of the children's semantic and syntactic development. Sometimes teachers may mediate the text by pausing after a new concept or label is introduced in the text and explaining the concept. Mediation may also occur in home settings, where a parent simplifies the explanation of a complex event such as a response to a child's question about why it rains.

Communication loops, shared reference, CDS, verbal mapping, questioning, linguistic scaffolding, and mediation all facilitate language development. Through these patterns of interaction, children's language development is enhanced. These interaction patterns are present in home, community, and school settings, although there may be some modifications due to the child's level of development and the interaction style of the adults or older children in the environment.

Parents often use language to mediate and support children's interactions with specific tasks or learning activities.

Home, Community, and School Settings

The settings in which children develop their language competencies vary in many ways. The patterns of interactions may vary along with the specific form of language that is used. Cultural diversity also increases the variations in communicative setting. Cultures develop their own distinctive language, which reflects the knowledge, belief systems, and phenomena within each culture. Languages also differ in terms of the five aspects of language knowledge: phonological, semantic, syntactic, morphemic, and pragmatic.

Even without considering social–cultural differences between distinct groups, home and school environments still vary in the ways communication occurs in those settings. At home, verbal interactions may have more of a focus on the immediate context of events, actions, and objects present in the home (Wells, 1986; Wilkinson, 1984). In home settings, children interact with a limited number of people with whom they have daily experiences. Their conversations with adults are more frequent and involve more "turns," or a wider range of topics, and involve more questions from the child (Tizard, 1981). At school, children interact with a much larger number of people, and their interactions are often governed by school rules or protocol (Geekie & Raban, 1994; Mehan, 1979).

Verbal interactions with children at home are more tailored for each child or, at most, shared with one or two other children. In contrast, at school, a child must often share the teacher in conversation with a group of students. The result is that children at school have less opportunity for conversations with adults. In addition, their relationship to the teacher is less personal, and the dialogue that occurs is often teacher directed to focus on specific instructional objectives and activities (Geekie & Raban, 1994). Verbal interactions at school often focus on events and objects not physically present in the classroom. This decontextualized speech is a contrast to the type of speech experienced by children at home. Further, in school settings, the wait time between adult questions and expected children's responses is also much shorter than that found in home settings.

Language development is also influenced by social routines. Routines may be linguistically patterned or more informal. They are usually culturally based, influenced by family, community, or both. In linguistically patterned routines, children are introduced to the routine through adult or teacher direction. Specific responses are expected (no open-endedness), and specific concepts and skills are taught directly. Children participate in a variety of formal or fixed linguistic routines from infancy on. Pat-a-cake and peek-a-boo are two common routines to which infants are often introduced. For older children, formal school-based linguistic routines may include saying the Pledge of Allegiance, taking attendance, greeting someone in the morning, and saying good-bye in the afternoon.

Informal, home-based routines may involve daily or weekly events in which the child may tag along on a trip to the grocery store or participate in routines involving being dressed, bathed, or fed. Informal linguistic routines also involve turn taking within communication loops. Recitational routines that occur in instructional settings are also informal linguistic routines. While the exact speech for these routines is not fixed (as it is in the Pledge of Allegiance), the turn-taking, question–answer interaction pattern is routinized.

Within routines, children experience each of the five aspects of language knowledge: phonological, semantic, syntactic, morphemic, and pragmatic. However, social routines emphasize pragmatic knowledge: knowledge of how to use language in different settings. Knowing when and how to say "please," "thank you," and "excuse me" is just one type of language-related knowledge learned through social routines. Home social routines that are also part of the larger society allow young children to learn how to interact successfully in school and community settings.

Sometimes vocabulary is also learned during routines. When her preschool teacher was taking attendance at the beginning of the school year, a little girl, Nicole, arrived late and went to the group circle and sat down. Nicole heard the other children saying "Present" when their names were called. When her name was called, Nicole replied, "Well, I'm here, but I don't have a present." Her teacher then explained that "present" also meant that she had come to school.

Recent Research on Nature–Nurture Connections and Language Development

Home, community, and school settings are also part of a multidimensional construct known as **socioeconomic status**. Socioeconomic status/SES is a "complex construct based on household income, material resources, education and occupation as well as related neighborhood and family characteristics" (Hackman et al., 2010, p. 651). Socioeconomic status is also associated with prenatal care (e.g., mother's health and nutrition), postnatal care, and cognitive stimulation. Each of these factors contribute to the context in which language develops.

Recently, researchers have explored the interaction between nature and nurture with respect to language development. This research has focused on the correlations between brain activation and development and socioeconomic status. Technological advances in the study of brain function and development involving brain imaging and activation have facilitated this exploration. For example, researchers have used neuroimaging to show differences in brain activation during language and reading tasks among children from different socioeconomic status groups (Farah et al., 2008; Hackman et al., 2010; Jednorog et al., 2012; Noble et al., 2006). When compared to children from middle or upper SES, children from low SES environments showed differences in brain activation during reading tasks involving phonological skills (Noble et al., 2006). Recent research has also begun to explore the connection between SES and the development of brain structures (Jednorog et al., 2012).

Implications of this research center on ways in which intervention programs may reduce or ameliorate the factors associated with low SES. For example, it is important that programs be implemented that address prenatal and postnatal nutrition and health as well as specific educational programs and community resources for children and their families (Hackman & Farah, 2009; Hackman et al., 2010; Jednorog et al., 2012).

Role of Early Childhood Teachers

An early childhood classroom teacher has a critical role in establishing a learning environment in which the language contexts provide opportunities for children to continue developing their language competencies. Through a teacher's understanding of the importance of verbal interaction and the ways in which it can be enhanced through curriculum planning and implementation, children's language development can be encouraged. Because informal learning activities are child directed and open ended, it may appear to observers such as parents, upper-grade teachers, and administrators that preschool and kindergarten children are "just playing" and are not engaged in any type of academic or cognitive work (DeVries, 2001; Honig, 2007).

As an early childhood teacher you will need to communicate to parents, colleagues, and administrators the specific aspects of your classroom curriculum and environment that will enhance children's language development. When this is done, parents, colleagues, and administrators will have a better appreciation of the ways in which children's educational and developmental needs are being met in your early childhood classroom. You will need to help parents and others understand that these informal learning activities are valuable because they provide an experiential basis for conceptual learning and language development due to active involvement of the learner in the classroom environment. You will also need to provide parents and family members with information on community resources as well as ways in which they can support their children's language development at home.

SUMMARY

Each theoretical perspective has added to our knowledge of the complexity of language development and to an awareness of the wide variety of language stimuli and contexts experienced by young children. The different theoretical perspectives vary in their focus on the role of nature and nurture as well as the emphasis on one or more of the five aspects of language knowledge. Throughout this text, the focus will be on the interactionist perspective, with its recognition of the ways in which nature and nurture interact. It provides a framework for understanding the complex ways children develop language competencies as they interact with people and objects in their environment.

The complex development of the brain plays a critical role in the development of language. While specific areas of the brain have been associated with specific language processing functions, neurolinguists agree that both hemispheres of the brain are involved in communication.

Children acquire language in a variety of settings and contexts. The ways language is used in each setting and the linguistic features of the language or dialect influence children's development of language. Through an understanding of the various interaction patterns and the characteristics of the different settings, teachers will be able to plan and implement appropriate language-related activities to enhance children's language development.

1. Key terms to review:

universal grammar	neurolinguistics	aphasia
language acquisition device (LAD)	central nervous system	Broca's aphasia
	peripheral nervous system	Wernicke's aphasia
hypothesis testing		shared reference
object permanence	neuron	communication loop
schemata	axons	child-directed speech (CDS)
preoperational stage	dendrites	
imitative speech	myelin sheath	verbal mapping
language acquisition support system (LASS)	axon terminal	linguistic scaffolding
	synapse	expansion
	cerebral cortex	recasting
zone of proximal development	cerebellum	strategic scaffolding
	hemispheres	mediation
developmental level	lateralization	

2. Distinguish between these theoretical perspectives: behaviorist, nativist, cognitive developmentalist, and interactionist. Name a theorist–researcher associated with each perspective. What are the implications of each theory for an early childhood education classroom?

3. Describe the zone of proximal development. How does this concept relate to language development?

4. Describe each of the following interaction patterns: child-directed speech, verbal mapping, questioning, linguistic scaffolding, and mediation.

Discussion

1. In what ways does brain development research document the influence of both nature and nurture on language development?

2. Reread the episode between Allison and her mother presented in this chapter. Determine which interaction patterns were present in this episode. In what ways did each interaction pattern facilitate Allison's verbal engagement?

Observation

1. Observe several activities in a preschool setting. Analyze the ways in which the activities were conducted for the types of language competencies enhanced in the activities. Include a detailed description of the activities and of the children's verbal and nonverbal behavior.

2. Observe an adult and an infant during feeding or dressing, during a child-care drop-off or pickup, or interacting in a grocery store or another public setting. Describe the verbal and nonverbal interaction with respect to shared reference and eye contact. Include a transcript of the verbal interaction.

CHAPTER 3

LANGUAGE DEVELOPMENT AMONG CHILDREN OF LINGUISTIC DIVERSITY

Learning Outcomes

After reading this chapter you should be able to

- Explain the relationship between language and culture
- Identify three types of language diversity
- Describe the factors influencing second language acquisition
- Describe the different programs for second language learners
- Discuss the guidelines for teachers in language and culturally diverse classrooms

Today was "parent storybook day" in Ms. Harper's preschool classroom. Parents of the preschoolers at the early childhood center were invited to come to read storybooks to the children informally. It was an event eagerly anticipated by all the children. Some children were even dressed up in special clothing for the event. Just before the parents arrived, Ms. Harper asked children to each select a storybook from the classroom library. The children enthusiastically selected their books. Several bilingual children selected Spanish-language storybooks. When parents arrived, they went to different areas of the room to sit down with small groups of children. Children whose parents had come made a special effort to sit close to their parents. As the storybook sharing progressed, children took turns giving their book to the adult, and having it read to them. Soon it became apparent that no Spanish-speaking parents had arrived. The Spanish-speaking children continued to hold on to their books and occasionally looked at the books independently.

Ms. Harper was also involved in the reading of storybooks to small groups of children. One of the bilingual Spanish children, Maria, approached her, handed her the Spanish-language version of *Clifford the Big Red Dog*, and asked her to read it. Ms. Harper replied, "I don't speak Spanish, but let's see, I'll try." She then read the text, pausing occasionally to ask Maria if she was saying it "right." Maria was clearly enjoying the story and also enjoying the opportunity to tell her teacher if the story in Spanish was being read correctly. Several times, Maria modeled different pronunciation of Spanish words that had been read. Since the story was supported by detailed illustrations, Ms. Harper was able to engage Maria in a conversation (in English) about the story events. When the other Spanish-speaking children in the room heard their teacher reading in Spanish, they came over to join in the story sharing.

This episode in Ms. Harper's classroom is representative of the status of linguistic diversity in many early childhood classrooms. Compared to previous times, there is an increasing likelihood that children of linguistic diversity will be in mainstream early childhood settings. In many classrooms, teachers will not be multilingual or represent diverse cultures, nor will they have received any special professional preparation to work with linguistic diversity (Rubinstein-Avila, 2006). In addition, attention to the linguistic and cultural backgrounds of the children may be limited and not incorporated into the classroom curriculum. To change this situation and provide more appropriate classroom environments for young language learners, it is important to understand basic concepts of linguistic diversity and second language acquisition.

CULTURE AND LANGUAGE

Language and culture are intertwined in a complex way. The system of symbols present in a language and the way in which a language is used to communicate have unique features for each particular culture or subculture.

The power of language to reflect culture and influence thinking was first proposed by an American linguist and anthropologist, Edward Sapir (1884–1939), and his student, Benjamin Whorf (1897–1941). The **Sapir–Whorf hypothesis** stated that the way we think and view the world is determined by our language (Anderson & Lightfoot, 2002; Crystal, 1987; Hayes, Ornstein, & Gage, 1987). Instances of cultural differences in language use are evident in languages having specific words for concepts and other languages using several words to represent those concepts. For example, the Arabic language includes many specific words for designating a certain type of horse or camel (Crystal, 1987). To make such distinctions in English, where specific words do not exist, adjectives would be used preceding the concept label, such as *quarter horse* or *dray horse.*

Cultural differences have also been noted in the ways in which language is used pragmatically. In U.S. culture, new skills are typically taught and learned through verbal instruction (Slobin, 1979) or through silent observation. A distinction has also been made between cultures that encourage independent learning and those that encourage cooperative learning (McLeod, 1994). These varied contexts for learning can be differentiated by the way in which language is embedded or isolated from the actual learning task or concept (Rogoff, Paradise, Arauz, Correa-Chávez, & Angelillo, 2003). For example, if a child questions his mother as she is planting vegetables in the garden, their language will be embedded in the activity and refer directly to the actions and objects present. In contrast, the language used in teaching a science lesson at school on the structure of plants may describe the same information out of context and be focused on learning lesson-specific facts from an oral lecture. In addition, the role of questioner will differ. At home, the child is often the questioner; at school, the teacher often serves as the primary questioner.

Differences in the social roles of adults and children also influence how language is used. Home and school contexts may represent different cultures, subcultures, or both, and may influence language development in noticeable ways. Nonverbal cues (e.g., facial expression) and contextual cues (e.g., shared experience) have different communicative roles in different cultures (Kaiser & Rasminsky, 2003). In some cultures, prelinguistic children (who are not yet verbalizing) are spoken about rather than spoken to (Heath, 1983). Children may be expected, and thus taught, to speak only when an adult addresses them. They are not encouraged to initiate conversations with adults or to join spontaneously in ongoing adult conversations. In addition, in some cultures, children who enthusiastically volunteer answers at school are considered show-offs (Peregoy & Boyle, 1993). In some cultural settings, children are not asked recitational questions. Instead, they are asked only questions of clarification or for new information. Thus, when these children experience recitational questions in a school setting, they may be confused as to the purpose of the questioning and the expected response. Further cultural differences in how language is used in educational settings have been documented by Tharp (1994). These differences include variations in how stories are told, the wait time given by teachers to students during questioning sequences, the rhythmic patterns of the verbal interactions, and the patterns of conversational turn taking.

Sociolinguistics

The field of **sociolinguistics** studies the "relationship between linguistic behavior and social situations, roles, and functions" (Meechan & Rees-Miller, 2003, p. 485). In recognizing the varied ways in which language is used in different settings and speech communities, there has also been an acknowledgment that people can develop linguistic flexibility that allows them to communicate effectively in different settings, using different dialects and communication styles (Stubbs, 2002). This perspective states that all forms of language have valid and authentic uses (Stubbs, 2002). Differences are simply differences, not deficiencies of language.

The recognition of the validity and authenticity of language variations within different cultures and communicative interactions came as the result of linguistic research in the 1970s and 1980s. One of the perspectives researched then was the **verbal-deficit perspective**. This perspective contended that anyone who did not use standard English did not have a valid language and thus was verbally deficient. Researchers explored how language was used in different social settings and documented the varied ways in which language differed with respect to vocabulary, phonological features, grammar, morphemic features, and pragmatic use (Bereiter & Englemann, 1966; Bernstein, 1971; Labov, 1979; Tough, 1977; Winch, 1990). This research provided a basis for recognizing that different ways of communicating and varied use of dialects do not indicate that a person is deficient in language.

Cultural Context of Families and Language Development

Further awareness of the role of cultural environments in the language development process was influenced in the 1980s by ethnographic research techniques that were used by language researchers. Ethnographic studies have contributed significantly to our understanding of linguistic diversity. **Ethnography** uses participant observation in real-life settings and focuses on individuals within their social and cultural contexts. In her ethnographic study, Heath (1983) explored children's development of language at home and school in two communities in the southeastern United States. She found differences in communication in working-class black and white families as well as among middle-class townspeople of both ethnic groups. Heath also described differences in story structures, language, and sense of "truth" (fiction vs. nonfiction) that children learned at home that were different from those expected at school. To be successful at school, these children had to be able "to recognize when a story is expected to be true, when to stick to the facts, and when to use their imaginations" (Heath, 1983, p. 294). This research documented valid and authentic differences in the ways language is used and in the ways in which children in those respective communities become competent language users. Heath concluded that the contrasts she found in language were not based on race, but on complex cultural influences in each community.

The importance of family context in language development was more recently described by Hart and Risley (1995, 1999). Findings from their longitudinal study document the significance of "talkativeness" in families in influencing language development rather than the family's socioeconomic status or ethnic group identity. Differences in language use were attributed to the complex family culture—not simply to socioeconomic status or ethnic group identity. Among the families studied, the most important difference was in the amount of talking. Children in families where there was more talking developed higher levels of language in the areas of vocabulary growth and vocabulary use. These differences were strongly linked to school performance at age 9.

Among these families, Hart and Risley (1995) identified five quality features in parents' language interactions with their children:

1. *Language diversity.* This is the variation and number of nouns and modifiers used by the parents.
2. *Feedback tone.* This is the positive feedback given to children's participation in an interaction.
3. *Symbolic emphasis.* This is the emphasis placed on focusing on names and associated relations of the concepts and the recall of those symbols.
4. *Guidance style.* This is parental interaction that uses *asking* rather than *demanding* in eliciting specific behavior from the child.
5. *Responsiveness.* This is parental responsiveness to requests or questions initiated by children.

Hart and Risley (1995) speculated that these categories may be "important for the language-based analytic and symbolic competencies upon which advanced education and a global economy depend" (p. 193).

A current hypothesis on why children from diverse linguistic backgrounds experience difficulty in school is the **socialization mismatch hypothesis**. This hypothesis "predicts that children are more likely to succeed in school when the home language and literacy socialization patterns are similar to those that are used and valued in school" (Faltis, 1998, p. 23). This hypothesis has been applied to children who speak a nonstandard English dialect as well as to children who are learning a second language. Home language socialization patterns may differ from those favored in the school classroom in the following ways (Faltis, 1998):

1. The amount of talk directed to preschool children
2. The participation of young children as conversation partners with adults
3. Opportunities children have to explain or give a personal interpretation of events
4. The types of questions asked of children during storybook sharing
5. The forms of narrative that are used (e.g., fiction, nonfiction, or ongoing narratives)

In addition, the social interaction patterns used in the classroom may vary from the home culture's with respect to expectations for competitive versus collaborative or cooperative activities as well as the "courtesies and conventions of conversations" (Tharp, 1994, p. 140).

Implications of cultural-linguistic diversities for early childhood classrooms. Children who come to your early childhood classroom will have developed their language competencies in the varied settings of their homes and communities. These speech communities may or may not reflect the way in which language is used in the more formal school setting. As an early childhood teacher, your role is to continue to enhance children's language development and to encourage children to develop linguistic flexibility so they can communicate effectively in a wide variety of settings. While you may think that your emphasis should be only on helping children develop language competencies that will contribute to their success in academic settings, it is also important for you to acknowledge the value of their other language competencies that will contribute to their effective communication in family and community settings (Delpit, 2002; Stubbs, 2002).

LANGUAGE DIVERSITY

This chapter focuses on three distinct types of linguistic diversity: differences in dialect, differences in registers, and differences in language. Each type of difference may affect learning in the classroom and require specific strategies on the part of the teacher. In addressing the needs of children with each type of linguistic diversity, it is important to remember that there are two common goals for all children: success at school and preparation for successful living. An initial step in understanding how to meet the needs of language-diverse students is to better understand the concepts and issues involved in both dialect usage and second language acquisition.

Dialect Diversity

Some language differences represent diverse **dialects**, or specialized variations of a language. Cultural and social differences and geographic locality influence the development of a dialect. Dialects develop in settings where a group of people communicate within their group more frequently and for a longer period of time than they do with outside groups. As a result of this geographic or social isolation, a specialized form of language develops that is unique to that context or cultural setting. For example, adolescent peer groups often develop their own dialects.

Characteristics of dialects. All dialects are characterized by distinct systematic features with respect to the five aspects of language knowledge: phonological, semantic, syntactic, morphemic, and pragmatic (Crystal, 1987; Freeman & Freeman, 2004; Van Herk & Rees-Miller, 2010). According to Labov (1995), nonstandard English dialects "show slightly different versions of the same rules [as standard English], extending and modifying the grammatical processes which are common to all dialects of English" (p. 54).

When dialects of the same language are represented in writing, there may be differences in spelling, grammatical structures, and punctuation, which will signal the use of the dialect. Sometimes a dialect is used in literature to represent the speech of a particular regional or social–cultural group. Dialects of the same language base are generally understandable by all speakers of the base language; however, communication between speakers of different dialects may be more effortful since the dialects may differ in one or more of the aspects of language, including semantics (vocabulary), syntax (grammar), morphemes (word structure), pragmatics (intent/context of language), or phonological (sound–symbol connections).

For example, phonological differences are heard in the way words are articulated. For example, the word *creek* may be pronounced with an extended *e* sound ("creek," as in *beet)* or with the short *i* sound (as in *pick*), as "crick." Semantic differences occur when different labels are used to refer to the same object or action. In some locales in the United States, a drinking fountain is referred to as a bubbler. Syntactic differences involve differences in the way sentences are structured. For example, "I don't got no time to help" and "I have no time to help" reflect syntactic differences. Morphemic differences are found in the way verb endings or other inflectional endings are used, such as *gonna* or *goin'* compared with *going to* and *going*. When people are communicating in different dialects, these differences may result in communication that requires more negotiation or clarification.

Pidgin languages.   In some areas of the United States, regional dialects have linguistic aspects that originated in pidgin languages. A **pidgin** is a language that developed in response to the interaction of two groups of people who did not initially share a language (Crystal, 1987). During the time of exploration, colonization, and settlement of North America, pidgin languages developed as a linguistic bridge between the natives and the explorers, traders, or settlers. For example, in the 1800s a pidgin language developed in Hawaii between the English-speaking explorers, settlers, and missionaries and native Hawaiians (Ogata, Sheehey, & Noonan, 2006).

Typically, pidgin languages have a small vocabulary, simple grammatical structure, and a narrower range of functions than the languages from which the pidgin was developed. Pidgin language use decreases and may even disappear when one group learns the language of the other or if the original reason for communicating, such as trading or selling goods, has ceased. In some situations, the pidgin develops into a **creole** language. This occurs when a pidgin language has been used across two generations, so that the children of the initial speakers of the pidgin learn or acquire the new language as their "mother tongue." As use of this language becomes more widespread and stabilized, it becomes a creolized language.

When a pidgin is creolized, linguistic features of the language are expanded, especially with respect to grammar–syntax, vocabulary–semantics, and function–style–pragmatics. For example, in the coastal area from Florida to South Carolina, the creolized language Gullah is still spoken in some localities. Gullah began as a pidgin language used among the slaves, who were brought to that coastal area from many different tribes along the western coast of Africa, and the plantation owners. Words and grammatical rules from English and the different African languages were combined into one language. This language made communication possible between the Africans and the plantation owners (Fishman, 1995; Fromkin & Rodman, 1998; Pollitzer, 1993). As Gullah was learned by successive generations, it became a creole.

Although some creoles are no longer used as languages, certain vocabulary and characteristic accents or pronunciations may have been incorporated into English and are still in use today. Teachers should be aware of the creoles historically used in their communities because the current dialect of English in use may have words, accents, or other linguistic features from those earlier languages.

Standard American English: a dialect.   Standard American English (SAE) is often referred to as the "most correct" form of language used in the United States and is the form of language considered appropriate in corporate, business, government, and formal educational settings. Standard American English is actually a dialect of English, and the use of the term *standard* is misleading (Durkin, 1995; Fromkin & Rodman, 1998; Meechan & Rees-Miller, 2003). The actual SAE dialect varies with the region of the United States. SAE, as described by grammarians, is not actually used by people; instead, speakers use a form of the SAE having more or less of the SAE features, depending on their social status, educational level, and the setting (Van Herk & Rees-Miller, 2010).

Throughout history, one variety of language has typically been used to communicate more broadly within any given culture (Gadda, 1995). This is not surprising because language plays a significant role in the development and advancement of any culture. Fromkin and Rodman (1998) caution against considering SAE (or any other standard dialect) as a superior form of language over other dialects or languages because the "standard dialect" is "neither more expressive, more logical, more syntactically complex, nor more regular than any other dialect or language. Any judgments, therefore, as to the superiority or inferiority of a particular dialect or language are social judgments, not linguistic or scientific ones" (p. 409).

Regional Dialects

In the United States, many regional dialects are present. People speaking a southern dialect are distinguishable from people speaking a Bostonian or New York dialect; however, people speaking different dialects of the same language generally can comprehend each other's speech. Even within a region, there are dialect differences. For example in the Midwest, dialect differences have been described for Chicago, Ohio, St. Louis, Michigan's Upper Peninsula, and the rural areas (Cameron, 2006; Flanigan, 2006; Frazer, 2006; Gordon, 2006; Murray, 2006; Simon, 2006).

Because we each have learned language in our early years within our home and cultural settings, we may grow up thinking that our way of speaking and using language is the "norm" (Gordon, 2006) and are surprised when someone suggests that we speak with a dialect. It is also important to remember that there are considerable variations within geographic regions and cultural groups with respect to dialect use. Even though a region or a cultural group may be characterized by a commonly used dialect, it is inappropriate to automatically assume that any speaker of that region or that cultural group will use that dialect.

African American English Dialect

One distinct example of a cultural dialect is African American/Black English. This section will describe some of the characteristics of African American English (AAE)/ Black English (BE). This description is included as an example of the richness and linguistic complexity of a dialect used by many Americans. AAE is a dialect used by a significant number of people of African American descent. It is also referred to as Black Vernacular English or Ebonics (Cloud, Genesee, & Hamayan, 2000). Varieties of AAE reflect urban and rural locales and regional dialects, as well as age, gender, and language context (Wheeler & Swords, 2006; Wolfram & Thomas, 2002).

The work of Labov (1979) contributed to a more accurate understanding of AAE as a linguistically complete, authentic dialect. For any language or dialect to endure, it must be functionally complete to support the communication needs of the community using it. AAE has endured in various areas of the United States for many decades. Its existence is evidence that it has served and continues to serve communicative needs, such as "cultural and linguistic transmission of tradition and history" and the "expression of pride in identity and community" (Orr, 2000, p. 1). Examples of some of the syntactic features of AAE contrasted to SAE are listed in Table 3.1.

AAE also has characteristic ways in which language is used in verbal interaction, referred to as **modes of discourse**. Smitherman (1995) described five distinctive

---

TABLE 3.1

Examples of Syntactic Contrasts Between Standard American English and African American English

Standard American English		African American English	
Possessive -'s	Get Uncle's coat.	Not required if word position indicates possession	Get Uncle coat.
Plural -s	She has ten dollars.	Not required with adjective indicating number	She get ten dollar.
Irregular past tense	This afternoon she came home.	Verb uninflected	This afternoon she come home.
Regular past tense	Yesterday I walked to town.	Not needed	Yesterday I walk to town.
Pronouns	Momma is sad.	Pronoun follows noun in apposition	Momma she sad.
Negation	I don't have anything.	Triple negation and use of *ain't* for don't, haven't, hasn't, isn't, and didn't	I ain't got nothing.

Source: Owens, Robert E., Jr. (2012). *Language Development: An Introduction* (8th ed., p. 406). Boston: Pearson. Copyright © 2012 by Pearson Education Inc. Adapted by permission of the publisher.

modes of discourse found among AAE speakers (see Table 3.2). These modes of discourse are part of pragmatic knowledge of AAE (i.e., how language is used differently in different situations). In each of these modes, the speaker is encouraged to use language creatively, symbolically, and figuratively while observing the established formulaic structure. These discourse structures are not found in SAE or in other English dialects. By recognizing and including these creative discourse structures in classroom activities, linguistic diversity is encouraged and validated (Tharp, 1994). It can also provide a basis for examining other types of discourse structures.

Controversy regarding AAE/BE has occurred in settings where assumptions have been made that AAE/BE is an obstacle to learning. In a 1978 court case, *Martin Luther King Junior Elementary School Children v. Ann Arbor School District Board*,

TABLE 3.2
Examples of Discourse Modes in Black English

Discourse Mode	Characteristic(s)	Examples
Call-Response	Verbal or nonverbal interaction between a speaker and a listener; contingent upon speaker's speech segments	Example responses to speaker's "calls": *Verbal:* Amen! Tell it! Yessuh! Rap on! *Nonverbal:* rolling eyes, clapping hands, shaking head
Signification	Verbal art of insult; also known as dropping lugs, joanin, capping, sounding	In addressing his congregation, Reben Nap said, "everybody talking bout Heaven ain goin there."
"The Dozens"	Set of responses in verse	Insult focuses on a person's relatives; typically person's mother as in "yo mamma ..."
Tonal Semantics	Voice rhythm and vocal inflection are used to convey meaning, including the use of repetition and alliterative word play	Rhythmic pattern to speech illustrated in speeches by Martin Luther King Jr., and Jesse Jackson
Narrative Sequencing	Forms: folktale, trickster tale, "toast." All forms involve an abstract point or general message within a concrete story; events are not objectively reported but are dramatized through voicing the facts along with the teller's personal emotional and social perspective on the facts.	"Brer Rabbit"—underdog animals who succeed in outsmarting their much larger enemies

Source: Durkin, Diane Bennett. (1995). *Language Issues: Readings for Teachers* (pp. 316–327). Boston: Allyn & Bacon. Copyright © 1995 by Pearson Education. Adapted by permission of the publisher.

parents charged that their children were being denied equal educational opportunities because the school was not helping their children overcome the language barrier of the children who spoke BE (Scott, 1995b). The court decision required the school district to help teachers acknowledge the home BE language and to incorporate this awareness and knowledge into reading instruction.

Responses to the court's decision have varied: providing in-service training for teachers in BE, directly teaching SAE, or teaching only BE; however, the decision did create awareness that students' use of BE in school settings often elicited negative attitudes from teachers. From these teachers' attitudes, further negative assumptions developed into low achievement expectations for BE speakers, which then became a self-fulfilling prophecy (Scott, 1995b).

Recognition of BE as a separate but authentic dialect of English is important in understanding the language background of many African American children. Similarly, it is important for teachers to recognize and value the home language or dialect of each child in their classrooms. Lisa Delpit (2002) described the important role of language in children's identity and development, referring to our home languages or dialects as "the skin that we speak" and noting that "our language embraces us long before we are defined by any other medium of identity" (p. xvii).

Bidialectism

Encouraging children to become linguistically flexible is critical for teachers in the development and implementation of curricula that will provide children with optimal learning opportunities. It is also important for teachers and parents to acknowledge the importance for children to develop the linguistic flexibility to be able to comprehend and use not only the dialect used at home and in their immediate communities but to also understand the form of English used in other social settings (Delpit, 1995). These children develop **bidialectism**, or the ability to use two dialects (Cloud et al., 2000; Ogbu, 1999). Children may develop the ability to use multiple dialects as they interact at home, in the larger community, and informally with peers. Children who are more linguistically flexible and can use more than one dialect will be able to communicate effectively in a wide variety of settings and interactions.

Language Registers

In addition to dialect differences, another way in which diversity is evident in our use of language is in the "registers" we use when communicating in a particular setting for a particular purpose (Crystal, 1987; Halliday, 2007; O'Grady et al., 2010). Children learn how to use language for specific purposes in specific settings as they experience different situations in their preschool and elementary school years. This is part of their pragmatic knowledge of language.

Children's use of different registers often is shown when they are role playing. For example, when they are pretending to be a clerk in a grocery store, or a doctor, or a teacher, they will use language in a way that reflects that role. When pretending to be a doctor, they might use specific terminology, engage in questioning the patient, give specific directions to the patient, or write out a prescription. When in the role of a teacher, they might use specific words and grammatical structures to get the students to pay attention, to follow directions, or to participate. They might "pretend" read using the pacing and intonation of conventional reading. During the preschool years, children are also encouraged to learn the register of politeness by saying "please," "thank you," "you're welcome," "excuse me," "I'm sorry." In some settings, "no problem" has replaced the use of "you're welcome"—which is evidence of the evolving nature of language use in specific social settings.

Academic English Register

In academic settings, language is used in specific ways for specific purposes. This register of language is referred to in English-speaking settings as **academic English**. The specific ways in which language is used (pragmatics) influences the semantic, morphemic and syntactic features of that language use. Although the focus here is on academic English, it is important to note that many other languages, for example French, German, and Spanish, also have academic registers.

Specific features of academic English.   Wong Fillmore (1999) characterized academic register as having these specific characteristics: a more technical, precise vocabulary; and specific "grammatical constructions and devices, rhetorical conventions, and discourse markers" (p. 15). The complexity of formal English and its decontextualized nature is evident in the types of learning activities present in educational settings (Grant, 1995). The three types of learning strategies that involve specific language competencies related to academic English register are:

1. *Cognitive strategies.* These strategies involve using language to interact with written and hands-on materials, using a range of cognitive processes, such as summarizing, deduction/induction, transfer, and inference.
2. *Metacognitive strategies.* These strategies involve using language to plan, monitor, and evaluate one's own learning.
3. *Social-affective strategies.* These strategies involve using language to interact with others (peers or teachers) in the learning process, such as asking questions for clarification or working collaboratively (Chamot & O'Malley, 1995).

Academic English register has both oral and written forms and is represented in educational materials as well as classroom discourse. Halliday (2007) describes the wide range of different registers used in school. For example, the way language is used in mathematics class differs from how it is used in English class or social studies. The emphasis placed here on academic English is not meant to imply that this is the only form of language used in the classroom. While learning activities in content areas such as science, math, and social studies use academic English, literature anthologies and creative writing assignments may involve other registers of English as a way of indicating a particular speech community or context (Wheeler & Swords, 2006). In addition, informal conversations in classrooms may occur in regional or cultural dialects in varying degrees; however, the main focus, particularly in upper elementary grades and beyond will be on using academic English. As grade levels increase, so does text-based instruction; thus, it becomes essential that children can effectively use academic English in both oral and written communication.

Another way of referring to the different language registers used by children in school settings is to simply refer to the registers as either informal English or formal English (Wheeler & Swords, 2006). This distinction between formal and informal English acknowledges that children come into classrooms speaking different forms of language that are linguistically valid and authentic. Thus, when children speak or write in their home/community dialect or a specific register, they are not making "errors" in English but are simply using a different form of language. Similarly, second language learners may transfer a grammatical pattern of their home language when speaking or writing English. This does not mean that children must unlearn their home language, dialect, or register, and use only academic English; instead, it means teachers must provide opportunities for children to develop linguistic flexibility, "choosing the language variety appropriate to the specific time, place, audience, and communicative purpose" (Wheeler & Swords, 2006, p. 38).

Importance of academic English register. Children's language competencies influence their educational opportunities and achievements. Educational activities involve specific types of communication and interaction. To be successful in academic settings, children must learn how to communicate effectively in those settings. They must learn how to use language in specific educational contexts and for specific purposes within those contexts. Differences in achievement in our schools may not simply reflect differences in academic potential but may represent complex differences in children's familiarity with the language of instruction, the academic English register. Students who develop competencies in using the academic English register will also benefit as they enter the work force. Academic English register, also referred to as **literate register** has also been identified as the "language of power" because it is used in many corporate and governmental environments (Delpit 1988, 1992, 2002; Purcell-Gates, 2002).

Teacher's role in encouraging acquisition of formal/academic English. Classroom teachers play a critical role in encouraging students to acquire academic English (Wong Fillmore, 1999). Throughout the early childhood years, developmentally appropriate language activities can gradually foster children's awareness of the language forms used in school settings. As language is used to accompany learning activities, initially through hands-on activities and increasingly through use of written materials with decontextualized language, children begin to acquire academic English. It is crucial that classroom teachers encourage children to begin to examine their own uses of language for different purposes and in different settings.

Rather than focus on correcting children's "errors" in grammar and pronunciation that reflect their informal English, home language, or specific register, teachers need to provide activities that build on children's general language knowledge as well as help them distinguish the features of academic English. Teachers must recognize the nature of children's linguistic confusions between their home language, dialect, registers, and academic English and provide an environment where children can develop flexibility and competency in using a variety of dialects and registers. In this way children will acquire the language skills needed to be successful in educational settings as well as in a broader range of environments and contexts as they move from childhood into adulthood (Fitts, 2001; Wheeler & Swords, 2006).

Wheeler and Swords (2006) encourage teachers to help children consciously "code-switch" between using informal English, regional dialect, or registers, and academic English. In their work with urban students who spoke a minority dialect, Wheeler and Swords found that the students could make a distinction between the terms *informal English* and *formal English*, comparing formal English to "dressing up" for a special occasion or event. In addition, this terminology did not carry with it a value judgment of their social–cultural heritage but simply indicated a different way of speaking in a different setting.

In encouraging children to become more familiar with academic English, Wong Fillmore (1999) advocated a continuous focus on "how language is being used and how it works" as well as providing opportunities for students to "use the language (oral and written) in more and more sophisticated ways in instructional activities" (p. 17). Wong Fillmore cautioned that although academic English is learned in the classroom, it will not be learned unless there are specific opportunities for students to focus on the features of academic English.

The acquisition of academic English is also critically important for second language learners; however, teachers need to remember that second language learners must first learn the target language in oral conversational form prior to being able to effectively acquire the academic register and written form used in educational settings. Acquisition of academic English, like the acquisition of any other language or dialect, is based on a child's first language or dialect (Cummins, 1995; Luke & Kale, 1997; Tough, 1985). In the section that follows, the processes involved in second language acquisition will be discussed. This will be followed by implications for classroom instruction for second language learners and culturally diverse students.

SECOND LANGUAGE ACQUISITION

During the past two decades, concern has increased in the United States over the educational needs of young children from non-English-speaking families. The challenge for educators is twofold:

- Provide opportunities for students to learn the necessary knowledge and skills.
- Provide opportunities for children to develop language competencies that will enhance and facilitate their opportunities to learn.

In your role as early childhood educator, you will need to understand the process of second language acquisition in order to provide appropriate learning opportunities for children from linguistically diverse families. This section will focus on the challenges faced by children learning a second language, the benefits of bilingualism, the sequence of second language acquisition, and the factors influencing how children develop and acquire a second language.

Becoming Bilingual

Students who have a home language (L1) other than English are faced with the challenge of learning a new or target language (L2) that has different features from their home language. The syntactic, semantic, morphemic, phonetic, and pragmatic aspects of the two languages may be significantly different. Languages from the same "language family" have similar characteristics and features, whereas languages from different language families are dissimilar (Crystal, 1987). For example, Spanish and French are both in the Indo-European (Romance) language family and have some similarities, such as the use of an alphabetic writing system and similar cognates/word stems. In contrast, Spanish and Chinese belong to different language families and are distinctly different in not only the writing system used but other aspects of language as well, including syntactic, semantic, pragmatic, and morphemic aspects. The ways in which aspects of language knowledge are similar or different between two languages influences second language acquisition. Children who are attempting to learn a language from a different language family will find it more difficult than if they were attempting to learn another language from the same language family. As the second language is learned, children build on their knowledge of language by making connections and comparisons between the home language and the target language. Target languages that are distinctly different from the home language will require more effort to learn.

Second language learners' efforts in distinguishing between the relevant language knowledge in two different systems are sometimes evident in their use of English in composing oral stories (Otto, 1987). Preschool children who are in the process of acquiring English language knowledge and distinguishing that knowledge from their first or home language may produce stories that are less fluent, less cohesive, or both. As a result, their stories might be assumed to be indicative of lower academic ability and language competency, when, in fact, a complex process of distinguishing between the various aspects of each language is occurring.

Children who are exposed to two languages at home acquire both languages as "first languages" (Piper, 1998). In some homes, each parent speaks a different language with the child; in other homes, the parents use one language with the child, and grandparents or other caregivers use a second language. In still other homes, both parents speak both languages to the child, mixing the two languages. It appears that children acquire bilingualism with less confusion when the languages are kept separate by the parent or caregiver who speaks them (Piper, 1998). If one parent speaks both languages, it is more difficult for the child to distinguish between the two languages and develop knowledge of the specific language's linguistic features.

Children learn additional languages more easily than do adults.

For example, in a home where both Spanish and English are used, one parent speaks only in Spanish and the other parent only in English, or perhaps English is used by both parents, and Spanish is used by grandparents who interact frequently with the child. This allows the child to more easily develop awareness of each language's systematic features, such as vocabulary, syntax, morphemes, and phonological distinctions.

Children acquiring two languages prior to age 3 is termed **simultaneous bilingualism** (Baker, 1996; Goodz, 1994). This type of bilingualism is usually found in homes where parents speak two (or more) languages. **Successive bilingualism** refers to instances in which children acquire their second language after age 3. In many respects, second language acquisition in successive bilingualism resembles first language development. Language is acquired through actively hypothesizing rules, analyzing language patterns, making errors, and revising the rules. The early stages of language development are similar for first and second language learners, with one-word utterances appearing initially, followed by two-word utterances and then multiword utterances (Genesee & Nicoladis, 1995). The rate of acquisition of vocabulary (semantic knowledge) of L2 learners is somewhat slower only during the preschool years (Bialystok, 1988; Genesee & Nicoladis, 1995).

As bilingual children acquire the home and target languages, they may mix the languages in the same communicative interaction. This phenomenon has been analyzed differently by various researchers. Some have documented what they call **language interference**, when children appear to confuse knowledge of one of the aspects of L1 with that of L2. For example, a child might use the vocabulary or syntactic structure of one language when attempting to communicate in the other language. Other researchers have questioned the existence of language interference, citing evidence that bilingual children appear to be able to distinguish between two language systems early on (De Houwer, 1990; Goodz, 1994; Lanza, 1992; Meisel, 1994).

Instances in which children appear to be mixing the two languages (also known as **code mixing**, or language mixing) may simply reflect their parents' use of two languages. It may also reflect attempts to maintain a conversation when knowledge of the second language is not sufficient to express the desired message (Baker, 1996; Goodz, 1994; Krashen, 1995). For example, if a child is attempting to communicate in English that she wants a drink of water, and she does not recall the word *water*, she may instead say, "Mommy, *agua* please," inserting a Spanish word in an English phrase to get her message across.

Codeswitching is distinguished from code mixing and language interference by the speaker's apparently conscious and deliberate use of two languages within the same sentence or from one sentence to another (Cloud et al., 2000; see also earlier section on language registers). Codeswitching is thought to be influenced by social or psychological factors, such as a desire to add emphasis or to show ethnic unity (Cloud et al., 2000; Lessow-Hurley, 2000). In some instances, isolated words of a language are "borrowed" and inserted into the communication by second language learners. This typically occurs when a concept label is not available in the language being used (e.g., a proper noun or new terminology, such as that referring to technology) or if a particularly specific shade of meaning is needed (Baker, 1996; Bhatia & Ritchie, 1996; Cloud et al., 2000; Lessow-Hurley, 2000).

Benefits of bilingualism. The U.S. educational community is now more aware of the benefits of bilingualism. In the past, especially prior to 1960, bilingualism was thought to be an educational handicap. It was believed that children could not learn a second language while still maintaining and refining their first language. Thus, children were strongly discouraged from speaking their first language and in many instances were made to feel ashamed of speaking a different language than English (Cummins, 1995). For some children, learning a second language also meant that they would lose the ability to speak their first language (Evans, 1994; Wong Fillmore, 1991). This phenomenon has been termed **subtractive bilingualism** because the result of acquiring a second language results in the loss of the child's first language. This result may have a negative impact on families as communication is disrupted. Transmission of cultural beliefs and parenting interactions require a shared language.

Prior to the late 1970s, bilingual children's academic failures were considered to be due to their bilingualism. Since that time, research has increased our understanding of the factors involved in second language acquisition, the ways in which second language acquisition can be facilitated and enhanced, and the ways in which the first language can be maintained. According to Wong Fillmore's (1991) research, "the timing and the conditions under which [children] come into contact with English" determine whether children will retain and continue to use their home language as well as influencing the acquisition of English (p. 323). Current approaches to bilingualism emphasize the acquisition of a second (target) language, with the continued development of the home language. This approach is also referred to as **additive bilingualism** because a child's language skills are enhanced in both languages.

Children who have acquired a level of fluency in two languages have been described as having the following increased language competencies (Ben Zeev, 1977; Genesee, Tucker, & Lambert, 1975; Goodz, Legare, & Bilodeau, 1987; Ianco-Worrall, 1972; Paneque, 2006; Thompson, 1999):

- higher levels of metalinguistic awareness
- greater and earlier awareness of language structure
- wider perspectives
- more social skills related to different communicative contexts

This body of recent research supports the conclusion that children acquire language knowledge not only at the linguistic level but at the metalinguistic knowledge level and the level of metalinguistic knowledge verbalization as well.

Challenges faced by second language learners.   When learning a new language, the learner must develop knowledge of the second language's features with respect to each of the five aspects of language knowledge: phonological, semantic, syntactic, morphemic, and pragmatic. This means the learner must develop knowledge of the systematic features of the new language and distinguish those features from their first or home language. This is a complex task and may be confusing to the young learner.

In this section, examples of the distinctions required of Spanish-fluent children learning English will be included to illustrate the complexity involved in second language acquisition. For second language learners, learning to read in English is a major goal and one required for success in English-speaking classrooms. Spanish-fluent children who are learning to read English are faced with the task of distinguishing between the two systems of sound–symbol correspondences as well as differences in syntax.

In Spanish, the correspondence between a symbol and the sound it represents is regular. English entails no such regularity. When vowel symbols and their corresponding sounds are compared between Spanish and English, there are distinct differences. Not only are English vowels more varied or irregular in the ways they are pronounced, but specific sounds associated with some English vowel symbols are in direct contrast to the Spanish pronunciation. For example, Spanish letter *i* has the sound of the English long *e*, and the Spanish letter *e* has the sound midway between the *e* in *let* and the *a* in *late* (Helman, 2004). Thus, when a Spanish-speaking child is participating in a phonics lesson in an English-speaking classroom, he may appear confused because the letter-sound connections in English are so different than the same letters used in Spanish.

TABLE 3.3
Example of English–Spanish Differences in Morphemes of Noun–Verb Agreement

English	Spanish
To come	*Venir*
I come	*Vengo*
You come	*Vienes*
She/he comes	*Viene*
We come	*Venimos*
You (plural) come	*Vienen*
They come	*Vienen*

Source: Joaquin Villegas, Northeastern Illinois University, personal communication, February 18, 2004.

Spanish-fluent children also must learn that English differs syntactically from Spanish. For example, in Spanish, the descriptive adjective is usually placed after the noun it modifies—as in *mesa redonda*, or "table round"—whereas in English the adjective is placed before the noun—that is, "round table." A second language learner needs to be aware of this difference when speaking, reading, and writing English. The Spanish language also uses specific endings and spelling changes to indicate not only verb tense but also the subject (*I, you, he, we, you* [plural], *they*) associated with the verb in a particular sentence. A second language learner must consider this difference when using English because English morphology has a different system for indicating subject–verb agreement (see Table 3.3).

Sequence of second language acquisition. Optimally, the acquisition of a second language will follow the same sequence as development of the first language, with receptive and expressive knowledge of the oral language developing first, followed by knowledge of the written language; however, learning difficulties may occur in classrooms where the curriculum expectations do not acknowledge the need to first acquire target language oral competency before instruction in target written language. A child who is orally fluent in his first language but not orally fluent in his second language (English) will have more difficulty learning to read in English than will a child who is orally fluent in both languages. Similarly, a child who can comprehend and read written academic language in his first language will learn to read academic language more successfully in the second language than will a child who cannot read in his first language (Cummins, 1994). Thus, a linguistic interdependence exists between first and second languages.

Factors Influencing Second Language Acquisition

A child's first language serves as a foundation on which the second language is acquired (Bruer, 1999; Cummins, 1979). Without this threshold of first language

FIGURE 3.1

Factors Influencing Second Language Acquisition

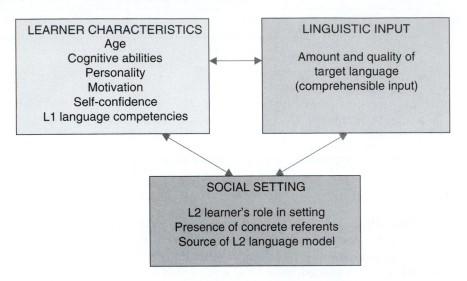

competencies, second language acquisition is difficult. Children first acquire a receptive knowledge of oral language; in other words, they comprehend oral language through listening and observing, followed by expressive knowledge, which enables them to use language to communicate. Second language learners typically have a "silent" period (Krashen, 1981, 1982, 1995; Santos & Ostrosky, 2003; Tabors, 1997) during which they appear to be working on acquiring receptive language knowledge. This can be seen among 6- and 7-year-old second language learners who do not speak spontaneously for several months, except for memorized phrases or sentences (Krashen, 1995). During the silent period, children may isolate themselves socially and take on the role of observer. This behavior does not signal a problem but should be understood as part of the process of learning how to communicate in a new language (Santos & Ostrosky, 2003).

Three major factors have a significant influence on second language acquisition: learner characteristics, social setting, and linguistic input. These factors are complex and interdependent. Figure 3.1 illustrates the interaction between learner characteristics, the social setting, and the linguistic input. The relationship between these factors is a dynamic one and varies with the specific situation in which the second language is encountered.

Learner characteristics. Age is a significant factor in second language acquisition. Before age 5, children's acquisition of an additional language resembles the first language development in both process and proficiency (Bialystok & Hakuta, 1994, cited in Lessow-Hurley, 2000). Not only do children learn language with more ease than adults, they also acquire productive phonetic knowledge at a level of near-native pronunciation, whereas adults who are second language learners are likely to speak with an accent (Bruer, 1999; Gass & Selinker, 2001; Lessow-Hurley, 2000; Schacter, 1996). Virginia Collier's work (1987, cited in Lessow-Hurley, 2000) focused on the acquisition of second language proficiency for academic settings; she concluded that children from ages 8 to 12 learn a second language more quickly than do children ages 4 to 7. Possible factors responsible for this difference include the older children's higher cognitive functioning (Baker, 1996) and their more developed first language, both of which facilitate second language acquisition. After age 12, the rate of acquisition slows down. With adults, the acquisition of a second language is also influenced by the ways in which the second language is similar to or different from their first language (Schacter, 1996). For example, it would be easier for an English-speaking adult to learn German than to learn Russian, due to the greater similarity between German and English. The more similar the two languages are with respect to the five aspects of language knowledge, the easier an adult will learn the second language.

Additional individual learner variables that affect second language acquisition include the learner's cognitive abilities, personality, motivation, self-confidence, and home language competencies (Cummins, 1994; Tabors, 1997). A learner's cognitive abilities influence how language input will be processed. Personality, motivation, and level of self-confidence determine the ways in which the learner will engage in language interactions. A shy child who lacks self-confidence will be less active in a language interaction than will an outgoing, confident child.

The social setting in which English language learners interact with speakers of the target (new) language is an important factor in second language acquisition.

Social setting.   The social setting in which interaction occurs with speakers of the target language is an important factor in second language acquisition (Hatch, Peck, & Wagner-Gough, 1995; Krashen, 1995). The social setting can be described in terms of three sets of variables: (1) the second language learner's role in the setting as a listener or an active participant; (2) the presence of concrete referents, which contribute to symbol formation and conceptual development; and (3) the person who is modeling the target language.

Linguistic input.   The quality and quantity of exposure to the target language is a significant factor in second language acquisition. Exposure to a second language is not sufficient for acquisition. The language input must be comprehensible to the learner (Cummins, 1994; Krashen, 1995, 2003). **Comprehensible input** occurs when the target/second language is used by a speaker at a level that is just slightly beyond the listener's current level of understanding (Krashen, 1995, 2003). This means that the language used is within the learner's zone of proximal development. Whether the linguistic input is comprehensible is a result of the interaction between the amount and quality of the target language received by the second language learner and the learner's individual attributes, such as age, cognitive abilities, home language competencies, personality, motivation, and self-confidence (Cummins, 1994). For example, in classroom settings where there is a focus on text-based instruction, lack of linguistic awareness by the teacher, lack of experiential learning, and a more complex level of English fluency and academic register, second language learners may not able to receive the comprehensible input needed for language learning.

Krashen (2003) recommends that teachers of second language learners provide comprehensible input by incorporating the following strategies in their classrooms:

1. Embedding the target language in context through pictures, realia, and movement
2. Modifying their speech to students by using a slower rate and less complex language
3. Organizing a curriculum not based on grammatical structure but based on language-rich activities, such as games, problem solving, and experiments
4. Encouraging but not forcing children to speak
5. Postponing the explicit, formal study of a language's grammar until much later than usual (high school)

PROGRAMS FOR SECOND LANGUAGE LEARNERS

As an early childhood teacher, you may not be responsible for providing a specific instructional program for second language learners; instead, children who are second language learners may be in your classroom for only part of their school day. For this reason, it is important that you be aware of the different types of programs that may be offered at your school to support children's acquisition of second language competencies. By understanding the different programs described in this section, you will be better able to design and implement your classroom curriculum to support these second language learners. Regardless of the specific language program for second language learners, collaboration between the special program teacher and the mainstream classroom teacher is essential. Joint planning and monitoring of student progress and areas of concern are critical to supporting all second language learners (Lewis-Moreno, 2007).

In accordance with the 1974 U.S. Supreme Court decision in *Lau v. Nichols*, schools must provide limited English proficient (LEP) students with "educational opportunities reflecting their language needs" (Burnett, 1993, p. 1). The Supreme Court decision did not specify the way in which this was to be done, leaving the implementation up to each school district. Decisions regarding the placement of second language learners in specific programs typically occur on entrance to school and at the end of each academic year. These decisions are based on an assessment of each child's level of English language proficiency. These placement decisions are critical to each child's success at school; however, the ways in which such decisions are made are complex and sometimes controversial (Rossell & Baker, 1988, in Burnett, 1993).

Many school districts use a home language survey (HLS) to determine a child's home language (J. Villegas, personal communication, July 19, 2004). An HLS typically asks questions that identify the language first learned by the child in the home and that language that used more frequently by both the child and the adults in the home (Burnett, 1993). Once it is determined that English is not the home language, the child's proficiency is then assessed using additional tests.

Two commonly used assessment tests are (a) the Measure of Developing English Language/MODEL (World-Class Instructional Design and Assessment/WIDA, 2005) assesses oral language skills in English and Spanish; and (b) Assessing Comprehension and Communication in English State-to-State for English Language Learners/ACCESS (Center for Applied Linguistics and WIDA, 2008). These language proficiency tests are used with students in grades K–12 and measure a wide range of the language competencies that will be needed for academic settings.

Conversational Proficiency and Academic Language Proficiency Needed

Assessing second language learners should involve both their conversational fluency and their fluency and understanding of academic English. If second language learners are assessed only on their conversational fluency prior to transitioning to English-only classrooms, they may still experience difficulty in succeeding in this classroom setting. Cummins (1984, in Del Vecchio & Guerrero, 1995) identified two distinct aspects of language proficiency required for second language learners to be successful in English-only classrooms: conversational fluency and academic English fluency. Conversational proficiency enables children to engage in social conversations effectively. In these everyday conversations, language is embedded in a context that provides support for developing the meaning of the communication. This proficiency is referred to as **basic interpersonal communication skills (BICS)**.

Proficiency in using academic English is referred to as **cognitive academic language proficiency (CALP)**. As described in an earlier section of this chapter, this involves using language to engage in academic tasks where the learner must rely on linguistic cues to develop meaning, such as in reading a textbook or listening to a teacher's direct instruction of a particular concept. This involves a much higher cognitive demand than that experienced in everyday, informal conversations. It is closely related to conceptual development and academic achievement. This is especially evident as children engage in content area subjects such as science, social studies, and mathematics.

In Cummins's (1994) review of research, he concluded that English language learners need 2 years to acquire age-appropriate conversational proficiency, and they need 5 to 7 years to acquire academic proficiency. The differentiation of these two types of proficiency and the difference in the time needed to acquire each type of proficiency means that when second language learners transition to English-only classrooms after acquiring conversational fluency in English, they may still need substantial language support for several more years. If there is no formal program at your school for providing this support, you will need to develop and implement learning activities and interactions in your classroom to meet their needs in acquiring academic register proficiency. Using comprehensive assessment measures such as the WIDA MODEL and ACCESS to monitor second language acquisition provides a more useful assessment of the full range of second language learners' linguistic competencies and areas of future growth.

Language Acquisition and Language Learning

Language acquisition refers to unconscious learning of language in naturalistic settings with a focus on meaning; in contrast, **language learning** refers to conscious rule learning in formal instructional settings with an emphasis on the form of language (Krashen, 1995, 2003). Specific programs for bilingual children can embody characteristics of language acquisition or language learning. Research on such programs indicates that those incorporating more naturalistic features of language acquisition settings are more successful than those focusing on language learning (Altwerger & Ivener, 1994; Krashen, 1995; Wong Fillmore, 1995).

Approaches to Second Language Acquisition and Learning

U.S. schools' responses to the challenge of educating nonnative speakers have taken several different approaches. These approaches reflect the social values placed on the native language and English and also reflect an expectation of the value of those respective languages to the students' futures. Research on past programs has documented the critical impact of such programs on family culture and communication. When young L2 students focus only on learning English and have little opportunity to use their native language, and when little value is placed on their first language in the larger culture, they lose their ability to speak their first language. In such settings, tragic disruptions of family relations have been reported (Wong Fillmore,

1991). When children can no longer communicate with their parents or extended families in their first language, social relationships break down.

Current educational approaches to linguistically diverse students include English as a second language (ESL) and several forms of bilingual education. Some programs focus only on students' acquisition of English to enhance and facilitate their success in educational settings; others seek to maintain and enhance learners' home language competencies. In addition, other programs introduce a new language to monolingual English students to develop second language acquisition. In the sections that follow, these educational approaches are described.

English as a Second Language (ESL)

ESL programs focus only on teaching English. Students' first languages are not a consideration, nor are their languages used in any aspect of classroom instruction. Teachers in ESL programs may not have any knowledge of, or fluency in, students' respective first languages. The goal of this approach is to foster the acquisition of English so that students can participate in English-only instruction.

In most schools, ESL programs involve intensive English instruction for part of the day and placement in regular classrooms for the rest of the day. Gradually, students transition to English-only classrooms while still receiving assistance from an ESL resource room in a pull-out program schedule. A "push-in" support program may also be used (J. Villegas, personal communication, October 9, 2000). This involves the ESL instructor working in the regular classroom along with the classroom teacher in meeting the needs of the language-diverse students. When successful, students are phased out of ESL assistance and are able to participate in English-only classrooms on a full-time basis.

One of the main challenges posed by the ESL approach is to develop and implement instructional strategies and techniques that foster English acquisition among students from diverse linguistic backgrounds. In some urban areas, ESL classrooms are composed of students coming from a wide range of linguistic diversity: Spanish, Russian, Polish, Greek, Chinese, French, Vietnamese, Bosnian, and Arabic. Specially trained ESL instructors are critical to the success of these classrooms. ESL programs are usually found in schools where there is a wide linguistic diversity without sufficient numbers of students with the same linguistic background to mandate bilingual education programs. Successful ESL programs provide frequent opportunities for peer interactions (Fassler, 2003). Through these peer interactions, students have access to comprehensible input as well as more opportunities to talk.

The emphasis on the acquisition of the academic register for ESL students in the upper elementary grades has been incorporated in the Cognitive Academic Language Learning Approach/CALLA (Chamot & O'Malley, 1995). By focusing on grade-appropriate content curriculum, ESL students are prepared to enter the regular classroom with the appropriate level of content knowledge. An emphasis on academic language acquisition provides ESL students with an opportunity to develop competencies in using the literate register found in the written materials used for instruction.

The Sheltered Instruction Observation Protocol/SIOP Model (Center for Applied Linguistics, 2012) provides a research-based set of components that guide teachers in designing and implementing lessons for English learners. This model supports teachers from beginning lesson preparation through implementation and then assessment.

Bilingual Education

In bilingual approaches, both the first language and the second language are emphasized, though in differing degrees. **Transitional bilingual education/TBE** has as its goal the gradual transition from the student's first language to English. This approach is used in self-contained classrooms where children are taught by a teacher who is fluent in both languages. Initially, content area instruction is in the child's first language. English is taught as a separate subject. Then English is gradually introduced and used during instruction (Genesee, 2001). Over a period of 2 to 3 years, the amount of English used in classroom instruction increases.

The transitional bilingual approach recognizes the need to begin instruction in the language in which children are fluent; however, the first language is not considered valuable to the children's long-term education; only English is valued. This approach does not consider the value of children's first language to their family culture or to the larger society's culture. In this way, transitional bilingual education may actually result in "subtractive bilingualism."

Developmental (maintenance) bilingual education is similar to transitional bilingual education in that both languages are also used in instruction; however, the similarities end at that point. Developmental bilingual education emphasizes both languages throughout children's education, so that fluency in both the first language and English are developed and maintained (Cloud et al., 2000; Genesee, 2001). This type of instruction also occurs in self-contained classrooms where the teacher is fluent in both languages and where all of the students have the same first language. This approach acknowledges and emphasizes the value and need for fluency and competency in using both the first language and English. Children who experience this approach to bilingual education develop authentic bilingualism. They are equally able to use both languages for purposes of learning and in their social environments. Thus, developmental bilingual education is an example of "additive bilingualism."

To implement transitional or developmental bilingual education programs successfully, schools must have a large enough number of students who speak the same first language and are at the same educational level, and they must employ professionally trained teachers who are fluent in both the first language and English. Some states, including Illinois and California, mandate bilingual programs for schools with 20 or more students who speak the same first language. Financial considerations often arise in schools with small numbers of students at different educational levels, which requires bilingual programs involving only five or six students at each level. This dramatically increases the cost of implementing a bilingual program.

Immersion Programs

In **immersion programs**, children are grouped according to their first language. Teachers in immersion classrooms must have fluency in both languages. Instruction in the language arts is provided in their first language. Instruction in all other areas of the curriculum is in the second language (Krashen, 1995). Typically there is no formal instruction of the second language. While most immersion programs have been for majority language children, such as English-fluent children learning Spanish, immersion programs can also be used with non-English-proficient students. For example, a class of Spanish-fluent children would receive instruction in language arts in Spanish, with content-area instruction—math, science, and social studies—in English.

Immersion programs vary with the grade level at which they are introduced (Piper, 1993). Early immersion programs begin in kindergarten, delayed immersion begins in third or fourth grade, and late immersion begins at sixth grade or later.

Two-way immersion programs, also known as **dual language programs**, are instructional programs designed to develop linguistic competency in more than one language (Genesee & Gándara, 1999). Half of the students come from homes where English is the home language and half from homes where a different language (e.g., Spanish) is spoken as the home language.

There are wide variations in how these two-way immersion programs are organized. In some programs, the majority language (English) is used 90% of the time, with the minority language (e.g., Spanish) used 10% of the time. In other dual language programs, there is a 50–50 split: half of the day in one language and half of the day in another language (Baker, 1996; Cloud et al., 2000). Students in each group serve as language models for each other (Cummins, 1998). In some situations, the entire elementary school follows a dual language program, while other dual language programs may involve specific grade levels, mostly at the primary level. Some schools institute a three-phase dual language program where the proportion of time the target language (e.g., English) is used gradually increases until each language is used 50% of the day (J. Villegas, personal communication, October 9, 2000). For example, in grades K–3, the Spanish/English proportion is 80/20; grades 4–6, 60/40; and grades 7–8, 50/50.

Second foreign language immersion programs are designed for language majority students (e.g., native English speakers). In these elementary classrooms, the second language, such as Spanish or Japanese, is used to teach 50% of the curriculum (Cloud et al., 2000).

Submersion Approach

When a school does not have a bilingual program for second language learners, these students then may be placed in a regular classroom along with other students who have English as their first language. This approach is called the submersion approach. The teacher may not be bilingual and may not have received any special training. The second language learners in the room may not all speak the same first language. Some may speak Spanish, others Polish, Chinese, Cambodian, Korean, or Russian.

The rationale for this approach relies on the assumption that second language learners will gradually acquire English through participating in an English-only environment. By their participation in this environment, it is expected that they will be able to acquire English, having heard it used in various learning activities, settings, or both. No value or consideration is given to their first language.

Submersion programs have been described as having a "sink or swim" approach (Baker, 1996; Faltis, 1998; Krashen, 1995), where the learner is likened to someone who, without knowing how to swim, is thrown into the deep end of a pool and is expected to either sink or struggle to swim. Submersion programs alone do not facilitate comprehensible input. Typically, the level of language used by both the teacher and the other students far exceeds the linguistic competencies of the second language learner. However, when a separate ESL pull-out class is added to a submersion program, second language learners are more likely to experience target language at a level they can comprehend (Krashen, 1995).

Foreign Languages in the Elementary School/FLES

In contrast to ESL and bilingual programs where the target language is used in content instruction, some elementary schools have a language program where English-speaking students are taught another language with the focus on the language as a subject. The most frequently taught languages in these programs are Spanish, German, and French (McLaughlin, 1985). Foreign Languages in the Elementary School programs range from 50 minutes of direct language instruction each day to 20 minutes of instruction three times per week (Piper, 1993). These programs have met with varying degrees of success in facilitating children's acquisition of a second language. Programs with an emphasis on rote, pattern drills, and grammatical lessons have had less success than programs emphasizing cultural awareness and oral communication. One of the key factors in FLES programs is the opportunity for students to use the target language in communicative settings at school and in their community environment. This contributes to fluency; unless a language is used functionally in daily conversations and learning activity dialogues or discussions, fluency cannot be achieved. An increase in FLES programs in the United States in recent years indicates an awareness of the importance of linguistic diversity to our students' futures.

GUIDELINES FOR TEACHERS IN LINGUISTICALLY AND CULTURALLY DIVERSE CLASSROOMS

As a classroom teacher, you have a critical role in creating opportunities for your students to develop and maintain their linguistic diversity, whether this involves a language or dialect difference. In addition to examining your own perspective toward linguistic and cultural diversity, you will want to create a positive classroom environment, build on children's first language competencies, and create a learning community in your classroom.

Examining Your Own Perspective

You will have a significant role in influencing your students' attitudes toward linguistic diversity and in enhancing their motivation to learn (Cary, 2007; Saracho & Spodek, 1995; Scott, 1995a). Initially, it is important for you to be aware that a child's home language is closely tied to his personal identity and culture (Delpit, 1990, 2006). When a teacher or a school implies that a child's home language is "wrong," the negative feeling extends to the child's family and culture. Instead, teachers should acknowledge and value the linguistic diversity that children bring to the classroom.

In the United States, most teachers are monolingual, with English as their only language. While they may speak more than one dialect, they may be unaware of issues related to language diversity. Unless they have traveled extensively to other countries or regions, lived in areas where another language is used, or formally studied another language, they may be unaware of the role of language in other cultures and of the cognitive, linguistic, and social demands of acquiring a second language.

As a first step in addressing the needs of children of linguistic and cultural diversity, each teacher must seriously reflect on her own attitudes and perspectives toward linguistic and cultural diversity. Recognition of the need to change one's own attitude is an initial step (Scott, 1995a). This recognition must be followed by taking advantage of opportunities to learn more about the languages and cultures represented in your classroom. A next step involves monitoring your own behavior for direct or indirect behaviors that might indicate low expectations for linguistically diverse students. Scott (1995a) recommended that small groups of teachers work together, "meeting periodically to discuss their observations, evaluations, and progress with monitoring [their] behaviors that communicate low expectations" (p. 277). Another step in the process of attitude change involves examining the ways in which linguistically diverse students are assessed. Scott (1995a) proposed that a "balanced data bank" be developed on each student's performance, including both strengths and areas of needed emphasis and resulting in a more complete profile of each student.

To become aware of the ways in which cultures may be similar or different, you will also need to examine your own culture and your students' culture with respect to these aspects: family structure, life cycle, interpersonal role relationships, discipline, time and space, religion, food, health and hygiene, and history, tradition, and holidays. It is important to acknowledge and understand one's own culture and language community as it provides a basis for becoming aware of one's identity and "cultural self" as well as beginning to understand other cultures and language communities (Zygmunt-Fillwalk & Clark, 2007). Teachers who have examined and reflected on their own attitudes toward linguistic and cultural diversity and acquired information about the respective cultures and languages represented in their classrooms are better able to create classroom environments that enhance the learning opportunities of all children. (See Figure 3.2 for a listing of teacher resources. See Figure 3.3 for a summary of ways to examine your own perspectives.)

FIGURE 3.2
Teacher Resources for Linguistic and Cultural Diversity

Boyd, F., Brock, C., & Rozendal, M. (2004). *Multicultural and multilingual literacy and language: Contexts and practices.* New York: Guilford Press.

Cary, S. (2000). *Working with second language learners: Answers to teachers' top ten questions.* Portsmouth, NH: Heinemann.

Cloud, N., Genesee, F., & Hamayan, E. (2000). *Dual language instruction: A handbook for enriched education.* Boston: Heinle & Heinle.

Delpit, L. & Dowdy, J. (Eds.). (2002). *The skin that we speak: Thoughts of language and culture in the classroom.* New York: The New Press.

Drury, R. (2007). *Young bilingual children talking and learning at home and school.* Sterling, VA: Stylus Publishing.

Eggers-Pierola, C. (2005). *Connections and commitment: Reflecting Latino values in early childhood.* Portsmouth, NH: Heinemann.

Helman, L. (2004, February). Building on the sound system of Spanish: Insights from the alphabetic spellings of English-language learners. *The Reading Teacher, 57* (5), 452–460.

Paley, V. (2000). *White teacher.* Cambridge, MA: Harvard University Press.

Santa Ana, O. (2004). *Tongue-tied: The lives of multilingual children in public education.* New York: Rowman & Littlefield.

Swiniarski, L., Breitborde, M., & Murphy, J. (2003). *Educating the global village: Including the young child in the world* (2nd ed.). Upper Saddle River, NJ: Merrill/Prentice Hall.

Tabors, P. (2008). *One child, two languages: A guide for preschool educators of children learning English as a second language.* Baltimore: Paul H. Brookes.

York, S. (2003). *Roots & wings: Affirming culture in early childhood programs.* St. Paul, MN: Redleaf Press.

Wheeler, R. & Swords, R. (2006). *Code-switching: Teaching Standard English in urban classrooms.* Urbana, IL: National Council of Teachers of English.

Wolfram, W. & Ward, B. (Eds.). (2006). *American voices.* Malden, MA: Blackwell Publishing.

FIGURE 3.3
Examining Your Own Perspectives

- Reflect on your own attitudes and perspectives toward linguistic and cultural diversity.
- Explore opportunities to learn more about the languages and cultures represented in your classroom.
- Examine the ways in which linguistically diverse students are assessed
- Examine your own culture thoroughly (e.g. family structure and roles, discipline, religion, food, health and hygiene, history, traditions

Creating a Positive Classroom Environment

One of the major ways that you can facilitate the development of linguistic diversity is by creating a classroom environment that acknowledges, values, and enhances that diversity. Guidelines for creating a positive classroom environment for linguistically diverse students include (see Figure 3.4 for a summary of these guidelines):

1. Selecting literature from different cultures and dialects in the classroom. During the past two decades, many high-quality trade books have been published on the folktales, legends, and customs of diverse cultures that introduce cultural characters (Beatty & Pratt, 2003). Using diverse literature increases the cultural awareness of students and encourages acceptance of diversity (Delpit, 1995).

2. Emphasizing that language use is determined by the culture in which it is used. Bring examples of other languages into your classroom in the form of books, newspapers, and other written materials as well as in songs.

3. Focusing on the pragmatics of language: how language is used differently in different situations and settings. Talk about the ways we use language in various social routines and settings, such as ordering at a fast-food restaurant, participating in a religious service, making a purchase at a store, and seeking information from a government office. Pragmatic knowledge of written language can be emphasized in exploring the ways language is used differently in fairy tales, mysteries, nonfiction, and poetry.

4. Modeling a curiosity and interest in other languages and dialects. Show your interest in other languages by bringing other languages into your classroom. Invite speakers (such as parents) of other languages to come to your class to share their language with your students. Encourage children to share their diverse language knowledge with you and their classmates.

5. Learning basic greetings and expressions in a variety of languages and dialects. Ask speakers of those languages in your classroom to help you with the articulation and inflection. This would be a good opportunity to involve bilingual parents in your classroom. Teach the greetings and expressions to your students. Use these greetings and expressions in daily communication in your classroom orally and in writing. (See Appendix for examples from several languages.)

6. Encouraging students in monolingual classrooms to develop an awareness of linguistic diversity through literature, guest speakers, media, and field trips to ethnically diverse communities. Students in classrooms that are monolingual can also benefit from opportunities to explore linguistic and cultural diversity. Such opportunities enhance students' conceptual development and their social–cultural awareness.

7. Incorporating a multicultural approach throughout the curriculum each day, not just a one-time unit or seasonal "tourist" approach.

8. Avoiding activities that perpetuate the concept that all people from a particular cultural group are the same (Derman-Sparks & ABC Task Force, 1989).

9. Selecting classroom materials that reflect diversity, such as ethnic dolls and role-playing attire.

FIGURE 3.4

Create a Positive Classroom Environment

---

1. Select literature from different cultures and dialects in the classroom.
2. Emphasize that language use is determined by the culture in which it is used.
3. Focus on how language is used differently in different situations and settings.
4. Model a curiosity and interest in other languages and dialects.
5. Learn basic greetings and expressions in a variety of languages and dialects.
6. Encourage students in monolingual classrooms to develop an awareness of linguistic diversity.
7. Incorporate a multicultural approach throughout the curriculum each day, not just a one-time unit or seasonal "tourist" approach.
8. Avoid activities that perpetuate the concept that all people from a particular cultural group are the same.
9. Select classroom materials that reflect diversity.

Building on First Language Competencies

As an early childhood teacher, you will also need to facilitate second language learners' use of their first language. This provides a basis for developing English oral competency and academic English register. This can be accomplished by (See summary of guidelines in Figure 3.5):

1. Acknowledging the student's first language or dialect as a valid form of communication. By sharing your positive attitude toward the student's dialect or language, you are enhancing the child's self-esteem and confidence.

2. Learning about the student's home language or dialect so that you are aware of potential language interference with respect to phonology, morphology, syntax, semantics, or pragmatics. This knowledge will help you assist the student in differentiating between the two language systems.

3. Acknowledging the student's need to develop receptive knowledge of Standard English before using English expressively. Provide many opportunities for students to hear storybooks and nonfiction books read aloud. Select books with illustrations that support the text by providing clear referents to the concepts presented. Be aware that second language learners will experience a "silent period" during which they will be actively listening but rarely will participate verbally in class interactions.

4. Providing many opportunities for students to engage in conversation/discussion. This will enhance their productive–expressive language. When these opportunities involve only two or three children in a conversation or discussion, L2 students are more likely to participate.

5. Allowing students to respond in their home language first, and then to focus on translating their responses into English. This does not mean that the monolingual teacher must be able to assist L2 students in making the translation; however, the teacher should allow time for L2 students to process the message in both languages and to assist each other in communicating.

6. Providing second language learners with cues, letting them know when to anticipate being called on or when their turn will be. If L2 students can anticipate their turn and are aware of the type of response needed, they will be able to participate more successfully in class discussions and recitations.

7. Providing content-area books that have clear illustrations of the main concepts presented in the text. With the main concepts illustrated, second language learners can identify concepts they already have in their first language and then learn the concept label in the second language. Second language learners can also benefit from being encouraged to use the illustrations to predict the upcoming text.

8. Providing opportunities for students to work together with other ESL students and with English-fluent students. Through group activities, students learn how to focus on a task, how to use language to accomplish the task, and how to work together. Cooperative learning opportunities will often draw out students' conceptual knowledge and cognitive competencies, which can be shared through problem-solving strategies.

9. Using songs, nursery rhymes, and finger plays to emphasize the sound–symbol system and phonemic awareness. These activities facilitate children's awareness of sound similarities and differences. The rhythm of the language also promotes a memory for the song or rhyme.

10. Providing opportunities to learn through hands-on, exploratory, experiential activities. Concept development is enhanced through hands-on activities. As concepts develop, conceptual schemata develop, and the child acquires the new language labels for the concepts. Hands-on experiences support conceptual development and subsequent language acquisition.

Creating a Learning Community

One way you can facilitate positive attitudes toward cultural–linguistic diversity is by creating a learning community in your classroom. At the center of each learning community is a teacher's deep respect for each child in her classroom. This means that the teacher's interactions with her children clearly communicate that "regardless of color, heritage, socioeconomic level, etc., all children in the class will have equal access as well as equal responsibility" (Miller & Pedro, 2006, p. 296). This can be accomplished by (See summary of guidelines in Figure 3.6):

1. Encouraging all students to participate verbally in the learning activities and class discussions in a nonthreatening, supportive manner. This involves intervening immediately when negative interactions occur so that students know that everyone is to be valued and respected (Wessler, 2003).

2. Responding positively to each student's contribution.

3. Making explicit the expectations for behavior and responses during large and small group discussions so that everyone understands what behavior is appropriate.

4. Encouraging students to use written text as a source of their knowledge during oral discussions and in opportunities for critical thinking.

FIGURE 3.5
Build on First Language Competencies

1. Acknowledge the student's first language or dialect as a valid form of communication.
2. Learn about the student's home language or dialect.
3. Acknowledge the student's need to develop receptive knowledge of Standard English before using English expressively.
4. Provide many opportunities for students to engage in conversation/discussion.
5. Allow students to respond in their home language first, and then to focus on translating their responses into English.
6. Provide second language learners with cues, letting them know when to anticipate being called on or when their turn will be.
7. Provide content-area books that have clear illustrations of the main concepts presented in the text.
8. Provide opportunities for students to work together with other ESL students and with English-fluent students.
9. Use songs, nursery rhymes, and finger plays to emphasize the sound–symbol system and phonemic awareness.
10. Provide opportunities to learn through hands-on, exploratory, experiential activities.

FIGURE 3.6
Creating a Learning Community

1. Encourage all students to participate verbally.
2. Respond positively to each student's contribution.
3. Clarify the expectations for class time behavior and responses.
4. Encourage students to refer to written text during oral discussions.
5. Provide a variety of opportunities for students to engage in small group activities.
6. Encourage students' creativity through open-ended activities.
7. Welcome parents to visit your classroom.
8. Encourage parents to share their cultural knowledge.
9. Create a lending library in your classroom for children and parents.

5. Providing a variety of opportunities for students to engage in small group activities within formal and informal settings.

6. Encouraging students' creativity through open-ended activities.

7. Welcoming parents to visit your classroom for open house and informal visits and to participate in class field trips.

8. Encouraging parents to share their cultural knowledge with your classroom.

9. Creating a lending library in your classroom for children and parents.

By encouraging students to communicate with each other in a wide variety of ways and for a wide variety of purposes, teachers can enhance students' understanding of each other by developing shared experiences and interactions.

SUMMARY

Linguistic diversity in languages and dialects is a common characteristic of urban U.S. settings and some rural areas where groups of recent immigrants have settled. Different languages and dialects represent authentic and valid forms of communication for specific cultures, locales, and families. Children who come to your classroom will have developed their language competencies in the varied settings of their homes and communities. Your role is to continue to enhance children's language development and to encourage children to develop linguistic flexibility so they can communicate effectively in a wide variety of settings. One aspect of this linguistic flexibility involves becoming fluent in the literate register, academic English.

Acquisition of a second language involves the same processes, interactions, and aspects of language knowledge as the development of the first language. Three major factors have a significant influence on second language acquisition: learner characteristics, social setting, and linguistic input. These factors are complex and interdependent. In the United States, public elementary schools are required to provide specific language programs (e.g., bilingual education and/or English as a Second Language/ESL) to support children of linguistically diverse homes.

The acquisition of linguistic competencies and linguistic flexibility among children with language or dialect differences can be enhanced by modeling positive teacher perspectives, creating a positive learning environment, building on first language competencies, and developing a community of learners. Language knowledge continues to be acquired long after basic conversational fluency is attained as children experience and participate in more complex educational tasks and varied social situations.

✳ ✳ ✳   CHAPTER REVIEW

1. Key terms to review:

Sapir–Whorf
   hypothesis

sociolinguistics

verbal-deficit
   perspective

ethnography

socialization
   mismatch
   hypothesis

dialect

pidgin

creole

Standard American
   English (SAE)

modes of discourse

bidialectism

academic English

literate register

simultaneous
   bilingualism

successive
   bilingualism

language
   interference

code mixing

codeswitching

subtractive
   bilingualism

additive
   bilingualism

comprehensible
   input

Basic Interpersonal
   Communication
   Skills (BICS)

Cognitive Academic
   Language
   Proficiency
   (CALP)

language
   acquisition

language learning

transitional	bilingual	dual language
bilingual	education	program
education (TBE)	immersion program	second foreign
developmental	two-way immersion	language
(maintenance)	program	immersion program

2. What are the benefits of bilingualism?

3. How is acquisition of a second language related to first language acquisition?

4. List and explain factors that influence second language acquisition.

5. What is the role of the teacher's perspective in a culturally and linguistically diverse classroom?

✳ ✳ ✳ CHAPTER EXTENSION ACTIVITIES

Observation

Observe in a bilingual preschool or primary classroom for to 2 hours. Describe how first and second languages are used in formal and informal communication.

Curriculum Development

Select a children's trade book (fiction or nonfiction) that focuses on a non-English language or diverse culture. Review the book. Explain how you would use this book in an early childhood classroom, describing the learning activities that would be based on the book.

4

Language Development
of Infants and Toddlers

Learning Outcomes

After reading this chapter you should be able to

- Explain the role of adult responsiveness in communicating with infants
- Describe the phonological development of infants and toddlers
- Explain the connection between concept development and semantic knowledge
- Provide several examples of a toddler's telegraphic speech
- Describe how infants begin to use gestures to show communicative intent
- Describe how toddlers begin to use language differently in different settings

Miriam looked at her newborn as she held him in her arms. He was alert, his eyes were open, and he seemed to be looking intently at Miriam's face. "Hello there, little one," Miriam said. "What a handsome boy you are. The nurse even put a blue bow on your hair. And such a tight grip you have. . . . Uh-oh! Was that a hiccup I heard?" In response to her voice, her newborn turned his head slightly, reestablishing eye contact. "Oh," Miriam responded, "it was a hiccup. How did you get the hiccups?" After patting him gently on the back, she looked at him and said, "There, there. Are you feeling better now? Did you get rid of those hiccups?" After a short pause in which no more hiccups occurred, Miriam said, "Yes, all better now. No more hiccups."

Miriam's verbal interactions with her newborn illustrate the beginning of communication for many young infants. Through their interactions with adults and older children, infants learn how language works. Language development begins when language speakers assume that an infant is a participating partner in conversational settings, even though it is months before the child is able to begin using conventional words. In this chapter, we will first focus on the early contexts in which children begin to participate in communicating with others. Later sections of the chapter will describe infants' and toddlers' language development in each of the five aspects of language knowledge: phonological, semantic, syntactic, morphemic, and pragmatic.

EARLY COMMUNICATION CONTEXTS

Beginning at birth, children are part of a social environment. It is within this social environment that language development begins. In the opening vignette, Miriam responded to her newborn as if he were a conversational partner. Although he did not respond verbally, she interpreted his nonverbal behaviors as if he had spoken. For example, when Miriam held her newborn in the hospital, and heard him hiccup, she responded as if he had spoken when she said, "Oh, was that a hiccup I heard?" She continued to respond to his nonverbal behaviors as if he was verbally communicating with her.

Key interaction patterns.   This opening vignette illustrates two key interaction patterns that enhance language development: eye contact/shared reference and communication loops. After establishing eye contact with her newborn son, Miriam created a communication loop by speaking, listening, and then responding to her newborn's nonverbal behavior. This process of getting an infant's attention and maintaining that attention is critical to creating a setting in which linguistic exchanges can occur (Cleveland, Schug, & Striano, 2007; Karmiloff & Karmiloff-Smith, 2001). Another critical aspect of communication that children experience as newborns is the pattern of turn taking or interactive dialogue (Tronick, Als, & Adamson, 1979). As infants participate in turn taking, whether nonverbal or involving speech, they become part of a communicative dialogue. According to Bruner (1990), "language is acquired not in the role of spectator but through use. Being 'exposed' to a flow of language is not nearly so important as 'using it' while 'doing'" (p. 70).

At about 8 months of age, an infant will follow his parent's gaze so that when his parent looks away the infant's gaze will follow in the same direction. Then, at about 10 to 12 months, the infant will be able to adjust his gaze to follow when his parent points in the direction of an object or event and then reestablish eye contact with his parent in response to this shared attention on the object or event (Johnson, Myers, & Council on Children with Disabilities, 2007).

Infants' continued participation in eye contact/shared reference and communication loops is critical to later language development and social interaction. A recent publication from the American Academy of Pediatrics (Johnson et al., 2007) identifies deficits in eye contact/shared reference as "one of most distinguishing characteristics of young children with autism spectrum disorder (ASD)" (p. 1191). This does not mean that every child who does not engage in eye contact and shared reference by late infancy is going to develop ASD; however, it does indicate that additional professional screening and evaluation should be considered.

Focus on meaning in early interactions.   Adults and older children talk to and interact with infants from the day they are born. Underlying these interactions is the assumption on the part of adults and older children that infants' behavioral responses and spontaneous verbal utterances are meaningful. This assumption initiates and sustains communicative interaction between infants and their families and other caregivers. The ways in which parents and caregivers direct young children's attention to ongoing events and the meaning of those events also has an important role in language development (Zukow-Goldring & Ferko, 1994). Individual differences among children in the rate of word learning have also been attributed to the frequency of parental speech directed to children as well as the variety of words used and the way in which the new words are presented (Karmiloff & Karmiloff-Smith, 2001).

Importance of adult responsiveness.   An important factor in early social interactions is the responsiveness of adults to an infant's behaviors (nonverbal and verbal). Higher levels of maternal responsiveness have been associated with children's later comprehension of speech (receptive language) (Paavola, Kunnari, & Moilanen, 2005). In their study of African American children (ages 18 to 30 months) from low-income families, Roberts, Burchinal, and Durham (1999) reported that "children from more stimulating and responsive homes . . . [had] larger vocabularies, [used] more irregular nouns and verbs, [used] longer utterances, and [had] increased rates of acquiring irregular forms . . . than children from less responsive and less stimulating homes" (p. 101).

The type of responses made by adults to infants (9 months of age) during interactions involving shared reference has been associated with children's later language competencies. When adult responses to children were contingent and focused on the meaningful content of the interaction, there was a positive relationship with infants' use of vocabulary as toddlers (Rollins, 2003).

The context of the interaction with toddlers also appears to be characterized by different types of language used by teachers as well as mothers. Researchers have found that the type of utterances used by teachers in interacting with toddlers varies with the context of the play in the classroom. For example, O'Brien and Xiufen (1995) compared teachers' language in various areas of a toddler classroom. In the doll/house area, teachers used a wider range of vocabulary and asked questions, while in the block/truck area, teachers asked fewer questions and made more suggestions. Similarly, Wiley, Shore, and Dixon (1989) reported that during book sharing, mothers focused on labeling and describing while during free play their utterances focused on the child's action. Mothers focused on maintaining shared reference in both the book sharing and free play contexts.

Differences in the contexts of communicating with infants and toddlers have also been documented in cross-cultural studies. For example, Karmiloff and

A critical aspect of communication for infants is the pattern of turn taking or interactive dialogue.

Karmiloff-Smith (2001) described specific cultures where parents spoke minimally to their children when they were prelinguistic, talking directly to their children only after they were capable of actually producing speech. Regardless of the parental and cultural interaction pattern, children in all cultures eventually learn to speak fluently. As research on the contexts of early communication continues, we will develop a clearer understanding of cultural and social interaction patterns and the various ways children develop language competencies.

In addition to eye contact/shared reference and communication loops, additional interaction patterns are embedded in a variety of contexts that enhance language development during infancy and toddlerhood. These include verbal mapping, child-directed speech, linguistic scaffolding, and questioning. Examples of these interaction patterns will be embedded in subsequent sections of this chapter as different aspects of language development are described.

Critical periods for language development.   It is only through interaction in the environment that language is acquired. Studies documenting severe language deprivation, such as Genie (Curtis, 1977, in Obler & Gjerlow, 1999) and among institutionalized orphans (Bruer, 1999), have provided evidence of the importance of nurturing young children's language development. In addition, the quality and quantity of the stimuli in the linguistic environment in which an individual interacts have a major impact on the development of language (Eliot, 1999). Further, the timing of environmental interactions is also important because some aspects of language development appear to be tied to critical periods, or "windows," of development (Bruer, 1999).

For example, the development of knowledge of phonemes, syntax, and morphemes appears to have critical periods for development. For phonological knowledge, the time from birth up to about age 10 is the optimum time for development. Syntactic and morphemic knowledge appear to have a critical period from birth up to puberty (age 12 to 14). However, Bruer cautions that there is evidence to suggest that not all learners are affected by these critical periods and they are able to acquire native mastery of a second language after the "critical period" has passed (p. 138). Bruer states "experience-dependent brain changes continue to occur throughout [a] child's life" (p. 187). In contrast, semantic knowledge (vocabulary) does not appear to be limited by a critical period of development (Bruer, 1999). Individuals continue to acquire semantic knowledge throughout their lives as learners. In addition, pragmatic knowledge appears to have no critical period of development.

ASPECTS OF INFANTS' AND TODDLERS' LANGUAGE DEVELOPMENT

Each of the five aspects of language knowledge is present in young children's receptive and expressive language behaviors. Receptive language develops first and provides a basis for later expressive language. In the sections that follow, each of the aspects of language will be described, along with examples of oral language behaviors that illustrate the receptive and expressive behaviors during infancy and toddlerhood. Within each section, an overview of the connection between oral language development and emergent literacy will be presented.

Examples and approximate ages will be given in this chapter and the next to illustrate language development and emergent literacy behaviors. These examples and references to specific ages should not be used as benchmarks for measuring or judging specific children. While developmental patterns may exist, universal, fixed ages for achieving those stages are nonexistent and are highly influenced by environmental settings and sociocultural interactions. It is also important to remember that variations in the development of language (both oral and written language) have been observed within the same child, fluctuating from day to day, with a variety of contexts, and between children of the same age or level of maturation.

In addition, it is important to keep in mind that each aspect of language knowledge does not develop in isolation from the other four aspects; instead, their development is interrelated. For the purposes of describing infant and toddler development in each of these areas, phonological language knowledge will be described first, followed by semantic, syntactic, morphemic, and pragmatic development. Of these five aspects, phonological knowledge has been the subject of the earliest research during a child's pre-birth and newborn phases.

PHONOLOGICAL DEVELOPMENT IN INFANCY

In acquiring language, an infant must first begin to "sort out" the speech sounds that are used by others in his environment (Werker & Desjardins, 1995). Small differences in speech sounds often distinguish big differences in meaning, such as *pat* and *bat*. Receptive language knowledge of the sounds of a language begins to develop as the infant hears the speech of others around him (Monastersky, 2004). Researchers have documented the perception of speech sounds beginning during the late prenatal period throughout infancy. In the section that follows, specific findings from that research will be described, along with an overview of the methods researchers have used to determine perception of speech.

Receptive Phonological Knowledge

Research methodology. In determining infants' perception of speech sounds, a variety of research techniques have been used. Researchers exploring sound perceptions by fetuses measured the differences in heart rhythms when new speech sounds were introduced. When a new sound was introduced, a fetus's heart rate decreased; as the specific sound was repeated, the fetus became accustomed to the sound, and the heart rate resumed its normal rhythm (de Boysson-Bardies, 1999). Research with newborns and young infants has used nonnutritive sucking intensity as a way to determine their perception of novel sounds as well as the perception of familiar speech sounds. With older infants, beginning around 4½ months, nonnutritive sucking is no longer a workable technique; researchers then monitor infants' eye gaze and head turning to determine speech and sound perception.

Researchers have also implemented recent technological advances in studying brain waves. By attaching electrodes to different areas of an infants' scalp, researchers are able to monitor the brain waves that occur during speech sound perception (Cheour et al., 1998; Conboy & Kuhl, 2011; Dehaene-Lambertz & Gliga, 2004; Kuhl, 2005). Analysis of these patterns of brain wave activity provides evidence of the perception of phonemes as well as larger units of speech.

In utero. Research on children's perception of speech and the development of the auditory system in utero has determined that the fetus can perceive sounds beginning with the 25th week of gestation (de Boysson-Bardies, 1999). At 35 weeks' gestation, a fetus's hearing acuity is at a level similar to an adult's. Thus, during the last months of pregnancy, a fetus can hear her mother's voice and perceive other sounds in the environment.

Knowledge of infants' perceptual abilities related to language is closely intertwined with research on brain growth and neurological development. Bergen and Coscia (2001) noted that brain research supports the view "that the capacity for basic language development is 'wired' into the anatomical structure of the brain" (p. 29).

At birth. Children are born with specific predispositions to pay attention to language and people in their environments. Infants can perceive differences in sound (Wolff, 1966) and have been found to prefer the human voice over any other sound, including environmental sounds (Condon & Sander, 1974; Eisenberg, 1976; Jensen, Williams, & Bzoch, 1975). As early as 4 days after birth, infants seem "to prefer to listen to their mother tongue over certain other languages," though they do not respond differently to other unfamiliar languages (Karmiloff & Karmiloff-Smith, 2001, p. 44). This indicates a biological readiness to perceive and process the sounds of language (Reich, 1986). In addition, research has documented infants' ability to distinguish their mother's voice from other voices within 3 days after birth, even showing a preference for their mother's voice over other female voices (DeCasper & Fifer, 1980; Karmiloff & Karmiloff-Smith, 2001).

Early infancy. DeCasper and Spence (1986) found that infants show preference for the acoustic characteristics found in a speech recited by the mother when pregnant rather than an unfamiliar speech not read during pregnancy. Further evidence of children's predisposition to attend to and process language comes from research that has documented children's ability to distinguish between specific sounds of language (phonemes) as early as 1 month of age (Aslin & Pisoni, 1980). Thus, children can evaluate and compare auditory stimuli beginning in early infancy. This perceptual ability facilitates children's responses in their interactions with people in their environment.

Research with very young infants has concluded that they can distinguish nearly all the phonemic contrasts represented in natural language (Cheour et al., 1998; Jusczyk, 1985). Children can distinguish specific phonemes as early as 1 month of age (Aslin & Pisoni, 1980). In addition, at 5 months, infants recognize and categorize the same phonemes, regardless of changes in speakers and intonation (de Boysson-Bardies, 1999; Jusczyk, 2003). Babies can also distinguish between sequences of syllables (Bijeljac-Babic, Bertoncini, & Mehler, 1993). Researchers are also beginning to document the relationship between phonological perception and speech segmentation during infancy and later language development at 2 years of age (Newman, Ratner, Jusczyk, Jusczyk, & Dow, 2006; Tsao, Liu, & Kuhl, 2004).

Role of prosody. The role of prosody in infants' language perception has been explored. **Prosody** refers to the pitch, loudness, tempo, and rhythm of speech (Crystal, 1987). From early on, infants are able to categorize utterances from different languages, based on the rhythmic (prosodic) patterns of the utterances (Jusczyk, 2003; Kuhl, 2005). The rhythm of an infant's home language is a very salient feature (Karmiloff & Karmiloff-Smith, 2001). Researchers have reported that 2-month-old infants detected changes in phonemes when the phonemes were part of short sentences rather than in word lists (Mandel, Jusczyk, & Kemler-Nelson, 1994).

de Boysson-Bardies (1999) concluded that prosody is "a perceptual glue that holds together sequences of speech" and that "the natural prosody of the language of infants' mothers commands their listening attention" (p. 28). Motherese, also known as child-directed speech, has more exaggerated intonation and clearer articulation. This may provide opportunity for infants to hear more closely the specific speech sounds and begin to make distinctions between similar-sounding phonemes (Kuhl, 2005) as well as distinguish word units (Thiessen, Hill, & Saffran, 2005). Thus, prosody appears to have a significant role in attracting the attention of infants and supporting their perception of speech sounds.

Late infancy.   Between 8 and 10 months, infants begin to pay more attention to phoneme–sound contrasts that exist in their home language, while they pay little or no attention to phoneme–sound contrasts found in other languages (Cheour et al., 1998; Jusczyk & Hohne, 1997, in Jusczyk, 2001; Kuhl, 2005; Palmer, Fais, Golinkoff, & Werker, 2012). This is interpreted to indicate that infants are beginning to pay particular attention to the sounds of the language surrounding them; a language that they will begin to use as they interact with family and others in their community.

Infants in homes where two languages are spoken also begin to discriminate between the phonemes used in each language. Researchers who studied infants from bilingual homes by measuring brain activity during linguistic processing found that these children showed neural discrimination between Spanish and English phonemes at 10 to 12 months of age (Garcia-Sierra et al., 2011). Such research provides evidence that important developments in children's early phonological development occur during infancy and before children are able to speak. Further, the language environments in which infants reside influence this development (Conboy & Kuhl, 2011).

Speech Development

Although infants perceive a wide range of phonemes and environmental sounds, their production of speech sounds is limited by their immature physiology. Speech requires coordination of the vocal tract, including the larynx, glottis, hard and soft palate, jaw, lips, and tongue. In addition, breathing needs to be coordinated with the vocal cords in order to have sufficient air available for speech production.

As physical maturation occurs during the first year of life, infants gain more control of the speech mechanism and begin to speak. This maturation involves significant changes in the physiology of the speech mechanism. For example, in newborn babies, the "larynx is high and close to the oral cavity, and the tongue is proportionally much larger than it is for the adult" (Cairns, 1996, p. 37). This means that a young infant's vocal tract is small. As maturation occurs during the first year, the larynx position moves lower. In addition, during the first 4 months of infancy, the curve of the vocal tract changes from a slant to the right-angle curve found in adults. These maturational changes influence the production of sounds, making it possible for the infant to produce a wider variety of sound patterns (Cairns, 1996; de Boysson-Bardies, 1999).

Infants' production of speech sounds and sound patterns is also influenced by the development and maturation of neural pathways in the brain. For example, infants' production of patterns of sound (i.e., babbling) occurs during the time that myelination of the axons is taking place in the brain cells controlling motoric activity (Cairns, 1996). During the myelination process, a protein sheath or covering develops along the axon which insulates it and keeps the nerve impulse traveling along that axon from short-circuiting other nearby neurons. Thus, the neurological development of the brain plays a significant role in infants' production of speech sounds, initially in babbling and later in more complex forms of utterances.

Early vocalizations.   Early infant vocalizations are initially reflexive and later on nonreflexive vocalizations develop (Stoel-Gammon, 1998). **Reflexive vocalizations** come from the infant's physical state. Crying, coughing, hiccupping, and burping are examples of reflexive vocalizations. Between 6 and 8 weeks, many infants spontaneously produce cooing sounds (Reich, 1986; Wolff, 1966). Cooing, and later on, babbling are **nonreflexive vocalizations**. **Cooing** sounds are extended vowel sounds such as *ooo*, *ahhh*, *eee*, and *aaaa* and are often made in relative isolation of each other. These sounds involve less complex production than consonants that involve the lips and teeth, such as *b*, *p*, *t*, *m*, and *c*. Later on, cooing sounds are "strung together, often 10 or more at a time. These strings are not pronounced in a rhythmical way; there are no clear intonational contours" (Crystal, 1987, p. 236).

The cooing stage is important because during this time, infants begin to manipulate their tongues and mouths in producing sounds. These actions are precursors to actions required for later speech production. Cooing is followed by a period of **vocal play**, during which the vocalizations begin to show a wider range of consonants and vowels and a range of articulation aspects (e.g., a nasal quality) and day-to-day variations (Crystal, 1987). Infants appear to be exploring and practicing how to produce, repeat, and vary sounds.

Babbling.   At about 4 to 6 months, babbling appears (Clark & Clark, 1977; Reich, 1986; Sachs, 1989; Segal, 1983; Stoel-Gammon, 1998). **Babbling** involves the production of consonant–vowel sounds of varying intonation. Babbling is essentially reduplicated sounds, such as *ba-ba-ba-ba*. In contrast to the variations observed in vocal play, babbling involves the production of less varied sounds with greater frequency. Some of the sounds produced in early babbling have been found to be representative of phonemic distinctions different from those found in the specific language culture of the infant (Reich, 1986). Sachs (1989) cited evidence that infants also produce a relatively small subset of sounds that are similar across different languages, such as English, Arabic, and Chinese. Only when longer babbling segments with intonational cues were analyzed could listeners accurately identify which infants were from specific language cultures.

At about 8 to 10 months, a child's babbling develops an echolike quality. This type of babbling, termed **echolalic babbling**, appears to echo the rhythm and phonation of adult speech in the child's environment (de Boysson-Bardies, 1999). It may sound as if the infant is carrying on a conversation with someone. This type of babbling has also been described as **jargon** (Sachs, 1989) and **intonated babble** (Stoel-Gammon, 1998).

The universality of the babbling stage is underscored by research with infants who are deaf (de Boysson-Bardies, 1999). Prior to 6 months of age, a child who is deaf vocalizes the same way as a child who can hear. After 6 months, children who are deaf do not progress to vocalizing syllables or a series of syllables, and vocalization decreases. When a baby who is deaf is 1 year old and has developed some muscular control over lip movements, vocal babbling occurs again. Further evidence of babbling as a stage in language development is documented by research indicating that babies who are deaf and are raised with sign language babble with their hands at 6 to 10 months of age (de Boysson-Bardies, 1999; Fisher, 1974, in Prinz & Prinz, 1979; Lillo-Martin, 1999; Masataka, 1996), manipulating the "elements of signs, much like the babbling stage of hearing infants" (Petitto & Marentette, 1991, in Armstrong, Stokoe, & Wilcox, 1995, p. 123).

An infant's exploration and production of vocal sounds is often accompanied by encouragement from the infant's family and caregivers. In some early face-to-face interactions, the adult imitates the sound made by the infant and then pauses, waiting for the infant to respond. This resembles a follow-the-leader vocal game. Occasionally, as a child produces a different sound, the adult responds with an imitation of the new sound. **Selective reinforcement** occurs when children are encouraged to produce and repeat the sounds that are appropriate and necessary for their home language, though Sachs (1989) cautioned that the use of this term may be an oversimplification of the language development process that is actually occurring. At about 11 to 12 months, infants may begin to produce word-like units that have relatively consistent sound patterns. A small number of conventional words may also be produced, such as "no." Further description of invented and conventional word used by infants is presented in the later section on semantic knowledge. The highlights of phonological development in infancy are presented in Figure 4.1.

FIGURE 4.1
Timeline of Phonological Development in Infancy

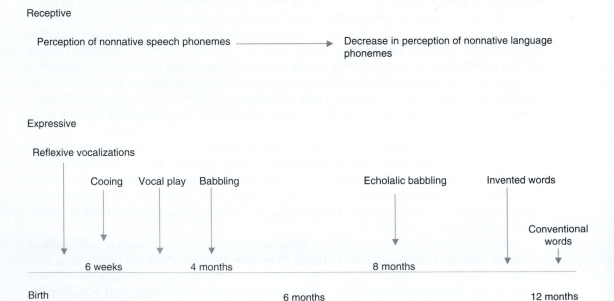

Early book sharing with infants and phonological development. In literate cultures, awareness of phonological distinctions may develop as infants engage in picture book sharing activities with parents or caregivers (Baghban, 1984). Parents may engage their infants in looking at the pictures by using wide variations in sounds and intonation. For example, animal sounds ("The cow says 'mooooo'"), rhyming text, songs, and environmental sounds (e.g., sounds of fire trucks, train engines). In this way, picture book sharing stimulates auditory perception and phonological awareness related to spoken and written language.

In a case study of an 11-month-old child, Otto (1994) described a young child's attempts to reproduce her mother's varied intonation and expressive sounds during the infant's independent picture book interactions. Although the infant was not yet speaking in words, the intonation of her vocalizations resembled the pitch, stress, and rhythm of her mother's speech during picture book sharing. Early picture book experiences appear to stimulate a child's awareness of the sounds of language and to develop an association between the sounds of language and illustrations in books. This association is the beginning of a child's **emergent literacy**, a gradual acquisition of knowledge about written language and the process of reading.

PHONOLOGICAL DEVELOPMENT IN TODDLERHOOD

Children's perception and production of phonemes becomes especially evident during toddler years, as they begin to speak a range of words. Initially, pronunciation of a child's first words is not stable, varying from day to day or even more often (Clark & Clark, 1977; Reich, 1986). Variations have also been documented between children in terms of the specific sounds mastered (Reich, 1986).

Toddlers are aware of speech sounds they cannot make (Ferguson, 1978) and may avoid or refuse to pronounce words containing those sounds. Children appear to have several ways of dealing with words whose sounds are too difficult to pronounce. Menn (1989) provided a detailed linguistic description of the ways children approach the pronunciation of difficult phoneme patterns. One of these ways is by reducing the sounds of consonant clusters (e.g., sp, bl, st) to one sound. Thus, instead of saying *spill*, the toddler says *pill*, and *store* becomes *tore*. When one child changed *blanket* to *banke*, she omitted the initial consonant cluster and left off the last consonant. Toddlers' avoidance of difficult sounds is also evident when adults ask them to imitate or repeat someone's name. If toddlers perceive difficulty in pronouncing the name, they may refuse, either verbally, by remaining silent, or nonverbally, by shaking their heads or looking away.

Adults may engage in imitating sounds made by toddlers to initiate a turn-taking, game-like interaction. For example, Ryan's mother described the following episode when he was 15 months of age (Otto, 1980):

As we were riding in the car, Ryan was sitting in his car seat in the back seat. He started making /sh/ sounds, as in *sh-sh-sh*. I repeated the sounds he made. He would wait a few seconds and then make repeated /sh/ sounds. This turn taking repeated four times, going back and forth. He would smile and make eye contact (in the mirror) as I made the sounds. Then it would be his turn. Then I tried making several /sh/ sounds and then saying a word with that sound, such as "shoes." Ryan did not respond with any /sh/ sound or attempt to say the word; however, when I would go back to saying only /sh/ sounds, he would then repeat or mimic those sounds. After about 10 minutes, he lost interest in the game.

Evidence of toddlers' awareness of sound similarities and patterns also occurs when toddlers express delight, respond nonverbally with body movement, or both while poetry or rhythmic prose is read or when action songs or finger plays are performed.

Phonological awareness and experiences with print.   Literacy-related phonological awareness begins to develop during toddlerhood, when children associate sounds and sound patterns with print in their environment. This development is based on a child's general level of phonological perception and production. For example, *Richard Scarry's Word Book* was a favorite book of Ryan's when he was 21 months old. While sharing the book with his mother one day, Ryan pointed to letters of the alphabet in the cover pages and verbalized. Then his mother started to give the correct phoneme as he pointed to each letter. He continued to point to letters randomly, and his mother gave the corresponding phoneme. In this way, Ryan explored the specific sounds that are associated with each alphabetic letter (Otto, 1980).

During the toddler years, children may also begin to explore letter and sound connections by manipulating magnetic letters displayed on their family's refrigerator or in their early childhood classroom. For example, a child might place the letters D and B on the refrigerator and say, "Daddy, bee" as well as naming the letters as they use them.

HEALTH PROBLEMS AND PHONOLOGICAL KNOWLEDGE DEVELOPMENT

When infants and toddlers experience health problems related to their perception or production of speech sounds, the development of phonological knowledge will be influenced. In this section, two specific health problems will be described: ear infections and physical malformations in the speech mechanism.

Ear Infections: Otitis Media

A child's speech and hearing mechanisms are sometimes affected by health problems during the early years. The onset and recurrence of ear infections is an all-too-frequent health problem of young children that can significantly impair language and speech development. Early childhood teachers and caregivers need to be aware of the characteristics and significance of this illness so that they may assist parents in safeguarding the health and development of young children.

Prevalence.   **Otitis media** refers to inflammation of the middle ear (Allen, 1993; Williams, 1994). Middle ear infections and fluid in the middle ear represent a common illness among young children; 85% to 90% of all children in the United States experience at least one ear infection before age 6 (Robinshaw, 2007; Williams, 1994). Otitis media is the second most frequent illness among children in the United States, second only to the common cold (Strauss, 1993). Almost 70% of all U.S. children will develop otitis media while they are toddlers (Brooks, 1994). Some children experience few ear infections; others have recurring, chronic infections during their toddler and preschool years. Children who attend group care or preschool during their early years experience more ear infections as they are exposed to more respiratory viral infections (Allen, 1993; Daly, 1997; O'Neill, 1999). (See Figure 4.2 for a diagram of the ear.)

Young children are more likely to have ear infections than older children or adults because of the angle of their **eustachian tube**, which connects the middle ear with the throat (pharynx). In young children, the eustachian tube has a horizontal orientation. This changes to become a 45° incline in older children and adults (MedicineNet.com, 2012).

FIGURE 4.2
Ear Diagram

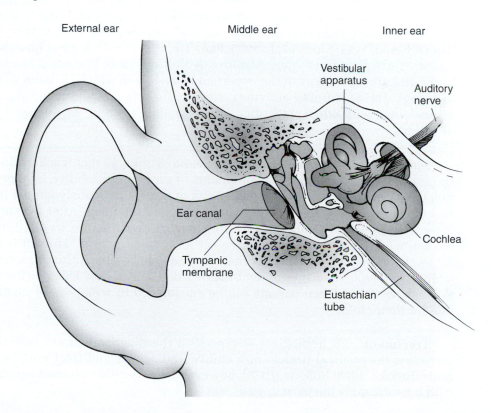

Effects of ear infections.   Speech perception is impaired by the presence of fluid in the middle ear because the fluid keeps the tympanic membrane from vibrating normally. When ear infections recur during infancy and the toddler years, this may affect a child's ability to recognize and distinguish between phonological characteristics essential for learning to speak and understand language (Mody, Schwartz, Gravel, & Ruben, 1999). For example, the buildup of fluid in the middle ear distorts language sounds and may result in a child's having difficulty distinguishing between /b/, /p/, /t/, and /d/. As a result, *bad*, *pad*, *dad*, and *Tad* may all sound alike (Given, 2002). Children with histories of ear infections during their first year of life have been found to have reduced consonants in their babbling (Luloff, Menyuk, & Teele, 1992, in Mody et al., 1999).

Severe, chronic cases of otitis media have long-term effects. It is the most common cause of acquired hearing loss among young children and is also associated with impairment in learning and language skills (Brooks, 1994). Cognitive development is influenced by stimulation from each of the senses. According to Allen (1993), "Sensory input may stimulate a greater number of interconnections between neurons in the brain" (p. 3). Allen further indicated that, in instances where sensory loss is long-term, delays in speech and reading development occur and general intelligence is affected, even though the hearing loss is eventually corrected.

Longitudinal studies of children with varying degrees of otitis media have documented the long-term effects of ear infections in young children in the domains of language and cognition and also in their interactions with others (Feagans, Kipp & Blood, 1994; Mody et al., 1999; Paradise, 1997; Teele, Klein, Chase, Menyuk, & Rosner, 1990; Vernon-Feagans, Manlove, & Volling, 1996; Wallace & Hooper, 1997). These areas involve many of the important behaviors in which children must be able to engage during learning activities, such as listening, comprehending, speaking, getting along with others, attending, concentrating, reading, writing, and following directions.

Symptoms of ear infections.   Otitis media symptoms that teachers and parents should watch for include fever, complaints of ear pain, irritability, lethargy, inattention to verbal stimuli, or lack of perception of sounds previously known (indicating loss of hearing). Children may pull at their ears or rub them. After the ear pain and fever have gone away, children's hearing may still be impaired by fluid in the middle ear, which may be retained in the ear for several months. Thus, it is important for teachers to watch for behavior that may indicate hearing difficulties, such as irritability, listlessness, or intermittent inattention (Denk-Glass, Laber, & Brewer, 1982; Robinshaw, 2007). Then parents can be encouraged to seek prompt medical attention for their child.

Treatment.   Technological advances in the diagnosis of ear infections have increased the medical profession's ability to diagnose and treat middle ear infections (Brooks, 1978; Roberts, 1976); however, there is little universal agreement as to which treatment is the most appropriate.

Antibiotics are the most common form of treatment for middle ear infections. Children typically take an oral antibiotic for approximately 2 weeks, followed by an additional visit to the doctor to check on the condition of the ear(s); however, the use of antibiotics is controversial (Marcy, 2001). Use of antibiotics has been associated with impaired immunity and recurring ear infections (Center for Medical Consumers, Inc., 1995) as well increases in resistant bacteria (Williams, 1994).

Another type of treatment for chronic middle ear infection involves surgically inserting a very small tube through the eardrum into the middle ear (referred to as a pressure equalization tube) (Allen, 1993; Feldman et al., 2003; Strauss, 1993), to ventilate the middle ear and prevent the fluid (effusion) from accumulating. This type of treatment is often done in children for whom ear infections recur frequently. The tube usually stays in the eardrum from several months to 2 years. Sometimes the tubes fall out on their own; in other instances, they are removed by a surgeon. The tubes do not prevent future occurrences of otitis media; instead, they provide drainage of the fluid that accumulates during any future episodes of otitis media. Tube insertion does, however, decrease the incidence of acute otitis media; because the fluids are drained away, severe infection is less likely to occur.

Physical Malformations in the Speech Mechanism

Physical malformations in the speech mechanism, such as a cleft palate, cleft lip, or a tongue abnormality, hamper a child's acquisition of specific speech sounds because the production of sounds is impaired. In many of these cases, corrective surgery is appropriate and effective. In some instances, speech therapy is needed during the "catch-up" period following surgery (Bellenir, 1997).

SEMANTIC DEVELOPMENT IN INFANCY

Children's perception of the sounds of language often occurs during events or interactions that add meaning to the sounds and sound patterns they hear. Although infants' stable use of speech units with meaning does not usually occur until about age 1 or later, infants may begin to participate in communicative settings shortly after birth.

Early Associations Between Speech and Meaning

Early interactions between parents and infants are often in response to the infant's cries. Young infants' crying and fussing occurs as an expression of their physiological and emotional status (Lederman et al., 2002; Soltis, 2003). Wolff (1969, in Santrock, 2001) described three types of cries: (a) a basic cry, (b) an anger cry, and (c) a pain cry. These types of cries are distinguished by pitch, rhythm, and intensity.

The ways in which an infant's parents and caregivers interpret and respond to the infant's crying often creates interactions in which the adult's language exposes children to the way meaning is developed and communicated. Our discussion of semantic development begins here with the topic of infants' cries because their cries elicit a parental or caregiver response that nearly always involves language and the assumption that the cries "mean" something. This assumption of meaning leads to the inclusion of children in interactive dyads (adult and child), which promotes communication.

When adults interact with crying infants, they assume that the infants have a particular need (Bell & Ainsworth, 1972). Often the context of the crying provides a clue. Perhaps a fire engine speeds by, noisily blasting its siren and waking the infant from sleep. An adult might presume that the child was startled by the noise and attempt to calm the infant. The soothing behavior of the adult most likely would include speech low in volume, using terms of endearment. If the infant is not quieted, the adult may test other possible sources of discomfort, such as a soiled diaper, hunger, change of position, or temperature of the sleeping area. These attempts are usually also accompanied by speech directed to the infant. The adult directly monitors the infant's verbal and nonverbal responses and interprets them as indications of the child's continued need or satisfaction. In these early infant–adult interactions, children are introduced to meaningful communication.

Concept Development and Receptive Semantic Knowledge

When meaning is attached to words or sequences of speech sounds, young children begin to develop semantic knowledge. Semantic development is closely tied to concept development. Children develop semantic knowledge through their experiences in varied environmental contexts that foster concept development (Harris, 1990). The first concepts children learn represent important objects, people, or actions in a culture (Menyuk, 1988). From those experiences, children develop ideas or notions of the ways in which stimuli, such as objects, actions, and other phenomena, are similar, different, or interrelated. As children process this information cognitively, they develop ways of categorizing these stimuli into abstract conceptual groupings, or schemata. Concept knowledge may develop before language labels (words) are attached to the concept. However, when children begin to attach conventional words to those concepts, they are on their way to understanding the speech of others and to communicating their thoughts and ideas (Vygotsky, 1962).

Direct and vicarious experiences.   Two types of experiences facilitate concept and semantic development: direct and vicarious. **Direct experiences** occur from birth on, as infants experience objects and events in their world as a direct participant— touching, tasting, smelling, seeing, and hearing. During this time, interaction with adults or older children serves to assist a child in safely exploring the environment through the senses and provides the child with object or action labels. Vicarious experiences begin to occur when a child acquires symbolic representation and begins to use and comprehend language in late infancy. **Vicarious experiences** occur when children interact with concepts through visual representations (such as pictures or print) or through verbal description alone without the actual referent being present. For example, listening to a book read about trucks is a vicarious experience, whereas riding in a truck or watching a big garbage truck rumble down the street is a firsthand experience. In infancy, many of children's experiences are essentially all firsthand, or direct. While direct experiences have a greater impact on concept development, both direct and vicarious experiences make valuable contributions to concept development.

Affective experience and concept development. One aspect of concept development relates to an individual's affective experience. The emotional content or functional intent of linguistic interactions also contributes to concept development. "New words take on meaning and become part of the child's vocabulary only when attached to emotion or intent" (Greenspan, 1997, p. 78). Children learn words that represent significant items or actions in their environments, such as the names of family members, the family pet, or specific foods. The emotional bond they have with their parents and other adults provides the motivational context for developing concepts and words relating to their immediate setting. When these interactions are pleasurable and reciprocal, children are motivated to acquire the spoken symbols, which makes communication possible.

Symbol formation: Associating speech sounds with meaning. When adults share objects with young children, they connect the present object or **referent** with the verbal symbol (i.e., a word) for that object (e.g., "rattle," "ball"). Through repeated experiences beginning in infancy, children acquire receptive knowledge of language symbols and their referents that are important in their respective environments. This pairing between a word and its referent has also been described as a mapping of the language onto the object or specific meaning (Hirsh-Pasek & Golinkoff, 1996). Infants appear to be using this principle of reference as they develop semantic knowledge.

The association of specific words (i.e., labels) with objects and actions in their environments is explained by the process of **symbol formation**. Four components are present in symbol formation: the addressor (adult or older child), the addressee (young child), the object or referent (e.g., rattle, ball, bottle), and the symbolizer's means for representing the referent (word or gesture; see Figure 4.3).

At first, the actual object or action must be in the immediate environment for the child to comprehend or produce the concept label. After repeated experiences that pair the object/referent with the symbolic medium (oral word), the word alone will elicit the concept for the child. When this occurs, symbolic representation has developed because the presence of the symbol alone elicits the concept. In Werner and Kaplan's (1963) description of symbol formation, this process of **distancing** the presence of the actual object or action (referent) from the use of the concept label (word–symbol) is a significant step in symbol formation (see also Sigel & Cocking, 1977). For example, the process of distancing is evident when a parent says, "Go get your ball," and the child responds by going to another room, retrieving the ball, and bringing it back. Before children can use concept labels (i.e., words), symbolic thinking and symbol formation must occur.

Symbol formation is also present in the following example: A parent repeatedly pairs the word *cracker* with an actual cracker so that the infant gradually begins to

FIGURE 4.3
Components of Symbol Formation

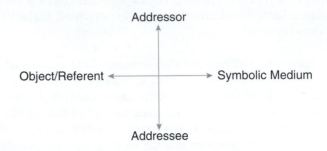

associate the word with the item. Initially, a parent asks, "Do you want a cracker?" as the parent holds a cracker for the infant to see. Over time, these repeated pairings result in the infant's responding when the word *cracker* is heard with no visible snack present.

Concept labels (i.e., words) and schemata are culture and language specific. A child's home language is the language she learns first. Thus, a child whose home language is different from English might have a similar concept of ball with respect to what a ball looks like and what it does; however, the word referring to that concept might be quite different. The *ball* schema would be different for people living in other cultures because each culture may use balls differently and in different activities. Children's use of words to indicate culturally common concepts is evidence that they are acquiring semantic knowledge.

Semantic development, then, first occurs in an infant's understanding of others' words and actions and object associations. Between 8 and 12 months, most infants can comprehend numerous words (de Boysson-Bardies, 1999; Jewell & Zintz, 1990; White, 1978). The average receptive vocabulary of a 10-month-old infant is 50 words (Golinkoff & Hirsh-Pasek, 2006). An infant's perception of suprasegmental elements of language (i.e., intonation: stress, pitch, and juncture) also adds to semantic development as meaning, attitude, and emotion are communicated through these elements before the words themselves are comprehended (Stewig, 1982).

Key interaction patterns in symbol formation. Three types of interactions are important to children's development of conceptual knowledge and vocabulary: turn taking, eye contact/shared reference, and verbal mapping. The turn-taking process, involving an adult or older child engaging a child in a conversation-like interaction, encourages a child to attend to the object or action and to respond to the speaker's verbal behavior, actions, or both.

Another important type of interaction is eye contact/shared reference of an object or action by both a child and an adult. This interaction pattern underlies symbol formation—that is, the association between the verbal label (word) and the referent. Gradually, as a child matures cognitively, the verbal symbol (word) for an object elicits the concept without the presence of the actual referent; however, eye contact remains important to early communicative contexts.

Verbal descriptions provided by adults enhance a child's awareness of her environment.

Verbal mapping is another interaction pattern that facilitates the development of semantic knowledge. When a parent is describing an ongoing action or event for her child, she is mapping the language onto the action. For example, a mother holds her 5-month-old infant while standing at a window in their home, looking at the bird feeder out in the yard. A cardinal comes to the feeder. The mother says to the infant, "Oh, look at the bird! It's a pretty red birdie. See, he's coming to eat. Look at the birdie! He's eating now. Oops, he flew away. Bye-bye, birdie." Different versions of this scene may be repeated throughout the following months in varied settings with varying verbal descriptions. For example, a mother might describe a bird as it flies by as they are riding in a car. She might also describe a bird they see while walking in the park or a bird in a tree in the backyard. Verbal descriptions or mapping provided by adults and older children enhance infants' understanding of how language can represent events and objects.

Expressive Semantic Knowledge

At about the age of 1 year, children may, with some degree of consistency, begin to use distinct vocal units to refer to specific objects or actions. It is important to keep in mind that some children will begin several months later and will eventually acquire language competency the same as the early talkers. Menn (1989) referred to children's early invented words as **protowords**, and others refer to them as **idiomorphs** (Reich, 1986; Werner & Kaplan, 1963). According to Reich (1986), idiomorphs develop from four different sources: (a) straining sounds that accompany gestures of need; (b) imitation of environmental sounds such as those made by keys, motors, and animals; (c) self-imitation sounds that occur naturally and then are repeated when a certain outcome is desired, such as "Achoo" meaning "I need a handkerchief"; and (d) imitation of adult speech.

The development of idiomorphs is important for three reasons:

1. Idiomorphs are children's first consistent sound patterns that have relatively stable referents.
2. Idiomorphs are evidence of children's ability to create and develop their own language.
3. Parents and teachers who learn the meaning of children's idiomorphs encourage children's verbal interactions by, in effect, learning each child's unique language.

As a child makes the transition from idiomorphs to more conventional words, the idiomorphs may be used with adult-like inflection, combined with other adult words to make compound words, or combined with an adult form of the same word (e.g., /ba/ *sheep*; /muh/ *cow*). Some children switch back and forth between using idiomorphs and adult forms for a period of time (Reich, 1986).

In a review of research describing children's first words, Owens (2012) noted that most of their words refer to people or animals in their immediate environment or objects young children can manipulate. Nouns are usually acquired before verbs (de Boysson-Bardies, 1999). Most young children develop a core vocabulary of frequently used words (Shatz, 1994). The realization that everything has a name marks an important event in a young child's language development (Vygotsky, 1978). This realization is usually followed by a toddler's intense interest in having objects in their environment labeled.

In addition to using one-word utterances that refer to people, objects, or actions in their environment, children in this stage may use utterances to express more complex thoughts. This one-word stage is also referred to as the **holophrastic stage**, because one word is used to convey a whole thought and is accompanied by distinct intonation, stress, pitch, or vocal rhythm. For example, the word *mama* may convey a variety of messages when spoken with varying stress and pitch. It may very well be intended to communicate any of the following:

- "Come pick me up!"
- "I'm scared."
- "Oh, I'm glad you're back home."
- "I'm uncomfortable."

Semantic knowledge of infants and emergent literacy. The development of semantic knowledge related to emergent literacy occurs as infants and adults participate in picture book interactions. During this activity, adults typically use gesture and finger pointing to establish a shared reference before labeling the character or object pictured.

Adults select for naming and labeling those pictured items that are entities in the child's environment and often those whose referents are visible at that time, such as a ball, chair, cat, or toy train. In repeated readings of storybooks, adults encourage greater participation from young children in labeling concepts pictured and in expanding the number of items named. In some instances, an adult reading a storybook emphasizes the sound made by an item pictured, such as a growling lion, and the child then uses an idiomorph (invented word) for the lion pictured based on the growling sound.

Children who have been included in storybook sharing events since early infancy, beginning at about 4 to 5 months, often show that they are predicting the meaning of upcoming text by their verbal and nonverbal behavior. In a case study of emergent reading among infants, Otto (1995) documented an 11-month-old girl's anticipation of upcoming story text. In this study, a mother and her 11-month-old daughter were sharing a book that they had shared repeatedly over previous months. The text pattern on successive pages was "touch your nose," "pat your head," and "wiggle your toes." Just seconds before the mother read "pat your head," the little girl reached up and patted her own head. When the mother turned to the page where the text was "wiggle your toes," the little girl's toes began to wiggle. During this interaction, the little girl's attention was focused on the storybook, and she appeared to be listening to her mother's speech.

In another instance, this same pair was sharing a book about animals whose pictures were under small flaps on successive pages. The mother had established a routine of making noises for each animal pictured. When they came to the lion page and the monkey page, the little girl made the respective sounds slightly ahead of her mother. In both of these examples, this 11-month-old was attributing meaning to specific content in a storybook, an early form of emergent literacy.

SEMANTIC DEVELOPMENT IN TODDLERHOOD

Between 1 and 2 years of age, a child has 20 to 170 words in his productive vocabulary but understands many more (Biehler, 1976; de Boysson-Bardies, 1999; Morrow, 1989; Owens, 1988). There is considerable variation among individual children because their vocabulary will reflect their individual family contexts and experiences. While idiomorphs will still be part of a young toddler's expressive vocabulary, there is a gradual transition to conventional words.

Toddlers are busy people. Having achieved locomotion through crawling and walking, they eagerly investigate all available aspects of their environment. When they discover that everything has a name, they often eagerly seek names for objects and people in their environment. Toddlers may also use language in ways that increase their opportunities to learn about their world by repeating what others say, asking questions, or using repetition to clarify meaning (Shatz, 1994).

A toddler may also show an increased interest in staying close to her primary caregiver and frequently bringing objects to her for comment (Cawlfield, 1992). A typical interaction involves a child's question, "What's that?" pronounced quickly as "whadat?" or "whadis?" or, more simply, "dis?" with rising intonation. When the adult responds with the label, the child may repeat it spontaneously. The child may then continue the conversation by asking about another entity in the environment.

As objects and events in children's environments are repeatedly labeled, both the receptive (listening) and expressive (productive) vocabularies increase; however, the listening vocabulary is still larger than the productive vocabulary (Owens, 1988). The productive vocabulary of older toddlers (18 to 30 months) may range from 200 to 300 words, with a much more extensive listening vocabulary. A toddler usually maintains only one word per referent in his or her productive vocabulary. A child may experiment with a specific word and switch to another if the first word is not successful in referring to the desired object, action, or event (Reich, 1986).

Some adults, aware of children's increasing comprehension, start spelling words to communicate with another adult without the children comprehending, as in "Shall we go for a r-i-d-e?" This works for a while, though through repeated exposure, children quickly learn what the spelling sequence means. It is important for teachers and parents to realize that although children's speech production is limited, comprehension of others' speech is much higher.

Children may begin to use a specific word while engaged in a related activity, which indicates the importance of having present the referent for the concept related to that word. For example, at 18 months, Ryan's first spontaneous use of the word *ball* occurred when he was playing independently with a ball. Ryan's mother noted, "Ryan said 'ball,' /ba/ /1/, today. He was holding a ball when he said it. He repeated it several times while dropping the ball and running to pick it up" (Otto, 1980).

At times, children appear to learn some words quickly with only a few exposures and without specific feedback reinforcement. This is known as **fast mapping** (Carey, 1978; Gopnik, Meltzoff, & Kuhl, 1999; Owens, 2001). This rapid word learning has been documented in research with toddlers, preschoolers, and older children (Bloom, 2000; Crais, 1992; Markson, as cited in Bloom, 2000; Markson & Bloom, 1997). While the initial association between a referent and a word is learned after only one or two exposures, relating that concept to the child's other concepts occurs much later (Cairns, 1996). Researchers have also documented the ability of toddlers to learn new vocabulary after overhearing the words used by others (Akhtar, Jipson, & Callanan, 2001). This demonstrates toddlers' active role in acquiring new vocabulary.

One aspect of semantic development involves children's acquisition of categories, which organize phenomena into groups of shared characteristics. Gelman's (1998) research indicated that children as young as 2½ years are starting to make "broad generalizations about categories . . . these generalizations increase rather dramatically between two-and-a-half and four years" (p. 24). These generalizations may be evident in toddlers' semantic overextensions and underextensions as they develop schemata with general and specific concepts (e.g., "cats, dogs, squirrels are all animals").

The context of a child's speech provides clues to the intended meaning of one- and two-word utterances. When talking, toddlers rely on suprasegmental elements—the stress, pitch, and juncture of intonation—and gestures to get their message across in their one- and two-word utterances. In responding to toddlers, parents and teachers rely on contextual factors to assist them in interpreting the child's message. For example, when a toddler points to the light switch and says "Yes! Yes!" the child is indicating that she wants the light turned on. A child's statement "Mommy milk" can have a variety of meanings based on different pauses, intonation, and gestures, such as:

1. "Mommy, you're drinking milk, too."
2. "My milk's all gone, Mommy."
3. "Oh, look Mommy, I spilled the milk."
4. "Mommy, I want some milk."

Complex thoughts are also evident when toddlers say "all gone" and "uh-oh!" "All gone" indicates that the child has awareness that something that existed is no longer present visually. This is clear evidence that the child has acquired object permanence. "Uh-oh" is an expression that indicates something did not go as expected (D'Arcangelo, 2000). When Brad, age 2 years, 11 months, was playing independently, he often used the phrase "Oh, man!" to express his awareness that something was not going as he wanted it to. It is possible that Brad had heard one of his parents or extended family members use this phrase, and he interpreted the meaning of the phrase from the context and then applied it to his own play setting.

Semantic knowledge of toddlers and emergent literacy.   Semantic knowledge related to emergent literacy continues to expand during the toddler years, as children develop an awareness of environmental print and meanings, such as stop signs, McDonald's logos, and labels on food packaging. If you observe a mother and her toddler as they shop for the family groceries, you will often see that the toddler can easily pick out the cereal package he wants even though the specific print is not yet read. Further semantic development also occurs during storybook reading as words and their referents are paired and emphasized in narrative and nonfiction books.

When Alyssa was eating a strawberry at her family's kitchen table, she saw a strawberry pictured in the food flyer that came with the daily newspaper. She said /sta/ when looking at the picture in the flyer and then pointed to the strawberry she was eating and said /sta/. This shows her awareness of the connection between the real strawberry she was eating and the one pictured in the food flyer (Otto, 2012).

Among some children of toddler age, exploration of drawing and writing begins. Various researchers have described detailed study of the emergence of writing (Baghban, 1984; Clay, 1987; Sulzby, Barnhart, & Hieshima, 1989; Temple, Nathan, & Burris, 1982). Early on, children seem to begin to distinguish between drawing and writing in both form and function, indicating that writing is "read." The attachment of meaning to graphic representations is an important development in children's inter-actions with written language. By observing adults as they use paper and pencil and interact with print in the environment, children learn that graphic marks carry mean-ing. As toddlers make marks of their own on paper, they may turn to an adult to ask or confirm what meaning their writing has or may label it themselves (Baghban, 1984).

Children's awareness that written symbols carry meaning is often evident in the way they interact with printed or written materials in their home environments. For example, at 1 year, 9 months, Ryan picked up a letter from his grandmother (writ-ten in cursive) (Otto, 1980). As he looked at it, he began to verbalize /ladeladelada/. This similar verbalization also occurred when Ryan picked up and looked at infor-mational brochures, his parents' mail, and food cartons. Occasionally, he would ask one of his parents to read the print by asking, "Wha da say?"

The dynamics involved in young children's explorations of written language and meaning are illustrated in this example of a toddler who participates in cre-ating his family's grocery list (Otto 1980). One day Ryan, age 2 years, 11 months, approached his mother while she was writing out her grocery list. When asked what he wanted from the store, he replied "raisins." She then wrote it down on her list. A few moments later, she asked Ryan if he needed anything else from the store. He said "raisins" again. His mom replied that she'd already written it down. At that point, Ryan took the pencil from her hand and said, "Me write raisins." He then made some marks on the grocery list, along with some dots. Then he handed the paper back to his mother.

Throughout infancy and toddlerhood, children are active learners in building their concept knowledge and vocabulary. Daily interactions with people, objects, and actions in their environment provide direct and vicarious experiences that enhance children's development of semantic knowledge. When children have opportunities to observe parents and teachers interacting with written language and to participate in those interactions (via storybooks, grocery lists, mail, and newspapers), semantic knowledge related to written language is also enhanced.

Research suggests that children's sensitivity to the way in which words are ordered in language (i.e., syntax) also affects semantic development (Gleitman & Gilette, 1999). For example, verbs occupy a systematic or set place in English phrases and sentences. Children appear to perceive this "special place" as indicating that words used in this manner indicate actions and not objects. In this way, syntactic knowledge narrows down possible meanings of new words, thus facilitating seman-tic development.

SYNTACTIC DEVELOPMENT IN INFANCY

Syntactic development during infancy is not readily evident because infants do not begin to use expressive language until the later part of infancy and then only in the form of idiomorphs and single words. However, research with infants has documented their ability to "detect changes in the order of sounds" (Karmiloff & Karmiloff-Smith, 2001, p. 90; see also Gervain, Berent, & Werker, 2012). Children's receptive knowledge of syntax is developing during infancy as they observe and begin to participate in the communicative contexts around them.

Although children may be at the one-word stage in their productive language, research suggests that they are perceiving and processing language in five- to six-word segments. Children at the one-word stage appear to indicate "that words presented in strings are not isolated units but are part of larger constituents" (Hirsh-Pasek & Golinkoff, 1996, p. 73). This early awareness facilitates syntactic knowledge development. Comprehension of speech requires that children be able to process words, phrases, and sentences. They must be aware of the role of phrases and word order in determining meaning from speech. Research also indicates that infants may be attending to acoustic properties (prosody) in distinguishing phrasal units (Jusczyk, 1997).

Children develop receptive knowledge of syntax through speech directed to them and also by being listeners—observers in adult-to-adult interactions. Syntactically, adult-to-child speech is shorter in length and less complex grammatically. It contains repetitions, uses fewer subordinate clauses, contains fewer modifiers and pronouns, and has more content words and fewer verbs.

Mothers' speech to children has been studied more extensively than fathers' or caregivers' speech. There is some indication that mothers' speech to children changes syntactically during infancy (Clark & Clark, 1977; deVilliers & deVilliers, 1978; Harris, 1992; Snow, 1977). When speaking to 8-month-old children, mothers' speech is as long as it is to 28-month-old children; however, when a child enters the one-word stage, shortly after age 1, mothers' speech becomes shorter and focuses on eliciting verbal interaction from the child. Thus, it appears that, as children begin to talk, mothers simplify their speech and focus on encouraging their children to verbally participate. Then, after children reach a higher level of verbal production, at about 2 years, mothers' speech again becomes more complex. This is further evidence of mothers' sensitivity to their children's linguistic competencies and zones of proximal development.

Older infants' receptive knowledge of syntax is evident in their nonverbal responses to questions or directions such as "Where is your cup?" or "Go get the ball" or "Where is your nose?" When a child retrieves a cup or ball or points to his nose, comprehension of the question or request is evident.

Although infants' productive speech may involve single idiomorphs or one-word utterances, there is often an implied grammatical structure that indicates the sentence type. Through the use of intonation and gesture, children's one-word utterances are often perceived to be "questions," "statements," or "commands" (Crystal, 1987).

Syntactic knowledge of infants and storybook interactions. Infants who are involved in storybook interactions with adults are exposed to more complex syntactic structures than those present in daily conversational settings. As infants near their first birthday, they begin to participate verbally as well as nonverbally during storybook interactions. Adults intuitively appear to alter the exact text to fit the comprehension and linguistic competencies of children. They shorten the text, create their own version of the text, increase repetitions, ask questions, and add sound effects. These adaptations encourage more engagement from children. An example of this is found in the following transcription of a mother sharing *Where's Spot?* (Hill, 2000) with her 11-month-old infant (Otto, 1994). As you read through the transcription, notice the way in which this mother engaged her daughter in the storybook by repeating short phrases, pointing to the pictures, adding sound effects, asking questions, and creating her own version of the text. The child's familiarity with this book was evidenced by her active engagement in the book sharing. Note how the infant took charge of turning the pages, lifting the flaps to reveal the animals underneath, imitating the animal sounds made by her mother, and revisiting several pages after the book had been shared. Also note that the mother's speech involved a variety of syntactic patterns, from single words to short phrases to simple sentences. Book sharing experiences such as this provide opportunities for infants to hear and comprehend more complex syntactic patterns.

M=Mother C=child, 11 months of age

M: *(opens book) Where's Spot? (laughs)*

C: *(lifts flap revealing bear behind closet door)*

M: *Boo! That's a boo bear. (laughs)*

C: *(turns page, lifts flap to see snake inside clock)*

M: *Tick tock, here's the clock. No, oh, no! Tick tock, here's the clock. No, oh, no!*

C: *(turns page, lifts flap on piano to reveal hippo)*

M: *(singing) Yes, we have no pianos, No, oh, no!*

C: *(turns page, lifts flap to reveal lion under stairs; begins to open and close mouth)*

M: *Roarrr! There's a lion. (laughs)*

C: *(continues to open and close mouth)*

M: *That's a lion. Lions roarrrr!*

C: *(turns page, lifts flap to reveal monkey in cupboard; begins to make monkey noises)*

M: *Mon-key. (makes monkey noises) Mon-key. (makes monkey noises) He's having some bananas. (points to picture) He loves bananas. (more monkey noises)*

C: *(turns three pages at once; lifts flap to reveal puppy dog)*

M: *There's Spot. Wuf! Wuf! (laughs)*

C: *(flips back to page with lion and lifts flap; moves mouth open and shut)*

M: *Roarrr. There's a lion.*

C: *(points to telephone) /Umph/ (rising intonation as if asking question)*

M: *That's the lion's telephone. He has his own little telephone. (points to flowers) Pretty flowers.*

C: *(flips to page with puppy dog in basket)*

M: *There's Spot!*

C: *(turns to last page; puppy dog is eating from bowl)*

M: *Yum, yum. Spot likes to eat.*

C: *(closes book with a flourish)*

M: *That was a good book!*

SYNTACTIC DEVELOPMENT IN TODDLERHOOD

Children's speech during the toddler years is characterized by longer utterances and utterances with specific syntactic features. It is often referred to as telegraphic speech. **Telegraphic speech** is defined as the child's use of two or three content words in an utterance, with no function words, such as conjunctions, articles, prepositions, and inflections (Tager-Flusberg, 1997). Simple sentences or utterances involving two or three words are created, such as "Daddy come" and "Mommy coat." Grammatical (syntactic) relations are implied in these two-word combinations.

In the section that follows, specific examples of syntactic patterns in toddlers' speech will be described. It is important to remember that during these toddler years, a child's language environment continues to influence her development of language knowledge. Research by Huttenlocher, Vasilyeva, Waterfall, Vevea, and Hedges (2007) reported that caregiver speech patterns were found to vary with the adult's education level. Further research by Huttenlocher, Waterfall, Vasilyeva, Vevea, and Hedges (2010) reported that the diversity of syntactic structures used by caregivers when speaking to children was associated with growth in syntactic development.

Syntactic Patterns in Telegraphic Speech

Although telegraphic speech appears to be syntactically simple, detailed research exploring the contextual meaning of children's two-word utterances has indicated that word order expresses semantic relations not captured by simply identifying the parts of speech present in the utterance (Brown, 1973; Schlesinger, 1971; Slobin, 1979). Thus, telegraphic speech represents both syntactic and semantic language knowledge. Syntactic knowledge is represented in the word order patterns found in telegraphic speech; however, the word order patterns are closely tied to a child's semantic knowledge. Because we cannot directly ask young children how they decide to combine words in utterances, we must analyze their utterances to see what syntactic patterns are present.

Children appear to use this syntactic–semantic knowledge when speaking, using such word combinations as "more juice," "play more," " all gone," "kitty come," "dog go," "bye Gram," "all clean," "all fixed," and "bird fly." For example, in "Daddy come," a noun and a verb are used in sequential order. The noun functions semantically as an agent, and the verb functions to show action. Thus, the semantic relations in "daddy come" are agent + action.

In addition to the agent + action pattern, several other syntactic–semantic patterns have been documented in the telegraphic speech of toddlers (Brown, 1973):

Syntactic–semantic pattern	Example
action + object	play drum
agent + object	mommy hat
action + location	go bed
entity + location	sock floor
possessor + possession	daddy shoe
entity + attribute	cookie big
demonstrative + entity	dis coat

Although these syntactic–semantic patterns are found in children's telegraphic speech, no specific order of development has been documented (Braine, 1976, cited in Tager-Flusberg, 1997).

Toddlers' three-word utterances also provide evidence of syntactic knowledge as shown in the following examples: "put gate up," "me eat cake," "make orange juice," "Caillou on next," and "all by myself" (Otto, 2012).

Toddlers may string several utterances together that have the features of telegraphic speech, but the communication is more complex due to the relationship between the utterances used together. For example, when given water in a sippy cup instead of juice, a toddler said to her caregiver, "this not juice. this water. want whole bunch of juice" (Otto, 2012).

Gradually, toddlers' use of more complex syntactic patterns emerges. Children may mix simple syntactic patterns with more complex ones that have more conventional sentence structure. For example: "put juice right there," "Shadow [pet dog] make footprints [in the snow] . . . more footprints over there," "What you got in there?" "I went this way." Negation may be indicated by adding the word "no" to the utterance. For example, "No, do it all by myself," "Wipe face off no." In the following example, a toddler (2 years, 9 months) uses complex syntactic structures as she pretends to go shopping with her caregiver (Otto, 2012): "You close this (purse) up for me? (caregiver zips up purse opening) Let's go shopping. Here's my list (grabs piece of paper). Let's go get juice. Come with me to shop. (caregiver starts to walk with child in room) Thank you."

Acquisition of Pronouns

Even though children may be using multiple-word utterances as toddlers, they may have difficulty with pronoun use. Pronoun use is semantic in the sense that pronouns take the place of nouns in an utterance; however, the way pronoun reference works in a sentence or an utterance involves syntactic structure because a pronoun refers to a noun used earlier in the utterance or sentence, in a specific syntactic position.

For example, in the sentence, "The girl was riding her bike when it broke," both *her* and *it* are pronouns that refer to nouns. We can identify the referent for *her* because the noun *girl* precedes the pronoun; likewise for *it*, which was preceded by *bike*. When children learn to use pronouns, they learn how to identify or indicate the appropriate referent in the utterance or sentence by using both syntactic and semantic information.

The acquisition of pronouns begins during the toddler years and extends through preschool (Owens, 2001). This long period of acquisition reflects the complexity of pronoun use. Children need to learn that the form of a pronoun must reflect the syntactic position within the utterance. For example, one form of a pronoun may indicate the subject of an utterance (I, he, she), while a different form is used to refer to the utterance's object (him, her, me).

The acquisition of the pronouns *I* and *you* is particularly complex for toddlers because the use of these pronouns depends on the role of the listener (you) and speaker (I) (Owens, 2001; Warren & McCloskey, 1997). In a conversation, the roles of speaker and listener are constantly changing, so the referents for *I* and *you* are also constantly changing. Further, it is difficult for an adult to model the appropriate use of *I* and *you* without adding to the confusion. This confusion may explain why parents and other adults use labels like *Daddy's* or *baby's* instead of *my* or *your* for objects. For example, a father might tell his son, "Daddy's going to work" rather than saying, "I'm going to work" or "This is Daddy's hat" instead of "This is my hat." Gradually, toddlers learn to use the *I* and *you* pronouns appropriately; however, it is important for early childhood teachers to be aware of the initial confusion toddlers experience in acquiring these pronouns.

Toddlers are also learning to use the pronouns "I" and "me." They may appear to use both forms to indicate the "agent" position (utterance subject position). For example, saying "Me want dat" on some occasions and at other times saying "I want dat." Even though a toddler has heard others say, "Ready or not, here I come" when playing hide and seek, the toddler may say, "Ready or not, here me come" when it is her turn to look for her playmate.

Toddlers are also gradually acquiring the use of the reflexive pronouns such as myself, himself, and herself. In acquiring reflexive pronouns, toddlers may use their knowledge of the possessive pronoun to then form the reflexive pronoun (Otto, 2012). For example, a toddler who has used "his" to refer to someone's possession (e.g., his hat) may use "hisself" instead of "himself." For example, "He got down there all by hisself."

Emergent literacy and syntactic knowledge. When toddlers participate in storybook activities with adults, they are exposed to more complex sentence structure than in everyday conversations. With young toddlers, adults may intuitively continue to adapt story text to fit the toddlers' comprehension and attention span. This adapted text often models simple syntactic structures similar to adult-to-child speech. When sharing the story *Are You My Mother?* (Eastman, 1960), the text "A mother bird sat on her egg" may be adapted as "Look at the bird. See the nest" and accompanied by gestures, pointing to the illustrations, and eye contact between adult and child to ensure a shared reference. Sometimes toddlers develop a clear expectation that text is stable. Parents and teachers are often reminded of this when they are rereading a familiar storybook and fail to re-create the same adapted text they used during prior readings. Realizing the change in the text, a toddler may stop the adult's reading and insist that specific language or sound effects be included that were previously part of the story.

With older toddlers, parents and teachers may also alternate reading short segments of text with conversational comments that engage a child in talking about the illustrations or a related experience. Teachers and parents may also use a series of questions to encourage children to use more complex explanations instead of responding only by pointing to the picture. For example, in the following excerpt, a toddler room teacher shares a book with a child. As they looked at the page where Teddy Bear's bedroom is pictured, the teacher asked a series of questions that encouraged the child to use specific words instead of simply pointing to identify where Teddy Bear could find his pajamas.

Teacher:	*Teddy Bear is going to bed. He wants to wear his pajamas. Where could they be? [pause] Are they in the basket? Tell me. [pause] Where's Teddy Bear's pajamas? Are they on the chest? [pause]*
Child:	*No.*
Teacher:	*Where are they? Tell me.*
Child:	*Right there. [points to bed in illustration]*
Teacher:	*Right where?*
Child:	*Over there. [points to bed]*
Teacher:	*Right over where?*
Child:	*On there. [points to bed]*
Teacher:	*On where?*
Child:	*On the bed.*
Teacher:	*On the bed! Why do you think he needs his pajamas?*
Child:	*To go to sleep!*

This example illustrates the way teachers and parents engage toddlers in storybook sharing that facilitates toddlers' expression of their syntactic knowledge by using phrases and short sentences when responding to questions.

MORPHEMIC DEVELOPMENT IN INFANCY

The development of the morphemic aspect of language knowledge is influenced by phonemic awareness (Owens, 2001). The ability to perceive sound distinctions associated with inflectional morphemes (e.g., plurals, tense markers, possessives) is necessary for the development of morphemic knowledge. As infants listen to language around them, they begin to develop receptive knowledge of the meaning-changing aspects of morphemes. For example, "You may have one cracker" versus "You may have these crackers" signals significant differences for the young child. The development of morphemic knowledge becomes more evident as children begin to produce language during the toddler years.

MORPHEMIC DEVELOPMENT IN TODDLERHOOD

Pronoun usage begins during toddlerhood, with the use of *I, mine, my, it*, and *me*. This is important to the development of morphemic knowledge in the sense that noun–verb agreement in English influences the use of inflectional morphemes (e.g., *I go. He goes. We go.*). Children's production of verbs during the early toddler period is usually expressed in present tense or present progressive (e.g., *go–going*). At the end of the second year, children usually begin regularly using plural forms of nouns (Bellugi & Brown, 1964; Brown, 1973; Owens, 1988, 2001).

Research on the emergence of English morphemic knowledge among children has documented the order in which specific grammatical morphemes develop during the toddler to primary years (Brown, 1973; deVilliers & deVilliers, 1973). The first grammatical morphemes to appear include present progressive of verbs (*go–going*), plurality (*toy–toys*), and possessive (*dog–dog's*). The sequence of morpheme acquisition does not appear to be influenced by the frequency of parents' use of specific morphemes; instead, acquisition is thought to be related to the linguistic (syntactic and semantic) complexity involved in using the specific morpheme (Brown, 1973).

PRAGMATIC DEVELOPMENT IN INFANCY

During infancy, children begin to express communicative intent (Goldin-Meadow, 2007; Tomasello, Carpenter, & Liszkowski, 2007), which provides a foundation for language development. Infants' expression of communicative intent first appears in nonlinguistic forms, such as facial expression, gaze, and gesture. Earlier sections of this chapter have described the importance of eye contact and shared reference in children's early communicative interactions. In this section, the emergence of children's use of gestures to communicate will be described as one way that young children show communicative intent.

Using gestures to communicate.   Clark (2003) described the emergence of gestures during infancy as following this sequence:

- 7 to 8 months: Infant begins to show objects to adults, holding up object to adult.
- 9 months: Infant reaches out or up, using an open hand.

- 9 to 12 months: Infant uses pointing and reaching to attract adult attention.
- 10 to 14 months: Infant's gestures become more refined and precise, adding vocalizations to gestures.

During later infancy, children appear to use gestures to express two types of intent. Pointing gestures are used to indicate or draw attention to an object or entity, while reaching gestures are associated with requests (Clark, 2003). Pointing gestures may simply be referential; that is, a child may use such a gesture to indicate or draw attention to something she wants to "talk about" (Goldin-Meadow, 2007). Having established this shared reference, the response of the adult to the child's gesture sets up a turn-taking or communication loop. Researchers exploring these interactions found that when the shared reference/eye contact was not maintained by the adult, the infant often persisted by repeating the pointing gesture (Tomasello et al., 2007). If the adult repeatedly discontinued the eye contact/shared reference, the infant's pointing gestures decreased, as if he decided that this adult was not a suitable "conversation partner."

Symbolic gestures. **Representational/symbolic gestures** are consistent actions used by a child in referring to events or objects. For example, a child might use a "sucking" action to refer to her pacifier or a dancing action to request that a radio be played (Casadio & Caselli, 1989, in Clark, 2003). Representational/symbolic gestures are used similarly to the way words are used—that is, a gesture is used in different contexts to refer to the same object, event, or request (e.g., the action of holding one's arms out as a symbolic gesture for airplane or a sniffing gesture to refer to a flower).

In a longitudinal study of infants beginning at 11 months and continuing to 24 months, Acredolo and Goodwyn (1988) described young children's spontaneous use of symbolic gestures to communicate a variety of intents or functions. These included noting the presence of a specific object, making a request, describing an attribute of an object, replying to a question, and referring to an event noted. The use of symbolic gestures occurred about the same time as children's first words; however, for some children, symbolic gestures provided a way to express communicative intent if they were not yet producing words (Acredolo & Goodwyn, 1988; Goodwyn & Acredolo, 1993). Children's symbolic gestures have also been referred to as **homesigns** (Goldin-Meadow, 2007) because the gestures come from each child's interactions in the home environment and are unique to that child and communicative context.

It is important to remember that infants' use of gestures and the development of symbolic gestures take place in social interaction with their families and others in their environment. As with all verbal communication with young children, nonverbal communication is successful only if the people involved in the interaction are engaged in eye contact and shared reference. Children who are in contexts where their gestures are interpreted with meaning (either referential, requesting, or representational/symbolic) by those around them will have their communicative intent realized.

For example, if an infant waves her arm toward an object and produces a sound, an adult, noticing this gesture, might respond, "Oh, you want to play with this?" and give the object to the infant. Infants begin to develop an awareness or understanding of how language is used and whether an outcome or intent has been achieved. If certain gestures and vocalizations resulted in being fed, comforted, or entertained, the child is likely to repeat communicating in this way. Social routines involving greetings and farewells and ritualized games of peek-a-boo and pat-a-cake also contribute to infants' development of pragmatic knowledge of language.

Dialogic turn taking. As infants interact with those around them, they begin to participate in dialogic turn taking. This dialogic turn taking contributes to children's awareness of how language is used for different purposes or intents in a specific context. For example, when infants and parents or teachers are engaged in picture book sharing, the way in which the book is shared may communicate awareness that books have meaning (Joyner & Ray, 1987). When sharing books with infants, parents and teachers often engage in labeling and commenting as well as providing sounds for animals, objects, or actions pictured.

As a book is shared, children have opportunity to develop a sense of how language expresses communicative intent. With repeated opportunities to engage in sharing the same book, infants will show a memory for book content and the words used by their parents or teachers to label the pictures or describe actions or indicate animal sounds (Otto, 1994). Infants may also participate in making the animal sounds associated with those animals pictured in the book. A child may learn that his vocalizations accompanied by rising intonation ("questioning") resulted in further speech from the parent or teacher. In this way, infants become aware of how books are associated with meaning and communicative intent.

PRAGMATIC DEVELOPMENT IN TODDLERHOOD

The toddler years are characterized by continued development of referential and symbolic gestures, along with increasing use of invented and conventional words to express communicative intent during interactions with those around them. Gradually, as toddlerhood progresses, children begin to use language for a greater variety of purposes or intents (Halliday, 1975, 2007; Menyuk, 1988). Initially, language is used instrumentally to satisfy a need. Then, the child also begins to use language in regulation of others' behavior. "No" is a word that some toddlers frequently use to influence others. The interactional function of language can be seen as toddlers begin or maintain a dialogue. A child's exclamation to "Look!" after building a block structure is an example of the personal function, drawing attention to his uniqueness or abilities. Language serves a heuristic function as children ask questions (e.g., "What's this?" "Why?"). The imaginative function of language is observed as children pretend and role-play. The last developing function of language used by children is informative. Children who relate information to others ("I have a turtle") are using language in an informative way.

Routine expressions.   In every culture, there are routine ways of greeting and departing. In the following example, Ryan's mother details Ryan's (16 months old) acquisition of saying "bye-bye" and waving (Otto, 1980):

Today as I was telling someone good-bye as they left our house, Ryan flexed his left hand and said "bye-bye." It was the first time he had done this. Then he began to play in the living room with his toys. About every 5 minutes, he stopped his play and said "bye-bye" and flexed his fingers on his left hand. He was smiling and seemed pleased with this new skill. This repeating occurred four or five times, after intervals of about 5 minutes. It was as if he was practicing what he had learned, without it being in the actual context of someone leaving the house. The next morning, when Ryan's father left for work, Ryan did not say bye-bye and wave until his father had walked down the sidewalk and almost out of view.

Conversations.   When they are toddlers, children begin to respond more verbally in conversational settings and take a few turns in maintaining the interaction

When infants and parents or caregivers enjoy storybooks together, their joint focusing on the book develops an awareness that books have meaning.

(Owens, 1988). Older toddlers introduce or change the topic of conversation. In addition, toddlers may use some attention-getting words and gestures (Owens, 1988). Gestures are used to increase the semantic content of what is said; however, as children's productive vocabulary increases during toddlerhood, they begin to rely less on gestures and gesture less during conversations.

Toddlers' pragmatic knowledge and emergent literacy. In literate cultures where children interact with print and texts, their behaviors may indicate that they are becoming aware of certain ways in which written language is used to communicate intent or purpose (Phillips & McNaughton, 1990; Snow, 1983). Toddlers may crawl up on a parent's or caregiver's lap as the adult is reading a newspaper or book and begin to ask questions or comment (e.g., "Whada write?" "Whada say?" "Whada name?"). Other toddlers eagerly bring the mail to parents, asking them to read it.

Teachers and parents who engage in storybook sharing with both infants and toddlers (Honig & Shin, 2001) provide opportunities for children to experience the way in which books communicate meaning. Storybook interactions with toddlers may continue for only a few minutes due to the limited attention span and distractability of toddlers. In the example that follows, a mother describes a short storybook interaction with her son (Otto, 1980):

> Ryan (17 months old) came over to me as I was reading the paper. He had a storybook in one hand. He gave me the storybook. I put the paper down, picked him up onto my lap, and started reading the story. He turned the pages before I had read each page so I then just talked about the animals on each page. Ryan then started jabbering as he turned the pages and then turned the book over, upside down, and backwards. Then he was off to play elsewhere. The total time he was interested in the book was 1½ minutes.

As described in this example, during toddlerhood, children may be learning how to hold a book and turn the pages. When Ryan, was about 1½ years old, he was observed experimenting with how to hold a book. On several occasions, after first holding a book upside down, he turned the book right side up before continuing to page through it (Otto, 1980). Ricky, another toddler, also indicated his awareness of print and reading in his interactions with storybooks by jabbering with a "reading" intonation and pointing to specific letters (Shatz, 1994). Shatz also described Ricky's "reading" of a fortune from a fortune cookie. Toddlers may also be learning what books are not used for in their environments (throwing, chewing, tearing). These are all parts of developing pragmatic knowledge of literacy and literacy-related events.

The way in which adults interact during storybook sharing may influence a child's awareness that books contain information and knowledge. In storybook sharing, a zone of proximal development is often created between the adult and child. DeLoache (1984; DeLoache & DeMendoza, 1985) explored mothers' storybook interactions with their toddlers (12 to 18 months of age) and documented several ways mothers focused on meaning while supporting and facilitating the interactions. Mothers adjusted their comments and questioning to reflect the linguistic and cognitive levels of their children. With younger children, they focused on vocabulary development, while they encouraged older children to respond to questions. In situations in which a child's

The drama corner is often the setting for conversations between older toddlers as they engage in imaginative play.

response was not completely correct, the mothers typically used indirect ways to hint at the correct answer or responded positively to what the child said while providing the correct answer. Some mothers referred to real-life events and objects as a way of relating to a pictured object or action. Mothers also added gestures or dramatizations as a way of explaining the meaning of the book text to their children.

The supportive scaffolding provided by the mothers in DeLoache's study gave their children the opportunity to engage in enjoying books at a higher level than they would be capable of independently. The children could not access the information and knowledge of the book independently, but with the scaffolding provided by their mothers, the children became more aware of the value of books and the enjoyment of reading. If an adult insists on reading the text of a story that is above a child's level of comprehension, thus disregarding the zone of proximal development, the child will often respond by ignoring the adult's reading, attempting to turn the pages, becoming restless, or simply closing the book and walking away.

Toddlers' knowledge of written language begins with experimenting and exploring how to make marks on paper. When he was 18 months old, Carlos's caregiver described his exploration of writing as follows (Otto, 1980):

> I was using a pen and writing some notes. Carlos was playing nearby. He came over and took my pen and began to mark on the paper. As he did so, he squealed in delight, looking at the line he had drawn. He also smiled and made eye contact with me. He

Toddlers learn how to handle books and turn pages
by having frequent opportunities to explore books.

fingered the pen, turned it over in his hand, and made some more marks on the paper, giggling all the while. He looked at each end of the pen and then turned it point down to use it.

I then took him to the table and got the box of crayons and a large sheet of paper. He took out the crayons slowly. After selecting a color, he drew a short line and laughed and squealed when he saw the mark on the paper. He tried out different colors. He tried out the pink one, but when it did not make a visible mark, he put it down and picked up a darker color. He usually had the crayon point down rather than blunt end down.

He also tried marking on a plastic pencil case. No mark appeared, so he then went back to marking on the paper. When I would take a crayon to write with, he would get excited when he saw me writing and reach out to grab the crayon. The marks he made on the sheet were 2–3 inches long, and horizontal.

Toddlers may show that they are learning about the communicative intent in printed text when they pick up printed items (e.g., cards, brochures, books, mail) and verbalize as if they were reading the print, though their reading is best described as imaginative jargon. Parents have described children's spontaneous participation in other literacy events, such as grocery-list making and letter writing. For example, when Ryan was 1 year, 7 months old and his mother was busy writing a letter, he went to his mother, crawled up on her lap, grabbed the pen, and scribbled on the letter (Otto, 1980). His mother then took his hand and the pen in hers and helped him write a short message. As this occurred, he watched as the message appeared on the page. In this example, Ryan was welcomed as an "emergent writer," contributing to the letter in his own manner and with mediation from his mother. As infants and toddlers participate in contexts where oral and written language are used, they begin to develop their pragmatic knowledge of how language is used in various settings and for various purposes.

Toddlers' responses to print may indicate an awareness that "print is different from pictures and is associated with meaning in a particular way" (Walton, 1989, p. 52). For example, a toddler who indicates that her wavy-line scribble says her name is indicating this awareness, as is a toddler who hums when she sees a page with music printed but talks only on a text page (Shatz, 1994). Another example of print awareness and meaning comes from a toddler (2 years, 9 months) who was looking at a Cheerios cereal box that had both text and a photo of a heart-shaped bowl of Cheerios with sliced strawberries in it. When her caregiver pointed to the print and asked, "What does this say?" the child replied "strawberries and milk for Cheerios" while pointing to the print (Otto, 2012).

SUMMARY

During infancy and toddlerhood, children's language competencies develop in five areas of language knowledge: phonological, semantic, syntactic, morphemic, and pragmatic. Developments in each area form the foundation for later, more complex development of language knowledge. During infancy, receptive knowledge of language occurs, with expressive language usually appearing at the end of infancy. Due to increased mobility, toddlerhood is characterized by energetic exploration of the surrounding environment and the language present in those environments. Significant growth occurs in each of the five aspects of language knowledge as toddlers become more active participants in a wider variety of communicative contexts.

✳ ✳ ✳   CHAPTER REVIEW

1. Key terms to review:

prosody	nonreflexive vocalizations	vocal play
reflexive vocalizations	cooing	babbling
		echolalic babbling

jargon	direct experience	idiomorphs
intonated babble	vicarious	holophrastic stage
selective	experience	fast mapping
reinforcement	referent	telegraphic speech
emergent literacy	symbol formation	representational/
otitis media	distancing	symbolic gesture
eustachian tube	protowords	homesign

2. Describe an infant's auditory perceptual competencies.
3. What is the value in adult–toddler storybook sharing?
4. When does language development begin?
5. At what age do children typically begin to use single words?

✳ ✳ ✳   CHAPTER EXTENSION ACTIVITIES

Research

Interview a pediatrician about the incidence and treatment of ear infections among infants and toddlers. Prepare a written summary of your interview and present a brief oral report to your class.

Discussion

Develop a chart summary based on the information in the chapter. The class could be divided into five groups, with each group developing the chart summary for one of the five aspects of language knowledge (see below).

Aspect of Language Knowledge	Infant Development	Toddler Development
Phonological		
Semantic		
Syntactic		
Morphemic		
Pragmatic		

CHAPTER 5

ENHANCING LANGUAGE DEVELOPMENT IN INFANTS AND TODDLERS

Learning Outcomes

After reading this chapter you should be able to

- Explain the concept of developmental appropriateness as it applies to infant and toddler classroom activities
- Identify important caregiver–infant interaction patterns that enhance language development
- Explain the ways in which language development is enhanced through story-book sharing with infants and toddlers
- Explain the value of using symbolic gestures with toddlers for communication
- Describe three exploratory activities in a toddler classroom and explain how the activities enhance language development

Kari was a teacher in an infant room of a day-care center. As she approached Robby's crib, she noticed that he was looking up at the teddy bear mobile hanging over his crib. Looking at Robby, she said, "Bears. See the bears?" Robby first looked at Kari and then at the bears. Kari said, "Yes, see the bears. Here they go. See them dance," and she jiggled the mobile to make the bears dance. Robby smiled and looked at Kari.

Children's language development is influenced by their surrounding environment and the opportunities for interaction in that environment. Kari's interaction with Robby illustrates how early interactions with infants can begin to encourage children to participate in conversations and eventually more complex communications. Although Robby did not respond verbally to Kari, the shared reference and turn taking that occurred supported a communicative interaction.

One of the basic tenets of early childhood education involves the planning and implementation of learning environments for young children that enhance their development. In this chapter, we will consider guidelines for interacting with infants and toddlers along with specific aspects of early childhood curricula that enhance language development. An emphasis will be placed on the rationale for selecting certain activities and teachers' roles in facilitating the activities. In this chapter, the use of the terms *infants* and *toddlers* is not meant to indicate only chronological age but refers to developmental level. *Infant curricula* will describe the appropriate learning activities for young, nonwalking children, and *toddler curricula* will focus on children from the time they are walking until they are 2½ to 3 years old.

Infants develop receptive language as they begin to interpret and comprehend the messages communicated by people around them. Children also begin to participate in communicative interactions through their use of gesture and preword vocalizations. Thus, during infancy, learning activities should focus on developing receptive language and establishing communication with infants through their use of gesture and preword vocalizations.

Toddlers begin to use language in two- or three-word utterances for a variety of purposes and are beginning a period of rapid growth in all aspects of language knowledge. Thus, toddlers need a curriculum that provides opportunities to explore and interact verbally as well as nonverbally in a range of activities.

The learning environment of infant and toddler settings is critical. It is important to consider all aspects of the environment—the physical environment, the cognitive environment, and the social–emotional or interpersonal environment—when seeking to enhance language development.

DEVELOPMENTAL APPROPRIATENESS OF CURRICULA

The concept of **developmental appropriateness** is based on the recognition that learning activities within specific contexts (e.g., home, school) should reflect children's developmental needs: physical, emotional–social, and cognitive–linguistic (Copple & Bredekamp, 2009; Kostelnik, Soderman, & Whiren, 2010). Developmental appropriateness means that the right experiences are provided at the right time for each child. Developmental appropriateness can be applied as a key criterion in evaluating the potential effectiveness of various contexts on children's language acquisition. Language development activities that are developmentally appropriate should be integrated throughout the curriculum and should be exploratory and interactive in nature. Children's individual developmental needs and their individual interests should be reflected throughout the curriculum. Hands-on activities that stimulate conceptual development and vocabulary acquisition are critical. Opportunities for frequent conversation, both in small groups and one-on-one, should be present throughout the day. Teachers need to respond promptly and directly to children's efforts to communicate.

Role of Teachers

A classroom teacher has a critical role in establishing a learning environment in which the language contexts are developmentally appropriate. Through a teacher's understanding of the importance of verbal interaction and the ways in which it can be fostered through curriculum planning and implementation, children's language development can be enhanced. As a teacher of infants and toddlers, you will need to communicate to parents, colleagues, and administrators how specific aspects of the classroom curriculum and environment will enhance children's language development. When this is done, parents, colleagues, and administrators will have a better appreciation of the ways in which children's educational and developmental needs are being met in your classroom.

Developmentally appropriate curricula that focus on language development are characterized by the following (Bredekamp & Copple, 1997):

- Recognition of the developmental levels of children
- Incorporation of language development activities throughout the curriculum
- Embedded conceptual development in a predominance of hands-on activities with authentic materials
- Flexibility in meeting the needs of individual children

Curricula for infant and toddler settings are not just simplified versions of curricula for preschool rooms; instead, each curriculum has specific, unique features that meet the developmental needs of infants and toddlers (Lowman & Ruhmann, 1998). The curriculum needs to be flexible so the unique needs of each young child can be met. This curriculum planning should include a specific focus on the ways in which the activities will enhance the development of language. Preplanning also enhances a teacher's role as a facilitator, guide, and observer of young children's development.

Culturally Appropriate Practices

One aspect of developmentally appropriate curriculum involves the awareness that classroom learning activities need to build on the language and social–cultural experiences of all children in a classroom (Bowman, 1992; Kostelnik, Soderman, & Whiren, 2010). Each teacher needs to be aware of the diverse languages and social–cultural environments represented in her classroom. For example, infant and toddler teachers need to acknowledge and value the language competencies children bring to their classrooms, whether it is a different language or a different dialect. In addition, learning materials need to reflect the cultural diversities represented in each classroom. This allows children to build on what they already know. For example, when selecting books for the library corner, select books that have familiar content and illustrations. The key to providing a culturally and developmentally appropriate curriculum is in a teacher's deep understanding of children's development as well as their individual cultural–linguistic home and community environments.

INFANTS

General Guidelines for Interactions with Infants

Four patterns are particularly relevant for interactions with infants: eye contact and shared reference, communication loops, verbal mapping, and adult-to-child talk (see summary chart in Table 5.1). Teachers should frequently engage infants in one-on-one conversations, using simple language and establishing eye contact and shared reference, such as the example of the interaction between Kari and Robby at the beginning of this chapter. According to Vukelich, Christie, and Enz (2002), "neuroscientists agree that a child's language capacity is dependent upon the quality of

TABLE 5.1
Important Caregiver–Infant Interaction Patterns

Interaction Pattern	Characteristics	Example
Eye contact and shared reference	Adult establishes and maintains eye contact with child along with joint attention to an object or action	Adult and child have eye contact; adult shakes rattle, both child and adult look at rattle
Communication loop	Adult and child take turns responding verbally, nonverbally, or both	Adult says "peek-a-boo"; child responds by laughing. Adult repeats. Child laughs again.
Verbal mapping	Adult describes to child what is happening	Adult who is dressing child says, "Here is your shirt. First it goes over your head. Oh, we need to put your arm here. Good job!"
Adult-to-child talk	Adult speech is short, not syntactically complex, and has repeated words	Adult says "Look at the bird. See it go up, up, up."

language input" (p. 18). Engaging infants in conversation-like turn taking establishes the patterns for future, more complex conversations and helps children develop the neural networks in the brain that contribute to language competencies.

Eye contact and shared reference.   Through eye contact and shared reference, teachers engage infants in communication about events or objects. In establishing eye contact, teachers need to position themselves so that the infant can see the teacher's face as he or she talks (Birckmayer, Kennedy, & Stonehouse, 2010). This means that the teacher would probably be in one of the following positions:

- Sitting on the floor with knees bent up and the infant held in a sitting position on the knees
- Lying on the floor (on side or stomach) with the infant close by
- Sitting on the floor while the older infant (9 months) is sitting in a small chair or on a cushion (Weitzman & Greenberg, 2002)

These face-to-face positions provide opportunity for the teacher to closely observe a child's facial expressions and level of attentiveness. Children benefit from being able to see how the teacher's mouth moves in forming words as well as from shared eye contact (Manolson, 1992).

Timing one-on-one interactions.   Timing the interaction with infants is also important. This is "key to helping the infant see the connection between language labels and the things they refer to [referents]" (Fowler, 1990, p. 26). For example, when showing a new object to an infant and labeling it, you first establish eye contact and then manipulate the object to draw the child's attention while labeling the

Brightly colored, soft books provide infants with visual stimulation and opportunities to manipulate the pages.

object. You also need to monitor the infant's verbal and nonverbal responses to the object. Does the infant attempt to reach for the object? Does the infant vocalize or attempt to imitate the sounds in the object's label? Does the infant turn away and look at another event in the room? By monitoring the infant's response, you can determine whether the interaction can be extended or whether it should be tried again later.

Observing, waiting, and listening. A teacher's observation of the infant's response to the interaction is critical. Manolson (1992) recommended that teachers "observe, wait, and listen" (p. 12) when interacting with infants. By closely observing a child's focus of attention and facial expressions, teachers are able to interpret and understand the child's interests and feelings better. When the teacher waits several moments before responding, it gives the child a chance to express his needs and interests (Kovach & Da Ros-Voseles, 2011).

For example, Lani, a teacher of infants, was in the process of dressing Katie (4 months of age) after changing her diaper. Lani was making funny faces and sounds. She laughed at herself and then said, "Funny? Is Lani being funny?" She paused and waited. Katie laughed. Then Lani asked, "Lani do it again?" After a moment or two, Katie wiggled and laughed. Seeing Katie's response, Lani continued to make the funny faces and sounds. Teachers who listen closely for a child's response, whether it be simply cooing, babbling, or vocal play, give recognition to the child's efforts at communicating.

Infant teachers need to be sensitive to each infant's approach to learning (Honig & Lally, 1981). Some infants thrive with more frequent stimulation from their teachers, whereas other infants need periods of "free time" to explore the environment on their own, at their own pace, without constant adult interaction.

When conversing with infants, it is important to use speech that is expressive and varied in intonation because it extends the child's attention and interest. In addition, adult speech that is syntactically simpler is easier for the infant to understand. Repeating words or phrases increases infants' understanding. Teachers should also use consistent concept labels rather than call a cat *cat* one time and *kitty* the next (Fowler, 1990).

Verbal mapping. Verbal mapping occurs when a teacher talks to an infant about what is going to happen, what is happening, or what has happened. When verbal mapping is appropriately provided during times when the child is alert, it can enhance an infant's receptive language by drawing attention to the teacher's speech and the ongoing events or actions (Kovach & Da Ros-Voseles, 2011). It is important for teachers to be sensitive to individual children's responses to verbal mapping. Continuous or too-frequent verbal mapping may be overwhelming to some infants. By monitoring an infant's eye contact, shared reference, and verbal and nonverbal responses, you can determine whether the verbal mapping is too frequent and overstimulating. Using simple sentences and repeating key words also facilitates verbal mapping.

Responding quickly to infants' physical and emotional needs. Infants' cries or calls of distress should always be given a quick response. Infants need the security of knowing that their physical and emotional needs will be met by their teachers. This sense of security builds a trusting relationship between infants and their teachers and provides a foundation for positive personality and social development that is essential for optimal cognitive development (Wortham, 1998). Teachers should praise infants for sitting up, shaking a rattle, vocalizing, and other accomplishments. This increases their positive feelings and encourages them to continue to respond to their environment.

General Guidelines for Infant Classroom Settings

Infant classrooms should be cheerful and contain a variety of colorful pictures of familiar objects, friendly animals, and people's faces displayed at the child's level. The room setting should be "rich in sensorimotor and social experiences" (Weiser, 1991, p. 21) without being overwhelming. Toys should focus on the sensorimotor needs of infants. For example, bells, balls, large snap-locking beads, nesting bowls, music boxes, or squeeze toys should be easily accessible. Toys need to be safe for infants to explore through grasping, chewing, or manipulating. Books should be of cardboard or padded plastic, with colorful, clear pictures of familiar objects. A variety of music should be played to enhance listening through exposure to a range of rhythm, pitch, and musical tone.

INFANT CURRICULA

Three types of activities predominate the curriculum in a developmentally appropriate infant room: exploratory activities, teacher-mediated activities, and routine activities. Each of these types of activities involves informal learning activities within a thoroughly and thoughtfully prepared environment. The daily schedule is planned around infants' physical needs and is individualized to accommodate each child's needs for eating, sleeping, and physical care, along with activities to engage children during their "alert" time.

Exploratory Activities

The focus of exploratory activities in the infant classroom is on encouraging children to engage independently in sensorimotor activities. These activities are based in sensory perception, involving sight, sound, taste, touch, and smell. According to Piaget (Brainerd, 1978), infants develop cognitively through their sensory and movement experiences while interacting in various settings. Piaget's description of the sensorimotor stage focuses on the importance of children's exploring objects and their actions on those objects. From these experiences, children develop ways of organizing sensory information so that it makes sense (Goodman, 1993). These activities are critical for concept formation as firsthand, direct experiences provide the basis for the development of concepts. During the course of a child's first year, labels for concepts begin to become attached to this experiential basis. These experiences provide the foundation for symbol formation and receptive language knowledge.

Exploratory activities for infants are accompanied by more teacher monitoring and mediating guidance than are activities for older children, due to the necessary concern for infants' safety and well-being. In addition, teacher mediation can provide labeling and verbal mapping, which are important to children's developing receptive language knowledge (Fowler, 1990). However, teachers should not feel compelled to engage in constant labeling or verbal mapping. Infants need time to explore on their own and at their own pace.

Crib-based activities.   Young infants in group-care settings spend some alert time each day in their cribs, though it is not recommended that children be left alone in their cribs when awake for extended periods of time. Crib time should be accompanied by opportunities to explore a variety of objects. Manipulative toys

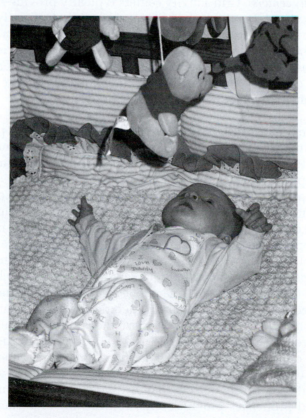

When placing a mobile, consider the view from the child's line of sight.

or toys that are visually engaging and safe are appropriate for crib-based activities, such as mobiles, crib activity centers, and other suitable objects.

Mobiles. Select crib mobiles that are visually engaging, with moving items and contrasting colors or patterns on the items. When deciding to use a mobile, be sure to examine it for safety features and to view the mobile from the child's perspective. Some mobiles are effective only when viewed from a sitting position.

Young infants benefit from their own observations and interactions with mobiles; however, it is also appropriate for teachers to occasionally provide basic labels for the items on a mobile and to describe the movement of the items. When labeling or talking about an item, a teacher should touch the item in question and check to be sure the child is also focusing on the item, engaging in shared reference. High-quality mobiles are generally easily attached and removed so that when teachers want to provide this type of visual and cognitive stimulation, a mobile can be mounted on the crib for a specific time period.

Crib activity centers. Crib activity centers typically provide a variety of activities that stimulate visual, tactile, and auditory perception. Crib activity centers are designed to be manipulated safely by infants. If an activity center is securely attached to the side of a crib, it may be left up for an extended time, provided that it is checked on a daily basis for safety. When infants are interacting with an activity center, teachers may occasionally mediate infants' interactions, similar to the way they mediate interactions with a mobile.

Crib-appropriate objects. Crib toys need to be visually or perceptually engaging so that the infant is interested and attempts to reach for and manipulate the object (Maxim, 1990). A teacher should verbally introduce an item by labeling it and showing any appropriate action. For example, a teacher would shake a rattle and pause, then repeat the action several times before leaving it in the crib. Plastic balls or other shapes with bells or noisemakers inside are appropriate crib toys. However, teachers must make sure that an object is securely made so it will not come apart. When an infant seems to have got tired of the object, exchange it for another similar or slightly familiar object or move the object to a different position. Changing the position of an object is particularly important if perception of the object changes with the position. Placed in different positions, many objects take on new shapes and perspectives.

Stuffed animals are not usually included in infant centers because they are difficult to sanitize and thus may increase the spread of illness. For this reason, some states have restrictions against the use of stuffed animals in child-care facilities.

With older infants who are able to sit up and move around independently by crawling or scooting, crib-based activities should involve objects they can hold and manipulate. Selecting objects that have a variety of textures, shapes, colors, and functional properties provides opportunities for important concept development. Objects with properties of sound such as rattles and balls with bells or squeakers inside encourage infants to repeat actions that create those sounds. All the items used in crib-based activities need to be able to be sanitized easily so that illnesses will not be spread when the objects are moved from crib to crib.

Young infants benefit from being placed in an infant seat for short periods of time so that they can observe people and activities in the room and the environment in general (Wortham, 1998). During the time an infant is positioned in an infant seat, the teacher needs to monitor the child's comfort level frequently and occasionally engage the infant in conversation or other short interactions.

Room-based exploratory activities.   When infants can sit up independently and move around by scooting or crawling, exploratory activities are more appropriately room based. This increases the perceptual range for infants. The infant room needs to be arranged and furnished so that all items within children's reach or mobility are appropriate and free of safety hazards.

Infants need time and opportunity to interact with objects at their own pace. The role of a teacher is to provide an appropriate environment and to monitor and mediate children's interactions, providing verbal mapping and labeling that is sensitive to each child's individual learning approach. Exploratory infant activities enhance language development through stimulating concept development, which leads to semantic knowledge.

Infancy is a time of receptive language development, as children hear language used by adults and begin to establish communication routines through shared reference and communication loops. Infants begin to learn that all objects have names. They also learn that certain actions on objects produce certain results: if you push a ball, it will roll; if you pick up a ball and throw it, it will go far away fast.

Balls and push–pull toys. Toys that move when touched or pulled encourage infants to move with or after the toys. These toys also encourage children to use their hands to move the toys. This helps children learn cause-and-effect relations and figure out how to repeat actions to create the same results. Teachers' verbal mapping and affective responses to children's actions stimulate conceptual development and encourage verbal (preword) interactions.

Music. During exploratory times, children's auditory perception can be stimulated by playing a variety of music. Music should be played at a moderate-to-low volume and only for short periods (10 to 15 minutes). Music with simple instrumentation and a strong rhythm is more appropriate than full orchestration with complex interwoven melodies and rhythms. Vocal music should feature distinct voices. Using instrumental or vocal music during exploratory activity time has value for older infants as well. Older infants who are moving around more independently may indicate their perception of rhythm and tone by their body movements. In addition, older infants are more responsive verbally and may babble or vocalize in response to vocal music. Music that has become familiar to them may evoke stronger responses.

Teacher-Mediated Activities

While mediation may occur when a teacher interacts with a child during exploratory activities (Weiser, 1991), more focused mediation occurs when a teacher sings a song to an infant, introduces an object to an infant, or shares a book with an infant. Teacher interaction in these instances also involves verbal mapping, labeling, linguistic scaffolding, and child-directed speech.

Songs and finger plays. When teachers sing simple songs to infants, they provide opportunities for children to become more aware of sound and rhythm. By using simple songs, you can focus on auditory sequencing and repetitive rhythms (Manolson, 1992; Maxim, 1990). In addition, listening skills and imitation of gestures are encouraged. Children may also begin to associate word labels with objects in their surroundings (Maxim, 1990). Action songs, also known as finger plays, are simple melodies that are accompanied by rhythmic gestures and movement. Although not always set to music, chants and nursery rhymes are also enjoyable because of the rhythmic language.

Selected objects and activities. One type of teacher-mediated activity occurs when a teacher selects a particular object or activity to be used with a specific child or several children, based on their developmental needs. This interaction is didactic in nature, with the teacher specifically selecting the learning materials and providing a flexible structure for the interaction. For example, to stimulate an infant's hearing, a teacher might select a rattle and hold it near the infant and shake it briefly, establishing eye contact and shared reference. Then the teacher would pause, waiting to see if the infant has any response, shake the rattle again, and pause. The teacher should respond enthusiastically to any response from the child, such as a change in facial expression, body movement, or vocalization. Labeling and verbal mapping could also be used. For example, "Look at this rattle. It makes this sound. [shake it] Did you hear it? [Baby waves arms, looks at rattle intently or smiles.] Yes, you did!" This should be followed with time for the infant to interact with the rattle alone, without teacher mediation.

Remember that an infant's curiosity and interest in objects or events is influenced by the way in which a selected object can be assimilated or accommodated into previous experiences. A child's interest is the greatest for objects or events that are only slightly different from previous experiences. Totally new experiences may be too overwhelming, resulting in the infant's ignoring the object or event or simply withdrawing (Weiser, 1991).

Object permanence is an important cognitive achievement of infancy. Teachers can provide opportunities for an infant to use this new awareness, such as playing peek-a-boo or uncovering a hidden object. The hidden object activity involves tying a brightly colored ribbon to a small toy (Wortham, 1998). The toy is then hidden under a small blanket or cloth. The teacher shows the infant how to find the toy by pulling the ribbon. By repeating these actions several times and praising the infant's responses and attempts to find the toy, the teacher encourages the infant to become actively involved in the game.

Teachers should carry infants around the room and talk to them about interesting objects or pictures in the room, using labeling and verbal mapping (Wortham, 1998). This verbal and visual stimulation encourages children to respond to objects and events in the room while in close contact with a watchful adult.

Books. Infants enjoy sharing and looking at books with their teachers. Book sharing with infants provides rich opportunities for both receptive and expressive language development that contributes not only to oral language development but to emergent literacy as well. It is important to be able to tailor the book sharing to a child's interests, while maintaining his eye contact and shared reference. This means that book sharing with infants will be done with individual children rather than in a group. It also means that book sharing will occur throughout a day, based on an infant's interests and level of alertness. The emphasis of the interaction is on a shared conversation about what is pictured rather than on the adult's reading the actual text (Honig & Lally, 1981; Honig & Shin, 2001).

Selecting books to share. Books for infants should be made of a durable material, such as cardboard, plastic, or cloth. The illustrations should be simple and large (Maxim, 1990). Books for babies may have a very simple story or sequence (e.g., Horacek, 2008. *Choo choo*), or may involve pictured concepts of familiar objects or animals (e.g., Priddy, 2001. *Happy baby colors*). Books with photo illustrations allow direct connections between what a child sees in his environment and what is pictured in a book (e.g., Ricklen, 1994. *Baby's neighborhood*). Board books with texts using nursery rhymes or songs are also engaging for infants because of the rhythmic language and melodies (e.g., Lear & Moroney, 2002. *Nursery songs*).

Sharing books with infants. Specific guidelines for teachers to observe in sharing books with infants include the following (Honig & Brophy, 1996; Honig & Shin, 2001; Im, Parlakian, & Osborn, 2007):

1. Select a quiet area in which to read, free of other sound or visual distractions.
2. Sit comfortably, with the infant in your lap.
3. Speak slowly.
4. Monitor the infant's eye gaze and any gestures to determine his attention to a particular picture. Take more time talking about pictures he is interested in.
5. Talk with expression, providing labels, adding sound effects, and using variations in intonation to encourage responses.
6. Continue the book sharing as long as the infant appears interested.

7. Encourage the infant to respond with sounds, vocalizations, and gestures appropriate to the book content (e.g., growling for a lion, meowing for a cat, patting a bunny).

8. Repeat sharing of the same book at different times. This repetition encourages infants to predict upcoming story content based on prior experiences with the book.

Routine Activities

At the infant level, significant portions of the day are devoted to feeding and other physical care routines. During these times, teachers can engage infants in conversation-like interactions, eye contact, and shared reference, and can provide verbal mapping. These interaction patterns help children understand what is happening or is about to happen (Manolson, 1992). Hearing the same words repeated in daily, routine activities also provides children with language that they will eventually use.

Feeding times can be accompanied by a teacher's talk about the types of food served and encouragement for the child's efforts in feeding. For very young infants, bottle feeding should occur while they are being held by their teacher in a semi-upright, slanted position. Teacher talk should accompany the feeding and burping sequence. With older infants, teachers can verbally encourage the child's hand-feeding attempts and talk about the food being served.

Diaper changing and dressing times should also be accompanied by teacher talk or singing. Because the child and teacher are face-to-face, these activities provide a good opportunity to establish eye contact and conversational turn taking through imitation of the infant's cooing and babbling responses and through verbal mapping, labeling, or singing. It is also an opportunity for an infant to observe up close her teacher's facial expressions and hear the variations in intonation of the teacher's speech and singing.

Incorporating an infant's name into a simple melody about dressing or incorporating the names of body parts, such as foot, arm, head, nose, and hand also provides infants with an opportunity to begin to associate word labels with themselves or parts of their bodies. Music can also be used to cue routines such as cleanup time or mealtime (Honig & Brophy, 1996).

Naptime also provides opportunity for language activities. Lullabies can be sung to help young children relax and fall asleep (Honig, 2005). The simple melodies, words, and repetitive refrains are comforting and reassuring. It is also beneficial to find out if specific lullabies are used at home and then use them in your classroom to add familiarity to naptime. You could also learn lullabies in different languages to share with the infants in your classroom.

Arrival and departure routines are also important times of verbal and nonverbal communication (Wilson, Douville-Watson, & Watson, 1995). These transition times are critical for supporting children's feelings of security and comfort. At arrival, teachers should touch, hold, and talk with each infant for a few minutes during the departure of the parent and for a few minutes after. Teacher talk can center on ongoing events, familiar toys, what the child is wearing, a favorite picture in the room, or what is observed from a window. In this way, a teacher mediates or supports a child's reentry into the classroom–center environment. Greetings such as "Hello, how are you?" or "Good morning" exchanged with parents serve to expose children to verbal social routines, developing their receptive pragmatic knowledge. A smile, giggle, or gesture from a child during these routines can be interpreted as a response, or turn taking, and should be verbally reinforced. Departure routines should also incorporate verbal interaction with infants and their parents. Sharing the significant and positive aspects of their infant's day with parents helps children transition back into parents' care.

While routine activities are often assumed to be "just routine" and not part of the planned curriculum, a teacher who carefully observes a child's behavior and provides ample time for the child's response, as well as actively listens to the child's communication efforts, can make these routine activities times of learning and enjoyment for the young child.

TODDLERS

General Guidelines for Interactions with Toddlers

The toddler age begins when a child achieves walking and ends when the child is 2½ to 3 years old. Children in this age span still enjoy sensorimotor play, such as touching, hearing, tasting, smelling, pushing, lifting, pulling, and dropping. They are also developing more complex ways of playing (Maxim, 1993), by using speech as a way of organizing their play and engaging in symbolic play. Toddlers' increased physical independence is accompanied by a desire to be more autonomous in deciding what they engage in and when.

Key interaction patterns. During the toddler years, adults' responsiveness to children's verbal and nonverbal communication is important in enhancing language development. The four interaction patterns developed during infancy (i.e., eye contact and shared reference, communication loops, child-directed speech, verbal mapping) are also important interaction patterns during toddlerhood.

Eye contact and shared reference. Eye contact and shared reference continue to be the basis for establishing a communicative interaction. This interaction becomes more complex due to toddlers' short attention spans and energetic exploration of their environment. A teacher must closely monitor a toddler's attention and make adjustments in the interaction to either maintain that attention or to allow the child to move on to another activity. For instance, when an adult is sharing a storybook with a toddler, the toddler may lose interest in the interaction after only a minute or two. In the example that follows, Lisa, a toddler teacher, is sharing a board book on animals with Joey.

Lisa: *Oh, look! Here's a lion. GRRR GRRR! [pause]*

Joey: *[smiles, points to lion]*

Lisa: *Yeah, grrr. A big yellow lion. Let's see the next page. [turns page] Oh, here's the monkey. [makes monkey sounds; pause]*

Joey:	*Eee eee. [turns page]*
Lisa:	*Oh, look at the lamb. Baa baa. [pause]*
Joey:	*[points to lamb] Baaaaa. [hears garbage truck rumble by outside the center, looks at window; turns book over to back cover and starts to leave]*
Lisa:	*All done! That was a good book!*

In this example, Lisa accepted Joey's decision to end the storybook sharing. Lisa realized that Joey's short attention span was characteristic of his developmental level and accommodated it during her interaction with him.

Communication loops. Lisa and Joey's storybook interaction illustrates a pattern of establishing communication loops, as Lisa paused after speaking to provide opportunity for Joey to respond verbally and nonverbally. Lisa's speech was characteristic of child-directed speech because it was short and not syntactically complex. She also focused on items pictured in the book rather than talking about events or animals not in the immediate context.

During an adult–toddler interaction, providing wait time is critical to encouraging a toddler to respond. When toddlers do not respond quickly to an adult's utterance, the adult's reaction may be to "fill in the blanks, answer all the questions, and even comment without leaving a pause" (Manolson, 1992, p. 7). This lack of sufficient wait time discourages a child from responding.

Maintaining a communication loop with toddlers requires specific techniques because toddlers are only beginning to carry on longer conversations. Teachers can use the following techniques to keep the conversations going (Manolson, 1992):

- Use facial expressions to show you are waiting for the child to take a turn.
- Lean close to the child to show the child she has your attention.
- Point to the activity or object of interest for the child's response.
- Use words like, "Look," "Your turn," and "What's happening?"
- Repeat what you said with a questioning intonation.
- Use questions that show your interest or encourage the child to extend his thinking.

Part of the challenge in maintaining a communication loop is interpreting the child's response. When you have difficulty understanding a child's response, try one of the following strategies to clarify the child's response and keep the communication going:

- Observe carefully the immediate context. Where is the child's focus? What just happened? Guess at the child's meaning based on what has just occurred.
- Repeat what the child just said but with a questioning intonation: "You want?"
- Ask the child to "show me what you want."

Child-directed speech. In child-directed speech, the adult tailors the conversation to the child's level of comprehension. When the language of the conversation becomes

Maintaining the communication loop with toddlers requires specific techniques to keep them engaged in the verbal interaction.

too complex, toddlers will disengage. Here are some ways to structure your conversations to enhance toddlers' comprehension and response (Kratcoski & Katz, 1998; Weitzman & Greenberg, 2002):

- Say less. Use shorter sentences and less complex grammar and vocabulary.
- Use prosody and intonation.
- Repeat specific words and phrases.
- Speak slowly and distinctly.
- Establish joint reference. Talk about events and objects in the immediate environment and use gestures in referring to the events and objects.

Verbal mapping. Verbal mapping is frequently used with toddlers to connect language with ongoing events. When you use language to describe an ongoing event, children learn the language needed to refer to the event and to begin to attach labels to the concepts and schemata. For example, in her toddler classroom, Lisa was sitting at a table with two toddlers, Sarah and Robby, who had just been given a lump of play dough and a roller. As Sarah and Robby began to manipulate the play dough, Lisa described their actions: "Look at Robby stretch the play dough. It is getting longer and longer." "Sarah is rolling her play dough. She is making it smooth."

Mediation. In addition to the interaction patterns just described (i.e., eye contact and shared reference, communication loops, child-directed speech, verbal mapping), mediation is another interaction pattern that enhances children's language development during the toddler years. Mediation occurs when a toddler's teacher uses language to simplify a complex event, such as altering the text when sharing a storybook that has a text that is too complex for the toddler to understand. This mediation is individualized for each specific child and book sharing event. When sharing *Corduroy* (Freeman, 1968) with Westley, a 2½-year-old, Lisa altered the text as follows: "This is Corduroy [points to bear]. He lives in a toy store. Oh, look! See the clown [pauses and points], the rabbit [pauses and points], the doll [pauses and points], the giraffe [pauses and points]." In changing the text to fit Westley's developmental level, Lisa simplified the text to increase Westley's understanding of the book, based on her awareness of his listening comprehension. As teachers use mediation along with the other interaction patterns of eye contact and shared reference, communication loops, child-directed speech, and verbal mapping, complex linguistic scaffolding develops that supports and encourages toddlers to actively participate in communicating.

Interacting with toddlers who are English language learners. When you are interacting with toddlers who are learning English as their second language, you can use the same key interaction patterns just described: eye contact/shared reference, communication loops, child-directed speech, verbal mapping, mediation, and linguistic scaffolding. Here are some guidelines to follow when interacting with toddlers who are English language learners:

- Begin your communication by establishing eye contact and shared reference. Continue to monitor the child's eye contact and shared reference throughout your interaction with him.
- Provide ample wait time for the toddler to respond either verbally or nonverbally to what you say or to the ongoing actions or event.
- Monitor the toddler's facial expressions and nonverbal behavior for signs that he comprehends what you or others say.
- Use child-directed speech that is simple in syntax and use vocabulary familiar to the toddler. You may find it useful to learn key words in the child's home language, such as *please*, *yes*, *no*, *thank you*, *drink*, *eat*, *quiet*, *sleep*, *help*, *more*, and *finished*.
- Combine gestures and actions in your conversation to support the meaning of what you say (see the following section on using symbolic gestures).
- As you engage in mediation and linguistic scaffolding, use your knowledge of each child's prior experiences and vocabulary to provide comprehensible input.

Using Symbolic Gestures with Toddlers

In addition to the interaction patterns described in the previous section, another way of communicating with toddlers involves using symbolic gestures, or "signs," when speaking, along with encouraging children to use these gestures to express their wants and needs. Although young toddlers have developed a listening vocabulary and show comprehension through their nonverbal responses, their expressive vocabulary is quite small. Toddlers are just beginning to produce word-like units (idiomorphs, or invented words) and a few conventional words. There is considerable variation among children's expressive language as they begin their second year of life. Some young toddlers will be using around six words; others may not begin saying recognizable words until several months later (Bates et al., 1994; Clark, 2003).

Benefits of using symbolic gestures.   Using symbolic gestures with toddlers may provide these children with an additional way of communicating. Toddlers' frustration is often reduced when they can communicate their needs and wants more directly (Beyer, 2007; Goodwyn & Acredolo, 1993). When a preverbal toddler uses signs to communicate her needs, teachers and parents no longer need to engage in a guessing game to determine why the child is upset or unhappy. In addition, as a result of encouraging the use of symbolic gestures, the noise level in a toddler room may decrease because children can communicate their needs without crying. Another benefit of using symbolic gestures in a toddler classroom is that it enhances the communication of children who may be hard of hearing or deaf, including children whose hearing is temporarily impaired due to ear infections. Hearing children who learn to use symbolic gestures are also able to communicate with parents, siblings, or classmates who may be hard of hearing or deaf.

Although additional research is needed to determine the long-term effects of using signing with young children (Sachs, 2009), some researchers and early childhood educators recommend using symbolic gestures with all toddlers and contend that children's use of these gestures does not delay oral language development and, in fact, enhances and reinforces language development (Beyer, 2007; Daniels, 1996; Goodwyn & Acredolo, 1993; Goodwyn, Acredolo, & Brown, 2000; Sign2Me, 2003).

Guidelines for using symbolic gestures, or signs, with toddlers.   If you decide that you want to introduce signing in your toddler classroom, you will need to become familiar with the different resources available. Figure 5.1 lists various resources. Some of the resources are based in American Sign Language, while others use signs that have been reported in observational studies of children's spontaneous use of symbolic gestures (i.e., home signs). Figure 5.1 also lists several board books designed to be used with toddlers that show pictures of toddlers using various signs.

After you have decided which signs to begin to use with toddlers in your classroom, there are several additional guidelines to keep in mind (Beyer, 2007; Acredolo & Goodwyn, 2009; Sign2Me, 2003):

- Remember that not all toddlers may be interested in using signs.
- Establish eye contact and shared reference as you speak and use the symbolic gestures.
- Introduce symbolic gestures slowly, focusing on only one or two signs.
- Choose signs that represent key activities or descriptors present in their daily activities, such as *more, finished, eat, help,* and *stop.*
- Use the signs regularly in daily activities. For example, "all done" could be signed by holding your arms out with both palms up and then turning them over and repeating the action while you say "all done."

FIGURE 5.1
Resources for Using Symbolic Gestures with Toddlers

Just for Teachers and Parents

Acredolo, L., & Goodwyn, S. (2009). *Baby signs: How to talk with your baby before your baby can talk*. Boston: McGraw Hill.

Anthony, M. & Lindert, R. (2009). *Signing smart: My first signs*. New York: Cartwheel Books/ Scholastic.

Beyer, M. (2007). *Teach your baby to sign: An illustrated guide to simple sign language for babies*. Beverly, MA: Fair Winds Press.

Chafin, S. (2009). *Knack baby sign language: A step-by-step guide to communicating with your little one*. Guilford, CT: Morris Publishing Group/Globe Pequot Press.

Heller, L. (2006). *Baby fingers: I want . . . Teaching your baby to sign*. New York: Sterling Publishing.

Murray, C. (2007). *Simple signing with young children: A guide for infant, toddler, and preschool teachers*. Beltsville, MD: Gryphon House.

Rosenberg, K. (2006). *Baby sign language: Find out what's on your baby's mind*. New York: Barnes & Noble.

Websites

www.babysigns.com
www.sproutingnewbeginnings.com

Board Books to Share with Children

Acredolo, L., & Goodwyn, S. (2002). *Baby signs for mealtime*. New York: HarperCollins.

Heller, L. (2004). *Teaching your baby to sign*. New York: Sterling Publishing.

Kubler, A. (2004). *My first signs*. Auburn, ME: Child's Play International Ltd.

- Look for ways to incorporate signing into your circle time activities through songs, stories, or games. This encourages children to participate in using signs.
- If you decide to use one of the board books listed in Figure 5.1, be sure to incorporate the signs shown in the book into your daily interactions with children.
- Be consistent in how you form and use each sign. Only through consistency and repetition will toddlers begin to associate a specific meaning with a sign.
- Check with children's parents to determine whether any symbolic gestures or signs are used at home. If so, incorporate these signs into your communication with the specific children involved.
- Expect that a child's initial use of symbolic gestures will be approximate rather than an exact imitation of your gestures.

TODDLER CURRICULA

Toddlerhood is a time of energetic exploration of the environment and of dramatic changes in receptive and productive language. Classrooms need to be furnished and activities planned with active explorers in mind. The curriculum should reflect toddlers' increasing independence and their need for opportunities to practice and refine their newly acquired physical skills and their new linguistic competencies. Hands-on experiences within a variety of learning activities foster continued growth in conceptual development, which supports language development. More specific learning activities may occur occasionally, when teachers interact with a small group of toddlers.

Three types of activities compose a typical day in a toddler room: exploratory activities, teacher-mediated activities, and routine activities. In each type of activity, it is important that toddlers not be rushed through the activity or pressured to respond in a particular way. Because toddlerhood is a time of developing autonomy, it is critical that the curricula in toddler rooms provide for sufficient time and opportunity for children to be more independent (Trawick-Smith, 1997). In each type of activity teachers can provide opportunities that will enhance children's language competencies.

Exploratory Activities

Exploratory activity time should provide toddlers with an opportunity to engage in hands-on activities and to interact creatively with a variety of materials and objects. The materials selected should be multipurpose so children can use them in a variety of ways. Toddlers benefit from exploring the possibilities of using basic items, and to engaging in symbolic play. A large box can become a car, a train engine, a house, a store, or an airplane.

This time of hands-on conceptual development provides opportunities for both receptive and productive language development. Toddlers do more than just "play." They engage in trial-and-error learning, they test hypotheses about how things work, and they explore cause-and-effect relations. They also develop social interaction skills and begin to carry on short conversations with their classmates.

Time allotted for exploratory activities depends on the developmental level of the children involved. Generally, the range of time for each exploratory activity period is about 20 to 30 minutes. Sufficient time should be allotted for children to engage in a variety of activities without feeling rushed; however, the time period should not extend beyond toddlers' energy levels. Depending on the total time in the program, there may be several exploratory activity periods.

During exploratory activity time, teachers should actively monitor individual children's behavior and involvement in the various activities. Teachers should circulate around the room and occasionally engage children in conversation and dialogue about their respective activities. Taking this active role is a positive way for teachers to monitor, model, and mediate children's interactions with materials and with each other.

The listening skills of teachers also are a factor in children's language development. Teachers should listen actively, establishing eye contact with the toddler who is speaking and giving interested attention to what is being communicated (Honig, 1982). By listening carefully to toddlers' comments and questions, teachers can provide the linguistic scaffolding needed to help toddlers express themselves. This active listening by the teacher also serves as a model to the child.

Active monitoring and conversation with children provides teachers with an opportunity to anticipate difficulties that may arise and to deal with them before the problem has reached a crisis stage. This also involves being aware of potential conflicts between children over using the same toy or picture book. In the sections that follow, specific exploratory activities appropriate for enhancing language development among toddlers are described, along with guidelines for teacher implementation and interaction.

Blocks and manipulatives.   Blocks and other manipulatives provide unlimited opportunities for symbolic play. A teacher should be available to monitor this area and enhance children's social–verbal relationships through mediation and by participating in child-initiated dialogues. Because toddlers may simply want to explore how blocks are stacked and manipulated, it is important that teachers carefully observe the block play and determine when it is appropriate to engage the child in conversation about his "building" or to mediate his interaction with others.

Book corner.   Toddlers enjoy looking at familiar books on their own, especially when the books are durable and have pages that can be turned easily, that is, board books. If you place books in the book corner that you have previously shared with children, they will be more interested in interacting with books. Having multiple copies of favorite books reduces the issue of taking turns or sharing, which is difficult for some toddlers.

Books should be stored within children's reach and on shelves that encourage children to return books when they are finished. Book racks or shelves that allow book fronts to be displayed will be more visually enticing than if only the book spines are visible. Comfortable seating areas near the books, such as pillows or small chairs, with a rug on the floor, will encourage children to share books with each other (Post & Hohmann, 2000). You can also encourage children to use this area by occasionally sitting in this area to be available for impromptu story sharing. Expect that you will have toddlers come to share books for different amounts of time.

Writing center.   Toddlers often show an interest in writing and drawing. This appears to stem from their observations of adults and older siblings. Providing an area with large sheets of paper and water-soluble colorful markers encourages toddlers to write. Adult supervision may be necessary to ensure that the toddlers' writing goes on the paper and not on tabletops or walls. It is important to

Toddlers enjoy looking at familiar books on their own.

remember that children's early writing is exploratory in nature. They are exploring how writing is made and how it has meaning. Researchers have described children's gradual construction of knowledge of written language through these explorations (Temple, Nathan, Burris, & Temple, 1988). Initially, toddlers engage in random scribbling and appear to focus on the "pleasurable physical action of the hand pushing and pulling a crayon or other writing implement across various surfaces" (Baghban, 2007, p. 21). Then, children begin to understand that marks can carry meaning.

Toddlers may fill a whole sheet with their scribble-like writings or may have only a small amount of writing on the sheet. They may announce the content or meaning of what they have written or may take it to a teacher to "read." When this happens, a teacher can instead request that the child read it for her or tell her about what was written. The important consideration here is that the child receive positive feedback for her attempts. When the child is finished with her piece of writing, you could print her name on the front, modeling the writing process and saying aloud each letter.

Discovery centers.   Discovery centers, also known as concept centers, are specific areas that have been designed and developed to facilitate experiences that support the development of specific concepts related to math, science, or social studies as well as general language knowledge. For example, a discovery center equipped with a magnifying glass and a small basket of seashells would encourage toddlers to observe the detailed textures of the shells and the delicate shapes. Another toddler discovery center could involve a collection of different types and colors of leaves along with a magnifying glass.

Teachers should provide opportunities for children to talk about their experiences in a discovery center either during their experience or shortly thereafter. The focus of the conversation would be on giving the child opportunity to talk about what was experienced or what actions occurred. In this way, discovery centers enhance semantic development and general verbal communication. Even at the toddler level, discovery centers can be effective; however, discovery centers at this level are less structured and more exploratory than centers in preschool classrooms.

Drama corner.   An area provided with dress-up clothes and accessories affords children opportunities to engage in symbolic, pretend play and use language as a part of that play. Clothes and other items should represent both genders so that this area is not gender restrictive. Both boys and girls should be encouraged to participate in this area.

In dramatic activities, children learn to verbally negotiate the roles they want to play.

The drama corner should include appropriate props, such as a telephone, a telephone book, empty boxes, chairs, a table, and the like. Some teachers may decide to create themed drama corners on a rotating basis. A grocery store, a home kitchen area, and a post office are typical themes for toddlers. These are contexts with which the toddlers may be familiar. Their respective experiences provide the creativity and frames of reference for engaging in dramatic play.

Children this age usually do not play cooperatively but may engage in parallel play. Teachers monitoring the drama activity area need to keep in mind that these children are just beginning to interact with each other. There may be times when a child is trying to engage in solitary play although she is in an area with other children. For this reason, you may find it better if only two or three children are in the drama corner at one time.

In assuming specific roles, children may communicate verbally with a specific role in mind. For toddlers, teachers may need to initiate a conversation ("Good morning, Mr. Mail Carrier. What letters do you have for me today?") and then extend that conversation to include other children in the area, thereby encouraging those children to respond verbally and become a part of the dramatic activity: "Thank you for my letters. What letters do you have for Jennifer today? Jennifer, come see what mail you have."

In dramatic activities, children learn to verbally negotiate the roles they want to play relative to the roles others around them want to play. With toddlers, you may expect that all of them want to be mail carriers or that all of them want to be the mother. Teachers should model for the children how to settle the issue verbally. For example, "We have two mail carriers. Let's pretend that each of you is on a different route. Pick someone different to deliver mail to." You can also expect that there will be wide variations in the time that children engage in this center. Some will come and go; others will stay for a longer period of time.

Sand and water table activities.   Sand and water tables allow children to have tactile experiences that contribute to their concept development. Toddlers need only a few accessories while at sand and water tables. Utensils for stirring and pouring encourage children to manipulate the sand or water. Using their hands to move the sand or water provides them with a better understanding of the basic properties of each of the substances. Toddlers need room to explore during this activity; thus, only two or three children should use the sand or water table at the same time. Similarly to other exploratory activities, your role as a teacher is to listen carefully to children's comments so that you can extend or clarify their understandings. You may decide to occasionally initiate conversation or use verbal mapping. This encourages the children to talk with the teacher and with each other. In this way, children's receptive and productive language will be enhanced.

Art activities.   Although art activities are closely monitored and facilitated by a teacher, the emphasis of art activities is always on a child's independent sensory exploration of the artistic medium. The focus is on the process rather than on the product. When toddlers are engaged in painting, their focus is often on mixing the colors and learning how to hold and move the brush. Pseudo-art activities that involve children pasting precut pieces onto paper or attempting to color or paint predrawn designs have little value for toddlers' concept development and creative expression.

Toddlers' curiosity in exploring painting and other artistic media will dominate their activities such that they often will not show an interest in naming or identifying what they have created. Some toddlers may resist painting or other art activities that appear to be overly messy; others seem to delight in those activities. By providing a variety of activities, teachers can meet the needs of both types of children.

When children's artwork is displayed in the room or sent home, teachers can help parents and other adults in interpreting the value of the activity and the product by focusing on the role of exploration in conceptual development and the process in using the specific media. A child's name should be written (printed) on the front (if possible) or on the back of the art paper. This models written language for the child and gives the child a sense of ownership.

Opportunities to explore outdoors provide toddlers with sensory experiences that contribute to conceptual and semantic knowledge.

Outdoor activities.   Toddlers are physically active and need regular times to be outside. Safe, developmentally appropriate playground equipment is crucial. There should also be room for exploration and space for movement activities (e.g., running, walking, trike riding). The outdoor area should be away from traffic and separate from older children's activities. A boundary fence eases monitoring children's movements and safety.

Outdoor activities provide opportunities for children to see and experience activities not present in the classroom. Outdoor activities also provide many opportunities for talking about what the children see, hear, and experience. When you are outside with toddlers, watch to see what interests them. Perhaps they see a butterfly, caterpillar, worm, bird, or squirrel. They might notice a big truck going by on the street. Follow their interest and comment on what you see or hear. You might follow your comment with a question, such as "Oh, look at the worm crawling on the sidewalk. Where do you think it is going?" Then pause to see if they continue the conversation with a comment or by asking you a question. Instead of standing near another teacher and visiting during the outdoor time, make yourself available to children's spontaneous conversations by slowly moving between the different outdoor activity areas and stopping to notice children's engagement in the various activities.

Teacher-Mediated Activities

Teacher-mediated activities at the toddler level involve a teacher's interacting with one or more children at a time, while reading a book, or sharing a new object or collection of objects, such as seashells. Large group activities are not usually successful because toddlers have limited attention spans and need to be actively engaged with the materials or books used (Birckmayer, Kennedy, & Stonehouse, 2009). Teacher-mediated activities need to be open-ended, exploratory, and sensitive to the interests and comments of the toddlers participating and of short duration. As opportunity presents itself, teachers can use some verbal mapping or linguistic scaffolding techniques.

Book sharing.   Book sharing with toddlers can enhance development of each of the aspects of language knowledge: phonological, semantic, syntactic, morphemic, and pragmatic. Two key factors in successfully engaging toddlers in book sharing are selecting appropriate books to share and using specific interaction strategies during book sharing. It is also important to remember that the focus of this activity is on *exploring the book* rather than *reading the text in the book*. Table 5.2 provides an overview of the developmental sequence for sharing books with infants and toddlers.

Selecting books. Selecting appropriate books is an important part of engaging toddlers in book sharing. Books should have clear, colorful illustrations of familiar objects and events. You will want to select books that represent the linguistic and cultural diversity of the toddlers in your room. Books with patterned text, nursery rhymes, or simple poems are enjoyed for their rhythmic language, which becomes memorable to toddlers. For example, *Brown Bear, Brown Bear, What Do You See?* (Martin & Carle, 1992)

TABLE 5.2
Developmental Sequence for Sharing Books with Infants and Toddlers

Level	Caregiver's Interaction	Example of Caregiver's Speech
Level 1	Points to objects pictured and labels objects. No attempt to read story line or to share the entire book.	"Cat. Dog. Bird"
Level 2	Points to objects pictured, labels objects, and may include descriptive language. No attempt to read story line or to share the entire book.	"See the yellow cat." "See the big brown dog." "Look at the blue bird."
Level 3	Describes actions or events pictured. No attempt to read story line; however, story events pictured on that page may be mentioned and referred to by pointing. More of book is shared due to increasing attention span.	"See the yellow cat run up the tree." "See the big brown dog chase the cat." "Look at the blue bird fly away."
Level 4	Incorporates more of story line in the verbal sharing. Story line is continued for several pages, if not the entire book.	"The yellow cat ran up the tree. Spot [points to dog] was chasing the cat. Let's turn the page and see what happens next. Oh, look, the birds got scared and flew away!"
Level 5	Increasing amounts of actual story text are read. This is dependent on the level of complexity of the story syntax and the story line.	"Sassy was a yellow cat that lived in a blue house. Spot was a brown dog that lived next door. One of Spot's favorite games was to chase Sassy up a tree. When Sassy ran up the tree, it scared the birds from their nests in the tree."

is a favorite of many toddlers. By sharing this book in the board book format, toddlers can more easily help turn the pages.

Books with simple plots or story lines can also be used. *The Very Hungry Caterpillar* (Carle, 1969) is an example of a book with a simple storyline that toddlers enjoy. However, you may find that when you initially share a book, toddlers may want to focus only on the illustrations rather than listen to the text being read. As children become familiar with the content pictured, you can insert segments of the text, building up to sharing the entire text.

Language development is enhanced when teachers coordinate the topics of books to actual events (Fowler, 1990). For example, if the street outside the toddler center is being repaired, books on trucks or building roads could be shared. A trip to a nature center could be followed up with a book about animals. Or it may be as simple as talking about the apples served for lunch when you are sharing a book that has a picture of an apple. For example, "That's an apple. What did we have for lunch today? Yes, we had apples" (Honig & Brophy, 1996, p. 61).

Concept knowledge is enhanced when this coordination between book topics and real events takes place, and it sets the stage for content-rich conversations between toddlers and teachers.

Interaction strategies for book sharing. The interaction strategies you use when sharing books with toddlers will depend on your awareness of each child's prior knowledge and level of language development (both receptive and expressive). This awareness provides you with knowledge of each child's zone of proximal development.

Toddlers need to be engaged in book sharing rather than passive listening. Children should be encouraged to participate by making spontaneous comments and responding to your comments and questions. Young toddlers may show a preference for randomly paging through a book, attracted by the pictures (Lawrence, 1998), or they may want to spend a long time looking at one particular picture (Honig & Brophy, 1996). When you focus on the illustrations in picture books, children are encouraged to "read the pictures" and talk about what they see.

As you share books with toddlers, you will find these additional suggestions useful:

- Monitor children's eye contact and shared reference. Be sure to point to pictures when you name or label the pictures. Use gestures to show action or to redirect a child's attention when she becomes distracted.
- Follow the children's lead on the duration of book sharing. If a toddler becomes restless, discontinue the book sharing. If you are with more than one child, allow the restless child to move to another activity.
- Be sure children can view the illustrations close-up. This is critical to their comprehension of book content. Pictures in books provide important visual referents to book content. In many instances, toddlers become disinterested in book sharing because they cannot see the illustrations close-up and are not able to comprehend the teacher's oral language without the visual referents provided by the illustrations. This is usually not an issue in one-on-one book sharing; however, in sharing books with three or more toddlers, it is a frequent occurrence.
- Use scaffolding techniques to involve children by using questioning and commenting. Build on children's comments and observations as well as their gestures or as they point to illustrations.
- Model animal sounds, sound effects, and gestures, as appropriate for the specific book. Encourage children to join in.
- When sharing a text that is patterned with a refrain, encourage children by pausing just before the repeated phrase so they can participate in the "reading."
- Extend comprehension by referring to a child's prior related experiences in the classroom or on the playground. This connection also enhances assimilation and accommodation of concepts and new vocabulary.

- Adapt each text to children's language and listening comprehension levels. Carefully observe children's verbal and nonverbal responses for evidence of comprehension and engagement. Depending on the listening comprehension level of the toddlers involved, you may be able to read portions of the text. If children have participated in book sharing since infancy, they will have a higher level of listening comprehension than if they are inexperienced in book sharing interactions.
- Respond positively to children's requests for repeated sharings, or "readings," of favorite books. Toddlers may request the same book be shared over and over again. Requests for repeated book sharings indicate toddlers' appreciation for the predictability of familiar pictures or the story text as well as their developing memory for story sequence and story language. With repeated sharings, toddlers may begin to actively participate more in describing the pictures or the story events.
- Expect toddlers to gradually participate more in the book sharing (Fowler, 1990). As a toddler becomes more familiar with books, you might extend the discussion and questioning to follow the story line that goes from page to page. At this point, you could say, "Look what's happening here. It looks

Songs and finger plays enhance children's awareness of rhythm and rhyme.

like . . ." and "Oh, now, see where. . . ." Gradually, over repeated interactions, and with a child's evident interest and comprehension, you will be able to share increasing amounts of the exact text.

Songs and finger plays.   Toddlers' language development can be enhanced by action songs and finger plays enjoyed at small group time or during daily routines. These activities encourage active listening and imitation, along with attention to rhythm, repetition, and expressive intonation (Squibb & Deitz, 2000). For example, the action song "Itsy-Bitsy Spider" combines rhythm and simple movements. Children first learn to listen to the song and begin to follow along with the actions. Gradually, with repetition, they are able to begin to sing along.

Introduce only one verse or song at a time. Through repeated opportunities to hear a song or rhyme, toddlers will begin to anticipate upcoming words and actions (Manolson, 1992). Toddlers can also be encouraged to begin to mark the rhythm of a song with sound shakers, clapping, or movement. In a group of toddlers, there will be a range of involvement, from simply listening to full verbal participation. Teachers' enthusiasm, eye contact, and clear enunciation of the song or rhyme will encourage toddlers' participation.

Teachers can also adapt familiar tunes to include the child's name or to focus on an ongoing activity. For example, the tune "Here We Go Round the Mulberry Bush" can be adapted to "This is the way we wash our face, wash our face . . ." (Manolson, 1992, p. 90). Creative adaptations of familiar tunes encourage children to listen and respond to rhythm through actions and by singing along.

Texts that rhyme also enhance toddlers' phonemic awareness because rhyming words emphasize the component sounds of words (Maclean, Bryant, & Bradley, 1987). For example, rhymes that pair such words as *fall*, *tall*, *ball*, *small*, *wall*, and *call* highlight the common sounds (*all*) found in each word.

Activity boxes.   Teacher-mediated activity boxes (Wilson, 1988) involve the manipulation and labeling of items contained in boxes with removable lids. For example, a peek-a-boo box encourages children to label what they see in the box's window (in the lid). After the toy is labeled (e.g., "cat") it is removed and held by the child. Then the teacher can encourage further receptive and productive language by asking questions or making simple requests: "Point to the cat's ears." "Where is the cat's tail?" "Point to the cat's eyes." Teachers should praise toddlers for their descriptions and their guesses.

Teachers facilitate children's interactions with items in the boxes by using verbal mapping, labeling, and linguistic scaffolding (extension and expansion) techniques. The activity can be continued until all the items are guessed. This activity is best done with only one or two children at a time so that each child can have more direct involvement in the activity.

A movement box can be used to familiarize children with action concept labels. For example, place a medium-sized soft ball and a long, colorful scarf in the box. Remove the ball and bounce it a couple times. Talk briefly with the children about the ball going up and down. Then suggest, "Let's bounce like a ball" (teacher jumps up and down and encourages children to do the same). Then put the ball back in the box and remove the scarf. Wave the scarf in the air. Then hand the scarf to a child and ask him to show the others how he waves it. Reinforce the child's actions verbally. Then the scarf can be given to another child and the request repeated.

Book-centered activity boxes include a familiar storybook and accompanying realia. For example, the book *Corduroy* (Freeman, 1968) could be accompanied by a brown teddy bear that is wearing overalls, several other stuffed animal toys, and a small flashlight. A book about trucks could be accompanied by several small toy trucks or different types of hats (fireman's hat, cowboy hat, mail carrier's hat, policeman's hat). You will need to allow ample time for a toddler to explore the realia and to talk about it. The addition of story-related objects encourages children's conceptual development and involves their active interaction in the story sharing. Additional teacher-mediated activities are described in the resource books listed in Figure 5.2.

Outdoor activities. Teacher-mediated outdoor activities focus on facilitating children's explorations and conversations about what they see, hear, or touch. For example, the teacher may sit at the side of the sandbox and encourage the children to explore how sand moves and is shaped by the different containers provided in the sandbox. You may find that by using verbal mapping, questioning, and linguistic scaffolding, you can extend children's conversations during their outdoor activities.

Seasonal outdoor teacher-mediated activities may include the following: watching bugs crawl across a leaf, collecting leaves, catching snowflakes, making a snowman or a snow angel, smelling flowers, and watching the clouds, tree branches, and leaves move in the wind. The key here is to carefully observe your toddlers to determine their interest and curiosity and then to mediate their interaction with that phenomenon. Avoid talking continuously or excessively, as it may overwhelm toddlers (Post & Hohmann, 2000). Instead, focus on acknowledging toddlers' interests and actions through responsive comments as you engage them in conversation.

FIGURE 5.2
Resource Books for Toddler Activities

Charner, K., Murphy, M. & Clark, C. (2006). *The encyclopedia of infant and toddler activities: Written by teachers for teachers.* Beltsville, MD: Gryphon House.

Levine, J. (2012). *The everything toddler activity book: Over 400 games and projects to entertain and educate.* Avon, MA: Adams Media.

Post, J., & Hohmann, M. (2000). *Tender care and early learning: Supporting infants and toddlers in child care settings.* Ypsilanti, MI: High/Scope Press.

Raines, S., Miller, K., & Curry-Rood, L. (2002). *Story s-t-r-e-t-c-h-e-r-s for infants, toddlers, and twos: Experiences, activities and games for popular children's books.* Beltsville, MD: Gryphon House.

Schiller, P. & Moore, T. (2006). *And the cow jumped over the moon: Over 650 activities to teach toddlers using familiar rhymes and songs.* Beltsville, MD: Gryphon House.

Routine Activities

Routines provide toddlers with a sense of security and predictability. Because of their familiarity with a routine, toddlers feel secure. In contrast to infants, toddlers are able to participate more independently in some of the routines of eating, dressing, hand washing, and toileting. In addition, toddlers can participate more actively in arrival and departure routines. The aspect of language knowledge encouraged in routines is pragmatic knowledge, which is an awareness of how language is used differently in different situations. As you engage toddlers in routine activities, you will want to make adaptations to the routines to respond to children's needs and to build in opportunities for conversation.

Arrival. During arrival time, it is important for you to call each child by name and to speak directly to the child and his parent. Also encourage children to respond to your greetings and then respond to any verbalization or gesture from the children. During this time, you will find it useful to begin a conversation with a child about a familiar object or event occurring in the room. This provides a focus as the child makes the transition to your classroom.

Snack time/mealtime. Toddlers enjoy feeding themselves, though their appetite may decrease during this period of development due to a slower rate of physical growth. It is beneficial for you to sit with toddlers as they eat, encouraging conversation and social routines of saying "please" and "thank you" and passing small serving dishes of food around the table. This is also a good time for children to become aware of new words. As you talk with children about the food that is being served, describe its appearance, texture, color, or taste (Wortham, 1998). For example, "Your applesauce is lumpy, bumpy, and cool." "Your mashed potatoes are warm and white. They stick to your spoon" (Honig & Brophy, 1996, p. 26).

As you talk with toddlers during snack time or mealtime, be sure to show interest in each child's contribution to the table conversation, regardless of how limited it might be (Fowler, 1990). It is important that each child feel included in the social–verbal interaction during snack time or mealtime. Toddlers should also be encouraged to help clean up their eating area when they have finished. This encourages them to learn to follow verbal directions.

Departure. At departure time, there are additional opportunities to engage children in conversation and routine dialogue. As toddlers ready themselves to leave your classroom, talk with each child briefly about the day's events. Be sure to position yourself at eye level with a toddler to direct his attention to you.

It is also useful to share information about a child's day with her parents. You will want to keep this sharing informative and positive. Toddlers' listening comprehension is at a higher level than their speech production, and they may comprehend and be influenced by a teacher's or parent's comments about them. These end-of-day conversations between teachers and parents set the stage for children's transitions back home. It is important that these transitions be positive and reassuring.

Family Connections

Positive school–home connections are important in supporting and enhancing all areas of children's development. In this section, the focus will be on ways in which school–home connections can support language development for infants and toddlers. As a teacher of these young children, it is important for you to establish close connections with each child's family. These close connections not only provide a sense of security and stability for children but also encourage parents and family members to see themselves as important partners in enhancing their children's growth and development.

General guidelines.   The following general guidelines are suggested as ways to create positive school–home connections that will foster children's language development:

- Establish rapport with family members. If your students' parents speak diverse languages, learn how to say the common greetings in their home languages. Always establish eye contact, be an active listener, and address the parents in a professional manner.

- Welcome parents into your classroom as they drop off and pick up their children. Also provide opportunities for parents to stay for a few minutes in the classroom and participate with their children in activities. This provides a smooth, gentle transition for infants and toddlers. It also reduces the stress that may occur as these transitions are made (Gallagher, 2005).

- Emphasize to parents the importance of talking with their infants and toddlers as they engage in routine activities at home and when they are involved in errands in their community. Encourage parents to use labeling and commenting as they engage their children in these activities as well as to support their children's attempts to label and comment in response to ongoing events or activities. For parents who speak a different language at home, encourage them to continue to use their home language with their infant or toddler.

- Encourage parents to become aware of their child's use of gestures (symbolic or referential). If you have used gestures in your classroom as a way of communicating with infants or toddlers, be sure to share these gestures with parents so they can continue this type of communication at home. They may discover that their children are less frustrated when they are able to communicate in this way. You will also want to share with parents the resources or books you have used for incorporating symbolic gestures in your classroom.

- Provide take-home activities involving language and book sharing. You could provide a book bag with two or three developmentally appropriate books that parents can check out to share with their children at home. As you begin this, you will want to establish a specific check-out and check-in procedure for your classroom library. When you allow parents to check out books from your classroom library, children can enjoy the same books at home that you have shared in your classroom.

- Encourage parents to share books with their infants and toddlers and to talk about the illustrations in the books by labeling, commenting, and asking simple questions. Emphasize to parents the importance of encouraging their children to respond to what is pictured in a book rather than expect their children to listen passively to the text being read.

- If you have children from diverse-language families, provide books in their home languages as well as in English. Provide information to parents about the availability of books in diverse languages available at your local public library or on the Internet. For example, www.languagelizard.com and www.mantralingua.com are two sources for books in a variety of languages.

- Encourage parents to each create an audiotape of a familiar story or a favorite lullaby or song that you can make available for children to listen to in your classroom. Parents who speak a different language at home can be encouraged to use their home language in making the audiotape.

- Share ideas for enhancing language development at home via a classroom newsletter (see Figure 5.3). To make your newsletter reader-friendly, focus on using bullet points rather than paragraphs.

FIGURE 5.3
Classroom Newsletter

Ideas for Sharing Books with Your Toddler
Why?
- Enjoy a special time with your child
- Help your child learn about the world
- Help your child develop listening and speaking skills

How?
- Choose toddler-level books
  - Board books
  - Simple illustrations
  - Familiar events and objects
- Talk about pictures and events in book
  - point to pictures
  - vary your voice and add sound effects or animal sounds
  - talk about child's related experiences
  - ask your child questions

When?
- Just before bedtime or naptime
- Any time your child is interested
- As often as you can

SUMMARY

The planning and implementation of developmentally appropriate curricula in infant and toddler rooms is important to a child's future development. Developmentally appropriate infant and toddler activities enhance the acquisition of each of the five aspects of language knowledge. Curricula for infants and toddlers focus on facilitating the development of receptive and expressive language. Sensorimotor, hands-on experiential activities are the basis for children's development of concept knowledge and for the acquisition of words for those concepts. Developmentally appropriate classrooms for infants and toddlers are characterized by opportunities to explore in a safe, well-planned environment with caring, observant teachers. As an early childhood teacher, you are the guide and facilitator for children as they explore and learn through the activities in your classroom and early childhood center.

Language development is facilitated when teachers use a variety of interaction techniques, including eye contact and shared reference, communication loops, child-directed speech, verbal mapping, labeling, questioning, and linguistic scaffolding. During daily arrival and departure times, teachers communicate with children and their parents, sharing information about children's development and learning activities as well as facilitating the transition between home and the early childhood center.

✳ ✳ ✳ CHAPTER REVIEW

1. What are the characteristics of developmentally appropriate curricula?
2. Describe three exploratory activities for an infant. Explain the way in which each of these activities enhances language development. Mention the specific aspects of language knowledge involved.
3. Explain how routine activities in an infant classroom can enhance language development.
4. Explain the value of object labeling and verbal mapping to toddlers' language development. State the specific aspects of language knowledge involved. Give two examples.
5. State three criteria for selecting books to place in a toddler's book corner.
6. Describe several techniques for sharing books with infants and toddlers.

✳ ✳ ✳   CHAPTER EXTENSION ACTIVITIES

Curriculum Development

1. Plan three activities for an infant or toddler room and describe the specific ways in which one or more aspects of oral language will be enhanced.

2. Using a website or one of the books listed in Figure 5.1, select five symbolic gestures to demonstrate to your college class. Explain how you would integrate these symbolic gestures into activities in a toddler classroom.

Observation

Observe outdoor time in a toddler center, focusing on the verbal interactions between the teachers and children. Pay attention to the characteristics of teachers' talk to children. Describe whether it follows the characteristics of child-directed speech.

CHAPTER 6

LANGUAGE DEVELOPMENT IN PRESCHOOLERS

Learning Outcomes

After reading this chapter you should be able to

- Describe how the order of phoneme development reflects the complexity involved in producing each phoneme
- Explain how vicarious and direct experiences enhance semantic development
- Describe ways in which preschool children's syntactic knowledge develops from three to five years of age
- Explain how instances of overgeneralization in preschoolers' use of morphemes provides evidence of their developing language knowledge
- Explain how preschoolers' speech during dramatic play provides evidence of developing pragmatic knowledge of language

Eric and Dylan were on trikes near each other. Dylan said, "Mine's outta gas and got a flat tire!" Eric added, "Mine, too!" Then Eric pantomimed filling the tires with air and filling the trike with gas. He said, "Pump, pump, pump" while filling the gas tank.

During lunch, Tammy identified many of the letters present in her alphabet soup. Several times she asked her teacher what they spelled.

While playing at the table with the small shape blocks, Maria picked up a star shape and said, "Twinkle, twinkle, little star."

Eric, Dylan, Tammy, and Maria provide evidence of the increasing complexity of children's speech during the preschool years in each of the five aspects of language knowledge: phonological, semantic, syntactic, morphemic, and pragmatic. While unfamiliar adults may have a difficult time understanding what a toddler is trying to communicate, they can more easily understand preschool children (Clay, 1991). Preschoolers can more accurately produce phonemes in their home language, observe adult word meanings, and use a larger vocabulary. Preschool children's syntax becomes more complex and conveys more precise communication than that of toddlers. They are able to participate verbally in conversation through turn taking. In these ways, children's language knowledge continues to develop during the preschool years. These increased language competencies provide children with greater facility in interacting with their environment.

Preschoolers continue to explore language. They explore how language sounds, how it communicates meaning, how word sequence influences meaning, what significance word endings have, how language is used differently in different settings, and what the relations are between oral language and written language. Children's explorations of language occur simultaneously with explorations of their environment. A dynamic interaction connects these two types of exploration. Language exploration and environmental exploration influence each other. Children's ability to ask questions and to use follow-up questioning to clarify others' communication enhances their explorations of language and their world.

Preschool children are not yet capable of private or internal speech (Bailey & Brookes, 2003). Their speech is a direct reflection of what they are thinking. They think aloud. Because preschool children are not yet able to process and retain information internally, they cannot delay expressing their thoughts. Thus, their interactions with others are characterized by spontaneous speech. For example, if a preschool teacher announces that she is going to read a story about a big red dog, children may respond with comments such as, "I have a dog. His name is Spot." "I saw a dog in the park today." "I saw a squirrel in the park." "Teacher, when are we going to play in the park?" It may seem to the teacher that the children simply are not "paying attention"; however, these verbal responses indicate that the children are simply expressing their thoughts and in many instances may be relating what the teacher said to their own personal experiences and interests. Telling preschool children to sit and just listen is essentially telling them to sit and not think. This explains why group story time needs to incorporate opportunities for children to talk as well as acceptance by the teacher of children's "divergent comments."

Preschool children's acquisition of language competencies is embedded in the environments in which the children interact, specifically their home environment and their preschool or child-care environment. Research has documented the importance of a supportive context for language acquisition both in the home environment and in the preschool or child-care environment (Beals, 2001; Hart & Risley, 1995, 1999; Hadley, Wilcox, & Rice, 1994; Henderson & Jones, 2002). The way in which their home and community environments support and guide their explorations influences not only children's language development but their cognitive development as well.

When parents share storybooks with children, they use language to describe the actions pictured and to tell or "read" the story, enhancing children's receptive language.

Within these environmental contexts, children are directly and indirectly encouraged to develop language competencies. Significant advances occur in language knowledge in each of the aspects of language: phonological, semantic, syntactic, morphemic, and pragmatic. In the sections that follow, preschool children's development of language knowledge in each of the five aspects will be described. The development of phonological knowledge will be described first because speech is the "primary way in which humans express themselves through language" (Dobrovolsky, 2005, p. 15).

In chapter 7, specific strategies for enhancing language development among preschoolers will be described.

DEVELOPMENT OF PHONOLOGICAL KNOWLEDGE

By preschool age, children's receptive awareness and production of language-related sounds (phonemes) are fairly well developed. While little agreement exists among researchers as to the universality of the onset of specific speech sound production prior to age 3, some consensus has been reached based on research with children after age 3 (Owens, 2012). Although general patterns of development have been identified, it is important to remember that considerable variation exists among children of similar ages.

Patterns of Development

The order of phoneme development reflects the complexity involved in producing each phoneme (Owens, 2012). For example, vowel phonemes are acquired earlier than consonants because vowel sounds require less specific coordination of the mouth and lips than do consonant sounds. In addition, the order of phonemic development for consonants reflects the manner in which the sound is produced. For example, the /m/ and /n/ phonemes are produced by closing the oral cavity (nasals), while the /p/ and /b/ sounds are produced by a sudden release of sound (plosives).

The location in the speech mechanism of the sound production also determines the order of acquisition. For example, the /p/ and /b/ sounds require the lips to come together, while the /k/ and /g/ sound is produced when the back of the tongue touches the soft palate. Sounds that are located in the initial position in words are acquired before sounds in the medial or last positions in words. Consonant clusters and blends such as /sh/, /ch/, /tr/, or /gl/ are more complicated to produce. For example, a preschooler might say /guvs/ instead articulating the blend /gl/ beginning the word "gloves." Although some consonant clusters may appear at about age 4, full acquisition of consonant clusters may not occur until about age 7 or 8.

Phonemic Awareness

During the preschool years, children's growing awareness of phonemes is often evident in how they use language. This metalinguistic awareness that words are composed of separate sounds that can be manipulated is termed **phonemic awareness**. When speaking, preschool children may begin to focus on and manipulate specific phonemes. Although they may not be able to name the different sounds in words or explain why the words rhyme, preschool children are developing an awareness that they can create words that have similar sounds and that sound manipulation is fun (Wasik, 2001). Phonemic awareness has been linked to later achievement in reading (Eldredge, 2004; Sensenbaugh, 1996).

Sound play. One of the types of language play identified by Schwartz (1981) is **sound play**, which consists of children's manipulating the phonemic elements and prosodic features of pitch, stress, and juncture. As infants, children engage in a form of sound play as they babble and explore sound production. As preschoolers, children focus on the sound similarities between words and consciously manipulating the sound elements in a word. This type of language play occurs when children are playing alone and with others.

Spontaneous rhyming is a type of phonemic sound play. As children play, rhyming chants may be expressed, as in "cat, fat, bat, mat, sat." Maclean, Bryant, and Bradley (1987) studied the development of phonological awareness in young children. They reported that children as young as 3 are aware of rhyme and alliteration and can respond to tasks that require them to orally identify words that rhyme and words that start the same as a target word. When children listen to stories or to poetry readings, they may also indicate their awareness of sound patterns and phonemic relations by anticipating upcoming text or contributing additional rhyming words. Children may also verbally comment on words that rhyme. For example, saying, "bat and cat sound the same. They rhyme."

Matching speech sounds to print.   Metalinguistic knowledge of phonemes also develops when children begin to focus on print in literacy-rich environments. As preschool children interact more with written language when adults read stories, and with environmental print, such as road signs and restaurant or store signs, they begin to associate initial letters with specific sounds (Clay, 1983). Ryan's mother, Barb, reported that whenever he would see the letter *B* present in print in his environment, he would say, "*B* starts your name, Mommy" (Otto, 1982). This occurred when he saw the words *bible* and *bank*, as well as also when he saw the letter *B* in an alphabet book. Although it is not clear whether Ryan was focusing on the sound of *b* or just the visual association, Ryan's comments indicated that he was beginning to pay attention to words and the graphic system for representing sounds in print. It is also possible that Ryan was remembering what his mother had told him previously when the letter *B* was singled out and associated with her name.

In a similar example, Greg, at age 4½ years, spotted the letter *G* engraved on the bottom of a flowerpot. After asking what the letter stood for, and being told it was the potter's name, he said, "I know *G,* 'cause that's what my name starts with."

Some preschool children begin to try to match speech to print and to explore ways of sharing ideas on paper (Bissex, 1980; Perlmutter, Folger & Holt, 2009; Purcell-Gates, 1996; Schickedanz, York, Stewart, & White, 1990; Shatz, 1994; Sulzby, 1983; Temple, Nathan, Burris, & Temple, 1988). Children's exploratory, hypothesis-testing behaviors are seen in monolingual as well as bilingual classrooms (Ballenger, 1996). As preschoolers attempt to figure out which letters to use for their names and messages and how to "say" what they have written or what someone else has written, their developing awareness of connections between sounds and print becomes evident. Initially, preschoolers typically use scribbling, letter-like forms, or strings of letters when writing and assign meaning to what they have written when "reading" it to a peer or adult, though no clear connections between the writing form and the sounds represented is evident. Gradually, children begin to associate specific sounds with letters and may use just one letter to represent a word (Perlmutter et al., 2009); for example, using the letter *D* to represent the word "Daddy."

For many children, one of the first words they learn to represent in writing is their own name. Thus, the letter–sound connections established in this context will reflect the children's individual names. Children may then transfer this knowledge of letter–sound connections when they are writing other words as well. For example, a child named Riley would transfer her awareness of the letter *R* and the sound associated with it to her writing attempts for the words *rock* and *rabbit.*

When preschoolers use a combination of writing-related strategies, they seem to be focusing on communicating their messages any way that "works" for them. For example, in Figure 6.1, Madeline (age 4) used a letter string OHTEFELLL along with early phonemic spelling of TARGET (two letters reversed) and ONT. When asked to read what she had written, Madeline gave the phonemic sound for each letter in the string and said "target" and "not." Although the letter string did not spell

FIGURE 6.1
Madeline's Writing

a word, the fact that she "read" it by giving the phonemic sound indicates that she was not simply giving an inventory of letters she could form but she was communicating a series of phonemic sounds she could represent by the appropriate letters. She also included drawn representations and labeled them "a comb" (lower left corner) and "that's the target" (lower right corner).

Then, in Figure 6.2, Madeline wrote ANDOIEMFOPAT. When asked to read what she wrote, she said "Andat (her teacher's first name) and M.F.O.P." She also used drawn representations of two people in her message. Madeline's work shows her exploration and experimentation as she develops knowledge of the phonological connections between oral and written language.

DEVELOPMENT OF SEMANTIC KNOWLEDGE

Children's vocabulary expands and becomes more refined or precise during the preschool years as children begin to develop more complex concepts. When children encounter new experiences, they have opportunities to expand their language as they refer to and respond to these new experiences. Receptive and expressive vocabulary grows rapidly. A preschool

FIGURE 6.2
Madeline's Writing

"Andat" "M. F. O. P"   11/29/11

child's expressive vocabulary has been estimated to range from 800 to 1,000 words (Crystal, 1987; Morrow, 1989; Owens, 2001).

Experiential Basis for Semantic Knowledge

Children develop concepts for those entities and ideas that are part of their cultural environment (Nelson, 1973). Concepts and their association with words develop through direct experiences and through vicarious (indirect/mediated) experiences. Figure 6.3 illustrates the connections between vocabulary development and experiences.

Assimilation and accommodation. Semantic knowledge develops through the processes of assimilation and accommodation. In **assimilation**, a new concept is incorporated into an existing conceptual schema. For example, a child has a concept of *cow* as having four legs and a long tail, making the sound "moo," eating grass, and being brown in color. On a trip to the zoo, this child sees a brown cow and a black-and-white cow. She learns from her teacher that this differently colored animal, too, is a cow. This new semantic knowledge is assimilated into the child's existing conceptual

FIGURE 6.3

Connections Between Vocabulary Development and Experiences

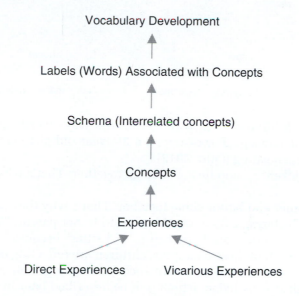

structure, within the color feature. The remaining features (tail, four legs, eats grass, says "moo") stay the same.

In **accommodation**, a cognitive structure or schema is changed to incorporate the new concept (Brainerd, 1978). Continuing with the zoo example above, at the same zoo, there is a horse next to the cow pen. When the child calls this new animal a cow, her teacher responds, "No, that's a horse. See how tall the horse is. And look at the long hair down its neck. The hair on his neck is called a *mane*." Now the child realizes that a horse is not a cow and must alter her cognitive structure to incorporate or accommodate this new concept. Her new schema for "four-legged animals" might look like the one shown Figure 6.4.

Gradually, through direct and vicarious experiences, children become aware of additional features that distinguish a cow from a horse; for example, horses say "neigh." In this way, through assimilation and accommodation, children's conceptual knowledge is expanded and refined. Accompanying this expansion and refinement of conceptual knowledge is the acquisition of vocabulary to allow more precise speech about these newly acquired concepts.

Semantic knowledge also develops as children communicate with adults and other children who expose them to new words within contextually rich settings. The context in which new words are introduced influences children's acquisition of vocabulary (Holmes, Holmes, & Watts, 2012). It is important to have the actual referent of the concept present in the immediate context (either in real life or pictured) in order to enhance semantic knowledge. Upon hearing a new word, some children will ask what it means or relate it to a word they already know. For example, when Riley's caregiver told her, "You might need a jacket. It's breezy out today," Riley asked, "Does that mean it's windy?" Her caregiver responded, "Yes, breezy means windy" (Otto, 2012).

FIGURE 6-4

Sample Schema for Four-Legged Animals

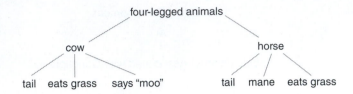

Preschool children may also reflect on the ways words are combined to represent a specific concept. For example, a 3½ year old girl made the following two observations when eating (Otto, 2012):

Child: "Chicken . . . noodle . . . soup go together. That's why they call it chicken noodle soup."

Child: "Peanut and butter come together. That's why they call it peanut butter."

In another instance, a 3½ year old girl said to her parent, "When I was a baby, I had babysitters. So now could you call it "kid sitter" because I'm a kid, not a baby" (Otto, 2012). In each of these examples, children are reflecting on word meaning and how words are combined to represent specific meaning. This also reflects developing morphological knowledge, which will be described later in this chapter.

Overextensions and Underextensions of Semantic Knowledge

As young preschoolers are acquiring semantic knowledge, overextensions and underextensions in using vocabulary may occur. **Overextensions** occur when children use the same word to apply to referents that may resemble the actual, appropriate referent in some way. For example, a child learns the concept of candy and begins using the word only to refer to candy. When he extends the use of that term to cherries or anything sweet, overextension has occurred. Another example is when a child first uses the word *kitty* to refer to a cat but later extends that term to refer to rabbits and other small, furry animals. A child who is familiar with videotapes and the meaning of "rewind" might overextend this word when asking that a book be re-read, for example saying, "rewind this book." **Underextension**, in contrast, occurs when a label or word is inappropriately restricted (e.g., the word *cat* is used only to refer to the neighbor's cat and not to other cats the child sees in the neighborhood). Throughout the preschool years, children's verbal interactions with adults and other children gradually refine the use of words, reducing instances of overextension and underextension.

Semantic Development and Book-Sharing Experiences

Conceptual development and vocabulary are also increased through book sharing with fiction and nonfiction texts (Elster, 1994). The written language of storybooks exposes children to more precise and varied vocabulary than they may experience in daily conversations. For many children, the appeal of storybooks and nonfiction books is in the variety of ways language is used to communicate a story or real-world information.

A child's pretend reading of a book can provide evidence of semantic knowledge and vocabulary growth.

Adult–child discussions during and after sharing books expand and refine children's semantic knowledge. These discussions enhance children's semantic development and also provide adults with a way of becoming familiar with children's developing conceptual knowledge. Children not only learn the literal meanings of words used in written texts but acquire more subtle meanings as well. For example, when Ryan was 3 years old, his mother had been reading him *Gus and the Baby Ghost* (Thayer, 1972) for several months (Otto, 1982). One night, he spontaneously acted out a scene from the book in which Mr. Frizzle runs down the stairs so quickly that his bathrobe is described (as well as pictured) as flying out behind him. That night, after Ryan had finished getting ready for bed and was wearing his bathrobe and pajamas, his mom started to tie his robe closed. He twisted away and hurried for the stairs. When his mom asked him where he was going, he replied, "I gotta run down the stairs with my bathrobe flying. Like Mr. Frizzle." Ryan proceeded to go down the stairs quickly, grinning all the while, so that his bathrobe "flew" out behind him. In fact, he repeated this scene several times that night.

Where the Wild Things Are (Sendak, 1963) is a favorite book of many pre-schoolers. The language used in this book and the relation of the illustrations to that language creates a vivid context for children and demonstrates how language is enhanced through storybook interactions. In this text, the following words are used and supported by dramatic illustrations: *gnashed*, *roared*, *mischief*, *rumpus*. These words are not typically used in children's daily oral conversations; however, within the context of this memorable story, children become acquainted with specific words that can be understood and incorporated into their receptive and, eventually, expressive semantic knowledge. A preschool teacher once described how several of her students first announced, and then began, their own "wild rumpus" while outside at the playground.

Semantic Knowledge and Figurative Language

Preschool children begin to understand figurative language. Examples of figurative language, such as similes and metaphors, may occur in daily conversations and may also be found in children's storybooks. For example, when a mother was getting her son ready to leave for preschool one day, she said, "Hop on over here and let's put on your shoes." He responded by hopping on both feet over to where his mother was sitting. He had a big smile on his face that seemed to indicate that he knew she was not expecting him to actually "hop" over. In such instances, young children are showing their awareness of figurative language; they are also demonstrating how they are refining their semantic knowledge by incorporating more specific vocabulary into their verbal interactions and responding to others' use of metaphoric language.

Preschool children may also encounter idiomatic expressions and be puzzled when they try to comprehend the literal meaning of the expression. For example, when Riley became upset when she could not find her fire engine toy to play with, her dad suggested that it would be okay, and that since they couldn't find it that night, she could "sleep on it" and in the morning they could find it (Otto, 2012). To this, Riley replied in a questioning tone, "Sleep on a fire engine?" Her dad then explained that "sleep on it" just meant that they would think about it as they went to sleep and in the morning maybe they could remember where the toy fire engine was.

Semantic Knowledge and Preschoolers' Narratives

Stories created by children provide evidence of their development of semantic knowledge. Children may incorporate specific phrases or vocabulary in their own stories that most likely come from their experiences with storybooks, such as "beautiful, handsome prince," "going to the parlor for dinner," "buried treasure." In these instances, the impact of storybook experiences on children's developing semantic knowledge is evident.

The development of semantic knowledge is closely related to the development of syntactic knowledge. Children's understanding of how words convey meaning is closely related to their knowledge of how to interpret or comprehend speech directed to them and how to arrange words in creating the messages they want to communicate.

DEVELOPMENT OF SYNTACTIC KNOWLEDGE

Preschool children's development of syntactic knowledge is evident in the length and structure of their speech. Children entering the preschool years (about 3 years of age) typically are in the telegraphic speech stage, speaking in short utterances of two to three words.

Mean Length of Utterance (MLU)

Although the sentence is considered a unit of structure in written language, oral language is often composed of smaller structural units, such as phrases composed of several words, and are referred to as "utterances." A more exact way of looking at the complexity of children's utterances is to consider the **mean length of utterance (MLU)**. This unit of measure was developed by Roger Brown (1973). It calculates the length and complexity of an utterance by counting the number of words and the number of grammatical markings (Karmiloff & Karmiloff-Smith, 2001). For example, "Mommy eat one carrot" has four words and an MLU of four. The utterance "Mommy eats carrots" is grammatically more complex because in addition to the three words, it has two grammatical markers. The -s on eats indicates third-person singular, and the -s on carrots indicates plurality. Thus, "Mommy eats carrots" has an MLU value of five. The calculation of MLU has allowed researchers to distinguish between children's utterances on the basis of complexity rather than just word count. MLU increases rapidly during the preschool years, from an MLU of about two to a value of eight or more (Karmiloff & Karmiloff-Smith, 2001).

The grammatical complexity of preschoolers' speech occurs in significant ways: increasing noun and verb phrase complexity, using negation (no, not), producing interrogative sentences (questions), and beginning to use passive forms of sentences (O'Grady, Dobrovolsky, & Aronoff, 1989). Each of these new structures contributes to the increasing linguistic complexity of preschool children's language.

Noun and Verb Phrase Complexity

Noun and verb phrase development occurs as sentence structures become more complex. Children begin to use subject–verb–object structure for sentences as well ("I ride train," "I do dat," "I need key"). Noun modifiers also appear ("I touch your hair"). Auxiliary verb use may appear, as in "her is going." Older preschool children also begin to use subordinating clauses. For example, "This is a secret passageway so I can get up here faster."

As children's ability to engage in monologues or extended speech develops, they begin to use more complex syntax when sharing stories and accounts of personal experiences. Noun and verb phrase complexity increases with the use of conjunctions (e.g., *and*) as well as with connectives (e.g., *because, then, so, if*; Puckett & Black, 2001). *And* is used as an all-purpose conjunction to string together speech in children's monologues. The use of the connective *because* typically develops toward the end of the preschool years. In the short story below, a 4-year-old boy used *because* and *and* to join his ideas together:

> Once there was a little mouse that can run fast *and* the cat was running after him *because* he took the cheese *and* he was too fast for the cat *and* he got to the mouse hole.

Negation

Preschool children begin to use the word *no* at the beginning of an utterance; later on, the negative word–element appears within sentences, as in "I no want milk." Gradually, contractions such as *don't* or *can't* appear. By the end of the preschool years, children are using negatives within sentences along with auxiliary verbs, such as *am*, *is*, *will*, *do* (e.g., "I'm not singing a song" or "It's not cold").

Interrogatives

Preschool children ask lots of questions. Some children seem to realize that, by asking questions, such as "why?" they can keep a conversation going. Questions are also formed by using rising intonation while still keeping subject-plus-verb order. For example, a young preschooler might ask, "Mommy hurt finger?" using rising intonation to indicate that a question is being asked. Gradually, preschoolers begin to use questions that have inverted order and auxiliary verbs (auxiliary verb + subject + verb). Thus, an older preschooler would ask, "Did Mommy hurt her finger?"

Passive Sentences

In passive voice sentence construction, word order is changed from that typically used, so that instead of the sentence being constructed in the active voice as agent–action–object ("The girl–threw–the ball"), the order is now object–action–agent ("The ball–was thrown–by the girl"). Preschool children are beginning to be able to comprehend passive sentences, though not consistently (O'Grady et al., 1989; Tager-Flusberg, 1997).

Preschoolers' comprehension appears to be related to whether the verb is an action verb. In most research that has explored children's understandings of passive sentences, comprehension was measured by children's responses when asked to act out the meaning of a sentence. Children seemed to be more influenced by the order of the words in the sentences and ignored *was* and *by* in comprehending the passive sentence. Spontaneous production or expressive use of passives by preschool children has been only rarely documented by researchers (Owens, 2001); however, research which involved increasing 4-year-olds' exposure to passive voice sentences reported an increase in children's production of passive sentences (Vasilyeva, Huttenlocher & Waterfall, 2006).

In summary, during the preschool years, significant changes occur in children's syntactic knowledge. At the beginning, children are likely to use simple two- and three-word utterances, whereas at the end of the preschool years, children use a wider variety of syntactic structures characterized by greater complexity, having embedded clauses (because . . .) and conjoined clauses (. . . and . . .). Syntactic complexity is also related to the development of morphemic knowledge about the linguistic units within words. As children acquire morphemic knowledge, their utterances also increase in complexity. In the next section, preschoolers' increasing morphemic knowledge and indications of greater linguistic complexity will be described.

DEVELOPMENT OF MORPHEMIC KNOWLEDGE

The preschool years are a time of significant development in morphemic knowledge. Children first develop knowledge of inflectional morphemes used to indicate plurality, possession, and verb tense. This typically begins between the ages of 2 and 4. Development of derivational morphemic knowledge begins later and takes longer (Kuo & Anderson, 2006). Derivational morphemes are morphemes added to words that change the part of speech or alter the meaning of the word, such as instruct–instruct*or*, comfort–comfor*table*, happy–*un*happy, quick–quick*est*, and quiet–quiet*ly*. Specific variations in the use of morphemes are also acquired by young children as they interact with adults and other children in settings where a dialect variation or different language is spoken.

Development of morphemic knowledge contributes to young children's linguistic competencies in providing a way of communicating meaning more precisely. By knowing how to change word structures to change meanings, children can communicate more effectively. Some words follow predictable patterns for using morphemes and are referred to as "regular." For example, with most nouns, the word is changed from singular to plural by adding an -*s*, as in *cats*. Regular verbs are changed from present to past tense with the addition of -*ed*, as in *walk*, *walked*. Possession is indicated by -*'s*. Comparatives are regularly formed by adding -*er* or -*est*, as in *fast*, *faster*, *fastest*. Words that do not follow the regular pattern for morpheme changes present a challenge to the process of language development. For example, *go* is an irregular verb. The past tense of go is *went*, not *goed*. *Child* is an irregular noun because the plural of *child* is *children*.

Role of Experimentation

Researchers have concluded that children do not learn morphology through simple imitation of adult speech; instead, children appear to experiment actively with language to determine how word endings are used to influence the meaning of a sentence (Carlisle, 2010). As children develop their morphemic knowledge, their use of morphemes provides evidence that they are learning the general or regular patterns for using morphemes to communicate meaning using grammatical and semantic markers as well as learning the exceptions or irregular patterns (Gopnik, Meltzoff, & Kuhl, 1999).

Observing Children's Experiments with Language

Children's experiments with language can be observed as they use language to tell stories or in conversations. **Overgeneralization** occurs when children use their morphemic rules for words that are not regular (O'Grady & Cho, 2005). For example, the past tense of regular verbs is formed by adding -ed to the word as in *walk–walked, jump–jumped,* and *want–wanted.* When using irregular verbs in the past tense, children may overgeneralize and use *falled* as a past tense for *fall, goed* for a past tense of *go, rided* for the past tense of *ride,* and *eated* for a past tense of *eat.*

The past tense morpheme -ed is pronounced one of two ways when it is attached to words. It may be pronounced as an additional syllable in *want–wanted*, or as a /t/ sound as part of the one-syllable word, as in *walk–walked.* Preschoolers may show evidence of overgeneralization of the way the -ed morpheme is pronounced. For example, the past tense of *like* might be pronounced as two syllables, *lik-ed.* Similarly, the past tense of *help*, might be pronounced *help-ed.*

Preschoolers also begin to use comparatives. Children are not yet able to determine which comparatives are regular and which are irregular, so overgeneralization may occur, as in *good, gooder,* and *goodest.* For example, when she was having trouble opening up bag of snacks, a 3½-year-old said, "I want it opener."

Similar overgeneralization may occur when preschoolers use adverbs. Regular adverbs are formed by adding -ly to the stem word, as in *quick–quickly.* When interacting with a storybook where the character was peddling fast on his bike, a preschool girl said, "peddle real fastly."

Preschool children may also experiment with creating noun forms. For example, "I know how to play chess. I am a great chess-ter" and "I like to tell jokes. I am a great joke-ster." When referring to toys that she and another playmate were moving around the play area, a preschool girl announced, "I am a puller and you are a carry-er."

Significant evidence of children's developing morphemic knowledge was documented by Berko (1958; cited in Genishi & Dyson, 1984). Berko used the "Wug Test" to elicit children's morphemic knowledge. This test used nonsense nouns and verbs that the children had to change to fit within a particular meaning or context. Preschool and first-grade children were shown picture cards with novel creatures and specific actions. A linguistic context was then provided, and the children filled in the linguistic gap. For example, "This is a wug. Now there is another one. There are two of them. There are two _____ (wugs)" (Berko, 1958; cited in Genishi & Dyson, 1984, p. 135). Berko concluded that children's ability to create the correct forms of nonsense words indicated that they had internalized morphemic rules and had not just learned them through simple imitation or memorization of known words.

Evidence of preschoolers' developing morphemic knowledge can be also found in children's narratives. In this 4-year-old boy's story, he used past tense fairly consistently for both regular and irregular verbs, except for the irregular verb *fall* (Otto, 1982):

> The queen wanted to fly, but actually she couldn't. For a few years she tried but she always fall down the mountain. But one day, she was on a side mountain and she flew. She thought of the other town with many windows, but then she decided to make a new town.

An analysis of this child's story shows that considerable morphemic knowledge is developing. Plural forms of nouns are used (*years*, *windows*). Two irregular verbs have correct past-tense forms (*flew*, *thought*). One negative contraction is used (*couldn't*). Three regular verbs have appropriate past-tense markers (*wanted*, *tried*, *decided*). There are two instances of infinitives (*to fly*, *to make*) and one example of using a form of "to be" as a main verb (*was*).

DEVELOPMENT OF PRAGMATIC KNOWLEDGE

During the preschool years, children begin to use language for a wider range of purposes than they have in the past. This development is supported by children's increasing semantic, syntactic, phonological, and morphemic knowledge.

Using Language Differently for Different Purposes

Children begin to use language to request permission, to invoke social rules, to express emotions, and to make judgments (Halliday, 2007; Owens, 2012). Language may also be used for jokes and teasing or to make an indirect request. Preschoolers gradually develop conversational competencies, increasing the number of conversational "turns" as well as a stronger topic focus.

Preschool children are developing awareness of how to use language differently when engaging young infants and older siblings (Berko Gleason, 1973; Clark, 2003; Shatz & Gelman, 1973) as well as adults. This awareness of a listener's needs is part of children's growing metalinguistic awareness, a conscious awareness. Preschoolers also begin to manipulate their speech to achieve a certain goals by using language differently with different audiences. For example, parents may be surprised when their child's teacher reports that their child is polite and does not whine at preschool, even though at home the child will resort to whining to achieve specific goals. Preschoolers are also developing awareness of how others use different registers in different settings (Wagner, Greene-Havas, & Gillespie, 2010), such as when talking with a teacher, talking with a peer, and talking with a baby.

The use of pragmatic language knowledge is evident when a 4-year-old wants a toy that another child is currently using. This message may be communicated in a variety of ways, using different levels of pitch, loudness, and tempo and nonverbal behaviors:

1. "It's mine." (grabs toy)
2. "Let's share." (suggests cooperative interaction with toy)
3. "Are you done with that?" (implying turn taking)
4. "Can I play with you?" (suggesting activity together of which the toy is a part)
5. "I want it!" (direct assertion of goal)
6. "Give me it!" (direct order, no negotiation)

The particular way the child communicates the message and the resultant success of the message further develop the child's pragmatic knowledge of language. Throughout frequent interactions with others, children gain experience in using language differently in different settings.

Evidence of Pragmatic Knowledge in Dramatic Play

Dramatic play activities can provide a further look at children's developing pragmatic knowledge as they negotiate and assume various roles and communicate with each other (Riley & Jones, 2007). In assuming a specific role, a child may use a specific variation of language or register.

Anderson's research (1992) explored in detail the pragmatic knowledge of a group of 18 children between the ages of 4 and 7. Five different registers were studied: babytalk, foreignertalk, classroom language–teachertalk, doctortalk, and gendertalk. Children were asked to provide the oral language for role-specific puppets in selected settings. The three settings included a family or home setting, a doctor's office, and a classroom. The classroom setting included a teacher puppet and two student puppets; one of the student puppets was described as a child who had just come to the United States and did not speak English well.

Anderson (1992) concluded that children's competence in language use was not consistent across settings. Children in her study seemed to acquire the family register the most easily, followed by the doctor register, and then the classroom register. Within the doctor setting, children used a register marked by technical jargon. Anderson also noted that the role-playing by older children indicated status differences between the doctor and nurse and between the medical staff (doctor and nurse) and patient. In the classroom context, how the children assumed the various roles differed according to age. The youngest children avoided the teacher role. The hardest register appeared to be the foreigner register, which involved assuming the role of someone who did not speak English well. The foreigner role was assumed only by the oldest children.

Anderson found that the children indicated the various roles first through prosodic features. Distinctions between the roles were indicated by voice pitch. Louder voices were used for male roles. When children assumed the foreigner role, they talked with a slower tempo and used syncopated speech. Another interesting finding was that children's topics of conversation and vocabulary varied with the setting. The oldest children had larger vocabularies and selected terms that were more appropriate for the setting than did the younger children. Role differences were also indicated by differences in the average length of the utterance. In some instances, children even corrected the experimenter's role-playing language to fit the register. Children also made self-corrections spontaneously. Most of these corrections were adjustments in pitch so that their pitch would fit the character role they were assuming. Self-corrections in vocabulary were not as frequent and were more characteristic of older children. Older children also made more self-corrections in syntax, such as changing a request from an imperative statement to a more polite question.

Gender differences were indicated as girls assumed more roles, spoke more, and modified their speech more to fit the specific contexts. Anderson speculated that boys were just as aware of gender register differences as girls were, but boys consciously avoided assuming inappropriate sex-typed language because they had been socialized against speaking like girls in any context.

Although Anderson's study is limited in its generalizability to all children due to its small sample and the sample's lack of ethnic and economic diversity, the study does provide evidence that children are acquiring pragmatic language knowledge during the preschool–primary years. This ability to tailor one's speech to fit the social and linguistic context is an important development in becoming able to communicate effectively in a variety of contexts.

Additional evidence of preschoolers' developing pragmatic knowledge is found in research focusing on block play and pretend telephone conversations. Cohen and Uhry (2007) studied preschoolers' language during block play and concluded that children used language to guide others and to verbally direct the ongoing episode. Research by Gillen and Hall (2001) noted the following pragmatic aspects of children's telephone conversations, which represent essential features in carrying on a conversation by phone: (1) a correct opening (such as "hello") in 70.9% of the calls; (2) a correct closing (such as "bye") in 45.3% of the calls; and (3) turn taking (listening pauses and speaking) in 51.3% of the calls. Children's use of language appropriate to the dramatic play setting was also noted in their "emergency" calls to the police, doctor, or fire department; their calls to order goods or supplies; and their calls to relatives or friends.

Evidence of Pragmatic Knowledge from Ethnographic Research

The development of pragmatic knowledge among preschool children was also documented in the ethnographic research conducted by Heath (1983) that took place over a 10-year period. In this research, Heath focused on two communities (identified as Roadville and Trackton) in the Piedmont area of the southeastern United States. Roadville was a white working-class community, and Trackton was a black working-class community; however, the focus was not on racial differences but on the ways in which cultural beliefs, practices, and social institutions influence children's development of language. Heath described the ways in which children learned to use language in various settings: home, school, and community. From infancy on, children in these two communities learned the specific ways in which language was used within their respective cultural settings. Heath's detailed account of children's experiences in acquiring language and learning how to use that language in various settings provides a wealth of evidence that pragmatic knowledge is an important aspect of language development.

While the findings from Heath's study were unique to the two communities involved, her study increased our awareness of the ways language development is shaped by the cultures in which it is used. As participants in specific cultures and their communities, children learn not only *what* to say but *how* and *when* to say it.

Pragmatic Development and Preschoolers' Oral Narratives

Research on the development of storytelling among young children provides a picture of how children develop language competency in using language to create monologues. Prior to the preschool years, children's linguistic behaviors occur in predominately dialogic interactions or short conversations with adults providing a structure or linguistic scaffolding within which the child participates (Reese & Fivush, 1993). Preschoolers gradually begin to engage in **monologues**, or settings where they are the main speaker to a listening audience. This shift between dialogue and monologue represents a significant change in the way language is used (Temple et al., 1988). Environmental support for this change is found in groups such as those described in Heath's (1983) study, where children's early stories occurred in scaffolded settings and gradually became more independent as the child acquired more monologic competency.

Miller and Mehler (1994) described young children's participation in personal storytelling events as going through several phases. First, children listen to stories or narratives and then begin to contribute to the narrative as a co-narrator. Gradually they are able to tell the narrative by themselves.

The narratives created by children follow the story structures and content appreciated by their cultures (Heath, 1983; Reese & Fivush, 1993). Heath (1983) documented differences in the way children from the two communities created and told stories. What constituted a "good" story was defined differently by each community. Children's stories reflected the aspects of "storyness" valued by their respective communities. Trackton stories, while based on real events, contained exaggeration and elaboration developed through the storyteller's creativity and entertaining manner. In contrast, the stories valued in Roadville were retold from a book's story, a factual account of a real event or a traditional story adapted to fit the situation (to make a moral or ethical point).

Evidence of Pragmatic Knowledge in Children's Interactions with Print

The pragmatic component of language development involves knowledge of the ways in which written language is used to communicate in different contexts. As children interact with written language in their world, inside and outside school settings, they learn how written language is used for various purposes. Pragmatic knowledge of written language builds on children's pragmatic knowledge of oral language. Children are active explorers in this process (Perlmutter et al., 2009).

The shift from dialogic interactions to oral monologues is also related to the development of pragmatic knowledge of written language. When a child develops the ability to engage in oral monologues, she is learning to use language in a more decontextualized manner. The nature of the relation between dialogue, oral monologue, and written text can be thought of as a continuum of decontextualization (shown in Table 6.1).

Conversational dialogue involves a reciprocal turn taking between participants who alternate listener–speaker roles. Meaning is negotiated through questioning, commenting, clarification, and repetition. The context of the conversation or

TABLE 6.1
Continuum of Decontextualization of Language

Dialogue	Oral Monologue	Written Text
Comprehension is tied to immediate context, negotiated through speaker–listener interaction	Comprehension is aided through speaker's use of intonation, gesture, and the immediate context	Comprehension is independent of immediate context through precise wording and complex syntactic structures

setting of the ongoing event adds meaning to the conversation. For example, imagine preschool children who are playing in the block center and who are having a conversation about what they are building. When one child from the block playing interaction tells a friend or his teacher about what they were building in the block center, his communication may take on the features of an oral monologue. In telling another person about what was built in the block center, the child would use intonation, gestures, and references to the physical surroundings (*there, that, this*) to communicate his message. His spoken words alone would not totally communicate the story of what was built; however, there would be more specificity and precise, descriptive language than would be typically used in a dialogic conversation. If the block play interaction would be described in a written story format, decontextualized language would be used. Written text "stands alone" in terms of being specific and not dependent on an immediate context outside the language used in the text. Thus, as preschool children begin to use monologues in telling stories or recounting personal experiences, they begin to decontextualize language, which enhances their understanding of how language is used differently in different contexts. In the example below, Riley engaged in an oral monologue in recounting her experience at preschool:

"Jason and Michael and I played Power Rangers. Then we had to sit in the thinking chairs and then they wanted to play Power Rangers again and I said, 'I'm not going to play that game!' And my teacher said I made a good decision."

When children have opportunity to dictate a familiar story, decontextualization may also be evident. Their comprehension and memory for the familiar story provides a basis for their dictated story. When she was 3½ half years old, Riley dictated this version of Goldilocks and the Three Bears.

The three bears went for a walk. Goldilocks (long pause) Grandpa Bear ate his porridge and it was too hot. Daddy Bear's porridge was too hot. Mama said it was too cold. Baby Bear ate his porridge and it was just right. Grandma Bear's porridge was, too, too hot. And they went for a walk. And Goldilocks ate all, all of their porridge. And her ran upstairs to see what her could see. And the bears came back home and they said, "Something fishy's going on." And they went upstairs to look at their beds. And Goldilocks ran down the stairs as fast as her can and her never came back.

Preschool children's curiosity about written language is evident when they pay special attention to print in their environment.

Although Riley's story version varies from the original in several ways, her dictation is characterized by features associated with decontextualized narrative text structure. For example, there is an introduction, specific mention of characters, sequence of key actions and events, and a final resolution.

Environmental print.   Children's interactions with written language occur in three ways: as observers of how written language is used in their environments, as questioners of adults who are engaged in literacy-related tasks, and as active explorer–experimenters with written language. In homes where literacy-related events occur frequently, children's observation of how written language is used may begin in infancy or toddlerhood. As preschoolers, children's observation and questioning are often characterized by increased energy, particularly in environments where literacy-related events occur frequently.

Preschool children's curiosity about written language is evident when they see print in their environment and question their parents or teachers about it. Here are two examples. When Ryan (age 3) and his mother went to a carnival and he got a balloon with words printed on it, he asked, "What does that say?" Earlier that day, Ryan was getting dressed, putting on shorts that had the word "PRO" printed on them. When he first put them on, he said, "Have name on" and looked for the word.

When he located it, he said, "Mom, what that say?" She replied, "PRO. P-R-O, PRO." Ryan then turned to his father and, pointing to the word, he said, "Dad, that say 'PRO,' that say 'PRO.'" His dad said, "Yes, it does!"

One day, Jon (3 years, 3 months) and his mother were looking at his baby album. On several pictures, his mother had written captions. Jon noticed the writing and asked, "What that say?" His mother asked him to point to what he meant. He pointed to the writing, again asking, "What that say? Why that there?" She read a couple of the captions for him and said, "I wrote it there so we'd know what the picture was about." Interactions such as these two examples show children's beginning understanding of how written language is used in different settings and what it means. In each case, a parent responded to the child's inquiry by explaining how print was used and what it "meant."

Early writing. Preschool children's early writing also provides evidence that children are learning about the different ways in which written language is shared for different purposes. Children's early explorations of writing often involve creating some writing and then giving it to an adult to be "read" (Schickedanz et al., 1990). Such requests indicate that the child is aware that writing has a purpose. Children also begin to use writing for personal purposes. Clay (1975) described children's writing that was like an inventory, listing letters or words they could write (see also Figure 6.1 and 6.2 of Madeline's writing earlier in this chapter). Other children have made signs for their classrooms or homes to tell certain specific information, such as "keep out." Clay (1987) described a preschool child who wrote jokes and stories for her dad. Baghban's (1984) daughter wrote letters to everyone she knew and wanted to mail them. Children's personal interests appear to influence the ways in which they use writing and how they engage in the writing process (Rowe & Nietzel, 2010). For example, socially oriented children use the writing activity as a way to interact with others at the writing table. Based on their personal interests, other children may focus more on using writing to communicate ideas, explore how writing is formed, or explore writing materials (e.g., how erasers work, how markers can be used). Thus, preschool children's early writing explorations contribute to their pragmatic knowledge of how language is used differently in different contexts and for different purposes.

Literacy-related drama. Preschool children's responses during dramatic play with literacy-related props also may indicate that they are developing pragmatic knowledge about how written language is used in classroom and out-of-classroom contexts. In their work, Morrow and Rand (1991), Vukelich (1990), and Neuman and Roskos (1990, 1991) documented preschoolers' dramatic play behaviors that provided evidence of children's knowledge of how written language is used in different settings, such as a doctor's office, business office, kitchen, and retail shop. Because children's use of language reflects the context of their dramatic play, it is important for preschool classrooms to provide a variety of contexts for creative drama (Umek & Musek, 2001).

When preschoolers participate in shared book interactions, they develop knowledge of how written language is used in books.

Pragmatic Knowledge and Storybook Experiences

Through preschoolers' experiences as observers and participants in shared book interactions, they develop knowledge of how written language is used in books. They gradually become aware of the left–right, top–down progression of texts. They learn how to orient a book and proceed through the book from the front to the back. They also become aware that the print, rather than the pictures, carries the real message of the story. Children with frequent storybook experiences also learn that the text is stable; they expect that what it says one day, it will say the next day. Parents and teachers often find this out when they do not read the text exactly the same way or with the same intonation during repeated readings. Their preschoolers will stop them, letting the adult reader know that what was said was not "right."

Children's early attempts to track print may be accompanied by their metalinguistic comments about the way written language works, providing further evidence of developing pragmatic knowledge. When 4-year-old Robbie was attempting to read *Where the Wild Things Are* (Sendak, 1963), he experienced difficulty in matching up the title he had memorized with his pointing to print. After trying several times unsuccessfully, Robbie concluded, "This book's not working right" (Schickedanz, 1981, p. 18).

Children's attempts at re-creating, or "reading," storybooks involve pragmatic knowledge because they indicate what the children know about how language is used in the process of reading. These reading attempts appear to follow a general developmental sequence. In Sulzby's (1985b) study of 2-, 3-, and 4-year-old children's attempted readings of familiar storybooks, she documented the ways in which preschool children begin to explore the process of reading, from simple labeling and commenting on the pictures to strategy-based reading.

Children's verbal interactions with each other as they share storybooks also provide evidence that preschoolers are learning how to use language in different ways. Tolentino's (2007) study of preschoolers' interactions during child-initiated reading activities described children's use of language to talk about the books they were sharing, incorporating their emerging concepts about print and exploring the ideas visually presented in their shared book. When information/nonfiction books were shared, more inquiry-based talk occurred.

Through understanding the significance of children's early explorations and experimentation in reading and writing, teachers will have a better awareness of the complex ways in which children's language knowledge is developing. Teachers can enhance children's further development by being available to answer preschoolers' questions and to welcome preschoolers' participation in literacy-related events throughout classroom activities.

SUMMARY

The preschool years are characterized by rapid development of each aspect of language knowledge. Children's articulation of speech becomes more understandable and, thus, preschoolers are more likely to be understood by people outside the family. Preschoolers' semantic knowledge increases as many more words are added to their receptive and expressive vocabularies. Sentence structure becomes more complex, allowing preschoolers to be more precise in what they are trying to communicate. Development of morphemic knowledge also contributes to preschool children's increasing linguistic competencies in creating more precise messages. Pragmatic knowledge is evident in preschool children's flexibility as they begin to use oral language differently in different situations.

Preschoolers' exploration of written language also provides evidence of developing pragmatic knowledge. Exploration of written language occurs for children who are in environments where literacy-related events occur frequently and where adults respond to children's inquiries about written language. Children begin to develop an awareness that letters can be associated with specific sounds and with particular words or meanings. Children's interactions with environmental print and their storybook interactions provide evidence that preschoolers are becoming aware of how written language works and how one goes about reading.

Each of the five aspects of language knowledge is an important area to consider in understanding language development among preschool children. This understanding of language development forms the basis for planning and implementing early childhood language curricula.

✳✳✳ CHAPTER REVIEW

1. Key terms to review:

phonemic awareness	accommodation	mean length of utterance (MLU)
sound play	overextension	overgeneralization
assimilation	underextension	monologue

2. Complete the following chart as a way of summarizing preschool children's developing knowledge of language.

Characteristics of Preschoolers' Language Development		
Aspect of Language Knowledge	**Receptive Language**	**Expressive Language**
Phonological		
Semantic		
Syntactic		
Morphemic		
Pragmatic		

✳✳✳ CHAPTER EXTENSION ACTIVITIES

Research

Record a preschool child's oral monologue. Analyze the child's speech for the presence of morphemic knowledge (inflectional and derivational morphemes).

Discussion

In what ways can shared storybook experiences with preschoolers enhance each of the five aspects of language knowledge?

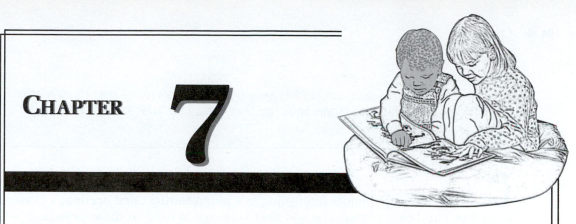

CHAPTER 7

ENHANCING LANGUAGE DEVELOPMENT IN PRESCHOOLERS

Learning Outcomes

After reading this chapter you should be able to

- Describe how linguistic scaffolding is used to enhance preschoolers' language development
- Describe how conflict resolution is used to enhance preschoolers' language development
- Identify several language-related goals for including a book center in a preschool classroom
- Describe interaction strategies used by effective teachers during book sharing
- Describe the ways in which routine activities can enhance preschoolers' language development
- Explain three guidelines for interacting with preschoolers who are English language learners

At lunchtime, Kristi and Tommy were visiting. Kristi put a piece of celery on her finger and said, "See my ring." Tommy asked her if she was married. She replied, "No, I'm not even an adult yet."

Just after Amber arrived at preschool, she approached her teacher and said, "Guess what I saw?" Her teacher said, "What did you see?" Amber replied, "A jingle bell, hanging on a wire." (It was the winter holiday season. Amber probably was referring to a holiday decoration she had seen.)

Jack was in the book corner when several other children joined him. He took one book out and said, "See my new book." He then opened the book and told the story to those around him.

Children's first experiences interacting in a group setting often occur at a nursery school or child-care center. The way that language is used in these preschool settings plays an important role in children's acquisition of language competencies and educational achievement (Cazden, 1996). This chapter will focus on the ways in which preschoolers' language development can be enhanced through specific interactions, approaches, and activities. It describes basic teacher–child interaction patterns appropriate for enhancing language acquisition in preschool classrooms, specific activities that enhance language development, and specific strategies to use with children who are English language learners. The chapter concludes with an example of a preschool newsletter to parents.

GUIDELINES FOR INTERACTIONS WITH PRESCHOOLERS

The ways in which teachers and caregivers interact with young children influence children's acquisition of language competencies as well as their general growth and development. These basic patterns of interaction are effective teaching strategies for enhancing children's acquisition of language knowledge in a preschool setting. This section will describe four teaching strategies that can be used throughout the preschool curriculum to facilitate and nurture the acquisition of language competencies:

1. Questioning
2. Linguistic scaffolding
3. Mediation
4. Conflict resolution

Some of these strategies are also appropriate for interaction with children at other ages; however, the use of each strategy differs with the developmental levels of the children. In this chapter, the focus will be on using the strategies with preschool children.

Questioning

Questioning is a key strategy that elicits a response from the listener. Teachers may consciously use questioning as a strategy to involve children in conversation and instructional dialogue. While this strategy composes a major part of the discussion dialogue between teachers and students at the primary level, it can also be used at the preschool level to encourage language development. The way a question is worded influences not only the comprehension of the question but also the language used by a child in response to the question.

Level of questioning.   Questions can vary with the level of knowledge required in the answer. At the preschool level, teachers' questions focus on two main levels: low-level questions involving rote recall or literal information and high-level questions involving interpretative, inferential, or open-ended responses. When children respond to these higher-level questions, they are "most actively involved mentally" and "use their language most powerfully for learning" (Lindfors, 1987, p. 314). More elaborate systems of classifying questions have been developed (e.g., Bloom, 1956). While it is important to include a variety of higher-level questions, such as those that support synthesis, evaluation, and application, most preschool teachers find it more useful to think in terms of two broad categories, low- and high-level questioning (Genishi & Dyson, 1984).

A teacher's decision about whether to use low-level or high-level questioning is influenced by the educational goal or purpose of the activity. Literal or low-level recall questions can be used to establish a basic level of comprehension or understanding. These questions can help determine whether a child is perceiving the same information in the environment or shared point of reference. For example, in the following dialogue, the teacher begins with literal questions and then progresses to higher-level questioning in the last line:

Teacher:	*What animal do you see on the ground by the tree?*
Child:	*A squirrel.*
Teacher:	*What is the squirrel doing?*
Child:	*Picking up a nut.*
Teacher:	*Why do you think he is doing that?*

The teacher's use of *why* in the last question asks the child to speculate a reason for the squirrel's actions. If squirrels and nut gathering had been mentioned earlier in the class (e.g., at shared book time), the teacher's question would have also elicited a comparison of the squirrel seen outside with the information about squirrels the children heard during their shared book time.

Spontaneous and preplanned questions.   While many questions are asked "on the run" during routine and exploratory activities, teachers need to take time to develop some questions for group activities in advance so that they can monitor the level and quality of the questions they ask. In preplanning questions, it is valuable to anticipate children's possible answers to the questions to determine whether the questions are appropriately worded and sufficiently related to the activity. Then, when activities are conducted and children are asked the questions, teachers are well prepared. Having questions and possible answers anticipated also helps teachers remain focused or return to the activity if any classroom disruption or unexpected events occur.

Varied purposes of questions. Questions are more effective if they require a more complex answer than just "yes" or "no." If yes/no questions are used, they can be followed up with a more open-ended question sequence. Open-ended questions enhance language development because when children compose their answers, they incorporate their knowledge of all five aspects of language knowledge (Wasik, 2010). Questions may also be developed to reflect the Socratic method. This type of questioning involves developing a series of questions that leads up to a logical conclusion or target answer. The initial questions in a Socratic series are simple and provide a basis for the subsequent questions.

Questions can vary in terms of the teacher's purpose for questioning. **Clarifying questions** are used when a teacher needs to understand more clearly the message or meaning of what a child said. This type of question reelicits part of a previous response to clarify what was originally said, as in "What did you say happened next?" Sometimes clarification questions have an echolike format, as in the following example:

Child: *I going owa nah.*

Adult: *You're going where?* (Reich, 1986, p. 97)

Recitational questions are asked when teachers want children to indicate their level of knowledge or awareness of a specific topic, such as "What is your name?" or "What color is this?" These questions are recitational because the teacher already knows the answer but is checking to see whether the child can produce the correct response to the question. Many of the questions teachers ask are recitational and are asked in order to check the comprehension or understanding by children on a particular task or about a specific event.

Recitational questions are frequently used in academic settings to determine children's comprehension of a story or an event. Not all children may experience recitation questions in their home environments due to differences in cultural interaction patterns. Thus, when asked this type of question at preschool, a child may be confused as to why the question is being asked of them (Meier, 2003).

Informational questions elicit information from a child that the teacher does not know but needs to know—for example, "Where did you put your coat?" or "What center do you want to work in today?"

Another type of questioning that occurs in preschools focuses on things or events that are not present in the immediate context, called **there-and-then questions** (Genishi & Dyson, 1984). These questions encourage children to think about past and future events and thus encourage their use of different verb tenses. This type of question also encourages children to use language to express their recall or to hypothesize what might happen. Throughout a typical day, there-and-then questions can be used at arrival time, departure, and story time as well as in conversations at snack time or on the playground. Children's original stories can also be elicited by there-and-then questions such as, "How did you learn to ride a bike?" (Sulzby, 1981).

Another way teachers may use questions at the preschool level is to stimulate children's curiosity by modeling wondering about the world around them (Lindfors, 1987). For example, a teacher might comment after seeing a squirrel run across the playground carrying a nut, "I wonder what that squirrel is going to do with that nut." In this way, teachers communicate to children exciting possibilities in learning about their environment and help children become aware of the teacher as a learner, someone who asks questions to find out new information.

Wait time.   A critical aspect in conversing with children and also with using any questioning strategy is the **wait time**, or the time given to a child to respond to the question or to take a turn in the conversation. Questions that are asked too quickly or impatiently discourage children from giving careful thought to the question and to their respective answers. It may also discourage children from responding at all. It is important for teachers to model being patient when waiting for children to respond. This modeling includes actively attending to the responding child's non-verbal behavior and facial expression as well as listening carefully to what the child says. When teachers model careful listening and sufficient wait time, it encourages children to be patient in their verbal interactions with their peers as well.

Cultural differences.   Wait times vary with specific cultures. In some cultures, the wait time is much longer than that used in Anglo classrooms (Tharp, 1994). The shorter wait time in Anglo classrooms may discourage children from another culture from participating in conversations and class discussions. In other cultures, there is a negative wait time, in which overlapping speech occurs when the responding speaker begins to talk before the first speaker has finished his "turn." In an Anglo classroom situation, the overlapping speech may be interpreted as rude behavior because turn taking was not observed. Teachers should be sensitive to the appropriate wait time needed in their respective classrooms to encourage all children to participate in conversations and in class discussions.

Responding to children's answers.   When teachers respond to children's answers to questions, they need to monitor their responses to what children have said as well as their facial expressions because both forms of feedback will have an impact on children's future class participation. To encourage children to participate in individual and group conversations, teachers should acknowledge each child's response (DiCarlo, Pierce, Baumgartner, Harris, & Ota, 2012). When a child's responses are repeatedly ignored, a signal is sent that her responses are not valued, and often the child begins to feel that the teacher does not want her to participate.

Positive feedback to children's responses should be more than just "That was a good answer" or "Yes, that's right." A teacher should confirm for the child (and the other children listening) the aspect of the answer that was appropriate and confirm the comprehension strategy used by the child. For example, in the following group discussion of *Are You My Mother?* (Eastman, 1960), the specific feedback to Matt's response confirmed for Matt why his response was correct:

Teacher:	*Why do you think the baby bird thought the airplane was his mother?*
Matt:	*Because it has wings, flies.*
Teacher:	*Yes, Matt, both birds and airplanes do have wings and they both can fly.*

Revising questions to encourage children's responses. Teachers should be prepared to simplify a question when children do not appear able to respond to it (Weitzman & Greenberg, 2002). If the question is too general or too open-ended, it can be made more specific to encourage a response. For example, if no response comes easily to the question "What do you think happened next in the story?" a more specific question would be "What do you think happened in the story after the train stopped at the station?" In a group setting, if the teacher's question elicits two or more incorrect responses, the question needs to be revised. To continue to call on other children is simply fishing for an answer. It takes away from the activity's focus and can lead to inattention on the part of young children. Poorly formed discussion questions rarely occur when teachers prepare questions and anticipate children's responses ahead of time.

In summary, the role of questioning as a teaching strategy is to facilitate development of children's receptive and expressive language. You will need to monitor the effectiveness of your questions. The types of questions you use and the way questioning occurs in your classroom will have a significant impact on your children's learning environment. Asking too many questions may result in class discussions becoming only times of recitation rather than times of sharing thoughts and developing knowledge. Asking too many questions of children when they are engaged in independent activities will interfere with their concentration and may interrupt cognitive processes. The key to successful questioning is to use a balance of questioning types and purposes, while constantly monitoring the impact the questioning has on the interaction in the classroom. A summary of the guidelines for questioning in preschool classrooms is located in Figure 7.1.

Linguistic Scaffolding

Due to preschoolers' increased language competencies, the linguistic scaffolding appropriate for interacting with preschool children is different from that used with infants and toddlers. The basic approach still involves recognizing the child's zone

FIGURE 7.1
Guidelines for Questioning in Preschool Classrooms

1. Use literal questions as well as higher level questions.
2. Plan group time questions in advance and anticipate children's responses.
3. Avoid questions that can be answered with yes or no.
4. Use a variety of question types: clarification questions, recitation questions, information questions, and there-and-then questions.
5. Be sensitive to the appropriate wait time that will encourage children's participation and thoughtful responses.
6. Positively acknowledge each child's response to the questioning through verbal and nonverbal recognition.
7. If a child's response does not fit the question, rephrase the question to clarify what is being asked.

of proximal development. This will help you support the child's participation at a higher level. As with the use of this strategy at other levels of development, linguistic scaffolding provides support for children as they communicate so that their messages are sent and received effectively. It is important that you use active listening strategies, along with linguistic scaffolding. This means that you will need to carefully observe and monitor the child's responses as well as take into consideration the child's level of prior knowledge and developmental level. In doing so, you will become more aware of the child's zone of proximal development and can provide appropriate linguistic scaffolding. Linguistic scaffolding may include the use of contingent questioning, expansion, repetition, or a combination of these.

Using contingent questioning. **Contingent questioning** involves using a series of questions that build on each other and engage a child's thinking and oral responses. In contingent questioning, a teacher takes into consideration the child's responses when formulating the follow-up questions. In maintaining this dialogue, the teacher is sensitive to the child's utterances and formulates her comments and questions based on what the child said (Trousdale, 1990) in both content and form. For example, in the following dialogue between Scott and his teacher during show-and-tell time, the teacher uses questioning to maintain the dialogue and support Scott's verbal participation. Without the use of this scaffold of questioning, Scott's verbal description of his truck would have been much briefer:

Teacher:	*Scott, it's your turn to share.*
Scott:	*[stands up, walks to front of the semicircle, stands near his teacher; holds up a toy fire truck; long pause]*
Teacher:	*Scott, what did you bring to share?*
Scott:	*A truck. [long pause]*
Teacher:	*What kind of truck is it?*
Scott:	*A fire truck. [long pause]*
Teacher:	*Yes, it is a bright red fire truck. [Teacher motions to the ladders on the truck] Scott, tell us what these are.*
Scott:	*Ladders.*
Teacher:	*Why do firefighters need ladders?*
Scott:	*To help people.*

Through the use of contingent questioning, this teacher engaged Scott in sharing more complete information about the truck he brought to show-and-tell. Without the questioning and linguistic scaffolding, Scott's verbal participation would have been limited. Her questioning was contingent because she used Scott's comment about ladders to then formulate a question about why firefighters need ladders.

Using expansion. Expansion is another part of linguistic scaffolding. It is used to "fill out" what a child says (Reich, 1986). Expansion is also a way to model more complex syntax, morphology, semantics, and correct pronunciation. In the following dialogue, expansion enhances syntax and morphology by creating complete sentences and adding inflectional endings and correct past-tense forms: [Cameron and Mark are playing at the outdoor sandbox. Their teacher is seated near the sandbox.]

Mark: *[finds a ladybug crawling in the grass near the sandbox] Oh, a bug!*

Teacher: *That looks like a ladybug. See it crawling through the grass. [pause]*

Cameron: *Look, it flyed over there.*

Teacher: *Yes, it flew over to the flower.*

Using repetition. Repetition is also a part of linguistic scaffolding. Repetition of specific words and phrases is a way to emphasize or focus on the key parts of the verbal interaction. In the previous example of dialogue between Mark and his teacher, his teacher repeated specific words to reinforce pronunciation and to confirm the meaning of what was said. A summary of guidelines for using linguistic scaffolding with preschoolers is presented in Figure 7.2.

Mediation

Mediation is a strategy that focuses on simplifying a learning stimulus or task and using language to facilitate comprehension and learning by a child. At the preschool level, mediation can occur in situations where a preschooler is putting a puzzle together or working at a water table and experimenting with objects that float or sink. As a teacher, you serve as a mediator between the child and the learning stimuli.

In mediation, the teacher's focus is on understanding the way in which children's responses to the activity indicate or fail to indicate their ability to learn from the task or activity. Blank (1973) emphasized the role of tutorial dialogue initiated by a teacher when interacting with a child. Through specific techniques involving both questioning and commenting, you can determine whether the child is comprehending the learning task. Then you can mediate or restructure the learning task by involving the child in a verbal exchange that increases the child's understanding of the activity or task. In this type of interaction, the child's response determines how you will proceed in the instructional dialogue. As you continue the interaction, you

FIGURE 7.2

Guidelines for Using Linguistic Scaffolding with Preschoolers

1. Develop an awareness of a child's independent level of verbal interaction.
2. Use active listening strategies to respond sensitively when interacting with the child.
3. Use contingent questioning to lead the verbal interaction forward with ongoing communication loops.
4. Use expansion to model specific vocabulary, word endings, grammatical structures, as well as pronunciation of unfamiliar words.
5. Use repetition to provide clarification and emphasize key words and phrases.

will focus on determining what confusion the child may have and how you can verbally mediate the child's interaction in the learning task.

Mediation may also be seen in the ways in which teachers alter texts as they share books with children. When teachers encounter a concept in the text that they feel is too difficult for children to understand, they change the text based on their understanding of their children's semantic and syntactic knowledge. Sometimes teachers may mediate the text by pausing after a new concept or label is introduced in the text and explain the concept through questioning or commenting using vocabulary children can comprehend.

When presenting conceptual information to children, teachers need to decide what information to present and how to present it so that it is comprehensible to children. In deciding how to present the information, teachers need to have an awareness of their children's prior knowledge and current conceptual understandings. Specific conceptual terms are not usually introduced until children are familiar with the general term; for example, the word *dog* is used to identify the larger class of animals before the specific term *cocker spaniel* or *Labrador retriever* is used.

It is also important to consider children's prior experiences when selecting a book to read. Sharing a book about collecting seashells would require different mediation and presentation to a group of children who have never been to a seashore than it would to a group of children who have vacationed at or live near an ocean. Likewise, sharing a book about farm animals would require different mediation with urban children than with children who live in a rural area. For example, sharing *The Animals of Buttercup Farm* (Dunn & Dunn, 1981) with a group of children from an urban school would require more attention to specific concepts and vocabulary, such as *meadows*, *barnyard*, *mare*, *spring foal*, *trotting*, *galloping*, *graze*, *nesting box*, *rooster*, *comb*, *gander*, and *goslings*. Children who live in a rural area would have a prior knowledge of these concepts and vocabulary words, so the amount of mediation would be different. A summary of guidelines for using mediation with preschoolers is presented in Figure 7.3.

Conflict Resolution

Usually, **conflict resolution** is considered a strategy for classroom management and discipline (Maxim, 1993), not language development. Yet, when conflict resolution is

FIGURE 7.3

Guidelines for Using Mediation with Preschoolers

1. Determine the child's level of prior knowledge and experience with the learning stimuli.
2. Simplify the learning task to encourage the child to participate in the learning interaction.
3. Use linguistic scaffolding to engage the child verbally in the learning interaction.
4. Continuously evaluate the child's level of participation and understanding to make adjustments in the way the interaction is mediated.

employed to encourage children to use language to express themselves and to solve or ameliorate social disagreements, it is another way of increasing language knowledge among young children. Children's conflicts often arise as they try to express and deal with negative emotions connected to events or experiences in the classroom.

At the preschool level, most children have acquired sufficient language competencies so that teachers can begin to use language-based strategies to help them express their emotions and begin to resolve their conflicts through verbal communication. Preschool children are better able to understand and consider alternative viewpoints than when they were toddlers (Wheeler, 2004). In disagreements over toys or turn taking, teachers can begin to help children verbalize their intents and wishes and lead them to some form of consensus or compromise.

For example, in a dramatic play area, two girls who want to be the mother have resorted to pushing each other. When the teacher intervenes, she suggests that one girl be the mother and the other one an aunt. By providing the children with alternative roles and helping them begin their role-playing, the learning and communicating value of the activity is enhanced. Without conflict-resolution strategies, the two girls probably would have chosen separate activities, ending their role-playing interaction.

In another example, Scott and John were outside on the preschool playground. Each boy was holding one end of a fire hose. For several minutes, Scott and John carried the hose around the playground. Scott said, "We're firemen." When they started to go around the playhouse, John was in the lead, with Scott at the end. Then Scott sat down, and it became a tug-of-war. John became upset and complained to a nearby teacher. When John said, "He won't let go," Scott just smiled and held on. The teacher suggested to John that he back up and go back around the playhouse. John did so and backed up to where Scott was. This seemed to break the impasse, and Scott got up, carrying his end of the hose, and ran after John.

Active listening. When supporting children's conflict resolution, teachers need to engage in active listening by acknowledging and accepting what children are communicating (Maxim, 1993). After the nature of the conflict is identified, teachers help children become aware of alternatives or possible compromises. Children are also encouraged to verbalize their feelings and identify others' feelings. As an active listener, a teacher acknowledges the emotional state of children while keeping a positive and balanced approach to resolving the conflict.

Immediate and long-term goals of conflict resolution. The immediate goal of conflict resolution is to have both sides of the disagreement accept the outcome or solution as a fair way to reduce the conflict while recognizing their individual needs and wishes. The long-term goal for conflict resolution is to provide children with the interpersonal communication skills that they need to resolve the conflict among themselves without teacher mediation. Teachers can begin to do this by modeling the use of key words and phrases for resolving conflict, such as "Are you okay?" "Can I help you fix it?" and "Let's work it out" (Wheeler, 2004, p. 228). Children can also be encouraged to clearly express their feelings with statements such as "I didn't like that."

Another way of supporting children in learning to use language to resolve conflicts is to share at story time books that focus on expressing emotions. A list of suggested books related to conflict resolution and emotions is found in Figure 7.4. It is important to share books that have this type of focus on a regular basis so that children become familiar with the words they can use in communicating their emotions and resolving conflict. Then, when a conflict or difficult situation arises, they will be better able to use the new words or ways of expressing their feelings.

Cultural differences. Cultural differences among children may explain conflicts that arise because children come to preschool with different expectations for "ownership, space, humor, or turn-taking" (Wheeler, 2004, p. 61). These differences may arise from differences in family interaction patterns as well as differences in cultural ethnicity or economic status. Teachers need to be sensitive observers of children's conflicts and the circumstances surrounding the conflicts as well as the ways in which children's expectations may influence the conflict. A summary of the guidelines for facilitating conflict resolution among preschoolers is presented in Figure 7.5.

Additional Guidelines for Conversations with Preschoolers

The four interaction strategies just described (questioning, linguistic scaffolding, mediation, and conflict resolution) are used when conversing with preschoolers. In addition

FIGURE 7.4

Suggested Books and Resources for Supporting Preschoolers' Conflict Resolution

Agassi, M. (2006). *Hands are not for hitting.* Minneapolis, MN: Free Spirit Publishing.

Aliki, (1986). *Feelings.* New York: HarperCollins.

Baker, J. (2001). *Social skills picture book: Teaching play, emotion, and communication to children with autism.* Arlington, TX: Future Horizons, Inc.

Boynton, S. (2007). *What's wrong, Little Pookie?* New York: Random House.

Kreidler, W. (1999). *Teaching conflict resolution through children's literature.* New York: Scholastic Teaching Resources.

Mayer, M. (2000). *I was so mad.* New York: Random House.

Meiners, C. (2005). *Talk and work it out: Learning to get along.* Minneapolis, MN: Free Spirit Publishing.

Parr, T. (2005). *Feelings book.* New York: Little, Brown Young Readers.

Polland, B. (2004). *We can work it out.* New York: Tricycle Press Random House.

Verdick, E. (2004a). *Feet are not for kicking.* Minneapolis, MN: Free Spirit Publishing.

Verdick, E. (2004b). *Words are not for hurting.* Minneapolis, MN: Free Spirit Publishing.

FIGURE 7.5
Guidelines for Facilitating Conflict Resolution Among Preschoolers

1. Encourage children's awareness that there are two or more sides to the problem.
2. Model key words and phrases to use in communicating and resolving the conflict.
3. Help children understand how each of their actions influenced the situation.
4. Suggest or brainstorm several possible solutions to the problem.
5. Decide how the solution will be put into practice.
6. Monitor the situation to see if further conflict resolution is needed.

to these specific strategies, teachers of preschool children are more effective in enhancing language acquisition if they observe the following guidelines (Miller, 2000):

- Establish eye contact and listen carefully to what the child says.
- Pay attention to the child's nonverbal responses and behaviors, which add meaning to what is said.
- When you cannot understand what a child has said, repeat the key word or phrase back to the child, using a questioning (but not threatening) intonation.
- Focus on the child's current interests and intent as a topic of conversation.
- Wait patiently and in a relaxed manner for the child to "take a turn" in the conversation.
- Respond to a child's comments by extending the conversation through added language and elaboration.

It is important to keep in mind that talk between teachers and children and between children is the basis for learning interactions in the preschool classroom (Snow, 2000). Because preschool children are not yet able to learn by independently reading, your mediation of children's learning experiences provides an important support as you engage them in specific learning activities. Talk in the classroom is vital. Preschool classrooms need to be structured and organized to provide for many opportunities to talk. In the next section, curricular activities for enhancing preschoolers' language development are described.

CURRICULAR ACTIVITIES FOR ENHANCING PRESCHOOLERS' LANGUAGE

A well-balanced preschool curriculum provides learning opportunities that enhance acquisition of phonological, syntactic, semantic, morphemic, and pragmatic language knowledge. As you become acquainted with the children in your preschool classroom, you will want to develop more specific goals in each area of language development to meet individual children's needs.

When you begin to plan and implement your curriculum, you should have a clear, educational rationale or purpose for each learning activity. Many sources of curricular ideas and activities describe how to conduct specific activities but do not indicate why those activities should be used. As a result, teachers may implement activities without having a full awareness of the potential for fostering language development. When teachers have a strong educational rationale for each learning activity, implementation of each activity is more focused and assessment of the learning outcome is more direct. When activities are implemented without a clear rationale or objective, the focus may simply be on keeping the children busy.

In the sections that follow, preschool learning activities and their potential for fostering language development will be described in three categories of activities:

1. *Exploratory activities.* Exploratory activities are independent, unstructured activities that are open ended and provide opportunities to explore ways of interacting with the materials provided.

2. *Teacher-guided activities.* These are structured, teacher-led activities for small and whole-class groupings.

3. *Routine activities.* Routine activities may occur on a daily basis in the classroom, such as attendance taking, arrival and departure routines, and snacks and mealtimes.

In each of these areas, specific activities will be described and analyzed for their potential contributions to language acquisition. In addition, guidelines are provided for using questioning, linguistic scaffolding, and other successful interaction strategies.

Encouraging Language Development Through Exploratory Activities

A developmentally appropriate preschool program will have several time blocks in which children can select from a number of unstructured, open-ended activities. These exploratory learning opportunities allow children to decide how they will interact with the materials provided.

Examples of exploratory activities include blocks and manipulatives, a drama corner (e.g., housekeeping, store, health office), a book center, a listening center, a writing center, concept centers, and an art center. Outdoor play is another unstructured activity during which time-specific aspects of language development can be encouraged. In each of these areas, it is important to remember that the exploratory nature of the activity requires that the children have an opportunity to interact independently with the materials, with only a minimum of adult guidance or intervention. In the following sections, language goals for these activities will be discussed, along with guidelines for teachers to observe when planning and implementing each area of exploratory learning. The guidelines for teachers' interactions in each of the areas should be implemented sensitively as opportunity arises.

Blocks and manipulatives.   Blocks and manipulatives are an important part of a preschool curriculum. General educational goals for using blocks and manipulatives include enhancing physical development, social interaction and collaboration, conceptual development, and problem solving (Bredekamp & Copple, 1997; Lindberg & Swedlow, 1980). Language development is embedded within these educational goals when children talk about their individual creations with others and when they collaborate with other children.

Language goals. Specific language goals for the blocks and manipulatives area include helping children learn to describe and label what was built and how they built it, helping children use language to solve problems, and encouraging children to ask questions about what they are building and describe how it relates to real-life structures or events. As children carry on conversations in this area, they use both receptive and expressive language.

Guidelines for enhancing language development.   When a block or manipulative area has a wide variety of building materials, language development can be supported in

For children in the block area, language conversation skills are enhanced when there are opportunities to talk about what they are building and when they work in collaboration with each other.

several ways. Silent support is given when teachers plan for sufficient time, space, and materials for block or manipulative play. The presence of a teacher in the block or manipulative area shows that the teacher is interested in that area (Lindberg & Swedlow, 1980). When you visit with children as they build, you can encourage them to describe verbally what they are building through extending, expanding, and repeating important segments of the children's comments. When children need direction, you might make a suggestion or ask a question as a way of providing or clarifying an idea related to the building activity.

It is critical, however, that you balance your involvement so that it enhances, but does not interfere with, children's exploration and creativity. There is a fine line between positive intervention and interference. Too much teacher direction, or too many questions, comments, or both, may result in the children losing interest in the activity. Teachers must be sensitive to children's needs for independent exploration and creativity.

Drama corner.   For people who have no background in early childhood education, activities in the drama corner look like they are simply fun activities but ones that have no connection to "real school learning." In reality, drama corner activities can contribute to children's language development in several ways. Dramatic play "is essential for the normal development of a wide range of social, cognitive, and language skills" (Sawyer, 2001, p. 35). Dramatic play activities provide opportunities for children to explore and practice using language in a variety of contextual situations. Dramatic activities also provide opportunities to engage in problem solving. Language is used during the negotiation of specific roles and common purposes that occur during the beginning of the dramatic play and throughout the joint interaction (Berk & Winsler, 1995).

In addition, children's experiences in dramatic play provide opportunities to participate in creating ongoing stories or narratives. These ongoing narratives are often characterized by a sequential structure and dramatic quality as well as by actors, actions, goals, and problems to solve (Glaubman, Kashi, & Koresh, 2001; Leong & Bodrova, 2012; Paley & Dombrink-Green, 2011). Dramatic play may reflect common everyday themes or may be a completely novel improvisation (Sawyer, 2001).

Language goals.   Language goals for dramatic play areas include helping children learn to use language to communicate or converse in their assumed roles and helping children learn to negotiate the role they want to assume. All five aspects of language knowledge are involved as children use receptive and expressive language to carry out their role-playing. Semantic knowledge is used to communicate the concepts conveyed in their conversations. Phonological knowledge is used in articulation. Syntactic knowledge is evident in the grammatical structures used in their speech. Plural word endings and verb tenses indicate morphemic knowledge. Pragmatic knowledge is evident as children tailor their speech to fit the dramatic setting, whether it be a restaurant, post office, or dinner table at home.

Dramatic play activities provide opportunities for children to explore and practice using language in a variety of contexts.

Guidelines for enhancing language development. In preparing a drama corner, teachers should attempt to include realistic materials, keeping in mind children's needs for safety and self-esteem. Sufficient amounts of drama materials are needed to allow several children to participate. Materials should be representative of both genders and promote multicultural diversity and acceptance. Gender-neutral roles should be encouraged, such as "server" rather than "waitress" and "mail carrier" rather than "mailman," because this opens up dramatic roles to both boys and girls (Sheldon, 1990).

Themed drama corners encourage children to begin to translate into behaviors their understandings of complex concepts involving written language (Morrow & Rand, 1991; Neuman & Roskos, 1990). For example, an office area, complete with a telephone, a typewriter, phone books, a calculator, message pads, file folders, writing utensils, desks, and chairs, draws on children's understanding of specific careers, literacy skills needed for office work, and adult communication skills. A post office might have letters ready to be processed, envelopes, stamps, a zip code book, and postcards. Children's interactions in this post office area would draw on their understandings of how written communications are sent in the mail. Examples of specific themes for dramatic play areas are provided in Table 7.1 (Morrow & Rand, 1991).

When providing materials for dramatic play, a teacher needs to consider the cultural background of children in his classroom and be sure that children are comfortable and familiar with the materials and the arrangement or organization of those

TABLE 7.1
Ideas for Themed Dramatic Play Corners

Theme	Props/Equipment
Fast-food restaurant	Order pads, pencil/markers, a cash register, recipes, lists of items/menu, newspapers for customers to read
Gas station/car repair shop	Sales receipts, repair orders, road maps, repair manuals, posters advertising equipment, newspapers for sale
Airport	Arrival and departure signs, tickets, boarding passes, safety messages, name tags for luggage, name tags for airline staff, magazines and newspapers for passengers
Supermarket/grocery store	Food packages, a cash register, shopping lists, receipts, coupons, advertising flyers, labeled shelves and sections

materials (Nourot & VanHoorn, 1991). For example, a grocery store theme should include food and household items that reflect children's community and home contexts. In addition, both high-realism and low-realism props are needed to accommodate the range of children's symbolic play (McLoyd, 1986, as cited in Nourot & VanHoorn, 1991). An example of low-realism props would be a series of large, open boxes provided for children to use in playing "train." An example of high-realism props would be an actual chef's hat and an apron for a restaurant-themed area. High-realism props for a grocery store area would include empty food packages, a toy cash register with an intercom device, and play money (coin and paper). Encouraging children to write a shopping list before entering the store would also add to the realism as well as encourage awareness of writing for a specific functional purpose.

Dramatic play activities are most beneficial when children can engage in a variety of roles and have sufficient time to explore the materials provided within that theme. Children need repeated opportunities to engage in dramatic play. From these repeated opportunities, children gradually begin to elaborate on the dialogues and interactions within that dramatic setting. When children's interest in a specific theme decreases and fewer children choose to interact in the dramatic play corner, a new theme should be selected and prepared. Teachers have found it valuable to introduce a new theme gradually so that children become familiar with the resources and props available in the new setting.

In many instances, it is valuable for the teacher to model specific ways of interacting with the themed materials. For example, in a veterinarian's office setting, the teacher could remind children to fill out appointment forms or prescription forms, to read to their pets in the waiting area, and to provide directions for the medications (Morrow & Rand, 1991).

Based on careful observation of children's interactions, a teacher can become aware of the need for an additional prop or piece of equipment. A teacher may also take advantage of the opportunity to encourage cooperation between children and facilitate their negotiation of purposes, roles, or both (Berk & Winsler, 1995). By observing children's interactions, teachers can also become aware of questions or misconceptions children might have about a particular concept or person's role. It is important not to interrupt a child's thinking (Lindberg & Swedlow, 1980) or to provide too much direction to children in the dramatic play area. Teachers who carefully observe children's verbal and nonverbal behaviors during dramatic play activities are able to recognize "teachable moments" when they can enhance children's understandings of concepts and interpersonal interactions (Owocki, 1999).

Book center. Most preschools have an area where children can interact with storybooks. Teachers can support and facilitate children's interactions in the book center by providing a variety of books and comfortable seating, along with monitoring children's book interactions. In some classrooms, better-quality books are tucked away on a high shelf or on the teacher's desk for "safekeeping"; however, for children to gain the most benefit from a book center, high-quality, interesting books must be present and accessible. Books should be stored in baskets or on open shelves in a way that allows children to easily see the book covers. This encourages them to select and interact with books. To maintain interest in the area, books should be changed periodically. Comfortable pillows and child-sized chairs or soft chairs, such as beanbags, contribute to children's interest in relaxing with a book. This area should have enough room for several children so they are encouraged to look at and talk about the books with each other.

Language goals.   Specific language goals for the book center area focus on encouraging children to talk about the pictures, orally re-create stories via pictures, develop a memory for story texts, increase vocabulary development, and learn to discuss or share a book with another child. Both receptive and expressive language knowledge are enhanced through children's storybook interactions.

Guidelines for enhancing language development.   Books placed in the book center should be familiar, having been shared previously at group story time. This provides children with an introduction to the book so that they can build on this introduction when they interact with the book independently in the book area. A range of genres should also be provided, such as poetry, including nursery rhymes; narratives; alphabet books; fairy tales; and nonfiction. This range provides children with exposure to a wide variety of language structures and vocabulary. It is also important to include books that represent a range of diverse cultures and families (Rowell, 2007).

By selecting books that are clearly illustrated and whose illustrations are directly related to the book's text, children's vocabulary development is enhanced. Picture dictionaries, wordless books, and concept books encourage children to look closely at the illustrations and to label the items or actions pictured. For example, in *Roads*

Encouraging children to write a shopping list before entering a dramatic play store area adds to the realism as well as encourages awareness of writing for a specific purpose.

(Harshman, 2002), the illustrations clearly support the text vocabulary, showing how roads connect and intersect bridges, buildings, and train tracks.

In keeping with the exploratory nature of the book center, teachers' monitoring should involve observing which books are used most frequently and the ways in which children interact with the books. For example, are they learning to "read" the pictures? Do they look only at the pictures when re-creating the story? Do they have a memory for the text or story line? Do they talk with each other about the story events or the illustrations? Teachers who take time to sit in the book center with children will find that their informal conversations about the books provide opportunities to further enhance expressive language and listening skills.

Listening center.   In a part of the room where quiet activities are planned, a CD player and headphone set can be placed along with storybooks and accompanying CDs. The storybooks used in this area should be familiar so children can follow the story easily. Multiple copies of each book will allow more than one child to hold the book and follow along with the recorded story.

Language goals. Language goals for this area include increasing children's listening comprehension and vocabulary and expanding children's ability to sequence story events.

Teachers who take time to sit in the book center with children will find that their informal conversations provide opportunities to further enhance expressive language and listening skills.

Guidelines for enhancing language development.   Because a listening center provides the opportunity for children to explore storybooks on their own by listening to the audio and manipulating the accompanying storybook, you will want to be sure that this area is prepared and equipped so children can use it without adult assistance. This means that you will want to be sure that the CD player is a durable model and the controls can be easily operated by children. You will need to take time to demonstrate how to use the CD player and headphones on several occasions so that children are comfortable and confident in using the equipment.

In addition to providing familiar stories, you will need to also provide predictable stories and rhyming texts (poetry and nursery rhymes). Predictable, rhythmic texts provide opportunities for children to hear the patterns of text and sound patterns in rhyme.

If you have children in your classroom who are English language learners, you will want to include some CDs of books in their home languages. This will provide opportunity for those students to enjoy stories using their first language

Preschool children's interactions with books are encouraged when books are displayed for easy access.

competencies and further enhance their listening comprehension and vocabulary development in their home language.

Another way of enhancing language development in a listening center is to provide story-based realia for children to use when listening to the CD. This realia might be a hat, a stuffed animal, or a small toy that is directly related to the story, such as a child-sized fireman's hat to go with a story about a fire truck. Providing this realia can enhance children's understanding of concepts and events in the story.

Although the listening center is for independent, exploratory activity, you will need to monitor this area, noting whether children are having any difficulty using the equipment or other materials. Occasionally, you may decide to engage children in brief, informal conversations about the audio stories as a way of encouraging them to talk about their book interactions.

Writing center.   In a writing center, children explore ways of communicating through creating pictures and print. Young preschool children communicate on paper through drawing and gradually begin to use scribble, letter-like forms, and conventional letters to create their messages. Through children's attempts in communicating on paper, they will gradually acquire receptive and expressive knowledge of how written language works. In addition, they will use drawing to supplement and complement their written messages.

Language goals. A writing center provides opportunities for children's language development to be enhanced in these areas:

- *Phonological.*   Awareness of the connections between speech sounds and written symbols and demonstration of emerging alphabet knowledge.
- *Semantic.*   Awareness that pictures and symbols communicate meaning and that print carries a message.
- *Syntactic.*   Awareness that messages can be created through using a range of preconventional (scribbling, letter strings, copied environmental print, and invented spelling) and conventional spellings (of high-frequency words).
- *Pragmatic.*   Awareness of the different forms and types of written communication, such as notes, greeting cards, lists, and personal stories.

Guidelines for enhancing language development.   The way in which a writing center is supplied and organized will influence children's interest and motivation in exploring writing. The center should be stocked with ample supplies of paper and writing implements (pencils, small felt-tip markers, and crayons), along with writing-related materials, such as envelopes, pretend stamps, alphabet letter stamps, and ink pads (with washable ink). Having a bulletin board in this area encourages children to share their creations with their classmates. Neither coloring books nor reading readiness

Preschool children become more engaged in writing-related activities when they have access to a variety of writing implements and paper.

workbooks should be a part of a writing center because neither activity encourages exploration and creative communication.

A writing center needs to have a child-sized table and several chairs, along with shelving units where the supplies are kept. There should be room for several children to use this center at the same time. Their conversations with each other often help them clarify and develop their messages or stories (Kissel, 2009).

The format or purpose of a child's writing in a writing center should be determined solely by the child. As their teacher, you may decide to visit a writing center to informally observe children's explorations, to model writing behaviors, or to offer encouragement (Neuman & Roskos, 1990). The emphasis should be on children's creative explorations of a wide range of preconventional forms rather than on learning to write with conventional spelling and penmanship.

When you visit the writing center, encourage children to talk about their writing and drawing. Some children may respond by talking about the pictures they have drawn. They may also refer to the letters, or letter-like forms they have used in their writing, and engage in reading-like behaviors, attempting to track print.

Concept centers.   Concept centers contain exploratory and game-like activities that one or more children can use independently. These centers may present specific content information, such as math, science, and social studies, or may have integrated content, such as math–science or social studies–language arts. Specific concept centers should be planned and implemented based on the current needs of the children in the classroom (Schickedanz, York, Stewart, & White, 1990). Some concept centers provide open-ended activities that are process oriented, while others have activities that are more product oriented. For example, a science center on magnetism that is process oriented might encourage children to test the magnetic properties of a variety of metal and nonmetal items. In contrast, another science center might have children match pictures of baby animals with pictures of adult animals by pasting the matched pictures on a piece of construction paper.

Concept centers are usually designed for only one child at a time because 3- and 4-year-olds developmentally are transitioning between solitary and parallel interaction patterns and are usually not ready for activities requiring cooperation. When children can interact cooperatively, concept centers may be designed for two or three children. In these situations, the concept center task may involve problem solving or another task requiring verbal interaction among children.

Language goals.   General language goals for concept centers include increasing children's conceptual development and vocabulary through hands-on activities, increasing children's ability to describe or verbalize concepts, using language in problem-solving tasks, and increasing children's question-asking behaviors.

Guidelines for enhancing language development.   In designing and developing concept centers, you will want to focus on concepts within classroom curricular themes. For example, for a seasonal theme of autumn, a concept center could provide a collection of leaves that children would examine with a magnifying glass; students could also complete a texture rubbing of the leaves and assemble a leaf collage.

It is important to select center activities that are self-correcting or open-ended so minimal monitoring is needed. Simply worded directions or illustrated steps support children's independent interactions in a center. Another way of encouraging language development is to provide a tape recorder and blank tapes in the concept center. This provides opportunity for your children to use language to describe and record what they have learned or what questions they have.

After children have interacted with a concept center over a period of time, you will want to monitor their interest level for indications that a new center needs to be introduced. To keep a center functioning smoothly, you will need to monitor the organization and equipment in the concept center to be sure the center is appropriately ready. Although concept centers are designed to be used independently by children, you will find it beneficial to stop by a center to respond to children's questions and comments. As you do this, you will support children's interactions in the center by using questioning, linguistic scaffolding, and mediation.

Art center.　Art activities provide an opportunity for children to explore independently the various mediums of artistic expression. Although art activities are visually expressive and communicative by nature, they also provide opportunities to enhance language development.

Language goals.　Language goals for art activities focus on encouraging children to develop conceptual knowledge related to art and to be able to verbally describe the colors, textures, or shapes with which they are working. In this way, children's semantic and syntactic knowledge of language is enhanced. Children should also learn the concept name of the particular technique they are using. Rather than label the technique as simply "painting," a teacher should explain the type of painting involved, such as sponge painting, string painting, finger painting, block painting, or brush painting. Semantic development is furthered as children learn other art-related concepts and vocabulary involving textures, shapes, and colors. When children have opportunities to share their comments and questions during the artistic process with you and with each other, their receptive and expressive language competencies are enhanced.

Guidelines for enhancing language development.　Teacher direction in art activities should be minimal; however, opportunities for conversation may occur during the creative process. Teachers should respond to children's comments and questions during art activities, using expansion and verbal scaffolding to clarify concepts or processes involved in the ongoing activity. However, too much teacher direction or conversation may interfere with a child's art experience.

For example, asking a child what he or she is creating takes away from the child's experience of using the media and places too much emphasis on the "product" created. To illustrate, Julie was a preschooler who was seated at a classroom table with crayons and paper. Her teacher asked her what she was making. Julie replied, "I don't know. I'm not done yet."

Computer center.   An exploratory activity found in many preschool classrooms is the computer center. Research, as well as practice, indicates that "computers can serve as catalysts for positive social interaction and emotional growth" (Clements & Sarama, 2003, p. 34).

Language goals.   The language goals associated with a preschool computer center include enhancing children's receptive and expressive competencies related to oral and written language. Software that encourages social interaction will provide opportunity for children to use language in their cooperative efforts. Software or online resources that involve interactive or animated stories will enhance children's listening comprehension (Lacina, 2007/2008; Lacina & Mathews, 2012) and encourage them to talk about the stories they hear and view. Software or online resources that can be used to create drawings and print will enhance children's use of graphic symbols and the alphabet (see further http://www.pbskids.org/teachers/connect/resources).

Guidelines for enhancing language development.   When setting up a computer center, be sure to place two chairs in front of the computer for children plus an additional chair at the side for you or your aide to use. Selecting appropriate software is a critical part of preparing a computer center for preschoolers. You will need to be aware of your children's ability to use the keyboard and the mouse, as well as their individual interests and ability to follow directions. Although this center is intended to be an independent area and not need constant supervision, you will want to visit this area occasionally to monitor children's success in using the software and in working together. As you interact with children in the computer center, you will find that by mediating children's interactions through demonstration, questioning, commenting, and prompting, you can increase their success in using the software. When the children are able to use the software independently, you will be able to reduce your involvement.

Outdoor play.   Outdoor play provides many opportunities for exploratory activities. Children benefit from having an outdoor play area where there are different types of play equipment, an all-weather play surface, and shade trees and other vegetation.

Language goals.   Language goals for outdoor play focus on enhancing children's communication with each other and with teachers as well as developing concepts through direct experiences. Children can be encouraged to describe natural events such as rain, snowfall, and wind. You can also encourage children to describe their experiences and the events they see and to ask questions about what they experience or see. Children should also be encouraged to use language to negotiate the use of equipment and to carry on conversations with peers and adults. Specific activities can be provided during outdoor play, such as using a sandbox, using a water table, playing with a parachute, and riding tricycles and other vehicles. Each of these activities is an opportunity to encourage children to use language to describe what they are experiencing and to comment and question during their exploration.

Guidelines for enhancing language development. It is important to remember that outdoor activities are most beneficial for preschool children if the activities remain exploratory, with only limited teacher guidance. However, by being aware of the concepts and vocabulary related to specific activities, you can enhance semantic development during informal conversations with children in outdoor activities or in recalling outdoor events during classroom discussions. Outdoor activities provide opportunities to engage children in spontaneous conversations as well as for children to talk more with each other. These longer conversations allow children to practice listening and responding to another person on topics of mutual interest and personal value.

Teachers can enhance children's language development by carefully considering how outdoor activities are set up and maintained. For example, a sandbox can provide opportunities to explore a variety of concepts and vocabulary related

A sandbox provides opportunities to explore a variety of concepts and vocabulary related to temperature, texture, shape, and different actions.

to temperature, texture, shape, size, and processes. Table 7.2 focuses on sandbox activities and illustrates the wide variety of concepts related to sandbox experiences. As you mediate preschoolers' interactions in the sandbox area, you can encourage children to focus on these concepts and vocabulary without impinging on the spontaneity of their exploration.

Another outdoor activity appropriate for preschool children is a parachute group activity. In this activity, a group of about 8 to 10 children, with their teacher(s), hold on to the edges of a colorful, circular parachute. A teacher leads the children in raising and lowering the parachute, catching currents of air. While this is a group activity, it is exploratory in the sense that the activity explores how a parachute moves, responding to currents of the air and specific manipulation. The activity contributes to conceptual and language development as a hands-on activity that provides opportunities to feel and see concepts such as up, down, high, low, wavy, twisting, floating, rising, and falling. As you interact with children in this activity, you will want to provide clear, simple directions and demonstrate how children should move the parachute. It is also important to verbally label your actions, such as *up, down, slow, fast, waving*, and *twisting*.

Language development is also enhanced when teachers and children take a walk outside together and talk about what they see (Bentley, 2012). This activity provides opportunities for children's spontaneous speech about ongoing events and objects they find interesting. When engaged in this activity, you, as their teacher, will want to be actively listening to what they say and what they are curious about. Your role is to listen carefully and provide linguistic scaffolding to the children's conversations, valuing and validating their observations and questions.

Encouraging Language Development Through Teacher-Guided Activities

In preschool settings, teacher-guided activities occur during large- or small-group times. Large groups generally involve all children; small groups usually involve three to five children. Small groups are more appropriate for the preschool age

TABLE 7.2
Concepts Related to Sandbox Activities

Temperature	Texture	Shape	Size	Processes
Hot	Rough	Round	Tall	Filling
Warm	Grainy	Square	Small	Dumping
Cool	Smooth	Pointed	Big	Packing
Cold	Bumpy	Hilly	Short	Pouring
		Flat	Tiny	Patting
			Huge	Shaking
				Spooning
				Pushing
				Smoothing

group because the children have more opportunities to participate and can better see illustrations or objects involved in the activity. Both large- and small-group activities are designed and directed by the teacher. The length and frequency of large-group or whole-class activities need to be limited for preschoolers because children at this age have a wide range of attention spans. Preschool children also vary in their listening comprehension skills and may not be able to attend to a teacher's speech directed to the whole group. Children's participation in large-group activities should remain voluntary. Children should be encouraged to join the group activity; however, they should not be disciplined if they choose not to join in, or stay with, the group. Four types of teacher-guided group activities will be discussed here with respect to encouraging language development: show-and-tell time, book time, oral storytelling, and poetry or music time.

Show-and-tell.   Show-and-tell is an activity that involves children taking turns to describe orally or comment on an object they have brought to share with their class or to tell about a recent event they experienced. According to Stewig (1982), this activity is one of the most abused practices when not planned and implemented with language development goals in mind.

Language goals.   Language-related goals for show-and-tell time include increasing listening comprehension and vocabulary, learning to focus on a topic or an object and to describe its distinguishing features, and learning to relate a sequence of events. Other goals are to encourage children to learn to take turns in this group setting and to generate their own questions about the object or topic being presented.

The show-and-tell activity potentially enhances development of each of the five aspects of language knowledge in both receptive and expressive modes. Receptive phonological knowledge is enhanced as children come to understand others' speech and articulation patterns. Expressive phonological knowledge is encouraged when children have an opportunity to communicate to a group of other children that involves speaking so that the volume and articulation of their speech contribute to clear communication. Receptive semantic knowledge is enhanced through hearing other children describe what they have brought, while expressive semantic knowledge is encouraged as children describe their object or experience. Morphemic knowledge is enhanced as children hear another's speech and contribute verbally to the discussion. A child's development of syntactic knowledge is fostered by exposure to various syntactic structures present in the verbal interaction occurring during show-and-tell. Pragmatic knowledge is enhanced as preschoolers learn how to use language in this specific setting: sharing an object or event of interest to the class and engaging in verbal interaction focusing on the object or event. Children's discourse in this activity may be monologic or may have the characteristics of a dialogue as they interact with those in the audience as well as their teacher. Show-and-tell time embodies the use of language to share information as a speaker and to obtain information as a listener.

Guidelines for enhancing language development.   Because preschool children's attention span may be limited to 10 or 15 minutes for group activities, many teachers have found that it is better to have five or fewer children participate as speakers in show-and-tell each day. The class is divided into groups so that over the course of a week, each child has an opportunity to participate as a speaker.

Teachers should give a carefully planned show-and-tell activity their undivided attention (Stewig, 1982) by providing the framework, scaffold, or mediation needed to help children share and talk about what they have brought or experienced. As you interact with your preschoolers during this activity, you will want to ask questions to stimulate further description by the children. Specific strategies that are useful include expansion and linguistic scaffolding. Summarizing or repeating what the children say is another way to enrich and extend the verbal interaction of this activity.

Instead of having children bring objects from home for show-and-tell, have children select a favorite toy or activity from your classroom to present during this time. This avoids the perception by some children (and parents) that a new toy is needed to bring in each time for show-and-tell.

Book sharing.   For many teachers and children, storybook time is a favorite part of their day. The benefits of including book sharing in the curriculum are many and have been well documented in studies of language acquisition and emergent literacy research. Storybook sharing is a social interaction routine that supports language development and "bridges the development of oral language skills and the emergence of print literacy" (Rice, 1995, p. 8). Children who have had early story-sharing experiences also have "greater success in learning to read and write" (Slaughter, 1993, p. 4).

Children's knowledge of each of the five aspects of language is enhanced through storybook sharing (Beauchat, Blamey, & Walpole, 2009; Christ & Wang, 2010; Morrow, 1989; Otto, 1996; Silverman & Crandell, 2010). As stories are read aloud and shared, children will have opportunity to develop:

- knowledge that language is used differently in different types of stories (pragmatic knowledge)
- awareness of the sound–aural system and the sound–graphic system of language (phonetic knowledge)
- receptive knowledge of how morphemes influence word meanings (morphemic knowledge)
- vocabulary knowledge through the rich and varied language in literature (semantic knowledge)
- knowledge of how thoughts are organized into sentences and phrases of book language, or literate register (pragmatic and syntactic knowledge)

Language goals.   Language-related goals for storybook time reflect our current knowledge of the benefits of storybook experiences for preschool children. These goals include increasing children's listening comprehension and vocabulary, helping children become aware of the connections between speech and print, and encouraging children to learn to sequence events and to recall sequences of events.

Guidelines for enhancing language development.   Basic guidelines for enhancing children's language development during shared book time involve (1) the selection of appropriate books and (2) the interaction strategies used during the book sharing.

Selection of appropriate books for book sharing.   The success and value of this activity is influenced by the characteristics of the books chosen to be shared. Book choices should reflect the developmental needs and interests of children in the classroom and the ongoing curriculum. Four main criteria for book selection are subject content, language complexity, quality of illustrations, and genre.

Subject content.   Books for preschool children should initially have subject content that concerns familiar concepts, actions, places, and people. This familiarity provides a basis for comprehension of the book's content. Gradually, as children's listening comprehension and receptive vocabulary increase, books can be selected that introduce new concepts as well as refine or elaborate existing concepts and vocabulary.

Language complexity.   Young preschool children with limited previous storybook experiences need to have simple story text or labeling books for their initial storybook interactions. With frequent story-sharing experiences and greater listening comprehension, more complex text (and storylines) can be introduced. Teachers need to constantly monitor the language complexity of the books read and determine whether children's listening comprehension can accommodate the level of syntactic complexity in the chosen book.

Illustrations.   In evaluating the quality of illustrations, teachers should determine whether the illustrations support the concepts, ideas, actions, and events portrayed in the text. Vocabulary acquisition is facilitated when illustrations directly and accurately support the text. Books for young children need to have simple illustrations. Complex illustrations make it difficult for children to determine the context or referent for the vocabulary introduced in the story. Illustrations need to be large enough to be visible when shared with a group of children. When children are not able to see the illustrations clearly, their comprehension of the story is impaired.

Genre.   In addition to considering subject content, language complexity, and illustration quality, teachers should also consider whether a book's genre will have benefits for children. **Genre** refers to the type of literature (Farris, Fuhler, & Walther, 2004). Preschoolers benefit from both fiction and nonfiction. In addition to the two main genres of fiction and nonfiction, there are more specific genres, such as fairy tales, mysteries, and folktales. Two special book types often used with preschool children are predictable books and alphabet books. Predictable books are books that have one or more of the following patterns of language (Slaughter, 1993): repetition of phrases or sentences (e.g., *The Gingerbread Man*, McCafferty, 2002); cumulative structures that repeat and expand phrases or sentences (*This Is the House That Jack Built*, Taback, 2002); rhythmic language or rhyme (e.g., *The Cat in the Hat*, Geisel [Dr. Seuss], 1957; or *Row, Row, Row Your Boat*, Goodhart, 1997); and sequential episodes (e.g., *Brown Bear, Brown Bear*, Martin & Carle, 1992). The characteristic patterns of language in predictable books encourage children to focus on the language. Memory for the text and content is enhanced by the predictability of these books.

Alphabet books represent a genre of children's literature that was first used in the United States in the late 1600s (Smolkin & Yaden, 1992). The format of alphabet books focuses on pairing each letter with a word or words that begin with that letter–sound. Illustrations represent the concept conveyed by the target word(s). In a longitudinal study of preschool children and their parents' interaction with alphabet books, Smolkin and Yaden (1992) reported that children were actively constructing six kinds of information about graphic systems:

1. Metalinguistic terms, such as *letter* or *word*, and using phrases such as "starts with" or "is for"
2. Directional concepts, such as left to right, top to bottom, and front to back
3. Letter orientation, such as distinguishing between *M*, *N*, and *W*
4. Feature analysis of letters: "This is *E*, with the three lines"
5. Letter symbol system and number symbol system, distinguishing between "numbers" and "letters"
6. Conventional sound–symbol relations, as in "*D* is for *dog*"

Smolkin and Yaden (1992) concluded that parents' interaction with their children was critical for the development of this knowledge of letter–sound connections.

When selecting alphabet books for preschoolers, you need to review the text to see if the labels used represent general concepts and not more specific concepts. For example, "*F* for *flower*" represents a general label, whereas "*R* for *rose*" is more specific and requires that a child have a conceptual hierarchy including both flowers and roses. Illustrations should also provide strong support for the concepts selected. For example, if the text says "*Y* is for *yogurt*," the yogurt illustrated should not look like an ice cream cone, or children may become confused.

Nonfiction books can be selected to represent specific themes related to science or social studies content, such as "animals," "weather," and "families." When using a nonfiction book during group time, you should focus on key vocabulary and the connections between concepts that are emphasized in the book. In this way, children's language knowledge is enhanced by opportunities to develop "vocabulary knowledge networks" (Pollard-Durodola et al., 2011/2012).

Interaction strategies used during book sharing. The way a teacher reads and shares a storybook with preschoolers influences the value of the experience. The focus of storybook sharing at the preschool level should be on developing listening comprehension, which is based on receptive knowledge of each of the five aspects of language knowledge. Books should not be read simply to take up class time or to provide a "holding" activity prior to or after lunch.

As you prepare to share a book with children, you will first need to read it thoroughly and examine the relationship between the illustrations and the text. This allows you to become familiar with the book's content and language. You then need to decide how to introduce the book and what aspects of the book you will focus while reading and when starting the discussion (Graham & Kelly, 1997, in Campbell, 2001; Roskos & Burstein, 2011). You might decide to focus on specific vocabulary or the sequence of events in the story. You will want to sit on a low chair and hold the book so that all the children can clearly see the illustrations. When reading, use clear pronunciation and vary your intonation and expression to reflect the characters or events in the story.

As you share a book with children, you may find that you need to mediate or alter the text to increase children's comprehension of the content. This may involve rephrasing and rewording the text to fit your preschoolers' level of understanding. You will also want to identify words the children might not know and decide if you will define the word, provide a synonym or relate the word to their prior experiences (Christ & Wang, 2012). For example, when reading the book *Snowy Day* by Ezra Jack Keats (1962), a teacher could ask, "What do you like to do on a snowy day?" as a way to encourage children to activate their prior knowledge and to predict what the child pictured will do in the story.

In repeated readings of a storybook, children's responses can be elicited to predict upcoming events or book language. By reading a segment of patterned text and pausing for a group response, you can encourage children to predict upcoming text based on their memory of text from previous readings. Through repeated readings, children become familiar with book language (literate register) and gradually may begin to focus on the connections between speech and print. With older preschoolers, you may decide to explicitly refer to the features of print that relate to the story or content, such as visible sound, for example, when the word *mooo* is written in large letters near a cow character in the story. When using alphabet books, you would point to the individual letters of the alphabet positioned on separate pages. This explicit attention to print during read-aloud time is referred to as **print referencing** (Zucker, Ward, & Justice, 2009). Print referencing further encourages children's awareness of the connections between speech and print.

Group story time can provide a setting in which you can encourage children to then create their own version of storybooks through group or individual dictation. For example, after reading *Goodnight Moon* by Margaret Wise Brown (1991), children can dictate their own version, replicating the pattern of the original text (Glazer, 2000). After you write their story dictation, you can transfer it into big book format. Children can add their own illustrations, and then the story can be enjoyed at group story time and placed in your classroom's book center.

Oral storytelling. Oral storytelling enhances the development of language knowledge among preschoolers. It shares many of the same benefits of story reading; however, story reading and storytelling have distinct differences. In storytelling, the story is communicated through speech and nonverbal behaviors, without supporting written text or illustrations. This places different demands on preschoolers and teachers. Because there are no illustrations to provide context for the story, children must rely on listening along with their interpretation of the teacher's gestures, facial expressions, and other nonverbal behaviors to comprehend the story (Berkowitz, 2011).

Language goals. Language-related goals for oral storytelling activities include increasing children's listening comprehension, visualization, and understanding of gestures and actions. Semantic and syntactic knowledge can also be enhanced by stories that build on children's prior story experiences and introduce new vocabulary.

Guidelines for enhancing language development. Oral storytelling is an art. It requires some different skills from teachers than those needed during story reading. More preparation time is required to tell a story because the story must be rehearsed until it can be told without using a text. Because there are no illustrations to create the mood, characters, and setting, you will need to communicate these facets of the story through thoughtful and dramatic use of language, intonation, and gesture.

In storytelling, eye contact and shared reference are critical to establishing and keeping the attention of your preschoolers. This allows you to closely monitor children's comprehension of the story and attentiveness. If children become restless and distracted, you can adjust either by increasing the dramatic features of the story (intonation, gesture) to attract their attention or by shortening the story. You could also increase children's engagement in the storytelling by encouraging them to respond physically (stomping their feet at appropriate times in the Three Billy Goats Gruff story) or verbally by joining in on the story's refrain, as in The Gingerbread Man story ("You can't catch me, I'm the Gingerbread Man") (Berkowitz, 2011).

One way of adding visual interest to oral storytelling is to use hand or finger puppets, felt-board characters, props, or musical instruments (Morrow, 1989). Each of these creative accompaniments helps create a visual context for your oral storytelling. This adds to the way in which story events are communicated and characters are introduced, enhancing comprehension of the story content. It is important for you to thoroughly rehearse using these accompaniments before you begin your storytelling.

With repeated experience in oral storytelling, you can build up your repertoire and confidence. When you use storytelling frequently in your classroom, your storytelling becomes a model for the children in their storytelling attempts. As an extension of your story reading and storytelling, you can encourage preschoolers to begin participating in retelling a story such as *The Little Red Hen* (Ottolenghi, 2002). After the children have become familiar with the story, they can be asked to provide sound effects or join in on the repeated refrain of the text. Stuffed animals or stick puppets can be handed to individual children to use when retelling their particular part of the story.

Poetry and song. Along with book sharing and storytelling, another type of teacher-guided activity involves sharing nursery rhymes, rhyming story texts, and songs in small- or whole-group settings. This typically occurs before or after book sharing or storytelling events in preschool classrooms and may last only for 5 or 10 minutes.

Language goals.   Poetry and song activities are characterized by language used in rhythmic and distinctive patterns. Language-related goals for poetry and song activities involve enhancing children's awareness of words that have sound similarities (Schickedanz, Pergantis, Kanosky, Blaney, & Ottinger, 1997) and rhythmic patterns. The rhythm and melody accompanying these activities also support children's verbal fluency. When gestures are incorporated to show actions embedded in the language of the poetry or song, children's comprehension is also enhanced (Arnold & Colburn, 2005).

Guidelines for enhancing language development.   When you are selecting a poem or song to use with preschool children, look for poetry or songs with a subject that is familiar to the children and for simple syntax. Whenever possible, select poetry or action songs to coordinate with a current area of your curriculum. For example, if your curriculum includes a unit on transportation or trains, you might decide to use an action poem about trains that involves actions of going forward and backward and vocalizing a train whistle.

By selecting poems and action songs that have a strong rhythm or rhyme, children's awareness of sound patterns will be enhanced. When you prepare to present a poem or song to children, decide which actions or movements should accompany the poem or song. Sometimes you might share the poetry or song using oral storytelling techniques; at other times, you might use a book version of the rhyme or song. Creating original story songs that use simple familiar tunes is another way to encourage language acquisition (Ringgenberg, 2003).

Start with poems or action songs that are relatively short and have simple wording. Later on, preschoolers will be able to learn longer and more complex poetry and songs. When you introduce a new poem or action song, repeat it several times before you expect your preschoolers to follow along. At the same time, demonstrate the appropriate actions. You may have some children who will participate in the actions before they begin to repeat the words of the song or poem. After you have used the poem or action song several times, you can ask general questions about the meaning or actions embedded in the poem or song (Silberg & Schiller, 2002). For example, in a poem about a train, you could ask, "How does the train move on the track?" "What noise does the train make?" This encourages children to think about the poem or song and what it describes.

When the children in your classroom are beginning to pay more attention to print, you can write their favorite poems or action songs on a chart or chalkboard. Then as you engage children in these poems or action songs, you can point to the words on the chart or chalkboard. This encourages them to begin to match their oral memory of the words with the printed text. In this way, sharing poetry and song with young children provides opportunities to develop knowledge of how oral and written language are connected.

Encouraging Language Development During Routines

Language enhancement opportunities in daily routines often go unrecognized. Routine activities are those activities that occur on a regular basis in preschool and serve an organizational (e.g., attendance) or physical (e.g., snack time and dressing to go outside) need. These activities are often excluded from consideration when planning curricula as they may not be credited with any opportunity for important learning. On the contrary, routine activities provide opportunity for acquiring important language knowledge. Specific language goals for routines may focus on developing conversational skills (pragmatic knowledge) and enhancing the other four aspects of language knowledge (phonological, semantic, morphemic, syntactic) through the communication that occurs during daily routines.

Arrival. During the time preschoolers are arriving at school, various language competencies can be encouraged. Pragmatic knowledge is enhanced as children participate in using oral language in routine greetings and in conversations with teachers and with peers. When children engage in routine greetings ("How are you?" "I am fine"), they are learning appropriate syntactic structures and common uses of language in social settings. When you greet each child by name (appropriately pronounced) and encourage children to address you and each other by name, you are fostering an awareness of the role that individual names have in the process of communication. Phonological knowledge is also enhanced when children learn to distinguish and pronounce each other's names.

Pragmatic aspects of written language can be introduced when children's names appear on coat racks or cubbies. Labeling the coat rack with children's names indicates where their coats should be hung. Attendance-taking procedures illustrate another function of written language—to record information. When children check

Attendance-taking procedures can illustrate another function of written language to record information.

in by selecting their name card and placing it on a display board or pocket chart, it helps them learn to recognize their name in print and begin to recognize others' names (Wilford, 2000). During arrival time, short previews of the day's upcoming events can be mentioned. For example, "We're going on a walk today" or "Today, Matt is going to bring his rabbit to visit class." Such statements model various sentence structures and provide semantic and morphemic information for children. As children respond verbally to the preview of upcoming events, they have an opportunity to use their expressive language knowledge.

Snack time/lunchtime. Many opportunities for language development can occur when children and teachers are gathered around a table to enjoy a snack or lunch. Conversational skills, one aspect of pragmatic knowledge, are encouraged during snack time/lunchtime as teachers and children talk informally about events or happenings in the classroom and in the outside world. Mealtimes provide a familiar setting to children, reminiscent of their mealtimes at home. Children's reception of others' speech and the expression of their responses foster their syntactic and morphemic knowledge. Phonological knowledge is also enhanced as children listen to each other and express their responses. When teachers expand and extend children's utterances, they are encouraging the development of syntactic knowledge by modeling more complex language structures.

It is important that a teacher is at each table and remains there for the duration of the snack time/lunchtime. When teachers attempt to multitask at this time by going from table to table or preparing for another activity, they are not be able to sustain the extended conversations that are so beneficial to young children's developing language competencies (Cote, 2001).

Snack time/mealtime also provides a good opportunity to introduce new vocabulary. You can do this by expanding or extending the speech of the children, incorporating new concepts, vocabulary, or both. For example, when the children are eating sliced apples, you could begin a conversation about apples, reminding them of a story they had shared about picking apples. Depending on student interest and response, you might go on to visit with the children about the parts of the apple (peel, stem, seeds), as well as its shape, color, and taste.

You can also encourage children to elaborate on their comments. For example, a child might say, "I saw a train today." You could respond, "Where did you see a train?" eliciting further response from the child. If you avoid asking questions that can be answered by a simple "yes" or "no," you will provide opportunities for children's extended responses. All of the other children at the table should be encouraged to participate. By observing children's facial expressions, eye contact, and verbalizations, you can encourage each child to participate. You also should monitor your involvement in the discussion, keeping in mind that you are the facilitator for children's conversations. Avoid dominating the conversation or turning it into a formal lesson.

By participating in discussions and conversations during snack time/mealtime, preschool children begin to learn how language is used in informal group interactions. Conversations at snack time/mealtime are less directed than in a teacher-led group

Snack time provides important opportunities to engage in conversations.

discussion about a storybook or an event. In fact, it is natural for conversations to develop between pairs of students during snack time as well as with the whole table of children.

Departure. Additional opportunities to extend preschoolers' language knowledge arise when they are preparing to go home. Pragmatic aspects of language can be emphasized through routine good-byes. In addition to a routine of saying "Good-bye. See you tomorrow!" children can be encouraged to label and talk about items they are taking home, such as artwork and books. Departure time is also a time when children appropriately communicate any specific need they have. For example, "I can't find my mitten" or "Where is my picture?"

At departure time, teachers may briefly review the highlights of the day and share them with children and their parents. This allows parents to be included in a conversation with their children about their experiences at school that day, easing the transition between school and home. Such conversations reinforce semantic information and may encourage children to express themselves in more syntactically complex utterances. The teacher may also use this time to relate the day's events and learning with future planned events. For example, "Today we wrote a story about our trip to the apple orchard. Tomorrow we will be making pictures to go with our story."

A teacher's awareness of the potential for language development in routine activities will contribute to children's opportunities to see language in use for communication, to find out information, to share information, and to engage in social dialogues.

Guidelines for Teachers of English Language Learners

Teachers can enhance children's linguistic diversity by creating a positive class-room environment, building on first language competencies, and creating a learning community. In this section, additional strategies and activities will be suggested for teachers of English language learners.

Supporting children's home language.   It is important to support children's first language competencies, because their home language is closely tied to their personal identity and is the basis for their communication and interaction with others. When you communicate to a child your positive attitude toward her home language, you are enhancing her self-esteem and confidence. Learn several key phrases in a child's home language, such as "hello," "please," "thank you," and "How are you?" (see examples in the Appendix).

It is beneficial to select books for the library center and for shared book time that represent children's home languages and cultures (Nemeth, 2009; see also International Children's Digital Library at http://en.childrenslibrary.org). You will also want to select other classroom materials that reflect diversity, such as ethnic dolls and role-playing clothes and accessories. Post labels in the children's home languages for key areas or learning materials, such as "book corner," "sink," or "table." You can create a positive classroom environment that welcomes English language learners by showing your interest and respect for other languages and cultures.

Children who are just beginning to learn another language, such as English, need to have time to develop their listening comprehension before they will be comfortable trying to communicate in the new language. This means that you will need to carefully observe language learners for signs they understand what is said.

Provide opportunities for teacher-guided small group picture book sharing. Sharing picture books in a small group or one-on-one with you will more actively engage English language learners than if their book experiences occur only in a large group setting. In a smaller setting, children are able to see the illustrations better and have a greater opportunity to ask questions and make comments. Allowing children to select the book for this activity also encourages them to take a more active role. You could also encourage them to turn the pages and point to the illustrations. Take your cues from each child and his interest in the book. If you notice that an English language learner child does not seem to be comprehending the book content, stop reading the text and focus on talking about the illustrations. Focus on establishing eye contact and shared reference, creating communication loops, and mediating the text so the child can comprehend the book content. You will also find it beneficial to share in a small group or one-on-one setting books that have been used in the large, whole-class setting. This repetition provides opportunity for the child to revisit book content or a story that was experienced earlier and have a greater opportunity to ask questions or ponder the illustrations.

Activate and build on English language learners' prior knowledge.   When you plan activities that build upon their prior knowledge, English language learners will become more engaged learners (Coltrane, 2003). In addition to observing how a child interacts in your classroom, you can learn about his prior knowledge through conversations with his parents and other family members. Then you can use the information you gather to plan book sharing, concept centers, themed dramatic play activities, and outdoor activities.

Family Connections

As a teacher of preschool children, you will want to establish close connections with each child's family through informal and formal communication. The goal is for parents and family members to see themselves as important partners in enhancing their children's growth and development. You can encourage this partnership by sharing information about your classroom's learning activities and how the activities enhance specific aspects of children's development. Since language development is a significant area of growth in the preschool years, you will want to share with parents and family members how your curriculum enhances language development and how they can support their children's language development at home and in their community. Informal communication about your curriculum can occur as you interact with parents/family members during arrival and departure times. More formal communication occurs at your preschool open house, parent conferences, or via newsletters. Your goal for both informal and formal communication with parents and family members is to describe how your curriculum benefits the development of their children as well as ways in which they can support this development at home (see Figure 7.6 for a sample newsletter to parents).

FIGURE 7.6
Classroom Newsletter

TALKING WITH YOUR PRESCHOOLER...

Preschoolers are busy, energetic language learners. During the preschool years, children's language develops in many important ways. You can support your child's language development by talking with your child and responding to her/his comments, questions, and observations about the world. When possible, try to ask questions that your child cannot answer by a simple yes or no. Ask, "what happened next?" or "what do you think about that?" or other questions where your child can use a lot of language.

- **At mealtimes** - Talk about the events of their day, the food that is being served, and upcoming activities or events.
- **At bedtime** - Share one or more story books. Encourage your child to talk about the illustrations, book content, and related experiences.
- **In the car** - Talk about where you are going, who you will meet, and what you will do there. Respond to your child's observations of what he sees as he rides in the car.
- **At the grocery store** - Talk about items or food you see and/or place in your shopping basket. Encourage talk about the shape, size, and flavor of fruits and vegetables as well as other foods.
- **At the playground** - Describe your child's actions when playing. For example: swinging (high, low, fast, slow) and sliding (zooming).

CURRICULUM PLANNING

To maximize the enhancement of preschool children's language acquisition, the curriculum throughout the day should have a consistent theme and a focus on language-rich activities. One example of a comprehensive language-theme curriculum is the "Language-Focused Curriculum" developed at the Language Acquisition Preschool at the University of Kansas (Bunce, 2008, 1995; Rice & Wilcox, 1995). This comprehensive curriculum incorporates child-centered and teacher-guided activities along with routine activities that focus on various aspects of receptive and productive language acquisition. This and other resources for curriculum planning are listed in Figure 7.7.

SUMMARY

Important language knowledge develops during the preschool years. The curriculum of the preschool classroom can foster language development through a wide range of exploratory, teacher-guided, and routine activities.

FIGURE 7.7
Teaching Resources for Enhancing Preschool Children's Language Development

Beaty, J. (2012). *50 Early childhood literacy strategies.* Boston, MA: Allyn & Bacon.

Bunce, B. (2008). *Early literacy in action: The language-focused curriculum for preschool.* Baltimore, MD: Paul H. Brookes Publishing.

Campbell, R. (2001). *Read-alouds with young children.* Newark, DE: International Reading Association.

Epstein, A. (2007). *Essentials of active learning in preschool: Getting to know the High/Scope curriculum.* Ypsilanti, MI: High/Scope Press.

Hohmann, M. (2002). *Fee, fie phonemic awareness: 130 Prereading activities for preschoolers.* Ypsilanti, MI: High Scope Educational Research Foundation.

Mackay, M. (2010). *Early childhood vocabulary development activities pre-K-1.* Huntington Beach, CA: Shell Educational Publishing.

Weitzman, E., & Greenberg, J. (2002). *Learning language and loving it: A guide to promoting children's social, language, and literacy development in early childhood settings* (2nd ed.). Toronto: The Hanen Centre.

A teacher's awareness of the potential for enhancing language development in all areas of the preschool curriculum provides many opportunities for children to see language in use. Specific teaching strategies that are effective in encouraging language development include questioning, linguistic scaffolding, mediation, and conflict resolution. Activities that incorporate books, poetry, and songs encourage children to develop receptive and expressive knowledge of written language and to further develop their receptive and expressive knowledge of oral language.

❋ ❋ ❋ CHAPTER REVIEW

1. Key terms to review:

clarifying questions	there-and-then questions	mediation
recitational questions	wait time	conflict resolution
informational questions	contingent questioning	genre
		print referencing

2. Explain the role of the questioning process in enhancing language acquisition among preschool children.
3. Describe how storybook sharing can enhance vocabulary development.
4. Define *linguistic scaffolding*.
5. How is language knowledge involved in conflict resolution?

❋ ❋ ❋ CHAPTER EXTENSION ACTIVITIES

Curriculum Development

Select one of the books suggested in Figure 7.4. Develop a lesson plan that identifies specific language goals for using the book. Also develop five to eight discussion questions, including both high-level and low-level questions.

Observation

Observe in a preschool classroom for a total of 30 minutes. Observe both unstructured and structured activities. Record in writing the questions that were used by the teachers or teacher aides. Categorize the questions as low- or high-level questions. Come to class prepared to discuss what you observed.

Research

Select one of the teaching resources for language development listed in Figure 7.6. Obtain a copy through your campus library. Review the teaching resource, identifying how the resource would be useful in planning a language development curriculum for a preschool classroom. Share your review with your college class.

CHAPTER 8

LANGUAGE DEVELOPMENT IN KINDERGARTNERS

Learning Outcomes

After reading this chapter you should be able to

- Describe the types of invented spelling that kindergartners use in their emergent writing

- Explain how kindergartners' use of figurative language and humor are related to semantic development

- Provide an example of kindergartners' increasing syntactic knowledge

- Explain how kindergartners' use of verb tense, possessives, and comparatives is related to development of morphemic knowledge

- Provide an example of kindergartners' increasing pragmatic knowledge of written language

Jack was the first to arrive in Ms. Kathy's kindergarten room. He walked in briskly, hung his coat in his cubby, and walked over to the science center. As he looked at the cups containing the bean seeds his class had planted, he said, "I see a sprout!" Just then, Marci came in. Jack called to her, "Come see the sprout!" Marci's comment was "Wow!" Ms. Kathy joined them and asked, "Jack and Marci, when we have circle time today, would you show the new sprout to our class?" Both Jack and Marci nodded their heads and began to walk toward the rug where circle time was held.

This chapter describes specific ways in which children's language develops during the kindergarten year with respect to each of the five aspects of language knowledge.

Teachers can expect children to exhibit a wide range of language competencies. It is important to remember that a child's language competencies upon entering kindergarten have been influenced by his home, community, and preschool environments. Thus, teachers need to be able to observe and document children's language competencies at kindergarten entrance so that appropriate activities can be planned to enhance language development. Included in this chapter are four checklists that kindergarten teachers may find useful in observing and documenting children's language development throughout the kindergarten year. A teacher's awareness of each child's oral and written language competencies is a key starting point for planning and implementing activities to enhance language development.

Although there are variations between children, the kindergarten year is a time when children continue to refine and expand their current knowledge of each of the aspects of language in both receptive and expressive modes. Children come from their preschool years with increased phonological knowledge, a rapidly expanding vocabulary, a greater understanding of syntactic and morphemic structure, and increased knowledge of how to use language differently in different settings. During this year, children may also become aware that different languages, dialects, and registers are spoken in different settings. Kindergarten children's knowledge of the five aspects of oral and written language is based in their experiences in their home, community, and school environments.

The language acquisition of kindergartners is also characterized by increasing metalinguistic awareness. Kindergartners become more aware of language as an object and language as a process (Rowe & Harste, 1986). In addition, they continue to develop the ability to reflect on how language works, both in speech and in writing.

DEVELOPMENT OF PHONOLOGICAL KNOWLEDGE

At kindergarten age, children are easily understood by most adults, having mastered the production of many phonemes (Allen & Marotz, 2009). You can expect to find some noticeable differences in children's production of specific speech sounds. Teachers do not need to be overly concerned when children's acquisition of speech sounds does not precisely follow that given in developmental charts; however, articulation difficulties that impact a child's speech intelligibility should be noted and monitored.

Phonological Knowledge of Oral Language

Children's awareness of sound similarities and contrasts and their ability to focus on these similarities and contrasts are evident in their verbal play. Children may spontaneously focus on verbal rhyme and rhythm when engaged in play with blocks, art materials, or other manipulatives. Chants, rhymes, action poems, and word games are a source of enjoyment and increase children's awareness of sound patterns and distinctions (Buchoff, 1994; Colgin, 1991).

The acquisition of phonological knowledge is also evident in kindergarten children's ability to distinguish similarities in beginning and ending sounds

(Kirtley, Bryant, MacLean, & Bradley, 1989). Children's awareness of alliteration (similarities of beginning sounds) and rhyme contribute to the acquisition of reading in two ways (Bryant, MacLean, Bradley, & Crossland, 1990): (1) perception of rhyme and alliteration are the forerunners of being able to distinguish phonemes, and (2) perception of rhyme helps children see similarities in spelling patterns.

Kindergarten children may also become aware of others' different pronunciations and may tease children who speak differently. Likewise, children who are experiencing difficulty may become less verbal, not risking failure or embarrassment. Teachers must be aware of these situations and encourage acceptance and communication among all children.

Phonological Knowledge of Written Language

Significant evidence of children's acquisition of phonological knowledge of written language may occur during the kindergarten year. Over the past 20 years, emergent literacy research has documented kindergartners' acquisition of receptive and expressive knowledge of written language through close observation of early attempts to read and write (Clay, 1982; McGee & Richgels, 1990; Sulzby, 1981, 1985a, 1986b; Temple, Nathan, Burris, & Temple, 1988). This body of research has focused on what children *do* when attempting to read and write and what they *say* about what they are doing.

Knowledge of the names of letters in the alphabet is related to the development of phonological awareness (Cardenas-Hagan, Carlson, & Pollard-Durodola, 2007). When kindergarten children create their own stories, they may comment on their process and their expectations for using print. When Emma was beginning to create her story, she announced, "Mine's gonna spell something." She then proceeded to write *THE LION* on the cover page of her book and said that was "the title." Jason, also a kindergartner, commented as he began his storybook creation, "I can write letters, but they won't spell anything." He then wrote letters of the alphabet in sequence from *A* to *K*. When asked to read his story, Jason responded:

> Once the bear jumped over the log, then, he climbed a tree and fell down the tree, and picked an apple from the tree and ate it. The end.

Jason's comment prior to creating his story indicated that he knew a system for writing used letters, but he was also aware that he did not know yet how to spell anything. The alphabet sequence he put to paper apparently was the "placeholder" for the story he wanted to share.

Evidence of phonological knowledge in reading attempts. Kindergarten children may show evidence of phonological knowledge in their attempts to read when they begin to focus on letter–sound connections (Clay, 1982; Otto, 1993; Sulzby, 1983; Sulzby, Barnhart, & Hieshima, 1989). When asked to "read" a familiar storybook, some children attempt an effortful "sounding out," focusing on the print. When they encounter difficulty, some children then refuse to read, indicating that although they know the print is the source of the message, they cannot decode it: "I don't know what that word says" or "I don't know this word." These print-related refusals are thought to indicate an awareness of the importance of decoding to "real" reading (Sulzby, 1983). Other children, while unsuccessfully attempting to decode print, frequently look to an adult researcher for confirmation that their attempts are "right" (Otto, 1984).

In the example that follows, a 5-year-old girl's attempt to read *Mr. Gumpy's Motor Car* (Burningham, 1973) indicates that she seemed aware that reading involved decoding the print (Otto, 1992). She stopped frequently to note that she could not "read that word." After reassurances that she was doing a good job, she continued on with the story, relying on her memory for the story text.

Child:	*Mr. Gumpy's Motor Car. There's his motor car. Mr. Gumpy was going for a ride in his motor car. He dr-dr-drove down the lane and out the gate. He got out—then—I can't read these words, they're too hard.*
Adult:	*That's okay. That's okay.*
Child:	*[turns page] The boy and the girl asked if they could come. The goat, the cow, the sheep and the hen, too. So did the pig. I can't read that part.*
Adult:	*Okay.*
Child:	*[turns page] And off they went. I do not like the—the—the way those clouds look. I do not like the way those clouds look. Wait, I can't read that page either.*

Evidence of phonological knowledge in writing attempts. Kindergarten children exhibit a wide variety of emergent writing behaviors that indicate that they are beginning to focus on the way print represents specific speech sounds. Children's early spelling attempts provide rich evidence of their acquisition of phonological knowledge about written language.

Children's early attempts to write in English are complicated by the varied ways in which sounds are encoded in English. Because the English alphabet has 26 letters and the English language is represented by approximately 44 phonemes (or standard sounds), children, not knowing standard spelling, "invent" a way to represent the sounds in words they want to use. An additional factor complicating children's early writing attempts is that the English language contains many words borrowed from other languages—French, Spanish, and Italian, to name a few—that follow a different system of sound–symbol relations. Children deal with these inconsistencies by developing their own system to represent sound–symbol relations through first focusing on letter-name and sound relations and then gradually beginning to represent more complete phonemic aspects of each word. Children's early spelling attempts have been classified into the following categories: prephonemic spelling, phonemic spelling, and transitional spelling.

FIGURE 8.1
Summary and Examples of Children's Early Writing

Category	Description	Examples
Prephonemic	Letters present with no consistent connection to sounds in message	XDMMXDXNEE "once upon a time" AlobartLouaLBN "this is a spring story"
Phonemic		
• Early	One or two sounds represented in each word	SW "Snow White"
• Letter-name	The letter name represents the sound.	LADE "lady"
• Later	Several sounds represented in each word	KAT "cat" RABT "rabbit" RAC "rock"
Transitional	Aspects of conventional spelling and consonant vowel patterns	OVR "over" gratful "grateful" askt "ask" muny "money"

Each category represents a different awareness of how specific speech sounds are encoded in print (see Figure 8.1 for a summary and examples).

Prephonemic spelling. **Prephonemic spelling** is characterized by the use of written letters that do not appear to have any relation to the specific sound usually associated with the letter (Temple et al., 1988). Children appear to select letters randomly without considering the specific sound(s) typically represented by the letter(s). Children may string a long line of letters together or group only three or four letters into word-like units.

Phonemic spelling. **Phonemic spelling** is characterized by evidence that children are attempting to encode phonemes. The three categories of phonemic spelling are early phonemic spelling, letter-name spelling, and transitional spelling (Temple et al., 1988). **Early phonemic spelling** refers to instances in which only one or two sounds per word are represented. For example, *Snow White* would be represented as "SW," and *big* would be represented as "bg."

In **letter-name spelling**, each letter name is used to represent a sound; no additional letters are included. For example, when *LADE* is written for the word *lady,* each of the letter names corresponds to the specific sound the child was trying to represent.

Transitional spelling is characterized by words that, while not spelled conventionally, have conventional features and consonant/vowel patterns (Temple et al., 1988). As children develop their awareness of letter and sound relationships, they appear to use a variety of strategies to create words and word-like units. Sometimes more than one category of invented spelling is present in a single writing sample.

Conventional spelling. Kindergartners begin to develop a small writing vocabulary of conventionally spelled words. Generally, these words are high-frequency words, such as *to, go, my, I, love, mommy, daddy*, and names of family members and pets, as well as their own name. Even when children have acquired conventional spelling for a number of words, they may use their invented spelling to overcome uncertainties they have when they are writing.

Digraphs use two letters to represent one sound, such as *ph* in phone. In writing words that contain digraphs, children search for letters they think represent the sounds needed. By observing how children represent digraphs in their early writing, a teacher can learn more about children's phonemic awareness.

It is important for teachers to appreciate the complexity children are facing when they begin to encode words. Children's beginning spelling attempts reflect the ways in which they focus on separating out the sounds that they hear in the words they want to write. Teachers who are aware of the challenges facing emergent writers in representing the specific sounds of words in their writing can better understand the amount of effort and concentration required. In addition, teachers can appreciate the value of observing children's early writing for evidence of children's developing phonological knowledge of written language.

Metalinguistic awareness of phonological knowledge. Children's conscious awareness of the sounds in words and how the sounds can be separated orally during language play or when attempting to create a written message are evidence of phonological awareness. This awareness is significantly related to learning to read and write (Melzi & Ely, 2009). Literacy-related instruction also influences the continued development of phonological awareness due to the focus of that instruction on letter-sound connections, phoneme segmentation of words, and spelling patterns.

DEVELOPMENT OF SEMANTIC KNOWLEDGE

Kindergarten children typically have a speaking vocabulary of 1,500 or more words (Allen & Marotz, 1994) and understand many more words (Piper, 1993). It is estimated that a child's listening vocabulary is four times larger than his speaking vocabulary (Jalongo & Sobolak, 2011). In most classrooms, teachers will note there are wide variations between children in the size of their listening and speaking vocabularies.

Vocabulary development is a major goal of language arts curricula in kindergarten as well as in the primary grades because vocabulary strength is associated with later reading comprehension and success in school (Jalongo & Sobolak, 2011). Expansion of children's semantic knowledge during the kindergarten year must involve not only adding new words and concepts but also further developing networks of vocabulary or schemata (Brabham, Buskist, Henderson, Paleologos, & Baugh, 2012). Existing concepts and vocabulary are further refined. Synonyms and antonyms are added, along with words representing shades of meaning.

Experience and Semantic Development

For kindergartners, vocabulary is acquired through direct and indirect experiences. Some vocabulary is learned through direct naming, or **ostensive naming** (Bloom, 2000). Vocabulary is also learned through conversational context as well as through literacy events where books are shared with children. Both conversational contexts and book sharing contexts provide supportive mediation, which is critical to vocabulary acquisition (Tabors, Beals, & Weizman, 2001).

Book-sharing experiences expose children to new concepts and vocabulary that they may not encounter in informal conversations. Children then may use this new knowledge in their creative writing, "trying out" the words they have heard used in the books. For example, after listening to a nonfiction book about peacocks in her class, Nora created a story about a peacock during her time at the writing center. Her story did not contain any print, only illustrations. When asked to share her story, Nora responded:

> Once there was a peacock, and, and he had, and his designs on his tail turned different colors. One day when they were all different colors, he met a brown rhinoceros and then his, his designs turned purple, and he met a purple turtle.

Defining Words

Researchers have focused on children's ability to define words as one way of exploring semantic development. Kindergarten-age children typically emphasize the appearance or function of the object when stating a definition (Allen & Marotz, 1994; Pease, Berko Gleason, & Pan, 1989). For example, in defining *ball*, children may emphasize "bounce," or the function of the ball. Definitions are now likely to begin to change from being based on individual experiences to having a more socially shared definition; however, children's definitions do not share the elaboration of an adult's definitions (Owens, 2001; Pan & Berko Gleason, 1997).

For example, in the dialogue below, Julie (5 years, 7 months) is asked about her favorite words and what they mean (Otto, 1979). Her definitions reflect her focus on function as well as the socially shared aspect of defining words.

Researcher:	*What is your favorite word?*
Julie:	*Red. That was my first word.*
Researcher:	*What does it mean?*
Julie:	*It's a color. Robbie's [her brother] favorite word is green.*
Researcher:	*What's another favorite word?*
Julie:	*Snack.*
Researcher:	*What does it mean?*
Julie:	*It's a meal you can eat anytime you want.*

Figurative Language

Children's understanding and use of figurative language, such as similes and metaphors, also provide evidence of semantic knowledge (Broderick, 1991; Waggoner & Palermo, 1989). When storybooks containing figurative language are shared and discussed, children are able to develop an understanding of the similes and metaphors. For example, in Eric Carle's *The Very Hungry Caterpillar* (1969), the cocoon is referred to as a small house. When sharing this book with children, you could mediate understanding of this figurative language by pausing in the reading and talking about the "house" concept and how the cocoon was like a house. Although direct, concrete similes and metaphors are most easily understood, there is some evidence that even kindergartners are beginning to understand more abstract comparisons (Waggoner & Palermo, 1989).

Humor

Kindergarten children's sense of humor is an indication of their semantic knowledge development. The riddles and jokes they create are often based in semantic comparisons or words that have multiple meanings (Honig, 1988). Knock-knock jokes are often popular among kindergarten children, though some children do not fully appreciate such jokes until they are in the primary grades. Knock-knock jokes have a predictable pattern and can be easily created. Sometimes their jokes do not make sense to adults, but still are thoroughly enjoyed by kindergartners. For example:

> "Knock, knock
>
> Who's there?
>
> Table.
>
> Table who?" (Poole, Miller, & Church, 2005, p. 31)

Kindergartners' enjoyment of knock-knock jokes and absurd riddles reflects their awareness of language patterns as well as their ability to manipulate words to create a humorous idea (Poole et al., 2005). Kindergarten-age children's humor also may show their awareness of incongruity; a situation is funny because of the discrepancy between what is supposed to happen and what happens. Incongruity may involve exaggerations of shape or size or misnaming (Cornett, 1986). Encouraging kindergartners' sense of humor can foster vocabulary enrichment (McGhee, 2004; Poole et al., 2005).

Because the increases in children's semantic knowledge during the kindergarten year are represented in words from many syntactic categories (e.g., nouns, verbs, adverbs, adjectives, conjunctions), the increase in semantic knowledge occurs concurrently with an increase in syntactic knowledge.

DEVELOPMENT OF SYNTACTIC KNOWLEDGE

Kindergarten-age children can construct basic sentences with little difficulty (McNeill, 1970). The average sentence length for 5-year-olds is five to seven words (Allen & Marotz, 2007). Children can comprehend others' speech that is more syntactically complex than the speech they produce. Kindergarten-age children's acquisition of syntactic knowledge continues as they begin to use more complex noun and verb phrase structures (Owens, 1988, 2001). Increases in syntactic knowledge allow children to communicate more complex ideas.

Pronoun Usage

Acquisition of more complex noun phrase structures may involve clearer use of pronouns. Most kindergarten-age children have mastered pronoun use for indicating subjects (*I, you, she, he, they*), and objects (*me, him, her, them*); however, they are just beginning to master the use of reflexives (*myself, himself, herself, themselves*) (Owens, 1988, 2001).

The relations between nouns and their referent pronouns are also indicated with more clarity during the kindergarten year. In Joshua's story, included previously, he used *his* to refer to the giraffe whose hair was sticking straight up. Not all uses of pronouns are that clear, however, which indicates that some children are still working on the relations between nouns and pronouns. An **unreferenced pronoun** is a pronoun whose noun referent is not clearly indicated by the pronoun and sentence structure. In oral speech, unreferenced pronouns may be clarified by the context in which they are used and by gesture; however, in written language, unreferenced pronouns interfere with comprehension.

Verb Phrase Expansion

Kindergarten-age children's speech is characterized by an increase in the number of adverbs used to expand verb phrases. Auxiliary verbs such as *have, do, will, was,* and *could* are also increasingly used throughout the kindergarten year.

Passive Sentences

Comprehension of sentences with passive voice requires that children change the way in which they process a sentence. This is because the syntax or structure of passive sentences varies from the more commonly used active voice sentence structure. Passive voice sentences are arranged in object–action–agent order ("The cat was chased by the dog"), which differs from the agent–action–object construction of most speech ("The dog chased the cat"). During the kindergarten year, children typically begin to comprehend passive sentence construction, although they may be able to produce only short sentences using passive voice (Owens, 1988, 2001).

Children appear to use passive sentences for specific linguistic or discursive purposes. Budwig (2001) proposed that children use passive voice to talk about an event where the agent is either not known or relevant or when they want to focus more on the consequences of the specific action than on the agent of the action. For example, when Steven approached his teacher and said, "The truck wheel got broke," he was using passive sentence construction that did not mention who broke the truck's wheel. It may be that Steven wanted to take the focus off who broke the wheel (perhaps he had!), or perhaps he just wanted to focus on the fact that it was broken and appeal to his teacher to fix the truck so he would be able to play with it.

DEVELOPMENT OF MORPHEMIC KNOWLEDGE

As the syntactic complexity of kindergartners' sentences increases, these children also begin to show an increase in their understanding of both inflectional and derivational morphemes. Inflectional morphemes are used to indicate verb tense, plurality, and possession. Derivational morphemes are used to show comparison and to change the grammatical category of a word (such as from verb to noun, as in *teach* to *teacher*). Throughout the kindergarten year, morphemic knowledge increases as children become more aware of morphemes in oral language.

Verb Tenses

Kindergartners continue to develop their awareness of how to show verb tense by using morphemes. With regular verbs, *-ed* is added to the word, as in *wanted* and *jumped*. More irregular verbs are mastered, such as *went, gone,* and *caught* (Allen & Marotz, 2007); however, kindergartners may still overgeneralize (e.g., *gived, singed*).

Comparatives and Superlatives

Increasing morphemic knowledge is evident in kindergartners' use of comparatives and superlatives. Kindergarten-age children appear to be aware that there are two ways of making comparatives and superlatives. One way is to add *-er* and *-est* to the root word; another way is to use *more* or *most* in front of the root word. Sometimes, it appears that children are trying out several hypotheses as to how comparatives and superlatives are formed. For example, a kindergartner might use both forms of making comparatives, as in "even more dirtier."

Noun Suffix *-er*

By age 5, most children have receptive and productive knowledge of the noun suffix *-er* (Owens, 1988, 2001). Children know that by adding this suffix to a verb, they can make the name for the person who does the verb action, as in *teach–teacher, bat–batter,* and *catch–catcher*. They may also create their own words. For example, upon noticing that a toy was broken, Sean told a classmate, "this needs to go to the *fixer-upper*."

DEVELOPMENT OF PRAGMATIC KNOWLEDGE

Along with continuing to develop knowledge of the phonological, semantic, syntactic, and morphemic aspects of language, kindergarten-age children are also continuing to acquire knowledge of how language is used differently in different settings.

Pragmatic Knowledge of Oral Language

In many respects, pragmatic knowledge will determine a child's competence in communicating and in participating in various social situations. Kindergartners use language for a wide variety of purposes. They use language to tell stories, direct peers, express pride, role-play, engage others as a resource for help or information, and gain and hold others' attention (Owens, 1988, 2001). Language may also be used indirectly to request help or regulate another's behavior. Teachers can expect to see differences between kindergarten-age children in their awareness and use of pragmatic knowledge for oral and written language. Children's pragmatic knowledge of language is influenced by not only the variety of social settings they experience but also the frequency of those opportunities and their interactions as listeners and speakers.

Varied contexts for oral language. The various social settings that children encounter during their kindergarten year can enhance acquisition of pragmatic knowledge. Children can learn how to respond during verbal interactions with their teachers and other school staff, such as the principal, assistant principal, janitors, secretaries, older children, teachers' aides, and guest speakers. Pragmatic knowledge involves not only knowing when one can speak and to whom but also the appropriate topics of conversation and cultural expectations for initiating, maintaining, and ending conversations.

Increasing conversational skills. During the kindergarten year, children's conversational skills continue to develop. Kindergartners gradually begin to consider and respond to the listener's perspective and to maintain a topic of conversation. Evidence of this growth is often seen in the conversations that occur during group story sharing. Early in the kindergarten year, children's comments about the story topic may appear "off task" or unrelated to the story; however, later on in the year, with supportive scaffolding from their teachers, children are able to participate in a shared conversation about the story topic or story events.

Informal conversations among children provide evidence that children are using language for different purposes. In fact, peer interactions may indicate pragmatic knowledge of language that is not evident in child–teacher interactions. For example, while peer interactions may involve nurturing, negotiating, persuading, arguing, and questioning, a child's speech with his teacher would not be likely to include these forms of language use (Cazden, 1988, in Fassler, 2003). Children who are English language learners may be able to use English for a variety of purposes in informal contexts with peers although they are not yet able to take an active part in group conversations and discussions.

Pragmatic Knowledge of Written Language

Kindergartners' emergent literacy behaviors indicate a growing awareness of the pragmatic aspect of written language. Kindergarten children can identify a wide range of functions for writing, including using writing to remember something,

Informal conversations among children provide evidence that children are using language for different purposes.

to communicate with others, to learn, and to express one's own ideas and stories (Freeman & Sanders, 1989).

Telling and dictating stories.   Kindergarten children's pragmatic knowledge of written language is evident in the different ways they use language when telling a story and when they are dictating a story for someone (usually an adult) to write down. In Sulzby's (1982) study of kindergarten children's told and dictated stories, she noted that the told stories were generally characterized by a conversational tone and voice-continuant intonation between sentences. In contrast, dictated stories were generally characterized by unit-by-unit (words, phrases, short sentences) phrasing and segmented intonation patterns. Some of the children in the study appeared to be pacing their dictation to match the scribe's writing.

Children's competencies in dictating stories or narratives are another component of pragmatic knowledge. Vivian Paley's (1981) yearlong chronicle of her kindergarten children's stories, *Wally's Stories*, documents the growth of children's language as they dictated original imaginative stories and retold and adapted familiar storybooks. Dictated stories provide children with an opportunity to use language to share personally important events and experiences (Paley, 2004). Experiences in dictating stories have also been associated with children's increasing awareness of the conventions of print, such as directionality, word spacing, punctuation, and letter–sound connections (Cooper, 2005). When story dictation is followed by experiences in dramatizing the story, children have opportunity to explore further how narratives are created, structured, and shared (Cooper, 2005).

Awareness of genre.   When creating their own original stories, children's knowledge of genre is shown by their creation of specific text types, such as fairy tales or alphabet books. When asked to create a fairy tale, many children begin their stories with "Once upon a time"; they may also close the story formally by announcing "The end." The format kindergartners choose when creating their books may indicate their awareness of how language is used. For example, a kindergartner might announce that it was just a picture book and therefore did not need any words.

Kindergarten children's re-creations of familiar storybook texts can also indicate their awareness of the different types of texts and the way in which language is used. Traditional storybooks are characterized by detailed descriptions, varied syntax, fully developed stories, and content-rich illustrations. In contrast, beginning reader texts are likely to have reduced vocabulary, simple syntax with repeated sentence patterns, limited story plots, and basic illustrations.

Through repeated opportunities to listen to these two types of text being read, kindergarten children may indicate their awareness of the structural characteristics of the two types of texts in their re-creations of the story (Otto, 1993). For example, compare the ways in which Misty used language in re-creating *Harry the Dirty Dog* (Zion, 1956), a traditional storybook, and *Stop!* (Crowley, 1982), a beginning reader text. Misty's re-creation of the two story texts shows that she has a strong awareness of the characteristics of the two texts. *Stop!* (Figure 8.2) is characterized by repetition and simple sentence structure. *Harry the Dirty Dog* (Figure 8.3) is characterized by more complex syntax and no repetitive pattern. Although both re-creations are only approximations of the actual texts, Misty's competency in reproducing texts with similar characteristics to the originals indicates her awareness of how language is used differently in these two storybooks.

FIGURE 8.2
Misty's Re-Creation of *Stop!*

Stop, said the man, but it kept going on.
Stop, said the boy, but it kept going on.
Stop, said the dog, but it kept going on.
Stop, said the postman. It kept going on.
Stop, said the policeman. It kept going on.
Stop, said the boy, but it just went on.
All milk come, fall out. The cats are happy.

FIGURE 8.3

Misty's Re-Creation of *Harry the Dirty Dog*.

He heard the water running so he took the brush, ran downstairs and hid it in the backyard. And run away from house, his house. He got all dirty, he got even more dirtier. He played catch with the other dogs. He got more dirty. He turned into a dog with black, he turned into white spots in with black body. He was hungry so he went home. They said, All the family looked out the window. There's a strange dog out there. He did everything to make them see that it's dirty dog. He did his tricks, but it never worked. He even put his, then, he even singed. He even put the flower on his nose. Wait a minute, he said. He ran up the stairs, the family was way a-hind him. Give me a bath, he washed as they, the father said, why don't you and your brother give him a bath? So the kids washed. Dad, Mom! In here right now! So he didn't want any more baths so he hid the thing under his pillow.

Children's memory for text and their expectations for the type of text associated with specific storybooks are aspects of pragmatic knowledge, which may become evident during the kindergarten year. This is most likely to occur in classrooms where children have numerous opportunities to interact with a wide range of books. Kindergarten-age children who experience a wide range of activities related to functional literacy will acquire specific pragmatic knowledge of how oral and written language are used differently in those varied settings.

Awareness of written conventions.   Throughout the kindergarten year, children become more aware of the way in which written language is formed, such as using punctuation, capitalization, and word spacing. For example, when asked if she could write, Jessi, a 5-year-old, confidently replied, "Yes." She then proceeded to print her name and explained, "I have to start my name with a capital letter. The rest are small letters." Jessi's awareness of letters and how to write her name was evident. In addition, her comments about the way she was writing her name, distinguishing between uppercase letters and lowercase letters, provided evidence of her developing meta-linguistic knowledge. Jessi's responses are typical of children who have experienced home and preschool environments that have language and literacy-rich interactions.

OBSERVING KINDERGARTNERS' LANGUAGE COMPETENCIES

As a kindergarten teacher, you can expect that when you meet your students in the beginning of the school year, they will represent a wide range of developmental levels and language competencies. While you will see some students exhibiting the language behaviors described earlier in this chapter, you will also see some students who do not show the same language competencies. For some children, kindergarten is the first experience they will have in a group instructional setting. Other children may have attended a day care or preschool for one or more years. The language competencies that children bring with them to your classroom will have been influenced by the children's home, community, and school environments during their early years.

As a kindergarten teacher, you will need to create a language-rich curriculum that will enhance each child's language development. One of the first steps you will take in creating this language-rich curriculum is to observe and document the language competencies of the children in your room. When you are aware of your children's language competencies, you can better plan and implement learning activities that further enhance their language development. Children's language development is integral to their learning and interactions with others. Your observations will also serve as a basis for suggesting specific ways parents and family members can enhance children's language development at home.

As a kindergarten teacher, you will also need to create and implement a curriculum that supports children's development in the areas identified in national and state standards for the language arts. For example, 51 states and U.S. territories have adopted the standards articulated in the Common Core State Standards Initiative (http://www.corestandards.org/the-standards/english-languagearts; http://www .nga.org/cms/home/news-room/news-releases). Throughout these states and territories, schools are expecting teachers to be accountable for addressing the standards through their instructional activities and assessments.

Key Areas to Observe

Observations of children's language competencies in four key areas will provide you with important information about your kindergartners' language development: (1) oral language: listening and speaking; (2) phonological awareness; (3) written language competencies; and (4) metalinguistic knowledge. A class-formatted checklist for each of these areas is provided in this chapter for your use (see Figures 8.4–8.7). Each checklist focuses on key behaviors and knowledges that represent the five aspects of language knowledge. These key behaviors and knowledges are also reflective of research cited earlier in this text that documents the connections between children's language development, literacy development, and school achievement. A brief overview of each checklist follows.

Oral language: Listening and speaking.   Children's listening and speaking competencies will influence the way they will interact with you as their teacher and with their peers. For example, does the child establish eye contact and engage in a turn-taking conversation with you as well as with other children? Does the child speak clearly? Does the child listen attentively at group time?

Phonological awareness.   Children's awareness of the specific sounds in words, sound similarities and differences, and how sounds can be manipulated represent important knowledge and competencies that are related to beginning decoding and

FIGURE 8.4

Observing Kindergartner's Listening and Speaking Competencies

	Children's names											
Does child												
Establish eye contact with speaker?												
Speak clearly and coherently?												
Respond appropriately to 1–2 step oral directions?												
Listen attentively at group story time?												
Participate by commenting or asking questions during group story time?												
Respond to teacher's questions about story content?												
Remember story content when books are shared repeatedly?												
Orally participate in finger play or action song during group time?												
Participate in conversations with teacher?												
Participate in conversations with peers?												

Symbol code: F = frequently, S = seldom, N = not observed

Reprinted with permission from: Otto, B. (2008). *Literacy development in early childhood.* Upper Saddle River, NJ: Pearson Merrill Prentice Hall, p. 178.

encoding of written language. For example, does the child orally identify rhyming words? When given a specific word, such as "ball," is the child able to separate out the beginning sound for that word?

Written language competencies.   While children's phonological awareness is related to their attempts in using written language to create stories and other writing, their understanding of the ways in which print functions in different settings and their early reading or reading-like behaviors represent further language knowledge and competencies related to school success. For example, does the child identify by

FIGURE 8.5

Observing Kindergartners' Phonological Awareness

	Children's names																								
Does child																									
Orally identify rhyming words?																									
Orally identify initial sounds in words?																									
Orally identify the ending sounds in words?																									
Identify two or more words that have the same initial sound (i.e. alliteration)?																									
Associate individual letters with specific sounds?																									
Use phonemic spelling when writing?																									

Symbol code: F = frequently, S = seldom, N = not observed

Reprinted with permission from: Otto, B. (2008). *Literacy development in early childhood.* Upper Saddle River, NJ: Pearson Merrill Prentice Hall, p. 187.

name individual letters of the alphabet? Does the child notice environmental print and attempt to read it? Does the child attempt to emergently "read" a familiar storybook?

Metalinguistic knowledge. Children's metalinguistic knowledge is related to their comprehension of instructional activities in the kindergarten year. Teacher-directed activities in kindergarten increasingly focus on specific language concepts, such as *word, sentence, beginning sound, rhyme, ending sound, letter, uppercase letter, lowercase letter, vowel, consonant,* as well as book parts, such as *title, page, author, illustrator.* By observing

FIGURE 8.6

Observing Kindergartner's Written Language Competencies

	Children's names																						
Does child																							
Seek out opportunities to interact with books independently?																							
Seek out opportunities to use drawing and writing independently?																							
Incorporate literacy-related events into creative drama?																							
Make comments while engaged in drawing/ writing about the content or purpose of his/her activity?																							
Dictate story or event sequence about personal experiences?																							
Use invented spelling or transitional spelling when writing																							
Understand that print communicates meaning?																							
Identify by name individual letters of the alphabet?																							
Attempt to track print when emergently reading a familiar storybook or own writing?																							
Write his/her name?																							
Write other known words? (e.g. names of family members, friends, or pets)																							
Write individual letters when dictated?																							

Symbol code: F = frequently, S = seldom, N = not observed

Reprinted with permission from: Otto, B. (2008). *Literacy development in early childhood*. Upper Saddle River, NJ: Pearson Merrill Prentice Hall, pgs. 180, 182, 184.

FIGURE 8.7

Observing Kindergartners' Metalinguistic Knowledge

	Children's names																						
Does child																							
Distinguish the front cover, back cover, and book title?																							
Distinguish between letters and words?																							
Indicate that print proceeds from left to right and top to bottom on each page?																							
Distinguish between author and illustrator roles?																							
Reflect verbally on reading and/or writing process?																							

Symbol code: F = frequently, S = seldom, N = not observed

Reprinted with permission from: Otto, B. (2008). *Literacy development in early childhood*. Upper Saddle River, NJ: Pearson Merrill Prentice Hall, p. 186.

children's beginning awareness of metalinguistic concepts early in the kindergarten year, you can better plan and implement your literacy curriculum. For example, does the child distinguish between letters and words? Does the child distinguish between author and illustrator roles?

Through the use of these or similar checklists, you can better understand how to plan and implement instruction that will further enhance kindergartners' language development in each of the five areas of language knowledge.

SUMMARY

Kindergarten children continue to refine and expand their current knowledge of each of the aspects of language in both receptive and expressive modes. Kindergartners are easily understood by most adults; however, a range of phonemic production is still present among children this age. Children's comments when creating their own stories may indicate their awareness of the writing process and their expectations for using print. Children's use of prephonemic, phonemic, transitional, and conventional spelling indicates their developing phonological knowledge.

Acquisition of semantic knowledge during the kindergarten year includes learning new vocabulary and the continued development of increasingly complex schemata. Kindergartners use more complex noun and verb structures and understand a wider range of syntactic structures than they can produce. Increases in kindergartners' morphemic knowledge are evident in their use of inflectional morphemes to indicate verb tense, possession, and comparatives. Kindergarten children's pragmatic knowledge of oral and written language is influenced by the social settings and school interactions they experience.

❋ ❋ ❋   CHAPTER REVIEW

1. Key terms to review:

   prephonemic spelling

   phonemic spelling

   early phonemic spelling

   letter-name spelling

   transitional spelling

   digraph

   ostensive naming

   unreferenced pronoun

2. What sounds have 5-year-olds not yet mastered?
3. What language knowledge is indicated by invented spelling?
4. Describe the types of invented spelling that kindergarten-age children may use.

❋ ❋ ❋   CHAPTER EXTENSION ACTIVITIES

Observation

Observe children's conversations in a kindergarten room during independent or learning center time. Identify the number of children engaged in each conversation. Record the length of the conversation and the number of turns in each conversation.

Research

Audiotape a kindergarten child's pretend storybook reading. Transcribe the tape. Analyze the child's language for syntactic and morphemic knowledge.

CHAPTER 9

ENHANCING THE LANGUAGE DEVELOPMENT OF KINDERGARTNERS

Learning Outcomes

After reading this chapter you should be able to

- Identify five curricular goals for kindergarten related to language development

- Describe how teachers can use a variety of questioning strategies to enhance language development in kindergarten

- Describe how a message/writing center can be implemented to enhance kindergartners' oral and written language

- Describe how group storybook time can be implemented to enhance kindergartners' oral and written language

- Describe the role of word study activities in enhancing children's metalinguistic knowledge and phonological knowledge

- Explain how routine activities can be implemented to continue to enhance children's language competencies

During the first two weeks of kindergarten, Ms. Sanchez observed her children's verbal and nonverbal responses during group story time. She noted that some children were very attentive and eagerly participated in discussing the shared stories, often asking questions related to the story events. Other children appeared to be easily distracted, were inattentive, and rarely made any comments or asked questions about the stories.

Based on these observations and her knowledge that shared storybook time provides important experiences in listening comprehension and verbal expression, Ms. Sanchez began to plan additional small group story times for book read-alouds for the children who were inattentive in the larger group as a way of engaging them more actively. When reading aloud in this small group setting, she closely monitored children's attention and listening comprehension. Ms. Sanchez also chose books to share that had simpler vocabulary and story lines. In the book corner, she established a "listening post" and supplied it with audiotapes and copies of books read during both the small group and large group story times. In both group story time settings, Ms. Sanchez began to use hand puppets to encourage children's participation in retelling stories shared during read-alouds. As the year progressed, Ms. Sanchez used a series of observational checklists to document children's language knowledge and competencies.

In the above example, Ms. Sanchez engaged in observational assessment of her kindergartner's language knowledge and competencies beginning early in the school year. Through her use of observational checklists she was able to develop a clear understanding of each child's language development and what language activities would be appropriate for each child.

Kindergarten teachers are faced with the challenge of providing a developmentally appropriate curriculum while addressing state language arts standards and accountability concerns (Lamme, Fu, Johnson, & Savage, 2002). This chapter begins with an overview of kindergarten curricula and interaction strategies. Subsequent sections describe examples of exploratory activities, teacher-guided activities, and routine activities that will enhance language development.

OVERVIEW OF KINDERGARTEN CURRICULA

Kindergarten: A Time of Transition

The kindergarten year marks a transition from home to school for most children. Even for children who have attended preschool or were in day care during the preschool years, kindergarten is often their first experience in a larger educational system. In addition to this transition to a larger school environment, in many school districts there is also a transition to a more formal, academic curriculum. For example, when compared with a typical preschool setting, in kindergarten there less time provided for free play as well as gross motor and outdoor play, while the time designated for group time and seatwork is increased (Dickinson, 2001). Such changes in children's social and learning environments are accompanied by changes in the way children are expected to communicate and the opportunities that occur for their continued language development.

Within the kindergarten environment there are also a variety of settings. The kindergarten may be a half-day or full-day program. Many states do not require kindergarten attendance, so not all children will attend kindergarten. Kindergartens also vary with respect to the inclusion of children with special needs.

Kindergarten Curriculum

The relation of the kindergarten curriculum to the elementary grade curriculum may vary from school to school. In some settings, the kindergarten curriculum emphasizes a strong hands-on, independent activity approach that is not closely aligned with the curriculum in the primary grades (grades 1–3). In other settings, the curriculum in kindergarten has a more academic approach, with blocks of time for seatwork involving paper-and-pencil activities and beginning reading instruction that are considered part of a formal reading and language arts curricula for grades K–3 (DeVault, 2003). The more academic approach to kindergarten curriculum appears to be driven by accountability concerns that state standards for student achievement are met beginning with the kindergarten year. Early childhood educators who believe that the academic approach is not developmentally sound argue that state standards can be met through developmentally appropriate curriculum as well.

This chapter's perspective on kindergarten curriculum focuses on "developmentally appropriate curriculum." This means that the curriculum in kindergarten is determined by the developmental levels of the children unique to each kindergarten classroom. Some kindergarten children may come to school having had no preschool experience, and others may have had 2 years of preschool. Due to these differences, there is likely to be a wide range in children's developmental levels. Some children may be ready for more direct instruction involving paper-and-pencil and print-based activities; others will not be able to benefit from this type of instruction until later in the kindergarten year. It is therefore important to have a developmentally appropriate curriculum so that individual children's needs are met through a variety of learning opportunities.

Providing a balance of whole group, small group, and independent and teacher-directed activities is important at the kindergarten level. While kindergartners' increased attention spans and listening vocabularies make it possible for them to participate more in group settings, it is still important to limit large group activities to a small part of the total schedule. Kindergarten teachers can determine the appropriateness of group size and activity length by trying out different group sizes with the different developmental levels of students present in the classroom.

The most successful kindergarten curricula provide a gradual transition from informal learning activities to learning activities involving direct instruction in whole group settings that characterize the primary grades. In the fall term of kindergarten, the learning activities resemble the informal learning activities of preschool settings. Gradually throughout the school year and in consideration of children's developmental needs, the learning activities may become more formal, involving direct instruction and paper-and-pencil activities. With this transition in mind, the learning activities described here include both informal and exploratory activities as well as teacher-guided learning activities. Teachers can enhance children's language development during the kindergarten year by providing a curriculum that is rich in opportunities for using and exploring language in both types of learning activities.

The opportunity to work together with manipulatives encourages children's conversational competencies.

Language-Related Curricular Goals

Curricular goals provide direction to teachers in selecting and implementing learning activities that are appropriate for children's levels of development. Specific goals for enhancing language development in kindergarten incorporate the five aspects of language knowledge and both oral and written language modes (see Figure 9.1). In addition, these goals can be used to provide a wide variety of learning activities that incorporate independent, exploratory experiences as well as teacher-directed activities (Otto, 1991).

FIGURE 9.1
Language Goals for Kindergarten

1. Increase children's ability to communicate orally in instructional and conversational settings.
2. Encourage an awareness of the purposes of reading and writing.
3. Increase vocabulary through conceptual development.
4. Increase listening comprehension.
5. Increase children's awareness of the process of communicating by using written language.

GUIDELINES FOR TEACHERS' INTERACTIONS WITH KINDERGARTNERS

In addition to providing a developmentally appropriate curriculum, kindergarten teachers should also develop oral language environments in which teachers' talk nourishes and supports language development. Teachers' classroom talk sets the stage for children's verbal participation and resulting language enhancement. According to Genishi (1992), "almost every activity presents an opportunity for talk when teachers allow it to" (p. 110). A summary of suggested guidelines for teachers' interactions with kindergartners is provided in Figure 9.2.

Use Key Interaction Patterns

Key interaction patterns that can be used strategically by kindergarten teachers include linguistic scaffolding, questioning, verbal mapping, and mediation. By kindergarten age, eye contact–shared reference and communication loop patterns are well established. In addition, the child-directed speech found in interactions with toddlers and preschoolers is less used with kindergartners because of their increased receptive and productive language competencies. While adults may slightly simplify their speech to kindergartners in terms of syntax or vocabulary, child-directed speech at the kindergarten level is much more complex than that addressed to a toddler or young preschooler and does not show the dramatic and varied intonation patterns used with younger children.

Linguistic scaffolding.   Linguistic scaffolding is used by kindergarten teachers to support and expand children's participation in personal conversations and class discussions. Verbal mapping and mediation are used when a teacher demonstrates how to use a learning center or explains a particular concept to kindergarten learners. Questioning has a key role in the oral language and conceptual–cognitive

FIGURE 9.2
Summary of Guidelines for Teachers' Interactions with Kindergartners

- Focus on nourishing and supporting children's language in each of the five aspects of language knowledge.
- Use linguistic scaffolding, verbal mapping, mediation, and questioning during interactions with kindergartners.
- Ask a variety of question types and question levels.
- Encourage children to represent their experiences through different modes of communication: oral language, written language, and art.
- Develop instructional conversation strategies to enhance children's understandings and content knowledge.
- Be an active listener, using follow-up questions based on the child's speech.

environment of kindergarten. Teachers' questioning techniques stimulate and guide children's thinking and their use of language. According to Copple, Sigel, and Saunders (1984), "expertise in the use of inquiry is one of a teacher's most valuable assets. It is difficult to acquire, and its proper exercise demands considerable sensitivity and perceptiveness" (p. 223). Skillful questioning not only motivates intellectual participation and provides direction for children in thinking through complex issues, but it also provides the opportunity for teachers to determine what children know and how they are thinking (Copple et al., 1984).

Use a variety of questioning strategies.   The opportunity to ask questions is essential for kindergartners. Questioning strategies at the kindergarten level incorporate literal and inferential questions along with recognition that some questions are asked for information, recitation, or clarification purposes.

In kindergarten, questioning is increasingly used to discuss more complex and more distant (nonpresent) phenomena. Teachers should use strategies that will "expand the child's ability to think and to represent" (Copple et al., 1984, p. 25). When children are encouraged to represent their concrete experiences through various modes of communication, such as oral language, written language, and art, they have the opportunity to reconstruct the experience mentally, which enhances cognitive and language development. Specific strategies that are effective in expanding children's thinking and representational competencies include asking questions, drawing attention to a puzzling situation such as a contradiction or an inconsistency, and appropriately challenging children to move beyond concrete experiences (Copple et al., 1984).

Foster instructional conversations.   Instructional conversations have a key role in establishing a communicative environment in kindergarten that enhances language development. In classrooms in which instructional conversations are fostered, teachers recognize children as conversational partners who have important thoughts to offer. Teachers plan activities that draw on children's prior knowledge and present new or more complex information, challenging and guiding children's thinking and conceptual development.

Teachers who engage in instructional conversations actively listen to what each child has to say, avoiding the tendency to listen only for "correct answers." While teachers may have a general idea of the questions they will use during a particular activity, the actual formulation and use of ongoing questions is contingent on the ways children respond to previous questions. Teachers who understand that children's responses reflect their thinking processes use this awareness to guide children's thinking and use of language through instructional conversations. Throughout kindergarten, instructional conversations play a key role in enhancing language development.

Verbal mapping and mediation.   Verbal mapping and mediation are interaction patterns that are often combined when interacting with kindergartners. For example, when demonstrating how to plant a bean seed in a paper cup, the teacher would use verbal mapping to describe exactly what is happening and how the seed is planted. The specific language that the teacher uses to simplify the process of planting the seed is an example of mediation.

Guidelines for Kindergarten Teachers of English Language Learners

Although your school may have special programs for English language learners, children who are learning English as a second language may be placed in your kindergarten classroom for part of the school day. If your school does not have a separate resource room or program for English language learners, you will have these students "immersed" in your regular kindergarten classroom.

In addition to using the interaction patterns and strategies just discussed, you will find the following suggested guidelines useful when interacting with kindergartners who are English language learners (Cary, 2000; Fassler, 2003; Mason & Galloway, 2012):

1. *Provide time and opportunities for meaningful talk.* Encourage children to talk with each other during the informal, exploratory activities in your classroom, such as during learning center activities, in the writing center, in the book center, and during snack time. This provides opportunity for children to use language to develop social relationships and to share their ideas and experiences with each other.

2. *Take time for one-on-one conversations with children during exploratory activity time.* In doing this, you can talk with children about their current activity and provide the linguistic scaffolding needed to support their oral communication. This also allows you to become better acquainted with each child and learn about their interests and experiences.

3. *Provide a welcoming environment where children can "try out" communicating in English.* Because children who are learning another language experience a "silent period" during which time their listening comprehension in their new language develops, it is important to provide a learning environment where they can develop their listening comprehension and begin to communicate in English using simple words and phrases. This means that you monitor their listening comprehension by closely observing their nonverbal behavior (e.g., eye contact, facial expression, gestures). If you sense that they want to respond to a question or make a comment, support their efforts to speak by providing ample wait time and active listening.

4. *Acknowledge and build upon the children's prior knowledge and experiences.* For example, if you find that one of your English language learners is involved in playing soccer or another sport, provide opportunities for that child to talk about his experiences. Also encourage him to write and illustrate a story about a recent game. Providing books in the book center that are related to children's sports or other activities will also build on their prior knowledge and experiences.

5. *Provide content-rich, engaging activities.* Direct experiences are important for concept development and vocabulary growth. By providing activities that incorporate direct experiences and hands-on activities, you will be creating an authentic context for children's learning. Wherever possible, use real artifacts, objects, and props to accompany these learning activities. For example, after reading *Popcorn* (Moran & Everitt, 2003) or *Popcorn Book* (de Paola, 1989), take time to show children how to make popcorn in your classroom. First show children the individual kernels (and an ear of corn, if possible) while talking about the way the kernels expand when heated and then burst open. Then use a popcorn maker that allows children to actually see the corn popping. You will want to provide opportunity for children to taste the popped corn as well.

LANGUAGE-ENHANCING ACTIVITIES THROUGHOUT KINDERGARTEN

Although the activities described in this section may be similar to those in a preschool classroom, a difference occurs in the way the children engage in those activities. Because kindergarten children are at a higher level of cognitive, social, and emotional maturity than when they were in preschool, and because their language knowledge is more developed, their interaction in those activities is more focused and complex. Kindergarten teachers who are sensitive to the ways in which children's language is developing can plan and implement learning activities that enhance children's language development. In the following sections, examples of three types of learning activities will be described: exploratory activities, teacher-guided activities, and routine activities.

EXPLORATORY ACTIVITIES

Exploratory activities provide opportunity for kindergartners to engage in informal learning at their own pace and motivation. These activities are generally open-ended and experiential. Exploratory activities in a kindergarten classroom include learning center activities and outdoor activities.

Learning Center Activities

Exploratory activities in learning centers need a generous time allotment to provide opportunities for children to fully engage in the exploration. Center activities at the kindergarten level may accommodate more than one child because most children can successfully interact with one to two other children. The learning centers should be set up to encourage conversation. You will want to periodically visit the various centers to verbally and nonverbally model ways to interact with materials. Avoid dominating or explicitly narrowing the ways in which children can interact with materials.

Learning centers at the kindergarten level can involve more problem-solving opportunities than at the preschool level. The class schedule should set aside time for children to share any outcomes of their center activities with the classroom. They could, for example, share a story they wrote or illustrated, share a piece of artwork, or show their block construction. Learning center activities at the kindergarten level may include a drawing/writing center, a book center, a science/math center, a computer center, and a drama corner.

Message center: Drawing and writing. Kindergarten children are active symbol makers (Dyson, 1990a). They communicate through both art and writing, symbolically representing their ideas and experiences (Behymer, 2003; Soundy, Guha, & Qiu, 2007). Thus, the focus of this center is on symbolic communication through both art and writing. By naming this center "the Message Center," children will know that the focus is on communicating their ideas, thoughts, and experiences with others through both drawing and writing. Teachers should expect that kindergartners will not only use a variety of illustration techniques but will also use a variety of forms of emergent writing, from scribble to letter strings to varied degrees of phonemic spelling. The forms used may vary from day to day or may be mixed in the same instance of writing (Casbergue, 1998; Sulzby, Teale, & Kamberelis, 1989). Hayes (1990) and Raines and Canady (1990) describe kindergarten classrooms where children are encouraged to engage in a wide range of writing-related activities throughout the curriculum for a variety of purposes. For example, in these classrooms, children are encouraged to use writing in their dramatic play, in signing their names to stories and artwork, and in signing up for activities or centers. In these settings, children acquire a greater awareness of the pragmatic or functional aspects of both oral and written language.

Materials and organization. Kindergarten message centers should be well stocked with a variety of writing implements, such as crayons, felt-tip washable markers, pencils, and pens, along with a variety of paper, including both lined and unlined and different shapes and colors. Providing a stapler and transparent tape encourages children to make books. Other ways of writing are encouraged when the writing center contains a typewriter, a chalkboard or slate and chalk, a computer, magnetic letters and a display board, or a combination of these.

In addition to having appropriate materials, kindergarten writing centers need to be organized so that children have opportunities to choose their own topic; ample time to create their illustrations, stories, or messages; and the chance to share what they created with their classmates, teachers, and families (Merenda, 1989).

Strategies. When monitoring a drawing/writing center, a kindergarten teacher should expect to see a range of pragmatic uses of writing that reflect children's cultural and community experiences (Bloome, Champion, Katz, Morton, & Muldrow, 2001; Dyson, 1992). Because a drawing/writing center is focused on the exploration of communication through symbols, children's attempts should be validated and encouraged by the teacher rather than "corrected."

Children should be encouraged to talk with each other while they are at the message center (Dyson, 1990b; Lamme et al., 2002; Throne, 1988). As they draw and write, children may engage in sociodramatic dialogue about the stories they are creating. This "talk" is important because it enhances the children's ability to manipulate and refine language and encourages them to use metalinguistic knowledge when they talk about their stories in progress. However, their final product may not clearly indicate the richness of their stories nor the discrete events that were discussed during the creation of their stories.

Kindergartners may also engage in "self-talk." Dyson (1989) described a kindergartner, Regina, who used self-talk to label the figures she had drawn as well as describe their characteristics, actions, and future events. By observing children's speech to self and others in a drawing/writing center, a teacher can better understand the contexts of children's early symbolic communication.

Giving children an opportunity to dictate stories individually in a drawing/writing center to an adult who serves as the scribe also enhances their development of language knowledge. In dictating a story, children observe the connections between speech and print as they observe the scribe (teacher's aide, teacher, or parent volunteer) writing down what they have dictated. When children dictate stories, they use vocabulary and syntactic structures they have mastered. Thus, children will be better able to reread their own dictated story because the story is based on their own language.

Book center. In preparing your book center, you will want to provide a wide variety of fiction and nonfiction (informational) books. Children's magazines should also be provided (Lesiak, 2000). At the kindergarten level, it is important to have wordless picture books as well as illustrated books with printed text. Compared to the books used at the preschool level, books selected for a kindergarten book center should have a more complex story plot and more text on each page. Supportive, complementary illustrations that enhance children's comprehension of the story or nonfiction content are still essential. Big books should also be provided because their format draws children's attention to print. Classroom big books created during circle time should also be featured in the book center, providing children with opportunities to enjoy the books individually. A few "easy reader" chapter books can be included for kindergartners who are already reading conventionally.

Books should be organized so that children have easy access. Many of the books should be stories the teacher has read at group story time. This familiarity will support children's attempts to recreate the stories for themselves independently (Martinez & Teale, 1988). A tape/CD player, headphones, and tapes/CDs of familiar storybook readings can also be included in the book center, along with copies of the book. Classroom read-alouds can be audiotaped and placed in this area for repeated listening. Audiotapes of story readings provide opportunities for children to listen to fluent reading and to become more aware of speech–print connections.

Books with enlarged print encourage children to focus on written language.

Science/math center. A science/math center involves hands-on exploration of concepts, with the introduction of related vocabulary. This center is most effective when it is related to concepts introduced at story time through nonfiction or fiction books. For example, if you read *Is This a House for Hermit Crab?* (McDonald, 1990) during group story time, then in the math/science center, you could set up an aquarium with a hermit crab. Talk with your kindergartners about ways to care for the crab. Then as children visit the center, have them write or draw their observations in a class journal.

Center activities using manipulatives that encourage children to collaborate can also be provided. For example, "In the Bag" encourages children to carefully observe and use language to describe an object. In this activity, a familiar object is placed in a paper bag. One child gives clues, and the other child guesses what is in the bag. The center is also set up with a poster that gives simple directions and shows a picture of the items that could possibly appear in the paper bag.

Computer center. A center equipped with a computer, appropriate software, and two or three child-sized chairs can be another tool for enhancing children's cognitive and language development. Encouraging children to work on computer software in pairs or threes provides opportunity to further develop social interaction skills as well as language competencies (Clements & Sarama, 2003). Kindergartners can also be encouraged to talk about their computer activities during group time, explaining and sharing what they have done or learned (Morrison, 2004). In selecting software and online resources to use in kindergarten, the major guideline to observe is to be sure that the program is developmentally appropriate and engaging. Interactive programs, such as that found in online storybooks, increase children's engagement and active learning (Lacina & Mathews, 2012).

Drama corner. In the drama corner, children use language in many different ways, thus enhancing their pragmatic knowledge of language. In dramatic play, language is used to plan, develop, and maintain interactions. The benefits of these enriched dramatic activities include an increase in vocabulary, syntactic complexity, and the total number of words used in conversation turns (Levy, Wolfgang, & Koorland, 1992). Dramatic play opportunities have been found to encourage greater linguistic elaboration through the use of explicit reference and adjectives or modifiers. Dramatic play also has been associated with expanding children's metalinguistic awareness as they negotiate with each other during dramatic play, deciding who should say what and how and when it should be said (Galda & Pellegrini, 1990). When puppets are included in the drama corner, children are encouraged to reenact favorite stories or to create their own original stories.

Kindergarten children will participate in the drama corner in a more elaborate way linguistically than they did at the preschool level. In dramatic play, children create, negotiate, and assume imaginary roles in imaginary settings through using language (Galda & Pellegrini, 1990; Owocki, 2001). They use words to match the identity of the roles assumed. For example, children assuming the roles of a mail carrier and postal clerk may no longer be addressed by their real names but by pretend names or titles of their assumed roles. Through language, the nature of objects is also changed; for example, a book bag becomes a mail pouch, and a rubber stamp becomes a postmark.

Theme-related drama (such as a post office, restaurant, or grocery store) provides opportunities for children to practice and master related vocabulary and supporting concepts. Literacy-related props can be added to themed dramatic play centers to encourage children to incorporate reading- and writing-related activities into their dramatic play. For example, a construction site might include paper and rulers for making blueprints, as well as road signs, warning signs, and trade magazines. (See Owocki, 2001, for extensive descriptions of literacy-enriched play centers.)

Dramatic activities will enhance language development more when children have some shared background information about the setting; when they have time, space, and props needed; and when an adult facilitates expanding their dramatic play (Levy et al., 1992). At the beginning of the kindergarten year, themed dramatic play centers should center on the social and cultural settings that represent the experiences of the children in the classroom. As the year progresses, and the class engages in group experiences through field trips, guest speakers, and shared literature, dramatic play centers can incorporate new themes that provide opportunity to enact their understandings through play. Through careful planning of the dramatic play centers, a teacher can provide important opportunities for further language development.

When puppets are included in the drama corner, children are encouraged to reenact favorite stories or create their own original stories.

Children's dramatic play activities can also be enhanced by providing direct (field trips) or vicarious (storybook or nonfiction) experiences in which children will see people in various roles. These experiences help children understand the social interaction and the language used in the specific settings that would foster more elaborate sociodramatic play.

While a classroom teacher carefully prepares a themed drama corner by providing the dramatic materials, her role is not to direct children's use of the materials or the roles they assume. Galda and Pellegrini (1990) reported that the presence of adult(s) in a dramatic play area may inhibit children's creativity and their use of language. Copple et al. (1984) offered these guidelines for teachers to follow when deciding whether to become involved in children's dramatic play:

1. Teachers should enter a child's dramatic play only when the child's play will not be disrupted.

2. When a child appears to need assistance to either enter the play or to continue in a particular role, a teacher may enter the play, giving suggestions for actions or speech.

3. If the play appears to be limited or restricted in terms of content, a teacher may enter the play, adding some information or ideas.

Diversity and dramatic play. Teachers may notice differences among children who come to kindergarten with diverse cultural and economic experiences. Smilansky and Shefatya (1990) documented instances in which differences were noted in how language was used in dramatic play between children from varied socioeconomic groups. While both the higher and lower socioeconomic status (SES) children used speech for management and role enactment, there was a difference in how they used speech for dialogue. The lower SES children did not use speech for the exchange of verbal make-believe, whereas the higher SES children "kept up a constant flow of chatter related to the roles being enacted" (p. 59). It is important to keep in mind that such differences do not reflect deficiencies, but instead reflect the differences in how language is used in varied contexts as well as children's prior experiences.

Outdoor Activities

Kindergarten children need opportunities for vigorous exercise to enhance their physical development; however, outdoor activities also provide opportunities for language development. Receptive and expressive language are encouraged in simple games with a few rules as well as in rules for using equipment and taking turns. Outdoor play offers opportunities for extended conversations between children and for teachers to talk with individual children. Encouraging children to observe weather conditions such as cloud formations and wind currents, as well as trees, flowers, birds, and other elements in natural surroundings, also helps children use language to describe what they observe. Taking a walk around the block with your kindergartners will also provide opportunities for observations and extended conversations.

TEACHER-GUIDED ACTIVITIES

Teacher-guided activities in kindergarten may involve whole-class or small group participation. In these activities, the teacher organizes and directs children's participation, engaging in instructional conversations with the children. The sections that follow will describe five types of teacher-guided activities that enhance children's language development: show-and-tell, storybook time, dictated and interactive writing, calendar time, and word study activities.

Show-and-Tell

At the kindergarten level, children's participation in the show-and-tell activity is expected to be longer and more elaborate than at the preschool level. Sometimes the oral sharing focuses on an object or it may simply be an oral narrative describing an experience or event.

"Y'All Know What?" is a form of sharing described by Pellegrini and Galda (1998), which may be more familiar to some young children than the show-and-tell label. In their classroom research, "Y'All Know What?" was used as a label for sharing time to encourage children to tell stories about their experiences. It draws on children's experiences in telling stories in home and community settings, where daily events are simply recounted or creatively exaggerated. Pellegrini and Galda described this approach as a way of transitioning children from a familiar speech event to more literate discourse patterns at school.

When planning for show-and-tell activities, you can structure the focus of the show-and-tell by assigning different themes or tasks for each show and tell time (Steen, 2011). For example, one week you might ask children to bring in a favorite book. Another week you might ask them to bring in a favorite stuffed animal. Whatever theme or task you assign, be sure that each child has the resources and family support to complete the assignment. For example, when asking children to bring in a favorite book, tell them they can select a book from the school/classroom library or from home.

During show-and-tell, kindergarten children are able to ask more questions of the presenter than are preschoolers. Another difference between the preschool and kindergarten levels is that kindergarten children typically need less prompting and linguistic scaffolding from the teacher when they present their show-and-tell. To provide more opportunity for discussion, a teacher may decide to schedule only three to five children each day to share, rather than trying to give everyone a turn to present on the same day. Keeping the sharing to only a few children each day encourages all the children to be more attentive and participate in the discussion more actively. Oral sharing or personal narratives may also be used as a basis for putting individual children's stories on paper through dictation and story illustration.

Storybook Time

Benefits.   When teachers read to kindergartners, they provide the children with an opportunity to learn more about language, the communication of meaning, and the varied purposes for reading (Taylor & Vawter, 1978). Frequent storybook reading has also been associated with increased knowledge of written language and of more specific concepts of letter-name knowledge and phonemic awareness (Neuman, 1999; Otto, 1996). If you have children in your classroom who are from home environments where storybook reading is not routine, it is especially critical to include frequent storybook times in your curriculum.

In classrooms where there is a formal literacy program and simple basal readers or primers are used with small groups of children, it is very important that kindergarten children continue to have opportunities to experience literature and trade books that are read aloud and discussed at group time. Compared to a basal reader, the language of "real literature" is more complex, the characters are more developed and realistic, and the story line is more elaborate. In this way, children's receptive knowledge of increasingly complex syntax and vocabulary is enhanced, which provides a foundation for their developing expressive language knowledge.

Strategies. Selecting the appropriate books for the children in your classroom is a key step in planning successful book sharing at group time. At the kindergarten level, stories are longer and more complex than the stories read in preschool classrooms. Books to include at group story time include fiction and nonfiction and should also involve a variety of genres, such as realistic fiction, fantasy (but not scary stories), poetry, fairy tales, and alphabet books. The selection of books to share should represent curricular connections in terms of conceptual knowledge as well as socialization. A curricular theme of "farm life" would include stories and nonfiction about life activities in a rural setting. A curricular theme of "friendships" would include stories that focus on making friendships and learning how to get along with others.

Wordless picture books are also valuable to share with kindergarten children at storybook time. Because wordless books contain no text, the focus of the sharing is on talking about the characters and events illustrated and the sequence of events. When sharing this type of book, it is critical for teachers to focus on the underlying story structure to help children make connections between the events and characters from page to page (Hough, Nurss, & Wood, 1987). Begin by taking the children on a picture walk through the book. Then go back through the book page by page, encouraging children to create an oral story to accompany the illustrations. This engages children in "active story construction" (Crawford & Hade, 2000, p. 8).

It is also beneficial to include books that involve humorous language play along with clear, relevant illustrations. This type of book further enhances and refines children's metalinguistic abilities (Zeece, 1995) because in comprehending a humorous situation, children become aware of the features of language, including multiple meanings, alliteration, rhythm, rhyme, and figurative language. Read-aloud books can also be selected to focus on sound similarities between words and phonemic awareness through texts characterized by rhyme and rhyming patterns, simple alliteration, and tongue twisters (Yopp, 1995). For example, consider the following books, which focus on specific sound patterns: *Tog the Dog* (Hawkins & Hawkins, 1986); *Roar and More* (Kuskin, 1990); *Buzz Said the Bee* (Lewison, 1992); *Moose on the Loose* (Ochs, 1991); *Moses Supposes His Toeses Are Roses* (Patz, 1983); and *Faint Frogs Feeling Feverish and Other Terrifically Tantalizing Tongue Twisters* (Obligado, 1983).

Because children's listening comprehension forms the basis for their later reading comprehension, storybook time is critical. Repeated readings of familiar and favorite books encourage children to develop a memory for story events and predictable language. This provides a basis for participating in the story reading through unison responses as well as participating in the discussion of the story. One way to encourage children's story involvement is to use "participation stories" (Neuman & Roskos, 1993). In this activity, children participate by repeating a refrain of the text, providing sounds of animals or events, or joining in a choral response.

Children who have not had many storybook experiences prior to kindergarten will especially benefit from opportunities for storybook reading individually with the teacher or with only a few children. In this smaller setting, there are more opportunities for asking questions and becoming involved in responding to the story and illustrations.

Kindergarten children may not rely on illustrations to understand the story as much as preschool children do because their vocabulary is more developed. This listening comprehension allows them to comprehend parts of a story without seeing the illustrations constantly. However, storybooks shared with kindergarten children still should have high-quality illustrations that support the story and theme. When kindergarten children attempt to re-create the story independently, they may use the illustrations as a way of recalling specific language of the text.

Big books.   In the kindergarten classroom, enlarged storybooks may be used as part of a formal early reading program. These enlarged books facilitate a focused emphasis on letter–sound connections and word decoding. When using a big book, it should be placed on a tripod book holder or other support to allow the teacher to easily turn the pages and to allow children to see the entire page without obstructions. Because the print is visible to the children, pointing to the words as you read helps children begin to track print. You will probably need to use a stick pointer or light beam pointer to effectively point to the print. When using a big book for the first time, introduce and read it following the general guidelines above for all read-alouds. Then on repeated readings, begin to point to the print as you read.

Effective strategies.   Children's comprehension of a storybook can be enhanced by the use of finger puppets or flannel board characters. Puppets or flannel board characters can be used as the storybook is initially read, or they can be used when reconstructing the story orally, without using the book. Children can participate by using the puppets to re-create characters' roles in speech and action.

Effective storybook reading techniques involve three parts: prereading, reading, and postreading (Lane & Wright, 2007; Mason, Peterman, & Kerr, 1989). Prior to reading a book, the teacher should introduce it to the children by talking about its title and encouraging children to predict what it is about. The teacher should also encourage children to listen with a purpose. While reading the story, the teacher should pause occasionally to ask comprehension questions or to involve children in predicting upcoming events or commenting on what has happened in the story. After the story reading is finished, the story events can be reviewed, and children can be encouraged to make connections between the story events and their own lives. They can also be encouraged to see how specific vocabulary introduced in the storybook is connected to their own schema of related concepts (Gregory & Cahill, 2010).

Story retelling.   Kindergarten story times can be extended by encouraging children to retell the story from looking at the pictures in the book and taking turns re-creating the story. Repeated readings of a story help children develop a memory for story events and dialogue that contributes to the accuracy of story retelling. As a book becomes more familiar, kindergarten children eagerly participate at group time in reconstructing the story line or sequence of events. Story retelling is an important activity because it encourages children to develop an awareness of a story event sequence and enhances their comprehension of the story. Gradually children will be able to retell the story on their own. Copies of favorite storybooks can be placed in the book center along with a tape recorder and blank tapes as a way of encouraging children to retell stories independently or in pairs during center time. Taped retold stories can then be shared at group time (Beatty & Pratt, 2003).

Story reenactment. Children's language competencies are enhanced by opportunities to reenact a familiar story through dramatization. This may take several forms. The teacher may begin by reading the story and having children act out different events nonverbally. Gradually, children's verbal participation can be increased to include unison responses, dialogue segments, or whole conversational interactions. The type of verbal participation that is encouraged is determined by the teacher's awareness of children's knowledge of the story and their language interaction competencies. Story reenactment can also be used with children's dictated stories (Groth & Darling, 2001; Paley, 1981, 1977, 1997).

Story-based writing and drawing. A good way of encouraging children's responses to shared books is to provide opportunity for them to draw or write as a follow-up activity to a read-aloud. For example, Ms. Lyons shared the book *Big Shark's Lost Tooth* (Metzger, 2006) with her kindergartners. The book is about a little shark, Chomper, who lost a tooth and wanted to put it under his pillow so the tooth fairy would come. Because Chomper lived at the bottom of the ocean with his mother, he was not sure the tooth fairy could find him. When Ms. Lyons came to the page where Chomper's mom was secretly writing a letter to the tooth fairy, she stopped reading and asked the children to work with a classmate in drawing or writing their own message to the tooth fairy that would help the tooth fairy find Chomper's home in the ocean. While many of the children drew pictures for the tooth fairy, two groups wrote printed messages along with their pictures. These are presented in Figures 9.3 and 9.4. As you look at these figures, note the phonemic spellings as well as the complex syntax of the sentences. Activities such as this provide opportunity for children to share their understanding of a story through drawing, reading, and writing. As a follow-up to their messages to the tooth fairy, Ms. Lyons finished reading the story to her kindergartners. (Yes, the tooth fairy did find Chomper's home!)

Dictated and Interactive Writing

Dictated writing and interactive writing are two ways children can participate in the writing process within their zones of proximal development. *Dictated writing* provides the most support to an emergent writer because the teacher writes down exactly what the children dictate. In *interactive writing*, the teacher explicitly involves the children in analyzing the sounds in words and in the encoding process (Brotherton & Williams, 2002). This requires that the teacher have a clear awareness

FIGURE 9.3
Kathleen, Christina, and Samantha's Tooth Fairy Story

of the emergent literacy and developmental needs of each child in his or her group. Teaching decisions must be "strategically planned" during interactive writing (McCarrier, Pinnell, & Fountas, 2000, p. 11). Experiences with these two types of writing encourage children to become independent writers as they transition to the primary grades (Bickel, Holsopple, Garcia, Lantz, & Yoder, 1999; Cicalese, 2003).

Dictated writing.   Opportunities to dictate stories encourage children to use their oral language competencies in creating a text. Because children are not constrained by the writing process, their stories have more elaboration and structure than their stories would if they were writing them down themselves. As the children dictate a story, the teacher writes it on chart paper or on the chalkboard. Each child contributes a sentence or thought. The teacher is careful to preserve the sentence structure or dialect of each child. After the story is completed, the teacher reads it back to the students, pointing to each word as it is read. Then the story is read a second time, with the children encouraged to join in unison or by reading their own sentences (Neuman & Roskos, 1993).

FIGURE 9.4
Lily, Mary, and Megan's Tooth Fairy Story

Benefits. Dictated stories provide many opportunities for language growth. Watching their teacher write in response to what they dictate helps children become aware of the connections between speech and print. Children also can watch the writing process, involving the mechanics of writing, such as punctuation and capitalization. Dictated stories also enhance syntactic and semantic knowledge as sentences are formed and specific vocabulary is used. Morphemic awareness is enhanced as teachers use and pronounce specific word endings to indicate verb tense or plurality of nouns. The process of creating a group story draws out children's expressive language. Children see how a narrative is constructed to share with others. The dictated story activity also provides opportunities for joint or unison reading. Repeated readings of the story foster children's memory for text and encourage them to begin to make the speech–print match. Further language opportunities arise when the dictated story is put in book form, laminated, bound, and placed in the reading center for individual enjoyment.

Picture-based and experience-based dictations. Dictation experiences can be used in two different ways in kindergarten. In the first type of dictated story, a teacher shows children one or more related pictures and leads them in creating a story to fit the pictures. Children find it easier to construct a story from a sequence of pictures than from one "busy" picture. In the latter instance, they are more likely to describe all the things seen in the picture rather than focus on a sequence of possible events or predict what would happen next (Hough et al., 1987). Sequenced pictures can be developed by a teacher or purchased from a teacher's supply store. Wordless picture books can also be used in creating a group story.

Another type of dictation activity is the language experience story. Language experience stories provide an opportunity for children to share in composing a narrative based on their common experience, such as a trip to the zoo or the arrival of the classroom pet hamster. In this activity, children put words to their experiences and see those words written down to be shared with others.

Some opportunities for dictated stories come from unexpected events in the classroom. For example, when Ms. Jackson's class heard noises over the school intercom during circle group time, one of the children said, "It sounds like there's a pig in the office." Other children chimed in. Ms. Jackson then asked them if they wanted to create a story about a pig's visit to the school office. There was a resounding "Yes!" from the children. Her prompt to the children was, "If a pig walked into school, what do you think it might do?" As the children dictated their story to her, Ms. O'Sullivan wrote it on the whiteboard nearby. After writing each sentence, she paused to re-read the sentence and then ask the children what would happen next in their story. When the story was finished, they read it in unison and had a class photo taken with the story. Then Ms. Jackson copied the story on chart paper so it could be posted in the room for children to reread as they wished.

Interactive writing. Similarly to dictated writing, interactive writing is also based on oral language (McCarrier et al., 2000); however, in contrast to dictated writing, interactive writing is characterized by explicit instruction that singles out language concepts such as letters, sounds, capitalization, punctuation, and directional-ity (Boroski, 2004). This explicit instruction is dialogic in nature, with the teacher asking children strategic questions about the sounds in words and how to write the words as well as the purpose of the writing (Bromley, 2000). Thus, interactive writing involves a higher level of participation by children than does dictated writing, and for that reason it may not be introduced until the later on in the kindergarten year.

For example, a teacher might decide to focus on the beginning sounds of certain words and encourage children to say the words slowly, suggesting what letter might be used to start the word. Gradually, then, at later times in the year, the teacher would move on to ending sounds and sounds in the middle of words.

Interactive writing involves both reading and writing because what is written is then read (Hall, 2000). Research has documented the value of interactive writing "for developing the phonological awareness and alphabetic knowledge children require for early reading" (Craig, 2003, p. 440). The explicit focus on language concepts during interactive writing also fosters the development of metalinguistic knowledge, because children have opportunity to focus on specific language concepts through supportive dialogue with their teacher and begin to be able to talk about and reflect on language.

Interactive writing may be used at group time as well as with individual children in the writing center (Yoder, 2001). A teacher may decide to encourage children to become involved in actually taking turns in writing known letters or familiar words or adding punctuation marks (Tompkins, 2000). The teacher then fills in and finishes the text as it is created so that it can be read easily. Interactive writing strategies can also be used in responding to literature and in thematic units to create lists, charts, poems, posters, and letters or other messages (Tompkins, 2000).

Calendar Time

Calendar time usually occurs as part of the group time in kindergarten. This typi-cally involves determining the day of the week and the number of the date, along with the month and sometimes the year.

Some children may not be able to understand *date*, *month*, and *year* because these temporal concepts are abstract rather than concrete in nature. The teacher may therefore need to focus on identifying the day of the week with a particular activity: "Today is Tuesday. This is the day we go to the school library." "Today is Friday. Today we go to the gym."

For some classrooms, a daily calendar time is not appropriate because children cannot fully comprehend the concepts involved. While they may be able to respond in rote fashion to saying the days of the week or the number of the date, there may be little understanding of the real concept. It may be enough to have calendar time for a few weeks, take a break for a month or two, and then start calendar time again.

Calendar time encourages children to begin to develop awareness of time concepts such as day, week, and month.

Word Study Activities

Word study activities in kindergarten are used to consciously focus children's attention on language units such as syllables or phonemes and to provide opportunities to begin to manipulate those units. For example, rhyming activities encourage children to recognize and produce words that have the same ending sounds. This conscious manipulation of language involves metalinguistic knowledge, which is a higher level of language knowledge.

Enhancing metalinguistic knowledge. Prior to kindergarten, language development involves mainly language knowledge at the linguistic or usage level. However, with the beginning of formal schooling in kindergarten, it is increasingly important for children to begin to develop metalinguistic knowledge of the aspects of language—most specifically, the phonetic, or sound–symbol, aspect. Systematic attention to a specific aspect of language knowledge, such as phonemic awareness and letter–sound connections, has been found to enhance reading achievement (Ball & Blachman, 1991; International Reading Association–National Association for the Education of Young Children [IRA–NAEYC], 1999). Reading and writing instruction in the primary and upper elementary grades requires children to consciously manipulate units of language—units of sound (e.g., phonemes, syllables, onset-rime) and units of syntactic or semantic meaning (e.g., morphemes, phrases, sentences).

While research has not identified one specific method as being effective with all children, successful approaches with beginning readers and writers involve "systematic code instruction along with meaningful connected reading" (IRA–NAEYC, 1999, p. 175). Word study activities that are based on children's literature, nursery rhymes, or songs can provide a meaningful basis for focusing on words and parts of words.

Focusing on phonemic awareness.   Kindergarten children are usually not yet ready for the paper-and-pencil activities used in the primary grades, but they can benefit from word study activities that focus on phonemic awareness or letter–sound connections in interactive and engaging ways (McGee & Ukrainetz, 2009; Yopp & Yopp, 2000). These activities can be introduced at group time, with repeated opportunities to engage in the activities in small group or individual settings. Initial word study activities should focus on developing children's listening skills since those skills are needed for later word study activities. Listening activities should encourage children to listen "actively, attentively, and analytically" (Adams, Foorman, Lundberg, & Beeler, 1998, p. 15).

Listening activities are followed by activities that focus on language in increasingly smaller units: from syllables to initial and final sounds (onset-rime) to phonemes (Adams et al., 1998; Yopp & Yopp, 2000). Teachers can support children's phonemic awareness by providing more explicit scaffolding as children begin to focus on phonemes (McGee & Ukrainetz, 2009). For example, the teacher emphasizes the first phoneme in a word orally, asks children to look at her mouth as she says the phoneme, and then asks children to repeat after her, such as "What is the first sound in boat? /b/b/b/boat. Look at my mouth, /b/b/b/boat. The first sound is /b/. Now you say it, /b/."

Word study activities may also involve different types of manipulation of sounds and word segments, such as matching, substituting, blending, segmenting, and deleting (Yopp & Yopp, 2000). For example, children are asked whether two words start with the same sound. They may be asked to focus on syllables, as in *sandbox* and *sandbag*; on onset-rime, as in *bat-cat-mat*; or on initial phonemes, as the /k/ in *car-cat*. It is also beneficial to use activities that focus on words and sentence units because reading and writing development "depends on a relatively secure notion of what is and is not a word" (Adams et al., 1998, p. 39).

Creating morning messages.   Using a "morning message" activity provides opportunities to focus on both oral and written language. This activity is based in a letter you would write to your students each day about the upcoming events in your classroom, the weather, school events, or an experience you have had. This letter provides the basis for focusing on the sounds of words as well as the way words are written. An example of a morning message is shown in Figure 9.5.

FIGURE 9.5
Sample of a Morning Message for Kindergarten

February 11, 2013

Dear Boys and Girls,

Good morning! Today it is sunny. We will go

Yes!

outside for recess. It will be fun to play outside.

Today I will read you a story about a

caterpillar. Have you ever seen a caterpillar?

Love,

Ms. White

When you are preparing a morning message to share with kindergartners, be sure to keep the following guidelines in mind (SchifferDanoff, 2001):

- Use a letter format with a greeting, date, and closing
- Use short sentences
- Use brightly colored felt-tip markers (e.g., blue, red, black, green)
- Include simple drawings or graphics to enhance comprehension
- Print using large letters that are well-formed and consistent

As children gather in front of the chart with your morning message, encourage them to look at the message before you begin to read it aloud. As they look at the message, ask them to tell you about the letters or words they see. Then as you read the morning message, use a pointer to help children follow as you read each word.

FIGURE 9.6

Teacher Resources for Kindergarten

Adams, M., Beeler, T., Lundberg, I., & Foorman, B. (2001). *Phonemic awareness in young children: A classroom curriculum.* Baltimore, MD: Paul H. Brookes.

Cecil, N. (2003). *Striking a balance: Best practices for early literacy.* Scottsdale, AZ: Holcomb Hathaway.

Hall, D., & Cunningham, P. (2008). *Making words kindergarten: 50 Interactive lessons that build phonemic awareness, phonics, and spelling skills.* Boston, MA: Allyn & Bacon Pearson.

Leu, D., & Kinzer, C. (2011). *Phonics, phonemic awareness, and word analysis for teachers: An interactive tutorial.* Boston, MA: Allyn & Bacon Pearson.

Scott, V. (2009). *Phonemic awareness: Reading-to-use lessons, activities, and games.* Thousand Oaks, CA: Sage Publications.

Tiedt, I. (2002). *Tiger lilies, toadstools, and thunderbolts: Engaging K–8 students with poetry.* Newark, NJ: International Reading Association.

Tompkins, G., & Collom, S. (2004). *Sharing the pen: Interactive writing with young children.* Upper Saddle River, NJ: Pearson Education.

You will also want to stop after each sentence to talk or ask questions about what you have read. After you have finished reading the morning message, select specific letters, letter patterns, or words for children to identify. Encourage children to come up to the chart to point to the location of the word or letter. Additional ideas for specific word study activities are found in the teacher resources listed in Figure 9.6.

ROUTINE ACTIVITIES

Each classroom has routines that occur daily or weekly. These routines provide opportunities to enhance children's pragmatic knowledge of language and their receptive and expressive knowledge of syntactic, semantic, morphemic, and phonetic features of language.

Arrival and departure. When children first begin to attend kindergarten, they will have already had an opportunity to establish arrival and departure greetings in their home and community environments; however, they may not be familiar with the specific routines established in more formal settings, such as classrooms. Arrival and departure routines are established during the first few weeks of school. The classroom teacher should greet children individually, calling them by name. During arrival time, children can also be encouraged to talk about their experiences.

Children can also participate in taking attendance. One strategy is to provide each child with a name card that is located in a pocket chart. When the children arrive in the classroom, they select their name card and take it to the rug area for the morning group time. Specific activities can be developed based on children's names and the letters used in their names, such as, "If your name starts with an *A*, stand up." This strategy encourages children to recognize their printed name and begin focusing on specific letters in their names and in other children's names.

Another version of this attendance-taking strategy is to write the children's names on T-shirt-shaped pieces of paper and hang them with clothespins from a line draped at the children's height. When children arrive in the classroom, they pick up their T-shirt, go to the gathering rug, and place their card nearby on the rug. As the class assembles there, the teacher leads the children in taking attendance, determining who is absent and participating in other name-related activities. At the end of the group time, children re-hang their T-shirt name card on the clothesline.

"Specials" Within the School Building

Kindergarten children may go as a class to other locations in the school for art and music or perhaps to the school library. Thus, they need to learn how to move as a class through the hallways. While it is important for children to learn to pass quietly through the hallways so as to not disturb other classes, there may be occasional opportunities for children to see and read printed signs or labeled doors in the school, such as OFFICE, JANITOR, or BAKE SALE. By encouraging children to read signs in their school environment, teachers increase children's awareness of the ways printed language is used for information, for identifying locations, and for other functional purposes.

FAMILY CONNECTIONS

Connecting with each child's family and supporting their role as partners in their child's education continues to be important during the kindergarten year. Three ways that you can connect with parents and family members of the children in your classroom are through book bags, family literacy packs, and classroom newsletters.

Book Bags

This activity involves organizing several book bags that are filled with one to three familiar books along with an unlined spiral notebook/journal and several washable felt-tipped markers. Then introduce each book bag at circle time and explain how children can check them out and use the book bag at home. Encourage them to share the books with their parents and other family members and then draw or write about their experience in the journal. When a book bag is returned, encourage the child to share their experience with the class. Before the book bag is checked out again, you will need to review the contents and replace any needed items.

This activity increases a family's accessibility to books that are appropriate for their kindergartner. It also creates a connection between books read at school and those shared at home. This repetition is important for emergent readers and writers. Parents are also able to observe their child's developing language and literacy.

To help parents and family members use the book bags, you might find it valuable to include a listing of the contents of the bag, including the due date, as well as some ideas for using the books. For example, "Talk about the pictures. Ask your child, "what do you see here?" "What do you think will happen next?" "What did you like about this book?" You will also want to help parents understand that reading aloud to their children and sharing books are important even after children are learning to read conventionally.

Family Literacy Packs

Family literacy packs are centered around a book and contain a range of other activities related to the book, along with a teacher-constructed board game (Hammack, Foote, Garretson, & Thompson, 2012). Similar to the book bag activity, family literacy packs also include a logbook or journal and a introduction letter to parents. Family literacy packs are also organized around specific learning objectives related to classroom curriculum. Throughout the year, different family literacy packs are introduced as a way of connecting the classroom curriculum to related activities in the children's homes.

This activity also increases a family's accessibility to books and provides related activities to extend and reinforce learning related to specific classroom curriculum. It also provides a way for parents to interact with and observe their children's learning and development. This strengthens parents' involvement as partners in their children's education.

Classroom Newsletters

Classroom newsletters are a way teachers can share information about the ongoing curriculum and events in their classrooms. Newsletters are also a way to provide parents and family members with ideas for interacting with their kindergartners to extend and enhance learning and development. When preparing your newsletter, focus on only a few main topics and use bullet points rather than paragraphs. This makes your newsletter content easy to read and remember. Figure 9.7 provides ideas for expanding kindergartners' vocabulary through home-based and community-based activities.

FIGURE 9.7
Classroom Newsletter

Ideas for Expanding Your Kindergartner's Vocabulary
As you and your child take time for these activities, be sure you talk about what you see and respond to your child's questions and comments.

Take family outings and field trips	Share books together

• Post office
• Grocery store
• Fire station
• Museums
• Zoo
• Farms
• Nature centers
	• Use your local library and our class' lending library
	
	• Choose books based on your child's interests and hobbies
	  ▪ Storybooks
	  ▪ Informational books
	
	• Talk about the illustrations as well as the book content

Make picture caption books	Write together
• Take digital photos of family, special events, or favorite toys • Create an online book or print out the photos and glue to several sheets of paper • Write down what your child says about each photo • Read what you have written • Encourage your child to 'read' with you or alone	• Have your child tell you a story about a recent experience or family event. • Write down what your child says. • Read what you have written. • Encourage your child to illustrate the story • Staple the pages together • Read the story aloud and encourage your child to echo read

SUMMARY

Kindergarten children's language development is enhanced through curricular activities that provide opportunities to use and explore language. Developmentally appropriate learning environments provide hands-on, informal learning activities along with teacher-guided activities that engage children in social and instructional conversations. The classroom teacher has a critical role in establishing the language environment of the classroom. Key interaction patterns in kindergarten include linguistic scaffolding, verbal mapping, mediation, and questioning. A well-balanced kindergarten curriculum includes exploratory, teacher-guided, and routine activities that incorporate many opportunities for children to use their developing knowledge of oral and written language.

✳ ✳ ✳   CHAPTER REVIEW

1. How is the learning and language environment in kindergarten different from the environment in preschool?
2. What are the key interaction patterns for kindergarten teachers?
3. Describe how questioning strategies are used at the kindergarten level.
4. Why are hands-on activities an important part of the kindergarten curriculum?
5. State five guidelines for selecting books to read at group story time in kindergarten.
6. Why should teacher read-alouds still be part of the curriculum when there is a formal reading instruction program?

✳ ✳ ✳   CHAPTER EXTENSION ACTIVITIES

Observation

Observe a kindergarten teacher reading to his or her class. Identify the ways in which the teacher focuses on vocabulary to enhance comprehension.

Curriculum Development

Select a children's illustrated storybook. Create flannel board characters or finger or hand puppets based on the story. Present the story to your college class, using the flannel board characters or puppets.

LANGUAGE DEVELOPMENT
IN THE PRIMARY YEARS

Learning Outcomes

After reading this chapter you should be able to

- Describe how phonological knowledge and metalinguistic awareness are related to children's reading development
- Describe how primary school children's direct and vicarious experiences can enhance vocabulary development
- Discuss how children's syntactic development is influenced by experiences with different text types and learning experiences
- Discuss how the use of academic English in primary classrooms is related to children's development of morphemic knowledge
- Describe how children's school and home experiences may enhance pragmatic knowledge during the primary years

In honor of her father's birthday, Young Liu, a first-grade student, wrote this story:

My fother!

When I see my fother hold my baby brother my fother
looks big and my baby brother looks small
I sgat with my fother and rolr blate with my fother
My fother like to woch TV

My fother goes to work all day

My fother like to cobe his hair

He works home too

My fother cos grass sometime . . . The End

During the primary school years (grades 1–3), children's language continues to develop in the five areas of language knowledge: phonological, semantic, syntactic, morphemic, and pragmatic. Young Liu's story illustrates the developing language competencies of a child in first grade. Phonological knowledge is evident in her invented and conventional spellings. Inflectional word endings indicate morphemic knowledge. Semantic knowledge is represented by the vocabulary she used. Syntactic and pragmatic knowledge are evident in the sentence structure and text structure of her story.

Children enter the primary grades with language competencies developed through their experiences in home and preschool–kindergarten settings. The primary years mark changes in children's language environment in three major ways: (a) children spend more time in nonhome settings with nonrelatives, (b) school settings increasingly involve formal instruction and academic English, and (c) children begin to read independently and thus experience new genres and written language structures. Each of these changes influences the variety of language styles children encounter. The increased emphasis on formal instruction requires that children acquire the pragmatic knowledge involved in learning how to participate verbally and to acquire the academic English (literate register). Instruction at the primary level in reading and language arts also often involves metalinguistic concepts, requiring that children consciously focus on specific linguistic concepts such as letter, word, punctuation, sound, blend, digraph, vowel, and consonant, as well as the way sentences and paragraphs are constructed.

Each of these changes in the linguistic environment influences the ways in which children's language development progresses. Recent research has documented the importance of providing opportunities for children to learn in collaborative settings with peers (Cicalese, 2003; Griffin, 2001). In these settings, "talk" between children surrounds reading and writing tasks, contributing to development of both oral and written language knowledge.

DEVELOPMENT OF PHONOLOGICAL KNOWLEDGE

The primary years are a time during which children achieve mastery over phoneme production. In addition, during this time, children's phonological knowledge is increasingly influenced by their experiences with reading and writing.

Oral Language Knowledge

During children's sixth and seventh years, they continue to increase in their ability to produce a full range of specific language sounds. By age 8, most children have complete phoneme production. A 6-year-old typically becomes able to articulate /Θ/ (*thin*) and /zh/ (*treasure*; Owens, 2001; Sander, 1972). The acquisition of consonant clusters (e.g., *str*, *sl*, and *dr*) may not occur until children are 8 years old. While some children may have acquired these articulations earlier than the ages cited here, it is important for teachers to hold off on referring slower-achieving children for speech remediation until they are well past those target ages for the respective sounds. For example, if a kindergarten child has difficulty with the /Θ/ sound in *thin*, speech remediation may not be appropriate until the child is about 7 years old.

Primary-age children also increase in their rhyming abilities and awareness of other sound patterns, such as onset and rime. **Onset** refers to the initial consonant (or consonant cluster) of a syllable that precedes the first vowel of a syllable; **rime** refers to the vowel and any remaining consonants of a syllable (Harris & Hodges, 1995; see Table 10.1).

Written Language Knowledge

Research investigating children's awareness of onset and rime patterns has documented children's use of this awareness when comparing known words with new words, figuring out the pronunciation, and decoding a new word by creating an analogy between the familiar word and the new word (Goswami, 1986, 1990; Goswami & Mead, 1992). Children appear to use this strategy regardless of their reading level (Goswami, 1986). For children to develop onset–rime awareness that contributes to their reading strategies, onset–rime activities must have both oral and written language components. This is because the English language has many alternative spellings for the same phonemes. For example, *go*, *show*, and *though* all have the same

---

TABLE 10.1
Examples of Onset and Rime

Word	Onset	Rime
cat	c	at
mat	m	at
light	l	ight
bright	br	ight
weed	w	eed
speed	sp	eed
thought	th	ought
sought	s	ought

TABLE 10.2
Examples of Orthographic Variations for Phonemes

Phoneme	Examples
[i]	bead, weed, cede
[σ]	all, caught, fought
[e]	hay, hey
[ε]	said, dead, red

vowel sound; however, the rime aspect of each syllable is spelled differently, precluding any productive analogy that might assist in decoding. Only through activities that combine oral and written language will children see the function that onset and rime patterns may serve in decoding. (See Table 10.2 for additional spelling variations of phonemes.) Other research with first graders has indicated that "phonemic segmentation scores . . . predicted overall performance in reading and spelling" (Foorman, Francis, Novy, & Liberman, 1991, p. 456).

Morris, Bloodgood, Lomax, and Perney (2003) identified a developmental sequence for reading that involves several levels of phonological knowledge and metalinguistic awareness. In their research of kindergarten and first-grade children over a 2-year period, they found that the following reading-related concepts or abilities emerged in this order (p. 321):

1. Alphabet knowledge
2. Beginning consonant awareness
3. Concept of word in text
4. Spelling with beginning and ending consonants
5. Phoneme segmentation
6. Word recognition
7. Contextual reading ability

The current controversy involving phonics instruction appears to center on two questions: (a) How much knowledge of letter–sound connections is necessary for the development of conventional reading and writing? and (b) Can sufficient phonological knowledge be acquired by children through informal, indirect instruction, or is formal, direct instruction in letter–sound connections necessary? (See Adams, 1990; Chall, 1967, 1983; Chomsky, 1972; Fields, Spangler, & Lee, 1991; Jewell & Zintz, 1990; McGee & Richgels, 2000; Menyuk, 1984; Schwartz, 1988; Teale & Sulzby, 1987.)

Instead of specifying a discrete body of phonological knowledge that is universally necessary for conventional reading, some educators contend that individual learning styles allow children to learn to read and comprehend text successfully even though their phonological knowledge varies. Others propose that the amount of time devoted to teaching phonics should be determined by an assessment of "children's knowledge of the alphabetic principle and their ability to use this knowledge when reading and writing" (Fox, 2004, p. 7). Continued research in the areas of emergent literacy and formal reading instruction promises to clarify these issues.

Primary children vary in their approaches to spelling. Some are just beginning to figure out the orthographic system. Other children are more sophisticated in their representations of phonemes. Thus, it is important for primary teachers to be aware of the developmental progression of orthographic–phonemic knowledge in young children. Prior to acquiring conventional spelling, primary grade children may go through one or more stages of phonemic spelling, as representations of phonemes become more consistent and complete.

Detailed study of children's invented spellings has been documented by Bissex (1980); Sulzby, Barnhart, and Hieshima (1989); Teale and Martinez (1989); Temple, Nathan, and Burris (1982); and Temple, Nathan, Burris, and Temple (1988). Each of these studies describes in more detail children's growing phonemic awareness and their transition to conventional orthography. In classrooms where children are encouraged to write using invented spellings, teachers can use these writings to examine children's growing phonological knowledge.

For example, look back at the opening vignette of this chapter to Young Liu's story about her father. As you read her story and compare her invented spelling with the conventional words, you can see that she was thoughtfully using her knowledge of the connections between letters and sounds to encode her story. Below are listed her invented spellings along with the conventional spelling of the words she used:

Fother	for	Father
rolr	for	roller
woch	for	watch
cos	for	cuts
sgat	for	skate
blate	for	blade
cobe	for	comb

Sometimes primary children's invented spellings just lack one or more letters to achieve conventional spelling. In many cases, the conventional spellings contain silent letters, vowel digraphs, or repeated consonants, such as *beter* for better, *usful* for useful, *truble* for trouble, *plese* for please, and *thoughtfull* for thoughtful. In other instances, children's spellings reveal an awareness of multiple syllables or many letters in a word but do not achieve conventional spelling, as in *symymoms* for synonyms and *antymoms* for antonyms.

In the following example, we see one child's attempts to communicate through invented spelling as he described a story he had just read. Connor (age 8) had just read Sharmat's (1978) book *Nate the Great and the Sticky Case.* When asked to write his response to the book, he wrote (punctuation and spelling are Connor's):

> I think that the Sticky case was funny. Also it was mistrais. In the biginy I did not know Where to start to find a cool. But as the case went on I thowt and thowt. But I still cood not crack the cace. Then all the cols started to come together. Then I know it was that fang (the dog) had it.

Several of Connor's invented spellings show highly developed phonemic awareness. For example:

mistrais	for	*mysterious*
biginy	for	*beginning*
cace	for	*case*
thowt	for	*thought*
cood	for	*could*
cols, *cool*	for	*clues*, *clue*

In each of Connor's invented spellings, he dealt with sounds that are represented in English in several ways (Temple et al., 1988). For example, in the word *case*, the /s/ sound can also be represented by *c*, as in *face*. Similarly, in *cood* for *could*, Connor used the same letter representations of sound used in *wood*.

Teachers can also observe the variations in how their primary students encode or represent specific words. For example, when a third-grade class wrote thank-you letters to a community organization that had donated individual copies of a thesaurus to them, their teacher noted wide variations in how her students spelled the word *appreciate*:

appriciate

appearcheate

apprieate

apresheate

appreshate

Primary-age children also become aware of the ways in which words are spelled differently in academic English than when represented in dialect. For example, in some dialects, the initial phoneme in *this* or *there* is pronounced *dis* and *dere*. In addition, as children begin to read a wider variety of texts, they come across unusual spelling patterns that do not follow previously learned letter–sound associations. For example, the word *bouquet* is pronounced "bow-kay" not "bow-kwet." Primary children also encounter words that sound the same when pronounced but have different meanings, such as *deer–dear*, *caught–cot*, and *wood–would.* Other words they encounter have similar-sounding endings, but the spelling pattern differs dramatically, such as in *though–row–toe–go.*

Children's experiences that contribute to their oral and written vocabularies and the ways they are encouraged to use and examine those words will influence their acquisition of orthographic knowledge (Henderson & Templeton, 1986). A key factor in this process appears to be opportunities children have to apply what they are learning about word spelling patterns to their reading and writing activities. Because English is a language with a wide variety of orthographic (spelling) patterns for phoneme representation, the acquisition of conventional spelling also involves a visual sense (does the word "look right"?) and the internalization of a large number of spellings (Wilde, 1992). Primary children's phonological knowledge continues to develop through these experiences.

DEVELOPMENT OF SEMANTIC KNOWLEDGE

During the primary years and continuing on in upper elementary grades, children's conceptual development and vocabulary grow significantly and are an important basis for reading comprehension. In this section, children's growth in vocabulary will be described, along with the ways in which their understanding of figurative language and humor provide further evidence of their developing semantic knowledge.

Vocabulary

While it is estimated that an average child will have a vocabulary of about 9,000 root words by the end of elementary school, there may also be significant differences among children within grade levels. Biemiller (2003) reported a range of 3,000 to 7,100 in estimated vocabulary size for second graders. Such differences in vocabulary size will impact the learning of individual students as well as the classroom curriculum. There is also evidence that children who begin the primary years with a larger vocabulary will continue to experience greater vocabulary growth than children who enter the primary years with a more limited vocabulary (Melzi & Ely, 2009; Nagy & Scott, 2000; Wasik, 2006).

During primary school years, elaboration and differentiation of concepts occur, along with the acquisition of labels attached to concepts. Semantic development continues to occur informally as children interact in conversations with family and friends and through exposure to various media as well as new experiences, such as family trips and vacations. Semantic development also occurs more formally in literacy-related instruction where children are introduced to specific words and encouraged to participate in discussing what those words mean. Such discussions of word meaning are metalinguistic in the sense that children are asked to focus consciously on meaning as an aspect of words.

Although children and adults share many of the same concept labels at this time, children's concepts in many instances are not as complete or elaborate as adults' concepts. This difference becomes evident in discussions where the concepts and their labels are topics of conversation, as in discussing a storybook or nonfiction book. During the primary years, children develop deeper, more complete concepts and become aware of synonyms and antonyms.

Figurative Language

Figurative language is a special aspect of semantic knowledge that begins to become more evident during the primary school years. Children's use and understanding of figurative language continues to increase during this time (Owens, 2012).

Comprehending and using figurative language requires a special understanding of semantic knowledge because the meaning of a word is used to create a comparison between two objects or settings. Similes (e.g., "she dances like a fairy") are more explicit in their comparison than are metaphors, which create an implied comparison (e.g., "she was a fairy, dancing across the stage"). In creating a metaphor, a child must be able to see the ways two objects or settings are similar on a more abstract or symbolic level (Hulit & Howard, 1993).

As preschoolers, children's thinking is more concrete and focuses on immediate contexts rather than the more abstract characteristics that form the basis for figurative language found in similes and metaphors. In contrast, primary children begin to realize that figures of speech are not always meant to be taken literally, and if they are taken literally, an amusing situation develops. Children this age are often fond of Amelia Bedelia books, such as *Amelia Bedelia Helps Out* (Parish, 2005), which focus on literal interpretation of figurative language, creating hilarious situations (e.g., "stealing home base" and "dressing the turkey").

A parent described the following instance in which her 7-year-old son used figurative language. He had accidentally discovered his birthday present hidden in a closet. When he saw his mother nearby and became fully aware of his discovery, the child said, "Uh-oh, looks like I just cooked my goose!" In their family, the phrase "cooked his goose" described people who had gotten themselves in predicaments. Realizing his similar situation, the boy used the figure of speech to express his awareness of his situation.

Another primary-aged child, Rebecca, described her younger brother as a "Silly Willie" when she saw him trying to walk with two shoes on one foot. Silly Willie was a character in a favorite book of Rebecca's. Through her familiarity with the concept of silliness portrayed in the storybook, Rebecca was able to use that concept in describing her younger brother's antics.

Humor

Semantic development is evident in primary-age children's appreciation of puns and riddles. This appreciation comes from children's ability to realize that words may have double meanings or may have a similar phonological sequence to other words (Pepicello & Weisberg, 1983). The riddles created by first and second graders tend to be completely nonsensical or too realistic and thus are not really riddles but "pre-riddles" (Sutton-Smith, 1975). During third grade, most children are able to grasp the double meanings of riddles simultaneously (McGhee, 1979). Throughout the primary years, children become more aware of possible double meanings and incorporate puns and riddles into their linguistic play.

Primary-age children appear to use their morphemic, phonological, and semantic knowledge in comprehending and creating riddles. Mahoney and Mann (1991) devised phoneme–morpheme riddles that were used in a riddle completion task. Children were directed to choose the response that answered the riddle's question in a "funny way" (p. 33). For example: "What goes 'oom oom'? (a) a cow walking backwards or (b) an old vacuum cleaner" (p. 33). In selecting (a) as the answer, children used their knowledge of sounds to figure out what the word would be if the sound a cow makes ("moo") were reversed ("oom"). In addition, children would need to use their semantic knowledge in selecting the funniest answer. In the following example, further use of phonemic and semantic knowledge in appreciating the humor of a riddle is evident: "Q: Why did the cookie cry? A: Because its mother had been a wafer so long" (Schultz, 1974, p. 100). In this riddle, "a wafer" is phonetically similar to "away for," and *cookie* and *wafer* have similar meanings, creating a surprise answer that is entertaining.

Specialized Vocabulary

Hobbies and special interests of primary children may provide opportunity to develop specialized vocabulary. For example, an 8-year-old who is an avid baseball fan would develop vocabulary related to this interest. This vocabulary might include such phrases as *hit a triple, pitch, struck out, pop-up, tagged up, grounder, line-drive out, inning, foul ball, home run.*

This vocabulary knowledge probably would not develop in a classroom simply because it is so specialized. Yet it is important to recognize that children's hobbies and special interests outside the classroom can have an impact on concept and vocabulary development. Teachers can recognize and acknowledge children's specialized vocabulary by providing opportunities for children to talk about and write about their home and community activities during language- and literacy-based activities in the classroom.

DEVELOPMENT OF SYNTACTIC KNOWLEDGE

During the primary years, children's language development is characterized by increasing syntactic complexity, a clearer understanding of how pronouns are used, and greater comprehension and use of sentences with passive-voice structure.

Sentence Complexity

Children's use of sentence structure becomes more elaborate and complex in both their oral and written language during the primary grade years. This syntactic development is influenced by language use in home, school, and community settings and by children's semantic language knowledge. Children who have been exposed to more complex language through a variety of genres, such as poetry, drama, nonfiction, and narrative stories, and who have many opportunities to create their own decontextualized texts will develop more elaborate syntactic knowledge. It is also important for children to have opportunities to participate in collaborative projects with their classmates as well as to participate in informal conversations and instruction-based discussions. Classrooms where most of the instruction occurs in teacher-directed large groups or where children work independently offer little opportunity for children to develop the linguistic competencies needed for complex language and literacy tasks (Raphael & Hiebert, 1996).

Primary-age children's knowledge of syntax is evident in their creation of both narrative and informational writing (Scott, 1995a). In her written story, "The Unicorn's Eyes," Ellie (a second-grade student) incorporated narrative structures; for example, "once there was," "one day . . ." She also used sequence clauses, such as "at dinner" and "the next day." She also created cause and effect structure; for example, "Sasha was very imaginative she was so imaginative that she won the imagination contest." Here is Ellie's story (punctuation and capitalization are hers):

> Once there was a girl named Sasha and two friends named Lila and Leesa, the twins. Sasha was very imaginative she was so imaginative that she won the imagination contest.
>
> One day her imagination went out of hand. People thought it was, At Acorn Hill top school the students were writing stories about things that start with U. Everyone was doing umbrella except for Sasha who was doing a unicorn. She said, "I wish I could see a unicorn," and she looked out the window and saw a real live unicorn. "Look a real live unicorn."
>
> Everybody stared at Sasha. Robby and Lila whispered "She's crazy." Suddenly the bell rang and the teacher had to say, "Sasha, I believe your imagination is out of hand." Sasha just cried and suddenly Lila gave the friendship bracelet back. "We liked the old you," they said together. Sasha walked and whispered to herself, "I knew I saw a unicorn, I knew I saw a unicorn."
>
> At dinner her mother was worried. "I cooked her favorite foods, spaghetti with meat sauce, but she is not eating." Her brother was happy because he was just a rascal. "Hey sis, did you loose your friends?" said Joseph. Sasha nodded. "Go to your room Scolded his mother." "So I hear you lost your friends honey." Sasha did not listen and walked away in tears.
>
> The next day she sat on the bench and saw the unicorn. "Hi, I am Daisy, I can be your pet but you have to show me to your friends." "Ok," answered Sasha. So she showed the unicorn to her friends and asked to be their friend again, and so they did.

Ellie's story contained several other complex grammatical features. These include:

- *Compound subjects.* "Robby and Lila whispered. . ."
- *Compound sentences.* "Once there was a girl named Sasha and two friends named Lila and Leesa." "So she showed the unicorn to her friends and asked to be their friend again, and so they did."
- *Subordinating conjunctions.* "I can be your pet but you have to show me to your friends."

Ellie's written story is clear example of the independent writing of a second grade student. Story dictation also provides opportunities to observe primary-age children's knowledge of grammatical structures and text features. Because the story is dictated, the child is free of the challenge of putting the story on paper.

Pronoun References

Primary-age children continue to develop a clearer understanding of how pronouns are used in oral and written language (Menyuk, 1988). When pronouns are used in oral language, their referents are often indicated by the context, the setting, or both, in which the speech occurs; however, in written language, pronoun referents need to be identified through specific syntactic features. **Anaphoric reference** is a term used to describe the way a pronoun refers back to a preceding noun (Owens, 2012). For example, in Ellie's story above, pronoun referents are clearly indicated through the grammatical structure of the text.

Passive Sentences

During primary grades, children are more accurate in understanding and producing passive sentences. Passive sentences require a different type of linguistic processing because passive sentences do not follow the expected subject–verb–object sequence. Children appear to use a variety of clues in understanding passive sentences: contextual support, the presence of action verbs, and the presence of a preposition such as *from* or *by* (Owens, 1988), as in "The window was broken by the ball."

Teachers can informally observe primary children's syntactic knowledge by providing opportunities for children to participate in creating their own written stories and participating in story dictation. Through careful observation, teachers can become better acquainted with children's current and developing syntactic knowledge of oral and written language.

Children's conscious or metalinguistic awareness of syntax becomes increasingly important as they are expected to manipulate syntactic features in such language arts tasks. These tasks include identifying complete (or incomplete) sentences, using spelling words in sentences (Scott, 1995a), or placing punctuation in paragraphs. Children's metalinguistic awareness of syntax appears to be enhanced during the process of learning to write when children begin to consciously manipulate language at the phrase, clause, and sentence levels (Scott, 1995a).

DEVELOPMENT OF MORPHEMIC KNOWLEDGE

During the primary years, children become more consciously aware of inflectional and derivational morphemes that are added to words to change the meaning of a word and/or to change the syntactic function of a word.

Inflectional Morphemes

In acquiring morphemic knowledge, children learn to distinguish between "regular" and "irregular" words because inflectional endings are used only with regular words. For example, the verb *go* is irregular, as its past tense is *went* and not *goed*. The noun *child* is irregular as its plural is *children*, not *childs*. Throughout the primary years, children acquire a greater awareness of when inflectional endings are appropriately used and when they are not. As their morphemic knowledge increases, children are able to communicate with more elaboration and preciseness.

Derivational Morphemes

While many primary-age children will have acquired most of the inflectional morphemes for marking plurality, possession, and past tense, their comprehension and use of derivational morphemes is still developing. **Derivational morphemes** are bound morphemes used with word stems that change the way a specific word functions in a sentence (Owens, 2012). For example, adding *-ly* to an adjective makes the word an adverb, as in *quick–quickly*. Adding *-ness* to an adjective makes it a noun, as in *good–goodness*. Derivational morphemes include both prefixes and suffixes. Examples of word stems with specific derivational morphemes are listed in Table 10.3.

During the primary grades, children begin to form adverbs by using the suffix *-ly* and may use other derivational morphemes as well, depending on the presence of such morphemes in their oral and written language environments. Josie's story demonstrates two instances of adverb use:

> I was riding my bike with the kids, and then *suddenly* a car came, and I stopped as *quickly* as I can.

TABLE 10.3
Examples of Free Morphemes and Derivational Bound Morphemes

Free Morpheme	Bound Morpheme	Changed Word
happy	un-	unhappy
happy	-ness	happiness
respect	dis-	disrespect
respect	-ful	respectful
quick	-ly	quickly
quick	-er	quicker

As children begin to use more derivational morphemes, they also become aware that some derivational morphemes change the pronunciation of the root word (Jarmulowicz, Taran, & Hay, 2007; Owens, 2001). While some derivational morphemes do not change pronunciation, as in *happy–happier* and *happy–happiness*, other derivational morphemes will change the placement of the accent, as in *active–activity* (Jarmulowicz et al., 2007). Still other derivational morphemes involve a change in the sound of the final consonant morpheme in the stem word, as in *electric* (from a /k/ sound) to *electricity* (a /c/ sound). Derivational morphemes may also involve a change in the last vowel in the word. For example, *divine* becomes *divinity*, and *explain* becomes *explanation* (Owens, 2001).

Classroom Instruction and Academic English

Children's oral language may not provide evidence of the same use of morphemic knowledge as their written language. When using oral language, such as slang and dialect, children may not observe the same use of inflectional endings as they do when using written language. For example, on the playground, a child might say, "I'm goin' skate-boardin' after school," whereas if the child was writing this in a story for a class assignment, he would write, "I am going to go skateboarding after school." This difference reflects the ways in which classroom instruction and exposure to academic English focuses on the use of both inflectional and derivational morphemes. As children enter and progress through the primary grades, they may encounter more formal morphemic instruction in reading and language arts classes, as decoding, encoding, and comprehension are emphasized. Teachers may emphasize the morphemic knowledge present in academic English when children participate orally in class discussions and conversations. Children also develop morphemic knowledge when decoding and comprehending written text and workbook exercises, such as studying prefixes, suffixes, and root words. Anglin's research (1993) indicated that primary-age children use their knowledge of morphemes (bound and free) to figure out word meanings. This research examined children's receptive vocabulary and found that children were using their knowledge of morphemes to develop clues about the meaning of a specific word.

Observing Children's Morphemic Knowledge in Their Written Stories

Primary-age children's morphemic knowledge can be observed in their early attempts at encoding their thoughts into words on paper. While this knowledge is related to children's phonemic knowledge, as discussed in an earlier section, it also provides evidence of their understandings of word formation and morphemes.

In her story, "Lazy Elves," Ellie (age 7) used a variety of inflectional and derivational morphemes. Her story follows, with words in italics to denote the presence of inflectional and derivational morphemes.

In the North Pole, at Santa's Workshop the *elves* were *busier* than ever! It was December 19th. Santa *checked* his list over and over again.

He was so happy. "It's just so wonderful that every single boy and girl was good over the year," said Santa.

Suddenly, "Honey, the elves want their football game!!!" said Mrs. Claus. "Ok!," said Santa. *Elves* love football and the *girls* do too. The *shyest* and *smartest* elf was *named* Amanda. The *tallest* and *laziest* elf was *named* Elferd. "Fifty two, fifty three, hut!!" *shouted* an elf. The same thing *happened* on December 20th.

Now on December 23rd when the elf said "Hut," Amanda *shouted*, "STOP, WE NEED TO MAKE THE *PRESENTS*!!" "NO!" said the elves. The next day the elves *wanted* to play football again and Amanda was so tired of *making* ten thousand *toys*.

Suddenly an idea came to her mind. "I can deliver the *toys*!" *Quickly* she got the reindeer and set off. When Amanda came back, she told Santa the whole *story* and he said "No more football for you *elves*!"

In Ellie's story, she used inflectional endings for past tense with regular verbs, such as *want–wanted, make–making, check–checked*. She also used the appropriate past tense form for several irregular verbs, such as *come–came, tell–told*. Plural forms of regular words are indicated by adding an -s. With some nouns, the plural form involves spelling changes. Ellie was aware of this, shown by her spelling of the plural of *elf*. Instead of just writing *elf*s, Ellie used the correct spelling of *elves*, changing the *f* to *v* and adding -*es*. Comparative suffixes, a form of derivational morphemes, were also used; for example, *busy–busier, shy–shyest, smart–smartest*. The derivational suffix -ly was used to change adjectives to adverbs, such as *sudden–suddenly, quick–quickly*. Through the use of inflectional endings, appropriate forms of irregular verbs, and derivational morphemes, Ellie was able to clearly communicate her story.

Throughout the primary years, children's morphemic knowledge continues to develop as they are engaged in informal conversations with others as well as in classroom activities that provide opportunities to hear, focus on, and use words containing inflectional and derivational morphemes.

DEVELOPMENT OF PRAGMATIC KNOWLEDGE

During the primary years, children may have increased opportunities to participate in a wider variety of activities and experiences. These may include opportunities to participate in sports or other extracurricular activities in the community, going on family vacations, visiting museums, and attending sporting events or religious-based events. In each of these activities, there may be specific ways in which language is used in terms of vocabulary, conversational patterns, and the use of an informal dialect or home language. In addition, the curriculum present in children's school classrooms during the primary years typically places a strong emphasis on becoming more metalinguistically aware of specific features of language. In this section, children's developing pragmatic knowledge of oral language, written language, and academic English will be described.

Oral Language

During the primary years, children begin to make specific requests for clarification and become increasingly more competent in conversations (Owens, 2001). They are better able to take into account what their listeners know when engaged in conversation. In Anderson's (1992) study, primary-age children indicated a wider range of registers and more complex modifications in their speech to fit in the various contexts of communication. Primary-age children are also better able to maintain a conversational topic, produce polite direct and indirect requests, and make adjustments in their speech in response to requests for clarification from others (Warren & McCloskey, 1997). Children now give more complete descriptions and comparisons when referring to specific objects (Menyuk, 1988).

Indirect requests.   An **indirect request** is meant to be interpreted as a request, even though it appears to be a yes/no question. For example, a direct request would be stated "Open the door," while an indirect request would be "Can you open the door?" This indirectness is considered a more polite way of requesting a particular action from another person. During the primary years, children become more aware of the intent of indirect requests and the appropriate response to such requests (Menyuk, 1988; Owens, 2001). Whereas 6-year-olds are likely to respond to an indirect request literally, responding with a "yes," 8-year-olds generally respond with the requested action (Owens, 2001).

Resolving conflict.   During the primary years, children's pragmatic knowledge of how to use language in different situations can facilitate resolving conflict. This flexibility in using language differently in different situations helps them work through conflict and express themselves more clearly. Primary children are able to reflect more on their actions as well as others' actions (Wheeler, 2004). Due to their increased thinking skills, children are now also able to generate different ways of solving problems. Teachers can provide opportunities in the classroom for children to develop a vocabulary as well as specific communication strategies for resolving conflict and maintaining friendships.

Written Language

Children's awareness of the pragmatic aspects of written language is influenced by the contexts surrounding them. During the primary years, a good part of each day is spent in a school setting. The ways written language is used and the opportunities for children to participate in a wide range of contexts influence the development of children's pragmatic knowledge. Children will show this awareness when they are given opportunities at home and at school to use writing in a variety of ways (Taylor & Vawter, 1978). Teachers who carefully observe the ways children engage in reading and writing can use these observations and new understandings to better develop and implement curricula (Dixon-Krauss, 1996).

In her detailed study, Bissex (1980) identified various forms or purposes of writing in her son's spontaneous writing during his kindergarten and primary years (ages 5–9). During that time, seven forms were used consistently: (a) signs, labels, and captions; (b) stories; (c) little books; (d) directions; (e) lists or catalogues; (f) newspapers; and (g) cards, notes, and letters. The three forms that appeared early but were discontinued by age 8 were (a) statements, (b) school-type exercises, and (c) riddles. Late-appearing (after age 6) forms included (a) rhymes; (b) charts, organizers, and planners; (c) diary; (d) quizzes (questions and answers); (e) information and observation notebooks; and (f) codes.

In Heath's (1983) ethnographic study, she noted the uses of literacy activities within the two communities referred to as Trackton and Roadville. In each community, reading and writing served a variety of purposes and functions. Preschool children in these environments learned the value of literacy from the interactions of those around them, and later when attending formal schooling, they learned the ways language is used to form written messages. Gradually, children began to incorporate features of stories they had read in their reading books into their own written stories. These features included character introduction, story parts, and chronological order. In a second-grade class observed by Heath, children were encouraged to note, categorize, and analyze the ways people spoke and the ways those people used reading and writing. The teacher also encouraged children to become aware of five different ways of talking: dialect, casual, formal, conversational, and standard. In this classroom, children's acquisition of pragmatic knowledge provided a framework for language learning in general. Children became aware of how they were using language and why.

Research by Dahl, Freppon, and McIntyre (1992) emphasized the importance of opportunities for primary-age children to engage in the writing process. Their study observed children's writing in classrooms that offered varied opportunities for writing. In classrooms that offered opportunities to write frequently as well as more social and instructional support for beginning writing, children showed more gains in being able to compose more complex writing.

Children's beginning writing and reading appear to be enhanced in classrooms that offer varied and frequent opportunities for children to talk with each other and with the teacher during literacy-related activities, such as talking, collaborating, and conferencing during story writing (Dahl et al., 1992; Galda, Pellegrini, Shockley, & Stahl, 1994–1995).

The variety of written text genres used in primary classrooms may influence the ways in which children construct their own texts (Chapman, 1995; Duke, 2000). While it is not known how much experience with a genre is needed to comprehend and then create a text in that genre, there is widespread agreement that substantial experience with a genre is needed. Chapman (1995) studied the types of texts (genres) created by first graders, along with the range of genres embedded in their classroom curricula. Children used a variety of genres, including simple and more complex narratives (i.e., recounting events, or "news"), notes, written dialogues, and verse or poetry. Chapman emphasized the need for primary teachers to examine

Children's beginning writing and reading appear to be enhanced in classrooms that offer varied and frequent opportunities for children to talk with each other and with the teacher.

the range of genres included in the classroom curriculum because children may be learning about genre through this immersion even though explicit instruction in the genre does not occur.

Duke's research (2000) documented the relative scarcity of informational texts used in first grade, with an average of only 3.6 minutes per day for activities involving written informational texts and a lack of informational text in the classroom environment on walls, bulletin boards, and shelves. This scarcity was even more pronounced in low-socioeconomic-status (SES) school districts, where the average time spent on informational texts was only 1.9 minutes per day. In this group, half of the low-SES classrooms experienced no informational texts.

Academic English

An important part of pragmatic language knowledge that is developed in the primary grades is an awareness of academic English as well as beginning to use academic English in learning contexts. Academic English involves pragmatic as well as semantic, morphemic, and syntactic features. For example, academic English is used in summarizing and making inferences when reading and interacting with hands-on materials. Academic English is also used metacognitively when children use language to plan, monitor, and evaluate their own learning. In addition, academic English is used during times when children are engaged in instructional conversations as they ask and respond to questions as well as when they interact with classmates during collaborative projects. To be a successful learner in settings where academic English is used, children need to develop an awareness of the specific ways in which academic English is used in cognitive, metacognitive, and social-affective strategies as a part of the learning process (Chamot & O'Malley, 1995). This also includes responding to writing assignments where informational text and narrative text are assigned.

The following two examples show a third grader's pragmatic knowledge of different text types in how she responded to two specific writing assignments. In the first example, Sarah uses informational text structure to describe what surprises might occur on an expedition. She had just read an informational book about the discovery of Machu Picchu (Young, 2012).

> Surprises can happen on an expedition. You can find ancient artifacts that you were not looking for. You can also get attacked by a wild animal. Last, you can disover things you never knew existed. These are some surprises that can occur on an expedition.

Sarah's paragraph is structured with an introductory, general sentence. This is followed by two sentences of examples of what might happen. Then one sentence more that begins with "last" to indicate the end of the sequence of examples. She ends her paragraph with a conclusive, summarizing sentence.

In the next example, Sarah was responding to an assignment to write a "tall tale" that included "a larger-than-life character and hyperboles" (Young, 2012). This assignment was a follow-up to the class's reading of a Paul Bunyan story. As you read this story, note the following features that are found in narrative fiction: setting, characters, use of character dialogue and dialogue markers, sequence of events, and problem resolution. Sarah's vocabulary is descriptive, and complex sentence structure is used. In addition, note her larger-than-life character and hyperboles.

> There once was a family that had twenty sons. But no daughter. One day the mother went to the boys holding a bundle. "Boys, I have a surprise for you," she said. "Is it another rock for our rock collection?" asked one. "No, it's another marble for our marble collection," said another. "No," the boys' mother said, laughing. "It is your newborn sister!" The boys groaned. They did not want a sister. Suddenly, the girl jumped out of the blanket. "Hey, y'all! My name is Mary Jane!" Mary Jane turned to the mother. "Thank you for bringing me home with you." She did not reply. The mother couldn't. She just stood there staring, dumbfounded, at Mary Jane. "Now," said Mary Jane, "I would like some exercise. Race through the forest and back!" Mary Jane ran through the forest at 250 mph. When she came back the boys were struggling over a fallen log in the front of the forest. Three hours later, the boys came back, gasping for breath. "I am starving!" yelled Mary Jane. "Whoever catches a boar with their bare hands first wins!" The boys went to bed, but Mary raced into the forest and

came back a second later with twenty boars, thirty does, and ten elk. "Hmm," said Mary, "this meat needs some sauce and a fire to cook it on." Mary went back into the woods. While she was there, a pack of eagles attacked her. Mary Jane sang a song to try and ward them away. That did not work. Quite on the contrary, in fact. She sang such a beautiful song, the eagles started dancing. They danced and danced until they knocked beehives on themselves. The honey pored all over them. Mary Jane, out of kindness, took the sticky eagles to the river to wash them off. Mary got the loose stuff off, But the eagles stayed golden. "My goodness, I have invented golden eagles!" exclaimed Mary Jane. Then, Mary told the eagles to gather honey and firewood. They obeyed. When Mary Jane and the eagles got home they cooked the meat and everybody stuffed themselves silly. And, just because they were her friends, Mary kept the eagles. THE END.

SUMMARY

In the primary years, children's language continues to develop and increase in amount and complexity with respect to phonological, semantic, syntactic, morphemic, and pragmatic knowledge. With increased time spent at school and with an increased emphasis on formal instruction, children's language environment in the primary grades changes dramatically from that of the preschool and kindergarten settings. Classroom interactions increasingly incorporate the academic English register, and children are expected to begin to manipulate language units consciously. Thus, primary-age children's metalinguistic language knowledge becomes important to their success at school.

❋ ❋ ❋   CHAPTER REVIEW

1. Key terms to review:

   onset   anaphoric reference   indirect request
   rime   derivational morpheme

2. How is the linguistic environment at the primary level different from a preschool or kindergarten language environment?

3. What two phonemes do children typically acquire during the primary years?

4. Give several examples of onset and rime.

5. Describe the central concerns of the current controversy regarding phonics instruction.

6. In what ways does invented spelling indicate a child's phonological knowledge?

✳ ✳ ✳ CHAPTER EXTENSION ACTIVITIES

Observation

Observe in a first-grade classroom writing center for 30 to 40 minutes. Describe children's use of phonological knowledge in their writing. Give specific examples.

Research and Assessment

Collect several second- or third-grade children's original stories. Look for instances of invented spelling. Are there consistencies in the way phonemes or sounds are represented? Give examples.

Curriculum Development

Read a book that features figurative language, such as an Amelia Bedelia book, to a group of primary-age children. Discuss with the children the figurative language. Record your observations about children's comprehension of the specific figurative language.

CHAPTER 11

ENHANCING LANGUAGE DEVELOPMENT IN THE PRIMARY YEARS

Learning Outcomes

After reading this chapter you should be able to

- Discuss the factors influencing the language environment in the primary grades
- Identify effective interaction patterns for primary classrooms
- Discuss the importance of curricular goals that incorporate each of the five aspects of language knowledge relating to oral and written language
- Explain the importance of developing listening competencies in primary classrooms
- Explain how word walls can be used to enhance phonological, semantic, and syntactic knowledge
- Discuss the ways in which interactive writing can enhance primary students' language knowledge and competencies
- Discuss the ways in which collaborative–cooperative projects can enhance primary students' language knowledge and competencies

In Mrs. C.'s first-grade classroom, the children were seated on the gathering rug with their insect research journals. Each child's journal reflected his or her individual exploration of insects through various nonfiction trade books from the classroom library. In addition to naming an insect and drawing a picture of it, the children included in their journals where the insect lives, what it eats, and one "amazing fact." Today, the children were meeting to orally share their journals with their class, taking turns to read and to show their information charts. After each student read his or her information, it was recorded by the teacher on a large summative chart. As the sharing continued, children often asked questions about the illustrations or about the insect studied.

By first grade, most children have developed a basic level of communicative competence. They can participate in conversations and use language to communicate their needs and wishes. At this level, there are increasing expectations that children will participate in the academic community of their school and classroom. In Mrs. C.'s first-grade classroom, described in the opening vignette, children's language development has been enhanced by opportunities to learn how to communicate both orally and in writing. Through the process of reading books on insects and writing about them in their journals, Mrs. C.'s students have had opportunities to increase their knowledge about language and how to share what they have learned orally and in writing.

FACTORS INFLUENCING THE LANGUAGE ENVIRONMENT IN THE PRIMARY GRADES

In the primary years (grades 1–3), the language environment is influenced by the curriculum of each classroom as well as the way in which it is implemented. In addition, a teacher's understanding of the importance of talk in the process of learning is also a factor.

Curricula and Standards

The curricula implemented in the primary grades are more formal and more firmly established than the curricula in kindergarten and preschool classrooms. Another strong influence on the curricula found in primary classrooms is the alignment of curricula to state and national standards (see Common Core Standards, 2012, http://www.corestandards.org/the-standards/english-language-art). While such standards exist for all areas of elementary curricula, the area of language arts standards is most relevant to this chapter. Most school districts adopt commercially developed curricula that are standards aligned. All teachers are expected to follow this formal curriculum and to implement lessons targeted to meet standards. While classroom teachers may not have control over the specific commercial curriculum that is selected for implementation, they do control the way the implementation occurs through the manner in which children are engaged in the curricular activities and experiences. The way a curriculum is implemented has a strong influence on the presence of talk in the classroom and the ways in which children become engaged in learning activities.

Implementation of Curricula

Curricula are often implemented in either of two ways: (a) task centered or (b) learner centered. In task-centered implementation, the focus is on adhering to the sequence and scope of learning tasks provided in the curricular materials. Learning activities strictly follow the predetermined sequence and duration. In contrast, learner-centered implementation focuses on children's individual needs, learning styles, and responses to instruction. Learner-centered implementation strives to fit the curriculum to the needs of the student. Thus, the sequence or duration of activities may vary, depending on a teacher's perception of her children's needs and learning styles. This approach recognizes that curricular planning should always reflect an awareness of children's developmental levels and learning styles rather than simply following a presequenced curriculum (Strickland, 1998).

Critical Role of Talk in the Learning Process

Lindfors (1990) challenged teachers to create "classroom communities" where children's talk is invited and sustained, allowing children "to connect with others, to understand their world, and to reveal themselves within it" (p. 38). A key component of classroom communities is talk—talk about what is being learned and about responses to the learning process. This awareness of the important role of classroom talk is a relatively recent development. In the past, a quiet classroom was considered the ideal, with students silently working independently on learning tasks. Talk was restricted to formal recitation exercises or oral reading. Researchers and classroom teachers have begun to question whether a quiet, ordered classroom is the best learning environment (Kasten, 1997; Raphael & Hiebert, 1996; Wells & Chang-Wells, 1996). When classroom talk is overly limited or restricted, children lose the opportunity to engage in focused conversations and do not learn how to express their thinking, clarify their misunderstandings, or question others' perceptions.

Teachers who understand the critical role of talk in the process of learning create classroom environments with a strong foundation for children's cognitive growth and the development of "higher mental processes that constitute reading and writing" (Raphael & Hiebert, 1996, p. 90). In these classroom environments, learning activities are planned and implemented to focus on enhancing children's oral and written language development in each of the five areas of language knowledge: phonological, semantic, syntactic, morphemic, and pragmatic.

INTERACTION PATTERNS FOR PRIMARY CLASSROOMS

At the primary level, the main interaction patterns used by teachers to enhance language development include linguistic scaffolding, mediation, and questioning. A teacher's active listening is an integral part of each of these strategies. Through active listening, teachers become aware of children's thinking and can maintain and extend their verbal participation. Only through active listening and observation can a teacher develop awareness of students' needs and learning styles.

Linguistic scaffolding provides a supportive verbal framework that sustains and encourages children's participation in both social and instructional conversations. Questioning, expansion, and repetition are specific ways in which linguistic scaffolding is created. At the primary level, teachers use linguistic scaffolding to support children's participation in a whole-class discussion, in small groups, and with individual children.

Mediation is an interaction pattern that teachers use to simplify a learning stimulus or task to facilitate student learning and participation. When reading a book, a teacher may substitute more familiar vocabulary as a way to begin to create connections to the more precise or technical vocabulary of the text. For example, when reading *The Magic School Bus: Inside the Human Body* (Cole, 1989), a teacher might make the following substitution of words to mediate the text to facilitate children's comprehension:

> Text: *"In the small intestine, food is broken down into molecules tiny enough for the body cells to use." (p. 10)*
>
> Teacher: *In the small intestine, food is broken down into very tiny pieces. These tiny pieces are called molecules. Then the cells in the body can use the food.*

Mediation also occurs when teachers engage in "thinking aloud" or "reflecting aloud" (Matthews, 1999, p. 36). For example, in reading *The Magic School Bus: Inside the Human Body* (Cole, 1989), a teacher might engage in the following "thinking aloud" as he introduces the book to his class:

> Teacher: *The title of this book is* The Magic School Bus. *Hmm, I wonder how a school bus could be magical. Maybe it is going to fly, or maybe it will travel somewhere very special.*

When teachers think and reflect aloud, they are verbalizing for their students their own thought processes. When this type of mediation is used in developing or completing a task, such as making applesauce or preparing to plant seeds, teachers make explicit what is happening and why or what worked in the past and what options may exist. In this way, teachers show children how language is used as a tool for learning. This type of verbal mediation is an inherent part of successful instructional interactions.

At the primary level, questioning most frequently takes place in instances in which children are expected to recite what they have learned. In this setting, questioning is used as a way to evaluate or monitor children's comprehension or learning. Teachers may use questions found in commercial curricula as the format for the expected recitation. While this recitational questioning serves a purpose in monitoring learning, primary teachers need to also use questioning to encourage children to expand their thinking through inquiry and discovery. Through actively listening to children's responses and comments, teachers can develop follow-up questions that will stimulate higher levels of cognitive processing such as compare–contrast, inference making, problem solving, generalization, and synthesis.

In developing questions to use, primary teachers may find it helpful to consider the **question–answer relationship (QAR)** (Hostmeyer & Kinsella, 2010; Kinniburgh & Shaw, 2009; Raphael, 1986). This refers to the relation between what information the question is asking for and where the answer is found. Some questions will ask for information that is "right there" in the text or in the immediate setting. For example, a teacher might point to the seashells on a table and ask, "Which of these seashells is round, like a ball?" Higher-level questioning uses a QAR in which the answer comes from either making an inference, drawing several pieces of information together, or perhaps from a child's general world experience outside of the classroom, such as, "What do you think happened to the creature that lived in this seashell?"

The amount of wait time after a question is asked is critical to the type of interaction that occurs and to the content of that interaction. Rowe's research (1986; as cited in Raphael & Hiebert, 1996) concluded that increasing the wait time from one to three seconds had significant beneficial effects. With three seconds of wait time, the development of ideas showed more continuity. While the volume of questions asked decreased when the wait time was increased, the questions asked became more cognitively complex. With the increased wait time, teachers incorporated more student responses into the instructional dialogue. This provided opportunity for more contingent questioning at higher levels of cognitive processing.

To be effective in encouraging children's responses during the increased wait time, teachers need to monitor their facial expressions and body language to avoid appearing impatient. Teachers should model thoughtful contemplation of the questions asked as well as thoughtful consideration of children's responses to questions.

OVERVIEW OF LANGUAGE-RELATED PRIMARY CURRICULAR GOALS

At the primary level, the main emphasis of the curriculum is often on the acquisition of reading, with little attention paid to the other language arts, such as listening, speaking, and writing. When the acquisition of reading is emphasized to the exclusion of other language forms, continued development of children's total language competencies becomes limited.

Primary curricula need to incorporate learning activities that address listening, speaking, reading, and writing. A balanced language development program will not only address the five aspects of language knowledge (i.e., phonological, semantic, syntactic, morphemic, and pragmatic) but will also focus on each of the areas of competency in using language (i.e., listening, speaking, reading, and writing).

The primary years are a time when children's language competencies can be developed in ways that foster effective lifelong communication. Children's long-term success in school is influenced by their ability to use language for many different purposes and in different settings. Pinnell (1996) encouraged teachers to engage in strategies and activities that promote children's awareness of, and experiences with, the whole range of language functions.

KEY ROLE OF LISTENING COMPETENCIES

Listening is a key factor in language development. Not only is it an integral part of conversation and instructional dialogue, it is also a necessary competency for understanding direct instruction. Children's listening competencies provide access to learning, particularly at the primary level, where students spend more time listening during the school day than they did in kindergarten. At the primary level, listening skills are essential because within this setting, children may be expected to listen for over half of their classroom activity time (Wilt, 1950, as cited in Wolvin & Coakley, 1985). Listening competencies are critical in facilitating the other language arts (speaking, writing, and reading) (Nation, Cocksey, Taylor, & Bishop, 2010). Children's ineffective listening strategies make learning tasks more difficult and often result in frustration.

In primary classrooms, children need to be able to listen effectively in a variety of contexts, including the following:

- Listening to and comprehending oral instructions or directions in a large-group setting
- Listening to and comprehending explanations of concepts from teachers or guest speakers
- Listening to peers in collaborative group work
- Listening to class discussion
- Listening when engaged in conversations with one or more others

Primary teachers can enhance children's listening comprehension by modeling effective listening strategies, such as active listening and sending feedback (Wolvin & Coakley, 1985). To be an effective listener, a child needs to (Lundsteen, 1990):

1. Receive the message
2. Focus on the language used
3. Discriminate what has been said
4. Assign meaning to what has been said
5. Monitor the ongoing communication
6. Remember what has been said
7. Respond to what has been said

As you encourage your students to be active listeners, you can observe their specific listening competencies. For example, a teacher might find that several children in her classroom need to be encouraged to remember more closely what the speaker has said and to use that knowledge to form their conversational response. Teachers can also explicitly encourage children to be active listeners who consciously focus on the message being spoken and then to give feedback to the speaker about whether they have comprehended the message.

Teachers who constantly repeat oral directions for their students may be doing their students a disservice with this repetition because it may not encourage careful listening. It may be better for a teacher to have another listener–student repeat the directions for other students rather than repeat the directions him- or herself. That way, another child provides a summary of the directions (Lundsteen, 1990).

In summary, to facilitate the development of children's listening competencies, teachers must first provide a model for effective listening during class discussions and during one-on-one conversations or conferences (Farris, Fuhler, & Walther, 2004). In addition, teachers should carefully observe how children take in and comprehend what is heard by noting both verbal and nonverbal responses. Primary students should have opportunities to continue to develop their listening skills because as they progress through elementary and secondary school, the amount of time they are expected to listen is likely to increase, depending on the specific class involved.

PLANNING ACTIVITIES TO ENHANCE PRIMARY-AGE STUDENTS' LANGUAGE DEVELOPMENT

Language-enhancing activities at the primary level include both exploratory discovery center activities and teacher-directed activities. Throughout exploratory and teacher-directed activities, children need to be encouraged to use language to learn, to reflect, and to inquire. Asking and answering questions is a critical part of classroom talk because it may stimulate curiosity and motivation to learn. Children need to have opportunities to ask questions and to seek answers to their questions through experiences and through focused classroom conversations. This process of asking questions and seeking out the answers through hypothesizing, collecting data, and analyzing the data is known as **inquiry learning**.

Inquiry learning is an approach that provides many opportunities to engage in questioning and conversations in the pursuit of new knowledge. Inquiry learning that integrates reading, writing, listening, and speaking into all areas of the primary curriculum can provide not only significant motivation to learn but also critical opportunities to learn how to use oral and written language in the process of gaining knowledge and solving problems. Teachers facilitate this language use through linguistic scaffolding, mediation, and questioning. Inquiry learning can take place through exploratory activities as well as teacher-directed activities.

In the sections that follow, specific activities will be described that can enhance language development in a variety of settings and can accommodate a range of learning styles through hands-on experiences, collaborative activities, small group and large group activities, and more formal, teacher-directed activities.

EXPLORATORY LEARNING ACTIVITIES

An important part of primary classroom activities is the provision of open-ended, hands-on learning activities (Bredekamp & Copple, 1997; Kostelnik, Soderman, & Whiren, 2010). While these activities resemble the exploratory activities recommended for preschool and kindergarten classrooms, primary-level exploratory activities present opportunities for more focused engagement and more complex interactions with the materials provided.

Exploratory learning activities at the primary level have been described as involving "investigative play" (Wassermann, 1990). These investigative activities are characterized by the following features:

- Are open-ended
- Provide opportunity to generate ideas
- Enhance the development of cross-curricular concepts
- Encourage children to be active learners
- Involve cooperative grouping

Classrooms with this focus are described as having a "can-do" perspective, in which children develop self-confidence in their abilities to interact effectively in their environment through successful risk taking and problem solving (Wassermann, 1990). Primary-age children are able to participate in generating the rules or directions for using each center. Posting the rules in each center provides opportunity for children to read and use language to direct their own interactions. It also encourages children to work independently (Sloane, 2002).

Three general areas of exploratory activities appropriate for primary classrooms are a classroom library center, a writing center, and content/concept learning centers, which focus on math/science, social studies/math, or science/social studies content. Other, more focused, centers can be developed; however, the focus of this section will be on these three types of centers. All children in a classroom should have an equal opportunity to engage in each center. Center activities should not be restricted to students who have finished their "seatwork." Procedures for using each center should be well explained as the teacher introduces the center to the class. Implementation of each center should be consistent and simple enough for children to be independent of teacher assistance. In the descriptions of possible center areas that follow, the emphasis will be on clarifying the potential of the activity to enhance one or more aspects of language knowledge.

Classroom Library Center

The classroom library is the focal point of the primary classroom. The materials provided in the library provide a foundation for the learning that occurs in the classroom. A wide range of genres should be provided: various types of fiction (realistic fiction, fables, fairy tales, mysteries), nonfiction (alphabet books, concept books), and poetry. Trade books and chapter books should also be included, as should copies of books used in the reading curriculum for the classroom.

At the primary level, it is still important for books to have frequent illustrations, because they provide important contextual information about the concepts presented in the books. First graders will use the classroom library more successfully if the teacher has featured some of the books from the center in class read-alouds. As children develop more independent decoding skills, they will enjoy new books without first having them read aloud by the teacher. Books should also be rotated through the classroom library to keep student interest and motivation high. It is also beneficial to introduce new books that will enhance topics of current focus in the curriculum, such as a unit on insects.

The books provided in the library center support the foundation for learning that occurs in the classroom.

Writing Center

The major goal of the writing center at the primary level is to facilitate the development of children's competencies in using written language to communicate for a variety of purposes. Children are encouraged to incorporate what they have learned throughout the classroom in their writing. Ideas generated during group shared story time or read-alouds or concept-development activities can become the focus of their writing. First-grade children may use more illustrations in their stories because illustrations can support their efforts in communicating a particular idea or action. Gradually, as they are able to use print more conventionally, illustrations play a lesser role.

Organizing a writing center. The setup of a writing center at the primary level is similar to that of writing centers in kindergarten, but a few differences should be noted. Primary-level writing centers are more likely to have lined paper available, along with plain paper. Additional materials are included for primary children to use in bookmaking, such as glue, scissors, a stapler, and a hole punch. In addition, a computer and printer or a typewriter may be included for children to use in creating their stories.

Journaling. Primary teachers may incorporate journaling into a writing center. In this approach, each child has his or her own notebook of paper, often a spiral notebook that is used to record daily events or stories. Children's writing in their personal journals is spontaneous, personal, and private (Tompkins, 2004a). One of the benefits of the journaling approach is that each child's writing is kept together, and children can see their writing as it develops and changes. Frequently, children are amazed by the amount of writing they have done over time (Tompkins, 2004a).

Encouraging talk in the writing center. In setting up a writing center, arrangement of furniture and supplies should accommodate and acknowledge the importance of ongoing conversations between the children in the center and occasional visits by their teacher. Dyson's study of children's self-talk and peer conversations during the process of composing have documented the importance of talk for self-direction, self-correction, and text development (Dyson, 1989, 2004). Teachers can carefully observe the talk that occurs in the writing center for insights into children's emerging competencies in putting thoughts on paper.

Sharing children's writing. Primary children benefit from opportunities to share with others what they have written. Two ways this can be done is through teacher–student conferences and by providing an author's chair where children can share what they have written with the whole class.

Teacher–student conferences. By conducting one-on-one conferences with each of your students, you will have an opportunity to learn more about their thoughts as they go through the writing process. The conferences should be conducted in a quiet area of your classroom where you can sit beside the student.

To begin a conference, ask the student to read aloud what he has written. This oral reading of the text provides a basis for the subsequent conversation you will have with the child about his writing. The focus of each conference needs to be on encouraging the child to talk about what he has written. You will want to ask questions that help a child focus on the meaning of what he has written. It is important to keep a conference short and focused (Cooper & Kiger, 2006).

Although there may be instances of unconventional spelling or grammar, it is important to focus initially on the meaning communicated and to validate the child's efforts in creating the written text. Young writers are easily overwhelmed and discouraged when the message in their writing is ignored and their writing is seen only as being "incorrect" or needing to be revised to meet a teacher's approval. This is especially important to remember when interacting with English language learners or children who speak a different dialect of English. This does not mean, however, that you avoid noticing instances of unconventional spelling and grammar. You can use this information as a basis for understanding children's zones of proximal development and plan your curriculum and future lessons to address these areas of potential learning.

As you note the relationship between what is read and what is written, you can better understand a child's developing phonological knowledge. In addition, by observing and reflecting on children's responses and comments during these one-on-one conferences, you can further determine which areas of the writing process or which particular skill to focus on as you plan future language arts lessons.

Author's chair.　You can designate (and label) a special chair as an "author's chair." During group time, individual children sit in this chair and share their creative writing with the class. Your role is to facilitate the children's sharing and engage the class in responding to the shared writing. In responding to a child's writing, you will want to encourage class members to focus on specific aspects of the writing they liked, questions they have about the story or text that they want to ask the author, and comments they have about the content of the writing (Tompkins, 2004b).

Because authors' chair activities involve all of the four language arts (listening, speaking, writing, and reading), such activities enhance the development of receptive and expressive language knowledge of all five aspects (phonological, syntactic, morphemic, semantic, and pragmatic). Author's chair activities are effective only if the audience (the rest of the class) can be attentive, active listeners for the author. Thus, it is important that a teacher be aware of attention-span limits. For this reason, author's chair activities may involve only two or three children each time.

In summary, creative writing center activities in primary classrooms enhance children's language knowledge in the following ways:

- Pragmatic knowledge is increased as children have the opportunity to see how written language is used to communicate for different purposes: invitations, thank-you notes, lists, personal narratives/stories, signs, and nonfiction texts on a particular concept or related concepts.

Journaling provides primary children with opportunities to create their own stories or to write about their daily and family events.

- Phonological knowledge and syntactic knowledge are increased through opportunities for children to put into print their experiences and thoughts. As they share their ideas through print, they gradually use more complex sentence and text structure to communicate.

- Children's productive semantic knowledge is enhanced as they have an opportunity to use their vocabulary in composing their written stories and other texts.

- Morphemic knowledge is enhanced through writing center activities as children use inflectional morphemes to indicate past tense, possession, and plurality.

Content/Concept Learning Centers

A content/concept learning center focuses on a concept or set of related concepts and is designed to encourage children to explore materials independently or to solve problems. For example, a math/science center might focus on measuring the lengths of different common objects. Related concepts, depending on the grade level, might include inch, centimeter, longer than, longest, shortest, and fraction. A social studies/science center might focus on matching pictures of animals or insects with pictures of their habitats. Related concepts for this center might include savanna, swamp, mountain, grassland, lake, ocean, rain forest, desert, and Arctic Circle. Content/concept centers enhance children's language development by focusing on increasing children's conceptual knowledge and vocabulary. They also provide an opportunity for children to use new vocabulary when responding to the tasks associated with the center.

In developing a content/concept center, teachers should label the materials with the appropriate vocabulary. Students will also benefit from having opportunities to discuss their learning center experiences when they gather in their classroom for circle time.

Word Walls

A word wall is a visual display of words that have been written on cards or large sheets of chart paper and mounted on a classroom wall. This visual display encourages children to focus on letter–sound connections and spelling patterns of words. Words selected to be included on the word wall are chosen based upon the way in which the word wall will support other classroom activities. Words placed on the word wall may represent children's high-frequency words that they are learning to read. The displayed words might also represent major content/concept words used in the learning centers (Tompkins, 2004b). Word walls can also focus on specific words from teacher-directed activities or books shared with the class. Other possible types of words displayed include spelling words, seasonal or holiday-related words, and words representing colors, shapes, or numbers (Kieff, 2003/2004; Williams, Phillips-Birdsong, Hufnagel, Hungler, & Lundstrom, 2009).

Usually, the words on a word wall are organized alphabetically by the first letter in the word; however, other ways of organizing the words may be used to show how words are related either conceptually or structurally. For example, words could be organized to represent selected words from a literature or science unit. Words might also be grouped to show word families (*cat, rat, mat, sat, hat*) or sound similarities (*fat, fun, fish, funny, furry*). You might decide to use different colors of paper or ink to distinguish specific groupings of words.

Word walls can be organized by word families.

When introducing a word wall, be sure that you have carefully selected the words to be placed on the word wall. The words should have significance to the students. For example, children's first names could be used for an initial word wall (Campbell, 2001) at the beginning of the school year. This would generate interest from the students as they see their name and their classmates' names on the word wall. Gradually, high-frequency words and names of characters from favorite stories could be added. Words should be added to the word wall slowly to avoid overwhelming the children with too many new words. Rasinski and Padek (2004) recommended introducing three to five new words per week during the primary grades.

Kieff (2003/2004) cautioned teachers to "make the word wall a teaching–learning tool, not just a display, by using it throughout the day . . . otherwise it just adds to the clutter of the room" (p. 84J). Word walls can serve as a focal point in teacher-directed word study activities. In addition, teachers can demonstrate how a word wall is used as a reference for writing and for reading. Word walls should be visible to the writing center area so that children can refer to the words during their writing activities (Casbergue, 1998). Students can be encouraged to create their own personal dictionaries based on words from the word wall. Games such as a form of bingo or "I Spy" can be developed to use with word walls (Kieff, 2003/2004).

Words displayed on a word wall can be added and deleted as students' needs for specific words change and develop. Once word cards are removed from the wall, they can be kept for individual student use in the writing center, perhaps on a ring or in a file box, or for use with a pocket chart.

Take-Home Exploratory Activities

Children may not have sufficient time at school to engage in exploratory reading and writing activities, or they may have limited literacy materials at home. One way to increase language-enhancing opportunities for children is to provide take-home suitcases (or book bags or backpacks) that are equipped for reading activities and/or writing activities.

A reading suitcase is equipped with one or more storybooks to be read either alone or with a parent (depending on the child's reading competencies). A spiral sketchbook is also included, along with drawing or writing implements. After a child has read a story (or listened to the story read aloud), she can draw or write her response to the story. When the reading suitcase is returned to the classroom after a day or two, the child may have the opportunity to share her written response with the class. As several children use the reading suitcase, a collection of responses is developed. The response book can be placed in the classroom library after all the children have had a chance to use the reading suitcase. Children will enjoy looking at and reading or rereading their own responses and other children's responses.

Opportunities to take storybooks home allow children
to explore and refine their interactions with written
language.

A writing suitcase is similar to a reading suitcase except that no storybook is
included. Instead, the suitcase contains a larger assortment of writing and drawing
implements (markers, chalk, pens, and pencils) and a variety of materials for making
different book formats: blank books, assorted papers in different sizes, scissors, transparent tape, a stapler, paper clips, construction paper for book covers, and a hand-
held hole punch. At the first-grade level, an alphabet card can be included to assist
children in letter formation. At the third-grade level, the letter card can be written in
cursive lettering. In using a writing suitcase, children might need to have the suitcase
for several days. Teachers might provide a theme or suggested story stems for children to use in their writing. When the writing suitcase is returned to the classroom,
each child should have an opportunity to share his writing with the class.

Through these two take-home activities, primary-age children will have extended
opportunities to explore and refine their language knowledge through reading and
writing. You could include a materials checklist in each suitcase so that the contents
can be easily determined as it is checked in and out.

TEACHER-DIRECTED ACTIVITIES

At the primary level, teacher-directed activities occur in both large and small group settings. Large group teacher-directed activities involve experiences in which the entire class can participate. Examples of large group language activities for primary grades described in this chapter include teacher read-alouds, oral discussions, creative drama, language experience and interactive writing, an author's chair, and media presentations on videotape or audiotapes. In this setting, the activities provide opportunity to develop a shared knowledge base and frame of reference for the entire class. This can facilitate children's sharing of ideas and also focus their communication on shared events.

Small group language activities are more focused on the specific needs of a subgroup of children or may focus on encouraging a higher level of involvement and group interaction between a few children. Suggested small group activities described in this chapter include word study activities, shared reading, literature circles, and collaborative–cooperative projects.

Teacher Read-Alouds

When a primary teacher reads to his class, children are encouraged to develop a shared knowledge of the concepts in the text, the sequence of the events, and the specific language used in the text. This shared knowledge provides children a common frame of reference on which they can focus their discussions and interactions.

Books selected to share during read-alouds should have a language level appropriate to the listening comprehension of children in the classroom. By selecting and using texts with different levels of complexity, you can develop your awareness of the texts appropriate for your students. The introduction of chapter books during teacher read-alouds is an effective way of enhancing children's ability to understand more complex story lines and characters. Chapter books enhance comprehension and story recall because the book is read over a period of time, and the story continues with each additional reading session. It is also important to include books that have dialect speech and other varied language styles, such as humor, figurative language, alliteration, and rhyme (Glazer, 2000).

Read-alouds can enhance language development in the primary grades in the following ways:

- Receptive phonological knowledge is increased as children hear your pronunciation of the words (and sounds) in the text. When big books are used, children can better see the relation between speech and print, which enhances their receptive phonological knowledge of written language.
- Receptive semantic knowledge is enhanced as new words are encountered in the text and when you take time to explain the meaning of the new

vocabulary. Be sure to refer to illustrations accompanying the text that enhance comprehension and provide opportunity to extend semantic knowledge.

- Receptive syntactic knowledge is increased as children hear the complex sentence and text structures contained in the shared books. Your fluent and expressive reading enhances children's processing of text that may be at a higher level of complexity than their current expressive syntactic knowledge.

- Receptive morphemic knowledge is enhanced through hearing you read the story text. Through your clear enunciation, children can become more aware of word structure and its relation to meaning. You can also pause to explain the meaning of words with specific inflectional or derivational morphemes.

- Receptive pragmatic knowledge is developed when a variety of genres is used during teacher read-alouds. Through the use of a variety of genres, children can develop different expectations for different texts, such as fairy tales, fables, narratives, poetry, mysteries, and nonfiction. This knowledge of text types may then be evident when children create their own stories, poems, or informational texts.

When big books are used at group story time, the text is more visible, encouraging children to focus on the print as well as the illustrations.

Oral Discussions

A teacher read-aloud is usually accompanied by an oral discussion related to the book just read. These discussions typically focus on determining children's comprehension of story events and concepts. It is important for teachers to use a variety of questions, both literal and higher level (inferential). Teachers should also use linguistic scaffolding to support and extend children's responses.

In these discussions, teachers are enhancing children's expressive language competencies. As children develop answers to specific questions, they are using their phonological, syntactic, semantic, morphemic, and pragmatic language knowledge. Based on class needs, teachers may also decide to focus the oral discussion on a particular aspect of language knowledge, such as letter–sound relations, vocabulary, word endings, or story genre or structure. This is more easily done when oversized or big books are used because the text is more visible to the children. Unison or choral reading may also be used to encourage children's expressive knowledge of written language.

Galda and Beach (2004) emphasized the importance of sharing responses to literature through oral discussions: "By creating opportunities for students to read and respond in the company of others, teachers foster their students' ability to make sense of text words and lived worlds" (p. 865). As children make connections between the experiences of the characters in the stories they read and their own experiences, they use oral and written language to learn about the world and to comment on it.

Oral discussions can be supplemented with the use of charts such as those suggested by Yopp and Yopp (2001): compare-and-contrast charts, semantic maps, and KWL charts. While these charts may be introduced prior to reading a story, they are also the basis of the poststory discussion. Compare-and-contrast charts focus on specific concepts portrayed in a story, such as good friends and bad friends, and may be used prior to reading or after the reading. Semantic maps encourage children to categorize words that are related concepts (see Figure 11.1).

When semantic maps are used with primary children, they need to be kept very simple, with only three or four main items. As this technique is used over time, more detail can be added. In addition, teachers should keep in mind that not all concepts presented in a text need to be represented in a semantic map. Instead, the main concepts or high-interest concepts can be the focus of a semantic map.

The KWL strategy, developed by Ogle (1986), is most successfully used with nonfiction texts. A three-column chart is created by the teacher. The first two columns are filled in prior to reading the text. In the first column, the *K* column, the teacher records what the children already know about the topic or concept. In the second column, the *W* column, the teacher records what the children want to know about the topic. Then, after the text is read, the third column, the *L* column, is where the teacher records what the children say they have learned from the reading. Figure 11.2 shows a completed KWL chart on "big cats."

FIGURE 11.1

Example of Semantic Map Based on the Nonfiction Book *One Big Ocean*

Source: Nichols, C. (2003). *One big ocean*. New York: Benchmark Books.

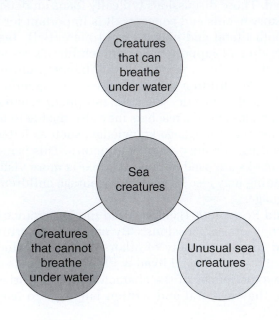

FIGURE 11.2

Big Cats KWL

What we Know:	What we Want to Know:	What we Learned:
- They have whiskers	- What different types of cats are there?	- Tigers live in Siberia + Asia
- Baby tigers are called cubs	- Where do they live?	- Lions live in Africa + India
- They have claws	- What do they eat?	- Leopards live in Africa, the Middle East + Asia
- They run very fast	- Which cat runs the fastest?	- Jaguars live in Mexico + Argentina
- They fight for their food		- Mountain Lions live in Chile + North America
- Lions have a mane		- Cheetahs live in Africa + the Middle East
		- Snow Leopards live in high-mountain areas of central Asia
		- Tigers eat fish + other prey
		- Lions eat zebras + antelopes
		- Cheetahs eat gazelles + impalas
		- Cheetahs are the fastest land animals

FIGURE 11.3
Water Cycle Diagram

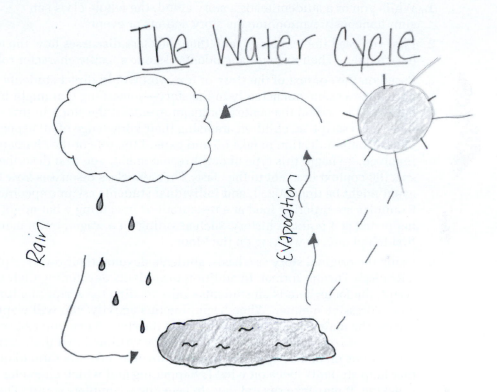

Informational text may also describe a sequence or process. This can be summarized and represented in a diagram format. For some students, such diagrams are a useful way of condensing information through visual representation and enhances their memory for that information. For example, Figure 11.3 was created after a book on the water cycle was shared.

Creative Drama

One way of enhancing primary-age children's language development is to use creative drama for story reenactment or event reenactment. Creative drama increases children's use of language to fit different contexts, their use of specialized vocabulary, and their experiences with different speech registers (Alber & Foil, 2003; Wagner, 1990). This type of activity is familiar to primary-age children because it resembles the spontaneous pretend play they may have engaged in during preschool or kindergarten.

Story reenactment can be conducted in these four ways:

1. While you or a student reads a story aloud, the whole class can simultaneously pantomime the story actions or events.

2. First you read the text aloud, and then the class discusses how the text can be acted out. Then individual students assume specific character roles.

3. Based on the context of the story or text, you would direct students to dramatize a scene not actually in the story—something that might have happened based on the context or major events in the story. In this strategy, there is no script, so children are using their knowledge of all aspects of oral communication to take on and extend the role of the character(s) involved. To begin this type of event reenactment, you first describe the specific context or event to the class. Then the class discusses how such an event might be dramatized, and individual students assume specific roles. Examples are ordering food at a restaurant or imagining what might have happened at a point in history, such as riding on a wagon train, using the first telephone, or walking on the Moon.

4. Using the original story as a basis, students develop their own script, using a Reader's Theater format. In addition to students developing their own script, the focus here is on students orally reading the script in a fluent and expressive manner. When beginning this activity, you will want to first review the main events and characters in the story. Then you can scaffold students' script writing in a group setting by writing down their script suggestions on chart paper. Your scaffolding may take the form of questions that help students focus on what is happening and which character is speaking. It may take several days to generate a complete script. Then you will need to make copies of the script for students, assign parts, and provide practice time before you have them perform their "Reader's Theater" version of the story.

In summary, creative drama provides the opportunity to enhance each of the five aspects of language knowledge, in both receptive and expressive modes: phonological, semantic, syntactic, morphemic, and pragmatic.

Morning Messages, Language Experience, and Interactive Writing

Morning messages, language experience stories, and interactive writing are used in primary classrooms to actively engage students in reading and writing processes through teacher mediation, linguistic scaffolding, and modeling. Each of these activities also provides a context for conducting minilessons on specific language concepts and competencies.

Morning messages.   When conducting a morning message activity, you will first develop a letter to your students on chart paper or white board and have it posted when students enter your classroom (SchifferDanoff, 2001). It is important to have the morning message focus on and reinforce a specific aspect of your language arts curriculum; for example, phonological knowledge, spelling, written conventions (such as punctuation), or high-frequency words.

As you read the message to your students, you will use a pointer and encourage students to echo read or read in unison with you. As you do this, you will stop to talk about the various language concepts that are the focus of your morning message. For example, in Figure 11.4, the morning message is centered on the letter *F* when it is used as the initial letter of words. This focus on initial sounds would be empha-

FIGURE 11.4
Initial Sound Morning Message

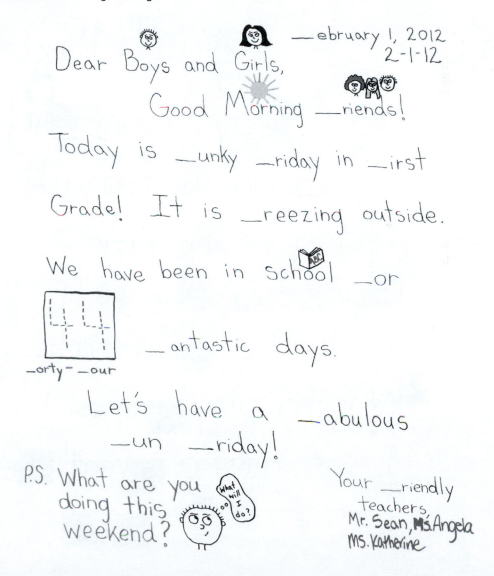

sized early in first grade as a way of reviewing what knowledge entering students bring with them from kindergarten. When sharing this morning message, you would encourage individual students to come up to the chart and write in the missing letter.

In contrast to Figure 11.4, the morning message in Figure 11.5 focuses on eight initial-letter sounds. This type of morning message could be used as a review before focusing on ending and middle sounds in words. The use of sticky notes for the missing letters is an additional way of engaging students. First, all of the sticky notes would be posted up at the top of the message. As the message is shared, individual

FIGURE 11.5
Review of Initial Sounds Morning Message

children would be called on to come select the sticky note letter and put it on the appropriate word.

Knowledge of the conventions of writing is a first-grade English language arts standard identified in the Common Core State Standards Initiative (http://www.core-standards.org/the-standards/language). The morning message found in Figure 11.6 focuses on a review of writing conventions. Since there is no punctuation or capitalization in this example, a teacher would use this type of morning message to engage

FIGURE 11.6
Morning Message on Punctuation and Capitalization

students in determining what punctuation (periods, commas, exclamation points) and capitalization (initial words of sentences, proper nouns) are needed.

It is important to understand that some children will be ready to actively participate in the morning message activity, while others will need time to observe their peers and benefit from seeing others participate. Be sure to keep the morning message time appropriate for your students' attention span. As needed, you may decide to continue a morning message activity on the following day. For additional examples and guidelines, see http://www.beaconlearningcenter.com/Lessons/397.htm; http://www.mrsnelsonsclass.com/teacherresources/teachingwriting.

Language experience stories. A central aspect of the language experience strategy is children's dictation of a text. The teacher, acting as a scribe, writes on chart paper, a chalkboard, or an overhead projector transparency exactly what children say. During the preschool and kindergarten years, children's dictation will typically be their oral language, which may contain aspects of their home dialects. At the primary level, children may dictate text that more closely represents the literate register, reflecting their knowledge of written language structure and decontextualization.

Teachers can encourage children's contributions during dictation by asking questions and providing comments to encourage further thought or response, such as:

- "Tell me more about . . . "
- "What did it remind you of?"
- "How did you feel about that?" (Mooney, 1990, p. 42)

The language experience strategy is used when teachers want to provide an opportunity for children to create a shared text and then share the reading of that text. Because the teacher assumes the writing of the text, children are not constrained by their lack of orthographic (spelling) knowledge. This strategy is a good way for teachers to observe the expressive language knowledge children have in the areas of semantic, syntactic, morphemic, and pragmatic knowledge. Based on this observation of students' language knowledge during language experience dictation, a teacher may develop and implement specific activities designed to enhance further growth in one or more of the five aspects of language knowledge.

Interactive writing. With interactive writing, the teacher focuses specifically on language concepts such as letters, words, or sounds and also focuses on specific vocabulary or sentence structure. Children are encouraged to contribute to the writing and spelling process. For example, as a first-grade teacher, you might decide that you want to emphasize that the first word of every sentence should be capitalized. Then, as your children dictate the sentences for your group story, you would stop before starting each new sentence to talk about the word that will start the sentence and the letter that begins the first word. Then you would ask for a volunteer to come to the story chart to write the capital letter to begin the word. At other times, you might decide to focus on parts of words, punctuation, or letter–sound connections.

It is important that the texts created in language experience stories and interactive writing be recopied in enlarged book form and eventually placed in the classroom library. This allows for individual student use during independent activity time.

At the primary level, students' group dictations can be used to create a wider variety of texts than in kindergarten classrooms. Whereas kindergarten children's dictated texts may focus only on a shared class event, primary children may be able to jointly create a fictional takeoff on a favorite storybook. Primary children's dictated texts may also be in the form of a nonfiction account of their knowledge about a set of related concepts (e.g., the weather), a list of words with similar characteristics, or a list of questions about a particular topic.

Media Presentations

Occasionally showing videotapes or DVDs can provide children with an opportunity to expand their listening vocabulary and receptive knowledge of syntax and semantics. Because there is no opportunity for children to have their questions answered or comments shared during the showing of the videotape or DVD, it is important that you take time just after the showing for children's questions and comments and to ask children questions to determine whether they comprehended the important ideas or concepts.

Audiotapes or CDs can also be used to enhance listening vocabulary, but only if the story is familiar to the children or if the story incorporates schemata already established. To comprehend an audiotape or CD story, children must be able to visualize the story characters and the events that occur. When children are inattentive during this activity, it may indicate that their listening comprehension is not sufficient to foster comprehension.

SMALL GROUP TEACHER-DIRECTED ACTIVITIES

Small group teacher-directed activities are planned to focus on the needs of a smaller group of students or to provide an opportunity for children to become more actively engaged in verbal interaction with several children. Four sample activities will be described in this section: word study activities, shared reading, literature circles, and collaborative–cooperative projects.

In organizing these activities, you will need to group students based on the children's specific needs or the purpose of the activity. For word study activities, children need to be able to focus on the selected linguistic concept (e.g., initial sounds, word endings). In literature circles, children need to have read the same story or text in order to be able to effectively discuss it.

Word Study Activities

Word study activities may focus on phonetic, morphemic, or semantic knowledge related to specific words (Bear, Invernizzi, Templeton, & Johnston, 2011; Burns, Roe, & Smith, 2002). In conducting a word study activity, the teacher first determines which children have a specific need for a focused activity and then selects an appropriate word study activity. Word study concepts are introduced in the format of a mini-lesson: an introduction to the concept, examples of the desired word analysis, and then an opportunity for children to practice the task cooperatively or independently, depending on their level of understanding.

Word families. Word family activities may focus on onset and rime (Johnston, 1999). In these activities, children sort words (written on cards) from two or more word families, such as *hop, stop, mop, map, tap,* and *cap.* Initially, the teacher guides the sorting process. Later on, children can work in pairs or alone. After sorting, words are written down in categories, and children are encouraged to add more words to each category on their own. When children can quickly and correctly read and spell the selected word families, the focus can change to new word families. Word family activities enhance language knowledge by encouraging children to identify and manipulate words, which enhances their phonetic knowledge of oral and written language.

Word banks. With word banks, children make a collection of the words they can read or vocabulary words they know. Usually, the words are placed on index cards and then used in word sort activities. Other types of word collections include word posters and word clusters (see Tompkins & Hoskisson, 1995). Additional word study activities are found in the resource books listed in Figure 11.7.

FIGURE 11.7
Resources for Word Study Activities

Bear, D., Invernizzi, M., Templeton, S., & Johnston, F. (2011). *Words their way: Word study for phonics, vocabulary and spelling instruction.* Boston, MA: Allyn & Bacon/Pearson.

Blachowicz, C., & Fisher, P. (2009). *Teaching vocabulary in all classrooms.* Boston, MA: Allyn & Bacon/Pearson.

Gunning, T. (2000). *Phonological awareness and primary phonics.* Boston, MA: Allyn & Bacon/Pearson.

McCormick, C., Throneburg, R., & Smitley, J. (2002). *A sound start: Phonemic awareness lessons for reading success.* New York: Guilford Publications.

Rush-Campbell, P. (2007). *Reading, writing and word walls: Strategies to boost literacy skills in all learners.* Peterborough, NH: Staff Development for Educators.

Tompkins, G. (2012). *50 literacy strategies: Step by step.* Boston, MA: Allyn & Bacon/Pearson.

Yopp, H., & Yopp, R. (2000). Supporting phonemic awareness development in the classroom. *The Reading Teacher, 54*(2), 130–144.

Shared Reading

In shared reading, children take turns reading to each other from individual copies of either basal readers or trade books. At the first-grade level, reading pairs are more effective than larger groupings. In second or third grade, children may be able to have shared reading in groups of three or four. The purpose of shared reading is to provide opportunities for children to read orally in an informal setting. Through repeated opportunities to read texts at their appropriate level of reading, children develop reading fluency.

Shared reading typically involves dividing the entire class into reading pairs or threesomes for a period of 10 to 15 minutes. The classroom teacher initially determines the composition of each reading group and then monitors children's participation. In this way, children have an opportunity to practice their oral reading with a peer. Children can be encouraged to share with each other their "detective strategies" in using clues from their word knowledge to decode and comprehend what is written. Shared reading may boost self-confidence and greater oral fluency.

Primary children also benefit from cross-age shared reading, which is typically referred to as "buddy reading" (Campbell, 2001). In this type of shared reading, students from upper grades visit a primary grade to read storybooks to two or three children at a time. This activity gives primary children an opportunity to increase their listening comprehension as well as their conversational skills.

Guided Reading

For this small group activity, children are selected by reading ability to read texts that have been designed for their reading level (Fountas & Pinnell, 2009). In this setting, the teacher provides different levels of scaffolding and mediation as individual children read the text. Decoding skills, oral fluency, and comprehension are emphasized in this activity. As the teacher guides the children through the text, she encourages children to think about how they read as well as the meaning of the text (Cole, 2006).

Literature Circles

With a literature circle, a small group of students meet to discuss a piece of literature (Galda, Cullinan, & Strickland, 1993; Owocki, 2001; Yopp & Yopp, 2001). For first grade, these discussion groups may follow a teacher read-aloud; in second and third grades, students may read their selections silently, prior to their discussions. This activity enhances children's oral language communication skills in each of the five areas of language knowledge. Children's comprehension is enhanced through peer discussions (Kasten, 1997). Their knowledge of the conventions of written language may also be enhanced as they refer to the text to support and clarify their discussion responses. Research studies have concluded that literature circles provide opportunity for primary students to develop more elaborate and complex responses to what they read through the process of orally sharing their thoughts and interpretations with each other (Morrow & Gambrell, 2002).

Cross-age shared reading enhances children's reading fluency and conversation skills.

Literature circles require specific communication skills that primary children may not yet have developed (Galda et al., 1993). Teachers should discuss with students which kinds of questions are appropriate for literature circles and for specific genres. When initiating this activity, teachers may decide to provide specific questions for the groups to use and then gradually encourage students to develop their own questions. Encouraging children to develop and use their own questions enhances their conversation skills (Newkirk & McLure, 1996).

Teachers must clearly communicate their expectations for the processes to be used in literature circles (i.e., thinking, reading, sharing meanings) and the ways in which students are to interact in terms of turn-taking or specific roles to be assumed (e.g., questioner, scribe/recorder). Students can also be encouraged to reflect on the success of their group in the discussion. Effective literature circles will develop over an extended period of time, with students gradually assuming more responsibilities in planning and conducting their discussions. When teachers of successive grade levels (e.g., first-, second-, and third-grade teachers) use this technique, students have repeated opportunities to continue to develop their oral discussion competencies and their ability to interact effectively.

Collaborative–Cooperative Projects

In the primary grades where themed cross-curricular instructional units are used, children may work in small collaborative groups. This may involve dramatic improvisation, role-playing, story retelling, or the creation of a mural or other hands-on project, such as a model or diorama. These projects may also involve exploring specific topics through a variety of library resources.

A wide variety of language skills are enhanced through collaborative–cooperative projects. In these projects, students use listening, speaking, reading, and writing to explore, create, and solve problems (Morrow & Gambrell, 1998). By working together on a project, children are encouraged to reflect on their thinking. The development of this "critical reflectiveness" contributes to literate thinking (Wells & Chang-Wells, 1996, p. 165).

Like literature circles, collaborative projects require social and interaction skills that students may need to acquire over an extended period. Teachers may need to introduce collaborative projects one step at a time, providing a supportive environment in which students can gradually assume more responsibility for planning and conducting their own projects.

FAMILY CONNECTIONS

Family–school connections can be strengthened by providing parents with specific activities and ideas for extending their children's learning at home. One of the key areas of language development in the primary years is vocabulary. Wasik (2006) described the following ways teachers can encourage parents to strengthen vocabulary development at home:

- Provide parents with a list of current vocabulary words, along with a brief definition. Include a note suggesting that the family use the words in conversations and talk about the meaning of the words.
- From your classroom library, provide photocopies of books you have created with your students using target vocabulary.
- Provide materials in a "writing book bag" to encourage parents and children to write their own stories using target vocabulary.

Your classroom newsletters to parents can also describe activities that parents and children can engage in that will enhance children's language development. Be sure to keep the newsletter easy to read and parent-friendly (see Figure 11.8).

SUMMARY

During the primary years, children continue to develop knowledge of oral and written language in each of the five aspects of language knowledge. Classrooms that encourage children's active explorations of language through hands-on, collaborative activities increase the depth and breadth of children's language competencies. At the primary level, teachers use linguistic scaffolding, mediation, and questioning to encourage children's expressive language. Children's listening competencies are

FIGURE 11.8
Primary Classroom Newsletter

Supporting Your Child's Learning at Home

Provide a quiet corner for your child to

- Share books and read for fun
- Complete schoolwork
- Create art projects

What's in a quiet corner?

- Small table or desk with storage containers or small boxes
- Writing materials
- Stapler, 3-hole punch, ruler, calculator, etc.
- Wastepaper basket
- Floor pillows or a beanbag chair

Together in your kitchen

- Read and prepare recipes together
- Start a collection of easy recipes
- Take digital pictures of what is made and enjoyed to make your child's personal cookbook

Preserving family memories

- Make a family scrapbook together
- Have your child write or dictate to you descriptions of events and trips
- Include your child's drawings
- Add digital pictures taken by you or your child with captions

Connecting with extended family

Encourage your child to send family members
- Thank you notes
- Written or email invitations
- Letters
- Stories and poems
- Invitations to Skype or Facebook to strengthen relationships and oral language capabilities

Parent resources:

Wilkes, A. (2008). *Children's quick and easy cookbook*. New York: DK Publishing, Inc.
Family Fun magazine. FFNcustserv@cdsfulfillment.com
Furgeson, L., & Taylor, S. (2001). *Family scrapbooking: Fun projects to do together*. New York: Sterling Publishing.
Bearnson, L., & Higgins, B. (2005). *Our family scrapbooks,* Bluffdale, UT: CK Media.
Zanzarella, M. (2004). *The good housekeeping illustrated children's cookbook*. New York: Hearst.

critical to their language development and success at school. Language-enhancing activities include both exploratory–discovery center activities and teacher-directed large and small group activities.

✳ ✳ ✳ CHAPTER REVIEW

1. Key terms to review:

   question–answer relationship (QAR)　　　　　　inquiry learning

2. What listening competencies do primary-age children need?
3. Select two of the recommended large group teacher-directed activities. Identify the aspects of language knowledge that could be enhanced by those activities.
4. What is the value of small group teacher-directed activities to language development? Give an example and explain its value.
5. How do content/concept learning centers enhance language development?

✳ ✳ ✳ CHAPTER EXTENSION ACTIVITIES

Observation

Observe a primary classroom for a morning. Which activities were teacher directed? Which activities were exploratory and independent? In what ways do both types of activities enhance language development?

Curriculum Development

Develop your own writing suitcase. Explain your rationale in selecting the materials for the writing suitcase. Also explain how you would introduce it to a second-grade classroom.

CHAPTER 12

LANGUAGE ASSESSMENT: OBSERVING, SCREENING, DIAGNOSING, AND DOCUMENTING

Learning Outcomes

After reading this chapter you should be able to

- Describe the strengths and limitations of using observation as a way of assessing children's language development

- Identify the criteria to follow when selecting a screening instrument

- Discuss the recommended procedures in setting up a prereferral conference with a child's parents

- Distinguish between screening and diagnostic testing procedures

- Discuss the ways in which portfolios may be used to document children's language development

- Describe how to share assessment information with parents

In planning her preschool curriculum, Ms. Sanchez seeks to engage in developmentally appropriate practice that reflects her children's levels of development. To do this, she conducts both informal assessments and more formal assessments of children's development. The informal assessments are observation based. Today, she plans to observe children's verbal interactions in the classroom book corner. As she sits in a small chair near the book corner, she uses a checklist to document children's interactions with each other—how they are interacting with the books and literacy-related props in the book center.

Assessment of children's development and learning is an important part of all early childhood programs. In order to plan appropriate learning activities and to respond to accountability concerns, teachers need to engage in ongoing and periodic assessments. To become aware of children's language competencies, you will need to assess children's language by using a variety of assessments and forms of documentation. In many instances, children with special needs will be included in regular early childhood classrooms. This means you will also need to become familiar with the types of assessments that speech pathologists and other specialists use to diagnose and document specific language disorders or developmental delays. This knowledge will allow you to understand the assessments used by these specialists and to participate more actively during assessment conferences for children with special needs who are enrolled in your classroom.

This chapter provides an overview of assessment techniques with a focus on three purposes: (1) documenting children's language development in the classroom as a basis for developmentally appropriate learning activities, (2) screening for language developmental delays, and (3) diagnosing children's language competencies for specific areas of difficulty.

Assessment measures can be grouped into two categories: informal and formal. These types vary in the specific information obtained through the assessment and the manner in which the information is collected. **Informal assessments** in early childhood are predominately observational, with children's language documented using checklists, anecdotal records, and audio or video recordings. **Formal assessments** involve eliciting children's responses to specific language tasks in a one-on-one or group setting. Formal assessments involve specific procedures for administration, scoring, reporting, and interpretation. Both types of assessments have strengths and weaknesses that influence their value in documenting children's language development. Informal assessments are used frequently in the classroom to document children's language development, while formal assessments are used to screen for developmental delay and to diagnose for specific areas of difficulty.

USING INFORMAL OBSERVATIONS TO DOCUMENT CHILDREN'S LANGUAGE DEVELOPMENT IN THE CLASSROOM

Two major responsibilities of early childhood educators are documenting the development and learning of the children in their classrooms and providing a developmentally appropriate curriculum. A range of informal assessment techniques can provide you with important insights into children's strengths and areas of potential development. In deciding which assessment techniques to use, you will need to first understand the types of informal assessments and the strengths and limitations of each type.

In early childhood settings, informal observational assessments of language focus on documenting children's developing competencies on an ongoing basis throughout the year. This ongoing assessment is referred to as **formative assessment**. From these ongoing assessments, a teacher's awareness of children's current language knowledge can be used to adjust classroom curricula to meet their needs. For example, if repeated observations indicate that children's vocabulary development is an area of concern, the curriculum can be modified to incorporate more concept-rich and vocabulary-focused experiences and activities.

Formative assessment is emphasized in the National Association for the Education of Young Children's position statement *Developmentally Appropriate Practices in Early Childhood* (Bredekamp & Copple, 1997). It specifies that assessments should (1) be "ongoing, strategic and purposeful" (p. 21); (2) primarily involve observation and description of children's development and sample work; and (3) reflect children's progress in attaining developmental goals.

Formative assessment is also incorporated into the concept of **authentic assessment**. This concept emphasizes assessment that has the following characteristics (Kostelnik, Soderman, & Whiren, 2010; Morrison, 2009):

- Occurs within a natural learning context of everyday activities
- Focuses on what children can do
- Is an integral part of the regular classroom curriculum

Morrison (2009) referred to authentic assessment as "performance-based assessment."

Observational Assessment

The process of observation requires that the observer know what to look for, how to record the behavior, and how the behavior should be interpreted or explained (Bentzen, 1985). A teacher's educational philosophy and professional knowledge form the basis on which observations of children's language behaviors are made. This process involving focused, yet naturalistic, observation has been termed "kid-watching" (Goodman, 1985; Owocki & Goodman, 2002).

A necessary part of observation, or kidwatching, is developing ways to document what is observed. This can be done by using checklists, anecdotal records, or audio or video recordings. The particular way in which a teacher decides to document observations will be based on the time involved and the ease in carrying out the documentation. Any type of documentation needs to contain certain identifying information, such as the child's first and last names, the date of the observation, the name of the observer, and length of time observed. As a group, observational measures have both strengths and limitations.

Strengths. Observations of children's ways of using language can be made while children are engaged in learning activities. You can observe children as they engage in solitary play, parallel play, or even small group cooperative play. Observing children when they are in a large group is also possible, especially if you are able to observe and not be involved in directing the activity. Observation provides opportunity to document children's use of language in naturalistic settings and does not interrupt or change the nature of their interactions with each other or with learning materials. Observations are flexible and can be adapted to specific situations in the classroom.

Limitations. Observations require that teachers have a clear understanding of the type of behavior or performance they are observing. If teachers do not know what specific behaviors or benchmarks to look for when conducting observations and how to interpret the behaviors observed, conclusions based on such assessments will be invalid and may result in inappropriate decisions. It is also important to keep in mind that repeated and frequent observations may be necessary before you can see a pattern of behavior or language use.

Another limitation of observations is the time needed to conduct them. Because an observation often involves focusing on only one child at a time, an extensive time commitment is required to conduct the same assessment on each child in the classroom.

Regardless of the format in which the observations are documented, using observations requires extensive record keeping. Data collected during observations must be organized and maintained over a period of time. It must also be interpreted and synthesized rather than simply filed away.

In addition, observational assessments are potentially limited by observer bias. When observations are unstructured and open-ended, teachers must make interpretations of children's performance or responses. This subjectivity may cause the assessment to become susceptible to observer bias (Smith, 1990). To overcome this weakness, more than one teacher should participate in conducting observations.

Another limitation of observational assessments is that they may not be well understood by administrators and parents because the outcomes of these assessments are descriptive and do not result in numeric ratings or give developmental percentiles or stages. Teachers may need to explain carefully to parents and administrators the nature of observations, interpretations, and conclusions arising from this type of assessment.

Specific Ways of Documenting Observations

Three frequently used ways of documenting observations are using checklists, anecdotal records, and audio and/or video recordings.

Checklists. Checklists are composed of lists of characteristics or behaviors that are the focus of an observation. Teachers may develop their own checklists

FIGURE 12.1

Example of a Checklist Format for Documenting Observations

Child's Name: Sarah T.	Date Observed: 2/15/02	
Age: 4 years, 8 months		
Oral Language Characteristic	Characteristic Present	Characteristic Not Present
Speaks confidently in group settings	✓	
Speaks distinctly enough for adults to understand	✓	
Speaks in expanded sentences		✓

or observation scales or may use checklists previously developed (Antonacci & O'Callaghan, 2004; Owocki & Goodman, 2002). When you develop your own checklist, it is important that the behaviors or criteria you include be representative of developmental competencies that have been identified in early childhood research and assessment literature. Before using a checklist, you need to review the checklist items to determine whether the characteristics listed are relevant to the information you need.

A basic format of a checklist is shown in Figure 12.1. In this format, the oral language characteristics are listed on the left, and the observer simply checks in the right column whether or not the characteristic was present during the observation on that specific day.

Checklists may also contain space for additional comments or for noting behaviors related to the target characteristics, and they may document observation over several weeks. The observation format shown in Figure 12.2 documents observations over a period of time and includes narrative examples. In this particular example, the observations were conducted in a child's home by a preservice early childhood teacher candidate (Jimenez, 2008). Ms. Jimenez conducted the observations over a three-week period because she wanted to observe this child's ways of using language over a longer time period. As illustrated in this detailed example, using observations is an important way teachers can begin to document children's early ways of communicating. Through repeated observations, specific areas of language development can be documented. From these observations, teachers can develop appropriate learning activities and experiences to enhance language development.

FIGURE 12.2

Observation of an Infant's Ways of Communicating[1]

Child's name: Charlie	Age: 5 months	Date(s) observed: February 2, 9, and 16		
Focus of observation	Questions to consider (be sure to indicate each speaker's identity, e.g. mother, sibling, observer):	Consistently	Occasionally	Not at this time
Attention to adult's speech	1. Does child look to speaker?		X	
	2. Does child turn to face the speaker?		X	
	3. Does child stop what he/she is doing and look to see who is talking?		X	
	Examples: *When the child was placed in his bouncer, his mother communicated with him. Although he was not consistent, Charlie would occasionally turn to and smile or babble at his mother; he would also stop bouncing and listen attentively.*			
Eye contact, shared reference	1. Does child respond to speaker's request to "look"?		X	
	2. Does child follow speaker's pointing gestures?		X	
	3. Does child make eye contact with speaker when he/she is talking and directly in front of or holding the child?		X	
	4. When presented with an object, does child first look at speaker and then at object?			X

(continued)

341

FIGURE 12.2 *(continued)*
Observation of an Infant's Ways of Communicating

Child's name: Charlie	Age: 5 months	Date(s) observed: February 2, 9, and 16		
		Consistently	Occasionally	Not at this time
Focus of observation	Questions to consider (be sure to indicate each speaker's identity, e.g. mother, sibling, observer):			
	Examples: Charlie was more likely to follow the request to look if his mother used a pointing gesture than if no gesture was used. He made eye contact when held directly in front of his mother but would turn away if not interested. When Charlie was lying on his back and presented with a new object, he immediately looked at the object, reached for it, grasped it, and put it in his mouth.			
Turn taking/dialogic participation	1. When adult speaks to child and then pauses, does child respond nonverbally?	X		
	2. When adult speaks to child and then pauses, does child respond verbally?	X		
	3. Does child "take turns" in listening and responding?	X		
	Examples: When his mother spoke and paused, Charlie would kick or move his arms. He would also babble back to his mother. Charlie would engage in a "conversation" if he was in a good mood and interested.			

Attention to ongoing events	1. Does child notice a new event in the room?		X
	2. Does child continue to watch ongoing events?	X	
	Examples: *If someone walked in or out of the room, the child consistently noticed and turned away from whatever he was engaged in. If the child was interested in the event, he would continue watching, but if he wasn't interested, he'd turn away.*		
Level of language	Which categories of expressive language were observed?		
	1. cooing	X	
	2. babbling	X	
	3. echolalic babbling	X	
	4. one-word (invented and conventional)		X
	5. two- to three-word phrases		X
	Examples: *Although the child occasionally appeared to experiment with echolalic babbling, he consistently engaged in babbling. When engaging in "conversation," he would say "baba" or "bubu."*		

Home use of language: ____ Non-English speaking _X___ Standard English speaking ____ Dialect of English

(continued)

FIGURE 12.2 *(continued)*

Observation of an Infant's Ways of Communicating

Child's name: Charlie	Age: 5 months	Date(s) observed: February 2, 9, and 16

Summary of child's ways of communicating (summarize each section): *Charlie is a 5-month-old boy who was observed on February 2, 9, and 16. He was observed at approximately the same time for all three observations: about noon. When he was placed in his bouncer, his mom sat in front of him. She communicated to him by asking him what he was doing or if he'd found his friend (a stuffed toy). Charlie would occasionally turn to look and face his mom. He would at times respond to the questions by babbling or smiling. When his mom got his attention, he would stop bouncing, listen attentively, and respond with a smile.*

When asked to look, Charlie was more likely to follow the request if it was followed with a hand gesture. Charlie has a series of pop-up books he seems to enjoy. During this observation, he was held by his mom as she read one of these books to him. If she pointed at something and said, "Look, Charlie!" he was more likely to respond to her request than if she just asked him to look. As the book was being read, Charlie did maintain eye contact, although it was not consistent. He would turn away once he seemed uninterested and would return to look at his mom if she changed her tone to a more excited one.

When his mom paused while she was engaged in a conversation with him, he would respond by kicking or moving his arms abruptly, as if requesting more conversation. At times, Charlie would respond to his mom's pause by babbling or filling in the pause with a sort of yell. Although the behavior is not consistent, the child does take turns in listening and responding. When his mom would babble to him, he would babble back. For example, when his mom said, "Charlie, ba-ba-ba," he responded with "ba-ba-ba" and so on. When someone else walked into the room, Charlie would turn his attention away from whatever he was doing to look at the new person. As he was being fed, Charlie would stop eating and observe the new person in the room for a while, until returning to eating.

His main way of communicating was through cooing and babbling; however, he did appear to experiment with echolalic babbling. Charlie seemed to indicate hunger or tiredness by crying. If Charlie woke up on his own from his nap, he would wake up babbling; however, if he was awakened by a loud noise, he would wake up crying and sometimes not go back to sleep.

Source: Data from Jimenez, S. (2008, April). Unpublished manuscript. Chicago, Illinois: Northeastern Illinois University. Format from Otto, B. (2008). *Literacy Development in Early Childhood: Reflective Teaching for Birth to Age Eight,* 1/e. published by Allyn & Bacon/Merrill, Boston, MA. Copyright © 2008 by Pearson Education. Reprinted by permission.

[1]A reproducible template for this observation format is provided in the Instructor's Manual, available online at Pearson Education.

In developing and using a checklist, you might find it valuable to use a format that provides separate documentation for each time you observe. This will allow you to more clearly notice the similarities and differences in a child's language over time and also preserves the integrity of each observation. Figure 12.3 provides a segment of an observation of a preschooler during shared book reading (Jimenez, 2008). Observations occurred on three different occasions, approximately one week apart.

Strengths and limitations.   The strength of a checklist is that it systematizes observation to focus on specific behaviors. When two or more teachers are observing several children or conducting repeated observations of one child, a checklist provides for a more uniform focus for the observations. Another strength of checklists is that they can be adapted and modified to include a specific focus.

Checklists are limited as a form of assessment because they may not provide information about the context of the behavior observed or the frequency or duration of the behavior (Puckett & Black, 2008). When a checklist provides only a yes/ no check-off for the observed behavior, complex behavior or learning may be oversimplified (McAfee & Leong, 2011). For example, a checklist with the item "uses new vocabulary" may not fully represent the complex development underlying this behavior. Because checklists target only specific behaviors, you may miss observing other important or related behaviors that occur (Beaty, 2006).

Anecdotal records.   An anecdotal record is a form of documentation that provides more detail than checklists. It is generally written in a narrative format, providing a descriptive account of language-related behaviors during a specified time. Although it may focus on a general area of language competency, such as vocabulary, an anecdotal record is more open-ended and less structured or systematic than a checklist-based observation.

Index cards or sticky notes are often used for anecdotal records (Kostelnik et al., 2007). While index cards and sticky notes are convenient for making anecdotal records during ongoing classroom activities, they need to be transferred and organized further in order to be useful. Many teachers have found it useful to transfer sticky notes to a file folder system in which each child has a separate file folder. Index cards can be filed alphabetically by child's last name into a small box. It's important to date each separate note so you will have a chronological order to your anecdotal records.

In preparing to develop an anecdotal record, you should first identify the purpose of the observation. Is it to record a child's conversational interactions with peers or to document vocabulary growth? It is also important that your interpretations of a specific language-related behavior be separate from the description of what you observe.

FIGURE 12.3
Observation of a Toddler's/Preschooler's Knowledge of How to Read During Shared Book Reading[1]

Child's name: Marissa		Age: 2 years, 2 months		
Focus of Observation	Questions to consider	Date: February 4 Book: Qué Rico!	Date: February 11 Book: Go Dog. Go!	Date: February 18 Book: Eyes, Nose, Fingers, and Toes
		Descriptive example:	Descriptive example:	Descriptive example:
Shared reference	Follows adult's gestures/pointing?	*As adult read and pointed to the words and pictures, Marissa looked and followed along. Sometimes she named the food on the page.*	*Marissa followed the adult's pointing, but would lift or push the adult's hand away from the book and point to the illustrations herself.*	*Marissa followed along and pointed to the parts of the body that were being talked about. She pointed to her own eyes, nose, etc.*
Turn taking/dialogic participation	Responds nonverbally? Responds verbally?	*Marissa Sometimes looked at the adult as the book was being read. Words were not pronounced 100% accurately, but one could make out what she was trying to say.*	*As Marissa sat on the adult's lap, she would look up at the adult. She observed the adult's mouth as she spoke. Marissa imitated the adult's reading throughout the book. "Go. Dog, go!" was repeated as "Doh da oh."*	*Marissa sat beside the adult while being read to. She made eye contact whenever the adult paused. She responded to a series of questions. "Where are your eyes?" Marissa responded, "Ee" and pointed to her eyes.*

Summary of each section of your observations (e.g., What similarities and differences were seen across the three sessions and with the three different books? What differences were seen for the first and second time a book was shared?).

Source: Data from Jimenez, S. (2008, April). Unpublished manuscript. Chicago, Illinois, Northeastern Illinois University. Format from Otto, Beverly, *Literacy Development in Early Childhood: Reflective Teaching for Birth to Age Eight, 1/e.* Published by Allyn & Bacon/Merrill, Boston, MA. Copyright © 2008 by Pearson Education. Reprinted by permission of the publisher.

---

[1] A reproducible template for this complete observation format is provided in the Instructor's Manual for this text, available online at Pearson Education.

FIGURE 12.4
Anecdotal Record of Pragmatic Language Behaviors

Child's Name	Responds to Routine Greetings/ Farewells	Expresses Needs or Wants
	Observer/Teacher: _____ J. Smith _____	
1. Heather	9/7 *Good morning, Miss Smith.*	9/15 *Can I have more milk?*
2. Teddy	10/2 *When asked how he was, Teddy replied, "I am fine." Then he asked me, "How are you?"*	11/30 *Asked teacher how to spell "happy" for him at the writing table.*
3. David	9/7 *"Good-bye, Miss Smith."*	*"Teacher, please tie my shoe."*
4. Marco	9/15 *"Hi, teacher."*	*"Teacher, I need help."*

The anecdotal record shown in Figure 12.4 focuses on specific children's pragmatic language behaviors. Note that this example shows the specific dates of the observations and details the relevant examples of children's verbal interactions. The value of this type of observation format is that it documents the expressive language of more than one child and provides the teacher with more specific assessment information to use in making curricular decisions and to share with parents regarding children's language acquisition.

Strengths and limitations.   Using anecdotal records is an effective way to describe children's language behavior within a classroom setting. These records can provide a record of detailed observations over time. Depending upon your assessment needs, you may find that anecdotal records provide you with important observations and insights that you might have overlooked when observing using a structured checklist. Or you might find that anecdotal records are limited by their lack of structure and their open-ended format. The actual content, wording, and nature of an anecdotal record are determined by the person writing/composing the narrative. Because anecdotal records are unstructured, they may be highly subjective, influenced easily by the attitudes and value systems of observers. One way of addressing this limitation is to distinguish between what was observed and how the observer interprets the child's behavior in the written anecdotal record. The anecdotal record presented in Figure 12.5 illustrates a way in which the observation is separated from the observer's interpretation of the child's behavior.

There may be little reliability or agreement between the anecdotal records made by multiple observers. When this occurs, teachers need to discuss their observations and attempt to reconcile their different interpretations before any conclusions can be drawn or decisions can be made about a child's language development.

FIGURE 12.5

Example of an Anecdotal Record on Vocabulary and Conceptual Development

Child: _____Teddy_____   Observer Teacher: _____Sue_____

Date: 10/2
Behaviors:
Teddy had the three larger plastic
    barrels at the table. After he had
    stacked them according to size, with
    the largest at the bottom, he said, "This
    is a caterpillar."

Comments/Interpretations:
*Teddy is able to see the similarity of
    the three barrels and a caterpillar. It
    also shows his developing
    conceptual and symbolic knowledge.*

Date: 11/20
Behaviors:
Teddy glued several pieces of white
    paper end to end. Then he added a
    triangular piece of green construction
    paper and said, "This is a kite."

Comments/Interpretations:
*Teddy is continuing to develop his
    awareness of the similarities of
    certain shapes to objects in the real
    world. We just read a story about
    kites this week. I wonder if the story
    helped Teddy to see the similarity
    between his creation and the kite
    pictured in the story. It was white and
    green, too.*

Another limitation of anecdotal records is the amount of time needed to create and maintain observational assessments using this format. To acquire an awareness of children's language development, a teacher must collect, review, and summarize a large body of anecdotal records. This may involve more time than is available to a classroom teacher. For these reasons, teachers in most classrooms use anecdotal records on only a limited basis.

Audio and video recordings.   Observations of children's communicative interactions can be captured on audio and video recordings. Videotaping provides a more complete language sample because nonverbal communication and the visual context can also be recorded.

Strengths and limitations.   Using audio or video recording as a way of documenting children's language development provides a full and rich sampling of verbal and nonverbal communicative behaviors. This form of documentation also has several limitations. First, it is essential that children's language behaviors not be influenced by the presence of the audio or video recording equipment or equipment operators. Second, some early childhood classrooms cannot afford to purchase the necessary recording and viewing equipment. A third limitation is the extensive time involved in reviewing the tapes and determining the evidence of language development present on the tape. If detailed written transcriptions are to be made, even more time will be required. Fourth, written parental or guardian permission is needed to record children. While you may not have time to use audio or video recording on a regular basis, you may find this form of documentation valuable for individual children for whom you want to make a closer, more extensive observation of their language development.

Summary. In summary, checklists, anecdotal records, and audio or video recording provide ways in which children's use of language can be documented during informal classroom observations. In deciding the purpose of your observations, determining how you will document them, and conducting your observations, you will increase your awareness of the language development of the children in your classroom.

SCREENING CHILDREN FOR LANGUAGE DELAYS

A form of assessment typically conducted and documented by early childhood teachers and specialists involves identifying children who may be at risk for developmental delays. Developmental screening is mandated by federal law in the Individuals with Disabilities Education Act (IDEA, 1975, reauthorized as PL 108-446 in 2004), which requires states to find and identify children who may need early intervention services (Allen & Cowdery, 2005). This process is referred to as **Child Find**. Each state develops its own procedures for this identification and screening process. Sometimes it involves early childhood centers; in other instances, specific agencies are involved. Early childhood development centers and schools may also decide to conduct developmental screening in order to better meet the needs of children enrolled in their programs.

A screening assessment may result in one of the following decisions (Meisels & Atkins-Burnett, 2005): (1) child's development is typical, and no further testing is needed; (2) results of screening are questionable or appear unreliable, and a decision is made to rescreen at a different time or in a different context; or (3) a referral is made for additional, more focused testing by one or more assessment specialists, such as a speech pathologist, an audiologist, an educational psychologist, or a physician.

Selecting a Screening Instrument

Because of the purpose of developmental screening, it is important to use an assessment instrument that involves only a brief series of developmental tasks lasting just 15 to 20 minutes (Meisels & Atkins-Burnett, 2005). The instrument should not involve tasks related to academic readiness. It is also important to select an instrument that has been commercially published and has undergone an extensive development process.

Validity and reliability.   During test development, the validity and reliability of the assessment instrument is established. Both of these properties are established during the professional development of the assessment instrument by using the instrument with sample populations as well as through various statistical procedures. **Validity** refers to the notion that the test actually measures what it is intended to measure. This means that the test items or tasks are carefully selected to represent key developmental milestones and behaviors.

Reliability indicates that a measure is designed to produce consistent, dependable, or repeatable scores (Mindes, 2011). Reliability must be established to assure teachers that they can be confident in the assessment results. Otherwise, the reported differences between children could be due to errors in test construction or administration. Information on a test's reliability and validity is usually located in the examiner's manual for that specific assessment or is available from the test publisher. Validity and reliability information is also published in test-review reference books, such as the *Mental Measurements Yearbooks* (Buros, 1938–) and *Tests in Print IV: An Index to Tests, Test Reviews, and the Literature on Specific Tests* (Murphy, Condey, & Impara, 1994). These sources are typically located in the reference section of a university or college library.

Standardized procedures.   Screening instruments are designed to be used on a large-scale basis in many classrooms and by teachers or other specialists. To ensure similar use, test developers specify the exact procedures for giving the assessment, scoring it, and interpreting the results. This uniformity gives confidence to the reliability of the test results across a classroom of students, between classrooms, and with multiple examiners. Established procedures for administration and scoring also reduce the possibility of bias due to examiner subjectivity or error.

Established norms for score interpretation.   A key aspect of professional test development is determining how a child's responses to the assessment tasks are scored and interpreted. Test developers determine what responses are typical and what responses indicate areas of concern or developmental risk. This process, referred to as **norming**, involves using the test with various sample populations to determine typical and atypical responses. Scores from a large number of subjects (children) are collected to provide a basis for comparing future test takers to this initial, norming sample (Wortham, 2008). Because these basic or normed scores are used to determine whether a child should be referred for additional testing, it is important that the norming process be thorough and appropriate.

The normative sample needs to represent the population with which the assessment will be used in terms of factors such as gender, age, geographic location, socioeconomic background, and ethnicity. If the normative sample is not representative of the students being assessed, the normed scores should not be rigidly applied when interpreting individual children's scores. For example, when a test contains items that focus only on knowledge or development specific to one culture and thus are inherently more difficult for children from other cultures, the test is said to be culturally biased.

It is important that you determine the similarity between the norming sample and your students prior to interpreting individual scores. Information on the composition of the norming sample (and other features of the assessment) can be found in either the examiner's manual or the technical manual available from the test publisher.

Language screening instruments. Most developmental screening instruments focus on several different developmental domains, such as cognitive, language, gross and fine motor, and social/personal. Developmental screening that occurs as part of the mandated Child Find process will use screening instruments that involve this wide range of domains.

In this section, the focus will be on language screening instruments. These instruments typically involve a series of stimuli, such as pictured items or objects used to elicit specific language responses. When selecting a developmental screening assessment for language, it is important to determine which of the five aspects of language knowledge are assessed and whether receptive and expressive language are both sampled. As with other developmental screening instruments, exact procedures are specified for administering and scoring these assessments. Personnel administering the tests must be properly qualified and have an understanding of young children's developmental needs during the assessment process. Test scores can be influenced by the way in which the test is administered. If the test is improperly administered, the test scores are not accurate representations of children's language knowledge and competencies. Table 12.1 provides an overview of six language screening instruments.

Assessing English language learners and children from diverse cultures. A screening instrument and procedures should take into consideration each child's linguistic and cultural diversity. Children's home or first language should be used during the assessment process. Assessment instruments that are culturally biased are not appropriate assessments for children from linguistically or culturally diverse backgrounds.

Using a child's home language during test administration ensures that the child understands better what is expected and how to respond to specific test items. In addition, when the purpose of the testing is to assess a child's knowledge of a second language, the person who administers the test should give the directions in the child's home language in case the child needs to have test procedures clarified.

Linking Screening to Follow-Up Referral and Services

The screening process needs to be linked to follow-up assessment and services. A screening measure serves to identify areas of concern; however, more assessment is needed to determine appropriate services or classroom placement. The linkage

TABLE 12.1
Language Development Screening Measures

Assessment	Age Level	Subtests/Sections	Language Areas Assessed	Time Needed
DIAL-4 (Developmental Indicators for Assessment of Learning), Mardell, & Goldenberg, (2011)	2yrs 6 mo-5yrs-11 mo	Motor: Gross and Fine, Language, Concepts, Self-help, Social Development	Phonological: articulation and phonemic awareness, Expressive naming, Receptive object and action naming	30–45 minutes
Fluharty-2 (Fluharty Preschool Speech and Language Screening Test, 2nd ed.), Fluharty, (2001)	3-0 through 6-11	Articulation Sentence repetition Following directions and answering questions Describing actions Sequencing events	Phonological Syntactic Semantic	10 minutes
KLST-2 (Kindergarten Language Screening Test, 2nd ed.), Gauthier, & Madison, (1998)	3-6 through 6-11	No specific subtests Receptive and expressive language in spontaneous speech Responding to questions and commands Repeating sentences Comparing and contrasting objects	Phonological Syntactic Semantic	10–15 minutes
PASS (Phonemic-Awareness Skills Screening), Crumrine, & Lonegan, (2000)	Grades 1 and 2	Rhyming Blending phonemes Deleting phonemes Isolating phonemes Substituting phonemes Segmenting phonemes Segmenting sentences Segmenting syllables	Phonological	15 minutes

Assessment	Age Level	Subtests/Sections	Language Areas Assessed	Time Needed
PLSS (Pre-Literacy Skills Screening), Crumrine, & Lonegan, (1999)	Prekindergarten	Rhyming Object naming Segmenting sentences Segmenting syllables Repeating multisyllabic words Repeating sentences Blending phonemes Naming letters Deleting phonemes	Phonological Semantic Syntactic	10–15 minutes
Denver II, Frankenburg, Dodds, Archer, Bresnick, Maschka, Edelman, & Shapiro, (1990)	Infancy (2 weeks) to age 6	Expressive and receptive language Other areas screened: Personal/social, fine motor/adaptive, and gross motor Also includes a parent questionnaire	Semantic Syntactic Morphemic	20–25 minutes (10–15 minutes for shortened version)

to appropriate follow-up is very important. Screening results and interpretations should be accurately and carefully explained to parents. This requires that teachers acquire knowledge of testing standards, procedures, and appropriate interpretations. Misinformation regarding children's test performance and how it should be interpreted can create negative effects for the children, their parents, and the school.

Although the purpose of screening measures is to identify children who need additional assessment, it is not appropriate to refer a child for further diagnostic assessment based on conclusions reached based on a single assessment measure. Instead, you should consider rescreening the child at a later date to check the consistency and reliability of the child's responses on more than one day. You should also use your informal observations along with the results of the screening to provide a more comprehensive understanding of the child's language development.

If it is necessary to make a referral for further testing or evaluation, it is important that you avoid alarming parents needlessly. When you recommend a referral, the emphasis should be on the need for more information that can be obtained through additional evaluation or testing. It is also important to share the belief that further evaluation will help you and the school better meet the child's needs. Because parental permission is needed for a referral, parents should feel comfortable with the referral and the potential benefits for their child. You should avoid prematurely labeling any child's difficulty because such a label may unnecessarily alarm parents. The purpose of the referral is to more thoroughly evaluate the child's development. Abbott and Gold (1991) described specific steps teachers should take in setting up, planning, and conducting a prereferral conference:

1. Contact the parents in person to set up a meeting, keeping in mind their availability. Tell the parents that you need to talk with them about their child but do not indicate their child is "failing."

2. Plan the meeting, choosing a private setting that has comfortable, informal seating. Be sure sufficient time is allowed. Assemble the documentation related to the child's learning achievements and challenges. This documentation may include work samples, anecdotal records, or both. List the modifications you have made in your program and curriculum in an attempt to better meet the child's needs and the outcome of those modifications. List the other professionals with whom you have consulted regarding this situation. Prepare a list of appropriate referral agencies or the school's referral professionals.

3. Conduct the meeting. Begin by welcoming the parents and telling them that you appreciate their coming. Have all materials ready. Describe the child's overall progress, specifically mentioning areas in which the child is meeting expectations. Encourage parents to share their observations of their child's learning at home. Begin to address the specific learning behavior that is of concern at school. Share the documentation you have regarding the situation and any concerns you have about the child's progress. Ask parents if they have noticed any similar behaviors at home. Be an active listener, allowing parents to express their concerns and feelings. Emphasize the need to find out more information so that the child will have the best possible learning environment. Communicate to parents what legal rights they have with respect to future testing and referral. Throughout the meeting, it is important for the teacher to focus on the shared concern with the parents for the best education for their child.

DIAGNOSING CHILDREN'S LANGUAGE COMPETENCIES FOR SPECIFIC AREAS OF DIFFICULTY

The screening process may result in identifying children for further assessment. When this happens, children are referred to specialists, who then conduct diagnostic assessments. Early childhood classroom teachers are unlikely to administer diagnostic tests because specialized training or specific advanced degrees are required (McAfee & Leong, 2011).

Purpose of Diagnostic Testing

Diagnostic tests are designed to identify more specifically the areas of difficulty and serve as a basis for planning an intervention program involving specific learning activities and experiences and services (McAfee & Leong, 2011). Diagnostic tests typically require more time to administer and comprise several different subtests that focus on specific areas of development. Diagnostic tests have been developed through extensive field testing and statistical measures. Validity and reliability of the tests have been determined, and specific procedures are set for administering, scoring, and interpreting scores using norming data.

Scope of Diagnostic Tests

Some diagnostic tests assess several developmental areas. These comprehensive measures may include subtests on cognitive functioning, language, quantitative concepts, physical motor development, and social development. For example, the McCarthy Scales of Children's Abilities (McCarthy, 1972) and the Gesell Preschool Test (Haines, Ames, & Gillespie, 1980) focus on several developmental areas. The McCarthy Scales of Children's Abilities is targeted for children ages 2 years, 4 months to 8 years, 7 months and includes subtests in these areas: verbal, perceptual–performance, quantitative, general cognitive, memory, and motor. The Gesell Preschool Test is for children ages 2 years, 6 months to 6 years, 0 months and includes subtests in the areas of motor, adaptive, language, and personal–social.

Another test, the Revised Brigance Diagnostic Inventory of Early Development (Brigance, 1991; Cohen & Spenciner, 1994) provides detailed information of development from birth to age 7 via specific subtests involving language: speech and language, general knowledge and comprehension, social and emotional development, basic reading, and manuscript writing. This specific language information can then be used in prescribing specific follow-up learning activities and experiences. Other subtests included in the Revised Brigance Diagnostic Inventory of Early Development assess preambulatory, gross, and fine motor skills; self-help skills; and basic math.

Table 12.2 provides an overview of several diagnostic assessments that focus more specifically on language development. The Peabody Picture Vocabulary Test–IV (Dunn & Dunn, 2010) assesses receptive vocabulary. Four tests reviewed in Table 12.2—the PLS–5, TELD–3, CELF–Preschool–2, and ITPA–3—are comprehensive in assessing language development because they elicit responses that involve four or more of the aspects of language knowledge. Assessments such as these, which elicit a more comprehensive range of language areas, will provide a more complete evaluation of a child's language development than do assessments that focus on only one area of language development.

TABLE 12.2
Overview of Selected Formal Assessments

Name of Test	Age Level	Focus	Subtests	Aspects of Language	Time Needed
Test of Early Language Development (TELD–3) (Hresko, Reid, & Hammill, 1999)	2 to 7 years	Oral language development	None	Semantic, syntactic, morphemic, pragmatic, phonetic* (*receptive only)	Untimed
Test of Language Development–Primary 4 (TOLD–P4) (Newcomer & Hammill, 2008)	4 through 8 years	Expressive and receptive language	Picture vocabulary, oral vocabulary, grammatical understanding, sentence imitation, grammatical completion, phonology	Semantic, syntactic, phonetic	1 hour
Clinical Evaluation of Language Fundamentals–Preschool (CELF–Preschool–2) (Wiig, Secord, & Semel, 2004)	Preschool–kindergarten	Receptive and expressive language	Receptive: linguistic concepts, sentence structure, basic concepts Expressive: recalling sentences, formulating labels, word structure	Semantic, syntactic phonological awareness	30–44 minutes
Preschool Language Scale–5 (PLS–5) (Zimmerman, Steiner, & Pond, 2011)	Birth through 7 years–11 months	Oral language—receptive and expressive	Articulation screener, language sample checklist, family interview Auditory comprehension, Expressive comprehension	Semantic, morphology, syntax, phonetic-articulation, pragmatic phonological awareness	20–30 minutes

Test	Age Range	Purpose	Subtests	Linguistic Components	Time
Peabody Picture Vocabulary Test III A & B (PPVT–4) (Dunn & Dunn, 2007)	2–6 to 90+ years	Receptive oral language (Standard English)	None	Semantic, syntactic	10–20 minutes
Expressive Vocabulary Test-2 (EVT–2) (Williams, 2007)	2–6 to 90+ years	Expressive vocabulary, and word retrieval	None	Semantic	10–20 minutes
Early Learning Milestone Scale, 2nd edition (ELM–2) (Coplan, 1993)	Birth to 36 months	General language development and speech intelligibility	Auditory Expressive Auditory Receptive Visual Language (nonverbal)	Prelinguistic expressive and receptive, semantic syntactic, phonetic	1–4 minutes
Illinois Test of Psycholinguistic Abilities, 3rd edition (ITPA–3) (Hammill, Mather, & Roberts, 2001)	5 years–0 months through 12 years–11 months	Spoken and written language	Spoken Language Analogies Vocabulary Morphological closure Syntactic sentences Sound deletion Rhyming sequences Written Language Sentence sequencing Written vocabulary Sight decoding Sound decoding Sight spelling Sound spelling	Semantic, morphemic, syntactic, phonetic, pragmatic	45–60 minutes

Using the Results of Diagnostic Testing

The results of diagnostic testing are used to plan an intervention program that addresses the child's areas of difficulty. The classroom teacher is part of the team that will be involved in planning and implementing the intervention program. To be an effective member of this team, you will want to thoroughly understand the results of the diagnostic testing and integrate those results with your classroom observations and assessments of the child. This understanding will provide you with important knowledge to use in implementing the intervention program as it relates to your classroom.

Taking time to review the diagnostic test. Even though you will not administer the diagnostic test, take time to review the test so you are familiar with the subtest areas and nature of specific items in the subtests. It is important that you are aware of the scope of information provided by test scores. In examining such scores, look at the types of subtests composing the measure as well as the nature of the specific test items or tasks.

Comparing results to your classroom observations and assessments. As you look at a child's diagnostic test results, compare them with the child's day-to-day behavior and responses in the classroom. When distinct differences between observed classroom behaviors and test scores occur, you need to share this information with the team. Be sure to provide any written documentation you have that is relevant to the areas assessed by the diagnostic test.

Looking at areas of low performance. When you receive a child's scores from a diagnostic test, take a closer look at items that were missed along with those that were correct. In doing this analysis, you will consider the type of language or information assessed by specific test items. For example, on a test that requires children to imitate or repeat target sentences such as "The hay was eaten by the cow," or "The dog and the cat ran across the park to the lake," assesses syntactic knowledge. Examine how closely children's imitated responses mirror the syntax of the stimulus sentence. What is missing? The subject? The verb? The subordinate clause? The prepositional phrase? The missing part of the target sentence indicates which syntactic structure has not yet been acquired.

Item analysis may also reveal instances in which regional variations in semantics may be responsible for errors. For example, if the stimulus word is *rig*, and the items pictured include an oil well structure and a semitrailer truck, children in locales where oil is not produced might select the semitrailer as a "rig" because they are not as familiar with oil wells. Thus, the resulting error may actually reflect cultural differences rather than linguistic deficits.

Considering the context of the testing. Many diagnostic measures involve individual testing in which the examiner and child are secluded in a separate room apart from the classroom. In many diagnostic measures, language information is obtained in isolated segments rather than through the natural dialogue or monologue that occurs in classroom interactions. Young children may find this isolated context intimidating and may not understand the nature of the testing tasks. The familiarity of the examiner to the child as well as the examiner's demeanor may have an impact on a child's responses in a formal testing situation.

It is important to keep in mind that the diagnostic testing typically occurs only on one day, and this limits it to representing a "snapshot" of the child's performance on that day. This is why you need to share your classroom observations and informal assessments that have occurred over a much longer time with the specialist to add a broader perspective on the child's development and achievements.

Sharing your questions and concerns with the specialist. Because you will be part of the team that implements an intervention program for a child, it is important for you to thoroughly understand the testing results as well as the specialists' interpretation of the results. The specialist who conducted the diagnostic tests will have had extensive experience with the specific test and will be able to assist you in understanding the test as well as the interpretation of the child's scores. When you take time to review the diagnostic test, compare the test results to your observations, look at areas of low performance, and consider the context of the test setting, you will be able to converse in meaningful ways with the specialist.

USING PORTFOLIOS TO DOCUMENT CHILDREN'S LANGUAGE DEVELOPMENT

Portfolios are often used as a way of organizing the documents resulting from a variety of assessment measures for each child (Martin, 1994). The term *portfolio* implies that the collection will be gathered in a type of portfolio or file folder. This approach to assessment has been implemented at all levels of education from early childhood through college. At each level, portfolios are implemented somewhat differently, based on the particular learning contexts in which they are used.

At the early childhood level, language development portfolios are usually composed of informal assessments and are formative in nature. As informal assessments and work samples are added to portfolios throughout the school year, changes in children's language become evident. For example, in Ms. Lyons's kindergarten room, portfolios were used to organize samples of children's early writing throughout the school year. Along with the samples, Ms. Lyons added anecdotal notes and children's comments or story dictations. In preparation for the upcoming year-end parent conferences, Ms. Lyons carefully reviewed each child's portfolio. As she reviewed Eric's writing, she noted a dramatic change in his knowledge of written language across the school year. In September, Eric mainly "drew" his stories and wrote only his name. Gradually, his stories incorporated more print, and letter–sound connections were more accurately represented, and the story lines became more complex. Now, at the end of the kindergarten year, Eric's stories were communicated through print, with his illustrations adding details to the context of the story. Ms. Lyons noted these changes in a written summary of Eric's portfolio and shared this information with his parents during their subsequent conference.

Using portfolios to organize multiple assessments of both receptive and expressive language development provides a broader understanding of children's development than that provided by only one or two assessments. The accompanying table lists the language assessment measures used in two preschool classrooms. Classroom A used only two assessments, whereas Classroom B had a portfolio system that included a wider variety of assessments.

Classroom A	**Classroom B**
Peabody Picture Vocabulary Test—IV	Peabody Picture Vocabulary Test—IV
Fluharty-2 Preschool Speech and Language Screening Test	Fluharty-2 Preschool Speech and Language Screening Test
	Pragmatic language checklist
	Anecdotal notes
	Six samples of child's emergent writing over four months

When teachers summarize the growth of the children in these respective classrooms, Classroom B will have richer, more comprehensive information on language development than will Classroom A.

A major challenge in using portfolios is managing the volume of information collected and using the information contained in the portfolio. The types and volume of materials to be included in the portfolio should be determined at the beginning of the school year, and a system should be established for organizing the portfolios as well as the contents of each portfolio. It is also important to attach a note to each assessment or work sample included in the portfolio that documents the child's name, the date, the context or setting of the assessment, and your comments on the significance of the assessment or work sample (McAfee & Leong, 2011).

The classroom teacher needs to first identify which language goals the early childhood curriculum will have for the upcoming school year. Then assessment measures can be selected to address specific language goals. Assessments conducted in the first part of the school year can be used as baseline information for planning specific curricular activities.

Provisions should be made for conducting assessments periodically throughout the year, typically every four to six weeks. These periodic assessments are usually informal in nature and may take the form of observation checklists, anecdotal records, or work samples. Children's work samples, such as drawing, invented spelling, writing, or dictated stories, should be carefully selected to represent significant work and evidence of change over time. In many classrooms, the decision to include a particular piece of work is a joint decision between the teacher and the child.

SHARING ASSESSMENT INFORMATION WITH PARENTS

As a classroom teacher, you will need to work closely with parents in sharing information on the specific assessments used in your classroom. While parental consent is required for developmental screening and referral, parents should also be aware of informal assessments used to document their children's development and learning. When sharing the results of assessments with parents, it is important for you to avoid overly technical language or premature diagnostic labels and to listen actively to parents' comments and questions.

When you meet with parents to talk about your assessment of their child's development, you should thoroughly explain the testing or assessment procedures used. In many instances, it is valuable to make an audio or video recording of the assessment so parents can observe and hear their child's spontaneous language and elicited responses. (Parental consent is necessary prior to audio or video recording.) Through the review of the audio- or videotape, parents have an opportunity to ask more specific questions and clarify other concerns they may have. This is also an opportunity to clarify the nature of any concerns you have for the child's language development.

Parents' observations of their children's language at home can make valuable contributions to the overall understanding and assessment of language development. Some teachers use specific parent questionnaires or checklists to obtain more information about the children in their classrooms. These questionnaires and checklists focus on the children's behavior at home and in their communities. For example, Owocki and Goodman (2002) developed a parent observation checklist called "My Child as a Language Learner" (p. 99). This checklist lists 12 different language-related behaviors, such as "enjoys listening to and telling stories." Parents are asked to indicate the frequency of behavior ("usually, sometimes, rarely"). Through this tool, teachers can gain more knowledge about the language competencies of the children in their classrooms.

SUMMARY

Assessment of young children's language development is an important part of early childhood education. Teachers who are aware of the strengths and limitations of specific types of assessments are better able to use assessments to create developmentally appropriate classrooms and learning activities. Knowledge of assessment procedures also assists teachers in identifying children who may need further referral to determine their language development needs.

✳ ✳ ✳ CHAPTER REVIEW

1. Key terms to review:

   formal assessment

   informal assessment

   formative
       assessment

   authentic
       assessment

   Child Find

   validity

   reliability

   norming

2. What are two strengths and two limitations of observational assessment?

3. Identify the value of using a checklist over using anecdotal records.

4. How do developmental screening assessment instruments differ from diagnostic instruments?

5. What is a portfolio? In what ways is a portfolio useful in assessing children's learning and development?

✳ ✳ ✳ CHAPTER EXTENSION ACTIVITIES

Assessment

1. Conduct a Storybook-Based Language Observation, following the guidelines and format presented in the Instructor's Manual.

2. Using the format of the observation form presented in Figure 12.2, conduct an observation of a young child and prepare a written summary.

Research

Interview a classroom teacher. Ask the teacher how children's language development is documented and shared with parents.

13

ENHANCING LANGUAGE DEVELOPMENT AMONG CHILDREN WITH COMMUNICATIVE DISORDERS

Learning Outcomes

After reading this chapter you should be able to

- Discuss the importance of using a team approach to helping children with communicative disorders
- Identify the behavior indications of hearing difficulties
- Describe techniques for enhancing language development among children with articulation disorders
- Describe techniques for enhancing language development among children who stutter
- Describe techniques for enhancing language development among children with delayed language
- Describe techniques for enhancing language development among children with autism

Ms. Thomas was concerned about the new child, Frankie, who was attending her preschool class. This was the end of the first week of his attendance, and she had observed some difficulties he was having in communicating with others in the preschool room. Frankie did not pay attention to someone who was talking to him unless that person first established eye contact with him. When specific noises occurred in the classroom (e.g., a chair falling over), he did not look around for the source of the sound. Frankie was not able to attend to a story when it was read aloud. Ms. Thomas also noticed that Frankie rarely spoke to other children during the independent activity times. Based on her observations, Ms. Thomas decided to talk with Frankie's parents to sense whether they noticed similar behaviors at home.

Not all children acquire language easily. An estimated 10% of elementary school children have some type of communicative disorder (Owens, 2001). Difficulties in acquiring language may stem from problems in reception of language, problems in production of language, or both. For example, children with hearing loss experience difficulty with language reception. Children who have problems producing specific sounds have difficulties with language expression. This chapter will focus on the special needs of children who have hearing loss, articulation disorders, fluency disorders, specific language impairment, cognitive impairment, and autism.

It is important for teachers to understand the distinction between communicative disorders and communicative differences (Piper, 1993). Different styles of speaking and communicating that are culturally based are not communicative disorders but simply different ways of communicating. Children who have communicative disorders use language in a way that significantly interferes with their ability to communicate with others who speak the same language and dialect. In some instances, they cannot effectively use language at all. Children who are becoming bilingual may not be able to communicate clearly in their second language; however, that is not a communicative disorder but only a developmental stage in the process of becoming fluent in two languages.

It is also important to remember that there are wide variations among normally developing children in the onset of language and vocabulary growth as well as the acquisition of specific grammatical structures (i.e., sentence length and complexity) (Karmiloff & Karmiloff-Smith, 2001). For example, some children may say their first conventional word at 12 months of age; for others, this will occur several months later. Because early childhood teachers interact with children who are in the process of developing communication skills, they need to be aware of the characteristics of specific communicative disorders as well as understand the normal range of language development so they can alert other teachers, administrators, and parents to potential difficulties.

Children who are at risk for speech and language disorders during the preschool years include those who (1) have had numerous ear infections, (2) do not talk or have limited speech, and/or (3) experience problems interacting (Patterson & Wright, 1990). Specific language disorders may be identified between birth and age 3 as well as during preschool screening programs and subsequent diagnostic testing. In some instances, intervention programs may be appropriate. If the problems persist until kindergarten and first grade, additional special services may be needed (Crowley, 1997, in Kostelnik, Soderman, & Whiren, 2010). At the elementary level, most school districts have a speech–language pathologist (SLP) who works with students who have been referred and identified as having mild to severe communicative disorders.

A TEAM APPROACH TO HELPING CHILDREN WITH COMMUNICATIVE DISORDERS

During all levels of early childhood education, it is important that a classroom teacher work with other specialists and children's parents in a team approach to address the needs of children with communicative disorders. The specific type of specialists included in this team approach will vary with the type of communicative disorder. For example, the following specialists might be included (Katz & Schery, 2006): audiologist (determines children's hearing levels and needed hearing aid devices), speech–language pathologist (diagnoses type of communicative disorder and is involved in establishing the intervention plan), deaf/hard-of-hearing teacher (provides additional classroom and family support), otolaryngologist (medical doctor specializing in surgical or other medical treatments related to speech–hearing physiology), counselor or social worker (provides support to the family and access to additional resources), and an interpreter (specialist skilled in communicating via sign language).

Sometimes children who are diagnosed as having mild speech or communication problems are placed in a "pull-out" program. In this approach, a child sees a speech–language pathologist for a specific time period during the day or week, depending on the severity of the speech problem. Another approach is for the speech teacher to come to the regular classroom and work with the child within the classroom setting (Owens, 1991). Sometimes this involves the classroom teacher and the speech–language pathologist in a team-teaching approach. In this setting, the classroom teacher works with most of the class, while the speech–language pathologist works with a smaller group of children who need specific teaching techniques or experiences.

In addition, the speech–language pathologist serves as a consultant to the regular classroom teacher, assisting in identifying children with language difficulties and describing specific ways these difficulties can be addressed in the regular classroom. The classroom teacher can also share her observations of the classroom behaviors and language interactions of a child with special needs with the speech–language pathologist. By clarifying the classroom expectations for participation and communication and the ways in which specific children are having difficulty meeting these expectations, the classroom teacher provides valuable insights to the speech–language pathologist about the needed intervention and language activities. Together they work to create a classroom environment that can foster growth in communication skills.

The following sections will describe communicative disorders that classroom teachers commonly face: hearing difficulties, articulation disorders, fluency disorders, specific language impairment (SLI), cognitive impairment, and autism. Behavioral indications of these communicative disorders will be described, along with strategies for enhancing language development in the classroom.

HEARING DIFFICULTIES

Sounds are measured with respect to pitch and loudness. The measurement for pitch is **hertz**, which refers to the frequency of the sound waves. The measurement for loudness is **decibels**, which refers to the pressure created by the sound waves. Normal hearing depends upon perception of both the pitch and volume of speech sounds. The normal range of hearing for humans is from 20 to 20,000 hertz (Hz); however, the range for human speech is from 500 to 4000 Hz (Vohr, 2003). Hearing loss may occur for specific frequencies within that range and at specific levels of loudness. Normal speech is typically about 60 to 65 decibels in loudness. Children who are unable to perceive sounds lower than 60 decibels usually do not develop spontaneous oral language (Ratner, 2009). When the ability to hear is reduced by more than 25 decibels in the frequency range for human speech, hearing loss occurs and language development is affected (Marschark, 1997).

Hearing loss that is situated in the physiology of the middle ear (e.g., the ear drum) is referred to as **conductive hearing loss** because the transmission of the sound vibrations is disrupted. Chronic ear inflections are associated with conductive hearing loss. **Sensorineural hearing loss** refers to hearing loss that is associated with the structures in the inner ear, such as the cochlea, or connections to the auditory nerve (Marschark, 1997).

Since the early 1990s, there has been a concerted effort to have all newborns screened for hearing loss in order to prevent later difficulties in language, academic achievement, and social skills. The American Academy of Pediatrics, the Joint Committee on Infant Hearing, and several federal agencies have been active in pushing for newborn screening for hearing loss (Hayes, 2003). Many states now require such screening. Some hospitals screen for hearing loss within the first three days (Vohr, 2003). Hearing losses that are identified during early infancy are referred to as **congenital hearing losses** because such losses were present at birth. Congenital hearing losses may be due to genetic (inherited) or prenatal conditions, such as in-utero infections (Roizen, 2003). About half of all permanent hearing loss is inherited (Reich, 1986; Vohr, 2003). Screening for newborn infants has benefitted from new technologies that measure an "infant's physiologic response to auditory stimulation" (Hayes, 2003, p. 65).

Children who have been identified during infancy as having congenital hearing loss will receive intervention services. Depending upon the nature and severity of their hearing loss, they may also be fitted with amplification devices (hearing aids) or cochlear implants. A cochlear implant is an "electronic device with electrodes that are surgically implanted in the cochlea, and an external unit that converts sound energy to an electric signal that stimulates the surviving auditory neurons" (Doyle & Ray, 2003, p. 101). Cochlear implants are used with babies who are deaf and with children for whom hearing aids are insufficient.

With older children, the amount of hearing loss is formally determined when an audiologist administers a hearing test that requires the child to visually signal when sounds are heard, thus determining the range of sound frequencies heard by each ear.

Hearing loss can be categorized as transient (temporary) or permanent. In addition to congenital hearing loss, other causes of permanent hearing loss include chronic inner ear infections and brain damage due to head or brain stem injury. Chronic ear infections are also associated with transient hearing loss, depending on the length and severity of the ear infection. Hearing loss may also result from infections associated with measles, meningitis, mumps, and scarlet fever (U.S. National Library of Medicine, 1997–2012).

When a young child has been diagnosed with a hearing loss and it is determined that an intervention program is needed, a family-centered approach is beneficial in helping the family members begin to interact and communicate with the child. The team of intervention specialists will work with the family in deciding which form of communication will be effective. For example, using American Sign Language, which combines signs, facial expression, and body language and movement would be one form of communication. Manually Coded English (MCE) is another option. MCE uses both a sign system and finger spelling (for the alphabet) (Gravel & O'Gara, 2003). The Total Communication System combines MCE with speech reading (also called lip reading) and auditory amplification (hearing aids or cochlear implants). It is important that intervention team specialists be sensitive to the preferences and communication styles of the hearing family members and that the decision about which communication option is chosen be made by the family. In addition, the family's preferences for a communication option should be reflected in the ways the classroom teacher communicates with the child.

Behavioral Indications of Hearing Difficulties

In your early childhood classroom, you may have children who have already been diagnosed with hearing loss and are in an intervention program. You may also have children in your classroom whom you suspect may have undiagnosed hearing problems. Through careful observation of a child's responses to oral speech and environmental sounds, a teacher can determine whether a hearing difficulty might exist (Cohen & Spenciner, 1994). Specifically, you would want to determine whether the child turns her head when a sound occurs or whether she startles at a loud noise. In addition, you should answer the following questions:

- Does the child respond only when being spoken to in close proximity and in face-to-face situations?
- Does the child respond when her name is called?

- Can the child follow one- or two-step directions without having multiple repetitions?
- Does the child ignore or misunderstand what others say?
- Does the child nod her head to a question or direction and then behave as if she did not hear? (Patterson & Wright, 1990)

In addition, if the child has a history of ear infections, colds, or allergies, either transient or permanent hearing loss may have occurred. Even a minor, transient hearing loss can have an effect on a child's interactions in the classroom (Harris, 1990). Whatever the reason for a hearing loss, the classroom teacher needs to be aware of the loss and make appropriate adjustments in implementing the classroom curriculum.

Techniques for Enhancing Language Development Among Children with Hearing Difficulties

When interacting with a child who is hard of hearing, you should:

1. Always speak to the child in close proximity and face to face.
2. In large-group settings, such as story time or circle activities, place the child nearby so that he can see the pictures and hear more clearly.
3. Use gestures to accompany any directions or conceptual explanations.
4. Use gestures to elicit children's attention during noisy activities or outdoor play.
5. Encourage the child to use the listening center, where earphones are used and the volume on the tape player can be adjusted to meet the child's needs.
6. Speak distinctly, using a moderate volume.
7. Encourage other children in the classroom to speak to the child in close proximity and in face-to-face orientation.
8. Allow ample response time so the child has time to process what you have said and then respond without hurrying.

Teachers should also provide visual and tactile aids through the use of illustrations, concrete objects, and hands-on activities, and they should continually check to be sure the child understands what has been said (Harris, 1990; Russell-Fox, 1999).

ARTICULATION DISORDERS

Speech production requires that the components of the physical speech mechanism (lungs, vocal cords, tongue, lips, teeth, soft and hard palate) work together in specific ways to produce the needed sounds. Articulation disorders result from difficulties in this coordination.

Indications of Articulation Disorders

Articulation disorders are indicated when a child's speech at age 3 cannot usually be understood by an unfamiliar adult, and at age 8, when errors in articulation are still evident (American Speech-Language-Hearing Association, 2012; Patterson & Wright, 1990). Some mispronunciations are typical among preschool children (Kostelnik et al., 2010). For example, consonant blends and digraphs may be mispronounced. *Spaghetti* may be pronounced "busketti," and *then* may be pronounced "ven" (Kostelnik et al., 2010) or "den." The amount, type, and duration of mispronunciations over time determine whether there should be a serious concern for a child's articulation.

In some instances, articulation problems may simply represent a delay in muscle development or coordination needed for articulating specific sounds. Articulation problems can also result from a child's chronic ear infections. Because the child could not clearly hear the speech sounds during the time in which the specific sounds were acquired, he may not have learned how to produce the specific sounds correctly.

In other instances, articulation problems may reflect specific physical impairment, such as cleft lip, cleft palate, or tongue-tie. Each of these physical impairments results from abnormalities that occurred during prenatal development and then affect articulation. **Cleft lip** is an incomplete fusion in the upper lip. When the roof of the mouth does not join correctly it is referred to as a **cleft palate**. Although the exact causes of cleft lips and cleft palates are not known, both genetic and prenatal environmental factors may be involved (Moller, Starr, & Johnson, 1990).

Tongue-tie, which is known as **restrictive lingual frenulum**, occurs when the fold of membrane (lingual frenulum) at the midline of the tongue's underside is too short (Tortora, 1992) or is "totally adhered to the floor of the mouth" (Boshart, 1999, p. 31). When the tongue is "tied," or restricted in its movement due to the shortened piece of membrane, articulation may be limited. Eating problems may also be evident. The medical term for the congenital condition resulting in tongue-tie is **ankyloglossia** (Tortora, 1992).

Because of their physical appearance, cleft lip and cleft palate conditions are usually recognized at birth, and surgery is performed during the first year. Depending on the severity of the condition, additional surgeries may be needed. Children with tongue-tie may not be identified until problems with eating or articulation are noticed. In each of these instances, surgery can correct the problem; however, depending on the age of the child and the severity of the original physical impairment, extensive speech therapy may still be needed. In severe cases of tongue-tie, postsurgery physical exercises may also be necessary (Bowen, 2000). Physical impairments such as cleft lip, cleft palate, and tongue-tie are associated with long-term problems if no intervention occurs.

When a teacher notices a child who may have continuing articulation problems, it is important for the teacher to share those observations with a speech–language pathologist so that a more focused assessment can be made and an intervention program can be developed and implemented by the classroom teacher and the speech–language pathologist.

Techniques for Enhancing Language Development Among Children with Articulation Disorders

The most important factor in enhancing language development among children who have articulation disorders is to create and maintain a positive classroom environment where children are encouraged to communicate and where any problems in communication are dealt with in a sensitive, caring manner. The classroom teacher should not embarrass a child who is having difficulty with a particular sound.

Children who do not have articulation difficulties will often notice when a classmate's speech exhibits articulation irregularities. Under no circumstances should children in the classroom be allowed to tease, imitate, or make fun of a child who has articulation difficulties. Instead, other children in the classroom should be encouraged to accept the sound approximations from the child with articulation problems. A teacher can also explain to the class that some children are learning how to make specific sounds or explain that the child does not hear all of the sounds that others may hear. In addition, the focus of the classroom language should be on the meaning of what is communicated instead of on a rigid standard for phoneme articulation. As mentioned earlier, it is also important for the classroom teacher and the speech–language pathologist to work closely in developing and implementing specific techniques or activities for children with articulation disorders.

Children with articulation problems may not participate in group discussions as readily as other children and may be more comfortable participating in small group activities where they are interacting in a conversational setting. In large groups, activities with unison responses (e.g., reciting an action poem, song, or refrain from a predictable book) provide children with articulation problems with an opportunity to participate verbally in a nonthreatening setting. Regardless of the activity, it is important for the classroom teacher and all the children in the classroom to respond positively to the child's attempts to communicate and to focus on the meaning of the communication rather than on the difficulties the child is having.

FLUENCY DISORDERS

Fluency disorders are characterized by interruptions or repetitions in the flow of speech. One category of dysfluency is associated with coordination of the speech mechanism, such as in stuttering (Olander, Smith, & Zelaznik, 2010). Another category is linguistic dysfluency, which involves interruptions or repetitions in speech associated with lexical, syntactic, or semantic variables (American Speech-Language-Hearing Association, 1999). While instances of speech dysfluency are found in adult speech interactions as well as in children's, not all dysfluencies indicate serious communication difficulties. Speech dysfluencies are common among preschool children as they explore and experiment with language production using their phonological, syntactic, semantic, morphemic, and pragmatic knowledges. Most dysfluencies disappear as children grow older (Weir & Bianchet, 2004).

Typically, children's dysfluencies show day-to-day and/or month-to-month variations that may depend on the communicative setting. Normal dysfluencies involve whole-word repetition ("that . . . that ball"), phrase repetition ("I want . . . I want the truck"), sentence revisions ("I went . . . we went to the store"), hesitations or grammatical pauses ("Mommy, I want . . . some cookies"), or interjections ("I saw . . . uh . . . the fire truck" (Gottwald, Goldbach, & Isack, 1985; Swan, 1993). These dysfluencies may simply reflect a heightened emotional state or hurried speech.

Indications of Fluency Disorders

Among young children, sound and syllable repetitions are more atypical, and, if persistent over time, may indicate that the child is at risk for stuttering. The most common speech dysfluency is stuttering (Culatta & Leeper, 1987). **Stuttering** involves an involuntary repetition of isolated sounds or syllables, prolonged speech sounds, or a complete halt in the flow of speech (American Speech-Language-Hearing Association, 1999; Cook, Tessier, & Armbruster, 1987). It often occurs at the beginnings of words. Stuttering indicates a "lack of coordination between linguistic intention and motor articulation as children learn to talk and think at the same time" (Weir & Bianchet, 2004, p. 1790).

Dysfluencies that may indicate the onset of stuttering include part of a word repeated more than twice ("b-b-b-ball") and sound prolongations of more than one second (Gottwald et al., 1985). In addition, frequent dysfluencies may also indicate that the child may be at risk for stuttering, such as when the child repeats more than two sounds or syllables in 100 words or when there are frequent sound prolongations (Yairi & Ambrose, 2005). Stuttering may be accompanied by facial grimaces or gestures, reflecting the speaker's emotional tenseness, and by a rise in pitch and loudness (American Speech-Language-Hearing Association, 1999; Weir & Bianchet, 2004). Stuttering may affect a child's social interactions, and some children may withdraw from verbally participating in conversations or discussions (Langevin, Packman, & Onslow, 2009). More than 50% of the children who develop stuttering as preschoolers recover within 12 to 18 months after the onset of stuttering (Bloodstein & Bernstein Ratner, 2007). When a child's speech dysfluencies are frequent and have the characteristics of stuttering, it is important for the teacher to consult with a speech–language pathologist to determine further appropriate intervention or remediation. For those for whom stuttering persists, specific speech therapy may be needed (Swan, 1993).

No specific factors—either hereditary, environmental, or organic factors (Ratner, 2009)—have been identified as the cause of stuttering; however, recent research indicates that stuttering may be associated with a complex interaction of these factors (Büchel & Sommer, 2004).

Techniques for Enhancing Language Development Among Children Who Stutter

In addition to receiving speech therapy, a child who stutters can benefit from specific techniques implemented by the classroom teacher. Because stuttering occurs during conversational interactions, teachers should interact with children who stutter in ways that reduce the conversational demands on the child. Teachers are encouraged to use a "Mr. Rogers" approach "by modeling slow, smooth speech, acknowledging when speech is difficult and creating special talk times" (Weir & Bianchet, 2004, p. 1791).

Children who are upset about their dysfluencies need reassurance that they are accepted and respected by the teacher and by others in the class. Teachers need to acknowledge that some words are difficult to pronounce. It is important that teachers discourage children from interrupting others and from trying to finish an utterance for someone who is having difficulty talking (Gottwald et al., 1985; Stuttering Foundation of America, 1991–2012). Teachers should also avoid telling the child to slow down, to start over, to think, or to take a deep breath because these requests indicate to the child that his speech is unacceptable and may increase his anxiety and dysfluencies (Gottwald et al., 1985). When talking with a child who is having fluency problems, a teacher should maintain eye contact with the child and be patient so the child does not feel that the teacher is uncomfortable talking with him (Weir & Bianchet, 2004).

Teachers may notice that a child who stutters becomes more fluent during group singing, choral responses, or choral reading. Recent neurological research has indicated that this type of speech is activated differently in the brain than the spontaneous speech that occurs in conversations (Büchel & Sommer, 2004). It is thought that the auditory cueing (i.e., through music or vocal cues) that precedes singing or choral speaking activates the brain's speech production process differently than when spontaneous speech is produced in conversations. Although this neurological process is not yet fully understood, these types of group vocal activities are effective in facilitating fluent speech. Thus, it is important to include these activities in early childhood classrooms because they provide opportunities for a child who stutters to participate in fluent speech.

At the primary grade level, children's stuttering and other dysfluencies may interfere more with their classroom performance than in the preschool years because learning activities in this context may require more group participation and more focused oral responses and oral reading. The Stuttering Foundation of America

(1991–2012) offers several guidelines for elementary teachers who are interacting with children who stutter or have frequent dysfluencies:

1. Ask the child questions she can answer with only a few words.
2. Call on the child early in a discussion, because tension and anxiety may increase as the child anticipates her turn.
3. Communicate to all students that they do not have to answer the question(s) in a hurry and that you want them to take their time and think about their answers.
4. Encourage children (not just the stutterers) to practice reading in pairs, taking turns or in unison.
5. Encourage children to practice reading their stories at home before they are expected to read individually in the classroom.
6. Encourage children to practice reading along with a taped version of the story at home or in the library center in the classroom before they are expected to read individually in the classroom.
7. Monitor the social interactions in your classroom so that peers do not tease or embarrass a child who stutters.

Stuttering among English language learners.   When children are learning a second language, they may experience stuttering or other dysfluencies as they learn to distinguish between the new language and their home language. For example, when speaking in the new language, a child may stutter as he experiences difficulty using new vocabulary or grammatical structures. If stuttering continues longer than six months, the child should be referred to a speech pathologist for additional screening and possible speech therapy (Shenker, 2008).

SPECIFIC LANGUAGE IMPAIRMENT (SLI)/DELAYED LANGUAGE

Specific language impairment (SLI) is a term that is used to refer to a child whose language development is substantially below age level and is not associated with any specific cause (Bishop, 1997); however, recent research has indicated that this disorder may be associated with the interaction of multiple genetic and environmental factors (Bishop, 2006). SLI has also been referred to as **delayed language**; however, the use of the term *delayed language* implies that the child is developing language but at a slower pace. While the linguistic characteristics are similar for both delayed language and SLI, delayed language is a more appropriate term for recognizing a preschool child's language difficulties, and SLI is thought to be more appropriate to refer to an older child (above age 5) who is experiencing this type of language difficulty (Whitehurst & Fischel, 1994).

Characteristics

Children with delayed language/SLI typically have normal-range hearing and nonverbal intelligence and no developmental disabilities, yet there are noticeable difficulties in both the receptive and expressive language competencies (Montgomery, 2002). They typically are able to score within the normal range on standardized nonverbal intelligence tests.

Linguistic characteristics of children with SLI involve limitations in each of the five aspects of language knowledge (Fey, Long, & Finestack, 2003; Owen, 2010; Yont, Hewitt, & Miccio, 2002). Phonological disorders have been documented among SLI children (Ziegler, Pech-Georgel, George, & Lorenzi, 2011). Semantic development may also be impaired (Yont et al., 2002). Compared to normally developing children's speech, the vocabularies of children with SLI are smaller (semantic), and their sentences are less complex, contain frequent grammatical errors, and show less variation (syntactic). A difficulty with the pragmatic aspect of language is also evident among children with SLI or delayed language, who are likely to have difficulty maintaining a conversation and may have problems understanding others or being understood. They are less likely to engage in dramatic play. In addition, children with delayed language are likely to focus talk on the here and now rather than the past or future, which may indicate a limitation of symbolic representation.

SLI or delayed language is usually first identified in the preschool years, when a child exhibits difficulty in conversational settings. As a child enters elementary school, further language impairment may be noted when the child experiences difficulty in comprehending and composing both oral and written language (Fey et al., 2003). In addition, difficulties in conversation may show up in general problems in interacting with other children at school and in the community.

Techniques for Enhancing Language Development Among Children with SLI or Delayed Language

As with other forms of communicative disorders, with delayed language/SLI, the classroom must be a positive language environment where the focus is on interactive communication. It is important for you to actively listen, truly listening to what each child is saying and responding to what is said. In this way, the conversations become child centered as you incorporate the child's topic into your responses (Dumtschin, 1988). Verbal mapping and linguistic scaffolding are techniques that you will find effective in encouraging interactive communication. Rather than try to directly teach language or correct usage, it is important to focus on the communicative intent of the child and follow up with verbal mapping or linguistic scaffolding to clarify the child's message.

Open-ended questions can also be used to elicit linguistic participation from a child, although you need to be sensitive to the level of questioning that is appropriate for each child. Children with delayed language or SLI may initially need to have lower levels of literal questioning to build up their self-confidence and also to build up their competencies in responding to questions (McNeill & Fowler, 1996). By using linguistic scaffolding techniques that involve a series of questions, children are encouraged to participate in longer conversations.

Storybook sharing in a one-on-one setting is another way to encourage children with delayed language or SLI to become more involved in using language to communicate their thoughts, questions, and ideas (McNeill & Fowler, 1996). During storybook sharing, you should closely observe and respond to the child's engagement with the story and with the illustrations. Use a variety of questions to elicit the child's responses to the book. Show enthusiasm for the child's involvement in talking about the pictures or about story content. You can also use expansion to elaborate on the child's comment or response.

Children with delayed language/SLI will also benefit from scaffolding during their unstructured (or "free play") activities. For example, you could sit down in the dramatic play area and, after observing the current setting, offer brief comments or questions or become a character or prop to support the child's interactions (Gould & Sullivan, 2005). Be sure to provide props and other dramatic play materials that are familiar to the child. It is also important to be an active listener and to provide ample wait time when you are engaging the child in conversation. Through these one-on-one interactions, teachers can facilitate conversational skills among children with delayed language or SLI. It is also important to facilitate social–linguistic interactions in all small groups and whole-class groupings to increase the pragmatic knowledge and skills, including using language to resolve conflicts.

COGNITIVE IMPAIRMENT

Children may experience cognitive impairment due to several factors. For example, genetic factors such as Down syndrome will impact language development. Brain injury due to a lack of oxygen during birth or traumatic brain injury in early childhood due to an accident or child abuse will also result in cognitive impairment that will impact language development. Environmental influences such as inadequate prenatal or postnatal nutrition will also result in cognitive impairment (Mastropieri & Scruggs, 2007).

Characteristics

Children who have a cognitive impairment may not process language effectively and may not develop the conceptual knowledge necessary for further language acquisition. They have difficulty paying attention to others' speech, processing it, and remembering what was said (Harris, 1990). They may be unable to sustain attention long enough to enjoy listening to a story and may have difficulty participating in conversations.

Techniques for Enhancing Language Development Among Children with Cognitive Impairment

In planning learning activities for children with cognitive impairment, you will need to focus on children's linguistic level rather than their chronological ages (Cook et al., 1987). It is particularly important to provide children who have cognitive impairments with opportunities to develop pragmatic language competencies for using language in their everyday settings to communicate their needs and wants to others in their homes, schools, and community environments (Ratner, 2009). Children with cognitive impairment will benefit from repeated experiences with the same storybook, song, action poem, or concept-building activity. This repetition provides additional time for children to integrate the information. It is also beneficial to monitor children's interactions and encourage them to ask questions or to seek assistance.

AUTISM

Autism is a complex neurological disorder that affects not only communication but other areas of development as well (Autism Society of America, 2012). Children with autism have difficulty with verbal and nonverbal communication, interacting with others (children and adults), and playing or enjoying other leisure activities.

Autism is classified as a **spectrum disorder**. This means that each child may be affected differently and with different levels of severity. Recent statistics from the U.S. Department of Education along with other government agencies indicate that the incidence of autism is 1 in 150 births and the incidence is increasing by 10% to 17% each year (Autism Society of America, 2007). Boys are four times more likely to be affected by autism than are girls. The incidence of autism does not appear to be associated with any racial, ethnic, social, or economic factors.

The diagnosis of autism is usually made between the ages of 18 months and 4 years (Greenspan, 1997). Because early intervention is critical in helping children with autism, the American Academy of Pediatrics (AAP) now recommends that all children receive screening for autism twice prior to age 2 (Autism Speaks, 2007). The first screening should occur at 18 months and the second at 24 months. The AAP also recommends that an intervention program be implemented when autism is suspected instead of waiting for a formal, definitive diagnosis. Early identification along with intervention is associated with improved outcomes for most young children with autism (Goin & Myers, 2004).

Early Signs

Identification of the early signs of autism has been documented in retrospective interviews with parents whose preschoolers were diagnosed with autism (Wimpory, Hobson, Williams, & Nash, 2000) as well as in research involving infants (Goin & Myers, 2004; Watson, Baranek, & DiLavore, 2003). Early signs that were associated with a later diagnosis of autism included the absence or lack of the following behaviors:

- Eye contact and shared reference
- Imitative behaviors involving actions and sounds
- Attention-seeking behaviors initiated through gestures, pointing, or sounds
- Preword turn taking using noises or gestures to communicate
- Responsiveness to own name
- Social smiling
- Pretend and functional play; instead repetitive play patterns occurred

It is important for teachers and parents to avoid overreacting when children exhibit one or more of the above behaviors; however, if multiple behaviors persist, screening for autism (and other developmental disorders) may be appropriate. Key behaviors that are red flags indicating that screening for autism should be considered include the following (Watson et al., 2003):

- No babbling, pointing, or gestures by 12 months of age
- No single words by 16 months of age
- No two-word spontaneous phrases at 24 months of age
- Loss of language or social skills at any age (pp. 207–208)

Techniques for Enhancing Language Development Among Children with Autism

As an early childhood teacher, you may have children in your classroom who have been diagnosed with autism, and you may have children who are beginning to exhibit autistic-like behaviors. For children who have been diagnosed with autism, an intervention plan will have been developed, and you will have an active role in implementing aspects of that plan in your classroom. While the interventions for children with autism will vary due to the specific child and the severity and individuality of the disorder, most intervention plans focus on increasing and enhancing children's communication and interaction competencies (Brown & Kalbli, 1997; Watson et al., 2003).

If you observe children who are exhibiting difficulty or delay in communicating through word or gesture or are experiencing difficulty in social interactions, you will want to adapt your curriculum and ways of interacting with these children to support their language development and social interactions. This means that you will carefully observe the child's responses to others in the classroom as well as the child's responses to your interactions with them. Based on your observations, you can better determine the ways in which you can support their communication and social interactions. You will also want to provide times when you interact with children one on one. For example, use shared storybook times to establish eye contact and shared reference as well as verbal and nonverbal turn taking. Be sure to choose a book that interests the child, or ask the child to select a book. You can also facilitate a child's social interactions with others by providing a verbal or behavioral scaffold that supports the child's interactions. Another area in which you can provide support is in dramatic play. To support the inclusion of an autistic child in dramatic play, you may need to enter the play setting and provide verbal mapping or dialogue that facilitates the child's interaction with another child.

As you focus on children with communicative difficulties, you will also want to talk with your school's special education teacher or other education specialists to become more aware of effective interaction strategies and techniques. Children with special needs and their families benefit from teachers and specialists who participate in a team approach to supporting and facilitating children's development.

MAKING REFERRALS FOR CHILDREN AT RISK FOR COMMUNICATIVE DISORDERS

Early childhood teachers who notice a child with communication difficulties should first observe the child's behavior in a variety of classroom interactions to determine the nature and extent of the difficulty. In addition, language-screening instruments can be administered to more thoroughly document the language and communication difficulties. It is also important to include parents as active participants and partners in the referral process. Referral to a specialist (e.g., pediatrician, speech–language pathologist) should be made only after the teacher has documented the difficulties over a period of time and only after the teacher has shared her concerns with the child's parents. For many parents, the referral process and follow-up intervention is often a time of intense emotional involvement and anxiety. As their child's teacher, you have an important role in supporting parents through this process. Figure 13.1 provides additional resources on communicative disorders.

FIGURE 13.1

Teacher Resources for Additional Information on Communicative Disorders

---

Autism

Autism Society of America
www.autism-society.org

National Center on Birth Defects and Developmental Disabilities
www.cdc.gov/ncbddd/autism/index.html

Cleft Lip and Cleft Palate

Centers for Disease Control and Prevention
http://www.cdc.gov/ncbddd/birthdefects/CleftLip.html

Cleft Palate Foundation
www.cleftline.org

Hearing Loss

American Speech-Language-Hearing Association (ASHA)
www.asha.org/public/hearing/disorders/types.htm

U.S. National Library of Medicine, NIH National Institutes of Health
http://www.nlm.nih.gov/medlineplus/ency/article/003044.htm

Stuttering

American Speech-Language-Hearing Association (ASHA)
www.asha.org/public/hearing/disorders/types.htm

The Stuttering Foundation
www.stutteringhelp.org

Tongue-Tie

Bowen, C. (2000). *Tongue-tie, ankyloglossia or short fraenum.* www.speech-language-therapy.com/tonguetie.html

U.S. National Library of Medicine, NIH National Institutes of Health
http://www.ncbi.nlm.nih.gov/pubmedhealth/PMH0002606

SUMMARY

Early childhood teachers have an important role in enhancing language acquisition among children who have special communication needs. Children who have hearing loss, SLI/delayed language, cognitive impairment, articulation difficulties, or speech dysfluencies or who are autistic, need classroom environments in which they can feel comfortable and are encouraged to communicate in a relaxed manner. Teachers can provide critical support to parents and family members during the process in which children are referred for additional assessments and intervention programs.

✻✻✻ CHAPTER REVIEW

1. Key terms to review:

   hertz
   decibels
   conductive hearing loss
   sensorineural hearing loss
   congenital hearing loss
   cleft lip
   cleft palate
   restrictive lingual frenulum
   ankyloglossia
   stuttering
   specific language impairment (SLI)
   delayed language
   spectrum disorder

2. Distinguish between communicative disorders and communicative differences.
3. Describe behavior of a child that might indicate a hearing impairment.
4. State three guidelines for interacting with primary-age children who stutter.
5. Describe the team approach to helping children with communicative disorders.

✻✻✻ CHAPTER EXTENSION ACTIVITIES

Research

1. Talk with a speech–language pathologist. Discuss the types of speech difficulties present in the school or school district; however, do not inquire about specific children or identify children by name in keeping with student confidentiality. Ask the speech–language pathologist to describe the techniques he or she recommends to teachers when interacting with children who have specific speech difficulties.
2. Select one of the resources listed in Figure 13.1. Thoroughly review the resource you selected and prepare a poster or PowerPoint presentation to share with your college/university class. In your report, evaluate the resource for use by beginning teachers as well as a resource for families.

14

FOSTERING LANGUAGE DEVELOPMENT THROUGH SCHOOL–HOME CONNECTIONS

Learning Outcomes

After reading this chapter you should be able to

- Identify goals for establishing school–home connections
- Discuss the factors influencing family/parental involvement
- Describe effective ways of communicating with parents
- Discuss ways parents can enhance children's language development through learning activities at home and in the community
- Describe the characteristics of effective parent programs

It was a special day at the child–parent center. Today was a parent read-aloud day. Parents were invited to come to their child's preschool to read storybooks to the children. On this particular day, five parents came. When they entered the room, they were enthusiastically greeted by the children, and each also received a special greeting from his or her own child. A few minutes later, the children had selected the books they wanted to have read and grouped themselves around each parent reader. For the next half hour, the five parents (along with the two teachers) read stories to the children.

Opportunities for parents to participate in their child's classroom, such as the read-aloud program described in the opening vignette, are just one of the ways to foster and encourage language development through school–home connections.

Children's families play a critical role in their language and literacy development. It is important for early childhood teachers to establish connections with each child's family unit and parental figures so that the lines of communication and mutual respect are strong. The "teacher provides the bridge from school to home" (McCaleb, 1997, p. 191). In this chapter, specific strategies and approaches for enhancing school–home connections will be described. Through your implementation of these strategies and approaches, you will encourage parents and family members to support and facilitate the language development of their children.

The ways in which teachers invite and engage parents in communicating with them and the school are critical to establishing positive connections. When teachers want to develop connections with children's homes, they must acknowledge and anticipate the diversity of the family units that may be involved rather than assume that all children come from families that are nuclear and traditional in membership. For some children, the family unit is composed of their birth parents and siblings. Other children's family units may be composed of one parent and/or one or more extended family members. Other children may live with their grandparents or with adoptive families. Still other children are in foster care. For the purpose of this chapter, the term *parent* will refer to a primary caregiver of a child, with the understanding that this primary caregiver may be a birth parent, a stepparent, a foster parent, an adoptive parent, or an aunt, an uncle, or a grandparent who has assumed the parental role for the child. The primary caregiver role may also be shared between two parents or other family unit adults.

GOALS FOR ESTABLISHING SCHOOL-HOME CONNECTIONS

Establishing positive school–home connections has the potential to significantly facilitate children's language development and other areas of development. Teachers should keep four general goals in mind when establishing school–home connections:

1. Increasing the teacher's/school's awareness and understanding of the child's home/family environment
2. Establishing a learning community
3. Increasing parents' awareness of their role in their child's language and literacy development
4. Increasing parents' awareness of the classroom's curriculum

Each of these goals contributes to the strength of school–home connections (Lilly & Green, 2004).

Increasing the Teacher's/School's Awareness and Understanding of the Home Environment

Children benefit from being able to make smooth transitions each day between home and school. The key to strong school–home relations, according to Vandergrift and Green (1992), is to know the parents well and to have a wide variety of options for parental involvement. When there are distinct cultural and linguistic differences between the home and the school or when a family experiences specific stresses (e.g., poverty, unemployment, divorce), children's ability to transition smoothly between home and school may be impaired. By becoming more familiar with the issues that your children's families face, you can more effectively address the needs of children in transitioning between home and school each day.

Children must see their school and teacher as valuing and respecting their home and family culture. Children's self-concepts are influenced by their perceptions that the larger society values and respects their home cultures. When there are significant differences in language and literacy between home and school, the school needs to concentrate more on bringing families into a closer relationship with the school (Diamond & Moore, 1995). Benefits of this closer relationship with families include children's stronger sense of self-identity and worth (Allen & Marotz, 1999; Lim, 2012).

Teachers' understanding of children's home/family cultural environment may be reflected in their implicit judgments of parents' levels of competence as parents (Elicker, Noppe, Noppe, & Fortner-Wood, 1997). Teachers need to avoid making culturally or economically biased judgments of parental competence based on a lack of understanding of the child's cultural–social home environment. They need to keep the lines of communication open and avoid stereotypic judgments. Teachers need to be respectful of the values and traditions of the families in which their students live and "guard against cultural and class arrogance" (Salinger, 1996, p. 71). Teachers should also avoid assuming that homogeneity exists among families of similar cultural or linguistic backgrounds because variations among families are likely to exist (Piper, 1993; Tutwiler, 2012).

When effective school–home communication is fostered, parents and teachers become partners in meeting the educational needs of children. To develop a partnership with parents, teachers must create effective ways of communicating with the family from the first day of attendance. School systems must develop ways to continually involve families in the life of the school in a wide variety of activities of varying participation.

Establishing a Learning Community

One way for you to involve families is to focus on developing a learning community. This learning community is manifested in your early childhood classroom and in the nature of the relationships you establish with children's parents and homes. **Learning communities** are characterized by mutual respect, cooperation, collaboration, and frequent, effective communication.

Mutual respect.   One aspect of a learning community is mutual respect. Parents need to be assured that their children's teachers are knowledgeable and compassionate. Teachers need to see parents as competent and need to understand their cultural perspectives. When there is frequent respectful communication with parents and when communication serves to inform parents of activities in their children's classrooms, parents are more likely to see their children's teachers as competent and welcoming. The availability of a translator to facilitate communication with parents who do not speak English is also an indication that the school respects and accepts the family's home language. In learning community classrooms, children are treated with respect and are encouraged to treat each other with respect.

Two important aspects of showing mutual respect involve observing confidentiality regarding family information and active listening. Confidentiality should be observed with respect to personal information about family relationships and other family matters (Cataldo, 1983). Such information should not be communicated to other staff or to other parents unless there are justifiable professional reasons for sharing the information.

Actively listening to parents involves listening closely to what they are saying and observing their nonverbal cues for additional meaning. According to Wilson, Douville-Watson, and Watson (1995), "Active listening involves objectively listening, in a non-defensive way, for the deeper message [of the parent]" and responding by giving feedback to the parent that clarifies the parent's message rather than judging or criticizing what the parent just communicated (p. 46). Through a teacher's active listening, parents feel that their opinions, ideas, and values are respected.

Cooperation and collaboration.   Learning community classrooms emphasize learning activities that occur in small groups (McCaleb, 1997). In these groups, children learn how to share, how to focus on common goals, and how to contribute to the learning task. This type of activity is not developmentally appropriate (or manageable) in infant and toddler classrooms or, to a certain extent, even in preschool classrooms. However, early childhood teachers who view cooperation and collaboration as a long-term goal for children's development can begin to encourage cooperation and collaboration through encouraging sharing and showing empathy and concern for each other.

When a partnership is created between the school/teacher and parents, one result is often a mutual sharing of educational goals for the children. Teachers become aware of specific learning goals parents might have for their children and vice versa. This partnership between school and home does not develop overnight or even after a few months. It is a result of long-term efforts in establishing and maintaining communication between school and home. The school–home relationships established when children are first enrolled in day care, preschool, or kindergarten programs may set the tone and expectations of the parents involved for years to come. Parents who feel welcomed into their children's first schools and who experience positive communicative relationships with their children's first teachers are more likely to continue to be more involved in their children's education.

Frequent communication.   Learning communities are characterized by frequent and effective communication. In the classroom, this means that the teacher and the children engage in frequent informal conversations as well as instructional, more formal dialogue that occurs during teacher-directed activities. The learning community that encompasses school–home connections also has regular, frequent communication with parents. It is important that the communication occur not only from teacher to parent but also from parent to teacher.

Increasing Parents' Awareness of Their Role

While most parents understand their role in supporting and caring for their children's physical and emotional development and well-being, they may not be fully aware of their potential role in their children's intellectual and language development.

Research studies have found a strong relation between the language and literacy activities engaged in at home and children's subsequent emergent literacy behaviors (Baghban, 1984; Bergin, Lancy, & Draper, 1994; Heath, 1983; Jordan, Snow, & Porche, 2000; Nord, Lennon, Liu, & Chandler, 1999; Taylor, 1983; Teale, 1986). There is evidence that parents should begin reading to their children in early infancy. Allison and Watson (1994) reported that "the earlier a parent began reading to their child, the higher the child's emergent reading level was at the end of kindergarten" (p. 68). In their research, Allison and Watson noted that some parents began reading to their children at birth.

Teachers can facilitate increasing parents' awareness by sharing with parents the importance of talking with their children, listening to them, reading to them, and reading with them. Teachers should also encourage parents to enhance children's conceptual development through activities at home and in the community. Additional suggestions for supporting parent–child activities will be introduced in a later section of this chapter.

Increasing Parents' Awareness of Classroom Curriculum

According to Piper (1993), "parents who understand what the teacher is doing and why are more likely to be supportive of what happens in the classroom" (p. 298). Teachers can enhance this awareness by communicating regularly with parents through informal conversations, open houses, and newsletters. Specific suggestions for these activities will be included in a later section of this chapter.

FACTORS INFLUENCING FAMILY/PARENTAL INVOLVEMENT

In addition to being aware of the characteristics of effective school–home relationships, teachers need to understand specific factors that may influence whether a family or parent decides to become involved in school–home connections. Figure 14.1 summarizes four factors that influence family/parental involvement.

FIGURE 14.1

Factors Influencing Family/Parental Involvement

- Parents' own experiences in school
- Cultural diversity
- Parents' work obligations
- Parents' perceptions of available opportunities for involvement

Parents' Own Experiences in School

Parents' memories of their experiences in school often have an impact on their level of comfort in attending school events and teacher conferences and in participating in their child's classroom (Coleman & Churchill, 1997; Jalongo & Isenberg, 2004; MacDonald, 2012). If their past experiences as a student were positive, they are more likely to feel comfortable at their children's school and in monitoring their child's schoolwork at home. Parents who did not experience success when they were in school may avoid contact with their child's teacher and school administrators because they associate school with negative feelings of failure, inadequacy, or low self-esteem. They may feel unable to help their children with their homework. When required to come to school for a conference, these parents may be defensive and uncommunicative. Particularly if the parents lack literacy or language competencies, it may be difficult for them to facilitate the necessary language and literacy competencies for their children's development. In these instances, the classroom teacher needs to focus on welcoming these parents so that they feel comfortable in the school.

It may be necessary to provide for someone to act as a translator for parent conferences with non-English-speaking parents; however, the translator should not be an older child in the family or an older student because that places both parents and the student–translator in a difficult situation. The teacher needs to help parents understand in what ways they can help their children at home, even if they are limited in their own language and literacy competencies.

While parents who have been successful in school usually have a positive orientation to school–home connections, they may also have unrealistically high expectations for their children's achievement, placing pressure on their children to perform, be "above average," and even be "gifted." In these instances, the classroom teacher needs to share with parents developmentally appropriate expectations and emphasize the importance of facilitating children's enthusiasm for learning and their curiosity rather than simply their performance of rote information or attainment of high achievement.

Cultural Diversity

As cultural diversity increases in classrooms, teachers become more aware of the different cultural orientations that influence parents' involvement in their children's education and interactions with teachers. Differences between home culture and school may become evident in several areas, such as holiday celebrations, discipline, timelines, or interpersonal mannerisms such as handshaking or touching (Jalongo & Isenberg, 2004). In some cultures, the school and its teachers are highly regarded as the experts; this orientation may discourage parents from "interfering" with teachers because education is thought to be the sole responsibility of the school. Parents with this orientation may also feel that all learning, or "schoolwork," should be done at school, under the supervision of the teacher. In these situations, teachers need to work more closely with parents so they understand the school curriculum and their role in enhancing their child's learning at home. Teachers should clearly establish the learning community partnership with parents in this regard rather than send parents the message that they must be "instructed" by the school and teacher as to what they need to do as parents.

Participation by parents of different cultures in school–home relationships is also influenced by the parents' perception of the school's and teacher's attitude toward their home language or dialect. Specifically, is the home language or dialect viewed as a deficit or as an asset? Will the school and their children's teachers pressure their children to assimilate mainstream American (i.e., White, middle class) culture (Piper, 1993)? Parents' participation is also influenced by their perception of how the school and teacher respond to instances of racism that may occur, in the form of name calling, bullying, or social rejection.

Parents' Work Obligations

The work schedule of parents and family obligations may make it difficult or impossible for parents to be available for daytime classroom visits and conferences. Thus, teachers should not assume that the parents' absence at a conference or classroom visit means that the parents are not interested in the educational progress of their children. It may mean that they are just unable to leave work at the scheduled time or have responsibilities for caring for other family members. The classroom teacher should provide parents with alternative times or ways to conference about their children's progress or to visit the classroom.

Parents' Perceptions of Available Opportunities for Involvement

Parents' decisions to be involved in their children's school are related to their own perception of the available opportunities to become involved (Hoover-Dempsey & Sandler, 1997; Hornby & Lafaele, 2011). If the only opportunities for involvement conflict with their work schedule or if the opportunities require a substantial time commitment, parents may decide that such involvement is not possible. Parents' perceptions of their own capabilities and talents are also a factor. For example, if their child's teacher is asking for parents to come to class to read stories to the whole class, some parents may not see themselves as having the literacy and speaking skills needed to feel comfortable in this role. For these reasons, teachers must offer a wide range of opportunities for parents to participate in school–home connections.

OPPORTUNITIES FOR PARTICIPATION AND INVOLVEMENT

All opportunities for participation and involvement contribute toward strong school–home connections. The wider the range of opportunities, the more likely a greater number of parents will be able to fit some school involvement into their busy schedules.

Types of Interaction in School–Home Connections

School–home connections involve three types of interactions. The first type is social participation of parents at the school through informal conversations with teachers, visiting the classroom, attending school events, or a combination of these. The second type of interaction occurs when parents engage in at-home learning activities that support the school curriculum. The third type of interaction occurs when parents participate in classroom activities, assisting the teacher in conducting specific learning experiences.

These types of interactions represent a continuum of involving parents from minimal involvement in social events to at-home activities supporting the curriculum and their child's learning to direct and active involvement in classroom learning activities. While this is a continuum, teachers should avoid expecting or assuming that involvement of parents in the classroom learning activities is the ultimate goal of establishing school–home connections. Instead, the main goal of establishing positive school–home connections is the enhanced learning and development of children. Furthermore, longitudinal research suggests that individualized connections—one-on-one relationships between the teacher and parent—may be more beneficial than focusing only on establishing parent involvement through group activities of parents (Seitz & Apfel, 1994; Seitz, Rosenbaum, & Apfel, 1985, cited in Powell, 1998).

ENCOURAGING PARENTS TO COME TO SCHOOL

When parents are encouraged to visit the school or classroom, they become more familiar with their children's teachers and the classroom curriculum.

Informal Conversations and Social Events

The initial step in creating a partnership with parents is to encourage parents to come to the school and to attend school events. At early childhood centers and most kindergarten classrooms, teachers and parents are in daily contact as parents bring their children into the school and pick them up at the end of the day. In these daily contacts, teachers can communicate in an informal way with parents, sharing information with parents about their children, the curriculum, and other important news.

A teacher's greetings to parents should be enthusiastic and friendly but brief because the teacher must usually greet many individuals. These brief conversations with parents are a good time to mention classroom projects or other events. When time permits, a teacher can also mention the purpose of such activities so that the parents are aware of the educational value or focus in the activities and can continue the focus at home. For example, "Today, we're taking the children on a walk to the park. We're going to be talking about color words." Parents might then talk with their children at home (or on the way home) about different colors.

If it is necessary to discuss a child's problematic behavior or developmental issues, it is important to set up a private conference. It is inappropriate to discuss a child's personal situation within hearing of other parents or school personnel who may be nearby. In this way, you are showing parents that you respect their family's and child's privacy.

Parent–teacher rapport is also enhanced when teachers can provide the opportunity for parents to visit the classroom for a longer time. This may take the form of a parents' day or parents' night where parents participate in learning activities with their children. Such participation is critical to parents' understanding of the process of learning and their child's active involvement in classroom learning activities. During these classroom visits, there are no "conferences" regarding student performance or development because the purpose of the classroom visit is simply to become more familiar with the curriculum, the children's daily activities, and their child's teachers. Some early childhood classrooms call these events "Bring Your Family to School," with the children serving as "tour guides" for their guests.

Other school events, such as student performances in music or drama, provide ways in which parents can be encouraged to come to school and be part of the school community. To encourage parent attendance, it is important that these events be held when parents are not working and that all members of the family and extended family be made welcome.

When teachers greet parents from families in which English is not the primary language, they must keep in mind that face-to-face communication may be the most difficult form of communication for these parents. Face-to-face communication requires that a response be formulated quickly, which in turn requires a high level of language fluency (Tabors, 1997). Thus, teachers should carefully word their questions and comments to parents to facilitate comprehension and encourage conversation. Teachers who take the time to learn the social greetings of another language, such as "Hello. How are you?" and "I'm glad to see you," enhance their rapport with parents. Parents who speak a different language will see the teacher's willingness to learn some of their language as an indication that their language and culture are accepted and valued. (See Appendix for basic greetings and expressions in different languages.)

Open Houses

The purpose of a school's open house is for all classrooms to share with parents the activities and content of the curriculum. Some open houses involve only classroom displays; others include a short, formal presentation by the classroom teacher on the rationale or purpose of various aspects of the curriculum. Teachers should focus on explaining the process of learning as well as the products that come from the processes. At this time, teachers can also emphasize the role that language contributes to lifelong learning and the role of oral language in the development of literacy competencies.

Open houses are not a time to focus on the specific difficulties of individual children. The focus of teacher–parent conversations should be on the positive aspects of children's participation in the classroom. Any children's work that is displayed should not have grades or evaluative comments or marks. Many teachers have found that parents enjoy having a guest book to sign and being given the opportunity to leave a note for their child in the child's cubby or desk. Children are delighted to find a note from their parents the following day.

Some schools encourage children to attend the open house with their parents and serve as guides, explaining the displayed schoolwork and activity centers. To facilitate this experience, open houses may be scheduled to give each family time and space to see all aspects of the learning environment.

Conferences

Several times a year, teachers set up specific times to meet with parents to discuss their children's progress. At the initial conference, teachers should focus on establishing positive rapport with the parents as this first meeting sets the tone for future communication (Diss & Buckley, 2005). In addition, teachers should encourage parents to do most of the talking at this first conference. This will give teachers a chance to learn parents' perspectives on school and their child.

If parents do not understand English sufficiently, a translator must be present. If possible, the translator should be another educator and not an older student or older sibling in the family because confidentiality is an issue in conducting individual conferences (Swiniarski, Breitborde, & Murphy, 1999).

During subsequent conferences, teachers share with parents descriptions of students' performance or examples of their work, explaining how the work was evaluated. The focus is on children's strengths and achievements, along with areas in which growth and development are needed. Parents should be asked for their interpretations of what teachers shared with them and how it corresponds with their children's behavior and performance at home. Teachers then need to describe to parents what they can do at home to enhance their children's learning, keeping in mind that parents may have time constraints or may be limited in their own literacy and language skills. Teachers should not overwhelm parents with extensive lists of what should be done at home but should instead focus on a few possible activities that parents and their children can engage in, such as those described in this chapter, in the section "At-Home Learning Activities," and in Figure 14.2. If a parent requests additional information, the teacher should conscientiously follow up the conference by contacting the parent with the requested information.

When a teacher is concerned about the learning difficulties a child may have, an important first step is to document those situations through the use of anecdotal

FIGURE 14.2

Tips for Parents in Supporting Children's Learning at Home

1. Arrange for your child to visit the public library regularly.
2. Share age-appropriate books with your child daily, or as often as possible.
3. Take time to visit with your child about the day's events.
4. Select child-appropriate electronic media and television programs to view with your child. Talk about the stories and events portrayed.
5. Provide opportunities to engage in creative activities at home with art/manipulative media, cooking, drama, and music.
6. Provide opportunities to participate in community outings and social gatherings.

records and work samples or other informal, performance-based measures. Before approaching parents with a request for further testing or referral, the teacher should also ask other teachers in similar classrooms or support professionals to unobtrusively observe the child's learning interactions in the classroom. The classroom teacher should also consider possible curricular or program modifications to determine whether that alone might address the learning difficulty.

Other Ways of Communicating with Parents

In addition to face-to-face contact with parents as they visit your classroom and school for open house, conferences, and special events, you can also communicate with parents via newsletters, home visits, and telephone calls or email.

Newsletters. The purpose of sending home a biweekly or bimonthly newsletter is to share with parents news from your classroom or school. A newsletter may contain information about school policies and upcoming events and an overview of curriculum and general child development (Bundy, 1991). Newsletters should be kept short, only one or two pages, and be reader friendly. DeMelendez and Ostertag (1997) offered four guidelines:

1. Use simple, clear language
2. Avoid using figurative language when parents represent different linguistic or cultural backgrounds
3. Use attractive, colorful paper
4. Organize the newsletter with clear headlines and sections

The tone of the newsletter should be conversational rather than academic. It is also useful to consider using a bulleted format instead of paragraphs. Professional jargon should be avoided. Form letters from commercially prepared curricula or books should also be avoided because such letters are impersonal and will not enhance school–home communication. When newsletters focus on upcoming curriculum or related events, parents are encouraged to reinforce the curriculum through their family's visits to the local library, area museums, or other family activities, such as picking apples, traveling, and doing home projects. In linguistically diverse classrooms, newsletters should be made available in other languages for homes in which English is not read.

Newsletters should be shared with children in the classroom prior to being sent home (Salinger, 1996). This sharing offers several benefits. Children become aware of the basic information in the newsletter so they know why it is being sent home. This also encourages the older children to read or "emergent read" the newsletter. Children are also more likely to encourage their parents to read the newsletter if they know what information it contains.

Home visits.　Some early childhood programs have found home visits a beneficial way to establish school–home connections (Bundy, 1991; Diss & Buckley, 2005; Wolfgang & Wolfgang, 1992). Others have experienced resistance from families who considered such visits an invasion of privacy (Maxim, 1993). Successful home visits focus on the opportunity for the teacher to introduce herself to the child and parent in the familiar surroundings of the family home. The visit should last only 15 to 20 minutes and, if possible, should be scheduled within the two-week period prior to the child's first attendance in the school/center. The visit should clearly focus on becoming socially acquainted with the child and parent. No personal questions should be asked of the parent about the family or the child. Instead, the teacher should share with the child and parent information about herself or her classroom and planned learning activities, such as "We're going to read stories about animals and then plan our trip to the zoo."

Telephone calls and email.　Teachers need to let parents know how to contact them at the school. Many school systems have phone-message or email systems that allow parents to leave messages for their teachers, indicating the best time to reach them. It is important for teachers, then, to respond to parents' questions or messages as promptly as possible. Teachers may make introductory telephone calls to parents early in the school year to establish communication with each family (Berger, 2004). These calls should be short and positive, focusing on introducing the teacher and classroom curriculum. While sending return email messages may be a very convenient way of responding to parents, face-to-face conversations or live telephone conversations are more effective when an extended conversation or dialogue is needed.

When teachers contact parents who may not be fluent in English, they need to realize that phone conversations may be a difficult form of communication for the parent. This is because the entire communication takes place auditorily and lacks the comprehension-enhancing nonverbal communication that takes place face to face, involving gestures, facial expression, body language, and other aspects of the conversational context. Telephone conversations also involve an instant response, which requires a higher level of language fluency. For this reason, teachers may find face-to-face conversations more effective with parents whose primary language is not English. In addition, it is much easier to include the services of a translator in a face-to-face conversation than in a telephone conversation.

AT-HOME LEARNING ACTIVITIES

Parents' conversations with their children from birth on significantly affect their children's development of language, as do their literacy-related interactions with their children at home and in their community (Pappano, 2008). While teachers may encourage parents to engage in specific at-home learning activities with their children, it is important that parents not be overwhelmed with a long list of "should do" activities. Much of the success of at-home activities depends on the parent's appropriate selection and implementation of the activities. If a given activity is not developmentally appropriate for the child, it will not benefit the child and may even negatively impact future learning or development. A relaxed, playful atmosphere is critical for at-home activities. Teachers also need to recognize the importance of including extended family members in opportunities for at-home activities (Au, 1993).

The focus of this section will be on the general ways in which parents can be encouraged to facilitate language and literacy development throughout the early childhood years. These general ways involve three basic communicative processes: conversations, modeling, and collaborative sharing. In each of these processes, parents are focusing on their children's individual zone of proximal development and providing the supportive scaffolding needed for development. (See Figure 14.3 for a list of recommended resources that provide more specific activities and experiences.)

Conversations

Parents of young children can facilitate their children's language development through the informal conversations that occur each day while doing errands or while riding in the car or on a bus (Nardi, 1992–93) or while engaged in activities at home, such as gardening, preparing food, eating together, or caring for a pet. Storybook sharing provides not only opportunity to develop an awareness of books but a context for talking about illustrations and using language to share ideas and stories. These conversations provide critical experiences for children in learning how to communicate. Researchers have documented connection between parents' conversations with their young children and later emergent reading and writing (Hart & Risley, 1995). Through the patterns of interaction, such as eye contact and shared reference, verbal mapping, questioning, linguistic scaffolding, mediation, adult-to-child speech, children's language development is facilitated and encouraged. Children benefit

FIGURE 14.3
Recommended References for At-Home Language/Literacy Activities

---

Bardige, B. (2009). *Talk to me, baby: How you can support young children's language development.* Baltimore, MD: Paul H Brookes.

Butler, D. & Clay, M. (2008). *Reading begins at home: Preparing children for reading before they go to school.* Portsmouth, NH: Heinemann.

Clinard, L. (2005). *Family time reading fun.* Dubuque, IA: Kendall/Hunt.

Fox, M. (2008). *Reading magic: Why reading aloud to our children will change their lives forever.* New York: Mariner Books.

Hallissy, J. (2010). *The write start: A guide to nurturing writing at every stage from scribbling to forming letters and writing stories.* Boston, MA: Trumpter.

Lilly, E. & Green, C. (2004). *Developing partnerships with families through children's literature.* Upper Saddle River, NJ: Merrill/Prentice Hall.

Pepper, J. & Weitzman, E. (2004). *It takes two to talk: A practical guide for parents of children with language delays.* Toronto: The Hanen Centre.

Pollard, C. & Chouinard, A. (2008). *Let's talk together: Home activities for early speech and language development.* Maple Grove, MN: Talking Child.

www.talkingchild.com/shops_DVDsCDsBooks.aspx

---

from these conversational opportunities at home because the conversational topics are based on prior experiences shared with family members, and conversations can be longer and involve more "turns" than conversations in a classroom setting.

Conversations in non-native-English-speaking families. Cultural factors sometimes influence parents' conversations with young children. The "good behavior" standard in some cultures does not encourage children to initiate conversations or to ask questions (Pappano, 2008). Parents may also be concerned that their children learn English and speak only English when talking with them; however, because the parents are not fluent in English, their language interactions are limited in vocabulary and complex grammar (Espinosa, 2008). Instead, parents should provide opportunities for their children to continue to develop competencies using their home language in singing, reading, telling stories, and conducting conversations in their everyday activities. A strong foundation in their first language provides a foundation for learning a second language.

Suggestions for parents. When you are talking with parents about the importance of engaging their children in conversations, you need to take into consideration the developmental level of the children's language (e.g., the one-word stage, the

Conversations about books and shared reading enhance children's developing language competencies.

telegraphic stage) and the interaction strategies that are most appropriate for that developmental level. Some basic ideas for parents in enhancing conversations with their children include the following:

- Start a conversation with your child by establishing eye contact and shared reference.
- Wait for your child to take a turn, responding to what you have said.
- Listen actively and patiently as your child talks or responds nonverbally.
- Use language that your child will comprehend.
- Respond to your child's questions and interests.
- Use gestures and pointing to add meaning to your speech.
- Encourage child-initiated conversations by responding to your child's spontaneous comments and questions.

Modeling

Parents show children how language is used every day as children accompany them on their errands and around their homes (Hannon, 1992). For example, children may see their parents using oral language to ask for information, to tell stories, to

When parents include their young children in literacy-related events, they are modeling ways of interacting with written language.

make appointments, or to find and purchase particular products. Similarly, children see their parents using print in the environment as they engage in reading to locate information in the telephone book, place an order at a restaurant, worship in religious ceremonies, locate a particular store in a shopping mall, follow a recipe, or assemble a bookshelf. When parents use writing, they are showing their children the way to produce written messages. Children may see their parents paying a bill by writing a check, writing a message in a greeting card, filling out a job application, using a word processing program on a computer, or making a shopping list.

Collaborative Sharing

When parents and children collaborate in a particular activity, a supportive scaffold is often created that provides further facilitation of language development. For example, when parents share storybooks with their children, children can be encouraged to participate in the story reading at their own level, perhaps through conversations about the illustrations, echo reading, or pretend reading. Sharing cooking tasks while following a recipe demonstrates the value of written language. Shared tasks also provide an opportunity for parent and child to engage in focused conversations on the task at hand, whether it be planting a garden, cleaning out a cupboard, washing a car, or making the list for weekly grocery shopping. While the shared task needs to be developmentally appropriate for the child, the critical aspect is the sharing and joint focus of the conversation between parent and child.

In two areas of family life, the collaborative sharing process may not always occur: watching television and using a computer. Both activities can be engaged in individually and inherently foster verbal passivity. Without parental monitoring, these activities can gradually dominate home life. Some parents find that watching television is an easy way to occupy young children's attention. This is dangerous because television is not interactive. Similarly, in some homes, using the computer may be an individual activity. This is especially true in homes where parents have provided a computer for their child's room. However, parents can facilitate language development at home through encouraging a more interactive approach to television watching and computer use in several ways.

Parents can use the many informative and entertaining programs on television as the focus of extended conversations and related activities. A particular television program might be followed up with a trip to the library or a museum, along with

Shared tasks, such as carving a pumpkin, provide rich opportunities for conversation and vocabulary development.

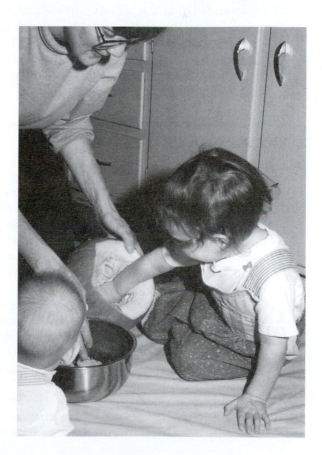

reading or writing activities. By monitoring what children are watching and even watching television with them, parents can use television as a starting point for a wide range of language-facilitating activities.

Parents can encourage a more interactive approach to using a computer by purchasing software that encourages joint participation of two or more people and by locating the computer in the room where family members gather for shared activities. Similarly, parents can facilitate language development by engaging their children in conversations based on information obtained through the software or through Internet sites. Related reading and writing activities can focus on a topic initially explored via the computer.

Not all parents can respond to teachers' encouragements to engage in at-home learning activities. Although computer use at home is increasing, many families do not have access to computers at home due to financial limitations or personal choice. Likewise, in some homes, few literacy-related materials are present. Allington and Cunningham (1996) reminded teachers that "all parents cannot read to their children" (p. 5), and some may struggle daily to physically care for their children in providing sufficient food, clothing, and housing. Allington and Cunningham also contended that the school curriculum needs to be developed and implemented in such a way that, when parental education and resources are lacking, children will not be placed further at risk. Thus, while at-home learning activities can facilitate language development, teachers need to acknowledge the realities some parents face and take them into consideration when developing the classroom curriculum and establishing school–home connections.

IN-CLASS PARTICIPATION

Benefits from parents' in-class participation include the parents' learning about classroom activities and the teacher's receiving some assistance in conducting activities. In some instances, the presence of their parents increases children's feelings of social confidence and comfort in the classroom (Tabors, 1997).

In some respects, in-class participation by parents is the highest level of parent involvement because it may involve a significant commitment in terms of time and talent. That said, teachers should avoid selectively paying more attention to parents who participate in classroom activities. Parents are quick to pick up on verbal and nonverbal cues that reflect a sense of respect, favoritism, or lack of respect from the teacher. With the increasing demands of work and other commitments, teachers may find few parents who are able to become involved in classroom activities. For those parents who can make the commitment to participate in their child's classroom learning activities, a wide variety of potential ways to become involved are available.

When encouraging parents to become involved, teachers need to share with parents the following types of information regarding their involvement: frequency of participation, opportunity for orientation and specialized training, special talents needed, and specific responsibilities. Some teachers have found it valuable to prepare brief descriptions of the specific volunteer assignments and to plan for volunteer orientations and training (Pryor, 1995).

Parents who make a commitment to participate in classroom activities on a regular basis, such as one or more times a week, might be invited to assist students in one of the classroom learning centers, work with individual students at the classroom computer, assist the librarian in helping students locate storybooks, and read books to children as they visit the library area.

Parents who are limited to participating in the classroom activities on an occasional basis might be invited to assist with a holiday party, chaperone a class field trip, assist with class plays or puppet shows, give a book talk, demonstrate a particular craft or skill, or read stories to children on an individual or group basis.

CHARACTERISTICS OF SUCCESSFUL PARENT PROGRAMS

Parent involvement refers to the wide range of possible avenues for participation in the school classroom, from parents attending social events and informal parent–teacher conversations to facilitating learning at home to becoming involved in classroom learning activities. In contrast, **parent programs** involve more specific arrangements and detailed organization. In many instances, specific parent programs have a strong "parental education" component and may even be mandated by the particular early childhood program, such as federal, state, or grant-funded programs (e.g., Head Start, Child–Parent Centers, or EvenStart at-risk early childhood programs). Enrollment of children in these programs may require a specific level of involvement from their parents.

Successful programs have these characteristics in common:

1. *A range of clearly communicated and organized opportunities encourages parent participation and involvement.* Early in the year, parents are given information on the ways in which they can become involved in their child's classroom and the opportunities they will have to participate in social events and interactions with their child's teacher and school.

2. *All levels of parent participation and involvement are valued.* Parents are welcomed warmly and respectfully, whether to attend an open house, parent conference, or potluck supper.

3. *Teachers are sensitive to parents' needs and life situations.* Special events for parents and families are scheduled to accommodate as much as possible their individual time constraints and life situations. Translators are arranged for parents who lack fluency in English.

Younger children are welcomed, or babysitting services are provided to facilitate parental participation or attendance at scheduled parent meetings or conferences.

4. *Teachers foster an atmosphere of mutual respect* (Morrow & Young, 1995; St. George, 2010). Parents are treated with respect for their cultural background and individually as partners in the classroom's learning community.

5. *Parents are part of the planning and decision-making process* (Galen, 1991; Rasinski, 1995). When possible, parents are included in the planning and decision-making process regarding parent involvement activities through the involvement of the school's parent–teacher organization, local school council, or other parent-based group.

EXAMPLES OF SUCCESSFUL SCHOOL–HOME CONNECTIONS

One successful parent program that was implemented in an inner-city child–parent center involved inviting parents to visit their child's preschool classroom once a month for an hour-long group "read-in" (Otto & Johnson, 1996). Parents who came selected a book from the classroom library, sat down in a child-sized chair, and were quickly joined by one or more children ready for the book sharing. The classroom had a large collection of big books, which facilitated enjoyment of the parents' reading by a group of several children. The classroom teachers also participated in the read-in. This program incorporated a classroom lending library and recognition for children who took books home to share with their families. Parents took turns in the classroom, helping to check books in and out. Some of the parents decided that it would be good to have special book bags for children to use and made arrangements to make a book bag for each child. Most parents went on to personalize their child's book bag with additional decorations or their child's name. The classroom teachers noted an increased interest in taking books home to read and also observed children's excitement and pride when their parents came to participate in the read-in.

Project EASE (Early Access to Success in Education; Jordan et al., 2000) included opportunities for parents to become involved in book-related activities with their kindergarten children at school every week. In addition, parent education sessions were held. Parents engaged their children at home in book sharing activities. The purpose of this program was to increase language and literacy interactions that would enhance language development. Follow-up studies of the children involved in Project EASE documented significant gains in vocabulary, story comprehension, and story sequencing.

Teachers can also collaborate with school librarians and administrators to offer family literacy events. Chance 2010 describes a collaborative program that involved teachers and a librarian along with strong administrative support. This program welcomed siblings and extended family members to daytime and evening literacy-related activities. Storybook read-aloud techniques were demonstrated by the teachers and librarian in two groups; one for Spanish-speaking parents and one for English-speaking parents. Then families participated in four different activities some of which were closely related to the read-aloud books. Refreshments followed. In addition, families were encouraged to visit the school library to check out books each Friday.

SUMMARY

The classroom teacher plays a critical role in establishing and maintaining positive school–home connections. While parent involvement and communication may be encouraged in many ways, each teacher needs to find out what works best for the families represented in his classroom. Throughout these efforts, it is important for the classroom teacher to focus on establishing mutual respect with parents and providing an opportunity for a wide range of activities that facilitate school–home communication. When this is done, everyone benefits—the children, their parents, their teachers, and the school.

❋❋❋ CHAPTER REVIEW

1. Key terms to review:

   learning   parent involvement   parent programs
     communities

2. List four goals for establishing school–home connections.
3. List and describe four factors that influence family/parental involvement at school.

❋❋❋ CHAPTER EXTENSION ACTIVITIES

Research

1. Visit an early childhood classroom for one day. Prepare a draft of a newsletter to parents that explains to them the day's learning activities.
2. Attend a parent–teacher organization meeting at an early childhood school or an elementary school. Write a summary of the types of activities planned and carried out by that organization.

APPENDIX

❋ ❋ ❋

BASIC GREETINGS AND EXPRESSIONS
IN DIFFERENT LANGUAGES

English	Spanish	Gujarati	Urdu	Japanese	Polish
Good morning	Buenos días	Su prabhatam	As-saalam-u-alaikum	Ohayo-gozaimasu	Dzien dobry
Good afternoon	Buenas tardes	(no expression)	As-saalam-u-alaikum	Kon-nichi-wa	Dzien dobry
Good evening	Buenas noches	Subh ratri	As-saalam-u-alaikum	Kon-ban-wa	Dobry wieczór
Hi/Hello	Hola	Namaste	Ad-aab or Kush-am-deed	Kon-nichi-wa	Cześć/Witam
How are you?	¿Cómo está Ud?	Ta-mai kem Cho?	Kai-se hai aap?	Ogenki desu ka?	Jak si**e**macie?
Thank you	Gracias	a-bhar	Shoo-kri-ya	Arigato gozaimasu	Dzi**e**kuj**e**
You are welcome	De nada	(no expression)	(no expression)	Dou itashimashite	Prosz**e**/ Nie ma za co
I'll see you tomorrow	Hasta mañana	Ta-ma-nay ka-lay Ma-li-su	Ka-al Mu-la-khat hogi or Ka-al Mi-len-gai.	Ashita o-as shimashou	Do jutra
It is very nice to meet you	Es un placer conocerla (fem.) Es un placer concerlo (masc.)	Ta-ma-nay mali ne Ba-huuj a-nand thayo.	Aap se mil kar khu-shi hui.	Oai-dekite ureshii desu	Milo mi Was poznać

English	Spanish	Gujarati	Urdu	Japanese	Polish
Please	Por favor	Ma-her-b-a-ni karo	Me-herb-a-ni	Onegai shimasu	Prosz**ę**
My name is . . .	Mi nombre es	Maru naam _____ che.	Mera naam _____ hai.	Watashi no namae wa _____ desu	Nazywam si**ę**
What is your name?	¿Cómo se llama?	Tamaru naam su che?	Aap-ka naam Kya hai?	O-namae wa nan desu ka?	Jak si**ę** nazywacie?

Source: Literacy Development in Early Childhood, p. 152, by Beverly Otto. Copyright © 2008 by Pearson Education. Reprinted by permission.

GLOSSARY

academic register the variation of Standard American English (SAE) that is used in educational and corporate settings; also known as *literate register* or *literate discourse*

accommodation the process in which a current cognitive structure or schema is changed to incorporate a new concept

activity boxes small boxes containing high-interest manipulative items used by a caregiver to enhance vocabulary and expressive language among toddlers

additive bilingualism an approach to bilingualism that emphasizes the acquisition of a second (target) language with the continued development of the home language

adult-to-child speech specific ways in which language is altered when communicating with young children; also known as *baby talk, motherese,* or *child-directed speech*

African American English (AAE) a dialect used by a significant number of people of African American descent

ankyloglossia the medical term for the congenital condition resulting in tongue-tie

aphasia the general loss of language due to brain damage

assimilation the process of incorporating a new concept into an existing conceptual schema

authentic assessment an assessment that occurs in a natural learning context and focuses on what children can do

axon part of the brain cell (neuron) that carries information away from the cell

axon terminal the end of the axon of a neuron in the brain, which branches out like a tree's branches and connects to the dendrites of an adjacent cell body

babbling the production of consonant–vowel sounds of varying intonation, usually involving reduplicated sounds such as *ba-ba-ba-ba,* that develops when a child is between 4 and 6 months old

Basic Interpersonal Communication Skills (BICS) conversational proficiency in a second language that enables effective engagement in social conversations

bidialectism the ability to use two dialects

bilingualism the ability to use two languages when communicating orally or in writing

blend when two or more phonemes (represented by consonant letters at the beginning of a word) are blended so that elements of each separate phoneme are still heard, such as in *cl*ear, *br*ing, *sk*ate, and *gr*eat

bound morphemes morphemes that must be attached to a free morpheme (e.g., -ly in slow*ly*)

Broca's aphasia the impairment of speech production resulting from damage to the lower area of the left frontal lobe of the cerebrum, referred to as Broca's area

central nervous system part of the nervous system composed of the brain and spinal cord

cerebellum the area in the lower back region of the brain that is associated with movement and coordination; transmits signals to the muscles that control the various parts of the speech mechanism to produce speech sounds

cerebral cortex the outer layer of the cerebrum, covering the brain like a cap and making up about 80% of the volume of the brain; plays a critical role in perception, thinking, and language

child-directed speech the specific language structures and discourse patterns that adults use with young children to increase their comprehension and participation in communication; also called *baby talk* or *motherese*

clarifying questions questions used to explain or elucidate something previously said

cleft lip a physical abnormality at birth that involves a separation or split in the upper lip

cleft palate a physical abnormality at birth that involves a split in the roof of the mouth

code mixing instances where a speaker appears to be mixing two languages; for example, vocabulary, idiomatic phrases

codeswitching distinguished from code mixing by the speaker's apparently conscious and deliberate use of two languages within the same sentence or from one sentence to another; is thought to be influenced by social or psychological factors, such as a desire to add emphasis or to show ethnic unity

Cognitive Academic Language Proficiency (CALP) the academic register of speech that involves higher cognitive demands and is related to conceptual and academic development

communication loop a circular or cycle-like exchanging of the roles of speaker and listener

comprehensible input when the target or second language is used by a speaker at a level that is just slightly beyond the listener's current level of understanding

conflict resolution the use of language dialogue to resolve disagreements

contingent questioning involves a series of questions designed to incorporate prior comments or questions from a child; the questions in the series build on each other and engage a child's thinking and oral responses

conversational skills specific ways communication is enhanced between two or more people; for example, turn taking, shared reference, establishing and maintaining eye contact, giving feedback

cooing extended vowel sounds, such as *ooo, ahh, eee, aaa,* often made in relative isolation of each other, usually beginning when an infant is 6 to 8 weeks old

creole a pidgin language that has been learned by a second generation of speakers

delayed language when a child's language development is significantly below age level without apparent cause

dendrites part of the brain cell that carries information to the cell body

derivational morphemes bound morphemes that may change the way a word is used in an utterance or sentence (e.g., happy–happi*ness*; construct–construc*tion*)

developmental level a child's independent competencies

dialects variations of a language that are characteristic of a particular social or geographical group (e.g., southern dialect, adolescent dialect, Bronx dialect)

digraph two consonant letters used together to encode a single phoneme not associated with either letter (e.g., *ch*icken, *ph*onics, *sh*are)

direct experiences "firsthand" experiences that contribute to the development of conceptual and semantic knowledge

discourse verbal interaction

discovery centers learning centers that encourage open-ended exploration of manipulatives, artifacts, or other concept-rich materials

distancing the gradual process in which a concept label becomes comprehended without the actual referent being present

early phonemic spelling a form of invented spelling where only one or two sounds per word are represented

echolalic babbling a type of babbling that appears to echo the rhythm and phonation of adult speech in a child's environment, developing when an infant is about 8 to 10 months old; also referred to as *jargon* or *intonated babble*

emergent literacy the gradual acquisition of knowledge about reading and writing through informal interactions with written language

eustachian tube a tube that connects the middle ear and upper throat area, which allows equalization of pressure on both sides of the eardrum

expansion an interaction pattern used by an adult to "fill out" what a child says; modeling of more complex syntax, morphology, semantics, and correct pronunciation

expressive language the language that a person is able to produce, as in speaking or writing

fast mapping when a child learns the label for a concept or entity quickly, with only a few exposures and without specific reinforcement

formal English a specific form of Standard American English used in school classrooms and educational materials; also referred to as academic English

formal settings settings in which aspects of language knowledge are isolated and directly taught

formative assessment a periodic assessment that tracks children's growth and development on an ongoing basis throughout the year

free morphemes morphemes that are used alone as a word

genre a form of literature

grammar a rule-governed system of sequencing linguistic units into oral speech and written sentences

hemispheres of the brain the two halves of the cerebral cortex, referred to as the left hemisphere and the right hemisphere

holophrasic stage in this state of language development, one word is used to convey a whole thought and is accompanied by distinct intonation, stress, pitch, and/or vocal rhythm

home signs symbolic gestures unique to individual home environments

hypothesis testing the process of learning language in which children try out different ways of manipulating language

idiomorphs see *protowords*

imitative speech involves the production of speech that approximates the speech of another person; may occur as a result of direct modeling or delayed modeling

indirect request a request in which the desired action is implied but not directly stated

inflectional morphemes bound morphemes that change a word to correspond to syntactic rules (e.g., cat–cat*s*; Mary–Mary'*s* hat; walk–walk*ed*)

informal assessments predominately observation-based assessments used to document children's behavior and learning

informal English a form of English used in informal conversations, such as at home, in recreational or community settings

informational questioning questions used to elicit information that the questioner does not know

inquiry learning   the process of asking questions and seeking out answers through hypothesizing, collecting data, and analyzing data

intonated babble   babbling that is expressed with marked variations in intonation; also termed *echolalic babbling* or *jargon*

intonation   the variations of pitch and accent used when speaking

invented spelling   individualized ways of spelling that reflect a child's knowledge of phonemes and letter–sound relations

jargon   see *echolalic babbling* and *intonated babble*

language   a system of oral or written symbols used for communication

language acquisition   unconscious learning of language in natural settings with a focus on meaning

language acquisition device (LAD)   an inborn mechanism described by Chomsky as aiding language development

language acquisition support system (LASS)   ways in which an environment supports children's language explorations

language arts   listening, speaking, reading, writing, viewing, and visually representing

language competencies   specific skills in using language to achieve success in communication

language interference   when a person appears to confuse knowledge of one or more of the aspects of his or her home language with the target language

language learning   conscious rule learning in formal instructional settings with an emphasis on the form of language

lateralization   the specialization of the two hemispheres of the brain that develops with the maturation and growth of the brain; each hemisphere develops certain cognitive functions

learning communities   learning-focused communities composed of students, teachers, and family members characterized by mutual respect, cooperation, collaboration, and frequent, effective communication

letter-name spelling   a form of invented spelling in which each letter name is used to represent a sound

linguistic level   unconscious knowledge of how language is used

linguistic scaffolding   language used to support a child's attempts to communicate; may involve questioning, expansion, and/or repetition

mapping   using language to represent an entity, action, or event

mean length of utterance (MLU)   a unit that measures the length and complexity of an utterance by counting the number of words and the number of grammatical markings

mediation   an interaction pattern in which an adult focuses on simplifying the learning stimulus or task to facilitate the language interaction with, and comprehension by, a child

metalinguistic knowledge   conscious knowledge of how language can be manipulated

metalinguistic verbalization   the highest level of language knowledge that involves verbally reflecting on one's language concepts

monologues   extended speech to a listener without conversational turn taking

morpheme   the smallest unit of meaning in language

morphemic knowledge   knowledge of word structure or how words are composed of one or more meaningful linguistic unit(s)

myelin sheath   the layer of fat cells that encases the axons in the brain; protects the nerve cells and makes it possible for the nerve impulses to travel faster

neurolinguistics   the field of research that has focused on the study of the relations between brain structure, cognitive processing, and language development

neurons the nerve cells in the brain composed of three main parts: a cell body, axons, and dendrites

nonreflexive vocalizations infant vocalizations that are not initiated as a result of a physical reflex; nonreflexive vocalizations include cooing and babbling

normed an average score or level determined by sampling a large, representative population

norming the process of determining normed scores

object permanence an awareness that an object continues to exist even when it is out of sight

onset refers to the initial consonant or consonant cluster of a syllable, which precedes the first vowel of that syllable (e.g., the *c* in *cat*; the *sp* in *speed*)

ostensive naming the process of naming a concept through direct reference to the object or event in the immediate context

otitis media inflammation of the middle ear

overextensions when a label or word is used inaccurately for referents that resemble the appropriate referent in some way; for example, labeling all vehicles "trucks"

overgeneralizations instances where a speaker assumes that a word follows a specific regular pattern or rule when it does not (e.g., go–*goed*, good–*goodest*)

peripheral nervous system involves the nerve pathways that connect the spinal cord with all parts of the body; carries out the actions signaled by the brain not only for language but for movement as well

phoneme the smallest linguistic unit of sound, which is combined with other phonemes to form words

phonemic awareness a conscious awareness of distinctive speech sounds

phonemic spelling characterized by evidence that children are beginning to encode specific sounds or phonemes

phonetic knowledge knowledge of sound–symbol relations and sound patterns represented in a language

phonics knowledge that alphabetic symbols (letters) are used to represent the specific sounds in words used in written language

phonological awareness conscious awareness of distinct speech sounds in language

phonological knowledge knowledge about sound–symbol relations in a language

pidgin a language that developed in response to the interaction of two groups of people who did not initially share a language

pragmatic knowledge knowledge of the different ways in which language is used in different settings and for different purposes

preoperational stage the second stage of cognitive development identified by Piaget that usually begins at about 2 years of age and extends to about 7 years of age; children in this stage begin to represent the world symbolically through words, images, and drawings

prephonemic spelling characterized by the use of letters in writing that do not appear to have any relationship to the specific sound typically associated with the letter

print referencing explicit attention to print during read-aloud time

productive language the language a person is able to express, as in speaking or writing; synonymous with *expressive language*

prosodic features the way in which a language is spoken during communication, involving intonation, loudness, tempo, and rhythm

prosody the pitch, loudness, tempo, and rhythm of speech

protowords early invented or individualized "words," also known as *idiomorphs*

recasting see *expansion*

receptive language the language a person is able to comprehend, as in listening or reading

recitational questioning questions used to determine a child's knowledge or awareness of a concept or action

reflexive vocalizations vocalizations that come from the infant's physical state (cries, coughs, hiccups)

referent an object or idea represented by a word

registers different ways of using a language in different contexts

reliability an assessment measure's consistency in producing dependable or repeatable results

restrictive lingual frenulum occurs when the fold of membrane (lingual frenulum) at the midline of the tongue's underside is too short; also known as *tongue-tie*

rime refers to the vowel and any remaining consonants of a syllable (e.g., the *at* in the word *cat*)

Sapir–Whorf hypothesis states that a person's language strongly influences the way he or she thinks about and views the world

schemata abstract cognitive structures stored in human memory to represent events, concepts, or relationships (*schema* is the singular form)

selective reinforcement when a child is encouraged to produce and repeat sounds that are appropriate and necessary for the language of people in his or her environment

semantic knowledge the aspect of language knowledge that involves word meanings and vocabulary

shared reference when two people (e.g., adult and child) attend to the same stimulus (event or object)

simultaneous bilingualism when children acquire two languages prior to the age of 3; usually found in homes where parents speak two or more languages

sociolinguistics the study of the varied ways in which language is used in different settings and speech communities

socialization mismatch hypothesis proposes that children will experience difficulty in school if their home language and literacy socialization patterns do not match the language and literacy socialization patterns present in the school classroom

sound play occurs when children manipulate the phonemic elements and prosodic features of pitch, stress, and juncture

specific language impairment (SLI) impairment in language development not attributable to any specific causal factor

Standard American English (SAE) a dialect of English used by the majority of Americans, which is often modified by regional variations

strategic scaffolding linguistic scaffolding that is used by an adult in a conscious way to encourage a child's language development

stuttering a fluency disorder involving involuntary repetition of isolated sounds or syllables or a complete halt in the flow of speech

subtractive bilingualism instances where learning a second language also means that a child will lose the ability to speak his or her first language

successive bilingualism when children acquire their second language after age 3

suprasegmental elements the use of pitch and stress to separate a stream of speech to communicate a specific meaning

symbol formation the process by which a specific oral or written symbol becomes associated with a referent through interaction between the addressor, addressee, referent, and symbolic medium

symbolic gesture consistent actions used to refer to events or objects

synapse the area of interconnection between the axon terminal of one neuron and the dendrites of another neuron

syntactic knowledge the knowledge of how words can be combined in meaningful sentences, phrases, or utterances

syntax the grammar of a language

telegraphic speech child's use of two or three content words in an utterance with no functor words

there-and-then questions a type of questioning that focuses on things or events that are not present in the immediate context

transitional bilingual education (TBE) an approach to bilingualism that has as its goal the gradual transition from the student's first language to English

transitional spelling characterized by words that have conventional features, such as consonant–vowel patterns, but are not yet spelled conventionally

underextension when a label or word is inappropriately restricted or limited in referring to objects/events

universal grammar the rule system that underlies all human languages

unreferenced pronouns pronouns whose noun referent is not clearly indicated by the pronoun and sentence structure

validity the notion that a test or assessment actually measures what it is intended to measure

verbal-deficit perspective contends that anyone who does not use Standard English does not have a valid language and thus is verbally deficient

verbal mapping the interaction pattern in which an adult verbally describes the object or action in a level of detail appropriate to the developmental level of the child

vicarious experiences experiences where the concept or action is experienced or communicated through visual representations or through verbal description alone without the actual referent being present

vocal play an infant's spontaneous vocalizations that show a wide range of consonants and vowels, a range of articulation aspects (e.g., a nasal quality), and day-to-day variations

wait time the amount of time between the end of a teacher's question and expected student responses; may also be referred to as *think time*

Wernicke's aphasia speech impairment associated with damage to a region of the brain in the area of the back and top of the temporal lobe referred to as Wernicke's area; comprehension is significantly impaired, as is the ability to construct meaningful sentences

written language modes the way written language is used expressively in writing and receptively in reading

zone of proximal development the difference between what a child can accomplish alone and what he or she can accomplish with an adult's mediation or assistance

REFERENCES

Abbott, C., & Gold, S. (1991). Conferring with parents when you're concerned that their child needs special services. *Young Children, 46*(4), 10–14.

Acredolo, L., & Goodwyn, S. (1988). Symbolic gesturing in normal infants. *Child Development, 59,* 450–466.

Acredolo, L., & Goodwyn, S. (2000). *Baby minds: Brain-building games your baby will love.* New York: Bantam Books.

Acredolo, L., & Goodwyn, S. (2009). *How to talk with your baby before your baby can talk.* Boston, MA: McGraw Hill.

Adams, M. (1990). *Beginning to read: Thinking and learning about print.* Urbana, IL: Center for the Study of Reading, University of Illinois at Urbana-Champaign.

Adams, M., Foorman, B., Lundberg, I., & Beeler, T. (1998). *Phonemic awareness in young children: A classroom curriculum.* Baltimore: Paul H. Brookes.

Akhtar, N., Jipson, J., & Callanan, M. (2001). Learning words through overhearing. *Child Development, 72*(2), 416–430.

Alber, S., & Foil, C. (2003). Drama activities that promote and extend your students' vocabulary proficiency. *Intervention in School & Clinic, 39*(1), 22–29.

Allen, K. E., & Cowdery, G. (2005). *The exceptional child: Inclusion in early childhood education* (5th ed.). New York: Thomson Delmar Learning.

Allen, K. E., & Marotz, L. (1994). *Developmental profiles: Pre-birth through eight* (2nd ed.). Albany, NY: Delmar.

Allen, K. E., & Marotz, L. (1999). *Developmental profiles: Pre-birth through eight* (3rd ed.). Albany, NY: Delmar.

Allen, P. (1993). *Understanding ear infections.* Whangarei, New Zealand: Dr. Peter Allen. Available from Hear You Are, Inc., 4 Musconetcong Ave., Stanhope, NY 07874.

Allington, R., & Cunningham, P. (1996). *Schools that work: Where all children read and write.* New York: HarperCollins.

Allison, D., & Watson, J. (1994). The significance of adult storybook reading styles on the development of young children's emergent reading. *Reading Research and Instruction, 34*(1), 57–72.

Altwerger, B., & Ivener, B. (1994). Self-esteem: Access to literacy in multicultural and multilingual classrooms. In K. Spangenberg-Urbschat & R. Pritchard (Eds.), *Kids come in all languages: Reading instruction for ESL students* (pp. 65–81). Newark, DE: International Reading Association.

American Speech-Language-Hearing Association. (2012). *Terminology pertaining to fluency and fluency disorders: Guidelines.* Available from www.asha.org/policy.

Anderson, E. (1992). *Speaking with style: The sociolinguistic skills of children.* London: Routledge.

Anderson, S., & Lightfoot, D. (2002). *The language organ: Linguistics as cognitive physiology.* New York: Cambridge University Press.

Anglin, J. (1993). Vocabulary development: A morphological analysis. *Monographs of the Society for Research in Child Development, 58*(10, Serial No. 238).

Antonacci, P., & O'Callaghan, C. (2004). *Portraits of literacy development: Instruction and assessment in a well-balanced literacy program, K–3.* Upper Saddle River, NJ: Merrill/Prentice Hall.

Armstrong, D., Stokoe, W., & Wilcox, S. (1995). *Gesture and the nature of language.* New York: Cambridge University Press.

Arnold, R., & Colburn, N. (2005). Sound advice. *School Library Journal, 51*(8) [online journal].

Asher, J., Kusudo, J., & de la Torre, R. (1974). Learning a second language through commands: The second field test. *Modern Language Journal, 58*(2), 24–32.

Asher, J., & Price, B. (1967). Learning strategy of Total Physical Response. *Child Development, 38,* 1219–1227.

Aslin, R., & Pisoni, D. (1980). Some developmental processes in speech perception. In G. Yeni-Komshian, J. Kavanaugh, & C. Ferguson (Eds.), *Child phonology: Vol. 2, Perception.* New York: Academic Press.

Atkinson, C. (1983). *Making sense of Piaget: The philosophical roots.* London: Routledge & Kegan Paul.

Au, K. (1993). *Literacy instruction in multicultural settings.* Fort Worth, TX: Harcourt Brace Jovanovich.

Autism Society of America. (2007). *Defining autism.* www.autism-society.org. Retrieved August 6, 2007.

Autism Society of America. (2012). About autism. www.autism-society.org/about-autism/. Retrieved July 16, 2012.

Autism Speaks. (2007). *Autism Speaks applauds new American Academy of Pediatrics guidelines for autism.* http://autismspeaks.org. Retrieved November 14, 2007.

Baghban, M. (1984). *Our daughter learns to read and write: A case study from birth to three.* Newark, DE: International Reading Association.

Baghban, M. (2007, January). Scribbles, labels, and stories: The role of drawing in the development of writing. *Young Children, 62*(1), 20–26.

Bailey, B., & Brookes, C. (2003). Thinking out loud: Development of private speech and the implications for school success and self-control. *Young Children, 58*(5), 46–53.

Baker, C. (1996). *Foundations of bilingual education and bilingualism* (2nd ed.). Philadelphia: Multilingual Matters Ltd.

Ball, E., & Blachman, D. (1991). Does phoneme awareness training in kindergarten make a difference in early word recognition and developmental spelling? *Reading Research Quarterly, 26*(1), 49–66.

Ballenger, C. (1996). Learning the ABCs in a Haitian preschool: A teacher's story. *Language Arts, 73*(5), 317–323.

Barac, R., & Bialystok, E. (2012). Bilingual effects on cognitive and linguistic development: Role of language, cultural background, and education. *Child Development, 83*(2), 413–422.

Barton, M., & Tomasello, M. (1994). The rest of the family: The role of fathers and siblings in early language development. In C. Gallaway & B. Richards (Eds.), *Input and interaction in language acquisition* (pp. 109–134). Cambridge, UK: Cambridge University Press.

Bates, E., Camaioni, L., & Volterra, V. (1975). The acquisition of performatives prior to speech. *Merrill-Palmer Quarterly, 21,* 205–216.

Bates, R., Marchman, V., Thal, D., Fenson, L., Dale, P., Reznick, J., Reilly, J., & Hartung, J. (1994). Developmental and stylistic variation in the composition of early vocabulary. *Journal of Child Language, 21,* 85–124.

Beals, D. (2001). Eating and reading: Links between family conversations with preschoolers and later language and literacy. In D. Dickinson & P. Tabors (Eds.), *Beginning literacy with language: Young children learning at home and school* (pp. 75–92). Baltimore: Paul H. Brookes.

Bear, D., Invernizzi, M., Templeton, S., & Johnston, F. (2004). *Words their way: Word study for phonics, vocabulary, and spelling instruction* (3rd ed.). Upper Saddle River, NJ: Merrill/Prentice Hall.

Beaty, J. (2006). *Observing development of the young child* (6th ed.). Upper Saddle River, NJ: Pearson/Merrill/Prentice Hall.

Beaty, J., & Pratt, L. (2003). *Early literacy in preschool and kindergarten.* Upper Saddle River, NJ: Merrill/Prentice Hall.

Beauchat, K., Blamey, K., & Walpole, S. (2009). Building preschool children's language and literacy one storybook at a time. *The Reading Teacher, 63*(1), 26–39.

Beed, P., Hawkins, E. M., & Roller, C. (1991). Moving learners toward independence: The power of scaffolded instruction. *The Reading Teacher, 44*(9), 648–662.

Behymer, A. (2003). Kindergarten writing workshop. *The Reading Teacher, 57*(1), 85–88.

Bell, S., & Ainsworth, M. (1972). Infant crying and maternal responsiveness. *Child Development, 43,* 1171–1190.

Bellenir, K. (Ed.). (1997). *Congenital disorders sourcebook* (Vol. 29). Health Reference Series. Detroit, MI: Omnigraphics.

Bellugi, U., & Brown, R. (1964). The acquisition of language. *Monographs for the Society for Research in Child Development, 29*(92), 1–191.

Bentley, D. (2012, May/June). Fire makers, barnyards, and prickly forests: A preschool stroll around the block. *Childhood Education, 88,* 147–154.

Bentzen, W. (1985). *Seeing young children: A guide to observing and recording behavior.* Albany, NY: Delmar.

Ben Zeev, S. (1977). The influence of bilingualism on cognitive strategy and cognitive development. *Child Development, 48*, 1009–1018.

Bereiter, C., & Englemann, S. (1966). *Teaching disadvantaged children in the preschool.* Upper Saddle River, NJ: Prentice Hall.

Bergen, D., & Coscia, J. (2001). *Brain research and childhood education: Implications for educators.* Olney, MD: Association for Childhood Education International.

Berger, E. (2004). *Parents as partners in education: Families and schools working together.* Upper Saddle River, NJ: Merrill/Prentice Hall.

Bergin, C., Lancy, D., & Draper, K. (1994). Parents' interactions with beginning readers. In D. Lancy (Ed.), *Children's emergent literacy: From research to practice* (pp. 53–78). Westport, CT: Praeger.

Berk, L., & Spuhl, S. (1995). Maternal interaction, private speech, and task performance in preschool children. *Early Childhood Research Quarterly, 10*(2), 145–169.

Berk, L., & Winsler, A. (1995). *Scaffolding children's learning: Vygotsky and early childhood education.* Washington, DC: National Association for the Education of Young Children.

Berko Gleason, J. (1973). Code switching in children's language. In T. Moore (Ed.), *Cognitive development and the acquisition of language.* New York: Academic Press.

Berko Gleason, J. (1989). Studying language development. In J. Berko Gleason (Ed.), *The development of language* (2nd ed., pp. 1–34). Upper Saddle River, NJ: Merrill/Prentice Hall.

Berkowitz, D. (2011). Oral storytelling: Building community through dialogue, engagement, and problem solving. *Young Children, 66*(2), 36–40.

Bernstein, B. (1971). A sociolinguistic approach to socialization with some reference to educability. In B. Bernstein (Ed.), *Class, codes and control* (Vol. I, pp. 165–192). London: Paladin.

Berthoud-Papandropoulou, I. (1978). An experimental study of children's ideas about language. In A. Sinclair, R. Jarvella, & W. Levelt (Eds.), *The child's conception of language* (pp. 55–64). New York: Springer-Verlag.

Beyer, M. (2007). *Teach your baby to sign: An illustrated guide to simple sign language for babies.* Beverly MA: Fair Winds Press.

Bhatia, T., & Ritchie, W. (1996). Bilingual language mixing, universal grammar, and second language acquisition. In W. Ritchie & T. Bhatia (Eds.), *Handbook of second language acquisition* (pp. 627–688). San Diego, CA: Academic Press.

Bialystok, E. (1988). Levels of bilingualism and levels of linguistic awareness. *Developmental Psychology, 24*, 560–567.

Bickel, D., Holsopple, S., Garcia, P., Lantz, M., & Yoder, D. (1999, December). Relationship of interactive writing to independent writing in kindergarten and first grade. Manchester, UK: Manchester University Press (ERIC ED 432015).

Biehler, R. (1976). *Child development.* Boston: Houghton Mifflin.

Biemiller, A. (2003). Vocabulary: Needed if more children are to read well. *Reading Psychology, 24,* 323–335.

Bijeljac-Babic, R., Bertoncini, J., & Mehler, J. (1993). How do four-day-old infants categorize multisyllabic utterances? *Developmental Psychology, 29,* 711–721.

Birckmayer, J., Kennedy, A., & Stonehouse, A. (2009). Using stories effectively with infants and toddlers. *Young Children, 64*(1), 42–49.

Birckmayer, J., Kennedy, A., & Stonehouse, A. (2010). Sharing spoken language: Sounds, conversations, and told stories. *Young Children, 65*(1), 34–39.

Bishop, D. (1997). *Uncommon understanding: Development and disorders of language comprehension in children.* Hove, East Sussex, UK: Psychology Press.

Bishop, D. (2006). What causes specific language impairment in children? *Current Directions in Psychological Science, 15*(6), 217–221.

Bissex, G. (1980). *GYNS at work: A child learns to read and write.* Cambridge, MA: Harvard University Press.

Blachowicz, C., & Fisher, P. (2002). *Teaching vocabulary in all classrooms* (2nd ed.). Upper Saddle River, NJ: Merrill/Prentice Hall.

Blank, M. (1973). *Teaching learning in the preschool: A dialogue approach.* Upper Saddle River, NJ: Merrill/Prentice Hall.

Blank, M., Rose, S., & Berlin, L. (1978). *The language of learning: The preschool years.* New York: Grune & Stratton.

Bloodstein, O., & Berstein Ratner, N. (2007). *A handbook on stuttering* (6th ed.), Clifton Park, NY: Cengage.

Bloom, B. (Ed.). (1956). *Taxonomy of educational objectives: The classification of educational goals* (Vols. I and II). New York: David McKay.

Bloom, L., & Tinker, E. (2001). The intentionality model and language acquisition: Engagement, effort and the essential tension in development. *Monographs of the Society for Research in Child Development, 66*(4), 1–101.

Bloom, P. (2000). *How children learn the meanings of words*. Cambridge, MA: MIT Press.

Bloome, D., Champion, T., Katz, L., Morton, M., & Muldrow, R. (2001). Spoken and written narrative development: African American preschoolers as storytellers and storymakers. In J. Harris, A. Kamhi, & K. Pollock (Eds.), *Literacy in African American communities* (pp. 45–76). Mahwah, NJ: Lawrence Erlbaum Associates.

Bohannon III, J., & Bonvillian, J. (1997). Theoretical approaches to language acquisition. In J. Gleason (Ed.), *The development of language* (4th ed.). Boston: Allyn & Bacon.

Bonvillain, N. (2008). *Language, culture, and communication: The meaning of messages*. Upper Saddle River, NJ: Pearson Prentice Hall.

Boroski, L. (2004). An introduction to interactive writing. In G. Tompkins and S. Collom (Eds.), *Sharing the pen: Interactive writing with young children*. (pp. 1–4). Upper Saddle River, NJ: Pearson Education.

Boshart, C. (1999). *Treatise on the tongue: Analysis and treatment of tongue abnormalities*. Austin, TX: PRO-ED.

Bowen, C. (2000). Tongue-*tie: Ankyloglossia or short fraenum*. www.speech-language-therapy.com/tonguetie.html. Retrieved May 19, 2008.

Bowey, J., & Patel, R. (1988). Metalinguistic ability and early reading achievement. *Applied Psycholinguistics, 9*, 367–383.

Bowman, B. (1992). Reaching potentials of minority children through developmentally and culturally appropriate programs. In S. Bredekamp & T. Rosegrant (Eds.), *Reaching potentials: Appropriate curriculum and assessment for young children* (Vol. I, pp. 128–136). Washington, DC: National Association for the Education of Young Children.

Boyd, F., Brock, C., & Rozendal, M. (2004). *Multicultural and multilingual literacy and language: Contexts and practices*. New York: Guilford Press.

Brabham, E., Buskist, C., Henderson, S., Paleologos, T., & Baugh, N. (2012). Flooding vocabulary gaps to accelerate word learning. *The Reading Teacher, 65*(8), 523–533.

Brainerd, C. (1978). *Piaget's theory of intelligence*. Upper Saddle River, NJ: Prentice Hall.

Bredekamp, S. (Ed.). (1987). *Developmentally appropriate practice in early childhood programs serving children from birth through age 8*. Washington, DC: National Association for the Education of Young Children.

Bredekamp, S., & Copple, C. (Eds.). (1997). *Developmentally appropriate practice in early childhood programs* (Rev. ed.). Washington, DC: National Association for the Education of Young Children.

Bredekamp, S., & Rosegrant, T. (1995). Reaching potentials through transforming curriculum, assessment, and teaching. In S. Bredekamp and T. Rosegrant (Eds.), *Reaching potentials: Transforming early childhood curriculum and assessment* (Vol. 2, pp. 15–22). Washington, DC: National Association for the Education of Young Children.

Brigance, A. (1991). *Revised brigance diagnostic inventory of early development*. Woburn, MA: Curriculum Associates.

Broderick, V. (1991). Production and judgment of plausible similes by young children. *Journal of Experimental Child Psychology, 51*, 485–500.

Bromley, K. (2000). Teaching young children to be writers. In D. Strickland & L. Morrow (Eds.), *Beginning reading and writing* (pp. 111–120). New York: Teachers College Press, and Newark, DE: International Reading Association.

Bronfenbrenner, U. (1979). The ecology of human development: Experiments by nature and design. Cambridge, MA: Harvard University Press.

Bronfenbrenner, U. (1989). Ecological systems theory. In R. Vasta (Ed.), *Annals of child development* (Vol. 6, pp. 187–251). Greenwich, CT: JAI Press.

Bronfenbrenner, U., & Evans, G. (2000). Developmental science in the 21st century: Emerging questions, theoretical models, research designs and empirical findings. *Social Development, 9*(1), 115–125.

Bronfenbrenner, U. (2005). Ecological systems theory. In U. Bronfenbrenner (Ed.), *Making human beings human: Bioecological perspectives on human development* (pp. 3–15). Thousand Oaks, CA: Sage Publications. (Original work published in 1992.)

Brooks, A. (1994, November 19). Middle ear infections in children: Brouhaha over treatment leads to consensus—For now. *Science News, 146*(21), 332–334.

Brooks, D. (1978). Impedance screening for school children: State of the art. In E. Harford, F. Booss,

C. Blueston, & J. Klein (Eds.), *Impedance screening for middle ear disease children* (pp. 173–180). New York: Grune & Stratton.

Brotherton, S., & Williams, C. (2002, Spring). Interactive writing instruction in a first grade Title I literacy program. *Journal of Reading Education, 27*(3), 8–18.

Brown, M., & Kalbli, J. (1997). Facilitating the socialization of children with autism. *Early Childhood Education Journal, 24*(3), 185–189.

Brown, M. W. (1991). *Goodnight moon.* New York: HarperCollins.

Brown, R. (1973). *A first language: The early stages.* Cambridge, MA: Harvard University Press.

Brownell, R. (Ed.). (2000). *Expressive one-word picture vocabulary test.* San Antonio, TX: Harcourt Assessment, Inc./PsychCorp.

Bruer, J. (1999). *The myth of the first three years.* New York: The Free Press.

Bruner, J. (1978). The role of dialogue in language acquisition. In A. Sinclair, R. Jarvella, & W. Levelt (Eds.), *The child's conception of language* (pp. 241–256). New York: Springer-Verlag.

Bruner, J. (1983). *Child's talk: Learning to use language.* Oxford, UK: Oxford University Press.

Bruner, J. (1990). *Acts of meaning.* Cambridge, MA: Harvard University Press.

Bryant, P., MacLean, M., Bradley, L., & Crossland, J. (1990). Rhyme and alliteration, phoneme detection, and learning to read. *Developmental Psychology, 26*(3), 429–438.

Büchel, C., & Sommer, M. (2004, February). Unsolved mystery: What causes stuttering? *PLoS Biology, 2*(2), 0159–0163. http://biology.plosjournals.org.Retrieved December 22, 2004.

Buchoff, R. (1994, May). Joyful voices: Facilitating language growth through the rhythmic response of changes. *Young Children,* 26–30.

Budwig, N. (2001). An exploration into children's use of passives. In M. Tomasello & E. Bates (Eds.), *Language development: The essential readings* (pp. 227–247). Malden, MA: Blackwell.

Bunce, B. (1995). *Building a language-focused curriculum for the preschool classroom: Vol. II. A planning guide.* Baltimore: Paul H. Brookes.

Bunce, B. (2008). *Early literacy in action: The language-focused curriculum for preschool.* Baltimore, MD: Paul H. Brookes.

Bundy, B. F. (1991). Fostering communication between parents and preschools. *Young Children, 46*(2), 12–17.

Burnett, G. (1993). The assessment and placement of language minority students. *ERIC/CUE Digest, 89,* ED357131.

Burningham, J. (1973). *Mr. Gumpy's motor car.* London: Penguin Books.

Burns, P., Roe, B., & Smith, S. (2002). *Teaching reading in today's elementary schools.* Boston: Houghton Mifflin.

Buros, O. (1938–). *Mental measurements yearbooks.* Highland Park, NJ: Gryphon Press.

Cairns, H. (1996). *The acquisition of language* (2nd ed.). Austin, TX: PRO-ED.

Camarata, S. (1995). A rationale for naturalistic speech intelligibility intervention. In M. Fey, J. Windsor, & S. Warren (Eds.), *Language intervention: Preschool through the elementary years* (pp. 63–84). Baltimore: Paul H. Brookes.

Cambourne, B. (1988). *The whole story: Natural learning and the acquisition of literacy.* Auckland, New Zealand: Ashton-Scholastic.

Cambourne, B. (1995). Toward an educationally relevant theory of literacy learning: Twenty years of inquiry. *The Reading Teacher, 49*(3), 182–190.

Campbell, R. (2001). *Read-alouds with young children.* Newark, DE: International Reading Association.

Cameron, R. (2006). Words of the windy city (Chicago, IL). In W. Wolfram & B. Ward (Eds.), *American Voices: How dialects differ from coast to coast* (pp. 112–117). Malden, MA: Blackwell Publishing.

Cardenas-Hagan, E., Carlson, C., Pollard-Durodola, S. (2007). The cross-linguistic transfer of early literacy skills: The role of initial L1 and L2 skills and language of instruction. *Language, Speech, & Hearing Services in Schools, 38*(3), 249–259.

Carey, S. (1978). The child as word-learner. In M. Halle, J. Bresnan, & G. Miller (Eds.), *Linguistic theory and psychological reality.* Cambridge, MA: MIT Press.

Carle, E. (1969). *The very hungry caterpillar.* New York: Philomel Books, Putnam & Grossett Group.

Carlisle, J. (2010). Effects of instruction in morphological awareness on literacy achievement: An integrative review. *Reading Research Quarterly, 45*(4), 464–487.

Cary, S. (2000). *Working with second language learners: Answers to teachers' top ten questions.* Portsmouth, NH: Heinemann.

Cary, S. (2007). *Working with English language learners* (2nd ed.). Portsmouth, NH: Heinemann.

Casbergue, R. (1998). How do we foster young children's writing development? In S. Neuman & K. Roskos (Eds.), *Children achieving: Best practices in early literacy* (pp. 198–222). Newark, DE: International Reading Association.

Castiglioni-Spalten M., & Ehri, L. (2003). Phonemic awareness instruction: Contribution of articulatory segmentation to novice beginners' reading and spelling. *Scientific Studies of Reading, 7*(1), 25–52.

Cataldo, C. (1983). *Infant & toddler programs: A guide to very early childhood education.* Reading, MA: Addison-Wesley.

Cawlfield, M. (1992, May). Velcro time: The language connection. *Young Children, 47*(4), 26–30.

Cazden, C. (1996). How knowledge about language helps in the classroom teacher—Or does it? (A personal account). In B. Power & R. Hubbard (Eds.), *Language development: A reader for teachers* (pp. 87–100). Upper Saddle River, NJ: Merrill/Prentice Hall.

Center for Applied Linguistics (2012). Sheltered instruction observation protocol/SIOP: Helping educators work effectively with English language learners. http://www.cal.org/siop/about/index.html. Retrieved April 5, 2012.

Center for Applied Linguistics and World-Class Instructional Design and Assessment/WIDA. (2005). *Assessing Comprehension and Communication in English State-to-State for English Language Learners/ACCESS.* http://www.wida.us/assessment/ACCESS/. Retrieved April 5, 2012.

Center for Applied Linguistics and World-Class Instructional Design and Assessment/WIDA. (2008).*WIDA MODEL.* http://www.wida.us/assessment/MODEL/. Retrieved April 4, 2012.

Center for Medical Consumers, Inc. Treatments worse than disease. (1995, April). *HealthFacts, 20*(191), 1–3.

Chafe, W. (1982). Integration and involvement in speaking, writing, and oral literature. In D. Tannen (Ed.), *Spoken and written language: Exploring orality and literacy* (pp. 35–54). Norwood, NJ: Ablex.

Chall, J. (1967). *Learning to read: The great debate.* New York: McGraw-Hill.

Chall, J. (1983). *Learning to read: The great debate* (Rev. ed.). New York: McGraw-Hill.

Chamot, A., & O'Malley, J. M. (1994). Instructional approaches and teaching procedures. In K. Spangenberg-Urbschat & R. Pritchard (Eds.), *Kids come in all languages: Reading instruction for ESL students* (pp. 82–107). Newark, DE: International Reading Association.

Chamot, A., & O'Malley, J. M. (1995). The cognitive academic language learning approach. In D. Durkin (Ed.), *Language issues: Readings for teachers* (pp. 160–175). White Plains, NY: Longman.

Chance, R. (2010). Family literacy programs—opportunities and possibilities. *Teacher Librarian, 37*(5), 8–12.

Chapman, M. (1995). The sociocognitive construction of written genres in first grade. *Research in the Teaching of English, 29*(2), 164–192.

Cheour, M., Ceponiene, R., Lehtokoski, A., Luuk, A., Aloik, J., Alho, K., & Näätänen, R. (1998). Development of language-specific phoneme representations in the infant brain. *Nature Neuroscience, 1*(5), 351–353.

Chomsky, C. (1972). Stages in language development and reading exposure. *Harvard Educational Review, 42,* 1–33.

Chomsky, N. (1965). *Aspects of a theory of syntax.* Cambridge, MA: MIT Press.

Chomsky, N. (1975). *Reflections on language.* New York: Pantheon.

Chomsky, N. (1982). *Lectures of government and binding.* New York: Foris.

Chomsky, N. (2002). *On nature and language.* New York: Cambridge University Press.

Christie, K. (2007). Learning to speak the world's languages. *Phi Delta Kappan, 88*(9), 645–647.

Christ, T., & Wang, X. C. (2010). Bridging the vocabulary gap: What the research tells us about vocabulary instruction in early childhood. *Young Children, 65*(4), 84–91.

Christ, T., & Wang, X. C. (2012, March). Supporting preschoolers' vocabulary learning: Using a decision-making model to select appropriate words and methods. *Young Children, 67,* 74–80.

Cicalese, C. (2003, November). *Children's perspectives on interactive writing versus independent writing in primary grades.* Unpublished master's thesis, Kean University, Union, NJ.

Clark, E. (2003). *First language acquisition.* New York: Cambridge University Press.

Clark, H., & Clark, E. (1977). *Psychology and language.* New York: Harcourt Brace Jovanovich.

Clay, M. (1975). *What did I write?* Auckland, New Zealand: Heinemann.

Clay, M. (1982). *Observing young readers: Selected papers.* Portsmouth, NH: Heinemann.

Clay, M. (1983). *Reading begins at home.* Exeter, NH: Heinemann.

Clay, M. (1987). *Writing begins at home.* Portsmouth, NH: Heinemann.

Clay, M. (1991). *Becoming literate: The construction of inner control.* Portsmouth, NH: Heinemann.

Clay, M. (1993). *An observation survey of early literacy achievement.* Portsmouth, NH: Heinemann.

Clay, M. (1998). *By different paths to common outcomes.* York, ME: Stenhouse.

Clements, D., & Sarama, J. (2003). Young children and technology: What does the research say? *Young Children, 58*(6), 34–40.

Cleveland, A., Schug, M., & Striano, T. (2007). Joint attention and object learning in 5- and 7-month-old infants. *Infant and Child Development, 16*(3), 295–306.

Cleveland, P. (1997). Language enhancing activities for toddlers. Unpublished manuscript, Northeastern Illinois University, Chicago.

Cloud, N., Genesee, F., & Hamayan, E. (2000). *Dual language instruction: A handbook for enriched education.* Boston: Heinle & Heinle.

Cochran-Smith M. (1984). *The making of a reader.* Norwood, NJ: Ablex.

Cohen, L., & Spenciner, L. (1994). *Assessment of young children.* New York: Longman.

Cohen, L., & Uhry, J. (2007). Young children's discourse strategies during block play: A Bakhtinian approach. *Journal of Research in Childhood Education, 21*(3), 302–315.

Cole, J. (1989). *The magic school bus: Inside the human body.* New York: Scholastic.

Cole, A. (2006). Scaffolding beginning readers: Micro and Macro cues teachers use during student oral reading. *The Reading Teacher, 59*(5), 450–459.

Coleman, M., & Churchill, S. (1997, Spring). Challenges to family involvement. *Childhood Education,* 144–148.

Colgin, M. (1991). *One potato, two potato, three potato, four: 165 Chants for children.* Mt. Rainier, MD: Gryphon House.

Collier, V. (1995). Acquiring a second language for school. *Directions in Language & Education, 1*(4), 1–12.

Coltrane, B. (2003). Working with young English language learners: Some considerations. ERIC Digest. ED 481690.

Common Core Standards (2012). http://www.core-standards.org/the-standards/english-language-art.

Conboy, B., & Kuhl, P. (2011). Impact of second-language experience in infancy: Brain measures of first- and second-language speech perception. *Developmental Science, 14*(2), 242–248.

Condon, W., & Sander, L. (1974). Neonate movement is synchronized with adult speech: Interactional participation and language acquisition. *Science, 183,* 99–101.

Cook, R., Tessier, A., & Armbruster, V. (1987). *Adapting early childhood curricula for children with special needs* (2nd ed.). Upper Saddle River, NJ: Merrill/ Prentice Hall.

Cooper, J. D., & Kiger, N. (2006). *Literacy: Helping children construct meaning* (6th ed.). Boston: Houghton Mifflin.

Cooper, P. (2005). Literacy learning and pedagogical purpose in Vivian Paley's "storytelling curriculum." *Journal of Early Childhood Literacy, 5*(3), 229–251.

Coplan, J. (1993). *Early language milestone scale* (2nd ed.). Austin, TX: PRO-ED.

Copple, C., & Bredekamp, S. (2009). *Developmentally appropriate practice in early childhood programs serving children from birth through age 8.* Washington, DC: National Association for the Education of Young Children.

Copple, C., Sigel, I., & Saunders, R. (1984). *Educating the young thinker: Classroom strategies for cognitive growth.* Hillsdale, NJ: Lawrence Erlbaum Associates.

Cornett, C. (1986). *Learning through laughter: Humor in the classroom.* Bloomington, IN: Phi Delta Kappa Educational Foundation.

Cote, L. (2001). Language opportunities during mealtimes in preschool classrooms. In D. Dickinson & P. Tabors (Eds.), *Beginning literacy with language* (pp. 205–222). Baltimore: Paul H. Brookes.

Cox, B. (1994). Young children's regulatory talk: Evidence of emerging metacognitive control over literary products and processes. In R. B. Ruddell, M. A. Ruddell, & H. Singer (Eds.), *Theoretical models and processes in reading* (4th ed., pp. 733–756). Newark, DE: International Reading Association.

Cox, B., & Dixey, B. (1994). Preschoolers doing "code-switching." In C. Kinzer & D. Leu (Eds.), *Multidimensional aspects of literacy research, theory, and practice* (pp. 162–171). 43rd Yearbook of the National Reading Conference. Chicago: National Reading Conference.

Cox, B., Fang, Z., & Otto, B. (1997). Preschoolers' developing ownership of the literate register. *Reading Research Quarterly, 32*(1), 34–53.

Craig, S. (2003). The effects of an adapted interactive writing intervention on kindergarten children's phonological awareness, spelling, and early reading development. *Reading Research Quarterly, 38*(4), 438–440.

Crais, E. (1992). Fast mapping: A new look at word learning. In R. Chapman (Ed.), *Processes in language acquisition and disorders* (pp. 159–185). St. Louis: Mosby Yearbook.

Crane-Thoreson, C., & Dale, P. (1992). Do early talkers become early readers? Linguistic precocity, preschool language, and emergent literacy. *Developmental Psychology, 28,* 421–429.

Crawford, P., & Hade, D. (2000, Fall/Winter). Inside the picture, outside the frame: Semiotics and the reading of wordless picture books. *Journal of Research in Childhood Education, 15*(1), 66–80.

Crowley, J. (1982). *Stop!* Auckland, New Zealand: Shortland.

Crumrine, L., & Lonegan, H. (1999). Pre-literacy skills screening. Austin, TX: PRO-ED.

Crumrine, L., & Lonegan, H. (2000). Phonemic awareness skills screening. Austin, TX: PRO-ED.

Crystal, D. (1987). *The Cambridge encyclopedia of language.* Cambridge, UK: Cambridge University Press.

Culatta, R., & Leeper, L. (1987). Disfluency in childhood: It's not always stuttering. *Journal of Childhood Communication Disorders, 10*(2), 95–106.

Cummins, J. (1979). Linguistic interdependence. *Review of Educational Research, 49,* 222–251.

Cummins, J. (1994). The acquisition of English as a second language. In K. Spangenberg-Urbschat & R. Pritchard (Eds.), *Kids come in all languages: Reading instruction for ESL students* (pp. 36–64). Newark, DE: International Reading Association.

Cummins, J. (1995). Underachievement among minority students. In D. Durkin (Ed.), *Language issues: Readings for teachers* (pp. 130–159). White Plains, NY: Longman.

Cummins, J. (1998). Linguistic enrichment in dual-language Spanish/English programs. *Leadership Letters: Issues and Trends in Bilingual Education.* Glenview, IL: Scott, Foresman.

Dahl, K., Freppon, P., & McIntyre, E. (1992, April). *A comparison of knowledge construction in writing by low-SES urban children in skills-based and whole language classrooms in the early grades.* Paper presented at the annual meeting of the American Educational Research Association, San Francisco.

Daly, K. (1997). Definition and epidemiology of otitis media. In J. Roberts, I. Wallace, & F. Henderson (Eds.), *Otitis media in young children: Medical developmental and educational considerations* (pp. 3–42). Baltimore: Paul H. Brookes.

Daniels, M. (1996). Seeing language: The effect over time of sign language on vocabulary development in early childhood education. *Child Study Journal, 26*(3), 193–208.

D'Arcangelo, M. (2000). The scientist in the crib: A conversation with Andrew Meltzoff. *Educational Leadership, 58*(3), 8–13.

Datta, L. (1975). Review of the Peabody Picture Vocabulary Test–R. In W. Frankenburg & B. Camp (Eds.), *Pediatric screening tests* (pp. 417–418). Springfield, IL: Thomas.

de Boysson-Bardies, B. (1999). *How language comes to children: From birth to two years.* Cambridge, MA: MIT Press.

DeCasper, A., & Fifer, W. (1980). Of human bonding: Newborns prefer their mothers' voices. *Science, 208,* 1174–1176.

DeCasper, A., & Spence, M. (1986). Prenatal maternal speech influences newborns' perception of speech sounds. *Infant Behavior and Development, 9,* 133–150.

Dehaene-Lambertz, G., & Gliga, T. (2004). Common neural basis for phoneme processing in infants and adults. *Journal of Cognitive Neuroscience, 16*(8), 1375–1387.

De Houwer, A. (1990). *The acquisition of two languages from birth: A case study.* Cambridge, UK: Cambridge University Press.

Del Vecchio, A., & Guerrero, M. (1995, December). *Handbook of English language proficiency tests.* Albuquerque, NM: Evaluation Assistance Center–Western Region, New Mexico Highlands University. www.ncela.gwu.edu/files/rcd/BE020503/Handbook_of_English.pdf. Retrieved December 23, 2004.

DeLoache, J. (1984, April). *What's this? Maternal questions in joint picture book reading with toddlers.* Paper presented at the annual meeting of the American Educational Research Association, New Orleans.

DeLoache, J., & DeMendoza, O. (1985). *Joint picturebook interactions of mothers and one-year-old children* (Tech. Rep. No. 353). Champaign, IL: University of Illinois, Center for the Study of Reading.

Delpit, L. (1988). The silenced dialogue: Power and pedagogy in educating other people's children. *Harvard Educational Review, 58*(3), 280–298.

Delpit, L. (1990). Language diversity and learning. In S. Hynds & D. Rubin (Eds.), *Perspectives on talk and learning* (pp. 247–266). Urbana, IL: National Council of Teachers of English.

Delpit, L. (1992). Acquisition of literate discourse: Bowing before the master? *Theory Into Practice, 31*(4), 296–302.

Delpit, L. (1995). *Other people's children: Cultural conflict in the classroom.* New York: The New Press.

Delpit, L. (2002). Introduction. In L. Delpit & J. L. Dowdy (Eds.), *The skin that we speak: Thoughts on language and culture in the classroom* (pp. xv–xxiv). New York: The New Press.

Delpit, L. (2006). *Other people's children: Cultural conflict in the classroom.* New York: The New Press.

DeMelendez, W., & Ostertag, V. (1997). *Teaching young children in multicultural classrooms: Issues, concepts, and strategies.* Albany, NY: Delmar.

Denk-Glass, R., Laber, S., & Brewer, K. (1982, September). Middle ear disease in young children. *Young Children,* 51–53.

de Paola, T. (1989). *Popcorn book.* New York: Holiday House.

Derman-Sparks, L., & ABC Task Force. (1989). *Anti-bias curriculum: Tools for empowering young children.* Washington, DC: National Association for the Education of Young Children.

DeTemple, J. (2001). Parents and children reading books together. In D. Dickinson & P. Tabors (Eds.), *Beginning literacy with language: Young children learning at home and school* (pp. 31–51). Baltimore: Paul H. Brookes.

DeTemple, J., & Beals, D. (1991, Fall–Winter). Family talk: Sources of support for the development of decontextualized language skills. *Journal of Research in Childhood Education, 6*(1), 11–19.

DeVault, L. (2003). The tide is high, but we *can* hold on: One teacher's thoughts on the rising tide of academic expectations. *Young Children, 58*(6), 90–93.

deVilliers, J., & deVilliers, P. (1973). A cross-sectional study of the acquisition of grammatical morphemes. *Journal of Psycholinguistic Research, 2,* 267–278.

deVilliers, J., & deVilliers, P. (1978). *Language acquisition.* Cambridge, MA: Harvard University Press.

DeVries, R. (2001). Transforming the "Play-oriented curriculum" and work in constructivist early education. In A. Göncü & E. Klein (Eds.), *Children in play, story, and school* (pp. 72–106). New York: Guilford Press.

Diamond, B., & Moore, M. (1995). *Multicultural literacy: Mirroring the reality of the classroom.* White Plains, NY: Longman.

DiCarlo, C., Pierce, S., Baumgartner, J., Harris, M., & Ota, C. (2012). Whole-group instruction practices and children's attention: A preliminary report. *Journal of Research in Childhood Education, 26*(2), 154–168.

Dickinson, D. (2001). Large-group and free-play times: Conversational settings supporting language and literacy development. In D. Dickinson & P. Tabors (Eds.), *Beginning literacy with language: Young children learning at home and school* (pp. 223–256). Baltimore: Paul H. Brookes.

Diener, M., Wright, C., Julian, J., & Byington, C. (2003). A pediatric literacy education program for low socioeconomic, culturally diverse families. *Journal of Research in Childhood Education, 18*(2), 149–159.

Diss, R., & Buckley, P. (2005). *Developing family and community involvement skills through case studies and field experiences.* Upper Saddle River, NJ: Merrill/Prentice Hall.

Dixon-Krauss, L. (1996). *Vygotsky in the classroom: Mediated literacy instruction and assessment.* White Plains, NY: Longman.

Dobrovolsky, M. (2005). Phonetics: The sounds of language. In W. O'Grady, J. Archibald, M. Aronoff, & J. Rees-Miller (Eds.), *Contemporary linguistics: An Introduction* (5th ed., pp. 15–56). Boston: Bedford/St. Martin's.

Doyle, K., & Ray, R. (2003). The otolaryngologist's role in management of hearing loss in infancy and childhood. *Mental Retardation and Developmental Disabilities Research Reviews, 9,* 94–102.

Duke, N. (2000). 3.6 minutes per day: The scarcity of informational texts in first grade. *The Reading Teacher, 35*(2), 202–224.

Duke, N., & Purcell-Gates, V. (2003). Genres at home and at school: Bridging the known to the new. *The Reading Teacher, 57*(1), 30–37.

Dumtschin, J. (1988, March). Recognize language development and delay in early childhood. *Young Children, 43,* 16–24.

Dunn, L. M., & Dunn, L. (2010). *Peabody Picture Vocabulary Test—IIIA and IIIB.* Circle Pines, MN: American Guidance Service.

Dunn, P., & Dunn, J. (1981). *The animals of Buttercup Farm.* New York: Random House.

Durkin, D. B. (Ed.). (1995). *Language issues: Readings for teachers.* White Plains, NY: Longman.

Dyson, A. (1981). Oral language: The rooting system for learning to write. *Language Arts, 58*(7), 776–784.

Dyson, A. (1989). *Multiple worlds of child writers: Friends learning to write.* New York: Teachers College Press.

Dyson, A. (1990a). Symbol makers, symbol weavers: How children link play, pictures, and print. *Young Children, 45*(2), 50–57.

Dyson, A. (1990b). Talking up a writing community: The role of talk in learning to write. In S. Hynds & D. Rubin (Eds.), *Perspectives on talk and learning* (pp. 99–114). Urbana, IL: National Council of Teachers of English.

Dyson, A. (1992). *Whistle for Willie,* lost puppies, and cartoon dogs: The sociocultural dimensions of young children's composing. *Journal of Reading Behavior, 24*(4), 433–462.

Dyson, A. (2004). Writing and the sea of voices: Oral language in, around, and about writing. In R. Ruddell & N. Unrau (Eds.), *Theoretical models and processes of reading* (5th ed., pp. 146–162). Newark, DE: International Reading Association.

Eastman, P. D. (1960). *Are you my mother?* New York: Random House.

Egan, K. (1996). Literacy and the oral foundations of education. In B. Power & R. Hubbard (Eds.), *Language development: A reader for teachers* (pp. 189–208). Upper Saddle River, NJ: Merrill/Prentice Hall.

Ehri, L. (1975). Word consciousness in readers and pre-readers. *Journal of Educational Psychology, 67*(2), 204–212.

Ehri, L., Nunes, S., Willows, D., Schuster, B., Yaghoub-Zadeh, Z., & Shanahan, T. (2001). Phonemic awareness instruction helps children learn to read: Evidence from the National Reading Panel's Meta-analysis. *Reading Research Quarterly, 36*(3), 250–287.

Eisenberg, R. (1976). *Auditory competence in early life: The roots of communicative behavior.* Baltimore: University Park Press.

Eldredge, J. L. (2004). *Phonics for teachers: Self-instruction, methods, and activities* (2nd ed.). Upper Saddle River, NJ: Merrill/Prentice Hall.

Elicker, J., Noppe, I., Noppe, L., & Fortner-Wood. C. (1997). The parent–caregiver relationship scale: Rounding out the relationship system in infant child care. *Early Education and Development, 8,* 83–100.

Eliot, L. (1999). *What's going on in there?* New York: Bantam Books.

Elster, C. (1994). "I guess they do listen": Young children's emergent readings after adult read-alouds. *Young Children, 49*(3), 27–31.

Espinosa, L. (2008, January). *Challenging common myths about young English language learners.* Foundation for Child Development Policy Brief: Advancing PK–3, No. Eight. www.fcd-us.org/sites/default/files/MythsOfTeaching ELLSEspinosa.pdf Retrieved May 21, 2008.

Evans, C. (1994). English-only children from bilingual homes: Considering the home–school connection. In C. Kinzer & D. Leu (Eds.), *Multidimensional aspects of literacy research, theory, and practice* (pp. 172–179). 43rd Yearbook of the National Reading Conference. Chicago: National Reading Conference.

Faltis, C. (1998). *Joinfostering: Teaching and learning in multilingual classrooms* (3rd ed.). Upper Saddle River, NJ: Merrill/Prentice Hall.

Farah, M., Betancourt, L., Shera, D., Savage, J., Giannetta, J., Brodsky, N., Malmud, El, & Hurt, H. (2008). Environmental stimulation, parental nurturance and cognitive development in humans. *Developmental Science, 11,* 793–801.

Farris, P., Fuhler, C., & Walther, M. (2004). *Teaching reading: A balanced approach for today's classrooms.* Boston: McGraw-Hill.

Fassler, R. (2003). *Room for talk: Teaching and learning in a multilingual kindergarten.* New York: Teachers College Press.

Feagans, L., Kipp, E., & Blood, I. (1994). The effects of otitis media on the attention skills of day-care-attending toddlers. *Developmental Psychology, 30*(5), 701–708.

Feldman, H., Dollaghan, C., Campbell, T., Colborn, K., Janosky, J., Kurs-Lasky, M., Rochette, H., Dale, P., & Paradise, J. (2003). Parent-reported language skills in relation to otitis media during the first 3 years of life. *Journal of Speech, Language, and Hearing Research, 46,* 273–287.

Ferguson, C. (1978). Fricatives in child language acquisition. In V. Honsa & M. Hardman-de-Baustita (Eds.), *Papers in linguistics and child language: Ruth Hirsch Weir Memorial Volume.* The Hague, the Netherlands: Mouton.

Fey, M., Catts, H., & Larrivee, L. (1995). Preparing preschoolers for the academic and social challenges of school. In M. Fey, J. Windsor, & S. Warren (Eds.), *Language intervention: Preschool through the elementary years* (Vol. 5, pp. 5–37). Baltimore: Paul H. Brookes.

Fey, M., Long, S., & Finestack, L. (2003, February). Ten principles of grammar facilitation for children with specific language impairments. *American Journal of Speech–Language Pathology, 12*, 3–15.

Fields, M., Spangler, K., & Lee, D. (1991). *Let's begin reading right: Developmentally appropriate beginning literacy*. Upper Saddle River, NJ: Merrill/Prentice Hall.

Fishman, A. (1995). Gullah. *Humanities, 16*(2), 45–49.

Fitts, E. (2001). Linguistic discrimination: A sociolinguistic perspective. ERIC ED 477 341. httlP://eric.ed.gov. Retrieved September 26, 2008.

Flanigan, B. (2006). Different ways of talking in the Buckeye State (Ohio). In W. Wolfram & B. Ward, *American voices: How dialects differ from coast to coast* (pp. 118–123). Malden, MA: Blackwell Publishing.

Fluharty, N. (2001). Fluharty-2 Fluharty preschool speech and language screening test (2nd ed.). Austin, TX: PRO-ED.

Foorman, B., Francis, D., Novy, D., & Liberman, D. (1991). How letter–sound instruction mediates progress in first-grade reading and spelling. *Journal of Educational Psychology, 83*(4), 456–469.

Fountas, I., & Pinnell, G. (2009). *The Fountas & Pinnell leveled book list*. Portsmouth, NH: Heinemann.

Fowler, W. (1990). *Talking from infancy: How to nurture and cultivate early language development*. Cambridge, MA: Brookline Books.

Fox, B. (2004). *Word identification strategies: Phonics from a new perspective*. Upper Saddle River, NJ: Merrill/Prentice Hall.

Fox, M. (2008). *Reading magic: Why reading aloud to our children will change their lives forever*. Boston, MA: Houghton Mifflin Harcourt.

Frankenburg, W., Dodds, J., Archer, P., Bresnick, B., Maschka, P., Edelman, N., & Shapiro, H. (1990). *Denver II technical manual*. Denver: Denver Developmental Materials, Inc.

Frazer, T. (2006). Introduction to Midwest English. In W. Wolfram & B. Ward, *American voices: How dialects differ from coast to coast* (pp. 101–105). Malden, MA: Blackwell Publishing.

Freeman, D. (1968). *Corduroy*. New York: Puffin Books.

Freeman, D., & Freeman, Y. (2004). *Essential linguistics: What you need to know to teach reading, ESL, spelling, phonics, and grammar*. Portsmouth, NH: Heinemann.

Freeman, E., & Sanders, T. (1989). Kindergarten children's emerging concepts of writing functions in the community. *Early Childhood Research Quarterly, 4*, 342–347.

Fromkin, V., & Rodman, R. (1998). *An introduction to language* (6th ed.). Fort Worth, TX: Harcourt Brace College Publishers.

Gadda, G. (1995). Language change in the history of English: Implications for teachers. In D. Durkin (Ed.), *Language issues: Readings for teachers* (pp. 262–272). White Plains, NY: Longman.

Galda, L., & Beach, R. (2004). Response to literature as a cultural activity. In R. Ruddell & N. Unrau (Eds.), *Theoretical models and processes of reading* (5th ed., pp. 852–879). Newark, DE: International Reading Association.

Galda, L., Bisplinghoff, B., Pellegrini, A., & Stahl, S. (1995). Sharing lives: Reading, writing, talking and living in a first-grade classroom. *Language Arts, 72*(5), 334–339.

Galda, L., Cullinan, B., & Strickland, D. (1993). *Language, literacy and the child*. Fort Worth, TX: Harcourt Brace Jovanovich.

Galda, L., & Pellegrini, A. (1990). Play talk, school talk, and emergent literacy. In S. Hynds & D. Rubin (Eds.), *Perspectives on talk and learning* (pp. 91–97). Urbana, IL: National Council of Teachers of English.

Galda, L., Pellegrini, A., Shockley, B., & Stahl, S. (1994, December–1995, January). Talking to read and write. *Reading Today, 12*(3), 32.

Galen, H. (1991). Increasing parental involvement in elementary school: The nitty-gritty of one successful program. *Young Children, 46*(2), 18–22.

Gallagher, K. (2005, July). Brain research and early childhood development: A primer for developmentally appropriate practice. *Young Children, 60*, 12–20.

Garcia-Sierra, A., Rivera-Gaxiola, M., Percaccio, C., Conboy, B., Romo, H., Klarman, L., Ortiz, S., & Kuhl, P. (2011). Bilingual language learning: An ERP study relating early brain responses to speech, language input, and later word production. *Journal of Phonetics, 39*(4), 546–557.

Gass, S., & Selinker, L. (2001). *Second language acquisition: An introductory course.* Mahwah, NJ: Lawrence Erlbaum Associates.

Gauthier, S., & Madison, C. (1998). Kindergarten language screening test (2nd ed.). Austin, TX: PRO-ED.

Geekie, P., & Raban, B. (1994). Language learning at home and school. In C. Gallaway & B. Richards (Eds.), *Input and interaction in language acquisition* (pp. 153–189). Cambridge, UK: Cambridge University Press.

Geisel, T. (1957). *The cat in the hat.* New York: Random House.

Gelman, S. (1998). Categories in young children's thinking. *Young Children, 53*(1), 20–26.

Genesee, F. (2001, September). *Practitioner brief #3: Some program alternatives for English language learners.* Santa Cruz, CA: University of California, Center for Research on Education, Diversity & Excellence.

Genesee, F., & Gándara, P. (1999). Bilingual education programs: A cross-national perspective. *Journal of Social Issues, 55*(4), 665–685.

Genesee, F., & Nicoladis, E. (1995). Language development in bilingual preschool children. In E. Garcia & B. McLaughlin (Eds.), *Meeting the challenge of linguistic and cultural diversity in early childhood education* (pp. 18–33). New York: Teachers College Press.

Genesee, F., Tucker, G., & Lambert, W. (1975). Communication skills of bilingual children. *Child Development, 46*, 110–114.

Genishi, C. (1992). Developing the foundation: Oral language and communicative competence. In C. Seefeldt (Ed.), *The early childhood curriculum: A review of current research* (pp. 85–117). New York: Teachers College Press.

Genishi, C., & Dyson, A. (1984). *Language assessment in the early years.* Norwood, NJ: Ablex.

Gentry, J. R. (1982). An analysis of developmental spelling in GYNS AT WRK. *The Reading Teacher, 36*(2), 192–200.

Gervain, J., Berent, I., & Werker, J. (2012). *Journal of Cognitive Neuroscience, 24*(4), 564–574.

Gillen, J., & Hall, N. (2001). "Hiya, Mum!" An analysis of pretence telephone play in a nursery setting. *Early Years, 21*(1), 15–24.

Gillon, G. (2004). *Phonological awareness: From research to practice.* New York: The Guilford Press.

Given, D. (2002). *Teaching to the brain's natural learning systems.* Alexandria, VA: Association for Supervision and Curriculum Development.

Glaubman, R., Kashi, B., & Koresh, R. (2001). Facilitating the narrative quality of sociodramatic play. In A. Göncü & E. Klein (Eds.), *Children in play, story and school.* New York: Guilford Press.

Glazer, J. (2000). *Literature for young children* (4th ed.). Upper Saddle River, NJ: Merrill/Prentice Hall.

Gleason, J. (1993). *The development of language* (3rd ed.). Upper Saddle River, NJ: Merrill/Prentice Hall.

Gleitman, L., & Gilette, J. (1999). The role of syntax in verb learning. In W. Ritchie & T. Bhatia (Eds.), *Handbook of child language acquisition.* San Diego, CA: Academic Press.

Goin, R., & Myers, B. (2004, Spring). Characteristics of infantile autism: Moving toward earlier detection. *Focus on Autism and Other Developmental Disabilities, 19*(1), 5–12.

Goldin-Meadow, S. (2007). Pointing sets the stage for learning language—and creating language. *Child Development, 78*(3), 741–745.

Golinkoff, R., & Hirsh-Pasek, K. (2006). Baby wordsmith: From associationist to social sophisticate. *Current Directions in Psychological Science, 15*(1), 30–33.

Goodhart, P. (1997). *Row, row, row your boat.* New York: Crown Publishers, Inc. Random House.

Goodman, K. (1993). *Phonics phacts.* Portsmouth, NH: Heinemann.

Goodman, Y. (1985). Kidwatching: Observing children in the classroom. In A. Jagger & M. T. Smith-Burke (Eds.), *Observing the language learner* (pp. 9–18). Newark, DE: International Reading Association, and Urbana, IL: National Council of Teachers of English.

Goodwyn, S., & Acredolo, L. (1993). Symbolic gesture versus word: Is there a modality advantage for onset of symbol use? *Child Development, 64*, 688–701.

Goodwyn, S., Acredolo, L., & Brown, C. (2000). Impact of symbolic gesturing on early language development. *Journal of Nonverbal Behavior, 24*(2), 81–104.

Goodz, N. (1994). Interactions between parents and children in bilingual families. In F. Genesee (Ed.), *Educating second language children* (pp. 61–81). New York: Cambridge University Press.

Goodz, N., Legare, M., & Bilodeau, L. (1987). The influence of bilingualism in preschool children. *Canadian Psychology, 28*, 218.

Gopnik, A., Meltzoff, A., & Kuhl, P. (1999). *The scientist in the crib.* New York: William Morrow.

Gordon, M. (2006). Straight talking from the Heartland (Midwest). In W. Wolfram & B. Ward, *American* voices: How dialects differ from coast to coast (pp. 106–111). Malden, MA: Blackwell Publishing.

Goswami, U. (1986). Children's use of analogy in learning to read: A developmental study. *Journal of Experimental Child Psychology, 42*, 73–83.

Goswami, U. (1990). A special link between rhyming skill and the use of orthographic analogies by beginning readers. *Journal of Child Psychology and Psychiatry, 31*(2), 301–311.

Goswami, U., & Mead, F. (1992). Onset and rime awareness and analogies in reading. *Reading Research Quarterly, 27*(2), 153–162.

Gottwald, S., Goldbach, P., & Isack, A. (1985). Stuttering: Prevention and detection. *Young Children, 41*(1), 9–16.

Gould, P., & Sullivan, J. (2005). *The inclusive early childhood classroom: Easy ways to adapt learning centers for all children.* Upper Saddle River, NJ: Pearson/Prentice Hall.

Grant, R. (1995). Meeting the needs of young second language learners. In E. Garcia & B. McLaughlin (Eds.), *Meeting the challenge of linguistic and cultural diversity in early childhood education* (pp. 1–17). New York: Teachers College Press.

Gravel, J., & O'Gara, J. (2003). Communication options for children with hearing loss. *Mental Retardation and Developmental Disabilities Research Reviews, 9*, 243–251.

Gregory, A., & Cahill, M. (2010). Kindergartners can do it, too! Comprehension strategies for early readers. *The Reading Teacher, 63*(6), 515–520.

Greenspan, S. (1997). *The growth of the mind and the endangered origins of intelligence.* Reading, MA: Perseus Books.

Griffin, M. (2001). Social contexts of beginning reading. *Language Arts, 78*(4), 371–378.

Groth, L., & Darling, L. (2001). Playing "inside" stories. In A. Göncü & E. Klein (Eds.), *Children in play, story, and school* (pp. 220–235). New York: Guilford Press.

Hackman, D. & Farah, M. (2009). Socioeconomic status and the developing brain. *Trends in Cognitive Sciences, 13*(2), 65–73.

Hackman, D., Farah, M., & Meaney, M. (2010). Socioeconomic status and the brain: Mechanistic insights from human and animal research. *Nature Reviews Neuroscience, 11*, 651–659.

Hadley, P., Wilcox, K., & Rice, M. (1994). Talking at school: Teacher expectations in preschool and kindergarten. *Early Childhood Research Quarterly, 9*(1), 111–129.

Haines, J., Ames, L., & Gillespie, C. (1980). *The Gesell Preschool Test.* Lumberville, PA: Modern Learning Press.

Haley, M., & Austin, T. (2004). *Content-based second language teaching and learning: An interactive approach.* Boston: Allyn & Bacon.

Hall, N. (2000). Interactive writing with young children. *Childhood Education, 76*(6), 358–364.

Halliday, M. (1975). *Learning how to mean: Explorations in the development of language.* London: Edward Arnold.

Halliday, M. A. K. (2007). *Language and education.* New York: Continuum.

Hammack, B., Foote, M., Garretson, S., & Thompson, J. (2012). Family literacy packs: Engaging teachers, families, and young children in quality activities to promote partnerships for learning. *Young Children, 67*(3), 104–110.

Hammill, D., Mather, N., & Roberts, R. (2001). *Illinois Test of Psycholinguistic Abilities* (3rd ed.). Austin, TX: PRO-ED.

Hannon, P. (1992, August). *Intergeneration literacy intervention: Possibilities and problems.* Paper presented at Adult Literacy: An International Urban Perspective, United Nations Headquarters, New York.

Harris, J. (1990). *Early language development: Implications for clinical and educational practice.* New York: Routledge.

Harris, M. (1992). *Language experience and early language development: From input to uptake.* Hillsdale, NJ: Lawrence Erlbaum Associates.

Harris, T., & Hodges, R. (Eds.). (1995). *The literacy dictionary: The vocabulary of reading and writing.* Newark, DE: International Reading Association.

Harshman, M. (2002). *Roads.* New York: Marshall Cavendish.

Hart, B., & Risley, T. (1995). *Meaningful differences in the everyday experience of young American children.* Baltimore: Paul H. Brookes.

Hart, B., & Risley, T. (1999). *The social world of children learning to talk.* Baltimore: Paul H. Brookes.

Hatch, E., Peck, S., & Wagner-Gough, J. (1995). A look at process in child second language acquisition. In D. Durkin (Ed.), *Language issues: Readings for teachers* (pp. 212–223). White Plains, NY: Longman.

Hawkins, C., & Hawkins, J. (1986). *Tog the dog.* New York: Putnam & Sons.

Hayes, C., Ornstein, J., & Gage, W. (1987). *The ABC's of languages and linguistics.* Lincolnwood, IL: National Textbook Company.

Hayes, D. (2003). Screening methods: Current status. *Mental Retardation and Developmental Disabilities Research Reviews, 9,* 65–72.

Hayes, L. (1990). From scribbling to writing: Smoothing the way. *Young Children, 45*(3), 62–68.

Heath, S. (1983). *Ways with words: Language, life, and work in communities and classrooms.* Cambridge, UK: Cambridge University Press.

Helman, L. (2004). Building on the sound system of Spanish: Insights from the alphabetic spellings of English-language learners. *The Reading Teacher, 57*(5), 452–460.

Henderson, E., & Templeton, S. (1986). A developmental perspective of formal spelling instruction through alphabet, pattern, and meaning. *The Elementary School Journal, 86*(3), 305–316.

Henderson, F., & Jones, E. (2002). "Every time they get started, we interrupt them": Children with special needs at play. In C. Brown & C. Marchant (Eds.), *Play in practice: Case studies in young children's play* (pp. 133–151). St. Paul, MN: Red Leaf Press.

Hill, E. (2000). *Where's Spot?* New York: Penguin Young Readers Group.

Hirsh-Pasek, K., & Golinkoff, R. (1996). *The origins of grammar: Evidence from early language comprehension.* Cambridge, MA: MIT Press.

Holmes, K., Holmes, S., & Watts, K. (2012). A descriptive study on the use of materials in vocabulary lessons. *Journal of Research in Childhood Education, 26,* 237–248.

Hornby, G., & Lafaele, R. (2011). Barriers to parental involvement in education: An explanatory model. *Educational Review, 63*(1), 37–52.

Honig, A. (1982). *Playtime learning games for young children.* Syracuse, NY: Syracuse University Press.

Honig, A. (1988). Humor development in children. *Young Children, 43*(4), 60–73.

Honig, A. (2005). The language of lullabies. *Young Children, 60*(5), 30–36.

Honig, A. (2007). Play: Ten power boosts for children's early learning. *Young Children, 62*(5), 72–78.

Honig, A., & Brophy, H. (1996). *Talking with your baby: Family as the first school.* Syracuse, NY: Syracuse University Press.

Honig, A., & Lally, J. (1981). *Infant caregiving: A design for training.* Syracuse, NY: Syracuse University Press.

Honig, A., & Shin, M. (2001). Reading aloud with infants and toddlers in child care settings: An observational study. *Early Childhood Education Journal, 28*(3), 193–197.

Hoover-Dempsey, K., & Sandler, H. (1997). Why do parents become involved in their children's education? *Review of Educational Research, 67,* 3–42.

Horacek, P. (2008). *Choo choo.* Somerville, MA: Candlewick Press.

Hostmeyer, P., & Kinsella, M. (2010). *Storytelling and QAR strategies.* Santa Barbara, CA: Teacher Ideas Press/ABC-CLIO.

Hough, R., Nurss, J., & Wood, D. (1987). Tell me a story: Making opportunities for elaborated language in early childhood classrooms. *Young Children, 43*(1), 6–12.

Hresko, W., Reid, D., & Hammill, D. (1981). *Test of early language development (TELD).* Austin, TX: PRO-ED.

Hresko, W., Reid, K., & Hammill, D. (1999). *Test of early language development* (3rd ed.). San Antonio, TX: Harcourt Assessment, Inc./PsychCorp.

Hudson, L., Chryst, C., & Reamsnyder, D. (1994). Goin' to Grandma's house: Using instructional conversation to promote literacy and reduce resistance in minority children. In D. Lancy (Ed.), *Children's emergent literacy: From research to practice* (pp. 265–284). Westport, CT: Praeger.

Hulit, L., & Howard, M. (1993). *Born to talk: An introduction to speech and language development.* New York: Merrill/Macmillan.

Huttenlocher, J., Vasilyeva, M., Waterfall, H., Vevea, J., & Hedges, L. (2007). The varieties of speech to young children. *Developmental Psychology, 43*(5), 1062–1083.

Huttenlocher, J., Waterfall, H., Vasilyeva, M., Vevea, J., & Hedges, L. (2010). Sources of variability in children's language growth. *Cognitive Psychology, 61*(4), 343–365.

Ianco-Worrall, A. (1972). Bilingualism and cognitive development. *Child Development, 43,* 1390–1400.

Im, J., Parlakian, R., & Osborn, C. (2007). Stories: Their powerful role in early language and literacy. *Young Children 62*(1), 52–54.

International Reading Association and National Association for the Education of Young Children. (1999). Learning to read and write: Developmentally appropriate practices for young children. In K. Paciorek & J. Munro (Eds.), *Annual editions: Early childhood education* (20th ed., pp. 166–183). Guilford, CT: Dushkin/McGraw-Hill.

International Reading Association and National Council of Teachers of English. (1996). *Standards for the English language arts.* Newark, DE: International Reading Association, and Urbana, IL: National Council of Teachers of English.

Jalongo, M., & Isenberg, J. (2004). *Exploring your role: A practitioner's introduction to early childhood education* (2nd ed.). Upper Saddle River, NJ: Merrill/Prentice Hall.

Jalongo, M., & Sobolak, M. (2011). Supporting young children's vocabulary growth: The challenges, the benefits, and evidence-based strategies. *Early Childhood Education Journal, 38*, 421–429.

Jarmulowicz, L., Taran, V., & Hay, S. (2007). Third graders' metalinguistic skills, reading skills, and stress production in derived English words. *Journal of Speech, Language, and Hearing Research, 50*, 1593–1605.

Jednorog, K., Altarelli, I., Monzalvo, K., Fluss, J., Dubois, J., Billard, C., Dehaene-Lambertz, G., & Ramus, F. (2012). The influence of socioeconomic status on children's brain structure. *PLoS ONE, 7*(8), e42486. doi:10.1371/journal.pone.0042486.

Jensen, P., Williams, W., & Bzoch, K. (1975, November). *Preference of young infants for speech vs. nonspeech stimuli.* Paper presented to the annual American Speech and Hearing Association Convention, Washington, DC.

Jewell, M., & Zintz, M. (1990). *Learning to read and write naturally.* Dubuque, IA: Kendall/Hunt.

Jimenez, S. (2008, April). *Observation of an infant's ways of communicating.* Unpublished manuscript, Northeastern Illinois University, Chicago.

Johnson, C., Myers, S., & Council on Children with Disabilities (2007, November). Identification and evaluation of children with autism spectrum disorders. *Pediatrics, 120*(5), 1183–1215.

John-Steiner, V., Panofsky, C., & Smith, L. (1994). *Sociocultural approaches to language and literacy: An interactionist perspective.* New York: Cambridge University Press.

Johnston, F. (1999). The timing and teaching of word families. *The Reading Teacher, 53*(1), 64–75.

Jordan, G., Snow, C., & Porche, M. (2000). Project EASE: The effect of a family literacy project on kindergarten students' early literacy skills. *Reading Research Quarterly, 35*(4), 524–546.

Joyner, R., & Ray, E. (1987). *Reading behavior in infancy: Developmental and attitudinal implications.* Paper presented at the annual conference of the Association for Childhood Education International, Omaha, NE.

Jusczyk, P. (1985). On characterizing the development of speech perception. In J. Mehler & R. Fox (Eds.), *Neonate cognition: Beyond the blooming, buzzing confusion.* Hillsdale, NJ: Lawrence Erlbaum Associates.

Jusczyk, P. (1997). *The discovery of spoken language.* Cambridge, MA: MIT Press.

Jusczyk, P. (2001). Finding and remembering words: Some beginnings by English-learning infants. In M. Tomasello & E. Bates (Eds.), *Language development: The essential readings* (pp. 19–25). Malden, MA: Blackwell.

Jusczyk, P. (2003). The role of speech perception capacities in language acquisition. In M. Banich & M. Mack (Eds.), *Mind, brain and language: Multidisciplinary perspectives* (pp. 61–86). Mahwah, NJ: Lawrence Erlbaum Associates.

Kaiser, B., & Rasminsky, J. (2003, July). Opening the culture door. *Young Children, 58*(4), 53–56.

Karmiloff, M., & Karmiloff-Smith, A. (2001). *Pathways to language: From fetus to adolescent.* Cambridge, MA: Harvard University Press.

Kasten, W. (1997). Learning is noisy: The myth of silence in the reading-writing classroom. In J. Paratore & R. McCormack (Eds.), *Peer talk in the classroom: Learning from research* (pp. 88–101). Newark, DE: International Reading Association.

Katz, L., & Schery, T. (2006, January). Including children with hearing loss in early childhood programs. *Young Children, 61*(1), 86–100.

Keats, E. J. (1962). *Snowy day.* New York: Viking Press.

Kempfer, G. (1993). *Rebecca's storybook-based language observation.* Unpublished manuscript, Northeastern Illinois University, Chicago, IL.

Kieff, J. (2003/2004, Winter). Winning ways with word walls. *Childhood Education, 80*(2), 84I–84K.

Kinniburgh, L., & Shaw, E. (2009, Winter). Using question-answer relationships to build reading comprehension in science. *Science Activities*, 19–28.

Kirtley, C., Bryant, P., MacLean, M., & Bradley, L. (1989). Rhyme, rime, and the onset of reading. *Journal of Experimental Child Psychology, 48*, 224–245.

Kissel, B. (2009). Beyond the page: Peers influence pre-kindergarten writing. *Childhood Education, 85*(3), 160–166.

Klenk, L. (2001, Spring). Playing with literacy in preschool classrooms. *Childhood Education, 77*(3), 150–157.

Kostelnik, M., Soderman, A., & Whiren, A. (2007). *Developmentally appropriate curriculum: Best practices in early childhood education* (4th ed.). Upper Saddle River, NJ: Pearson Merrill/Prentice Hall.

Kostelink, M., Soderman, A., & Whiren, A. (2010). *Developmentally appropriate curriculum: Best practices in early childhood education.* Upper Saddle River, NJ: Columbus, OH.

Kovach, B., & Da Ros-Voseles, D. (2011). Communicating with babies. *Young Children, 66*(2), 48–50.

Krashen, S. (1981). *Second language acquisition and second language learning.* London: Pergamon Press.

Krashen, S. (1982). *Principles and practice in second language acquisition.* New York: Pergamon Press.

Krashen, S. (1995). Bilingual education and second language acquisition theory. In D. Durkin (Ed.), *Language issues: Readings for teachers* (pp. 90–115). White Plains, NY: Longman.

Krashen, S. (2003). *Explorations in language acquisition and use.* Portsmouth, NH: Heinemann.

Kratcoski, A., & Katz, K. (1998, May). Conversing with young language learners in the classroom. *Young Children, 53,* 30–33.

Kuhl, P. (2005). Early language acquisition: Cracking the speech code. *Nature Reviews Neuroscience, 5*(11), 831–843.

Kuo, L., & Anderson, R. (2006). Morphological awareness and learning to read: A cross-language perspective. *Educational Psychologist, 41*(3), 161–180.

Kuskin, K. (1990). *Roar and more.* New York: Harper Trophy.

Labov, W. (1979). The logic of nonstandard English. In J. Alatis (Ed.), *Report of the Twentieth Annual Round Table Meeting on Linguistics and Language Studies* (*Monograph Series of Languages and Linguistics,* No. 22). In D. Durkin (Ed.), *Language issues: Readings for teachers* (pp. 281–313). White Plains, NY: Longman.

Labov, W. (1995). The study of nonstandard English. In B. Power & R. Hubbard (Eds.), *Language development: A reader for teachers* (pp. 50–54). Upper Saddle River, NJ: Merrill/Prentice Hall.

Lacina, J. (2007–2008). Computers and young children. *Childhood Education, 84*(2), 113–116.

Lacina, J., & Mathews, S. (2012, May–June). Using online storybooks to build comprehension. *Childhood Education,* 155–161.

Lamb, S. (1999). *Pathways of the brain: The neurocognitive basis of language.* Philadelphia: John Benjamins.

Lamme, L., Fu, D., Johnson, J., & Savage, D. (2002). Helping kindergarten writers move toward independence. *Early Childhood Education Journal, 30*(2), 73–79.

Lane, H., & Wright, T. (2007). Maximizing the effectiveness of reading aloud. *The Reading Teacher, 60*(7), 668–675.

Langevin, M., Packman, A., & Onslow, M. (2009). Peer responses to stuttering in the preschool setting. *American Journal of Speech-Language Pathology, 18*(3), 264–276.

Lanza, E. (1992). Can bilingual two-year-olds code-switch? *Journal of Child Language, 19,* 633–658.

Lawrence, L. (1998). *Montessori read & write: A parents' guide to literacy for children.* New York: Three Rivers Press.

Lear, E., & Moroney, T. (2002). *Nursery songs.* Scoresby VIC, Australia: Five Mile Press.

Lederman, D., Cohen, A., Zmora, E., Wermke, K., Hauschildt, S., & Stellzig-Eisenhauer, A. (2002). *Automatic classification of the cry of infants with cleft palate.* Paper presented at the 2nd European Medical and Biomedical Engineering Conference, Vienna.

Lempinen, E. (2012a). AAAS Briefing: Links between poverty, brain development raise key policy issues. Advancing Science Serving Society/AAAS News: News Archives. American Association for the Advancement of Science. http://www.aaas.org/news/releases/2012/0731early_brain.shtml. Retrieved July 2, 2012.

Lempinen, E. (2012b). Poverty can harm early brain development, researchers say. *Science, 337,* p. 428.

Leong, D., & Bodrova, E. (2012, January). Assessing and scaffolding make-believe play. *Young Children, 67*(1), 28–34.

Lesiak, J. (2000). Research-based answers to questions about emergent literacy in kindergarten. In R. Robinson, M. McKenna, & J. Wedman (Eds.), *Issues and trends in literacy education* (2nd ed., pp. 213–236). Boston: Allyn & Bacon.

Lessow-Hurley, J. (2000). *The foundations of dual language instruction* (3rd ed.). New York: Longman.

Levy, A., Wolfgang, C., & Koorland, M. (1992). Sociodramatic play as a method of enhancing the language performance of kindergarten age students. *Early Childhood Research Quarterly, 7,* 245–262.

Lewis-Moreno, B. (2007). Shared responsibility: Achieving success with English language learners. *Phi Delta Kappan, 88*(10), 772–775.

Lewison, W. (1992). *Buzz said the bee.* New York: Scholastic.

Lightbown, P., & Spada, N. (2006). *How languages are learned*. New York: Oxford University Press.

Lillo-Martin, D. (1999). Modality effects and modularity in language acquisition: The acquisition of American sign language. In W. Ritchie & T. Bhatia (Eds.), *Handbook of child language acquisition* (pp. 531–568). San Diego, CA: Academic Press.

Lilly, E., & Green, C. (2004). *Developing partnerships with families through children's literature*. Upper Saddle River, NJ: Merrill/Prentice Hall.

Lim, S-Y. (2012). Family involvement in education. In G. Olson & M. Fuller (Eds.), *Home and school relations: Teachers and parents working together* (pp. 130–155). Boston: Pearson.

Lindberg, L., & Swedlow, R. (1980). *Early childhood education: A guide for observation & participation* (2nd ed.). Boston: Allyn & Bacon.

Lindfors, J. (1987). *Children's language and learning* (2nd ed.). Upper Saddle River, NJ: Prentice Hall.

Lindfors, J. (1990). Speaking creatures in the classroom. In S. Hynds & D. Rubin (Eds.), *Perspectives on talk and learning* (pp. 21–40). Urbana, IL: National Council of Teachers of English.

Loban, W. (1976). *Language development: Kindergarten through grade twelve*. Urbana, IL: National Council of Teachers of English.

Loop, C. (2004). *Which tests are commonly used to determine English and/or Spanish proficiency?* National Clearinghouse for English Language Acquisition & Language Instruction for Education Programs. www.ncela.gwu.edu/expert/faq/25tests .htm. Retrieved July 27, 2004.

Lowman, L., & Ruhmann, L. (1998, May). Simply sensational spaces: A multi-S approach to toddler environments. *Young Children, 53*, 11–17.

Luke, A., & Kale, J. (1997). Learning through difference: Cultural practices in early childhood language socialization. In E. Gregory (Ed.), *One child, many worlds* (pp. 33–46). New York: Teachers College Press.

Lundsteen, S. (1990). Learning to listen and learning to read. In S. Hynds & D. Rubin (Eds.), *Perspectives on talk and learning* (pp. 213–225). Urbana, IL: National Council of Teachers of English.

Lyons, C. (2003). *Teaching struggling readers: How to use brain-based research to maximize learning*. Portsmouth, NH: Heinemann.

MacDonald, J. (2012). Teachers and parenting: Multiple views. In G. Olson & M. Fuller, (Eds.), *Home and school relations: Teachers and parents working together* (pp. 84–100). Boston: Pearson.

Maclean, M., Bryant, P., & Bradley, L. (1987). Rhymes, nursery rhymes, and reading in early childhood. *Merrill-Palmer Quarterly, 33*(3), 255–281.

Mahoney, D., & Mann, V. (1991). *Using children's humor to clarify the relationship between linguistic awareness and early reading ability*. Paper presented at the Biennial Meeting of the Society for Research in Child Development, Seattle.

Mandel, D., Jusczyk, P., & Kemler-Nelson, D. (1994). Does sentential prosody help infants organize and remember speech information? *Cognition, 53*, 155–180.

Manning, M., Manning, G., & Morrison, G. (1995). Letter-writing connections: A teacher, first graders, and their parents. *Young Children, 50*(6), 34–38.

Manolson, A. (1992). *It takes two to talk: A parent's guide to helping children communicate*. Toronto: The Hanen Centre.

Marcy, M. (2001, May). *Management of acute otitis media* (Evidence report/Technology Assessment No. 15, Publication No. 01-E010). Rockville, MD: U.S. Department of Health and Human Services, Agency for Healthcare Research and Quality. http://www.ahrq.gov/clinic/epcsums/otitisum. htm. Retrieved September 26, 2008.

Mardell, C. & Goldenberg, D. (2011). Developmental Indicators for Assessment of Learning/DIAL-4. San Antonio, TX: Pearson Psych Corp.

Markson, L., & Bloom, P. (1997). Evidence against a dedicated system for word learning in children. *Nature, 385*, 813–815.

Marschark, M. (1997). *Raising and educating a deaf child*. New York: Oxford University Press.

Martin, B. (1996). *Brown bear, brown bear, what do you see?* New York: Henry Holt.

Martin, B., & Carle, E. (1992). *Brown bear, brown bear, what do you see?* Orlando, FL: Harcourt Brace Jovanovich.

Martin, S. (1994). *Take a look: Observation and portfolio assessment in early childhood*. New York: Addison-Wesley.

Martinez, M., & Teale, W. (1988). Reading in a kindergarten classroom library. *The Reading Teacher, 41*, 568–572.

Masataka, N. (1996). Perception of motherese in a signed language by 6-month-old deaf infants. *Developmental Psychology, 32*(5), 874–879.

Mason, J. (1980). When do children begin to read: An exploration of four-year-old children's letter and word reading competencies. *Reading Research Quarterly, 15*, 203–227.

Mason, J., Peterman, C., & Kerr, D. (1989). Reading to kindergarten children. In D. Strickland & L. Morrow (Eds.), *Emergent literacy: Young children learn to read and write* (pp. 52–62). Newark, DE: International Reading Association.

Mason, P., & Galloway, E. (2012). What children living in poverty do bring to school: Strong oral skills. Let them talk! *Reading Today, 29*(4), 29–30.

Mastropieri, M., & Scruggs, T. (2007). *The inclusive classroom: Strategies for effective instruction* (3rd ed.). Upper Saddle River, NJ: Pearson/Merrill/Prentice Hall.

Matthews, L. (1999). Not just onions! Exploring layers of meaning in texts. In J. Hancock (Ed.), *The explicit teaching of reading* (pp. 29–38). Newark, DE: International Reading Association.

Maxim, G. (1990). *The sourcebook: Activities for infants and young children* (2nd ed.). Upper Saddle River, NJ: Merrill/Prentice Hall.

Maxim, G. (1993). *The very young: Guiding children from infancy through the early years* (4th ed.). Upper Saddle River, NJ: Merrill/Prentice Hall.

McAfee, O., & Leong, D. (2011). *Assessing and guiding young children's development and learning* (4th ed.). Boston: Pearson/Allyn & Bacon.

McCafferty, C. (2002). *The gingerbread man.* Columbus, OH: McGraw-Hill Children's Publishing.

McCaleb, S. P. (1997). *Building communities of learners: A collaboration among teachers, students, families, and community.* Mahwah, NJ: Lawrence Erlbaum Associates.

McCarrier, A., Pinnell, G., & Fountas, I. (2000). *Interactive writing: How language and literacy come together, K–2.* Portsmouth, NH: Heinemann.

McCarthy, D. (1972). *Manual for the McCarthy Scales of Children's Abilities.* New York: Psychological Corporation, Harcourt Brace Jovanovich.

McDonald, M. (1990). *Is this a house for hermit crab?* New York: Orchard Books.

McGee, L., & Richgels, D. (1990). *Literacy's beginnings: Supporting young readers and writers.* Boston: Allyn & Bacon.

McGee, L., & Richgels, D. (2000). *Literacy's beginnings: Supporting young readers and writers* (3rd ed.). Boston: Allyn & Bacon.

McGee, L., & Ukrainetz, T. (2009). Using scaffolding to teach phonemic awareness in preschool and kindergarten. *The Reading Teacher, 62*(7), 599–603.

McGhee, P. (1979). *Humor: Its origin and development.* San Francisco: W. H. Freeman & Company.

McGhee, P. (2004). The importance of nurturing children's humor. *Illinois AEYC Winter News, 4*(2), 8.

McLaughlin, B. (1985). *Second-language acquisition in childhood: School-age children* (Vol. 2, 2nd ed.). Hillsdale, NJ: Lawrence Erlbaum Associates.

McLeod, B. (1994). Linguistic diversity and academic achievement. In B. McLeod (Ed.), *Language and learning: Educating linguistically diverse students.* Albany, NY: State University of New York Press.

McNeill, D. (1970). *The acquisition of language: The study of developmental psycholinguistics.* New York: Harper & Row.

McNeill, J., & Fowler, S. (1996, Summer). Using story reading to encourage children's conversations. *Teaching Exceptional Children, 28,* 43–47.

Medicine Net. (1999). Definition of tube, Eustachian. http://www.medterms.com/script/main/art.asp?articlekey=8524. Retrieved May 3, 2012.

Meechan, M., & Rees-Miller, J. (2003). Language in social contexts. In W. O'Grady, J. Archibald, M. Aronoff, & J. Rees-Miller (Eds.), *Contemporary linguistics: An introduction* (5th ed., pp. 485–529). New York: Bedford/St. Martin's.

Mehan, H. (1979). *Learning lessons.* Cambridge, MA: Harvard University Press.

Meier, T. (2003). "Why can't she remember that?" The importance of storybook reading in multilingual, multicultural classrooms. *The Reading Teacher, 57*(3), 242–252.

Meisel, J. M. (1994). Code-switching in bilingual children. *Studies in second language acquisition* (Vol. 16, pp. 413–440). Bloomington, IN: Indiana University Press.

Meisels, S. (1989). *Developmental screening in early childhood: A guide* (3rd ed.). Washington, DC: National Association for the Education of Young Children.

Meisels, S., & Atkins-Burnett, S. (2005). *Developmental screening in early childhood: A guide* (5th ed.). Washington, DC: National Association for the Education of Young Children.

Melzi, G., & Ely, R. (2007). Language and literacy in the school years. In J. Berko Gleason & N. Ratner, (Eds.), *The development of language* (pp. 391–435). Boston: Pearson.

Melzi, G., & Ely, R. (2009). Language and literacy in the school years. In J. Berko Gleason & N. Bernstein

Ratner (Eds.), *The development of language* (pp. 391–435). Boston: Pearson/Allyn & Bacon.

Menn, L. (1989). Phonological development: Learning sounds and sound patterns. In J. Berko Gleason (Ed.), *The development of language* (2nd ed., pp. 59–100). Upper Saddle River, NJ: Merrill/Prentice Hall.

Menyuk, P. (1984). Language development and reading. In J. Flood (Ed.), *Understanding reading comprehension* (pp. 101–121). Newark, DE: International Reading Association.

Menyuk, P. (1988). *Language development: Knowledge and use.* Glenview, IL: Scott, Foresman/Little, Brown.

Merenda, R. (1989). "Me and Ethan": Celebrating the writer's choice. *Childhood Education, 65*(4), 217–219.

Metzger, S. (2006). *Big shark's lost tooth.* New York: Scholastic.

Miller, R., & Pedro, J. (2006). Creating respectful classroom environments. *Early Childhood Education Journal, 33*(5), 293–299.

Miller, P., & Mehler, R. (1994). The power of personal storytelling in families and kindergartens. In A. Dyson & C. Genishi (Eds.), *The need for story: Cultural diversity in classroom and community* (pp. 38–54). Urbana, IL: National Council of Teachers of English.

Miller, W. (2000). *Strategies for developing emergent literacy.* Boston: McGraw-Hill.

Mindes, G. (2011). *Assessing young children.* Boston: Pearson.

Mody, M., Schwartz, R., Gravel, J., & Ruben, R. (1999). Speech perception and verbal memory in children with and without histories of otitis media. *Journal of Speech, Language, and Hearing Research, 42*(5), 1069–1079.

Moerk, E. (1974). Changes in verbal child–mother interactions with increasing language skills of the child. *Journal of Psycholinguistic Research, 3*(2), 101–106.

Moller, K., Starr, C., & Johnson, S. (1990). *A parent's guide to cleft lip and palate.* Minneapolis: University of Minnesota Press.

Monastersky, R. (2004). Look who's listening. *Early childhood education annual editions 03/04* (pp. 31–33). Guilford, CT: McGraw-Hill/Dushkin.

Montgomery, J. (2002, February). Understanding the language difficulties of children with specific language impairments: Does verbal working memory matter? *American Journal of Speech–Language Pathology, 11,* 77–91.

Mooney, M. (1990). *Reading to, with, and by children.* Katonah, NY: Richard C. Owen.

Moran, A., & Everett, B. (2003). *Popcorn.* San Diego, CA: Harcourt.

Morris, D., Bloodgood, J., Lomax, R., & Perney, J. (2003). Developmental steps in learning to read: A longitudinal study in kindergarten and first grade. *Reading Research Quarterly, 38*(3), 302–323.

Morrison, G. (2004). *Early childhood education today.* (9th ed.). Upper Saddle River, NJ: Prentice Hall.

Morrison, G. (2009). *Early childhood education today* (11th ed.). Upper Saddle River, NJ: Merrill/Prentice Hall.

Morrow, L. (1989). *Literacy development in the early years.* Upper Saddle River, NJ: Prentice Hall.

Morrow, L., & Gambrell, L. (1998). How do we motivate children toward independent reading and writing? In S. Neuman & K. Roskos (Eds.), *Children achieving: Best practices in early literacy* (pp. 144–161). Newark, DE: International Reading Association.

Morrow, L., & Gambrell, L. (2002). Literature-based instruction in the early years. In S. Neuman & D. Dickinson (Eds.), *Handbook of early literacy research* (pp. 348–360). New York: Guilford Press.

Morrow, L., & Rand, M. (1991). Promoting literacy during play by designing early childhood classroom environments. *The Reading Teacher, 44*(6), 396–402.

Morrow, L., & Young, J. (1995). *Parent, teacher, and child participation in a collaborative family literacy program: The effects on attitude, motivation, and literacy achievement. Reading Research Report, No. 64.* Washington, DC: Office of Educational Research and Improvement.

Muhlstein, E., & Croft, D. (1986, September). *Using the microcomputer to enhance language experiences and the development of cooperative play among preschool children.* Cupertino, CA: DeAnza College.

Murphy, L., Condey, J. C., & Impara, J. (1994). *Tests in print IV: An index to tests, test reviews, and the literature on specific tests.* Lincoln, NE: University of Nebraska.

Murray, T. (2006). Spirited speech (St. Louis, MO). In W. Wolfram & B. Ward (Eds.), *American voices: How dialects differ from coast to coast* (pp. 124–129). Malden, MA: Blackwell Publishing.

Nagy, W., & Scott, J. (2000). Vocabulary processes. In M. Kamil, P. Mosenthal, P. D. Pearson, & R. Barr (Eds.), *Handbook of reading research.* (pp. 269–284). Mahwah, NJ: Erlbaum.

Nardi, W. (1992–1993). Nurturing our youngest learners: What American families can do at home to help their children succeed at school. *ETS Developments, 38*(2), 5–7.

Nation, K., Cocksey, J., Taylor, J., & Bishop, D. (2010). A longitudinal investigation of early reading and language skills in children with poor reading comprehension. *Journal of Child Psychology & Psychiatry, 51*(9), 1031–1039.

National Association for the Education of Young Children (NAEYC) (2004). Where we stand: On curriculum, assessment, and program evaluation. *Young Children, 59*(1), 51–53.

National Institute on Deafness and Other Communication Disorders. (2008). Otitis media (ear infection). http://www.nidcd.nih.gov/health/hearing/otitism.asp. Retrieved September 30, 2008.

Nelson, K. (1973). Structure and strategy in learning to talk. *Monographs of the Society for Research in Child Development, 38*(1–2, Serial No. 149).

Nemeth, K. (2009). Meeting the home language mandate: Practical strategies for all classrooms. *Young Children, 64*(2), 36–42.

Nemeth, K., & Erdosi, V. (2012). Enhancing practice with infants and toddlers from diverse language and cultural backgrounds. *Young Children, 67*(4), 49–57.

Neuman, S. (1999). Books make a difference: A study of access of literacy. *The Reading Teacher, 34*(3), 286–311.

Neuman, S., & Roskos, K. (1990). The influence of literacy-enriched play settings on preschoolers' engagement with written language. In J. Zutell & S. McCormick (Eds.), *Literacy theory and research: Analysis from multiple paradigms* (pp. 179–187). Chicago: National Reading Conference.

Neuman, S., & Roskos, K. (1991). Peers as literacy informants: A description of young children's literacy conversations in play. *Early Childhood Research Quarterly, 6,* 233–248.

Neuman, S., & Roskos, K. (1993). *Language and literacy learning in the early years: An integrated approach.* Fort Worth, TX: Harcourt Brace Jovanovich College Publishers.

Newcomer, P., & Hammill, D. (1997). *Test of language development—Primary* (3rd ed.). San Antonio, TX: Harcourt Assessment, Inc./PsychCorp.

Newkirk, T., & McLure, P. (1996). Telling stories. In B. Power & R. Hubbard (Eds.), *Language development: A reader for teachers* (pp. 132–138). Upper Saddle River, NJ: Merrill/Prentice Hall.

Newman, R., Ratner, N., Jusczyk, A., Jusczyk, P., & Dow, K. (2006). Infants' early ability to segment the conversational speech signal predicts later language development: A retrospective analysis. *Developmental Psychology, 42*(4), 643–655.

Newport, E., Gleitman, H., & Gleitman, L. (1977). Mother, I'd rather do it myself: Some effects and non-effects of maternal speech style. In C. Snow & C. Ferguson (Eds.), *Talking to children: Language input and acquisition* (pp. 109–149). Cambridge, UK: Cambridge University Press.

Nichols, C. (2003). *One big ocean.* New York: Benchmark Books.

Ninio, A., & Snow, C. (1999). The development of pragmatics: Learning to use language appropriately. In W. Ritchie & T. Bhatia (Eds.), *Handbook of child language acquisition* (pp. 347–386). San Diego, CA: Academic Press.

Noble, K., Wolmetz, M., Ochs, L., Farah, M., & McCandliss, B. (2006). Brain-behavior relationships in reading acquisition are modulated by socioeconomic factors. *Developmental Science, 9*(6), 642–654.

Nord, C., Lennon, J., Liu, D., & Chandler, K. (1999). *Home literacy activities and signs of children's emergent literacy, 1993–1999.* Washington, DC: U.S. Department of Education, Office of Educational Research and Improvement, NCES 2000–026.

Nourot, P., & VanHoorn, J. (1991). Symbolic play in preschool and primary settings. *Young Children, 46*(6), 40–50.

O'Brien, M., & Xiufen, B. (1995). Language learning in context: Teacher and toddler speech in three classroom play areas. *Topics in Early Childhood Special Education, 15*(2), 1–12.

O'Grady, W., Archibald, J., Aronoff, M., & Rees-Miller, J. (Eds.). (2005). *Contemporary linguistics: An introduction* (5th ed.). Boston: Bedford/St. Martin's.

O'Grady, W., & Cho, S. (2005). First language acquisition. In W. O'Grady, J. Archibald, M. Aronoff, & J. Rees-Miller (Eds.), *Contemporary linguistics: An introduction* (5th ed., pp. 361–398). Boston: Bedford/St. Martin's.

O'Grady, W., Dobrovolsky, M., & Arnoff, M. (1989). *Contemporary linguistics: An introduction.* New York: St. Martin's Press.

O'Neill, P. (1999, September 25). Acute otitis media. *British Medical Journal, 319*(7213), 833–836.

Obler, L., & Gjerlow, K. (1999). *Language and the brain.* New York: Cambridge University Press.

Obligado, L. (1983). *Faint frogs feeling feverish and other terrifically tantalizing tongue twisters.* New York: Viking.

Ochs, C. (1991). *Moose on the loose.* Minneapolis, MN: Carolrhoda Books.

Ogata, V., Sheehey, P., & Noonan, M. (2006). Rural Native Hawaiian perspectives on special education. *Rural Special Education Quarterly, 25*(1), 7–15.

Ogbu, J. (1999, Summer). Beyond language: Ebonics, proper English, and identity in a Black-American speech community. *American Educational Research Journal, 36*(2), 147–184.

Ogle, D. (1986). K-W-L: A teaching model that develops active reading of expository text. *The Reading Teacher, 39*, 564–570.

Olander, L., Smith, A., & Zelaznik, H. (2010). Evidence that a motor timing deficit is a factor in the development of stuttering. *Journal of Speech, Language, & Hearing Research, 53*(4), 876–886.

Orr, E. (2000). *Linguistic perspectives on African American Vernacular English and implications for the language arts classroom.* (ED 458811). eric.ed.gov. Retrieved November 5, 2012.

Otto, B. (1979). Unpublished research notes, Northwestern University, Evanston, IL.

Otto, B. (1980). Unpublished research notes, Northwestern University, Evanston, IL.

Otto, B. (1982a). [Toddler talk.] Unpublished raw data.

Otto, B. (1982b). A Vygotskian perspective on word concept development. *Northwestern University Psycholinguistic Newsletter, 7*(3), 15–33.

Otto, B. (1984). Evidence of emergent reading behaviors in young children's interactions with favorite storybooks (Doctoral dissertation, Northwestern University, 1984). *Dissertation Abstracts International, 45*, DA8423283.

Otto, B. (1985). Unpublished research notes, Northeastern Illinois University, Chicago.

Otto, B. (1987). Unpublished research notes, Northeastern Illinois University, Chicago.

Otto, B. (1991). Developmentally appropriate literacy goals for preschool and kindergarten classrooms. *Early Child Development and Care, 70*, 53–61.

Otto, B. (1992). *Storybook-based language observations.* Unpublished manuscript, Northeastern Illinois University, Chicago.

Otto, B. (1993). Signs of emergent literacy among inner-city kindergartners in a storybook reading program. *Reading & Writing Quarterly: Overcoming Learning Difficulties, 9*, 151–162.

Otto, B. (1994, September). *Emergent reading among infants and toddlers.* Paper presented at the Illinois Day Care Action Council Annual Conference, Rosemont, IL.

Otto, B. (1995a). [Young children's explorations of books.] Unpublished raw data.

Otto, B. (1995b, February). *Emergent reading behaviors among infants and toddlers.* Paper presented at the Chicago Association of the Education of Young Children Conference, Chicago.

Otto, B. (1996). Let's read a story: The role of storybook reading in young children's literacy acquisition. *Illinois Schools Journal, 76*(1), 5–18.

Otto, B. (2008). *Literacy development in early childhood: Reflective teaching for birth to age eight.* Boston: Allyn & Bacon/Merrill.

Otto, B. (2012). [A case study of language development]. Unpublished raw data.

Otto, B., & Johnson, L. (1996). Parents in your classroom: A valuable literacy link. *Teaching K–8, 26*, 56–57.

Ottolenghi, C. (2002). *The little red hen.* Columbus, OH: McGraw-Hill Children's Publishing.

Ovando, C., Collier, V., & Combs, M. (2003). *Bilingual & ESL classrooms: Teaching in multicultural contexts* (3rd ed.). Boston: McGraw-Hill.

Owen, A. (2010). Factors affecting accuracy of past tense production in children with specific language impairment and their typically developing peers: The influence of verb transitivity, clause location, and sentence type. *Journal of Speech, Language & Hearing Research, 53*(4), 993–1014.

Owens, R. (1988). *Language development.* Upper Saddle River, NJ: Merrill/Prentice Hall.

Owens, R. (1991). *Language disorders: A functional approach to assessment and intervention.* Upper Saddle River, NJ: Merrill/Prentice Hall.

Owens, R. (2001). *Language development: An introduction* (5th ed.). Boston: Allyn & Bacon.

Owens, R. (2008). *Language development: An introduction* (7th ed.). Boston: Pearson Allyn & Bacon.

Owens, R. (2012). *Language development.* Boston: Pearson.

Owocki, G. (1999). *Literacy through play.* Portsmouth, NH: Heinemann.

Owocki, G. (2001). *Make way for literacy! Teaching the way young children learn.* Portsmouth, NH: Heinemann and Washington, DC: National Association for the Education of Young Children.

Owocki, G., & Goodman, Y. (2002). *Kidwatching: Documenting children's literacy development.* Portsmouth, NH: Heinemann.

Paavola, L., Kunnari, S., & Moilanen, I. (2005). Maternal responsiveness and infant intentional communication: Implications for the early communicative and linguistic development. *Child: Care, Health & Development, 31*(6), 727–735.

Paciorek, K., & Munro, J. (Eds.). (1999). *Notable selections in early childhood education* (pp. 3–10). Guilford, CT: Dushkin/McGraw-Hill.

Paley, V. (1981). *Wally's stories.* Cambridge, MA: Harvard University Press.

Paley, V. (1990). *The boy who would be a helicopter.* Cambridge, MA: Harvard University Press.

Paley, V. (1997). *The girl with the brown crayon.* Cambridge, MA: Harvard University Press.

Paley, V. (2004). *A child's work: The importance of fantasy play.* Chicago: University of Chicago Press.

Paley, V., & Dombrink-Green, M. (2011, September). A conversation with Vivian Gussin Paley. *Young Children, 66*(9), 90–93.

Palmer, S., Fais, L., Golinkoff, R., & Werker, J. (2012). *Child Development, 83*(2), 543–553.

Pan, B., & Berko Gleason, J. (1997). Semantic development: Learning the meaning of words. In J. Berko Gleason (Ed.), *The development of language* (4th ed., pp. 122–158). Boston: Allyn & Bacon.

Paneque, O. (2006). Good intentions, bad advice for bilingual families. *Childhood Education, 82*(3), 171–174.

Pappano, L. (2008, May/June). The power of family conversation. *Harvard Education Letter.* www.edletter.org/insights/familyconversation.shtml. Retrieved May 21, 2008.

Paradise, J. (1997). Developmental outcomes in relation to early-life otitis media: Present and future directions in research. In J. Robert, I. Wallace, & F. Henderson (Eds.), *Otitis media in young children: Medical, developmental, and educational considerations.* Baltimore: Paul H. Brookes.

Parish, P. (2005). *Amelia Bedelia helps out.* New York: HarperCollins.

Patterson, K., & Wright, A. (1990). The speech, language or hearing-impaired child: At-risk academically. *Childhood Education, 67*(2), 91–95.

Patz, N. (1983). *Moses supposes his toeses are roses.* San Diego, CA: Harcourt Brace Jovanovich.

Payne, A., Whitehurst, G., & Angell, A. (1994). The role of home literacy environment in the development of language ability in preschool children from low-income families. *Early Childhood Research Quarterly, 9*(3–4), 427–440.

Pease, D., Berko Gleason, J., & Pan, B. (1989). Gaining meaning: Semantic development. In J. Berko Gleason (Ed.), *The development of language* (3rd ed., pp. 101–134). Upper Saddle River, NJ: Merrill/Prentice Hall.

Pellegrini, A., & Galda, L. (1998). *The development of school-based literacy: A socioecological perspective.* New York: Routledge.

Pepicello, W., & Weisberg, R. (1983). Linguistics and humor. In P. McGhee & J. Goldstein (Eds.), *Handbook of humor research: Volume 1. Basic issues* (pp. 59–83). New York: Springer-Verlag.

Peregoy, S., & Boyle, O. (1993). *Reading, writing, & learning in ESL: A resource book for K–8 teachers.* White Plains, NY: Longman.

Perlmutter, J., Folger, T., & Holt, K. (2009). Prekindergartners learn to write: A "play on words." *Childhood Education, 86*(1), 14–19.

Phillips, G., & McNaughton, S. (1990). The practice of storybook reading to preschool children in mainstream New Zealand families. *Reading Research Quarterly, 25*(3), 163–250.

Piaget, J. (1955). *The language and thought of the child.* New York: World.

Piaget, J. (1962). *Play, dreams and imitation in childhood.* New York: W. W. Norton.

Pine, J. (1994). The language of primary caregivers. In C. Gallaway & B. Richards (Eds.), *Input and interaction in language acquisition* (pp. 15–37). Cambridge, UK: Cambridge University Press.

Pinker, S. (1994). *The language instinct: How the mind creates language.* New York: Morrow.

Pinker, S. (2007). *The language instinct: How the mind creates language.* New York: Harper Perennial Modern Classics.

Pinnell, G. (1996). Ways to look at the functions of children's language. In B. Power & R. Hubbard (Eds.), *Language development: A reader for teachers* (pp. 146–154). Upper Saddle River, NJ: Merrill/Prentice Hall.

Piper, T. (1993). *Language for all our children.* Englewood Cliffs, NJ: Prentice Hall.

Piper, T. (1998). *Language and learning: The home and school years* (2nd ed.). Upper Saddle River, NJ: Merrill/Prentice Hall.

Pollard-Durodola, S., Gonzales, J., Simmons, D., Davis, M., Simmons, L., & Nava-Walichowski, M. (2011/2012). Using knowledge networks to develop preschoolers' content vocabulary. *The Reading Teacher, 65*(4), 264–274.

Pollitzer, W. (1993). The relationship of the Gullah-speaking people of coastal South Carolina and Georgia to their African ancestors. *Historical Methods, 26*(2), 53–69.

Poole, C., Miller, S., & Church, E. (2005). Don't forget to laugh: The importance of humor. *Early Childhood Today, 19*(5), 29–33.

Post, J., & Hohmann, M. (2000). *Tender care and early learning: Supporting infants and toddlers in child care settings.* Ypsilanti, MI: High/Scope Press.

Powell, D. (1998). Reweaving parents into the fabric of early childhood programs. *Young Children, 53*(5), 60–67.

Priddy, R. (2001). *Happy baby colors.* New York: St. Martin's Press.

Prinz, P., & Prinz, E. (1979, September). *Acquisition of American sign language and spoken English in a hearing child and a deaf mother and hearing father: Phase II—early combinatorial patterns of communication.* Paper presented at the Fourth Annual Conference on Language Development, Boston University, Boston.

Pryor, E. (1995). Parent volunteers: Partners in literacy. In T. Rasinski (Ed.), *Parents and teachers: Helping children learn to read and write* (pp. 179–184). Fort Worth, TX: Harcourt Brace & Company.

Puckett, M., & Black, J. (2001). *The young child: Development from prebirth through age eight* (3rd ed.). Upper Saddle River, NJ: Merrill/Prentice Hall.

Puckett, M., & Black, J. (2008). *Meaningful assessments of the young child: Celebrating development and learning* (3rd ed.). Upper Saddle River, NJ: Pearson/Merrill/Prentice Hall.

Purcell-Gates, V. (1989). What oral/written language differences can tell us about beginning instruction. *The Reading Teacher, 42*(4), 290–294.

Purcell-Gates, V. (1996). Stories, coupons and the *TV Guide*: Relationships between home literacy experiences and emergent literacy knowledge. *Reading Research Quarterly, 31*(4), 406–428.

Purcell-Gates, V. (2002). ". . . As soon as she opened her mouth!": Issues of language, literacy, and power. In L. Delpit & J. L. Dowdy (Eds.), *The skin that we speak: Thoughts on language and culture in the classroom* (pp. 123–141). New York: The New Press.

Raines, S., & Canady, R. (1990). *The whole language kindergarten.* New York: Teachers College Press.

Raphael, T. (1986). Teaching question–answer relationships, revisited. *The Reading Teacher, 39*, 516–523.

Raphael, T., & Hiebert, E. (1996). *Creating an integrated approach to literacy instruction.* Fort Worth, TX: Harcourt Brace College Publishers.

Rasinski, T. (Ed.). (1995). *Parents and teachers: Helping children learn to read and write.* Fort Worth, TX: Harcourt Brace & Company.

Rasinski, T., & Padek, N. (2004). *Effective reading strategies: Teaching children who find reading difficult* (3rd ed.). Upper Saddle River, NJ: Merrill/Prentice Hall.

Ratner, N. (2009). Atypical language development. In J. Berko Gleason & N. Berstein Ratner (Eds.), *The development of language* (7th ed., pp. 315–390). Boston: Pearson/Allyn & Bacon.

Reese, E., & Fivush, R. (1993). Parental styles of talking about the past. *Developmental Psychology, 29*(3), 596–606.

Reich, P. (1986). *Language development.* Upper Saddle River, NJ: Prentice Hall.

Reutzel, D. R., & Cooter, R. (2004). *Teaching children to read: Putting the pieces together* (4th ed.). Upper Saddle River, NJ: Merrill/Prentice Hall.

Ricciuti, H., White, A., & Fraser, S. (1993). Maternal and family predictors of school readiness and achievement in Black, Hispanic, and White 6–7 year olds. *Society for Research in Child Development Abstracts, 9*, 567.

Rice, M. (1995). Children's language acquisition. In B. Power & R. Hubbard (Eds.), *Language development: A reader for teachers* (pp. 3–15). Upper Saddle River, NJ: Merrill/Prentice Hall.

Rice, M., & Wilcox, K. (1995). *Building a language-focused curriculum for the preschool classroom, Vol. I: A foundation.* Baltimore: Paul H. Brookes.

Ricklen, N. (1994). *Baby's neighborhood.* New York: Simon & Schuster.

Riley, J., & Jones, R. (2007, Fall). When girls and boys play: What research tells us. *Childhood Education, 84*, 38–43.

Ringgenberg, S. (2003). Music as a teaching tool: Creating story songs. *Young Children, 58*(5), 76–79.

Roberts, J., Burchinal, M., & Durham, M. (1999). Parents' report of vocabulary and grammatical development of African American preschoolers: Child and environmental associations. *Child Development, 70*(1), 92–106.

Roberts, M. (1976). Comparative study of pure tone, impedance, and otoscopic hearing screening methods. *Archives of Otolaryngology, 102*, 690–694.

Robinshaw, H. (2007). Acquisition of hearing, listening and speech skills by and during key stage 1. *Early Child Development and Care, 177*(6–7), 661–678.

Rogoff, B., Paradise, R., Araus, R., Correa-Chávez, M., & Angelillo, C. (2003). Firsthand learning through intent participation. *Annual Review of Psychology, 54*, 175–203.

Roizen, N. (2003). Nongenetic causes of hearing loss. *Mental Retardation and Developmental Disabilities Research Reviews, 9*, 120–127.

Rollins, P. (2003). Caregivers' contingent comments to 9-month-old infants: Relationships with later language. *Applied Psycholinguisitcs, 24*(2), 221–234.

Roskos, K., & Burstein, K. (2011). Assessment of the design efficacy of a preschool vocabulary instruction technique. *Journal of Research in Childhood Education, 25*, 268–287.

Rowe, D., & Harste, J. (1986). Metalinguistic awareness in writing and reading: The young child as informant. In D. Yaden & S. Templeton (Eds.), *Metalinguistic awareness and beginning literacy: Conceptualizing what it means to read and write* (pp. 235–256). Portsmouth, NH: Heinemann.

Rowe, D., & Neitzel, C. (2010). Interest and agency in 2- and 3-year olds' participation in emergent writing. *Reading Research Quarterly, 45*(2), 169–195.

Rowell, E. (2007). Missing! Picture books reflecting gay and lesbian families. *Young Children, 62*(3), 24–30.

Rubinstein-Avila, E. (2006). Connecting with Latino learners. *Educational Leadership, 63*(5), 38–43.

Rush, K. (1999). Caregiver–child interactions and early literacy development of preschool children from low-income environments. *Topics in Early Childhood Special Education, 19*(1), 3–14.

Rushton, S., Eitelgeorge, J., & Zickafoose, R. (2003). Connecting Brian Cambourne's conditions of learning theory to brain/mind principles: Implications for early childhood educators. *Early Childhood Education Journal, 31*(1), 11–21.

Russell-Fox, J. (1999). Together is better: Specific tips on how to include children with various types of disabilities. In K. Paciorek & J. Munro (Eds.), *Annual editions in early childhood education* (20th ed., pp. 100–102). Guilford, CT: Dushkin/McGraw-Hill.

Ryval, M. (1995). Mommy, my ear hurts! *Chatelaine, 68*(3), 24.

Sachs, J. (1989). Communication development in infancy. In J. Berko Gleason (Ed.), *The development of language* (2nd ed., pp. 35–58). Upper Saddle River, NJ: Merrill/Prentice Hall.

Sachs, J. (2009). Communication development in infancy. In J. Berko Gleason & N. Ratner (Eds.), *The development of language* (7th ed., pp. 37–57). Boston: Pearson/Allyn & Bacon.

Salinger, T. (1996). *Literacy for young children*. Upper Saddle River, NJ: Merrill/Prentice Hall.

Salinger, T. (2002). Assessing the literacy of young children: The case for multiple forms of evidence. In S. Neuman and D. Dickinson (Eds.), *Handbook of early literacy research* (pp. 390–418). New York: Guilford Press.

Salvia, J., & Ysseldyke, J. (1998). *Assessment* (7th ed.). Boston: Houghton Mifflin.

Sander, E. (1972). When are speech sounds learned? *Journal of Speech and Hearing Disorders, 37*, 55–63.

Sandler, W., & Lillo-Martin, D. (2005). Natural sign languages. In W. O'Grady, J. Archibald, M. Aronoff, & J. Rees-Miller (Eds.), *Contemporary linguistics: An introduction* (5th ed., pp. 343–360). New York: Bedford/St. Martin's.

Santiago, R. (1994). The interdependence between linguistic and cognitive performance among bilingual preschoolers with differing home language environments. In D. MacLaughlin and S. McEwen (Eds.), *Proceedings of Boston University Conference on Language Development* (Vol. 19, pp. 511–520). Somerville, MA: Cascadilla Press.

Santos, R., & Ostrosky, M. (2003). *Understanding the impact of language differences on classroom behavior*. Nashville, TN: Center on the Social and Emotional Foundations for Early Learning. csefel.vanderbilt.edu/resources/wwb/wwb2.html Retrieved September 26, 2008.

Santrock, J. (2001). *Child development* (9th ed.). Boston: McGraw-Hill.

Saracho, O., & Spodek, B. (1995). Preparing teachers for early childhood programs of linguistic and cultural diversity. In E. Garcia & B. McLaughlin (Eds.), *Meeting the challenge of linguistic and cultural diversity in early childhood education*. New York: Teachers College Press.

Sawyer, R. K. (2001). Play as improvisational rehearsal: Multiple levels of analysis in children's play. In A. Goncu & E. Klein (Eds.), *Children in play, story and school* (pp. 19–38). New York: Guilford Press.

Scarborough, H. (1990). Very early language deficits in dyslexic children. *Annals of Dyslexia, 41,* 207–220.

Scarborough, H. (2002). Connecting early language and literacy to later reading (dis)abilities: Evidence, theory, and practice. In S. Neuman & D. Dickinson (Eds.), *Handbook of early literacy research.* New York: Guilford Press.

Schacter, J. (1996). Maturation and the issue of universal grammar in second language acquisition. In W. Ritchie & Tej Bhatia (Eds.), *Handbook of second language acquisition* (pp. 121–158). San Diego, CA: Academic Press.

Schickedanz, J. (1981, November). Hey! This book's not working right. *Young Children*, 18–27.

Schickedanz, J., Pergantis, M., Kanosky, J., Blaney, A., & Ottinger, J. (1997). *Curriculum in early childhood: A resource guide for preschool and kindergarten teachers.* Boston: Allyn & Bacon.

Schickedanz, J., York, M., Stewart, I., & White, D. (1990). *Strategies for teaching young children.* Upper Saddle River, NJ: Prentice Hall.

Schieffelin, B., & Ochs, E. (1986). Language socialization. *Annual Review of Anthropology*, *15*, 163–191.

SchifferDanoff, V. (2001). *Beyond morning message.* Jefferson City, MO: Scholastic Professional Books.

Schlesinger, I. (1971). Production of utterances and language acquisition. In D. Slobin (Ed.), *The ontogenesis of grammar.* New York: Academic Press.

Schultz, T. (1974). Development of the appreciation of riddles. *Child Development, 45,* 100–105.

Schwartz, J. (1981, July). Children's experiments with language. *Young Children*, *36*(5), 16–26.

Schwartz, J. (1988). *Encouraging early literacy: An integrated approach to reading and writing in N–3.* Portsmouth, NH: Heinemann.

Scott, C. (1995a). Syntax for school-age children: A discourse perspective. In M. Fey, J. Windsor, & S. Warren (Eds.), *Language intervention: Preschool through the elementary years* (pp. 107–144). Baltimore: Paul H. Brookes.

Scott, J. (1995b). The *King* case: Implications for educators. In D. Durkin (Ed.), *Language issues: Readings for teachers* (pp. 273–280). White Plains, NY: Longman.

Segal, M. (1983). *Birth to one year.* White Plains, NY: Mailman Family Press.

Seitz, V., & Apfel, H. (1994). Parent-focused intervention: Diffusion effects on siblings. *Child Development, 65,* 666–676.

Sendak, M. (1963). *Where the wild things are.* New York: Harper & Row.

Sensenbaugh, R. (1996). Phonemic awareness: An important early step in learning to read. www.ericdigests.org/1997-2/read.htm. Retrieved September 26, 2008.

Sharmat, M. (1978). *Nate the Great and the sticky case.* New York: Coward, McCann & Geoghegan.

Shatz, M. (1994). *A toddler's life: Becoming a person.* New York: Oxford University Press.

Shatz, M., & Gelman, R. (1973). The development of communication skills: Modifications in the speech of young children as a function of listener. *Monographs of the Society for Research in Child Development, 38* (Serial No. 152).

Sheldon, A. (1990, January). "Kings are royaler than queens": Language and socialization. *Young Children, 45*(2), 4–9.

Sheldon, A. (1993). Pickle fights: Gendered talk in preschool disputes. In D. Tannen (Ed.), *Gender and conversational interaction* (pp. 83–109). New York: Oxford University Press.

Shenker, R. (2008). *Stuttering and the bilingual child.* The Stuttering Foundation. www.stutteringhelp.org/Default.aspx?tabid=55. Retrieved May 30, 2008.

Sigel, I., & Cocking, R. (1977). *Cognitive development from childhood to adolescence: A constructivist perspective.* New York: Holt, Rinehart & Winston.

Sign2Me. (2003). *Signing in your infant/toddler program.* Northlight Communications. www.Sign2Me.com. Retrieved February 25, 2008.

Silberg, J., & Schiller, P. (2002). *The complete book of rhymes, songs, poems, fingerplays, and chants.* Beltsville, MD: Gryphon House.

Silverman, R., & Crandell, J. (2010). Vocabulary practices in prekindergarten and kindergarten classrooms. *Reading Research Quarterly, 45*(3), 318–340.

Simon, B. (2006). Saying ya to the Yoopers (Michigan's Upper Peninsula). In W. Wolfram & B. Ward (Eds.), *American voices: How dialects differ from coast to coast* (pp. 130–135). Malden, MA: Blackwell Publishing.

Sinclair-deZwart, H. (1969). Developmental psycholinguistics. In D. Elkind & J. Flavell (Eds.), *Studies* in cognitive development: Essays in honor of Jean Piaget. New York: Oxford University Press.

Skinner, B. (1957). Verbal behavior. Upper Saddle River, NJ: Prentice Hall.

Slaughter, J. (1993). Beyond storybooks: Young children and the shared book experience. Newark, DE: International Reading Association.

Sloane, M. (2002). Making the most of learning centers. In K. Paciorek & J. Munro (Eds.), Annual editions early childhood education 02/03 (pp. 160–163). Guilford, CT: McGraw-Hill/Dushkin.

Slobin, D. (1979). Psycholinguistics (2nd ed.). Glenview, IL: Scott Foresman.

Smilansky, S., & Shefatya, L. (1990). Facilitating play: A medium for promoting cognitive, socio-emotional and academic development in young children. Gaithersburg, MD: Psychosocial & Educational Publications.

Smith, J. (1990). Measurement issues in early literacy assessment. In L. Morrow & J. Smith (Eds.), Assessment for instruction in early literacy (pp. 62–74). Upper Saddle River, NJ: Prentice Hall.

Smith, M., & Dickinson, D. (1994). Describing oral language opportunities and environments in Head Start and other preschool classrooms. Early Childhood Research Quarterly, 9(3–4), 345–366.

Smitherman, G. (1995). "The forms of things unknown": Black modes of discourse. In D. Durkin (Ed.), Language issues: Readings for teachers (pp. 314–330). White Plains, NY: Longman.

Smolkin, L., & Yaden, D. (1992). O is for mouse: First encounters with the alphabet book. Language Arts, 69, 432–441.

Snow, C. (1977). Mother's speech research: From input to interaction. In C. Snow & C. Ferguson (Eds.), Talking to children: Language input and acquisition (pp. 31–50). New York: Cambridge University Press.

Snow, C. (1983). Literacy and language relationships during the preschool years. Harvard Educational Review, 53(2), 165–189.

Snow, C. (2000, October). On language and literacy development. Scholastic Early Childhood Today, 46.

Snow, C., & Ninio, A. (1986). The contracts of literacy: What children learn from learning to read books. In W. Teale & E. Sulzby (Eds.), Emergent literacy: Writing and reading (pp. 116–138). Norwood, NJ: Ablex.

Snow, C., Tabors, P., & Dickinson, D. (2001). Language development in the preschool years. In D. Dickinson & P. Tabors (Eds.), Beginning literacy with language: Young children learning at home and school (pp. 2–25). Baltimore: Paul H. Brookes.

Soltis, J. (2003). The signal functions of early infant crying. Behavioral and brain sciences. volume 27(4), 433–459

Soundy, B., Guha, S., & Qiu, Y. (2007). Picture power: Placing artistry and literacy on the same page. Young Children, 62(3), 82–88.

Squibb, B., & Dietz, S. (2000). Learning activities for infants and toddlers: An easy guide for everyday use. Washington, DC: Children's Resources International.

Stewig, J. (1982). Teaching language arts in early childhood. New York: Holt, Rinehart & Winston.

Stice, C., Bertrand, J., & Bertrand, N. (1995). Integrating reading and the other language arts. Belmont, CA: Wadsworth.

Steen, B. (2011). Promoting healthy transitions from preschool to kindergarten. Young Children, 66(2), 90–95.

St. George, C. (2010). How can elementary teachers collaborate more effectively with parents to support student literacy learning? Delta Kappa Gamma Bulletin, 76(2), 32–38.

Stocka, N., & Dennis, L. (2012). The daily dozen: Strategies for enhancing social communication of infants with language delays. Young Children, 67(4), 36–41.

Stoel-Gammon, C. (1998). Role of babbling and phonology in early linguistic development. In A. Wetherby, S. Warren, & J. Reichle (Eds.), Transitions in prelinguistic communication (pp. 87–110). Baltimore: Paul H. Brookes.

Strauss, R. (1993). Otitis media with effusion in children: Telltale clinical patterns, helpful diagnostic procedures. Consultant, 33(5), 85–88.

Strickland, D. (1998). Teaching phonics today: A primer for educators. Newark, DE: International Reading Association.

Stubbs, M. (2002). Some basic sociolinguistic concepts. In L. Delpit & J. L. Dowdy (Eds.), The skin that we speak: Thoughts on language and culture in the classroom (pp. 65–85). New York: The New Press.

Stuttering Foundation of America. (1991–2012). Notes to the teacher: The child who stutters at school. www.stutteringhelp.org/teachers.

Stuttering Foundation of America. (1993). *The child who stutters at school: Notes to the teacher* [brochure]. Memphis, TN: Author.

Stuttering Foundation of America. (2008). The child who stutters at school: Notes to the teacher. www.stutteringhelp.org.

Sulzby, E. (1981). *Kindergartners begin to read their own compositions: Beginning readers' developing knowledges about written language. Final report to the Research Foundation of the National Council of Teachers of English.* Evanston, IL: Northwestern University.

Sulzby, E. (1982). Oral and written language mode adaptations in stories by kindergarten children. *Journal of Reading Behavior, 14*(1), 51–59.

Sulzby, E. (1983). *Beginning readers' developing knowledges about written language. Final report to the National Institute of Education.* Evanston, IL: Northwestern University.

Sulzby, E. (1985a). Kindergartners as readers and writers. In M. Farr (Ed.), *Advances in writing research: Vol. 1. Children's early writing development* (pp. 127–199). Norwood, NJ: Ablex.

Sulzby, E. (1985b). Children's emergent reading of favorite storybooks: A developmental study. *Reading Research Quarterly, 20*(4), 458–481.

Sulzby, E. (1986a). Children's elicitation and use of metalinguistic knowledge about *word* during literacy interactions. In D. Yaden & S. Templeton (Eds.), *Metalinguistic awareness and beginning literacy: Conceptualizing what it means to read and write* (pp. 219–233). Portsmouth, NH: Heinemann.

Sulzby, E. (1986b). Writing and reading: Signs of oral and written language organization in the young child. In W. Teale & E. Sulzby (Eds.), *Emergent literacy: Writing and reading* (pp. 50–87). Norwood, NJ: Ablex.

Sulzby, E. (1991a). Roles of oral and written language in children approaching conventional literacy [Oralitá e scrittura nel percorso verso lalingua scritta]. In M. Orsolini & C. Pontecorvo (Eds.), *La costruzione dei primi testi scritti nel bambino* (pp. 57–75). Roma: La Nuova Italia.

Sulzby, E. (1991b). Assessment of emergent literacy: Storybook reading. *The Reading Teacher, 44*(7), 498–500.

Sulzby, E., Barnhart, J., & Hieshima, J. (1989). Forms of writing and rereading from writing: A preliminary report. In J. Mason (Ed.), *Reading and writing connections* (pp. 31–64). Needham Heights, MA: Allyn & Bacon.

Sulzby, E., Teale, W., & Kamberelis, G. (1989). Emergent writing in the classroom: Home and school connections. In D. Strickland & L. Morrow (Eds.), *Emergent literacy: Young children learn to read and write* (pp. 52–62). Newark, DE: International Reading Association.

Sutton-Smith, B. (1975). A developmental structural account of riddles. In B. Hirschenblatt-Gimblett (Ed.), *Speech, play and display*. The Hague, the Netherlands: Mouton.

Swan, A. (1993). Helping children who stutter: What teachers need to know. *Childhood Education*, 138–141.

Swiniarski, L., Breitborde, M., & Murphy, J. (1999). *Educating the global village: Including the young child in the world.* Upper Saddle River, NJ: Merrill/Prentice Hall.

Taback, S. (2002). *This is the house that Jack built.* New York: G. P. Putnam's Sons.

Tabors, P. (1997). *One child, two languages: A guide for preschool educators of children learning English as a second language.* Baltimore: Paul H. Brookes.

Tabors, P., Beals, D., & Weizman, Z. (2001). "You know what oxygen is?" Learning new words at home. In D. Dickinson & P. Tabors (Eds.), *Beginning literacy with language: Young children learning at home and school* (pp. 93–110). Baltimore: Paul H. Brookes.

Tabors, P., Snow, C., & Dickinson, D. (2001). Homes and schools together: Supporting language and literacy development. In D. Dickinson & P. Tabors (Eds.), *Beginning literacy with language: Young children learning at home and school* (pp. 313–334). Baltimore: Paul H. Brookes.

Tager-Flusberg, H. (1997). Putting words together: Morphology and syntax in the preschool years. In J. Berko Gleason (Ed.), *The development of language* (4th ed., pp. 139–191). Boston: Allyn & Bacon.

Tannen, D. (1982). The oral/literate continuum in discourse. In D. Tannen (Ed.), *Spoken and written language: Exploring orality and literacy* (pp. 1–16). Norwood, NJ: Ablex.

Tannen, D. (1990). *You just don't understand: Women and men in conversation.* New York: Ballantine.

Taylor, D. (1983). *Family literacy: Young children learning to read and write.* Portsmouth, NH: Heinemann.

Taylor, N., & Vawter, J. (1978). Helping children discover the functions of written language. *Language Arts, 55*(8), 941–945.

Teale, W. (1986). Home background and young children's literacy development. In W. H. Teale & E. Sulzby (Eds.), *Emergent literacy: Writing and reading* (pp. 110–121). Norwood, NJ: Ablex.

Teale, W., & Martinez, M. (1989). Connecting writing: Fostering emergent literacy in kindergarten children. In J. Mason (Ed.), *Reading and writing connections* (pp. 177–198). Boston: Allyn & Bacon.

Teale, W., & Sulzby, E. (1987). *Emergent literacy: Writing and reading.* Norwood, NJ: Ablex.

Teele, D., Klein, J., Chase, C., Menyuk, P., & Rosner, B. (1990). Otitis media in infancy and intellectual ability, school achievement, speech and language at age 7 years. *The Journal of Infectious Diseases, 162*, 685–694.

Temple, C., Nathan, R., & Burris, W. (1982). *The beginnings of writing.* Boston: Allyn & Bacon.

Temple, C., Nathan, R., Burris, N., & Temple, F. (1988). *The beginnings of writing* (2nd ed.). Boston: Allyn & Bacon.

Tharp, R. (1994). Research knowledge and policy issues in cultural diversity and education. In B. McLeod (Ed.), *Language and learning: Educating linguistically diverse students* (pp. 129–167). Albany, NY: State University of New York Press.

Thayer, J. (1972). *Gus and the baby ghost.* New York: William Morrow.

Thiessen, R., Hill, E., & Saffran, J. (2005). Infant-directed speech facilitates word segmentation. *Infancy, 7*(1), 53–71.

Thompson, L. (1999). *Young bilingual learners in nursery school.* Buffalo, NY: Multilingual Matters Ltd.

Throne, J. (1988, September). Becoming a kindergarten of readers? *Young Children, 43*, 10–16.

Tizard, B. (1981). Language at home and at school. In C. Cazden (Ed.), *Language in early childhood education* (pp. 17–27). Washington, DC: National Association for the Education of Young Children.

Tolentino, E. (2007). "Why do you like this page so much?" Exploring the potential of talk during preschool reading activities. *Language Arts, 84*(6), 519–528.

Tomasello, M. (2000). First steps toward a usage-based theory of language acquisition. *Cognitive Linguistics, 11*(1/2), 61–82.

Tomasello, M., Carpenter, M., & Liszkowski, U. (2007). A new look at infant pointing. *Child Development, 78*(3), 705–722.

Tompkins, G. (2000). *Teaching writing: Balancing process and product* (3rd ed.). Upper Saddle River, NJ: Merrill/Prentice Hall.

Tompkins, G. (2004a). *Teaching writing: Balancing process and product* (4th ed.). Upper Saddle River, NJ: Merrill/Prentice Hall.

Tompkins, G. (2004b). *50 literacy strategies: Step by step* (2nd ed.). Upper Saddle River, NJ: Merrill/Prentice Hall.

Tompkins, G., & Hoskisson, K. (1995). *Language arts: Content and teaching strategies* (3rd ed.). Upper Saddle River, NJ: Merrill/Prentice Hall.

Tompkins, P. (1998). Role playing/simulation. *The Internet TESL Journal, 4*(8). http://iteslj.org. Retrieved December 10, 2003.

Tortora, G. (1992). *Principles of human anatomy* (6th ed.). New York: HarperCollins.

Tough, J. (1977). *The development of meaning: A study of children's use of language.* New York: Wiley.

Tough, J. (1985). *Talk two: Children using English as a second language.* London: Onyx Press.

Trawick-Smith, J. (1997). *Early childhood development: A multicultural perspective.* Upper Saddle River, NJ: Merrill/Prentice Hall.

Tronick, E., Als, H., & Adamson, L. (1979). Structure of early face-to-face communicative interactions. In M. Bullowa (Ed.), *Before speech: The beginning of interpersonal communication* (pp. 349–372). Cambridge, UK: Cambridge University Press.

Trousdale, A. (1990). Interactive storytelling: Scaffolding children's early narratives. *Language Arts, 67*(2), 164–173.

Tsao, F., Liu, H., & Kuhl, P. (2004). Speech perception in infancy predicts language development in the second year of life: A longitudinal study. *Child Development, 75*(4), 1067–1084.

Tutwiler, S. (2012). Family diversity. In G. Olson & M. Fuller (Eds.), *Home and school relations: Teachers and parents working together* (pp. 39-62). Boston: Pearson.

Umek, L., & Musek, P. (2001). Symbolic play: Opportunities for cognitive and language development in preschool settings. *Early Years, 21*(1), 55–64.

U.S. National Library of Medicine, NIH National Institutes of Health, Medline Plus, (1997–2012). Hearing loss. http://www.nlm.nihgovmedlineplus/hearingdisordersanddeafness.html. Retrieved July 14, 2012.

Van Herk, G., & Rees-Miller, J. (2010). Language in social contexts. In W. O'Grady, J. Archibald, M. Aronoff, & J. Rees-Miller, (Eds.), *Contemporary linguistics: An introduction.* (pp. 485–526). Boston: Bedford/St. Martin's.

Vandergrift, J., & Green, A. (1992). Rethinking parent involvement. *Educational Leadership, 50*(1), 57–59.

Vasilyeva, M., Huttenlocher, J., & Waterfall, H. (2006). Effects of language intervention on syntactic skill levels in preschoolers. *Developmental Psychology, 42*(1), 164–174.

Vernon-Feagans, L., Manlove, E., & Volling, B. (1996). Otitis media and the social behavior of daycare attending children. *Child Development, 67,* 1528–1539.

Vohr, B. (2003). Overview: Infants and children with hearing loss—Part I. *Mental Retardation and Developmental Disabilities Research Reviews, 9,* 62–64.

Voss, M. (1988). "Make way for applesauce": The literate world of a three-year-old. *Language Arts, 65*(3), 272–278.

Vukelich, C. (1990, Summer). Where's the paper? Literacy during dramatic play. *Childhood Education,* 205–209.

Vukelich, C., Christie, J., & Enz, B. (2002). *Helping young children learn language and literacy.* Boston: Allyn & Bacon.

Vygotsky, L. (1962). *Thought and language* (E. Hanfmann & G. Vakar, Eds. and Trans.). Cambridge, MA: MIT Press.

Vygotsky, L. (1978). *Mind in society: The development of higher mental psychological processes* (M. Cole, V. John-Steiner, S. Scribner, & E. Souberman, Eds.). Cambridge, MA: Harvard University Press.

Waggoner, J., & Palermo, D. (1989). Betty is a bouncing bubble: Children's comprehension of emotion-descriptive metaphors. *Developmental Psychology, 25*(1), 152–163.

Wagner, B. (1990). Dramatic improvisation in the classroom. In S. Hyunds & D. Rubin (Eds.), *Perspectives on talk and learning* (pp. 195–211). Urbana, IL: National Council of Teachers of English.

Wagner, L., Greene-Havas, M., & Gillespie, R. (2010). Development in children's comprehension of linguistic register. *Child Development, 81*(6), 1678–1686.

Wallace, I., & Hooper, S. (1997). Otitis media and its impact on cognitive, academic, and behavioral outcomes: A review and interpretation of the findings. In J. Roberts, I. Wallace, & F. Henderson (Eds.), *Otitis media in young children: Medical, developmental and educational considerations* (pp. 163–194). Baltimore: Paul H. Brookes.

Walton, S. (1989). Katy learns to read and write. *Young Children, 44*(5), 52–57.

Warren, A., & McCloskey, L. (1997). Language in social contexts. In J. Berko Gleason (Ed.), *The development of language* (4th ed., pp. 210–258). Boston: Allyn & Bacon.

Wasik, B. (2001, Spring). Phonemic awareness and young children. *Childhood Education, 77,* 128–133.

Wasik, B. (2006). Building vocabulary one word at a time. *Young Children, 61*(6), 70–78.

Wasik, B. (2010). What teachers can do to promote preschoolers' vocabulary development: Strategies from an effective language and literacy professional development coaching model. *The Reading Teacher, 63*(8), 621–633.

Wassermann, S. (1990). *Serious players in the primary classroom: Empowering children through active learning experience.* New York: Teachers College Press.

Watson, L., Baranek, G., & DiLavore, P. (2003). Toddlers with autism: Developmental perspectives. *Infants and Young Children, 16*(3), 201–214.

Weir, E., & Bianchet, S. (2004). Developmental dysfluency: Early intervention is key. *Canadian Medical Association Journal, 170*(12), 1790–1791.

Weiser, M. (1991). *Infant/toddler care and education* (2nd ed.). Upper Saddle River, NJ: Merrill/Prentice Hall.

Weiss, A. (2004, January). Why we should consider pragmatics when planning treatment for children who stutter. *Language, Speech, and Hearing Services in Schools, 35,* 34–45.

Weitzman, E., & Greenberg, J. (2002). *Learning language and loving it: A guide to promoting children's social, language, and literacy development in early childhood settings* (2nd ed.). Toronto: The Hanen Centre.

Wells, G. (1986). *The meaning makers: Children learning language and using language to learn.* Portsmouth, NH: Heinemann.

Wells, G., & Chang-Wells, G. (1996). The literate potential of collaborative talk. In B. Power & R. Hubbard (Eds.), *Language development: A reader for teachers* (pp. 155–168). Upper Saddle River, NJ: Merrill/Prentice Hall.

Werker, J., & Desjardins, R. (1995). Listening to speech in the 1st year of life: Experiential influences on phoneme perception. *Current Directions in Psychological Science, 4*(3), 76–81.

Werker, J., & Tees, R. (1984). Cross-language speech perception: Evidence for perceptual reorganization during the first year of life. *Infant Behavior and Development, 7*, 49–63.

Werner, H., & Kaplan, B. (1963). *Symbol formation: An organismic approach to language and the expression of thought.* New York: Wiley.

Wertsch, J. (1991). *Voices of the mind: A sociocultural approach to mediated action.* Cambridge, MA: Harvard University Press.

Wessler, S. (2003). It's hard to learn when you are scared. *Educational Leadership, 61*(1), 40–43.

Wheeler, E. (2004). *Conflict resolution in early childhood: Helping children understand and resolve conflict.* Upper Saddle River, NJ: Merrill/Prentice Hall.

Wheeler, R., & Swords, R. (2006). *Code-switching: Teaching Standard English in urban classrooms.* Urbana, IL: National Council of Teachers of English.

White, B. (1978). *The first three years of life.* New York: Avon Books.

Whitehurst, G., & Fischel, J. (1994). Practitioner review: Early developmental language delay: What, if anything, should the clinician do about it? *Journal of Child Psychology* & *Psychiatry* & *Allied Disciplines, 35*(4), 313–349.

Wiig, E., Secord, W., & Semel, E. (2004). *Clinical evaluation of language fundamentals preschool* (2nd ed.). San Antonio, TX: Harcourt Assessment, Inc./PsychCorp.

Wilde, S. (1992). *You can red this!* Portsmouth, NH: Heinemann.

Wiley, A., Shore, C., & Dixon, W. (1989, April). *Situational differences in the type of utterances mothers use with thirteen-month-old children.* Paper presented at the Biennial Meeting of the Society for Research in Child Development, Kansas City, MO.

Wilford, S. (2000, October). Literacy: Building bonds through books and conversation. *Scholastic Early Childhood Today, 15,* 41–45.

Williams, C., Phillips-Birdsong, C., Hufnagel, K., Hungler, D., & Lundstrom, R. (2009). Word study instruction in the K–2 classroom. *The Reading Teacher, 62*(7), 570–578.

Wilkinson, C. (1984). Classroom status from a sociolinguistic perspective. In A. Pellegrini & T. Yawkey (Eds.), *The development of oral and written language in social contexts* (pp. 145–153). Norwood, NJ: Ablex.

Williams, R. (1994). Protecting little pitchers' ears. *FDA Consumer, 28*(10), 10–15.

Wilson, L. (1988). What's inside the box? Activity boxes that foster language development. *Scholastic Pre–K Today, 2*(4), 38–39.

Wilson, L., Douville-Watson, L., & Watson, M. (1995). *Infants and toddlers: Curriculum and teaching* (3rd ed.). Albany, NY: Delmar.

Wimpory, D., Hobson, R., Williams, J., & Nash, S. (2000). Are infants with autism socially engaged? A study of recent retrospective parental reports. *Journal of Autism and Developmental Disorders, 30*(6), 525–536.

Winch, C. (1990). *Language ability and educational achievement.* New York: Routledge.

Windsor, J. (1995). Language impairment and social competence. In M. Fey, J. Windsor, & S. Warren (Eds.), *Language intervention: Preschool through the elementary years* (Vol. 5, pp. 213–238). Baltimore: Paul H. Brookes.

Winsler, A., Diaz, R., & Montero, I. (1997). The role of private speech in the transition from collaborative to independent task performance in young children. *Early Childhood Research Quarterly, 12,* 59–79.

Wolfe, P. (2001). *Brain matters: Translating research into classroom practice.* Alexandria, VA: Association for Supervision and Curriculum Development.

Wolff, P. (1966). The natural history of crying and other vocalizations in early infancy. In B. Foss (Ed.), *Determinants of infant behavior IV.* London: Methuen.

Wolfgang, C., & Wolfgang, M. (1992). *School for young children: Developmentally appropriate practices.* Needham Heights, MA: Allyn & Bacon.

Wolfram, W., & Thomas, E. (2002). *The development of African American English.* Malden, MA: Blackwell.

Wolvin, A., & Coakley, C. (1985). *Listening.* Dubuque, IA: William. C. Brown.

Wong Fillmore, L. (1991). When learning a second language means losing the first. *Early Childhood Research Quarterly, 6,* 323–346.

Wong Fillmore, L. (1995). Individual differences in second language acquisition. In D. Durkin (Ed.), *Language issues: Readings for teachers* (pp. 224–247). White Plains, NY: Longman.

Wong Fillmore, L. (1999). *Reading and academic English learning.* Paper presented at the 1999 Regional Conference of Improving America's Schools, Chicago.

Wortham, S. (1998). *Early childhood curriculum: Developmental bases for learning and teaching* (2nd ed.). Upper Saddle River, NJ: Merrill/Prentice Hall.

Wortham, S. (2008). *Assessment in early childhood education* (5th ed.). Upper Saddle River, NJ: Pearson Merrill Prentice Hall.

Yairi, E., & Ambrose, N. (2005). *Early childhood stuttering: For clinicians by clinicians.* Austin, TX: PRO-ED.

Yoder, S. (2001). You write, I write: Using interactive writing as a means of authentic assessment. In L. Morrow & E. Asbury (Eds.), *Literacy activities for early childhood classrooms* (pp. 6–7). Boston: Allyn & Bacon.

Yont, K., Hewitt, L., & Miccio, A. (2002). "What did you say?": Understanding conversational breakdowns in children with speech and language impairments. *Clinical Linguistics, 16*(4), 265–285.

Yopp, H. (1995). Read-aloud books for developing phonemic awareness: An annotated bibliography. *The Reading Teacher, 48*(6), 538–543.

Yopp, H., & Yopp, R. (2000). Supporting phonemic awareness development in the classroom. *The Reading Teacher, 54*(2), 130–145.

Yopp, R., & Yopp, H. (2001). *Literature-based reading activities* (3rd ed.). Boston: Allyn & Bacon.

Young, K. (2012). Unpublished research notes. Chicago, IL: Northeastern Illinois University.

Young children immersed in media, says recent study. (2004, February/March). *Reading Today, 21*(4), 14.

Zeece, P. (1995). Laughing all the way: Humor in children's books. *Early Childhood Education Journal, 23*(2), 93–97.

Ziegler, J., Pech-Georgel, C., George, F., & Lorenzi, C. (2011). Noise on, voicing off: Speech perception deficits in children with specific language impairment. *Journal of Experimental Child Psychology, 110*(3), 362–372.

Zimmerman, I., Steiner, V., & Pond, R. (1992). *Preschool language scale-3.* San Antonio, TX: Harcourt Assessment, Inc./PsychCorp.

Zimmerman, I., Steiner, V., & Pond, R. (2002). *Preschool language scale* (4th ed.). San Antonio, TX: Harcourt Assessment, Inc./PsychCorp.

Zion, G. (1956). *Harry the dirty dog.* New York: Harper & Row.

Zucker, T., Ward, A., & Justice, L. (2009). Print referencing during read-alouds: A technique for increasing emergent readers' print knowledge. *The Reading Teacher, 63*(1), 62–72.

Zukow-Goldring, P., & Ferko, K. (1994). An ecological approach to the emergence of the lexicon: Socializing attention. In V. John-Steiner, C. Panofsky, & L. Smith (Eds.), *Sociocultural approaches to language and literacy: An interactionist perspective.* New York: Cambridge University Press.

Zygmunt-Fillwalk, E., & Clark, P. (2007). Becoming multicultural: Raising awareness and supporting change in teacher education. *Childhood Education, 83*(5), 288–293.

INDEX